CROSS
ON
LOCAL
GOVERNMENT
LAW

AUSTRALIA AND NEW ZEALAND
The Law Book Company Ltd.
Sydney : Melbourne : Perth

CANADA AND U.S.A.
The Carswell Company Ltd.
Agincourt, Ontario

INDIA
N.M. Tripathi Private Ltd.
Bombay
and
Eastern Law House Private Ltd.
Calcutta and Delhi
M.P.P. House
Bangalore

ISRAEL
Steimatzky's Agency Ltd.
Jerusalem : Tel Aviv : Haifa

MALAYSIA : SINGAPORE : BRUNEI
Malayan Law Journal (Pte.) Ltd.
Singapore and Kuala Lumpar

PAKISTAN
Pakistan Law House
Karachi

CROSS
ON
LOCAL
GOVERNMENT
LAW

by

Charles Cross, M.A., LL.B.,

of Gray's Inn and the Northern Circuit, Barrister

and

Stephen Bailey, M.A., LL.B.,

Senior Lecturer in Law, University of Nottingham

London   Sweet & Maxwell   1986

First Edition 1959
Second Edition 1962
Second Impression 1965
Third Edition 1966
Fourth Edition 1971
Fifth Edition 1974
Sixth Edition 1981
Seventh Edition 1986

Published by
Sweet & Maxwell Limited of
11 New Fetter Lane, London.
Computerset by Burgess & Son (Abingdon) Limited.
Reproduced, printed and bound in Great Britain by
Hazell Watson & Viney Limited,
Member of the BPCC Group,
Aylesbury, Bucks

British Library Cataloguing in Publication Data

Cross, C.A.
    Cross on local government law.—7th ed.
    1. Local government—Law and legislation—
    England and Wales
    I. Title   II. Bailey, S.H.   III. Cross, C.A.
    Principles of local government law
    344.202'9 KD4759

    ISBN 0–421–34190–4
    ISBN 0–421–34200–5 Pbk

PREFACE

Since the publication of the sixth edition of this book, the law concerning local government has undergone substantial change. There have been several consolidating measures—the Food Act 1984, the Building Act 1984, the Weights and Measures Act 1984 and the Housing Act 1985 and there has been much new legislative material. The Local Government Finance Act 1982 and the Local Government Act 1985 have brought about considerable change in structure and in the allocation of functions and finance. There has been much new case law, particularly in the area of local authority decision-making and in finance. These changes have called for much revision and re-writing.

This new edition bears a somewhat different title. It takes account of the fact that Mr. Stephen Bailey of the University of Nottingham, an Assistant Editor of the Encyclopedia of Local Government Law, has undertaken a very substantial amount of revision and re-writing. I am greatly indebted to him for his detailed work on the book and for applying his considerable scholarship to it.

Because of the ever widening scope of local government law I have, as in the last edition, obtained the help of specialist lawyers in relation to particular topics. Mr. Reginald Jones, the Financial Editor of the Encyclopedia of Local Government Law, undertook the revision of the chapters on finance, rating and grants; Mr. David Hoath of the University of Sheffield, the chapter on housing; Mr. Richard Jones of University College, Cardiff, the chapter on the social services; and Mr. R.N.D. Hamilton the chapters on land acquisition and planning. Mr. Harold Clarke, of the Chelmer Institute of Higher Education, an Assistant Editor of the Encyclopedia of Local Government Law, read the whole of the text and made comments on it, and revised the chapter on local government in Greater London. Each of these contributors are authors of distinction and I am greatly appreciative of their help.

The law stated is that in force on January 1, 1986, except that account has been taken of those provisions which are scheduled to come into force on April 1, 1986.

In general, the functions of the various Secretaries of State are exercisable, in relation to Wales, by the Secretary of State for Wales.

Reference is made throughout this book to the fines on the standard scale prescribed under the Criminal Justice Act 1982. At the time of going to press the fines as prescribed by the Criminal Penalties, etc., (Increase Order) 1984 (S.I. 1984 No. 447) were as follows:

Level 1	£50
Level 2	£100
Level 3	£400
Level 4	£1000
Level 5	£2000

December 31, 1985.   Charles Cross

CONTENTS

CONTENTS

TABLE OF CASES

[Paragraph references in **bold** type indicate a fuller treatment of the case.]

ix

1

li

liii

TABLE OF STATUTES

CHAPTER 1

THE LEGAL FRAMEWORK OF LOCAL AUTHORITIES

THE Local Government Act 1972 gave effect to the proposals contained **1-01**
in the White Paper "Local Government in England: Government
Proposals for Reorganisation"[1] and in the consultative document "The
Reform of Local Government in Wales," published in 1971. It created
new structures for local government and allocated functions among the
new authorities. It re-cast the law, modified and in simpler form, with
respect to the administrative working of local authorities. It replaced the
Local Government Act 1933, and it incorporated, with modification, the
provisions of the London Government Act 1963, relating to the
constitution of authorities in Greater London. The structure of London
government was not materially affected: fundamental reorganisation had
taken place in 1965 following the London Government Act 1963 under
which the Greater London Council and the London borough councils
had been established.[2]

Under the Act of 1972 new areas and new authorities were created in
England, outside Greater London, and in Wales.[3] Each country was
divided into counties and districts. In England, certain counties were
metropolitan counties and the districts within them were metropolitan
districts. In England many districts were divided into parishes and in
Wales all districts were divided into communities.

Changes were effected in Greater London and in the metropolitan **1-02**
counties by the Local Government Act 1985. That Act abolished, from
April 1, 1986, the Greater London Council and the metropolitan county
councils, giving effect to proposals contained in the White Paper,
"Streamlining the Cities."[4] It provided for the transfer of their functions
to other authorities—in the main, they were re-allocated, respectively, to
the London borough councils and the metropolitan district councils. Part
III of the Act established the Inner London Education Authority,
formerly a special committee of the Greater London Council, as a
directly elected authority.[5] Part IV provided for separate "joint authorities" to be established to act as (1) police, (2) fire and civil defence, and (3)
passenger transport authorities in the metropolitan counties, and as the

---

[1] Cmnd. 4584.
[2] Local government in Greater London is described in Chap. 28.
[3] Local Government Act 1972, s. 1.
[4] Cmnd. 9063.
[5] This authority was first established as the Inner London Interim Education Authority with
  effect from September 1, 1985. From the abolition date (April 1, 1986) it was known by its
  present title.

fire and civil defence authority for London.[6] Part VII established a "residuary body" in each area to deal with residual matters concerning the abolished authorities.

The areas of counties, districts and London boroughs are called principal areas and their councils are called principal councils. Parishes and communities have parish and community meetings and may have parish and community councils. The areas of metropolitan counties continue as local government areas for certain purposes, for example as the areas under the control of joint authorities.

Many districts bear the style of borough and their councils are called borough councils; certain parishes bear the style of town and their councils are called town councils. Some areas within districts which were formerly cities or boroughs have a body known as the charter trustees of the city or the charter trustees of the town as the case may be.

This, in briefest terms, is the formal structure of local government. The achievement of status and change of status is the subject of detailed statutory provision and this is described in Chapter 3.

1–03   The term "local authority" is applied to principal councils and to the councils of parishes and communities.[7] Joint authorities and residuary bodies are treated as "local authorities" for specified purposes.[8] All these authorities are corporate bodies and have the characteristics of corporations. In addition, two other bodies have corporate status, namely, the parish trustees of a parish not having a parish council, and the charter trustees of a city or borough.

1–04   One feature common to local authorities is their corporate status. A study of the principles of local government law must therefore begin with an examination of the nature of corporate status and the legal consequences which flow from incorporation.

Nature of a corporation

A corporation has been defined by a leading authority in the following terms[9]:

> A collection of many individuals, united into one body, under a special denomination, having perpetual succession under an artificial form, and vested, by the policy of the law, with the capacity of acting, in several respects, as an individual, particularly of taking and granting property, of contracting obligations, of suing and being sued.

The "collection of many individuals" becomes by incorporation one individual, an artificial person, having rights and duties, capable of suing

---

[6] These authorities were established with effect from September 15, 1985: see the Local Government Act 1985 (New Authorities) (Appointed Days) Order 1985 (S.I. 1985 No. 1283).

[7] Local Government Act 1972, s. 270(1): definition of "local authority," as amended by the Local Government Act 1985, Sched. 17.

[8] Local Government Act 1985, Scheds. 13, 14.

[9] *Kyd on Corporations* (1793–94) Vol. 1, p. 13.

and being sued, of holding property and making contracts. A corporation is a wholly different and separate entity from the individuals who compose it. It is the corporation as such, not its constituent members, which is liable for its obligations and in whom its property vests. It is a legal *persona*. This is perhaps the most significant feature of corporate status: its importance is seen more clearly when an examination is later made of contractual and tortious liability.

There are other characteristics of an incorporated body. It must have a **1–05** name, and all legal transactions must be effected in that name. It was held in *Knight* v. *Wells Corporation*[10] that a bond entered into by a corporation in its wrong name was void. Secondly, it has perpetual succession. Individual members who compose it may die or retire or be replaced by new corporators, but the corporation continues an unbroken existence. Obligations entered into whilst one group of persons makes up the membership bind the corporation even though the whole of the membership has changed. Finally, it has a seal. The acts and decisions of a corporation are authenticated by its seal, which in some respects is like the signature of a natural person. The corporate will is evidenced by the affixing of the seal to the document in which it is expressed. These characteristics are found in the common law rules as to corporations.

Local authority corporations

In the case of local authorities these rules are, for the most part, **1–06** expressed in statute. The Local Government Act 1972[11] provides that a principal council shall be a body corporate by the name of the county council or district council as the case may be. Similarly worded provisions apply to parish and community councils,[12] and to the Inner London Education Authority, joint authorities and residuary bodies.[13] So far as parish and community councils are concerned it is expressly stated that notwithstanding anything in any rule of law a council need not have a common seal and where it has no seal any of its acts which are required to be signified under seal may be signed and sealed by two members of the council.[14]

The doctrine of ultra vires

Perhaps the most important principle to be considered in relation to **1–07** corporate status is the doctrine of *ultra vires*. The term *ultra vires* means

---

[10] (1696) 1 Ld. Raym. 80.

[11] s. 2.

[12] ss. 14 and 33. In the case of a parish not having a separate parish council the chairman of the parish meeting and the proper officer of the district council are incorporated as "the parish trustees": s. 13.

[13] Local Government Act 1985, ss. 18(1), 24(1), 25(1), 26(1), 27(1), 28(1), 57(1).

[14] Local Government Act 1972, ss. 13(5), 14(3), and 33(3). As to the occasions where sealing is necessary, see § 10–07.

"beyond the powers." An act is *ultra vires* an authority if it is beyond its powers; the converse term is *"intra vires."*

1-08   The doctrine as applied to statutory corporations is stated in Lord Watson's speech in *Baroness Wenlock* v. *River Dee Co.*[15]:

> "Whenever a corporation is created by Act of Parliament, with reference to the purposes of the Act, and solely with a view to carrying these purposes into execution, I am of opinion not only that the objects which the corporation may legitimately pursue must be ascertained from the Act itself, but that the powers which the corporation may lawfully use in furtherance of these objects must either be expressly conferred or derived by reasonable implication from its provisions."

Unlike a natural person who can in general do whatever he pleases so long as what he does is not forbidden by law or contrary to law, a statutory corporation can do only those things which it is authorised to do by statute, directly or by implication. If such a corporation acts otherwise than in this way its acts are *ultra vires.* There must in all cases be statutory authority for what is done, and that authority must either be expressly given or reasonably inferred from the language of an Act of Parliament.

Application of the doctrine generally

1-09   This rule, if rigidly applied to statutory corporations, would greatly handicap their activities and would require empowering legislation to be burdened to an impossible extent by detailed provisions. The courts have therefore held that a corporation may do not only those things for which there is express or implied authority, but also whatever is reasonably *incidental* to the doing of those things. Lord Selborne said in *Att.-Gen.* v. *Great Eastern Ry.*[16]:

> "It appears to me to be important that the doctrine of *ultra vires* . . . should be maintained. But I agree . . . that this doctrine ought to be reasonably, and not unreasonably, understood and applied, and that whatever may fairly be regarded as incidental to, or consequential upon, those things which the legislature has authorised ought not (unless expressly prohibited) to be held by judicial construction to be *ultra vires.*"

1-10   This common law rule is given statutory force in section 111 of the Local Government Act 1972.[17] Authorities are there empowered to do anything (whether or not involving the expenditure, borrowing or lending of money or the acquisition or disposal of any property or rights) which is calculated to facilitate, or is conducive or incidental to, the discharge of any of their functions. In exercising this power authorities are required to comply with the provisions of the Act or any other existing or future enactment. This means, amongst other things, that authorities must keep

---

[15] (1885) 10 App. Cas. 354 at p. 362.
[16] (1880) 5 App. Cas. 473 at p. 478.
[17] This section applies to joint authorities and the Inner London Education Authority: Local Government Act 1972, s. 146A(1)(*a*), inserted by the Local Government Act 1985, Sched. 14, para. 16; and to residuary bodies: 1985 Act, Sched. 13, para. 12(*a*).

accounts of expenditure under this head in accordance with the provisions of Part VIII of the 1972 Act and Part III of the Local Government Finance Act 1982.

The words "incidental to" are not equivalent to the words "in connection with." They have a narrower meaning. This point emerged in *Amalgamated Society of Railway Servants* v. *Osborne*, where Lord Macnaghten said[18]:

> "The learned counsel for the appellants did not, as I understand their argument, venture to contend that the power which they claimed could be derived by reasonable implication from the language of the legislature. They said it was a power 'incidental,' 'ancillary' or 'conducive.' ... If these rather loose expressions are meant to cover something beyond what may be found in the language which the legislature has used, all I can say is that, so far as I know, there is no foundation in principle or authority for the proposition involved in their use."

These dicta were relied on in *Att.-Gen.* v. *Crayford Urban District Council*.[19]

In the application of the doctrine there are then three issues: first, **1-11** whether what is done is specifically authorised by statute; secondly, whether (if there be no specific authority) one can reasonably imply authority from the language of the statute; and, thirdly, whether an act for which no such direct or implied authority is found is reasonably incidental to the carrying into effect of a statutory purpose.

In the many cases which have come before the courts the question has usually centred on implied powers and incidental powers. It must be rare for an authority to perform an act for which there is no statutory authority at all but it has frequently happened that a council has extended and enlarged a service to a point where it is alleged that its statutory powers have been exceeded, and it has then been contended on behalf of the council that authority can reasonably be implied from the language of the statute as a whole. In other cases a council has engaged in some activity for which there is no clear authority in statute, but it has been argued for the council that this activity has been undertaken for the better carrying into effect of a statutory power or duty—the council has relied on the rule as to incidental powers.

Several of the more important cases relating to this topic are now given. **1-12** The first, the *Ashbury Railway Carriage* case, is of particular significance, since it is from this case that the rule in its modern application may be said to stem:

Ashbury Railway Carriage Co. v. *Riche*.[20] The company was incorporated under the Companies Act 1862 to make, sell or lend on hire all kinds of railway

---

[18] [1910] A.C. 87 at p. 97.
[19] [1962] Ch. 575.
[20] (1875) L.R. 7 H.L. 653. The rule in this case was expressly applied to the London County Council, as a statutory corporation, in *Att.-Gen.* v. *London County Council* [1907] A.C. 131.

plant. The company entered into a contract for the construction of a railway. *Held*, that the act of the company in entering into the contract was *ultra vires*. The Lord Chancellor said[21]: "Now . . . if that is the condition upon which the corporation is established (his Lordship was referring to the procedure of incorporation under the Companies Act) it is a mode of incorporation which contains in it both that which is affirmative and that which is negative. It states affirmatively the ambit and extent of the vitality and power which by law is given to the incorporation, and it states, if it were necessary to state, negatively, that nothing shall be done beyond that ambit, and that no attempt shall be made to use the corporate life for any other purpose than that which is so specified."

Att.-Gen. v. *Fulham Corporation*.[22] The metropolitan borough of Fulham was a statutory body created under the London Government Act 1899. The corporation, in common with many other authorities, provided facilities for residents to wash their own clothes in separate troughs under powers clearly conferred by the Baths and Washhouses Acts 1846 and 1878. In 1920, the corporation introduced a new scheme under which residents brought their washing to the wash-house, leaving it there to be laundered by employees of the council. A collection and delivery service was provided at a small additional charge. An action for a declaration that the scheme was illegal was brought by the Attorney-General at the relation of a ratepayer. It was argued for the corporation that what had been done was incidental to the use of its statutory powers; that it was not material that the washing was undertaken by council servants and not by the customers. *Held*, that the scheme was *ultra vires* the corporation, for there was no authority express or implied to enable the corporation to wash clothes for others as distinct from providing facilities enabling persons to come to the wash-house to wash their clothes.

Att.-Gen. v. *Manchester Corporation*.[23] The corporation had power conferred under a private Act to use its tramways "for the purpose of conveying and delivering animals goods minerals and parcels." The corporation proposed to establish a general parcels delivery service within and beyond the area covered by the tramways system, not confined to parcels and goods carried on their tramways. An action was brought by the Attorney-General at the relation of a ratepayer to restrain the corporation. The corporation contended that its acts were authorised by statute or if not fully authorised thereby were properly incidental or ancillary to the business for which statutory powers were available. (The corporation also argued that it was a common law corporation and could therefore act without statutory power—it failed on this point for reasons which no longer have relevance.) *Held*, the corporation had statutory power to carry on the business of common carriers upon their tramways and as ancillary to that business to do all things necessary for the collection and delivery of parcels or goods carried on the tramways; but the corporation had no power to carry on a general parcels delivery service apart from their tramways.

Att.-Gen. v. *Smethwick Corporation*.[24] The corporation passed a resolution providing for the establishment of a printing, bookbinding and stationery works for the purpose of executing work required by them. An action was brought by the Attorney-General at the relation of a ratepayer claiming a declaration that the proposal was *ultra vires*. *Held*, that the formation of a department to do the printing, bookbinding and stationery work of the

---

[21] At p. 670.
[22] [1921] 1 Ch. 440.
[23] [1906] 1 Ch. 643.
[24] [1932] 1 Ch. 562.

corporation was incidental to or consequential upon the carrying out of the corporation's statutory duties and was not therefore *ultra vires*. The Master of the Rolls quoted with approval the passage from Lord Selborne's judgment in *Att.-Gen.* v. *Great Eastern Ry.*[25]

R. v. *Greater London Council and Another, ex p. Westminster City Council.*[26] It was held that the maintenance of good staff relations was a proper function of a local authority and a decision to release staff for that purpose was within s. 111, subject to the *Wednesbury* test of reasonableness.[27] But if the object, or a major object, of the decision was to conduct a political campaign in opposition to government policy that was an irrelevant consideration and the decision would be invalid. On that basis a decision by the Inner London Education Authority to release one member of staff to a joint committee or body of trade unions made in the interests of good industrial relations was valid but a decision of the GLC to release seven members of staff with pay to the same body in support of the GLC's campaign against government policy was invalid.

Application of doctrine to procedural requirements

Parliament frequently prescribes the procedure which should be fol- **1-13** lowed in the making of a particular order or decision. This may be done in considerable detail in the relevant statute (or schedule). Alternatively, a minister may be empowered to lay down procedural rules in a statutory instrument. Even where there is a duty to observe a procedural step, non-observance will render the ultimate decision *ultra vires* only if it is a *mandatory* or *imperative* requirement. Failure to observe a *directory* re-quirement does not have that effect. There are many cases illustrating the distinction,[28] but the courts have been unable to formulate clear guidelines as to which steps are mandatory and which directory. Parliament very occasionally indicates the consequences which follow from the non-observance of particular requirements. An example of such an indication, in section 82 of the Local Government Act 1972,[29] reads:

> "The acts and proceedings of any person elected to an office under this Act or elected or appointed to an office under Part III or IV of the Local Government Act 1985 and acting in that office shall, notwithstanding his disqualification or want of qualification, be as valid and effectual as if he had been qualified."

A court is likely to hold a requirement to be mandatory where, for **1-14** example, it relates to the exercise of a right or a power rather than the performance of a duty,[30] or it provides an important safeguard to individual interests, such as a requirement to give prior notice of a decision or to hold a hearing,[31] or to give notice of rights of appeal,[32] or

---

[25] See § 1–09.

[26] *The Times*, December 27, 1984.

[27] As to the *Wednesbury* test, see § 12–20.

[28] See *Craies on Statute Law* (7th ed.), pp. 260–263; *Maxwell on the Interpretation of Statutes* (12th ed.), pp. 314–322.

[29] As amended by the Local Government Act 1985, Sched. 14, para. 4.

[30] *Montreal Street Railway Co.* v. *Normandin* [1917] A.C. 170; *Cullimore* v. *Lyme Regis Corporation* [1962] 1 Q.B. 718.

[31] *Bradbury* v. *Enfield London Borough Council* [1967] 1 W.L.R. 1311, *infra*.

[32] *Rayner* v. *Stepney Corporation* [1911] 2 Ch. 312; *London & Clydeside Estates Limited* v. *Aberdeen District Council* [1980] 1 W.L.R. 182.

rights to make objections,[33] or to give the prescribed period of notice of the implementation of a licensing scheme by council resolution,[34] or to consult appropriate bodies.[35] Similarly a requirement is likely to be mandatory where it reflects the need for justice to be seen to be done[36] or where the procedure leads to the imposition of a financial burden on a member of the public.[37] In *Howard* v. *Bodington*,[38] Lord Penzance stated[39]:

> "I believe, as far as any rule is concerned, you cannot safely go further than that in each case you must look to the subject-matter; consider the importance of the provision that has been disregarded, and the relation of that provision to the general object intended to be secured by the Act; and upon a review of the case in that aspect decide whether the matter is what is called imperative or only directory."

Bradbury v. *Enfield London Borough Council.*[40] The reorganisation of Enfield's schools on comprehensive lines involved changes which in the case of eight schools did not in the council's view amount to "ceasing to maintain" them. Accordingly, the requirements of s. 13 (1), (3) and (4) of the Education Act 1944 were not observed. These were that where a local education authority intended to "establish" a county school or "cease to maintain" a county or voluntary school, it was to submit proposals to the Minister, and give public notice so that objections could be made to him. The Court of Appeal held that changes in the age group or sex of the pupils did amount here to "ceasing to maintain" the existing schools. The requirements of s. 13 (1), (3) and (4) were applicable, and were mandatory. In addition, and in relation to all Enfield's secondary schools, the council had failed to comply with s. 13 (6) and (7) of the 1944 Act, which provided that after the general proposals were approved, the authority had to submit specifications and plans of the school premises to the Minister. The Minister would approve them if they were in conformity with prescribed standards. The Court held these requirements to be directory. The only remedy was to complain to the Minister under s. 99 of the 1944 Act. The court granted an injunction to restrain the council from implementing the changes only in relation to the group of eight schools.

Howard v. *Secretary of State for the Environment.*[41] By s. 16 (2) of the Town and Country Planning Act 1968 (now s. 88 (2) of the 1971 Act), an appeal against an enforcement notice "shall be made by notice in writing to the Minister, which shall indicate the grounds of appeal and state the facts on which it is based." The plaintiff gave notice of appeal within the 42 day period specified in the enforcement notice, but indicated the "grounds" and "facts" concerned after that period had expired. The Court of Appeal held that the section was mandatory as to the giving of notice in writing within the specified

---

[33] *R.* v. *Lambeth Borough Council, ex p. Sharp, The Times,* December 28, 1984.
[34] *R.* v. *Swansea City Council, ex p. Quietlynn Ltd., The Times,* October 19, 1983; *R.* v. *Birmingham City Council, ex p. Quietlynn Ltd. and other cases* (1985) 83 L.G.R. 461 at pp. 471–479, 512–514.
[35] *Agricultural, Horticultural and Forestry Industry Training Board* v. *Aylesbury Mushrooms Ltd.* [1972] 1 W.L.R. 190.
[36] *Noble* v. *Inner London Education Authority* (1983) 82 L.G.R. 291.
[37] *Per* Scarman L.J. in *Sheffield City Council* v. *Graingers Wines Ltd.* (1977) 75 L.G.R. 743 at pp. 748–749.
[38] (1877) 2 P.D. 203.
[39] *Ibid.* at p. 211.
[40] [1967] 1 W.L.R. 1311. See also *Lee* v. *Enfield London Borough Council* (1967) 66 L.G.R. 195; *Lee* v. *Department of Education and Science* (1967) 66 L.G.R. 211.
[41] [1975] Q.B. 235.

time, but directory only as to the contents of the notice of appeal. Accordingly, the Minister had jurisdiction to entertain the plaintiff's appeal.

There is some authority to the effect that failure to comply with a **1-15** directory requirement will only be excused where there has been "substantial compliance."

> *Cullimore* v. *Lyme Regis Corporation.*[42] The borough council prepared a works scheme under the Coast Protection Act 1949, whereby charges were to be levied for certain coast protection works. The scheme required the council within six months of completion of the work to determine the interests in the land benefited by reference to which charges were to be levied, and the amount of such charges. The council determined these matters almost two years after completion. Edmund Davies J. held that the charges were *ultra vires* and void on the grounds that either (1) the sixth month time limit was a mandatory requirement, or (2) even if it were a directory requirement, there had been nothing approaching substantial compliance.

It is not clear, however, whether "substantial compliance"means **1-16** substantial compliance with the particular procedural requirement that has not been observed or substantial compliance with the procedural code as a whole. In *London & Clydeside Estates Ltd.* v. *Aberdeen District Council,*[43] Lord Hailsham L.C. stated, *obiter*, that "a total failure to comply with a significant part of a requirement cannot in any circumstances be regarded as 'substantial compliance' with the total requirement. . . . "

A flexible approach to the effect of failure to comply with procedural requirements was suggested by Lord Hailsham L.C. in the *London & Clydeside* case[44]:

> "When Parliament lays down a statutory requirement for the exercise of legal authority it expects its authority to be obeyed down to the minutest detail. But what the courts have to decide in a particular case is the legal consequence of non-compliance on the rights of the subject viewed in the light of a concrete state of facts and a continuing chain of events. It may be that what the courts are faced with is not so much a stark choice of alternatives but a spectrum of possibilities in which one compartment or description fades gradually into another. At one end of this spectrum there may be cases in which a fundamental obligation may have been so outrageously and flagrantly ignored or defied that the subject may safely ignore what has been done and treat it as having no legal consequences upon himself. In such a case if the defaulting authority seeks to rely on its action it may be that the subject is entitled to use the defect in procedure simply as a shield or defence without having taken any positive action of his own. At the other end of the spectrum the defect in procedure may be so nugatory or trivial that the authority can safely proceed without remedial action, confident that, if the subject is so misguided as to rely on the fault, the courts will decline to listen to his complaint. But in a very great number of cases, it may be in a majority of them, it may be necessary for a subject, in order to safeguard himself, to go to the court for declaration of his

[42] [1962] 1 Q.B. 718.
[43] [1980] 1 W.L.R. 182.
[44] *Ibid.* at pp. 189–190. Lord Hailsham's observations were applied by Woolf J. in *R.* v. *Chester City Council, ex p. Quietlynn Ltd., The Times,* October 19, 1983.

rights, the grant of which may well be discretionary, and by the like token it may be wise for an authority (as it certainly would have been here) to do everything in its power to remedy the fault in its procedure so as not to deprive the subject of his due or themselves of their power to act. In such cases, though language like 'mandatory,' 'directory,' 'void,' 'voidable,' 'nullity' and so forth may be helpful in argument, it may be misleading in effect if relied on to show that the courts, in deciding the consequences of a defect in the exercise of power, are necessarily bound to fit the facts of a particular case and a developing chain of events into rigid legal categories. . . . "

Whether the applicant has been prejudiced may be relevant to the question of the effect of failure to comply with a procedural requirement; however, in appropriate cases an act or decision may be quashed even though the applicant has not been prejudiced.[45]

In areas where ordinary procedures for judicial review are ousted by a "statutory *ultra vires*" or "time limit" clause (see *infra*, paras. 12–42 and 12–46) the statute generally provides that a person substantially prejudiced by failure to comply with any requirement may apply to the High Court within six weeks for the ultimate order or decision to be quashed.

1-17   Breach of a directory requirement will not render the ultimate decision void, and may not even amount to an *intra vires* error of law which may be challenged on an appeal or on an application for certiorari to quash for error of law on the face of the record.[46] However, if he is in time, a person aggrieved may be able to obtain mandamus to compel observance of the requirement.

> *Brayhead (Ascot) Ltd.* v. *Berkshire County Council.*[47] The Town and Country Planning General Development Order requires that reasons be given by a local planning authority where it refuses planning permission or attaches conditions to a permission (the current provision is art. 7 (7) of the 1977 Order, S.I. 1977 No. 289). Winn J. held that failure to give reasons did not render a condition void, but that a court would normally grant mandamus to compel the reasons to be divulged.

In some cases, Parliament expressly allows defects to be corrected. For example, section 88A (2) of the Town and Country Planning Act 1971 provides that on an appeal against an enforcement notice, the Secretary of State may correct any informality, defect or error in the notice, or give directions for varying its terms, if he is satisfied that the correction or variation can be made without injustice to the appellant or to the local planning authority. Section 88A (3) provides that he may disregard the fact that a person entitled to be served with the notice has not been so served if neither he nor the appellant has been substantially prejudiced by

---

[45] [1980] 1 W.L.R. 182 at p. 183, *per* Lord Hailsham L.C: compare the position in respect of failure to comply with natural justice: below § 12–30. Failure to comply with a mandatory procedural requirement is fatal even where there is no prejudice: *R.* v. *Birmingham City Council, ex p. Quietlynn Ltd. and other cases* (1985) 83 L.G.R. 461 at pp. 471–479.
[46] See *Mountview Court Properties Ltd.* v. *Devlin* (1970) 21 P. & C.R. 689.
[47] [1964] 2 Q.B. 303.

the failure. If, however, the notice is a nullity for any reason, the defect cannot be corrected under section 88A.[48]

Other aspects of the ultra vires doctrine

Many of the cases on the application of the *ultra vires* doctrine to local   **1-18** authorities have concerned issues as to whether a particular project could lawfully be undertaken. However, the *ultra vires* doctrine may also be invoked to control the *methods* by which decisions are reached. Accordingly, in *Anisminic Ltd.* v. *Foreign Compensation Commission*,[49] the House of Lords came near to holding that any error of law in the course of decision making will infringe the *ultra vires* doctrine. The courts have also held that powers are exceeded if exercised in bad faith, for improper purposes, where a legally relevant consideration has been ignored, where a legally irrelevant consideration has been taken into account, or where the decision is so unreasonable that no reasonable authority could act in such a manner. A discretion may not be fettered improperly by any contract or undertaking, by the creation of an estoppel, or by any rigid policy rule. Local authorities must not act under the dictation of any other body in the exercise of functions in the absence of express or implied statutory authority. Finally, the courts may hold that there is an obligation to observe natural justice or to act fairly. These are limitations which the courts, in the appropriate context, deem Parliament to have intended to impose, in the absence of express provision to the contrary. These aspects of the *ultra vires* doctrine are considered in Chapter 12.

Legal consequences of a breach of the ultra vires rules

There are two important consequences which may follow from a   **1-19** breach of the *ultra vires* rule. First, legal proceedings may be commenced in the High Court. A person aggrieved may apply for "judicial review" of a local authority's decision under Order 53 of the Rules of the Supreme Court. The court may in an appropriate case grant one or more of a number of remedies, some of which are peculiar to public law (the prerogative orders of certiorari, prohibition and mandamus), and the other ordinary remedies also applicable in the private law context (injunction, declaration and damages). The former group may only be sought under Order 53; the latter may also be sought in ordinary High Court proceedings, although the courts will normally require an applicant to proceed under Order 53 if the case is within the scope of that Order. Thus, a remedy may be available to quash an *ultra vires* decision that has been made (certiorari), to prohibit *ultra vires* action which is about to take place (prohibition, injunction), to compel performance of a public duty (mandamus, injunction), or simply to make the legal position clear (declaration). These remedies are considered in Chapter 12.

---

[48] See *Miller-Mead* v. *Minister of Housing and Local Government* [1963] 2 Q.B. 196.
[49] [1969] A.C. 147.

Where unlawful expenditure is concerned, the ordinary procedure has been for an action to be commenced in the High Court for a declaration or for a declaration coupled with an injunction. This is what happened in *Att.-Gen.* v. *Fulham Corporation*,[50] discussed earlier. In a similar way a rate-payer in Birmingham obtained a declaration that the council had acted *ultra vires* in granting free bus travel to old-age pensioners,[51] and in Cardiff tenants of council houses unsuccessfully sought a declaration that a differential rent scheme was *ultra vires*, arguing that a charge based on ability to pay was not within the Housing Act 1936.[52] Such proceedings would now normally be brought by way of an application for judicial review.

1-20   An action in the High Court is costly, and in relation to local authorities a more effective check is exercised through statutory audit.[53] Where it appears to the auditor that any item of account is contrary to law he may apply to the court for a declaration to that effect, unless the expenditure has been sanctioned by the Secretary of State. Where the court makes the declaration asked for, it may order repayment by the person concerned and may order the rectification of accounts, and in some cases disqualification from membership of the local authority follows.

1-21   Any person interested may inspect documents of account and any local government elector may question the auditor about them and may raise an objection to an account.[54]

These matters are considered in more detail in Chapter 7. But the point is noted here that if an authority oversteps its powers or if members (or officers) are responsible for expenditure which is *ultra vires* they are likely to be called to account through the system of statutory audit.

1-22   There is the further practical point that an authority cannot engage in a major scheme or project without involving in some way, and generally at an early stage, one of the Ministries, and Ministries always must be satisfied, before giving any consent required of them, that adequate statutory authority exists for what is proposed. Some services are grant-earning, and grants are customarily given only in respect of "approved" expenditure, that is to say, approved by a government department. When a local authority needs to acquire land compulsorily it must always rely on a clearly applicable statutory power. In initiating larger schemes, therefore, an authority is in any event unlikely to engage or be able to engage in activities which are *ultra vires*.

Recent trends

1-23   Parliament has given several widely-drawn powers to local authorities, powers which enable them to act for the good of their areas in ways not

---

[50] [1921] 1 Ch. 440.
[51] *Prescott* v. *Birmingham Corporation* [1955] Ch. 210.
[52] *Smith* v. *Cardiff Corporation* [1955] Ch. 159.
[53] Local Government Finance Act 1982, Part III.
[54] *Ibid.* s. 17.

specified by statute. These general powers do not negative the *ultra vires* rule but they do soften its application. Section 6 of the Local Government (Financial Provisions) Act 1963 enabled a local authority to incur expenditure up to a 0.4p rate for any purpose which in its opinion was in the interests of the area or its inhabitants, provided such activity was not subject to other statutory provision. This provision was important because of its novelty. It was re-enacted in section 137 of the Local Government Act 1972 in somewhat wider terms. Up to the product of a 2p rate may be spent for the benefit of the area or a part of it or for the benefit of all or some of the inhabitants. Section 139 gives a power to local authorities to spend money on gifts donated for the benefit of the inhabitants of the area, and a gift may be unrelated to any statutory purpose. Section 137 also gives authorities power to contribute to certain charitable funds and appeals related to the United Kingdom, and section 138 authorises expenditure in dealing with actual or imminent or apprehended disasters and emergencies affecting an area or its inhabitants. Sections 120 and 124 enable local authorities to purchase land for the benefit, improvement or development of their areas; and section 2 of the Local Authorities (Land) Act 1963 empowers local authorities, for the benefit or improvement of their areas, to erect buildings or to construct or carry out works on land. Here again is the concept of benefit to the area generally.

But there has been a converse tendency as well, a tendency to **1-24** particularise, and to particularise in such a way that generally implied or incidental powers are curtailed, not only in the field in which the restriction takes place, but at large, since it can be argued that if a particular power is required by statute in one field, it is required in another. There is, in fact, one example of this in the section which extends the scope and activity of local authorities in a generalised way and the two tendencies are seen within one provision. Where an authority develops land for the benefit of the area under section 2 of the Local Authorities (Land) Act 1963, it has power to repair, maintain and insure the buildings or works and generally deal with such buildings or works in the proper course of management. This is not a new kind of provision. It is found in section 124 (5) of the Town and Country Planning Act 1971 (a provision originally derived from the 1944 Planning Act). But it can be argued that if an authority has power to put up a building it can, under the doctrine of implied and incidental powers, or under the subsidiary powers conferred by section 111 of the Local Government Act 1972,[55] deal with it in the proper course of management, and indeed one would have thought that there would have been a bounden duty on the authority to do this and to keep the building in repair. There are other statutory provisions enabling authorities to erect buildings and there is no reference in them to insurance. Is it to be assumed in those cases that to

[55] See § 1–10.

effect insurance is *ultra vires*? This particular enabling power is perhaps more restrictive than enabling.

1-25   The Royal Commission on Local Government in England[56] took the view that all of the main authorities which they proposed should be established should have a general power to spend money for the benefit of their areas and inhabitants, additional to their expenditure on services for which they would have statutory responsibility. The Commission referred to the precedent under section 6 of the Local Government (Financial Provisions) Act 1963. They suggested that the only limit on the use of new power should be the wishes of the electors and such restrictions as have to be placed on local government expenditure in the interests of national economic and financial policy. The White Paper "Reform of Local Government in England"[57] stated that the Government of the day were sympathetic in principle to this proposal.[58] But practical difficulties were noted; for example, unconditional powers, not restricted by any financial limit, might lead to wasteful duplication or to local action which could conflict with national objectives in important fields of policy. In the event, only the "free 2p," and the subsidiary powers referred to above, emerged as law.

[56] Vol. I, para. 323.
[57] Cmnd. 4276.
[58] *Ibid.* para. 69.

CHAPTER 2

ACQUISITION OF POWERS

THE powers of local authorities are all derived from statute, from public   **2-01**
Acts and local Acts. The numerous powers referred to in this book all
stem from public Acts, but individual authorities may supplement these
general powers and acquire additional powers by means of local
legislation. There are, in addition, powers *available* under the general law
which cannot be exercised until some formal steps are taken—these
powers may be acquired by the adoption of "adoptive" Acts, under
provisional order procedure, and under special parliamentary procedure.

Local authorities have an influence in fashioning the powers which
Parliament gives them. A note of this appears in the final paragraphs of
this Chapter.

A. LOCAL LEGISLATION

Procedure in Parliament

The rules governing the promotion of local Bills (and private and   **2-02**
personal Bills) are found in the standing orders of each House. The first
step is the giving of public notice and the presentation of a petition for
leave to introduce the Bill to Parliament. Notice of intention is published
in the Press and in the *London Gazette*, and if land is to be acquired notice
is given to owners, lessees and occupiers. A copy of the Bill is deposited in
the Committee and Private Bill Office (of the Commons), with the Clerk
of the Parliaments (in the House of Lords), and with the government
departments affected. The dates by which these and subsequent steps are
to be taken are given in standing orders. Normally, Bills should be
deposited by November 27 each session.

Each House has an officer, called an Examiner, to check that all
formalities have been observed. The petitioners must prove to one of the
Examiners that procedure has been rightly followed, and this may be
challenged by any party by presenting a memorial. If the Examiner finds
that formalities have not been observed, he reports to each House and a
decision is made as to whether to strike out the petition or waive the
requirements of standing orders. A decision as to the House in which a
private Bill shall proceed is made at a meeting between the Chairman of
Committees in the House of Lords or his counsel, and the Chairman of
Ways and Means in the House of Commons or counsel to Speaker.

Where a private Bill proceeds first in the House of Lords, it has a first   **2-03**
reading, a purely formal process, and a second reading which is normally
formal, but which may be opposed. If it passes the second reading, any

opposed clauses (*i.e.* clauses against which a Petition or Petitions have been received) are committed to a Select Committee of five Lords. The House may agree to an Instruction to the Committee, usually to the effect that the Committee should have regard or be satisfied on certain matters before passing a provision in the Bill. An Instruction may go beyond the scope of any of the Petitions against a particular provision.

Procedure in this Committee largely follows the pattern of a judicial proceeding. A case is put by the promoters and objectors (or "petitioners"), through counsel practising at the Parliamentary Bar, and witnesses may be called. Government departments may also make representations. If there is opposition to the general principles of the Bill as they appear in the preamble, these arguments are normally taken first. If the Committee refuses to sanction the preamble, a report is made to the House and no further proceedings may be taken in that session unless the Bill is recommitted. If the preamble is approved, then each contested clause is argued and objectors may press for the inclusion of clauses to safeguard their interests.

2-04   Unopposed clauses (the great majority) are usually considered by the Committee on Unopposed Bills. This technically consists of the Lord Chairman of Committees and such Lords as think fit to attend, but usually there is simply an informal meeting conducted by the Lord Chairman with the assistance of his counsel. The promoters are represented by a parliamentary agent rather than counsel. Witnesses do not give evidence on oath. Representatives of government departments may attend. The Committee ensures that the promoters prove the requisite need for the provisions sought. A clause is disallowed (*a*) if the clause embodies a policy which does not commend itself to the Committee; (*b*) unless the clause is needed to such an extent as to counterbalance the presumed undesirability of enacting it; or (*c*) if the clause is wholly or partly covered by a public general Act. Unopposed clauses may instead be referred to a Select Committee. This is thought appropriate, for example, where the House agrees to an Instruction, or where important issues of principle are concerned.

The Bill is then reported to the House, with any amendments made in Committee, and given its third reading; it is then passed to the House of Commons, where all the stages are repeated. Proceedings in the House of Commons are very similar to those in the House of Lords, but there are some differences in detail. The Bill becomes an Act of Parliament on receiving the Royal Assent. The full details of this procedure are given in Erskine May, *Parliamentary Practice.*[1]

Validity of local legislation

2-05   Once a local Act has been passed its validity cannot be impugned on

---

[1] 20th ed., Part III.

the grounds that it had not passed through the proper procedure or that it was improperly obtained.[2]

> *Pickin* v. *British Railways Board*.[3] Section 18 of the British Railways Act 1968 (a private Act) stipulated that provisions in a large number of pre-1845 Railway Acts, whereby on abandonment or discontinuance of a railway the land was to revert to the owners for the time being of the adjacent land, should not apply to property of the board. P. sought a declaration that he was the owner of part of the land of a disused branch line. Part of his argument was that section 18 was ineffective to deprive him of his rights, on the grounds that standing orders had not been complied with, and that the board had fraudulently concealed certain matters from Parliament and its officers and thereby misled Parliament into passing the section. *Held*, the courts had no power to disregard an Act of Parliament, whether public or private, and could not examine Parliamentary proceedings to determine whether there had been any irregularity or fraud.

Enabling powers to promote or oppose legislation

A power to oppose a local or personal Bill is available to all local **2–06** authorities and joint authorities and the Inner London Education Authority, and a power to promote such a Bill is available to all authorities except parish and community councils.[4] A Bill may not be promoted to change a local government area or the Inner London Education Area, or an area's status or electoral arrangements.[5] A resolution to promote or to oppose a local or personal Bill requires a majority of the whole number of the council members. In the case of the promotion of a Bill 30 days' clear notice of the meeting and of the proposal must be given in the local press, and in the case of a proposal to oppose a Bill the period is 10 days. This is in addition to the ordinary notice.[6] Where the proposal is to promote a Bill, a further meeting must be called as soon as may be after the expiration of 14 days from the deposit of the Bill in Parliament. This second meeting is convened in the same way as the first and unless a majority of the whole members confirms the propriety of promoting the Bill it is withdrawn. A residuary body may oppose a local or personal Bill without complying with these requirements.[7]

A local Bill promoted by the council of a London borough may include provisions requested by another London borough council or by the Common Council; a Bill promoted by the Common Council may include provisions requested by any London borough council; and a Bill promoted by a metropolitan district council may include provisions requested by another metropolitan district council in the same county.

---

[2] *Edinburgh and Dalkeith Ry.* v. *Wauchope* (1842) 2 Cl. & F. 710; *Lee* v. *Bude and Torrington Junction Ry.* (1871) L.R. 6 C.P. 576.
[3] [1974] A.C. 765.
[4] Local Government Act 1972, s. 239, as amended by the Local Government Act 1985, Sched. 14, para. 32.
[5] *Ibid.* s. 70, as amended by the Local Government Act 1985, Sched. 14, para. 1.
[6] *Ibid.* Sched. 12.
[7] Local Government Act 1985, Sched. 13, para. 12(*h*).

The same requirements as to meetings apply to a requesting council as apply to a promoting council. The requesting council may contribute to the expenses of promotion.[8]

Clauses acts

2-07 In the earlier part of the nineteenth century, a very great number of private Bills were presented to Parliament and an attempt was made to secure a measure of uniformity by the provision of "model Bills" containing clauses usually found in private Acts of a given class, and setting out a convenient order. These models were not incorporated into standing orders and were not in any way formally recognised, but they were printed with the sanction of the Speaker and served as a guide to parliamentary agents.[9] A greater degree of uniformity was made possible by the introduction of the Clauses Consolidation Acts of 1845 and 1847, and the promotion of private legislation in particular fields was simplified and cheapened. The Clauses Acts contained a standard set of provisions which could readily be incorporated into any private Act—and indeed into any public Act. The Waterworks Clauses Act 1847, in the words of its preamble, consolidated " . . . in One Act certain Provisions usually contained in Acts authorising the Making of Waterworks for supplying Towns with Water." An undertaker requiring statutory authority to supply water would promote a "special Act" which authorised the construction of works and incorporated some or all of the provisions of the Waterworks Clauses Act. The provisions of the Town Police Clauses Act 1847 and the Towns Improvement Clauses Act 1847 similarly became operative by incorporation with a private Act, but some of the sections were incorporated into the Public Health Act 1875 and extended to all urban districts. The Lands Clauses Consolidation Act 1845 and the Cemeteries Clauses Act 1847 are further examples of statutes providing a set of provisions for incorporation into private legislation.

Construction of private Acts

2-08 In construing private Acts the rule is to interpret them strictly against the promoters, and liberally in favour of the public.[10] In *Altrincham Union Assessment Committee* v. *Cheshire Lines Committee*[11] Lord Esher M.R. said[12]:

> "Now it is quite true that there is some difference between a private Act of Parliament and a public one, but the only difference which I am aware of is as to the strictness of the construction to be given to it when there is any doubt as to the meaning. In the case of a public Act you construe it keeping in view the

---

[8] Local Government Act 1985, s. 87.
[9] H.C. (1847–48), 556 Qns. 226–228.
[10] *Bristol Guardians* v. *Bristol Waterworks Company* [1914] A.C. 379, and see *Craies on Statute Law* (7th ed.), Part IV, especially pp. 565–569.
[11] (1885) 15 Q.B.D. 597.
[12] At p. 602.

fact that it must be taken to have been passed for the public advantage, and you apply certain fixed canons to its construction. In the case of a private Act, which is obtained by persons for their own benefit, you construe more strictly provisions which they allege to be in their favour, because the persons who obtain a private Act ought to take care that it is so worded that that which they desire to obtain for themselves is plainly stated in it. But when the construction is perfectly clear, there is no difference between the modes of construing a private Act and a public Act, and, however difficult the construction of a private Act may be, when once the court has arrived at the true construction, after having subjected it to the strictest criticism, the consequences are precisely the same as in the case of a public Act. The moment you have arrived at the meaning of the legislature, the effect is the same in the one case as in the other."

Local legislation and local government reorganisation

Section 262 of the Local Government Act 1972 provides that local **2-09** legislation in force on April 1, 1974, remains in force, unless specifically dealt with, in the area to which it applied before that date, but the Secretary of State or any appropriate Minister may, by order, extend it to the whole of the new local government area. In order to encourage the rationalisation of the vast amount of local legislation all local Acts ceased to have effect in metropolitan counties at the end of 1980 (the end of June 1981 for Greater Manchester),[13] and will cease to have effect elsewhere in England and Wales outside Greater London at the end of 1986.[14] The Secretary of State or other appropriate Minister may, however, exempt a local provision from repeal or postpone the date on which local powers cease to apply.

The Secretary of State stated in DoE Circular 14/74 that there was a great deal of local legislation

"which should have been repealed many years ago, because it has been overtaken by general law, because it is no longer applicable in modern circumstances, because the powers are spent or because the provisions in question represent the sort of law that Parliament would not now be inclined to pass.... For the exercise to be worthwhile the process of pruning and redrafting must be drastic. From earlier experience it is thought that most local authorities will not need to re-enact more than a very small percentage of the legislation which they are inheriting...."

It was strongly recommended that county councils should co-ordinate the review of local legislation in their area, and that district councils should avoid submitting Bills.

The rationalisation process, and indeed private legislation procedure generally, has been considered by the House of Lords Select Committee on Practice and Procedure.[15] The Committee recommended (i) that further Miscellaneous Provisions Bills or Bills on particular topics should

[13] Metropolitan Counties (Local Statutory Provisions) Order 1979 (S.I. 1979 No. 969); Greater Manchester (Local Statutory Provisions) Order 1980 (S.I. 1980 No. 1845).
[14] Non-Metropolitan and Welsh Counties (Local Statutory Provisions) Order 1983 (S.I. 1983 No. 619).
[15] First Report, 1977–78 H.L. 155.

be introduced as public legislation; (ii) that consideration should be given to the possibility of making Miscellaneous Provisions Bills subject to a special procedure for non-controversial Bills; (iii) that local authorities should discuss the timetable of their promotions with the House authorities and the Department of the Environment at an early opportunity; (iv) that the arrangements for reaching agreement on common clauses should be continued and extended; and (v) that the modified procedure for the consideration of clauses common to more than one Bill by a single Select Committee should be used in future cases if the exercise in the 1977–78 session[16] proved successful. Otherwise, there was no need for fundamental change in private legislation procedure although a number of small reforms were desirable.[17] The Committee rejected proposals from counsel to the Lord Chairman of Committees which would in effect, although not in theory, have restricted the right of individual local authorities to petition for private legislation, with requests for additional legislation being channelled through a single local authority agency and a joint committee of the two Houses. These proposals were opposed by the local authority associations.

2-10   In 1973, the Department of the Environment set up a group on an informal basis to consider proposals for public legislation on local authorities' general powers, and the process of rationalising local legislation. This group consists of representatives of government departments, local authority associations and parliamentary agents, counsel to the Lord Chairman, and counsel to Mr. Speaker. It participated in the discussions leading to the Local Government (Miscellaneous Provisions) Act 1976. The House of Lords Select Committee on Practice and Procedure recommended that the powers of this group should be continued and expanded. It should be enabled to instruct parliamentary counsel to draft bills on agreed topics, subject to the demands of the Government's main legislative programme. This would assist the introduction of further public Miscellaneous Provisions Acts, a proposal which seems to be generally accepted as more appropriate for the development of local government than reliance on local legislation. A number of provisions of the kind found in local Acts were included in the Local Government (Miscellaneous Provisions) Act 1982.

B. Adoptive Acts

2-11   There are several statutory provisions which are effective within an area only after formal adoption by the authority concerned. The tendency in recent years has been to incorporate the provisions of adoptive Acts in legislation having general application. Many of the adoptive provisions of the Public Health Acts Amendment Act 1890 were incorporated in the

---

[16] See Report of the Select Committee, 1977–78 H.L. 137.
[17] 1977–78 H.L. 155, pp. x–xii.

Public Health Act 1936; and the Local Government Act 1972 extended (with few exceptions) the adoptive provisions of the Public Health Acts 1875 to 1925 to the whole of England and Wales whether adopted or not.[18] The following are examples of adoptive provisions which still remain:

  (a) Public Health Act 1925. The provisions with regard to the naming of streets.[19]
  (b) Highways Act 1980. The advance payments code.[20] Under the Local Government Act 1972 the code continued to apply where it previously applied: it can now be made to apply elsewhere in parishes and communities by resolution of the county council.[21]
  (c) Private Places of Entertainment (Licensing) Act 1967. This provision enables a licensing system to be administered by the adopting authority.
  (d) The provisions of the Local Government (Miscellaneous) Provisions Act 1976 which deal with hackney carriages and private hire vehicles.[22]
  (e) Unoccupied property rating provisions.[23]
  (f) Local Government (Miscellaneous Provisions) Act 1982. A number of the powers may be adopted by resolution.[24]

C. PROVISIONAL ORDERS

Provisional order procedure has been largely superseded by the use of **2-12** orders subject to special parliamentary procedure, and reference to it is therefore brief. It was introduced in the last century primarily to save local authorities and statutory bodies the expense involved in promoting private Bills, and many statutes made powers available by way of orders made by a Minister and confirmed by Parliament. The procedure to be followed in the making of a provisional order under the Local Government Act 1972, or any enactment passed on or after June 1, 1934, is contained in section 240 of the Local Government Act 1972. Publicity is given by the applicants, objections are considered by the Secretary of State, and a local inquiry is held unless he considers one to be unnecessary. It is open to the Secretary of State to make a provisional order and to submit it for confirmation to Parliament. If while the confirmation Bill is pending, a petition against the order is presented, the petitioner may appear before the Select Committee to

---

[18] Sched. 14, para. 23.
[19] ss. 17–19; Local Government Act 1972, Sched. 14, paras. 24 and 25.
[20] ss. 219–225.
[21] Highways Act 1980, s. 204(2)(c).
[22] Part II, ss. 45–80.
[23] General Rate Act 1967, s. 17.
[24] e.g. s. 1(2) (licensing of public entertainments); s. 2 (control of sex establishments); s. 3 (street trading).

which the Bill is referred and he may oppose the order as if it were a
private Bill. An order which extends the area for which any local
statutory provision is in force must be provisional only.[25] An example of
such an extension is the Royal County of Berkshire (Public Entertainment) Provisional Order Confirmation Act 1976. The procedure which
applies to the making of orders under statutes before June 1, 1934, is
given in those statutes.

D. ORDERS SUBJECT TO SPECIAL PARLIAMENTARY PROCEDURE

2-13   The Statutory Orders (Special Procedure) Act 1945[26] introduced a
simpler way of acquiring powers. An order is first made by the
Minister concerned, and when the preliminary proceedings in the
enabling Act have been complied with it is laid before Parliament. The
procedural requirements include the giving of notice in the *London
Gazette*, and, where the order relates to any particular area, in at least
one newspaper circulating in that area. The notice must state how
objections may be lodged, and if objections are raised and not
withdrawn the Minister must consider them, holding a local inquiry
unless satisfied that there are special circumstances which render this
unnecessary.

When the order is laid before Parliament, petitions against it may be
lodged within 21 days of its submission. Petitions of objection are of
two kinds: petitions for amendment, praying for particular and specific
amendments, and petitions of general objection, praying against the
order generally. All petitions are referred to the Lord Chairman of
Committees of the House of Lords and the Chairman of Ways and
Means of the House of Commons. In due course they report to each
House whether objections have been presented against the order, and,
if there have been objections, whether they are proper to be received,
and whether they are petitions for amendment or petitions of general
objection. If within 21 days of this report either House resolves that the
order be annulled it becomes void and no further proceedings may be
taken with respect to it. If no such resolution of annulment is passed
then one of three things may happen. If there is no petition against the
order it comes into operation at the end of the resolution period; if
there is a petition for amendment the order stands referred to a joint
committee of both Houses; if there is a petition of general objection it
stands referred to the joint committee, unless either House resolves to
the contrary.

Where an order is referred to the joint committee, the committee
may report the order with or without amendment. If it is without

---

[25] Local Government Act 1972, ss. 254(8) and 262(10).
[26] As amended by the Statutory Orders (Special Procedure) Act 1965 and the Local
    Government Act 1972, s. 240.

amendment the order comes into operation on the day the report is laid before Parliament; if the order contains an amendment it will take effect as amended on a day fixed by the Minister, but if the Minister considers it expedient he may withdraw the order or may cause it to be submitted to Parliament for further consideration by means of a Confirmation Bill.

E. The Influence of Local Authorities in the Legislative Field

There are two important ways in which this influence is exerted. First, **2-14** over many years individual local authorities have promoted private Bills giving them powers not otherwise available, and other authorities, recognising the general usefulness of some of these provisions, have written them into their private Bills. The inclusion of common form clauses is facilitated by the existence of a code of Model Clauses prepared by a committee appointed by the Chairman of Committees of the House of Lords and the Chairman of Ways and Means of the House of Commons. Many of these clauses have ultimately found their way into general legislation. The Highways Act 1980 contains a number of provisions formerly in a Model.[27] Examples are the provisions in the Act relating to crossings over footways[28] and to the prevention of evasion of private street works charges.[29]

Secondly, the local authority associations exert a constant influence in legislative matters, by formal process and informally. This influence is exercised in the following ways:

(a) in bringing to the notice of government departments alleged defects in the law affecting directly or indirectly the status or the work of local authorities;

(b) in examining proposals for new legislation, whether sponsored by the Government, private members or other bodies, and making representations in what is conceived to be the general interest of the member authorities represented;

(c) in furthering what is considered by the associations to be the right kind of relationship between the central government and local authorities, both generally and in particular instances of administrative practice; and

(d) in taking part in that informal process of government—the "sounding" process where senior civil servants informally discuss in the broadest terms ideas for projected legislation and administrative arrangements.

No major change in law or administrative practice which concerns local government is introduced without consultation with the local

---

[27] Report of the Committee on Consolidation of Highway Law, Cmnd. 630, para. 9.
[28] Highways Act 1980, s. 184.
[29] *Ibid.* s. 235.

authority associations, taking the form of an exchange of memoranda or the submission of observations or the holding of conferences. When proposed legislation has reached Bill form it is examined by the associations clause by clause, and new clauses and amendments to existing clauses are submitted and deletions urged. A Bill is rarely the subject of discussion before it is laid on the table, though doubtless the substance of particular clauses is settled in general consultations.

Chapter 3

LOCAL AUTHORITY AREAS AND STATUS

This chapter deals with the following topics: areas and status; provisions **3-01** as to alteration in area and status; electoral areas; miscellaneous related provisions; financial and other adjustments; changes in name; re-organisation of status and functions under the Local Government Act 1985.

A. Areas and Status

Counties and districts

The Local Government Act 1972 divided England and Wales **3-02** (excluding Greater London) into 53 counties and 369 districts. Six of the counties are metropolitan counties and the districts within them, 36 in number, are metropolitan districts.[1] The areas and names of counties appear in the Act: the areas of metropolitan districts also appear in the Act and their names were given by the Secretary of State by order.[2] The areas of districts in Wales are given in the Act and their names in an order made by the Secretary of State.[3] Non-metropolitan districts were defined and named by order.[4] The Local Government Act 1985 abolished the metropolitan county councils with effect from April 1, 1986, and redistributed their functions among the metropolitan districts and a number of joint authorities established to undertake specific functions. The areas of metropolitan counties continue as local government areas for certain purposes, for example as the areas under the control of the new joint authorities.

The councils which govern the areas of non-metropolitan counties and all districts are principal councils, a term which includes London borough councils.[5]

Parishes

Where rural parishes, whether separate or grouped, were in existence **3-03** before April 1, 1974, they continued to exist from that date by the name

---

[1] ss. 1 and 20. England does not include what was formerly the administrative county of Monmouthshire or the county borough of Newport: s. 1(12). As to London, see Chap. 28.

[2] Sched. 1 and Metropolitan Districts (Names) Order 1973 (S.I. 1973 No. 137).

[3] Sched. 4 and Districts in Wales (Names) Order 1973 (S.I. 1973 No. 34).

[4] English Non-Metropolitan Districts (Definition) Order 1972 (S.I. 1972 No. 2039); English Non-Metropolitan Districts (Names) Order 1973 (S.I. 1973 No. 551).

[5] Local Government Act 1972, s. 270 (definition of "principal area") as amended by the Local Government Act 1985, Sched. 15, para. 8(*b*).

of parishes, and a rural borough, created under section 28 of the Local Government Act 1958, ceased to be a borough but continued in the status of a parish.[6] Provision is made in the Act for a further category. The Local Government Boundary Commission for England (this body is referred to at paragraph 3–13) was required in 1973 to consult existing local authorities with a view to making proposals to the Secretary of State for the constitution of parishes by reference to the areas of existing boroughs and urban districts, areas which were to be merged with other units in local government reorganisation.[7]

3–04   The Secretary of State's guidelines to the Commission contained the following paragraph:

> "When making proposals in accordance with these provisions the Commission should have regard to the policy of the Government, now reflected in the Act, with regard to statutory authorities at parish level. The Act provides for the retention of existing rural parishes with their parish councils or parish meetings. The Government's further view, as explained in Parliament, is that small towns which are at present boroughs or urban districts should retain elected councils at parish level where such towns are broadly comparable in size and character with other small towns or villages which at present have rural parish councils. But it is the Government's view that statutory authorities should not be established at parish level (at any rate for the present) for areas which are essentially parts of larger towns or of continuously built-up areas.... No absolute maximum figure is prescribed but the limited range of functions available to parish councils and the fact that much of their importance lies in the fact that they act as the focus for local opinion, do not point to the desirability of large units at this level: many towns of the order of 10,000–20,000 (as well as those below this range) might well qualify."

The recommendations of the Commission were accepted by the Government and promulgated by order and the councils of these authorities became successor parish councils.[8] Each order provided that as from the date of its operation members of the existing councils also became parish councillors.[9]

3–05   Every parish is required to have a parish meeting.[10] In general terms a small parish may have a parish council if it chooses, a large parish is obliged to have a parish council, and parishes whether large or small may be grouped under a common council if they so agree. The detailed rules are as follows. The district council is required to establish a parish council by order if a parish has 200 electors or more, or if the meeting of a parish with more than 150 and less than 200 electors so decides. The district council has a discretion to establish a parish council in a parish with less than 150 electors where the parish meeting so requests. A district council may by order create groups of

---

[6] Local Government Act 1972, s. 1.
[7] Local Government Act 1972, Sched. 1, Part V.
[8] Local Government (Successor Parishes) Orders 1973 (S.I. 1973 No. 1110, S.I. 1973 No. 1939) and 1974 (S.I. 1974 No. 565).
[9] The enabling power is in the Local Government Act 1972, Sched. 3, para. 13(2).
[10] Local Government Act 1972, ss. 9–12.

parishes with a common council at the request and with the consent of the parish meetings concerned.

Where the population of a parish has no more than 150 local government electors the parish meeting may ask the district council to dissolve the parish council and the district council may do so. If the application is rejected two years must elapse before a fresh request may be made.

Communities

Districts in Wales are divided into communities. These are the areas **3-06** of what were formerly the boroughs, urban districts and rural parishes in Wales, and certain divided parts of former urban districts. The names of the communities are those of the areas which they succeeded except in the case of the divided urban districts—their names appear in statute.[11]

A parish council existing on March 31, 1974, automatically became a community council on April 1, 1974. An existing borough or urban district council could apply before 1973 to the Secretary of State for an order creating a community council for the area and where this was done the Secretary of State was obliged to accede to the request. It was open to the Secretary of State to make such an order, after such consultations as he thought proper, if an application was received after 1972 or if the existing council refused to make an application. This provision did not apply to six large towns—Cardiff, Merthyr Tydfil, Newport, Port Talbot, Rhondda, and Swansea.[12]

A district council is obliged to establish a community council if the community meeting so resolves and it must dissolve a community council if the meeting so requests.[13]

Joint authorities

Part IV of the Local Government Act 1985 established for each of the **3-07** six metropolitan counties (1) a metropolitan county police authority; (2) a metropolitan county fire and civil defence authority; and (3) a metropolitan county passenger transport authority. They are referred to collectively as "joint authorities." Each is a body corporate. With one exception, each is known by the name of the county, with the addition of the relevant description. The exception is the Northumbria Police Authority, which is the authority for the metropolitan county of Tyne and Wear and the non-metropolitan county of Northumberland. Part IV also established a London fire and civil defence authority.[14]

---

[11] Local Government Act 1972, s. 20(4), Sched. 4, Part III.
[12] *Ibid.* s. 27.
[13] *Ibid.* s. 28.
[14] Local Government Act 1985, ss. 23–28.

Residuary bodies

3-08   Part VII of the Local Government Act 1985 established a "residuary body" for London and for each of the six metropolitan counties. Each residuary body is a body corporate and consists of between five and ten members appointed by the Secretary of State. They have various responsibilities arising out of the abolition of the Greater London Council and the metropolitan county councils, including the making of redundancy and compensation payments, pensions and the custody of property for which provision is not otherwise made.

The status of borough

3-09   A district council may petition Her Majesty for the grant of a charter conferring upon the district the status of borough.[15] The resolution authorising the petition requires a two-thirds majority at a specially convened meeting of the council. Where Her Majesty by the advice of the Privy Council grants a charter the district becomes a borough, the district council becomes the borough council and the chairman and vice-chairman of the council are entitled to the style of mayor and deputy mayor respectively.

The status of town

3-10   The council of a parish or community, by a simply majority, may resolve to adopt the status of town.[16] The council becomes the town council and the chairman and vice-chairman are known as town mayor and deputy town mayor respectively.

Privileges of former cities and boroughs

3-11   The Act makes provision for the retention of some of the privileges and dignities of former local authorities.[17] Although it abolished boroughs and cities as units of government and accordingly brought to an end the rights to borough status conferred by royal charter, these charters were neither abrogated nor surrendered. All other rights and privileges belonging to a borough or city were specifically preserved, subject, of course, to any contrary provision appearing in the charter granted to the district of which the borough or city was part, and subject to any contrary provision in the Act itself. An obligation is put on any authority to whom charters and insignia of an abolished borough are transferred to preserve them, so far as practicable, in the area of the former authority.[18]

There are several ways in which former rights and privileges survived. First, many former boroughs and cities virtually became the new districts and those new districts were able to incorporate within the new charter

[15] Local Government Act 1972, s. 245.
[16] *Ibid.* s. 245.
[17] *Ibid.* s. 246.
[18] *Ibid.* s. 254.

many of the inherited rights and privileges. Secondly, many smaller boroughs became successor parishes and their councils adopted the status of town. Thirdly, the Act made provision to enable a former borough, in a district which does not petition for a charter conferring borough status on it, to retain an identity through charter trustees, a body corporate consisting of the district councillors representing the former borough. If the number of councillors is less than three, the district council may make up the difference by appointing local government electors for the area of the former borough. The charter trustees are enabled to elect one of their number as city mayor or town mayor as the case may be.[19]

Where the area of any charter trustees becomes comprised in a borough, upon the grant of a charter under section 245, the charter trustees continue in being without alteration of their powers, and the privileges and rights of the inhabitants of that area are unaffected.[20]

A part of the preserved rights are those concerned with the appointment of local officers of dignity—these would include sheriffs of cities and towns, high stewards, honorary recorders and the like.[21] The status and rights of freemen are undisturbed.[22]

Prerogative titles and armorial bearings

Many former authorities bore the title of city or royal borough, and 3-12 their mayors were variously addressed, in some cases by the prefix "the right honourable," or "the right worshipful," and in some cities the mayor held the title of lord mayor. A continuation of these titles lies within the royal prerogative, exercised by the Queen on the advice of the Secretary of State for the Home Department. Such titles are conferred by Letters Patent.

Specific provision is made for the transfer of armorial bearings from the former authorities to the newly created authorities.[23]

B. ALTERATIONS IN AREA AND STATUS

Part IV of the Local Government Act 1972 established permanent 3-13 machinery for the review of local government areas. Two Commissions were set up, the Local Government Boundary Commission for England and the Local Government Boundary Commission for Wales.[24] Both are bodies corporate. The first consists of a chairman, deputy chairman and not more than five members: the second consists of a chairman, deputy chairman and not more than three members, and one of them must be Welsh speaking. Membership of the Commissions is an office of profit

---

[19] Local Government Act 1972, s. 246. See also the Charter Trustees Order 1974 (S.I. 1974 No. 176).
[20] *Ibid.* s. 246, as amended by the Charter Trustees Act 1985.
[21] *Ibid.* s. 246.
[22] *Ibid.* s. 248. As to honorary freemen, see § 27–26.
[23] *Ibid.* s. 247, and orders made thereunder.
[24] *Ibid.* ss. 46 and 53, and Scheds. 7 and 8.

under the Crown—this means that their members cannot sit in the House of Commons. The Commissioners are empowered to delegate to others the work of any particular investigation.

This is the third set of Commissions in the post-war period. There was first the Local Government Boundary Commission of 1945, brought to an end by the Local Boundary Commission (Dissolution) Act 1949, and secondly the Local Government Commission for England and Local Government Commission for Wales set up in 1958 and dissolved by the Local Government (Termination of Reviews) Act 1967. It is noted in passing that the bodies established to deal with parliamentary constituencies, the Boundary Commission for England and Boundary Commission for Wales, established in 1944, are still in operation.

The Commissions are basically advisory bodies. Their recommendations are submitted to the Secretary of State and become effective when contained in an order made by him.

The English Commission

3-14   The Commission is under a duty to undertake a regular review of certain areas at intervals of not less than 10 years and not more than 15 years, subject to directions given by the Secretary of State. These are the non-metropolitan counties in England, all metropolitan districts, all London boroughs, and the boundaries between Greater London and the counties adjoining it, between the City of London and adjacent London boroughs and between each of the metropolitan counties and the non-metropolitan counties adjoining it. It is open to the Secretary of State to vary the interval between reviews either for a whole review or for a particular case or class of case. A variation is made simply by a direction of the Secretary of State.[25] Between periodic reviews the Commission may carry out an ad hoc review of any particular area. In the case of non-metropolitan districts there is a broad duty to keep them under review and no timings are given. Any local authority or parish meeting may invite the Commission to undertake a review.

As will be noted later it is the duty of districts to keep the boundaries of parishes under review but it is open to the Commission, in certain circumstances, itself to take the initiative.

The Secretary of State is empowered to direct the holding or postponement of reviews.[26] He may order a review of a district or a review of the principal areas in England as a whole or a review of one or more

---

[25] Local Government Act 1972, s. 48, as amended by the Local Government Act 1985, Sched. 16, para. 5. The Secretary of State has varied the first interval so that the first review must be conducted not less than ten or more than eighteen years after April 1, 1974: DoE Circular 12/84. This was necessitated by the postponement of reviews in metropolitan areas: *infra* n. 26.

[26] *Ibid.* s. 49. The Secretary of State has directed the English Commission not to undertake any review of the areas and boundaries of authorities affected by the abolition of the Greater London Council and the metropolitan counties: DoE Circular 12/84.

areas or parts of areas. Similarly, the Secretary of State may direct the Commission not to undertake during a specified period a review of any one or more areas or parts of areas.

The object of all reviews is to consider if change is called for and, if it is, to formulate proposals. The proposals may be far-reaching. The Commission is to have in mind "the interests of effective and convenient local government," a phrase drawn from Part II of the Local Government Act 1958 and referred to again later in paragraph 3–26. There is a wide variety of means by which change may come about. The Commission may recommend any of the following steps or a combination of any of the following steps[27]:

(*a*) the alteration of a local government area;

(*b*) the constitution of a new local government area of any description outside Greater London by the amalgamation of two or more areas of the like description or by the aggregation of parts of such areas of the like description or by the separation of part of such an area of the like description;

(*c*) the abolition of a principal area of any description outside Greater London and its distribution among other areas of the like description;

(*d*) the constitution of a new London borough by the amalgamation of two or more London boroughs or by the aggregation of parts of London boroughs or by the separation of part of a London borough;

(*e*) the abolition of a London borough and the distribution of its area among other London boroughs;

(*f*) the constitution of a new parish by—
  (i) the establishment of any area which is not a parish or part of one as a parish; or
  (ii) the aggregation of the whole or any part of any such area with one or more parishes or parts of parishes;

(*g*) the abolition of a parish with or without the distribution of its area among other parishes;

(*h*) a change of electoral arrangements for any local government area which is either consequential on any change in local government areas proposed under the foregoing, or is a change which is independent of any change in local government areas so proposed—this latter kind of change is known as substantive change and is referred to later in paragraph 3–25.

The English Commission is required to submit a report to the Secretary **3-15** of State following a review, and there is provision for interim reports. A report will contain the Commission's proposals or will state that having carried out the review it has no proposals to make. No provision is made for public inquiries, statutory consultations and conferences by the Secretary of State as applied under earlier legislation but he may not give effect to proposals put to him until six weeks have passed from the time he received them. This enables objections to be made to the Commission's proposals. The Secretary of State may by order give effect to the Commission's proposals with or without modification. If he decides to

---

[27] Local Government Act 1972, s. 47, as amended by the Local Government Act 1985, Sched. 16, para. 4 and Sched. 17.

make an order with modification he may, if he chooses, ask the Commission to conduct a further review and to make revised proposals. An order made by the Secretary of State is by statutory instrument: it is subject to negative resolution of either House of Parliament if it alters the areas of any authority other than a parish, or abolishes any authority other than a parish.[28]

3-16   The Secretary of State is empowered to give the Commission directions for guidance in conducting reviews. Where a direction concerns all reviews, or reviews of any class or a single review of all or any class of principal areas in England, the Secretary of State must first consult the local authority associations. A direction may be given to the Commission with respect to the order in which a review of areas is to be undertaken.

The Welsh Commission

3-17   The first major task of the Welsh Commission was to undertake a review of Wales with a view to the making of changes in the areas, councils and electoral arrangements of communities and with respect to the initial review of electoral arrangements for counties and districts in Wales.[29]

3-18   It is the continuing duty of the Welsh Commission to keep under review all counties and districts in Wales. It is not related to specified periods of time.[30] The Secretary of State for Wales may give directions as to the holding of reviews, but, unlike the arrangement in England, he is not empowered to give directions not to undertake reviews during a specified period. As is the case in England, the Secretary of State for Wales may give directions to the Welsh Commission for their guidance in conducting reviews.[31] If a direction concerns all reviews, or reviews of any class or a single review of all or any class of the principal areas in Wales, the Secretary of State must first consult the appropriate local authority associations. A local authority may ask for a review to be carried out.

3-19   If the Commission considers it desirable in the interests of effective and convenient local government, it may make proposals for change to the Secretary of State. The Commission's proposals may consist of any of the following or a combination of one or more of them.

(*a*) the alteration of a local government area;

(*b*) the constitution of a new local government area of any description by the amalgamation of two or more such areas of the like description or by the aggregation of parts of such areas of the like description or by the separation of part of such an area of the like description;

(*c*) the abolition of a local government area of any description and its distribution among other areas of the like description;

---

[28] *Semble* an injunction will not lie to restrain the Secretary of State from submitting an order alleged to be *ultra vires*: *Harper* v. *Secretary of State* [1955] Ch. 238.
[29] Local Government Act 1972, s. 64 and Sched. 10.
[30] *Ibid.* ss. 54, 55.
[31] *Ibid.* s. 59.

(*d*) the constitution of a new community by—
  (i) the establishment of any area which is not a community or part of one as a community;
  (ii) the aggregation of the whole or any part of any such area with one or more communities or parts of communities;
(*e*) a change of electoral arrangements for any local government area which is either consequential on any change in local government areas proposed under the foregoing or is a substantive change. Arrangements for substantive change are referred to later at paragraph 3–25.

Whenever a review is undertaken, the Commission must have regard to **3-20** the system of community councils and is required, *inter alia*, to consider whether to make a proposal for the constitution or dissolution of a community council.[32]

The rules as to the submission of reports by the Commission to the Secretary of State for Wales and the rules as to their implementation correspond to those which apply in England,[33] and an order altering the area of a county or district or abolishing it is subject to a negative resolution of either House of Parliament.

The duties of district councils

It is the duty of each district council in England to keep the whole of its **3-21** district under review for the purpose of considering whether or not to make proposals to the English Commission as to the constitution of new parishes, the abolition of parishes, or the alteration of parishes. A parish council may ask the district council to undertake a review and it must consider the matter unless in its opinion to do so would impede the proper discharge of its general functions in the matter of review.[34] The duty of review relates to the whole of a district including areas not within parishes. The power of the Secretary of State to direct the holding or postponement of reviews, referred to above, applies equally to districts as to the Commissions. When a district has carried out a review it submits a report to the Commission and the Commission, in turn, may make proposals to the Secretary of State, with or without modification. If the Commission thinks the proposals submitted, even with modification, are not apt for securing effective and convenient local government, or where the district has reported that it will not recommend the Commission to make proposals, the Commission itself may undertake a review. The Commission's proposals, whether its own or those of the district council which it accepts, are submitted to the Secretary of State and he may make an order to give effect to them, either with or without modification.

A similar duty falls to the councils of districts in Wales to keep their areas under review in order to consider recommendations for the constitution of new communities, the abolition of communities, and the

---

[32] Local Government Act 1972, s. 55(5).
[33] *Ibid.* s. 58.
[34] *Ibid.* s. 48(8),(9).

alteration of communities.[35] A district council is obliged to consider a request made by a community council or community meeting to undertake a review, though the council may refuse the request if in its opinion to do what is asked would impede the proper discharge of its functions in relation to review. Subsequent procedure is similar to that which applies in England, except that if a district council intends to make a recommendation for a change in a local government area, it must also consider the community council arrangements.

Procedure for reviews

3-22   The procedure applies alike to England and Wales.[36] A Commission or district council proposing to conduct a review is required to take a number of steps to see that interested parties are aware of what is proposed to be done, and each must take account of representations made. There must first be consultations with all local authorities whose areas are affected and with any other local authorities and public bodies which would appear to be concerned. There must additionally be consultations with bodies representative of staff employed by local authorities who have asked to be consulted and consultations with such other persons as the Commission or district council thinks fit. Steps must be taken to see that persons who may be interested in the review are informed of draft proposals or recommendations and of the place where the relevant documents may be inspected. The Commission or council must then take account of representations which are made within the period of deposit, and a final decision must take account of them.

Where recommendations are made by a district council following a review, the Commission may consult the council of any other local government area affected and such other bodies and persons as it thinks fit.

If a commission or a district council wishes to hold a local inquiry it may do so, and in that event the provisions with regard to subpoena, penalty for failure to attend and the award of costs would apply.[37]

3-23   Particular procedural rules apply to the alteration in boundaries between English and Welsh counties.[38] Joint proposals may be made by the English and Welsh Commissions with the consent of the counties concerned. Before making proposals they are obliged to give publicity to the proposed review, to prepare draft proposals, available for public inspection, and to receive objections, holding a local inquiry if thought fit. Powers were not available under earlier legislation to the former Local

---

[35] Local Government Act 1972, s. 55(2),(3).

[36] *Ibid.* s. 60. Regulations may be made prescribing procedure. The Secretary of State has indicated that he does not intend to make such regulations, in order to leave the Commission as much flexibility in their arrangements as possible: DoE Circular 12/84, para. 15.

[37] *Ibid.* ss. 61 and 250.

[38] *Ibid.* s. 62, as amended by the Local Government Act 1985, Sched. 16, para. 6.

Government Commissions for England and Wales to propose an alteration to the boundary between the two countries.

C. ELECTORAL AREAS

Part IV of the Local Government Act 1972 provides permanent **3-24** machinery for the review of electoral areas through the Local Government Boundary Commissions of England and Wales.

Arrangements for review [39]

It is the duty of each Commission to carry out periodic reviews for the **3-25** purpose of making proposals for changes in electoral areas. The Commissions must do this at intervals of not less than 10 years or more than 15 years, but an authority or other person may ask the Commission to carry out a review at any time. When the Commission has finished its review, it submits a report and recommendations to the Secretary of State for the Home Department, and he may make an order giving effect to them as they stand or with modification, in the same way and subject to the same rules which apply to the making of orders as to boundary and other changes.

It is the duty of a district council in England to review the electoral arrangements of parishes within the area and it may make appropriate orders. The council must consider a request for a review made by a parish council or by at least 30 electors in the parish. A request by a parish council or by at least 30 electors may be made to the Commission and where this is done the Commission may send recommendations to the district council, who may make an order accordingly, or with such modifications as the Commission may accept. If the district council does not agree with the Commission or defaults in making a recommended order, the Commission may make its own proposals direct to the Secretary of State for the Home Department.

Similarly expressed provisions apply to Wales and to communities in Wales.

The changes here described are "substantive changes." A substantive change is defined as a change in electoral arrangements for any local government area which is independent of a change in the boundaries of that area. [40]

Factors relevant to change

There are a number of rules to be observed in considering electoral **3-26** arrangements. [41] In the case of counties, the number of electors in each electoral division is to be roughly the same, electoral divisions may not be

---

[39] Local Government Act 1972, ss. 50 and 57.
[40] *Ibid.* s. 78.
[41] *Ibid.* Sched. 11.

split between districts and parishes and communities may not be split as between electoral divisions. In the case of London boroughs and districts there must be, as nearly as may be, an equal number of electors per councillor in each of the wards, but this principle is overridden by the requirement in section 47(1) of the Act that changes should be "in the interests of effective and convenient local government."[42] In parishes and communities, before deciding whether to introduce wards, regard must be had to the question whether the number and distribution of electors is such as to make a single election of councillors impracticable or inconvenient, and to the desirability of any areas being separately represented on the council.

Whenever changes are being considered, thought must be given to local ties and to the production of easily identifiable boundaries.

D. Miscellaneous Provisions

3-27 The Secretary of State has a general power under section 266 of the Local Government Act 1972 to revoke by a later order any order made under the Act. But there is a limitation to this power so far as orders made under Part IV of the Act are concerned. The power is limited to the supplementary provisions in the order, and before a change of this kind is made certain procedural steps must be taken.[43]

A restriction is placed on the promotion of private Bills. No authority has power to promote a Bill for forming, abolishing or altering any local government area or the Inner London Education Area or for the alteration of status or for the alteration of electoral arrangements.[44]

The Act brought certainty into the matter of seaward boundaries. In the case of some authorities, seaward boundaries were fixed by local Act, but generally speaking they were fixed by reference to the limit of medium tides. The matter is now brought within the review of the Commissions.[45]

E. Financial and Other Adjustments[46]

3-28 The Secretary of State has power to make regulations of general application to deal with consequential and transitional arrangements which are needed following the making of orders under Part IV of the

---

[42] *Enfield London Borough Council* v. *Local Government Boundary Commission* [1979] 3 All E.R. 747.
[43] Local Government Act 1972, s. 69.
[44] *Ibid.* s. 70, as amended by the Local Government Act 1985, Sched. 14, para. 1.
[45] *Ibid.* s. 71. As to accretions from the sea, see s. 72; as to the alteration of boundaries where the line of a watercourse changes, see s. 73.
[46] *Ibid.* ss. 67 and 68.

Local Government Act 1972.[47] The regulations may deal with the transfer of property, rights and liabilities, functions and staff. Other matters (the name of a new area and its constitution, for example), may be dealt with in local orders. Agreements may be entered into by the bodies involved to deal with property and finance, and provision is made for arbitration where agreement is not reached.

F. CHANGES OF NAME OF LOCAL AUTHORITY AREAS[48]

The council of a county, district or London borough may change its name **3-29** by a two-thirds majority at a specially convened meeting of the council.[49] The name of a parish and the name of a community may be changed by the district council at the request of the parish council, or parish meeting where there is no parish council, or at the request of the community council, or community meeting where there is no community council.

G. RE-ORGANISATION OF STATUS AND FUNCTIONS UNDER THE LOCAL GOVERNMENT ACT 1985

As has already been noted, the Local Government Act 1985 abolished **3-30** the Greater London Council and the six metropolitan county councils. Provision was made under this Act for the transfer of functions, and the new arrangements are set out in this book in the Chapters on specific functions. Provision was also made for the transfer and compensation of staff[50] and the transfer of property. Most functions were transferred to London borough councils and metropolitan district councils respectively. In London and in each metropolitan county, the successor councils were required to establish a joint committee to co-ordinate arrangements for the transfer of functions. Such committees were required, *inter alia*, to consider whether any of those functions could with advantage be discharged jointly by those councils or any of them by virtue of arrangements made under section 101 of the Local Government Act 1972,[51] and to consult and co-operate with the new joint authorities, the Inner London Education Authority, any other body to which functions or property were transferred, and the staff commission.[52] Furthermore, it was the express duty of both the abolished and successor authorities and their officers to co-operate with each other and generally to exercise their functions so as to facilitate

---

[47] See Local Government Area Changes Regulations 1976 (S.I. 1976 No. 246) as amended by S.I. 1978 No. 247, and Local Government (Changes in Electoral Arrangements) Regulations 1985 (S.I. 1985 No. 110).
[48] Local Government Act 1972, ss. 74–76.
[49] In February 1980, Salop County Council resolved to change the name of the county to Shropshire.
[50] See § 4–39.
[51] See. §§ 4–48, 4–59.
[52] Local Government Act 1985, s. 95.

the implementation of the 1985 Act and any transfer of functions, property or staff.[53]

The Secretary of State had power to make orders before the abolition date for the transfer on that date of property, rights and liabilities.[54] He may at any time by order make such incidental, consequential, transitional or supplementary provision as appears to him necessary or expedient.[55]

The Secretary of State has special powers of control over joint authorities and the Inner London Education Authority.[56] These powers are to be exercised

> "with a view to securing that the functions of a new authority are discharged economically, efficiently and effectively in the period beginning with its establishment and ending three years after the abolition date...."

3-31　The Secretary of State may, by regulations,[57] provide for the submission to him by the authority, or the making by him, of schemes with respect to the discharge of the authority's functions so far as concerned with:

(a) the number of persons employed by the authority, or employed by it for a particular purpose;

(b) the authority's arrangements for obtaining services, supplies or facilities;

(c) the authority's organisation and its arrangements for managing its affairs;

(d) in the case of a police authority, the number of persons constituting the establishment of the police force maintained by it; and

(e) in the case of a fire authority, the number of persons constituting the establishment of any fire brigade maintained by it.

The authority must in this initial period discharge its functions in accordance with any scheme approved or made by the Secretary of State.

3-32　The Secretary of State also had special powers of control over the Greater London Council and metropolitan county councils in the period leading up to abolition. These required his consent for:

(a) financial and other assistance to local authorities after July 24, 1984[58];

---

[53] *Ibid.* s. 97.
[54] *Ibid.* s. 100.
[55] *Ibid.* s. 101.
[56] *Ibid.* s. 85.
[57] See the Police Authorities (Establishment and Support Services Schemes) (Metropolitan Counties and Northumbria Police Area) Regulations 1985 (S.I. 1985 No. 1302); the Fire and Civil Defence Authorities (Establishment, Support Services and Management Schemes) Regulations 1985 (S.I. 1985 No. 1303).
[58] Local Government Act 1985, s. 91 and Sched. 15.

(b) expenditure after April 1, 1985 under section 137 of the Local Government Act 1972[59];

(c) disposals of land after July 31, 1984[60];

(d) the entering of certain contracts after July 31, 1984[61]; and

(e) arrangements after March 21, 1985, for the assumption of certain liabilities.[62]

Finally, there is provision for the Secretary of State to reorganise the allocation of functions transferred to joint authorities under the 1985 Act.[63] For example, he may by order constitute a metropolitan district council as a police authority, and a metropolitan district council, London borough council or the Common Council as a fire authority. He may allocate passenger transport functions to a metropolitan district or London borough council.

[59] Local Government (Interim Provisions) Act 1984, s. 7.
[60] *Ibid.* s. 8.
[61] *Ibid.* s. 9 and the Local Government Act 1985, s. 93.
[62] Local Government Act 1985, s. 92.
[63] *Ibid.* s. 42.

CHAPTER 4

THE ADMINISTRATIVE MACHINERY OF LOCAL AUTHORITIES

4-01　THE subject-matter of this Chapter is considered under the following headings: the constitution of councils, joint authorities and committees; meetings; members; officers; the disposal of local authority business; publication of information and the Commissions for Local Administration for England and Wales.

A. CONSTITUTION OF COUNCILS, JOINT AUTHORITIES AND COMMITTEES[1]

4-02　A principal council consists of the chairman and councillors. The council's members are elected at local elections.[2] The chairman is elected annually by the council from among its members and his election is the first business to be transacted at the annual meeting. The council is required to appoint a vice-chairman, and, subject to standing orders, he may undertake whatever is required to be done by the chairman. The council may pay to each a reasonable allowance to cover the expense of office.[3] Similar rules apply to the chairman and vice-chairman of a joint authority.[4] The chairman of a district council has precedence in his district but not so as prejudicially to affect Her Majesty's royal prerogative. Where a district council has been granted a charter the chairman and vice-chairman have the style of mayor and deputy mayor respectively.

A parish council consists of the chairman and members of the council. The council's members are elected at local elections. The chairman is elected annually by the council from among its members and his election is the first business to be transacted at the annual meeting. A vice-chairman may be appointed by the council from among its members. An allowance may be paid to the chairman, but not to the vice-chairman. Similar rules apply to the constitution of community councils. In certain circumstances the chairman and vice-chairman of a parish or community

---

[1] Local Government Act 1972, ss. 2–5, 13–15, 33, 34. As to the particular rules which apply to London authorities, see Chap. 28; and as to joint authorities and residuary bodies, see the Local Government Act 1985, Parts IV and VII.
[2] See generally Chap. 13.
[3] The power to make an allowance must be exercised in good faith: see *Att.-Gen.* v. *Blackburn Corporation* (1887) 57 L.T. 385 and *Att.-Gen.* v. *Cardiff Corporation* [1894] 2 Ch. 337. In the latter case an increase was made in the mayor's salary. The additional amount was not paid to the mayor but carried to a separate account and expended under the direction of a committee to celebrate a royal event. It was held to be a valid payment.
[4] Local Government Act 1985, ss. 24–28, 34.

council may hold the title of town mayor and deputy town mayor respectively.[5]

The members of a joint authority (other than a police authority) are   **4-03** members of the "constituent councils" appointed by those councils to be members of the authority. The constituent councils are the councils of the metropolitan districts in the county and, in the case of the London Fire and Civil Defence Authority, the London borough councils and the Common Council. The number of members to be appointed by each constituent council is specified in Schedule 10 to the Local Government Act 1985. These numbers may be changed by order of the Secretary of State, who must have regard to the number of local government electors in the areas of the constituent councils and must consult the constituent councils before making such an order.

The arrangements for police authorities are similar, except that some members are appointed by a joint magistrates' courts committee consisting of such number of representatives from each of the magistrates' courts committees in the area as those committees may agree. In default of agreement, the number may be determined by the Secretary of State. Appointments by the joint magistrates' courts committee must be made in accordance with a scheme made by the committee and approved by the Secretary of State. The Secretary of State may also prescribe the times, manner and terms of such appointments.[6]

A constituent council may at any time terminate the appointment of a person appointed by it to a joint authority and appoint another person in his or her place.[7] The appointment also terminates if the member ceases to be a member of the constituent council.[8] In this event, or if a vacancy arises for some other reason, the constituent council must appoint a replacement, normally within one month.[9] Each constituent council must, so far as practicable, exercise its power to make or terminate appointments so as to ensure that the balance of parties for the time being prevailing in that council is reflected in the persons who are for the time being members of the authority, and for whose appointment the council is responsible.[10]

Authorities may appoint committees as they think fit[11] and in certain   **4-04** cases the appointment is obligatory. For example, the Education Act 1944 requires local education authorities to appoint such education committees as they consider expedient for the efficient discharge of

---

[5] Local Government Act 1972, s. 245(6); and see § 3–10.
[6] Local Government Act 1985, s. 24.
[7] *Ibid.* s. 31.
[8] *Ibid.* s. 32(1).
[9] *Ibid.* s. 32(2)–(8).
[10] *Ibid.* s. 33.
[11] Local Government Act 1972, ss. 101 and 102. These provisions apply to joint authorities (other than police authorities) by virtue of s. 101(13), as amended by the Local Government Act 1985, Sched. 14, para. 15, and to police authorities, with modifications, by virtue of s. 107.

their functions.[12] Authorities for the purposes of the Local Authority Social Services Act 1970 must appoint a social services committee,[13] and non-metropolitan county councils must appoint police committees.[14] In general, where a statute requires the appointment of a committee, the authority may not act (unless the matter is urgent) otherwise than on a recommendation or report of the committee.[15] An authority may, however, empower an officer to discharge the relevant function.[16]

Membership of committees is fixed by the council and (except in the case of a committee controlling the finance of the local authority) may include persons not members of the authority, but the number of co-opted members on any committee may not exceed a maximum of one-third of the total membership.[17] In a limited number of cases, the composition of a particular committee is dealt with by statute. The police committee of a non-metropolitan county consists of members of the county council and magistrates, and one-third of the total must be magistrates.[18] At least a majority of members of a social services committee must be members of the authority, and where a sub-committee is established, at least one member must be a member of the local authority.[19] An education committee must include persons experienced in education, and may contain a number of co-opted persons less than one-half of the total membership.[20]

A member cannot be compelled to serve on a committee against his wish[21] and it is open to a council to dislodge a member from a committee although appointed for the ensuing municipal year. In *Manton* v. *Brighton Corporation*[22] it was held that as the council had power to revoke the authority of a committee as a whole it also had power to revoke the authority of any single member before the end of his prescribed period of office. Furthermore, in *R.* v. *Rushmoor Borough Council, ex p. Crawford*[23] it was held that the majority party on a council could exclude other members from all committees by passing an appropriate resolution complying with standing orders.[24]

---

[12] Sched. I, Part II; Local Government Act 1972, s. 101(9). For a complete list of statutory committees, see Local Government Act 1972, s. 101(9), as amended by the Health and Social Services and Social Security Adjudications Act 1983, Sched. 29, and the Local Government Act 1985, Sched. 17.

[13] s. 2; Local Government Act 1972, s. 101(9(f)); Local Government, Planning and Land Act 1980, s. 183.

[14] Police Act 1964, s. 2(1),(2), as amended by the Courts Act 1971, s. 53(5), the Local Government Act 1972, Sched. 27, para. 18 and the Local Government Act 1985, Sched. 11, para. 1(2)(3); Local Government Act 1972, s. 101(9)(c).

[15] See § 17–07.   [16] Local Government Act 1972, s. 101(10).

[17] *Ibid.* s. 102(3).   [18] Police Act 1964, s. 2(2), as amended (see n. 14, *supra*).

[19] Local Authority Social Services Act 1970, s. 5.

[20] Education Act 1944, Sched. I, Part II.

[21] *R.* v. *Sunderland Corporation* [1911] 2 K.B. 458.

[22] [1951] 2 K.B. 393.   [23] *The Times,* November 28, 1981.

[24] On the facts, the resolution did not so comply and was held *ultra vires.* Cf. *R.* v. *Sheffield City Council, ex p. Chadwick, The Times,* December 19, 1985.

Where an authority appoints a representative to *another* body,[25] that person holds office in accordance with the terms creating the other body.[26] Where this provides for a fixed term of office with no provision for rescinding the appointment, a local authority may not replace the member in order to reflect a change in its political complexion.[27] Provision may, however, be made enabling an appointment to be rescinded.[28]

B. MEETINGS

This topic is considered in three parts: the law relating to the calling and **4-05** conduct of meetings; the law of defamation as applied to local authority and committee meetings; the rights of the public and Press.

(1) The calling and conduct of meetings

The rules governing the meetings of local authorities and committees are found, first, in statute—in the main in Schedule 12 to the Local Government Act 1972.[29] Part I of the Schedule regulates meetings and proceedings of all principal councils, Part II those of parish councils, and Part III of parish meetings. Parts IV and V cover community councils and meetings respectively, and Part VI contains general provisions relating to all councils. Part IA applies the provisions of Part I to joint authorities and the Inner London Education Authority, with minor modifications. Secondly, they are found in standing orders. An authority may make standing orders to regulate its proceedings and business, and may vary or revoke them. Standing orders generally contain rules of debate and other procedural matters in respect of which there is no specific statutory provision. Thirdly, recourse may be had to the common law rules as to meetings. These come into operation only where a point is not covered by statute or standing orders. Thus, if standing orders are silent on such matters as the ejection of unruly members, the adjournment of meetings, the powers and duties of chairmen, then the issue will be decided on common law principles.

Principal councils

Schedule 12 requires a principal council and the Inner London **4-06** Education Authority to hold an annual meeting and such other meetings as the council or authority thinks necessary. The annual meeting in an election year is to be held on the eighth day after the retirement of councillors or on a day within 21 days immediately following the day of

---

[25] There is no direct general power enabling this to be done, but such power may be implied from the Local Government Act 1972, s. 177(2): see § 4–25.

[26] *R.* v. *Peak Park Joint Planning Board* (1976) 74 L.G.R. 376.

[27] *R.* v. *Lambeth London Borough Council, ex p. Parker, The Times,* March 1, 1983.

[28] *e.g.* Local Government Act 1985, s. 31(1): see § 4–03.

[29] As amended by the Local Government Act 1985, Sched. 14, para. 35, and Sched. 17.

retirement. In a year when there is no election the annual meeting may be held in either March, April or May. These rules apply to a joint authority as they apply to a principal council in a year where there is no election.

The chairman of a council may call a meeting of the council at any time, and he may be required to call a meeting on the requisition of five members (three in the case of a joint authority and ten in the case of the Inner London Education Authority). If the chairman after a requisition refuses to call a meeting or fails to call it within seven days of receiving the requisition, any five members (or three in the case of a joint authority and ten in the case of the Inner London Education Authority) may themselves do so as soon as he refuses or on the expiration of the seven days. Notice of the time and place of any meeting of the council is to be published at the council offices three clear days[30] before the meeting, and where the meeting has been called by members the notice is required to be signed by them and it must specify the business.

A summons to attend a meeting, specifying the business and signed by the proper officer of the council, must be sent to each member, and again three clear days' notice is required. No business may be transacted at a meeting unless it is specified in the summons or is urgent business brought before the meeting in accordance with standing orders. If a summons is not served on any member the validity of the meeting is not affected.

The chairman presides at the meeting. In the absence of the chairman the vice-chairman (or deputy mayor where the chairman is a mayor) presides. In London boroughs, the deputy mayor presides if at the time he is still a councillor and the members present choose him. If these are absent, another member of the council is chosen.

The quorum for a principal council, a joint authority or the Inner London Education Authority is one quarter of the body—provision is made for exceptional situations where more than a third of the council are disqualified.

Parish councils and community councils

4-07   The rules are similar to those which apply to principal councils but are rather more detailed. It is obligatory to hold an annual meeting and at least three other meetings in a year. They may not be held in licensed premises unless there is no other reasonable alternative. An extraordinary meeting may be called at any time by the chairman or members—the rules follow those which apply to principal councils except that two members only are required to sign the requisition.

The law with respect to community councils is marginally different from the law which applies to parish councils. For example, it is

---

[30] The day on which notice is given and the day of the meeting is to be excluded: *R.* v. *Herefordshire Justices* (1820) 3 B. & Ald. 581.

obligatory only to hold an annual meeting: other meetings are held as the council thinks necessary.

The quorum is one-third of the members of the whole council and provision is made to meet exceptional circumstances in which one-third of the council are disqualified, but the quorum is never less than three.

Parish meetings

The parish meeting is required to assemble annually between March 1   **4-08** and June 1. Other meetings are held as fixed by the parish council, or where there is no council by the chairman of the parish meeting. Where the parish does not have a separate parish council the parish meeting is required to assemble at least twice a year. Proceedings may not begin before 6 p.m. and may not be held on licensed premises unless no reasonable alternative is available. A parish meeting may be convened by the chairman of the parish council, or any two councillors for the parish or any six local government electors for the parish. Where there is no council, a meeting may be convened by the chairman of the parish meeting or any person representing the parish on the district council. Seven days' public notice must be given of the meeting and the notice must specify the time and place of it and the business to be transacted.

Matters discussed at a parish meeting are decided by a majority of those present and voting. The decision of the person presiding as to the result of the voting is final unless a poll is demanded. Such a poll may be demanded before the end of the meeting on any question arising at the meeting.[31] It is open to the person presiding or to the meeting to consent to a poll. If such consent is not given, a poll must be held if demanded by not less than 10, or one-third, of the local government electors present at the meeting, whichever is the less.

Community meetings

The rules are somewhat different from those which apply to parish   **4-09** meetings since community meetings are not continuing bodies with executive functions. There is, for example, no requirement as to regular meetings. Where a community has a community council the chairman of that council, if present, presides at the community meeting. In any other case the meeting appoints the chairman, but for that meeting only. As in the case of parish meetings, matters are decided by a majority of those present and voting, and a poll may be demanded.[32]

Committee meetings

Rules for the calling of committees and the procedure to be followed in   **4-10** committee are generally found in standing orders—section 106 of the

---

[31] Parish and Community Meetings (Polls) Rules 1973 (S.I. 1973 No. 1911 as amended by S.I. 1976 No. 2067 and S.I. 1983 No. 1151).
[32] *Ibid.*

Local Government Act 1972[33] confers a general power on local authorities to make standing orders respecting the quorum, proceedings and place of meetings of committees and joint committees, and subject to the standing orders these matters are determined by the committee itself. But the general provisions with regard to the conduct of meetings, referred to in the paragraph which follows, apply to meetings of committees as well as to meetings of local authorities.

General provisions

4-11   Except where otherwise provided by statute, decisions are taken by a majority of members present and voting, and the person presiding has a second or casting vote if there is no majority. The names of those present must be recorded.

The minutes of the meeting are entered in a book kept for that purpose, and the book may consist of loose leaves consecutively numbered. They are signed at the same or next following meeting of the authority by the person presiding thereat and a minute purporting to be so signed is received in evidence without further proof.

The minutes of a principal council and its committees and sub-committees are available for inspection by members of the public.[34] The minutes of a parish or community council and a parish meeting are available for inspection by electors[35] or by an agent for an elector.[36]

(2) Defamatory statements in council and committee

4-12   Statements made in council and committee are subject to the general principles of law relating to defamation. A person who issues a defamatory statement (one exposing a person to hatred, ridicule or contempt, or which causes him to be shunned or avoided, or which has a tendency to lower him in the estimation of right thinking members of society generally or injure him in his office, profession or trade) commits a tort, and is liable for the consequences which flow from such an act.

It may be noted in passing that a local authority has a "governing" reputation which it is entitled to protect by a defamation action. In *Bognor Regis Urban District Council* v. *Campion*[37] the council successfully

[handwritten margin note: a civil wrong the remedy for which is a common law action for damages of a decree of the court.]

[handwritten note: + Derbyshire CC v Times Newspapers Ltd (March 1991)]

[33] This provision applies to joint authorities and the Inner London Education Authority: s. 101(13), as amended by the Local Government Act 1985, Sched. 14, para. 15, and s. 107.

[34] Local Government Act 1972, ss. 100C, 100E, inserted by the Local Government (Access to Information) Act 1985, s. 1. See also § 4–16. Formerly, there was no general right of access to the minutes of committees and sub-committees (*Wilson* v. *Evans* [1962] 2 Q.B. 383), except where the minutes of a committee exercising referred powers were submitted to the council for approval (*Williams* v. *Manchester Corporation* (1897) 45 W.R. 412) or where this was expressly required by statute (*e.g.* Education Act 1944, Sched. 1, para. 9: education committees). For rights of access to documents concerning local authority accounts, see § 7–17. The right to take copies is not a right to be provided with copies: *Russell-Walker* v. *Gimblett* (1985) 149 J.P. 448.

[35] Local Government Act 1972, s. 228 as amended by the Local Government (Access to Information) Act 1985, Sched. 2, para. 6.

[36] *R.* v. *Glamorganshire County Council* [1936] 2 All E.R. 168.   [37] [1972] 2 Q.B. 169.

brought an action against a ratepayer who had published a leaflet defamatory of the council.

Defence of privilege

It is a general defence in an action for defamation to show that the **4-13** statement was made on a "privileged occasion," being made in such circumstances as to be exempt from the rule that a man attacks the reputation of another at his own risk. "Privileged occasions" are of two kinds.

As to the first, the privilege is absolute, and the motive prompting the author of a defamatory statement is not material. Absolute privilege attaches to certain proceedings (*e.g.* judicial and parliamentary) and where it is present there is a complete bar against an action. It does not attach to meetings of local authorities, even where functions are exercised which attract an obligation to act judicially and fairly.[38] Communications between a Local Commissioner and a local authority are, however, absolutely privileged.[39]

As to the second, the privilege is qualified, and the "relevant occasion," to use the words of Lord Atkinson in *Adam* v. *Ward*,[40] is

> " . . . an occasion where the person who makes a communication has an interest or a duty, legal, social or moral, to make it to the person to whom it is made, and the person to whom it is so made has a corresponding interest or duty to receive it."

An essential feature of qualified privilege is the absence of malice.

Qualified privilege will accordingly frequently attach to statements **4-14** made in council and committee. Where it is pleaded in an action for defamation the author of the defamatory statement must prove (a) a duty or interest to make the statement, and (b) a duty or interest on the part of the recipient to receive it. If these things are proved the plaintiff will not succeed unless he proves malice on the defendant's part.

So long as a person believes in the truth of what he says malice cannot normally be inferred.

Horrocks v. *Lowe*.[41] Councillor Horrocks issued a writ against Alderman Lowe, each of the Bolton Council, claiming damages for slander. At a meeting of the authority the alderman made a speech defamatory of the councillor. The alderman claimed, *inter alia,* that the words were spoken on a privileged occasion. By his reply the councillor pleaded that the alderman was actuated by express malice. The trial judge held that the occasion was privileged, that the alderman had honestly believed that what he had said was true but that he had shown such gross and unreasoning prejudice as to constitute malice in law

---

[38] *Royal Aquarium etc., Society* v. *Parkinson* [1892] 1 Q.B. 431; *cf. R.* v. *London County Council, ex. p. Akkersdyk* [1892] 1 Q.B. 190: meetings held to consider applications for music and dancing licences.
[39] Local Government Act 1974, s. 32.
[40] [1917] A.C. 309 at p. 334.
[41] [1975] A.C. 135.

sufficient to destroy the privilege. An appeal by the alderman to the Court of Appeal was allowed. The councillor appealed to the House of Lords. The House of Lords *held*, dismissing the appeal, that the defendant not having misused the privileged occasion by using it for some purpose other than that for which the privilege was accorded to it in the public interest his positive belief in the truth of what he said entitled him to succeed in his defence of qualified privilege. Lord Diplock stated[42] that, save in the exceptional case where a person may be under a duty to pass on, without endorsing, defamatory reports made by some other person, "what is required on the part of the defamer to entitle him to the protection of the privilege is positive belief in the truth of what he published, or, as it is generally . . . termed, 'honest belief'. . . . Even a positive belief in the truth of what is published on a privileged occasion—which is presumed unless the contrary is proved—may not be sufficient to negative express malice if it can be proved that the defendant misused the occasion for some purpose other than that for which the privilege is accorded by law." Examples of improper purposes or motives include giving vent to "personal spite or ill-will" or obtaining "some private advantage unconnected with the duty or interest which constitutes the reason for the privilege." However, where there is a positive belief in the truth of the statement, it is only where the defendant's "desire to comply with the relevant duty or to protect the relevant interests plays no significant part in his motives for publishing . . . that 'express malice' can properly be found."

The second element mentioned above—the duty or interest to receive—has the effect of greatly limiting the extent of publication if qualified privilege is to be preserved.

De Buse v. *McCarthy*.[43] The town clerk of Stepney sent out a notice convening a meeting of the council to consider, *inter alia*, a report of a committee regarding the loss of petrol from one of the council's depots. Included in the notice was a long agenda of business, and a complete copy of the report of the committee. Copies of the notice were sent to the public libraries in accordance with long-established practice. *Held*, that the extent of the publication of the report destroyed the privilege otherwise attaching to it. There was no common interest between the council and the ratepayers to be informed in what was only a preliminary stage in an investigation.

As will be noted below, under the Public Bodies (Admission to Meetings) Act 1960, s. 1, and the Local Government Act 1972, Part VA, the Press and public must on request be allowed access to or, in certain circumstances, be supplied with agenda and certain other documents relating to matters before local authorities and other bodies. Where such matter is made available to the Press or to the public, the agenda and other documents are privileged unless publication is proved to have been made with malice.[44] Qualified privilege therefore attaches to them. However, this statutory privilege covers only the publication to the Press or member of the public. Whether further publication by the Press or members of the public is protected by qualified privilege depends on the common law and section 7 of the Defamation Act 1952.[45]

[42] At pp. 150–151.
[43] [1942] 1 K.B. 156.
[44] 1960 Act, s. 1(5); 1972 Act, ss. 100H(5)(6).
[45] *Infra*.

Other defences

Certain other defences are available. Justification can be pleaded if the words are true, and justification provides a complete answer. It is also a good defence to show that what was said was a fair comment on a matter of public interest,[46] honestly believed to be true, relevant and not inspired by malicious motive, and that the statements of fact on which the comment was based were materially true.

4-15

Defences of apology and fair reporting are open to newspapers. Under section 2 of the Libel Act 1843 it is a good defence to prove that a statement was published without actual malice or gross negligence and that the earliest opportunity was taken to publish an apology. The defendant must, when filing his defence, make payment into court by way of amends. Section 7 of the Defamation Act 1952 provides that fair and accurate reports of meetings of local authorities and their committees are privileged, unless the publication is proved to be made with malice. This qualified privilege does not extend to meetings to which the public and the Press are denied admission. To secure the benefit of this provision the newspaper must publish a reasonable letter by way of explanation or contradiction if so requested. A copy or fair and accurate report or summary of any notice or other matter issued for the information of the public by or on behalf of any local authority is similarly protected. Section 7 of the 1952 Act also applies to broadcasts from a station within the United Kingdom.

A local authority may in principle be liable in respect of defamatory statements made by an officer within the scope of his authority.[47]

(3) Rights of public and Press

The Public Bodies (Admission to Meetings) Act 1960 provided that meetings of local authorities and certain other bodies which exercise public functions should be open to the public. A list of these bodies was given in the Schedule to the Act, and included as well as local authorities, joint boards, joint committees of local authorities, parish meetings and education committees. Section 100 of the Local Government Act 1972 applied the Public Bodies (Admission to Meetings) Act 1960 to committees, joint committees and advisory committees appointed by local authorities under sections 101 and 102 of the Act, except in so far as the provisions of the 1960 Act already applied. The Local Government (Access to Information) Act 1985 introduced a new regime providing greater public access to local authority meetings, reports and documents. The Public Bodies (Admission to Meetings) Act 1960 continues to apply to parish and community councils, parish meetings, health authorities

4-16

---

[46] The administration of local affairs by authorities is a matter of "public interest": *Purcell* v. *Sowler* (1887) 2 C.P.D. 215.

[47] *Glasgow Corporation* v. *Lorimer* [1911] A.C. 209. The corporation was held not liable on the facts.

and certain other bodies. The two sets of provisions are considered separately.

Local Government (Access to Information) Act 1985

4-17   Section 1 of this Act inserts a new Part VA (sections 100A—100K) in the Local Government Act 1972. It applies to any principal council, which term includes the councils of non-metropolitan counties, districts and London boroughs,[48] and, for the purposes of Part VA, the Inner London Education Authority, a joint authority, the Common Council of the City of London, joint boards and joint committees of two or more principal councils, a combined police authority which is a body corporate, and a combined fire authority.[49] It also applies, with some modifications, to committees and sub-committees of such bodies.[50]

Meetings of the bodies subject to Part VA must normally be open to the public. However, the public *must* be excluded from a meeting during an item of business whenever it is likely that confidential information would otherwise be disclosed to members of the public in breach of an obligation of confidence. For this purpose "confidential information" means (1) information furnished to the council by a government department on terms which forbid the disclosure of the information to the public, and (2) information the disclosure of which to the public is prohibited by or under any enactment or by a court order. Moreover, a council *may* by resolution exclude the public from a meeting during an item of business whenever it is likely that "exempt information" would otherwise be disclosed to members of the public. The resolution must identify the proceedings, or the part of the proceedings, to which it applies, and state the description, in terms of schedule 12A, of the exempt information in question.[51] The descriptions of information which are for the time being exempt information are found in this Schedule, and the descriptions may be varied by order of the Secretary of State. Part I of the Schedule lists 15 descriptions of exempt information. These are subject to qualifications contained in Part II. Part III contains provisions for interpretation of the Schedule. The descriptions in Part I include information relating to particular persons, such as employees, former employees, council tenants and applicants for or recipients of services or financial assistance; information relating to the adoption, care, fostering or education of any particular child; information relating to the financial or business affairs of any particular person; the amount of proposed expenditure on the acquisition of property or the supply of goods or services; any terms proposed or to be proposed in the course of

---

[48] Definition of "principal council" in the Local Government Act 1972, s. 270(1), as amended by the Local Government Act 1985, Sched. 15, para. 8.
[49] Local Government Act 1972, s. 100J.
[50] *Ibid.* s. 100E.
[51] *Ibid.* s. 100A(1)–(5). *Cf. R.*v. *Liverpool City Council, ex p. Liverpool Taxi Fleet Operators' Association* [1975] 1 W.L.R. 701: *see* § 4–20.

negotiations for a contract for the acquisition or disposal of property or the supply of goods or services; the identity of the authority or a person as the person tendering for a contract for the supply of goods or services; information concerning legal proceedings; information which would reveal that the authority proposes to serve a notice, or make an order or direction under any enactment; any action taken or to be taken in connection with the prevention, investigation or prosecution of crime; and the identity of a protected informant.

Public notice of the time and place of a meeting of a body subject to **4-18** Part VA must be published at the offices of the body three clear days before the meeting, or when the meeting is convened if called at shorter notice. While the meeting is open to the public, the council does not have power to exclude members of the public from the meeting, and duly accredited Press representatives must, so far as practicable, be afforded reasonable facilities for taking a report and (unless the meeting is not held on council premises or the premises are not on the telephone) for telephoning the report at their own expense. However, these provisions are without prejudice to any power of exclusion to suppress or prevent disorderly conduct or other misbehaviour at a meeting.[52]

Copies of the agenda and any reports for a meeting must be open to public inspection at least three clear days before the meeting, or when the meeting is convened, if convened at shorter notice. Part or the whole of a report may be withheld if it relates only to items during which, in the opinion of the proper officer, the meeting is likely not to be open to the public. Late items must be open to inspection from the time they are added to the agenda. Copies of a document are not, however, required to be open to public inspection until copies are available to council members. An item of business may not be considered at a meeting unless either the rules as to publication of the agenda are complied with or, by reason of special circumstances, which must be specified in the minutes, the chairman of the meeting is of the opinion that the item should be considered as a matter of urgency. At a meeting, a reasonable number of copies of the agenda and relevant reports must be available for the use of the public. If the Press so request they must be supplied with a copy of the agenda and relevant reports, such further statements or particulars as are necessary to indicate the nature of the items included in the agenda and, if the proper officer thinks fit in the case of any item, copies of any other documents supplied to members of the council in connection with the item.[53]

After a meeting, certain documents must be open to public inspection **4-19** at the council's offices for six years:

(1) the minutes, or a copy of the minutes, of the meeting, excluding so

[52] Local Government Act 1972, s. 100A(6)–(8). *Cf. R.* v. *Brent Health Authority, ex p. Francis* [1985] Q.B. 869: see § 4–20.
[53] *Ibid.* s. 100B.

much of the minutes of proceedings during which the meeting was not open to the public as discloses exempt information;

(2) a summary prepared by the proper officer which provides a reasonably fair and coherent record of proceedings without disclosing exempt information, in circumstances where the exclusion of part of the minutes means that the part published does not provide such a record;

(3) a copy of the agenda; and

(4) a copy of so much of any report for the meeting as relates to any item during which the meeting was open to the public.[54]

If and so long as copies of the whole or part of a report for a meeting are required to be open to public inspection, copies of a list of the background papers for the report or the part of the report and at least one copy of each of the documents included in that list must also be open to public inspection. This applies both before and after the meeting, except that the relevant period after the meeting is four years, not six. Nothing in these provisions requires any document which discloses exempt information to be included in the list, and nothing requires or authorises the inclusion in the list of any document which includes confidential information within the meaning of section 100A. "Background papers" are those documents which disclose any facts or matters on which, in the opinion of the proper officer, the reports or an important part of the report is based and which have, in his opinion, been relied on to a material extent in preparing the report. They do not, however, include any published works.[55]

A document directed by any provision of Part VA to be open to inspection shall be so open at all reasonable hours. No payment may be required except in the case of access to background papers, in which case a reasonable fee may be required for the facility. A person entitled to inspect a document may make copies of or extracts from it or require a photocopy to be supplied, upon payment of a reasonable fee. This does not, however, require or authorise any infringement of copyright, except that where the owner of the copyright is a principal council, nothing done in exercise of these rights shall constitute an infringement of copyright. Where any accessible document for a meeting is open to public inspection, or is supplied for the benefit of a newspaper, the publication thereby of defamatory matter contained in the document is privileged, unless the publication is proved to be made with malice. The rights conferred by Part VA to inspect, copy and be furnished with documents are in addition, and without prejudice, to any such rights conferred by or under any other enactment.[56]

---

[54] Local Government Act 1972, s. 100C.
[55] *Ibid.* s. 100D.
[56] *Ibid.* s. 100H.

Public Bodies (Admission to Meetings) Act 1960

As from April 1, 1986, this Act applies only to parish or community **4-20**
councils, the Council of the Isles of Scilly and joint boards or joint
committees which discharge functions of any of those bodies (or of any of
those bodies and of a principal council, the Inner London Education
Authority, a joint authority or the Common Council of the City of
London); parish meetings; the Land Authority for Wales; regional, area
or district health authorities, community health councils, and, if the order
establishing a special health authority so provides, that authority; family
practitioner committees as regards the exercise of their executive
functions; and other bodies with power to levy a rate, other than bodies
subject to Part VA of the Local Government Act 1972.[57] The 1960 Act[58]
applies to committees of parish and community councils by virtue of
section 100 of the 1972 Act.

Power is given to exclude the public from meetings whenever publicity
would be prejudicial to the public interest because of the confidential
nature of the business or for other special reasons stated in the resolution
excluding the public and arising from the nature of the business. One
particular ground for exclusion is specifically given, but without prejudice
to the generality of the broad rule. A body may treat the need to receive
or consider recommendations or advice from sources other than
members, committees or sub-committees of the body as a special reason
why publicity would be prejudicial to the public interest, without regard
to the subject or purport of the recommendations or advice. A body is
able under this provision to exclude the public and Press when receiving
advice from its officers. The following case relates to these general
provisions.

R. v. *Liverpool City Council, ex p. Liverpool Taxi Fleet Operators'
Association.*[59] Forty members of the public wished to attend a committee
meeting, but there were only 14 seats available for Press, public and those
making representations to the committee. The chairman suggested that the
public be excluded because of the limited seating, and because it was desirable
that those making representations be heard privately. The committee resolved
to exclude members of the public apart from the Press "in view of the
limitations of available space and in order that the business of the committee
may be carried out satisfactorily." The applicants sought an order of certiorari
to quash the council's decision in the matter considered at the committee
meeting on the ground of non-compliance with the Public Bodies (Admission
to Meetings) Act 1960. *Held,* (1) the reasons for exclusion amounted to "special
reasons" within the Act, (2) the requirement that the reasons be stated in the
resolution was directory and not mandatory. Accordingly, the fact that the
second reason was expressed too vaguely to meet that requirement did not
invalidate the resolution.

[57] Public Bodies (Admission to Meetings) Act 1960, Schedule, para. 1, as amended, *inter alia,*
by the Local Government (Access to Information) Act 1985, Sched. 2, para. 4.
[58] As amended by the Local Government (Access to Information) Act 1985, Sched. 2,
para. 6.
[59] [1975] 1 W.L.R. 701.

Furthermore, these provisions are without prejudice to any power of exclusion to suppress or prevent disorderly conduct or other misbehaviour at a meeting.[60] At common law, there is a power to exclude during a meeting anyone whose behaviour is disruptive or disorderly and, indeed, a power to prevent the entry of the public in circumstances where disruption or disorderly conduct is apprehended. In either case the power may be exercised where exclusion is necessary for the carrying on of the authority's business.[61]

Where a meeting is required to be open to the public, notice of the time and place of the meeting must be published at the offices of the body at least three clear days before the meeting, or when the meeting is convened if called at shorter notice. If the Press so request they must be supplied with a copy of the agenda, together with such further statement or particulars as are necessary to indicate the nature of the items on the agenda. There is no provision for access to background papers.

C. Members

4-21   There is little statute or common law regarding individual members of local authorities. This is to be expected, for it is an incident of corporate status that the corporation, rather than the individuals who comprise it, has legal significance. A member in his individual capacity has no executive powers and can exercise no lawful authority. This is the position in law. There are, of course, a number of conventions and commonly accepted practices which govern the rights and powers of members in their individual capacities. Sometimes these matters are covered by standing orders—for example, they frequently give members a qualified right of inspection of land and premises owned by the local authority.

The principal legal rights relate to the inspection of documents and to the payment of allowances. The principal duty consists of an obligation to disclose any pecuniary interest a member may have in a matter before the council. Reference is also made in the following paragraphs to the statutory requirement as to attendance, insurance of members, and the procedure for challenging validity of office.

(a) Inspection of documents

4-22   At common law, a member is entitled to see such documents as are reasonably necessary to enable him to carry out his duties. He has no right to a roving commission to examine the books or documents of a corporation—a mere curiosity or wish to see them is not sufficient.[62] Mandamus to compel disclosure will be refused if a member is not

---

[60] Public Bodies (Admission to Meetings) Act 1960, s. 1(8).
[61] *R. v. Brent Health Authority, ex p. Francis* [1985] Q.B. 869.
[62] *R. v. Southwold Corporation, ex p. Wrightson* (1907) 5 L.G.R. 888.

actuated solely by his public position but is inspired by an indirect motive, for example, a desire to assist a person in litigation with the council.[63]

R. v. Barnes Borough Council, ex p. Conlan.[64] A councillor strongly opposed his authority's decision to defend an action. He demanded access to the draft case prepared for council before it was submitted. *Held*, the common law right arises from a councillor's common law duty to keep himself informed of all matters necessary to enable him properly to discharge his duty as a councillor. The common law right is accordingly limited to access to such documents as might reasonably be necessary to enable him properly to perform his duties. The court refused to compel disclosure in this case.

R. v. Lancashire County Council Police Authority, ex p. Hook.[65] In 1976, a county council police committee received a report on complaints about the conduct of the Chief Constable. In 1977, H. was elected as a county councillor and appointed to the police committee. The committee subsequently dismissed the Chief Constable in the light of the findings of an independent tribunal. However, only an abridged form of the original report was released to the committee as then constituted. H. requested to see the unabridged report. The committee refused the request, acting on the advice of leading counsel to the effect that the suppressed parts of the report contained damaging and potentially defamatory matters of rumour and gossip that were not relevant to the committee's remaining statutory duties and might not now be protected by qualified privilege. The Court of Appeal (Waller and Dunn L.JJ., Lord Denning M.R. dissenting) *held* that though a councillor had an undoubted right in law to see council documents reasonably necessary to enable him to perform his duties, it was for the police committee in the exercise of its discretion to determine whether there was such reasonable necessity. Its decision here was based on proper advice and was not one which no reasonable authority could have made. *R. v. Barnes Borough Council, ex p. Conlan* (*supra*) was approved.

R. v. Birmingham City Council, ex p. O.[66] A councillor, in her capacity as chairman of the housing committee, obtained information which led her to doubt the suitability of a married couple to adopt a child whom they had been fostering. The councillor, who had no direct connection with the social services department, was held by the Court of Appeal to be not entitled, on the grounds of confidentiality, to see the files of the social services department relating to her case. However, this decision was reversed by the House of Lords, which *held* that she was entitled to see the files. A councillor, by virtue of her office, was entitled to have access to all written material in the possession of the local authority as long as she had good reason. In the case of a committee of which she was a member she would normally have good reason for access to all that committee's written material. In the case of other committees a "need to know" had to be demonstrated, and the matter in the last resort was for the council to determine, subject to judicial review under the *Wednesbury* principles. The council had decided to allow access and this decision had not been shown to be *ultra vires*.

---

[63] *R. v. Hampstead Borough Council, ex p. Woodward* (1917) 15 L.G.R. 309.
[64] [1938] 3 All E.R. 226.
[65] [1980] Q.B. 603.
[66] [1983] 1 A.C. 578, H.L. See also *R. v. Hackney London Borough Council, ex p. Gamper* [1985] 1 W.L.R. 1229, where Lloyd L.J. held that there was no logical distinction between access to documents and attendance at meetings.

— meetings

County District + London Borough

4-23   The Local Government (Access to Information) Act 1985 creates a statutory right of access to documents for members of "principal councils" as defined for the purposes of Part VA of the Local Government Act 1972.[67] Any document which is in the possession or under the control of a principal council and contains material relating to any business to be transacted at a meeting of the council or a committee or sub-committee of the council is to be open to inspection by any council member. However, there is no right of inspection where it appears to the proper officer that a document discloses certain classes of exempt information. Ten of the fifteen descriptions of exempt information specified in Part I of Schedule 12A to the 1972 Act[68] apply here. The Secretary of State may vary this list by order. This right of inspection is expressly stated to be in addition to any other rights that a member may have.[69]

The accounts of a local authority or joint authority and the Inner London Education Authority and of any proper officer may be inspected by any member and he may make a copy of them or take extracts from them.[70]

FARTS : Financial loss
Attendance Allowance
Responsibility Allowance
Travelling + Subsistence

(b) *Monetary payments*

4-24   The Local Government Act 1972[71] authorises the payment of allowances in respect of attendance, financial loss, travelling and subsistence to members of local authorities, joint authorities, the Inner London Education Authority and other bodies such as local valuation panels, joint committees, joint boards and other prescribed bodies, where the members are engaged on approved duties. In certain circumstances a responsibility allowance may be paid.

A member who is a councillor of the authority from which payment is claimed[72] is entitled to an attendance allowance of such reasonable amount, not exceeding the prescribed amount, as the authority may determine. Co-opted members of local authorities may claim a financial loss allowance where they necessarily lose earnings or are necessarily put to additional expense on account of an approved duty. Payments under these provisions may not be made to parish or community councillors in respect of duties performed within the parish or community or grouped parish or grouped community.

---

[67] See § 4–17.

[68] *Ibid.*

[69] Local Government Act 1972, s. 100F, added by the Local Government (Access to Information) Act 1985, s. 1.

[70] Local Government Act 1972, s. 228, as amended by the Local Government Act 1985, Sched. 14, para. 24.

[71] ss. 173–178, as amended by the Local Government, Planning and Land Act 1980, ss. 24–26, the Miscellaneous Financial Provisions Act 1983, s. 7 and the Local Government Act 1985, Sched. 14, paras. 18–20, and Sched. 17.

[72] *Hopson* v. *Devon County Council* [1978] 1 W.L.R. 553 (district councillor appointed to committee of the county council not entitled to claim attendance allowance from the county council).

A member is also entitled to travelling and subsistence allowances in respect of expenditure necessarily incurred in the performance of approved duties. Except in the case of parish and community councils travelling expenses are payable in respect of all approved duty, whether within or without the area of the authority, and with no minimum distance, and a subsistence allowance is payable to a member where the expenditure on subsistence is necessarily incurred by him. In the case of parish and community councillors, travelling expenses and subsistence allowances are not payable unless the duty lies outside the parish or community or grouped parish or grouped community.

A councillor may by notice in writing opt to receive a financial loss allowance instead of an attendance allowance. If notice is given by a member within one month beginning with the day of his election, then he is entitled to receive financial loss allowance for the performance of any approved duty after his election. If notice is given otherwise, the allowance is payable for the performance of any approved duty after the end of the period of one month beginning with the day on which the notice is given. If a financial loss allowance notice is withdrawn, by a further notice in writing, the allowance ceases to be payable in respect of any duty performed after the day on which notice of withdrawal is given.

A principal council, a joint authority and the Inner London Education Authority may pay any member an allowance in addition to other allowances if he has special responsibility in relation to the discharge of the functions of the council.

Maximum rates of payment are specified or prescribed by the Secretary of State for the Environment.[73]

A local authority has power to defray travelling and other expenses reasonably incurred by or on behalf of any members in making official and courtesy visits, whether inside or outside the United Kingdom, on behalf of the council,[74] and an authority operating a public service vehicle undertaking may give travel concessions to members of the authority in the performance of approved duties.[75]

The term "approved duty" is defined in section 177 of the Local **4-25** Government Act 1972, as attendances at meetings and the doing of other things, or classes of things, for the purposes of the authority or body and approved by that authority or body. It also includes service on or for other prescribed bodies to which a member is nominated or appointed by the council under some statutory power of duty.

The allowances referred to above may be paid to members attending a conference or meeting convened by any person or body (except a

---

[73] Local Government (Allowances) Regulations 1974 (S.I. 1974 No. 447) as amended.

[74] Local Government Act 1972, s. 176, as amended. The section also authorises expenditure on the reception and entertainment of distinguished persons visiting the area.

[75] Public Service Vehicles (Travel Concessions) Act 1955; Travel Concessions Act 1964; and see *Litherland Urban District Council* v. *Liverpool Corporation* [1958] 1 W.L.R. 913.

commercial or political organisation) to discuss matters which in the council's opinion relate to the interests of the area or its inhabitants.

There are several specific provisions as to conferences—section 83 of the Education Act 1944 enables local education authorities to organise and participate in conferences relating to education.

(c) *Disclosure of interest*[76]

4-26   The principal duty imposed by statute on members relates to their interest in matters before the authority. A breach of this duty exposes a member to criminal proceedings. If a member has a pecuniary interest, direct or indirect, in any contract or proposed contract or other matter and is present at the meeting when it is discussed, he must disclose the fact and refrain from discussion and voting. An authority may, by standing orders, provide for the exclusion of such members, and this is commonly done, with a proviso that the member may remain if the majority of those present at the meeting so decides. A member has an indirect interest if:

  (a) he or any nominee of his is a member of a company or other body with which the contract is made or is proposed to be made or which has a direct pecuniary interest in the matter under consideration; or

  (b) he is a partner, or is in the employment, of a person with whom the contract is made or is proposed to be made or who has a direct pecuniary interest in the matter under consideration.

This does not apply to membership of or employment under a public body. In the case of married persons living together the interest of one is deemed to be the interest of the other if known to the other. Where the indirect pecuniary interest of a member arises from his beneficial interest in securities which he or his wife holds, then if the total nominal value of these shares does not exceed £1,000 (or one-hundredth part of the total nominal value of the issued share capital, whichever is the less), then whilst the member must declare his interest he is not precluded from speaking and voting.

4-27   It was a generally held view that the maxim *de minimis non curat lex* could not be applied to the interest provisions and that members were under an obligation to declare an insignificant and trifling interest. The matter was cleared up by the Local Government (Pecuniary Interests) Act 1964, which provided that a member should not be treated as having a pecuniary interest by reason only of any interest (a) of that member, or (b) of any company, body or person connected with him, which was so

---

[76] Local Government Act 1972, ss. 94–98. These provisions apply to local authorities, joint authorities and the Inner London Education Authority: s. 98(1A), inserted by the Local Government Act 1985, Sched. 14, para. 13. See also the National Code of Local Government Conduct (Department of the Environment Circular 94/75). See § 4–34.

remote or insignificant that it could not reasonably be regarded as likely to influence him in discussion and voting. This rule now appears in section 97(5). The section also excludes an interest which a member has merely as a ratepayer, inhabitant of the area, or water consumer, or as a person entitled to participate in any service offered to the public.

There has been a good deal of case-law on this topic, and indeed this is **4-28** to be expected, for the statutory provisions are expressed in broad terms and without precise definition. The body of case-law helps in two ways. First, because the statutory provisions are in broad terms, the courts have looked at the mischief which the provisions were intended to prevent and have enunciated certain underlying notions. Lord Esher M.R. said in *Nutton* v. *Wilson*[77]:

> "I adhere to what I have before said with regard to provisions of this kind. They are intended to prevent the members of local boards, which may have occasion to enter into contracts, from being exposed to temptation, or even to the semblance of temptation."

Secondly, in applying the law to particular cases the courts have stated and developed a number of rules—to take one example, pecuniary interest means more than pecuniary advantage, and voting in a matter which is to the financial detriment of a member is therefore illegal. The first of the two cases which follow illustrate this rule; in the second the words "or other matter" in section 94 are considered.

Brown v. *Director of Public Prosecutions.*[78] A motion was submitted to the **4-29** Northampton County Borough Council to abolish a levy charged on council tenants who took in lodgers or sub-let, except in the case where council members were the tenants. An amendment was put to delete the exception, and six members who were tenants voted against the amendment. Three of the six took in lodgers. All six were found guilty of an offence against section 76(1) of the Local Government Act 1933. They appealed to the Divsional Court, claiming that they had no pecuniary interest in the matter, but were merely subjecting themselves to a specific pecuniary detriment. Their appeal was dismissed. Lord Goddard C.J. said[79]: "It seems to me that section 76 (this is now section 94 of the Act of 1972) is drawn in such terms that it does not matter whether the result of the vote would be to the pecuniary interest or disinterest of the person voting. Parliament has not said that they may vote against their interest and not for their interest: it has said that they must not vote on any matter in which they have a pecuniary interest."

Rands v. *Oldroyd.*[80] R., a building contractor and a member of a local authority, decided in 1956 that his company, in which he had a controlling interest, would not in future tender for building contracts for the council. In 1957 a motion came before the council that when public tenders were invited the borough engineer should tender on behalf of his department, and that, where necessary, the direct labour force should be augmented. An amendment to delete that part of the motion dealing with an increase in the labour force succeeded, R. voting for the amendment. It was argued on behalf of R., *inter*

[77] (1889) 22 Q.B.D. 774 at p. 747.
[78] [1956] 2 Q.B. 369.
[79] At p. 375.
[80] [1959] 1 Q.B. 204.

alia, that "or other matter" in section 76 was to be construed *ejusdem generis* with "contract or proposed contract", or was at any rate to be construed as meaning a *specified* transaction or matter which, like a contract or proposed contract, gave rise to rights and liabilities. This argument did not prevail. Lord Parker C.J. said[81]: "I find it impossible to give any satisfactory narrower meaning, even if I were so minded, to these words 'any contract or proposed contract or other matter.' . . . the more one does consider the matter the more difficult and impossible it is to cut down those words 'or other matter' to something which was definable and which was a limitation on what appear to be general words. Bearing in mind the mischief aimed at by this Act, I do not think those words are to be read in other than a very general way, and I see no ground for introducing a limitation which, as I said, is one which cannot satisfactorily be defined."

4-30 *Declaration of interest.* A member may disclose his interest in two ways. He may give a general notice of some interest to the proper officer of the authority or he may give particular notice as the occasion arises. A general or particular notice must be recorded, and the book in which the record is kept must be open for inspection by members of the authority.[82]

4-31 *Breach of the rules.* A member may commit one or more of three offences: he may fail to disclose an interest, he may take part in consideration or discussion, and he may vote. There is no *duty* upon the proper officer to advise members who are in doubt as to their position, or to warn members who may be putting themselves in jeopardy of proceedings, but it is customary for him to put his specialised knowledge at a member's disposal if he is asked for guidance.

Failure to comply with the law renders a person liable on summary conviction to a fine not exceeding level 4 on the standard scale, unless he can prove that he did not know that the matter in which he had an interest was being considered. A prosecution cannot be instituted except by or on behalf of the Director of Public Prosecutions.[83]

There is no precise rule as to where responsibility lies for bringing alleged infringements to the notice of the Director of Public Prosecutions. Anyone may start inquiries simply by reporting the matter to the police, and it would equally be open to a council to resolve that the Director be informed of any incident in which members have apparently contravened the law. But it appears to be a fairly widely accepted view that a responsibility rests with the proper officer or chairman of a council to report a manifest contravention to the chief constable, who in turn will lay the facts before the Director of Public Prosecutions if in his view such course is warranted.[84]

4-32 *Removal of disabilities.* The Secretary of State is empowered by section 97 to remove the disability imposed on members where the number of members disabled at any one time is so great as to impede the transaction

---

[81] At p. 212.
[82] Local Government Act 1972, ss. 94(1), 96.
[83] Local Government Act 1972, s. 94(3).
[84] See hereon Report of Bognor Regis Inquiry, 1965.

of business or where it appears to him that it is in the interests of the inhabitants of the area that the disability be removed. General dispensations have been granted to enable council house tenants to speak and vote on matters of general housing policy,[85] to enable parents of a child in full-time education to speak and vote on questions concerning school refreshments and transport,[86] and to enable members to speak and vote on matters concerning special responsibility allowances under the Local Government Act 1972, s. 177A.[87] In the case of parish or community councils it is the district council which may exercise this dispensing power.

The disability of interested members is twofold: they may not take part in the consideration or discussion of the matter and they are precluded from voting. The Secretary of State or district council granting a dispensation may choose to remove only the first disability, enabling a member to give his view but not his vote.

A person may discuss, and vote on, an application for a dispensation even though he is one of the members concerned; and the chairman, vice-chairman or deputy chairman of a principal council is not to be regarded as having a pecuniary interest in the allowance paid him, nor is a member to be so regarded in relation to travelling, subsistence or attendance allowances.[88]

Validity of votes cast by interested persons. A difficult situation arises **4-33** where a member is clearly under a disability yet persists in speaking and voting. The matter is by no means free from doubt but it is submitted that if the member is manifestly interested the chairman would be justified (and indeed may be under an obligation) to refuse to count his vote, for the "vote" has been cast illegally and therefore can be said not to be a vote at all. An authority for this view is found in *Nell* v. *Longbottom.*[89] In this case the mayor-elect of Louth voted for himself: it was held that his vote was invalid and could not therefore be regarded as having been cast. It would appear that where a council acts in a quasi-judicial capacity a vote cast by a member having an interest may render the decision void as contrary to natural justice on account of bias.[90]

The National Code of Local Government Conduct. The Redcliffe-Maud **4-34** Committee on Local Government Rules of Conduct[91] recommended that existing rules, embodied in statutes and standing orders, should be supplemented by a nationally agreed code of conduct. A code was

---

[85] DoE Circular 105/73.
[86] DoE Circular 5/80.
[87] DoE Circular 8/82.
[88] Local Government Act 1972, s. 94.
[89] [1894] 1 Q.B. 767. This case was decided on the somewhat different provisions of the earlier law.
[90] See *R.* v. *London County Council* [1892] 1 Q.B. 190; *R.* v. *Hendon Rural District Council, ex p. Chorley* [1933] 2 K.B. 696 and § 12–31.
[91] Cmnd. 5636 (1974).

subsequently agreed by central government departments, the local authority associations in England and Wales and the Convention of Scottish Local Authorities.[92] The code is a guide for all councillors whether elected or co-opted. It emphasises, *inter alia*, that compliance with the law, standing orders and the code is the personal responsibility of each councillor. It is not enough to avoid actual impropriety; each councillor should at all times avoid any occasion for suspicion or the appearance of improper conduct. Although the law requires disclosure of pecuniary interests, non-pecuniary interests, such as kinship, friendship or membership of an association, can influence a councillor's judgment and give the impression that he might be acting for personal motives.

> "A good test is to ask yourself whether others would think that the interest is of a kind to make this possible. If you think they would, or if you are in doubt, disclose the interest and withdraw from the meeting unless under standing orders you are specifically invited to stay."

Interests should also be disclosed at party group meetings. Where a councillor's business or personal interests are closely related to the work of one of the council's committees (or sub-committees), he should not seek or accept the chairmanship of that committee (or sub-committee) and should seriously consider whether membership would involve him in disclosing an interest so often that he could be of little value to it or would weaken public confidence in its impartiality. The code also notes that it is a grave betrayal of trust to use confidential information for personal advantage and that the receipt or offer of gifts should be reported to the chief executive.

The national code may be incorporated into standing orders. Furthermore, a failure to comply with the code may be regarded by the Commission for Local Administration[93] as maladministration by the authority, whether or not the code has been incorporated in standing orders.[94]

(d) *Attendance*

4-35   A member who for six months fails to attend any meeting of the authority or its committees or sub-committees or joint committees or joint boards with which it is linked ceases to be a member unless within that period his absence is approved by the authority. Time begins to run from the date of the member's last attendance. There are exceptions to the general rule in the case of military personnel in time of war or emergency.[95]

---

[92] See DoE Circular 94/75.
[93] *Infra.* §§ 4–64 — 4–70.
[94] See Annual Reports of the English Commission for 1980–81, paras. 27–32; 1981–82, paras. 42–48; 1982–83, paras. 29–40 and Appendix 5.
[95] Local Government Act 1972, s. 85. This section applies to local authorities, joint authorities and the Inner London Education Authority: s. 85(4), inserted by the Local Government Act 1985, Sched. 14, para. 7.

(e) *Insurance*

An authority may insure members against personal accident suffered **4–36** whilst engaged on the authority's business.[96]

(f) *Validity of office*

A procedure is available under section 92 of the Local Government **4–37** Act 1972, by which an elector can challenge the right of a person to act as a member of a local authority on the grounds that he is disqualified in law. Proceedings may be instituted in either the High Court or a magistrates' court where the person challenged has in fact acted as a member, and in the High Court only where the person challenged merely claims to be entitled to act. If it is proved that a defendant has acted whilst disqualified, a penalty not exceeding £50 (in the High Court) or level 3 on the standard scale (in a magistrates' court) may be imposed for each occasion on which he acted. If the case is heard by the High Court the court may declare the office vacant and grant an injunction restraining the defendant from acting further. Proceedings must be commenced before the expiration of six months from the date on which the defendant acted as a member—the period begins to run from the earliest date on which he acted.[97]

Where the issue is merely a claim to be entitled to act, the High Court may, if it finds that the member is disqualified, make a declaration to that effect and declare that the office is vacant, and it may grant an injunction restraining him from so acting.

Where proceedings are begun in a magistrates' court and the magistrates consider that the matter in question would be more properly dealt with by the High Court, they may order the discontinuance of the proceedings before them; and it is open to a defendant to apply to the High Court for an order that the proceedings in the magistrates' court be discontinued.

D. OFFICERS

The following matters are considered in this section: appointment; tenure **4–38** and remuneration; responsibilities; superannuation; interest, corruption and accountability.

---

[96] Local Government Act 1972, s. 140, as amended by the Local Government (Miscellaneous Provisions) Act 1982, s. 39, Sched. 7. This power is available to residuary bodies, joint authorities and the Inner London Education Authority: Local Government Act 1985, Sched. 13, para. 12(*d*) and Sched. 14, para. 16.

[97] *Bishop* v. *Deakin* [1936] Ch. 409.

Appointment

Section 112 of the Local Government Act 1972[98] requires an authority to appoint such officers as it thinks necessary for the proper discharge by the authority of its functions and for carrying out commitments on behalf of other authorities. The former obligation to appoint particular officers was considerably modified by this section. Where an officer is appointed for a particular purpose or to discharge a particular function he is referred to in the Act as the "proper officer." But the freedom not to appoint prescribed officers does not extend to committees of local authorities of which some members are required to be appointed by a body or person other than a local authority. This is the effect of subsection (3) and it means that chief constables, deputy chief constables, and assistant chief constables must be appointed under the Police Act 1964, National Park officers must be appointed under Schedule 17 to the Act of 1972, and fishery officers under the Sea Fisheries Regulation Act 1966. Secondly, five statutory requirements as to the appointment of particular officers are preserved in subsection (4).[99] They are as follows;

(a) Chief education officers appointed under section 88 of the Education Act 1944.

(b) Chief officers and other members of fire brigades maintained under the Fire Services Act 1947.

(c) Inspectors of weights and measures appointed under section 72 of the Weights and Measures Act 1985.

(d) Agricultural analysts and deputy agricultural analysts appointed under section 67(3) of the Agriculture Act 1970.

(e) Directors of social services appointed under section 6 of the Local Authority Social Services Act 1970.

Thirdly, the full discretion in appointment does not extend to persons appointed by a local authority to perform a specified function, a category which includes public analysts appointed under section 76 of the Food Act 1984.

4-39   Sections 257 and 258 of the Local Government Act 1972 made provision for the establishment of two staff commissions, one for England and one for Wales. Their objectives were to promote arrangements for the transfer of staff from former authorities to new authorities on an equitable and efficient basis, to encourage the best means of recruitment and appointment of officers, and to safeguard the interests of the staff concerned. The commissions had no mandatory powers but advised the Secretary of State, and he in turn had power to give directions to any authority.

---

[98] Sections 112–119, concerning staff, apply to local authorities, joint authorities and the Inner London Education Authority (s. 146A, inserted by the Local Government Act 1985, Sched. 14, para. 16) and (except for s. 116) to residuary bodies (1985 Act, Sched. 13, para. 12(*b*)).

[99] As amended by the Local Government Act 1985, Sched. 7.

The transfer of staff on reorganisation was governed by regulations made under section 255 of the Local Government Act 1972.[1] Section 259 of the Act required the Minister to make regulations for the payment of compensation to persons who suffer loss of employment or loss or diminution of emoluments which is attributable to provisions of the Act or delegated legislation made under it.[2] The loss must be attributable to the legislation and not to changes of policy by the new authorities.[3]

The transfer of staff on the abolition of the Greater London Council and the metropolitan counties is governed by Part VI (ss. 50–56) of the Local Government Act 1985. The Secretary of State is advised by the London and Metropolitan Government Staff Commission, first established under the Local Government (Interim Provisions) Act 1984. The Secretary of State may by order designate a person or a class or description of employees for the purposes of their being transferred to the employment of a successor authority. Any person who at any time after July 16, 1985, is in the service of:

(a) the Greater London Council, a metropolitan county or district council, a London borough council or the Common Council of the City of London, or

(b) a new authority or a residuary body,

and who suffers loss of employment or loss or diminution of emoluments which is attributable to any provision made by or under the 1985 Act, is entitled to compensation.

A parish council and community council may, under section 112(5) of the Local Government Act 1972, appoint one or more persons from among their number to be officers of the council, without remuneration.

4-40 A member of an authority cannot be appointed by that authority to any paid office, other than chairman or vice-chairman, and this bar continues for 12 months after membership ceases.[4] The bar applies notwithstanding that the service is given in an honorary capacity.

> *Att.-Gen.* v. *Ulverston Urban District Council.*[5] A member of the urban district council was appointed clerk of the council on an offer by him immediately to resign his membership and to serve in an honorary capacity for twelve months from the date of his appointment. *Held*, the appointment was to a "paid office."

Tenure and remuneration

4-41 Officers appointed under the Local Government Act 1972 hold

---

[1] Local Authorities, etc. (Staff Transfer and Protection) Order 1974 (S.I. 1974 No. 483) as amended.

[2] Local Government (Compensation) Regulations 1974 (S.I. 1974 No. 463). See also S.I. 1974 No. 54) (fire services); S.I. 1974 No. 759 (police); S.I. 1975 No. 353 (coroners).

[3] *Mallett* v. *Restormel Council* [1978] I.C.R. 844; *Harper* v. *North-West Water Authority* [1978] I.C.R. 884; *Walsh* v. *Rother District Council* [1978] I.C.R. 1216; *Fleming* v. *Wandsworth London Borough Council* (1984) 83 L.G.R. 277.

[4] Local Government Act 1972, s. 116.

[5] [1944] Ch. 242.

office on such reasonable terms and conditions, including terms of remuneration, as the authority appointing them thinks fit.[6] The more specific provisions in the Local Government Act 1933 were not repeated in the Act of 1972: officers are therefore directly subject to the general enactments relating to employment, in particular the Employment Protection (Consolidation) Act 1978, and to the terms of the contract of employment into which they have entered.

Special rules apply to particular groups. The remuneration and conditions of service of police officers are regulated by statutory provisions.[7] Similarly, discipline and dismissal in the fire services are the subject of statutory provisions.[8]

4-42   The statutory discretion of local authorities to appoint officers on such terms and conditions and remuneration as they think fit is in practice substantially curtailed. The principle of fixing wages and salaries by means of joint negotiating machinery has extended as much to local authorities as to industry. There are over 40 separate negotiating councils or committees. The activities of the employers' side of local government wage-negotiating organisations are co-ordinated by the Local Authorities' Conditions of Service Advisory Board (LACSAB), which also provides a joint secretariat for these bodies, maintains liaison with other employers and obtains and disseminates information on service conditions. This is a non-statutory body, and its members are appointed by the local authorities' associations and the employers' sides of negotiating bodies.

The recommendations of joint negotiating committees are, however, not necessarily to be taken as the measure of "reasonableness" when the authority's discretion is being exercised. In *Carr* v. *District Auditor for No. 1 Audit District (Alston-with-Garrigill)*[9] Slade J. stated[10]:

> "I think that the sole function of any such recommendations can be, and can only be, to give guidance to the members of the council as to what may be considered to be objectively reasonable. It is only if a remuneration ... is objectively unreasonable that it becomes unlawful."

That payments in excess of national wage settlements are not necessarily *ultra vires* was confirmed in *Pickwell* v. *Camden London Borough Council.*[11]

4-43   The payment of gratuities to serving officers is illegal.

---

[6] Local Government Act 1972, s. 112.
[7] Police Act 1964, ss. 44 and 46; Police Negotiating Board Act 1980; and the regulations made thereunder. Members of police forces are excluded from the operation of much of the Employment Protection (Consolidation) Act 1978, such as, for example, the provisions as to unfair dismissal: 1978 Act, s. 146(2), (3).
[8] Fire Services Act 1947, ss. 17, 18 and Fire Services Act 1959, ss. 5, 14, 29 and the regulations made thereunder.
[9] (1952) 50 L.G.R. 538.
[10] At p. 545. In the view of Lord Goddard C.J. and Parker J., the question turned on whether certain fees were or were not to be regarded as part of the clerk's salary.
[11] [1983] Q.B. 962. See § 7-18.

Re Magrath.[12] Durham County Council increased the county treasurer's salary by £100 in 1925. In 1931 the council paid him £700 apparently in respect of additional work which had come to him in 1920 and which had not been recognised from 1920 to 1925. The district auditor disallowed the sum of £700 and surcharged the members who voted for the payment. The Court of Appeal held that the district auditor was right in disallowing it as being retrospective and without consideration. Lord Maugham said[13]: "It is, I think, clear that the local authority cannot out of public moneys give gratuities to their officers or servants over and above their fixed salaries and wages.... Different considerations might well apply to a case where the officer or servant was asked to perform extra services in respect of a specified job or undertaking, on the understanding that as soon as the work was complete the authority would determine the amount of his special remuneration."

Responsibilities

The responsibilities of officers to their councils and to the public at **4-44** large have been the subject of judicial comment. The first (as to clerks) appear in *Re Hurle-Hobbs, ex p. Riley and Another* (1944),[14] the second (as to treasurers) in *Att.-Gen.* v. *De Winton*[15] to which reference is made in Chapter 7.

Re Hurle-Hobbs, ex p. Riley and Another. The auditor surcharged interest amounting to £1,024 paid under an agreement which the auditor held had been entered into by the council as a result of the negligence and misconduct of an alderman of the council and the town clerk, both of whom the auditor found had withheld from the council material information which might have deterred the council from entering into the agreement. Lord Caldecote C.J. said: "Notwithstanding the strenuous contention of counsel on his behalf, the town clerk seems to me wholly to misconceive his duty when he says that although he thought that the matters I have discussed ought to have been disclosed to the council, he was entitled to stand by without taking such steps as were open to him merely because he would otherwise have been liable to dismissal from his office without notice.... The office of town clerk is an important part of the machinery of local government. He may be said to stand between the borough council and the ratepayers. He is there to assist by his advice and action the conduct of public affairs in the borough, and if there is a disposition on the part of the council, still more on the part of any member of the council, to ride roughshod over his opinions, the questions must at once arise as to whether it is not his duty forthwith to resign his office or, at any rate, to do what he thinks right and await the consequences. This is not so dangerous or heroic a course as it may seem. The integrity of the administration of public affairs is such that publicity may be safely relied upon to secure protection for anyone in the position in which the town clerk was said to have been placed."

It is common practice for officers to give advice to members of the **4-45** public regarding prospective slum clearance, road-widening schemes and

---

[12] [1934] 2 K.B. 415.

[13] At p. 435.

[14] This case is not reported but a full note of it appears in the appendix to *Hurle-Hobbs on District Audit*. For a critical discussion on this case, see Report of the Bognor Regis Inquiry, paras. 233 *et seq.* Today an officer would have the additional security of the unfair dismissal provisions of the Employment Protection (Consolidation) Act 1978.

[15] [1906] 2 Ch. 106.

the like. A responsible officer answering such an inquiry may well owe a duty of care towards the inquirer, so that if he negligently gives wrong information he and the authority may be sued for damages.[16]

Superannuation

4-46   Employees of local authorities are subject to the provisions of the Superannuation Act 1972[17] and the detailed regulations made thereunder.[18] Whole-time officers of local authorities and certain joint boards and joint committees are compulsorily superannuable, and there are provisions as to the admission into superannuation of part-time officers and manual workers. Superannuation funds are maintained by the contributions of employees, at prescribed percentages of remuneration, and equivalent contributions are made by employing authorities. Funds must be actuarially valued quinquennially and where a fund is deficient a further payment is required from the local authority. Superannuable employees may transfer from one local authority to another and to and from certain nationalised industries without detriment to their superannuation rights. The regulations provide for retirement pensions, retiring allowances, widows' pensions, children's pensions, short service pensions and death gratuities. Benefits are based on years of service and on pensionable remuneration.[19]

Interest, corruption and accountability

4-47   If it comes to the knowledge of an officer that a contract in which he has a direct or indirect pecuniary interest (other than a contract to which he himself is a party) has been or is proposed to be concluded by the authority he must disclose this fact in writing.[20] An officer is forbidden, under colour of his office or employment, to exact or accept any fee or reward other than his appropriate remuneration.[21] An officer who fails to disclose an interest or accepts a reward is liable on summary conviction to a fine not exceeding level 4 on the standard scale. An officer is under duty to account for money and property committed to his charge.[22]

An authority is under an obligation to take security in relation to officers likely to have control of money and may take security for other officers.[23] Security may also be taken for other persons not employed by the authority but likely to have control of money or property.

---

[16] See §§ 10–41—10–42.
[17] See especially ss. 7–9. The schemes for local authority officers and for teachers are separate: *Secretary of State for the Environment* v. *Cumbria County Council* [1983] I.C.R. 52.
[18] Local Government Superannuation Regulations 1974 (S.I. 1974 No. 520) as amended.
[19] See S.I. 1974 No. 520, Part E1.
[20] Local Government Act 1972, s. 117(1).
[21] *Ibid.* s. 117(2). See also the Public Bodies Corrupt Practices Act 1889 and the Prevention of Corruption Acts 1906–16.
[22] *Ibid.* s. 115.
[23] *Ibid.* s. 114.

E. Disposal of Local Authority Business

Part VI of the Local Government Act 1972[24] (and more particularly **4-48**
section 101) makes provision for the way in which local authorities may
arrange for the discharge of their functions. All authorities (including
parish and community councils) may discharge their functions through a
committee, a sub-committee, through another authority, through joint
committees and through officers, including officers loaned by another
authority. In certain cases functions may be discharged through a joint
board. There is no power to delegate to a member.[25]

Committees

An authority has a general power to arrange for a committee or a sub- **4-49**
committee to discharge any of its functions. The term "to discharge a
function" is used in the Act of 1972 in place of the word "delegation" in
earlier legislation. There is, in practice, still a division in decision-making
into two groups: in the first are those decisions which are subject to
confirmation of the council (the power to make such decisions will be
spoken of here as "referred powers"), and in the second group are those
which are effective as soon as they are made by the committee (the
powers to make such decisions are referred to here as "delegated
powers"). Technically, the former situation whereby matters are "referred" involves the delegation of a part only of the decision-making
process, usually the part that consists of the investigation of the factual
background, the consultation of interested parties and the receipt of
expert advice. In *some* circumstances, this information must be fully
summarised so that it may be considered by the council.

> *Osgood* v. *Nelson*.[26] Allegations of neglect in the performance of his duties as
> Registrar of the Sheriff's Court of The City of London were made against O.
> The Court of Common Council of the City referred the matter to a committee,
> which heard evidence and submissions and reported that in their opinion
> irregularities had occurred. The council resolved to dismiss O. They had before
> them the committee's report and a full transcript of evidence. *Held*, this mode
> of proceeding was perfectly fair, and did not constitute a violation of the rule
> against delegation.
> *Jeffs and others* v. *New Zealand Dairy Production and Marketing Board*.[27] The
> Board had power to define zones from which particular factories could get

---

[24] Part VI (ss. 101–110) applies to local authorities, joint authorities (apart from police
authorities) and the Inner London Education Authority: s. 101(13) amended by the Local
Government Act 1985, Sched. 14, para. 15.

[25] *R.* v. *Secretary of State for Education and Science, ex p. Birmingham City Council* (1984) 83
L.G.R. 79. The Act cannot be construed as permitting a committee of one: *R.* v. *Secretary
of State for the Environment, ex p. Hillingdon London Borough Council, The Times,*
November 20, 1985. *Cf. KLF (UK) Ltd.* v. *Derbyshire County Council, The Times,* August
21, 1985, where it was held that a council could be bound by statements made by a
member.

[26] (1872) L.R. 5 H.L. 636.

[27] [1967] 1 A.C. 551.

cream and milk. The Board set up a committee of three of its members to investigate the question of supply to two factory-owning dairy companies. The committee acting on its own initiative held a public hearing at which farmers and other interested parties gave evidence and made oral and written submissions. The farmers opposed zoning. The committee made a written report, and recommended certain zonings, which were accepted by the Board without alteration. The report did not record, even in a summary form, the evidence given at the hearing, but did state the submissions that had been made. The Board conceded that it was under a duty to act judicially in determining zoning questions affecting the rights of individuals. The Privy Council held that the Board acted in breach of natural justice in failing to hear the interested parties, but that they would have complied with natural justice had the evidence and submissions been fully summarised. The appointment of a person or persons to hear evidence and submissions was appropriate where the credibility of witnesses was not involved.

R. v. Chester City Council and others, ex p. Quietlynn Ltd.[28] The applicant challenged the decisions of a number of authorities to refuse sex shop licences under the Local Government (Miscellaneous Provisions) Act 1982, on a variety of grounds. One ground raised against Chester City Council was that the committee that decided to refuse the licence had delegated the task of conducting the hearing required by para. 10(19) of Schedule 1 to the 1982 Act to a panel or sub-committee of five members: all that was before the committee was the recommendation of the panel that a licence should be refused on the grounds that the grant of a licence would be inappropriate having regard to the character of the locality and that the number of sex establishments appropriate for the locality was nil. Woolf J. held that this procedure would not have been adequate had the statute contemplated a judicial hearing. Similarly it would not have been adequate for the majority of quasi-judicial hearings. Conversely, it would be sufficient in respect of purely administrative matters. The consideration of an application for a licence was not a purely administrative matter and there was a duty to act fairly: in the ordinary way it would be preferable for the committee to be provided with a summary of the applicant's representations as well as the sub-committee's recommendation. However, on the facts of the case there was no actual unfairness to the applicants: the committee's decision was substantially one of policy, based on the characteristics of the locality which could be expected to be known to the committee; there was no suggestion that the applicants had made any representations to the panel which were relevant to the actual grounds for refusal; the members of the panel were members of the committee and present at the committee meeting and could have provided further information had it been sought. This ground of challenge failed. Woolf J.'s decision on this point was reversed by the Court of Appeal. Stephen Brown L.J. held that the appellant's representations should have been considered by the committee and since no report of any kind had been made to it there was a procedural irregularity which could not be cured by the fact that members of the committee could have been expected to know the characteristics of the locality and that they could have asked if they wished for details from the panel members present.

In other circumstances decisions taken under referred powers when confirmed become in all respects the decisions of the council and whatever consideration was given to matters in committee is deemed to have been given them by the council.

---

[28] *The Times*, October 19, 1983 and (1984) 83 L.G.R. 308. Applied in *R. v. Birmingham City Council, ex p. Quietlynn Ltd.* (1985) 83 L.G.R. 461, 491–492, 501–502.

Goddard v. *Minister of Housing and Local Government.*[29] The plaintiff sought to challenge the validity of a compulsory purchase order and put forward two contentions, one of which was this: that the council never applied its mind to the issue, for the resolutions of the committees concerned were merely "rubber-stamped," whereas the council were obliged by statute to "satisfy themselves." This point did not succeed. The court held that the council, *acting through their committees*, were satisfied.[30]

Where a council delegates specific matters to committees (where, in the **4-50** terms of the Act, a council discharges any of its functions by a committee) the decision of the committee is effective forthwith.[31] It is specifically provided that an arrangement of this kind does not prevent the authority itself from exercising the relevant function. This right to withdraw delegation must, of course, be subject to any third party rights which have come into being (by way of contract, for example) in consequence of a committee's decision. Where an authority has delegated a function to a committee then, unless it otherwise directs, the committee may in turn delegate that function to a sub-committee or to an officer. The maxim *delegatus non potest delegare* has no longer any significance in this context.

There are two limitations on an authority's power to delegate which apply in relation to the discharge of functions whether by a committee, a sub-committee, an officer or some other authority. The power to levy a rate or issue a precept or borrow money and the power to approve schemes for local lotteries may be exercised only by the authority.[32] There may also be circumstances in which it is implicit in a statute that action can only be taken by the authority, *e.g.* the adoption of a local plan under section 14 of the Town and Country Planning Act 1971 requires a resolution of the council.

The exercise of delegated powers by committees is illustrated in the case which follows:

Battelley v. *Finsbury Borough Council.*[33] The local authority had appointed a works committee and by its standing orders it was provided: "The works committee shall be responsible for... appointment and management of the staff of the borough engineer's department." The plaintiff, having applied for the post of assistant road superintendent, was interviewed by the works committee which resolved that the plaintiff should be appointed to the post. He was notified by the town clerk that he had been selected "subject to confirmation." Subsequently the committee appointed someone else. The plaintiff brought an action for breach of contract. *Held*, on the true construction of the standing orders the local authority had delegated to the works committee the power to appoint the plaintiff to the post, and the committee, having entered into a contract to that end, was in breach.

---

[29] [1958] 1 W.L.R. 1151.
[30] See further, de Smith, *Judicial Review of Administrative Action* (4th ed.), p. 299, where it is noted (note 27) that the local authority in *Goddard* was not obliged to hold a hearing as to the matters of which it had to be "satisfied."
[31] A council may delegate to a "sub-committee": *Southwark London Borough Council* v. *Peters* (1971) 70 L.G.R. 41.
[32] Local Government Act 1972, s. 101(6); Lotteries and Amusements Act 1976, s. 6(3).
[33] (1958) 56 L.G.R. 165.

It will be noted that a standing order was the instrument of delegation and that the words "shall be responsible for" constituted an act of delegation.

Joint committees

4-51   Authorities are enabled to discharge their functions through joint committees,[34] and such committees have a power to co-opt to their membership. Expenses of a joint committee are defrayed by local authorities in such proportions as they may agree. If they cannot agree, it is for the district council to determine the proportions if the joint committee is appointed by the councils of parishes or communities or groups of parishes or communities in the same district. If the appointing authorities are all principal authorities or if the councils of parishes or communities are situated in two or more districts then, if the parties cannot agree, the apportionment is determined by an arbitrator agreed by the authorities or, in default of agreement, by an arbitrator appointed by the Secretary of State.[35]

4-52   The constitution of a joint committee is generally contained in a formal agreement entered into by the authorities concerned. The agreement commonly prescribes the number of members of the joint committee, the number of members which each authority may appoint, the terms of office, and other related matters. The joint committee has no corporate status and it cannot therefore hold property. Any property which it uses vests in one of the constituent authorities which holds it in trust for the rest. Alternatively, the constituent authorities may hold the property jointly. A member of a local authority appointed to a joint committee of which the authority forms part ceases to be a member of that committee when he ceases to be a member of the authority. There is a specific power to appoint joint advisory committees.

Several statutes make provisions for the appointment of joint committees for specific services—for example, joint education committees may be established under the Education Act 1944,[36] and children's regional planning committees must be established for planning areas (for the purposes of planning community homes for children in care and the preparation of schemes of intermediate treatment for children and young persons under court orders) defined by the Secretary of State for Social Services under the Child Care Act 1980.[37]

Joint boards

4-53   A joint board is fundamentally different from a joint committee. There is no general power to create joint boards. Specific powers are contained

[34] Local Government Act 1972, s. 102.
[35] *Ibid.* s. 103.
[36] Sched. 1, Part II; Local Government Act 1972, Sched. 30.
[37] s. 31.

in a number of statutes and in each case the rules as to the constitution are stated in the enabling statute. A power is contained in the Local Government Act 1972, enabling the provisions of the Act to be extended to joint boards, so that the affairs of joint boards may be administered in much the same way as the affairs of local authorities.[38] A joint board is a corporate body, created by order of a Minister, requiring in many cases the approval of Parliament. It has perpetual succession, a common seal, and it can hold land. Unlike a joint committee a joint board cannot be dissolved by agreement. It has independent financial powers, including the power to borrow, and obtains the money it needs from constituent authorities by means of precepts. The term of office of members of a joint board depends on the provisions of the Order by which it is established.[39]

The following are examples of joint boards. The Public Health Act 1936[40] empowers the Secretary of State for the Environment by order to create a united district under a joint board for any of the purposes of that Act, and certain other public health statutes. A board constituted in this way is declared by the statute to be a corporate body by such name as the order determines, having perpetual succession, a common seal and a power to hold land. Expenses are defrayed out of a common pool to be contributed by the constituent authorities in proportion to their rateable values, and a power is given to issue precepts on the constituent authorities for the amounts due. Section 1 of the Town and Country Planning Act 1971 empowers the Secretary of State to create a joint planning board to act as the local planning authority over the areas of a number of planning authorities, but unless the councils agree he must hold a public inquiry and the order he makes must be laid before Parliament. If either House within forty days resolves that the order be annulled, then it ceases to have effect. A somewhat similar provision is contained in Schedule 1 to the Education Act 1944, respecting the creation of joint education boards.

Delegation to officers

The Local Government Act 1972 for the first time gave a general power **4-54** to local authorities to discharge any of their functions through officers. Several earlier statutes had enabled certain officers to take decisions on behalf of a local authority. Section 17 of the Public Health Act 1961, for example, gave summary powers to medical officers of health and public health inspectors to deal with stopped-up drains, and section 64 of the Town and Country Planning Act 1968 enabled a local planning authority to delegate certain of its decision-making powers to named officers. The implication was, of course, that, in the absence of a direct statutory

---

[38] Local Government Act 1972, s. 241.
[39] *R. v. Peak Park Joint Planning Board* (1976) 74 L.G.R. 376: member appointed to the board by the county council could not be removed by the council before expiry of the term of office specified in the Order.
[40] s. 6; Local Government Act 1972, s. 181 and Sched. 30; Water Act 1973, Sched. 9.

power, an officer could not act except with the authorisation of his council. This situation made nonsense of the administrative system, but there was a widely accepted practice that whatever action an officer took within the scope of his general authority, or within the terms of a policy settled by the council, would be taken as the act of the council itself. This practice worked sensibly enough on the assumption that the act would be ratified by the council should ratification be necessary. Indeed, as will be seen in Chapter 10, an authority may be bound even against its will by a contract entered into by an officer within his ostensible authority.

4-55   It is now the practice of authorities to specify areas of decision-making which fall to specified officers,[41] but the practical question will remain as to the binding effect of an officer's act beyond the scope of formal delegation. These matters are considered at paragraphs 12-12 to 12-14.

Ratification

4-56   According to the law of agency, where an agent purports to act on behalf of a principal, but in fact lacks power to bind the principal, the principal may nevertheless be bound by that act, with retroactive effect, if he subsequently ratifies it. The basic conditions are:

(1) the principal must be in existence and capable of being ascertained at the time of the act;

(2) the principal must be competent at the time when the act was done by the agent;

(3) it must be shown that the agent was acting on the principal's behalf.[42]

The extent to which these principles are applicable to the acts of an officer or member purportedly taken on behalf of a local authority is uncertain. It is clear that they do not apply where the act is *ultra vires* the authority.

> *Co-operative Retail Services Ltd.* v. *Taff-Ely Borough Council*.[43] The Clerk to the council erroneously took the view that a resolution of the council amounted to a grant of planning permission for a Tesco superstore. In fact the resolution indicated that while the borough council favoured the application, it was a "county matter" and so had to be referred to a joint meeting with the county council.[44] Without consulting the council or the planning committee, he issued the standard notice, backdated, which stated that the council had granted permission. The council subsequently resolved that "the action taken by the clerk in issuing the planning consent be confirmed." The Court of Appeal held that the council had not granted planning permission originally; that the notice issued by the clerk was a nullity; that the "confirmation" had not amounted to a "ratification" but was simply a confirmation of his action in issuing a document

---

[41] Principal councils are obliged to maintain a list, open to public inspection, of powers delegated to officers: s. 100G(2), (4); § 4-61, *infra*.

[42] See *Bowstead on Agency* (15th ed.), pp. 51-84.

[43] (1979) 39 P. & C.R. 223.

[44] See the Local Government Act 1972, Sched. 16, para. 15.

giving notice of a non-existent resolution to grant permission; and that, in any event, an act that was *ultra vires* could not be ratified. This decision was subsequently confirmed when the House of Lords unanimously dismissed an appeal by the borough council: *Att.-Gen. ex rel. Co-operative Retail Services* v. *Taff-Ely Borough Council*.[45]

Furthermore, they do not apply where an authority purports to ratify the decision of a person to whom there is no power to delegate. In *Barnard* v. *National Dock Labour Board*,[46] dock workers were suspended by a port manager. The Court of Appeal held that this power was only exercisable by the local dock labour board. There was no power of delegation. The court also rejected an argument that the suspensions had been ratified by the board. Denning L.J. stated[47]:

" . . . if the board have no power to delegate their functions to the port manager, they can have no power to ratify what he has done. The effect of ratification is to make it equal to a prior command; but just as a prior command, in the shape of a delegation, would be useless, so also is a ratification."

The position with respect to the ratification of an officer's act in **4-57** commencing legal proceedings is unclear. In the following cases it was held that prior authorisation is necessary:

St. Leonard's Vestry v. *Holmes*.[48] A notice was served by a sanitary inspector without authority; and, later, a second notice was served by him after consultation with some members of a sub-committee. But no consideration was given by the vestry before the work was undertaken. After the work was completed, the action of the sub-committee and of the inspector was approved by resolution of the vestry. In proceedings to recover from the owner the cost of executing the work, the vestry failed. Day J. said[49]: "It is important that the vestry should exercise a discretion in each case, and it is not enough that the inspector does what he pleases, and then relies on his acts being afterwards approved by the vestry."

Bowyer, Philpott & Payne, Ltd. v. *Mather*.[50] Proceedings were begun by an inspector. He had not been authorised to institute these particular proceedings and he had received no general authority to prosecute. *Held*, subsequent ratification by the authority was not sufficient.

These cases were, however, distinguished by the majority of the Court of Appeal in the following decision:

Warwick Rural District Council v. *Miller-Mead*.[51] The authority's solicitors issued a writ against the owner of a caravan site under section 100 of the Public Health Act 1936, which enabled proceedings to be taken in the High Court where "the authority are of the opinion that summary proceedings would afford an inadequate remedy." Three days after the issue of the writ the council met and considered a report of its officers on the prevailing conditions. The

---

[45] (1982) 42 P. & C.R. 1.
[46] [1953] 2 Q.B. 18. The decision of Forbes J. in *R.* v. *Brent Health Authority, ex p. Francis* [1985] Q.B. 869 appears to be inconsistent on this point.
[47] At p. 40.
[48] (1885) 50 J.P. 132.
[49] At p. 134.
[50] [1919] 1 K.B. 419.
[51] [1961] Ch. 590.

council authorised proceedings in the High Court "being of opinion that the summary proceedings would afford an inadequate remedy." The preliminary objection was taken that at the date of the issue of the writ there was no resolution of the council. *Held*, the proceedings were correctly instituted for the authority could ratify by its subsequent resolution the earlier act of its servant. The court observed that at the date of the issue of the writ, the authority, had it applied its mind to the question, was capable of issuing the writ.

This decision was affirmed by the Court of Appeal,[52] but on narrower grounds. The court looked at the precise terms of section 100 rather than to the general rules of ratification. The Master of the Rolls said[53]:

> "I do not think that the terms of the section should be so strictly construed as to require in all cases that the formal expression of the local authority's requisite opinion should have preceded in time the issue of the writ, provided, at any rate, that such formal opinion is expressed before any effective stage in the proceedings comes before the court; and, if I were wrong in that view, I think that, on the facts of the present case, including the recorded minutes ... the court should properly hold that the opinion formally expressed ... had been held in truth three days before; and that the council so intended to record."

His Lordship distinguished *St. Leonard's Vestry* v. *Holmes* and *Bowyer, Philpott & Payne Ltd.* v. *Mather*[54] on the following grounds.[55]

> "We are not, as I think, here concerned with the authority of some person or persons to institute proceedings on behalf of the council or in the council's name, but with the much narrower and distinct point not covered by any direct authority, namely: whether the cause of action which the council asserted in the indorsement of the writ was a cause of action which the council could have possessed at any relevant time. Since the writ was issued in the council's name by its duly constituted solicitors, no such question arises as that debated in *Bowyer* v. *Mather*, and if the only question was as to the solicitors' authority to institute proceedings in the council's name, which the council was itself perfectly competent to bring, then it would in my judgment be clear, upon principle and authority, that subsequent ratification of the solicitors' action by the council would relate back to the date of the issue of the writ.... [N]o question here arises of the authority of the solicitors acting for the council to issue a writ in the council's name, for no evidence before the court was directed to that point.... I accept Mr. Francis' submission that the council, being a *persona ficta* established by section 32 of the Local Government Act 1933, is competent in the ordinary course to institute legal proceedings in its own name and the solicitors for the council regularly appointed as such are entitled prima facie to act in that capacity in connection with such proceedings."

Accordingly, the case is essentially an authority on the interpretation of section 100. It is submitted that the suggestion that the doctrine of ratification would apply to the subsequent approval of the solicitors' act in issuing a writ (1) was *obiter*, given that there was no evidence on the point, and (2) is inconsistent with *St. Leonard's Vestry* v. *Holmes* and

---

[52] [1962] Ch. 441.
[53] At pp. 455–456.
[54] *Supra.*
[55] At pp. 450–451.

Bowyer, Philpott & Payne Ltd. v. *Mather*[56] unless a distinction is to be drawn between the subsequent approval of an act of an officer and the subsequent approval of an act of a solicitor. It is suggested, however, that a local authority is no more entitled to delegate a decision to institute proceedings to a solicitor than the authorities were entitled to delegate such decisions to inspectors in the two cases cited. The remarks of Danckwerts L.J. were similarly directed to the interpretation of section 100. Willmer L.J. dissented, holding that the only way in which the opinion of a local authority can be expressed is by way of a resolution; and that the opinion that summary proceedings would afford an inadequate remedy must be so expressed before the commencement of proceedings. The case was indistinguishable in principle from *St. Leonard's Vestry* v. *Holmes* and *Bowyer, Philpott & Payne* v. *Mather.*[57]

Warwick Rural District Council v. *Miller-Mead*[58] was applied by the   **4-58**
Court of Appeal in *Stoke-on-Trent City Council* v. *B. & Q. Retail Ltd.*[59] The council instituted proceedings for an injunction to restrain the defendants from opening their shops on Sunday contrary to the Shops Act 1950. They relied on section 222 of the Local Government Act 1972 as authority for the institution of proceedings without seeking the consent of the Attorney-General for a relator action.[60] The court held that the council was so entitled, provided they considered whether the action proposed was expedient for the promotion or protection of the inhabitants in their area, as required by section 222. On the facts, the sub-committee that had originally caused the proceedings to be instituted in the council's name had given no thought to these limitations. However, the policy committee, which subsequently resolved that the proceedings "be prosecuted and continued" did consider these matters. The Court of Appeal held that this constituted a valid "ratification."[61]

There are two other cases where subsequent ratification has been permitted:

Firth v. *Staines.*[62] Section 58 of the Metropolis Management Act 1855 empowered any metropolitan vestry to appoint a committee ... for any purposes which in the discretion of the ... vestry would be better regulated and managed by means of such committee. . . . Provided always that the acts of every such committee shall be submitted to the ... vestry ... for their approval." The committee, in whom public health powers were vested, directed an inspector to serve a notice requiring abatement of a nuisance, and in default to take proceedings. The inspector subsequently started proceedings, and a summons was issued. After the summons was issued but before the proceedings were heard, the vestry approved the committee's action. The defendant argued

---

[56] (1885) 50 J.P. 132 and [1919] 1 K.B. 419.
[57] *Ibid.*
[58] [1961] Ch. 590.
[59] [1984] Ch. 1.
[60] See § 12–47.
[61] See Lawton L.J. at pp. 23–24; Ackner L.J. at pp. 29–30. Oliver L.J. agreed with Lawton L.J.: p. 35.
[62] [1897] 2 Q.B. 70.

that prior approval was necessary. *Held*, the vestry's action constituted a valid ratification. *Per* Hawkins J.[63]: "... if at each step in the execution of their powers the committee are first to obtain the sanction of the vestry, the whole object of their appointment is lost...."

It will be noted that this case turns entirely on the interpretation of the 1855 Act as authorising delegation, provided that acts are subsequently ratified. It was followed in the next case:

R. v. *Chapman, ex p. Arlidge*.[64] A by-law of a sanitary authority provided that the chairman of a committee might, when the sanitary authority was in vacation, give instructions with respect to urgent matters, provided that such acts should be reported to the sanitary authority. The chairman of the public health committee directed, during the vacation, that a notice be served on A. requiring abatement of a nuisance. His action was subsequently approved at the next meetings of, respectively, the committee and the authority. A complaint was then made against A. for default in complying with the notice, and a magistrate made an order requiring abatement. A. argued that the notice had not been validly served. The Divisional Court *held* (Atkin J. dissenting) that the notice had been validly served. *Firth* v. *Staines*[65] was applied. *St. Leonard's Vestry* v. *Holmes*[66] was distinguished on the ground that "in that case there was nothing resembling by-law 130 and giving the inspector authority to act as he acted in that case." It was noted that by-law 130 "has not been suggested to be *ultra vires*...."[67]

Accordingly, it appears that this case was decided on the basis that there was lawful authority for this arrangement, and is on all fours with *Firth* v. *Staines*.[68]

It is impossible to discern any clear principle from the cases on ratification other than that they "turn on the implications of various statutory provisions: there is no rigid rule. But in general the court is likely to be more strict where the issue is one of substance as opposed to formality."[69]

Finally, it should be noted that arrangements whereby a committee chairman is authorised to take urgent action between meetings provided that this is subsequently ratified are of doubtful legality. It will be noted that there is no power under section 101 of the Local Government Act to delegate to members,[70] and the decision in *Barnard* v. *National Dock Labour Board*[71] is against the doctrine of ratification applying in such circumstances. However, delegation to an officer is permissible under section 101, and it would be possible to authorise an officer to take action in consultation with the chairman. Moreover, approval of urgent

---

[63] At p. 74.
[64] [1918] 2 K.B. 298.
[65] *Supra*, n. 62.
[66] *Supra*, n. 48.
[67] [1918] 2 K.B. 298 at p. 308.
[68] *Supra*, n. 62.
[69] H. W. R. Wade, *Administrative Law* (5th ed.), p. 324. See also D. Lanham, "Ratification in Public Law" (1981) 5 Otago Law Review 35.
[70] See § 4–48.
[71] [1953] 2 Q.B. 19. See also cases cited at § 17–07.

chairman's action by the council (or a committee acting under delegated powers) would render the action authorised *from that time*, even if not retrospectively.

Other authorities[72]

An authority may discharge any of its functions by another authority **4-59** under what is commonly called an agency arrangement. The statutory responsibility for the function remains with the authority to whom the function is statutorily allocated.

There is clear scope for this device in a system where executive functions in any particular area lie with at least two authorities—the county council and the district council. Perhaps the best example is seen in highway administration. The county council is the highway authority, with power to plan, construct, and subject to the district council's strictly limited powers, maintain all highways other than trunk roads, and it exercises all traffic powers. The district council may maintain urban unclassified roads and may construct and maintain footpaths and bridleways. Both authorities may provide off-street car parks, the district council's powers being exercisable with the consent of the county council. The advantage of agency arrangements in this situation is clear.

One authority may place its staff at the disposal of another local authority or health authority,[73] and under the Local Authorities (Goods and Services) Act 1970, local authorities may enter into agreements with other authorities for the supply of goods or materials, the provision of administrative, professional or technical services, the use of plant or the carrying out of works of maintenance, but not construction.[74]

Apart from the general limitation that an authority cannot delegate the power to issue a precept or levy a rate or borrow money, there is the specific restriction that an authority cannot discharge its functions under the Diseases of Animals Act 1950 by any other authority.[75]

F. Publication of Information

Part II of the Local Government, Planning and Land Act 1980 places on **4-60** local authorities a duty to publish information about the discharge of their functions and other matters. For this purpose the Secretary of State may issue a code of recommended practice. The code, which may be revised from time to time, may specify that publication be made in

---

[72] Local Government Act 1972, s. 101.

[73] *Ibid.* s. 113, as amended by the National Health Service Reorganisation Act 1973, s. 57, Sched. 4, and the Health Services Act 1980, s. 1, Sched. 1.

[74] These powers are available to joint authorities and the Inner London Education Authority (s. 146A, inserted by the Local Government Act 1985, Sched. 14, para. 16) and to residuary bodies (1985 Act, Sched. 13, para. 12(*b*)).

[75] Local Government Act 1972, s. 101(7). The provisions of the Diseases of Animals Act 1950 have been consolidated in the Animal Health Act 1981.

periodical reports or in any other specified manner and may also indicate the occasions and form of publication. In particular, the code may provide for the publication of information with or included in rate demands or in statements of accounts prepared under section 23 of the Local Government Finance Act 1982 for inspection by members of the public at an authority's offices or elsewhere and, where the information refers to the cost of discharging functions, the way in which the cost is determined. Different codes may be issued covering different classes of information, different kinds of authority or areas or different forms and occasions of publication. Before issuing a code, the Secretary of State must consult such local authority associations as appear to him to be concerned. In practice, the codes are published with the agreement of the Consultative Council on Local Government Finance. Codes have been issued concerning the publication of (1) rate demands and supporting information[76]; (2) annual reports and financial statements[77]; and (3) manpower information.[78]

If he considers it necessary, the Secretary of State may make regulations by statutory instrument, subject to annulment by either House of Parliament, requiring authorities to publish information in accordance with the code. Regulations have been made to require observance of the codes for the publication of manpower information.[79] A number of authorities either refused to publish information or were not publishing information quarterly in accordance with the code of practice.

4-61   Section 100G of the Local Government Act 1972[80] provides that every principal council, as defined for the purposes of Part VA of the 1972 Act,[81] must maintain a register stating the name and address of every member of the council for the time being and the ward or division which he or she represents, and the name and address of every member for the time being of a committee or sub-committee.

Each council must also maintain a list specifying the powers which, for the time being, are exerciseable by officers and stating the title of the officer by whom each power is exercisable. Arrangements for the discharge of a power by an officer for a specified period not exceeding six months are excluded from this requirement. Thirdly, a summary must be kept of the rights to attend meetings and the rights of access to documents conferred by Parts VA and XI of the Local Government Act 1972, and such other enactments as are specified by the Secretary of State. All these documents must be open to inspection at the council's offices.

---

[76] 1980: *see Encyclopedia of Local Government Law,* §§ 6–01—6–04.
[77] 1981: see *ibid.* §§ 6–13—6–18.
[78] Local Government (Publication of Manpower Information) (England) Code 1983: see DoE Circular 3/83. For Wales, see Welsh Office Circular 7/83.
[79] Local Government (Publication of Manpower Information) (England) Regulations 1983 (S.I. 1983 No. 8); for Wales, see S.I. 1983 No. 615.
[80] Inserted by the Local Government (Access to Information) Act 1985, s. 1, with effect from April 1, 1986.
[81] See § 4–17.

Apart from these duties to make certain classes of information **4-62** available to the public, there is a general power under section 142 of the Local Government Act 1972 for a local authority to make, or assist in the making of, arrangements whereby the public may obtain information concerning the services provided in the area by the authority, other authorities, government departments, charities or voluntary organisations, and other information as to local government matters affecting the area. This section was considered in the following case.

> R. v. *Inner London Education Authority, ex p. Westminster City Council.*[82] It was held that a decision of ILEA under section 142 to retain an advertising agency to conduct a compaign with the object of informing the public of the effect of rate-capping and of persuading the public to the view held by the authority was invalid, because in reaching its decision the authority was pursuing an unauthorised purpose, namely that of persuasion, which had materially influenced the making of the decision. Glidewell J. said that the following all came within "information on matters relating to local government": (a) an account of the various facilities provided by and the activities engaged in by authority; (b) a description of proposed or even hoped for improvements in or increases in those facilities and activities; (c) the cost of the various facilities and activities present and anticipated for the future; (d) an explanation of the effect of legislation, including the Rates Act 1984; (e) a description of the extent to which ILEA's activities and facilities would probably have to be curtailed if the Secretary of State's maximum expenditure was to be achieved, including estimates or suggestions of particular facilities or activities which would be affected in this way.
>
> But the decision of the authority was intended to serve two purposes, information and persuasion. Where a decision was intended to achieve two purposes for one of which there was no authority, the tests to be applied were as adopted by Megaw J. in *Hanks* v. *Minister of Housing and Local Government,*[83] namely (i) what was the true purpose for which the power was exercised; and (ii) if any purpose was unauthorised, had it materially influenced the decision? If it had, then the decision was invalid because irrelevant considerations had been taken into account.

The council of a non-metropolitan county may conduct, or assist in the **4-63** conducting of, investigations into, and the collection of information relating to, any matters concerning the county or any part of it. It may also make arrangements whereby any such information or the results of any investigation are made available to any other local authority in the county, any government department or the public.[84] These powers may also be exercised by a London borough council the Common Council and a metropolitan district council. Furthermore, a scheme may be made for these purposes for Greater London or a metropolitan county by the constituent councils. One of the councils is to be designated to carry out the work, although if two-thirds of the constituent councils so decide, any

---

[82] [1986] 1 W.L.R. 28. See also R. v. *Greater London Council and another, ex p. Westminster City Council, The Times,* December 27, 1984 (see § 1–12), and R. v. *Greater London Council, ex p. Westminster City Council, The Times,* January 22, 1985.

[83] [1963] 1 Q.B. 999.

[84] Local Government Act 1972, s. 141.

or all of them may be required to carry out specified tasks. Expenses incurred with the approval of two-thirds of the councils may be recovered from all of them in proportion to their population.[85]

Finally, there are various powers whereby a Minister may require local authorities to provide him with information. For example, every local authority, joint authority, joint board, joint committee and residuary body and the Inner London Education Authority must send the Secretary of State such reports and returns and give him such information with respect to their functions, as he may require or as may be required by either House of Parliament.[86] The Secretary of State has power to require information to be provided by the Greater London Council, the metropolitan county councils and their officers, to him and to the bodies and authorities to which functions were transferred under the Local Government Act 1985.[87]

G. COMMISSIONS FOR LOCAL ADMINISTRATION

4-64   Part III of the Local Government Act 1974 introduced the "ombudsman" principle into the context of local government. The Act established two Commissions for Local Administration, one for England and one for Wales, with powers similar to those of the Parliamentary Commissioner for Administration in relation to the Civil Service. England is divided into three areas, with one Local Commissioner responsible for each area. From time to time, the areas are adjusted to achieve an even distribution of the work load among the Commissioners. There is one Local Commissioner for Wales. The Parliamentary Commissioner for Administration is a member *ex officio* of each Commission.

The Secretary of State was required by the Act[88] to designate a "representative body" for England, and one for Wales.[89] The English body includes representatives of the Associations of County Councils and District Councils, the Association of Metropolitan Authorities and the Water Authorities' Association.[90] The bodies are to receive and publish reports from the respective Commissions, and the reports made by individual Commissioners under section 23(11). They may comment on the reports. They also receive estimates of the Commission's expenses for the next financial year. Any observations concerning the estimates must be considered by the relevant Commission, and if the amount eventually decided upon is considered by the representative body to be excessive, the matter may be referred to the Secretary of State.[91]

[85] Local Government Act 1985, s. 88.
[86] Local Government Act 1972, s. 230, as amended by the Local Government Act 1985, Sched. 14, para. 26; 1985 Act, Sched. 12, para. 12(*g*).
[87] Local Government (Interim Provisions) Act 1984, s. 5; Local Government Act 1985, s. 96. See also § 11–27, *infra*.
[88] s. 24.
[89] S.I. 1974 Nos. 683 and 707.
[90] Annual Report of the English Commission 1983–84, para. 99.
[91] Local Government Act 1974, Sched. 4, paras. 10 and 11.

A Local Commissioner may investigate written complaints made by or **4-65** on behalf of a member of the public who claims to have sustained injustice in consequence of maladministration, in connection with action taken or default first arising after April 1, 1974.

The authorities subject to investigation are: **4-66**

(1) any local authority, defined for the purposes of this Act as county councils, district councils, London borough councils, the Common Council of the City of London and the Council of the Isles of Scilly;

(2) any joint board the constituent authorities of which are all local authorities;

(3) the Land Authority for Wales;

(4) any joint authority established by Part IV of the Local Government Act 1985;

(5) any other police authority, except the Secretary of State;

(6) the Inner London Education Authority; and

(7) any water authority.[92]

Any reference to an authority includes a reference to the members, officers, committees and sub-committees of that authority, to persons or bodies acting on their behalf under sections 101 or 110 of the Local Government Act 1972, and to any appeal committee constituted under the Education Act 1980, Sched. 2.[93]

Complaints must be referred through a member of the authority **4-67** concerned. If a member fails to refer a complaint, the Local Commissioner may receive it directly. Where a complaint is received directly, but without prior reference to a member, it was the practice of the Commissions to send a copy to the authority concerned with a view to settlement locally, and to inform the complainant of the proper procedure.[94] This procedure was changed as from June 1, 1984.[95] It is now the practice for the Commission to send all complaints received directly to the Civic Head of the local authority with a request that he or she seek to obtain a satisfactory local settlement of the complaint within a reasonable time, or else refer it to the Local Ombudsman for consideration. The initial result of the change was a marked increase in the number of direct complaints becoming properly referred through a member.[96] In the absence of special circumstances, a complaint must be made to a member within 12 months of notice to the person aggrieved of the matters alleged in the complaint. Before investigation by the Commissioner, the

---

[92] Local Government Act 1974, s. 25(1), as amended by the Community Land Act 1975, Sched. 10, para. 9(1), the Local Government, Planning and Land Act 1980, Sched. 22, para. 14(2) and the Local Government Act 1985, Sched. 14, para. 51.

[93] *Ibid.* s. 25(4), (5); (subs. (5) was inserted by the Education Act 1980, s. 7(7)).

[94] Annual Report of the English Commission 1977–78, paras. 46–50.

[95] Annual Report of the English Commission for 1984–85, paras. 94–97 and Appendix 4, paras. 25–28.

[96] *Ibid.* para. 96.

authority concerned must have notice of the complaint and a reasonable opportunity to investigate and reply to it. The complaint must specify the action alleged to constitute maladministration, although it is sufficient to specify the action taken by the authority in connection with which the complaint of maladministration is made.[97]

The expression "maladministration" appears also in the Parliamentary Commissioner Act 1967, s. 5(1)(a), but is defined in neither the 1967 Act nor the 1974 Act. In the second reading debate on the Parliamentary Commissioner Bill, Mr. Richard Crossman stated that the characteristics of maladministration include "bias, neglect, inattention, delay, incompetence, ineptitude, perversity, turpitude, arbitrariness and so on."[98] The Commission's booklet, "Your Local Ombudsman," stated that the term refers, for example, *to the way* in which a decision has been taken, and that it covers action or inaction based on improper considerations or conduct, including arbitrariness, malice, bias, unfair discrimination, neglect, unjustifiable delay, incompetence, failure to observe relevant rules or procedures, failure to take relevant considerations into account, failure to establish or review procedures or the use of faulty systems.[99]

4-68   The authority and persons concerned must have an opportunity to comment on any allegations. Investigations are to be in private, but the Commissioner otherwise has a discretion as to the procedure to be adopted. A Local Commissioner has wide powers to require persons to furnish information or disclose documents, although a Minister of the Crown or an authority may give written notice that disclosure of specified information would be contrary to the public interest, in which case there are limitations on the disclosure of that information by the Commissioner to other persons.[1]

A report of the results of an investigation or of the reasons for a decision not to conduct one must be sent to the member who referred the complaint, to the complainant, and to any authority or person alleged to be responsible for the action of which complaint is made. Persons are not normally to be named or identifiable. Reports are to be open to public inspection for three weeks, and public notice of this is to be given. Where the Local Commissioner is of the opinion that injustice has been caused in consequence of maladministration, the authority concerned comes under a duty to consider the Commissioner's report, and to notify him of the action which has been or will be taken. If no such notification is

---

[97] 1974 Act, s. 26(2)(a); *R.* v. *Local Commissioner, ex p. Bradford Metropolitan City Council* [1979] Q.B. 287, 312–313 (Lord Denning M.R.) and 315–316 (Eveleigh L.J.).

[98] H.C. Deb. Vol. 754, c. 51 (1966).

[99] See also N. Lewis and B. Gateshill, "The Commission for Local Administration," pp. 17–29; Annual Report of the English Commission for 1977–78, paras. 111–113, 146; *R.* v. *Local Commissioner, ex p. Bradford Metropolitan City Council* [1979] Q.B. 287 at pp. 311–312, 314, 319.

[1] 1974 Act, s. 32(3), as amended by the Local Government, Planning and Land Act 1980, s. 184. See hereon *Re a Complaint against Liverpool City Council* [1977] 1 W.L.R. 995 and *Gaskin* v. *Liverpool City Council* [1980] 1 W.L.R. 1549.

received within a reasonable time, or the Commissioner is not satisfied with the authority's response, he is to make a further report. Where a Commissioner has made a report, an authority has power to incur expenditure in making a payment or providing a benefit to a person who has suffered injustice.[2] Authorities are not obliged by law to accept the views of the Local Commissioner. At March 31, 1985, in 6 per cent. of the 1,534 cases where injustice had been found, the authority failed to take action satisfactory to the Commissioner. Only one in five further reports had the desired effect.[3] The local authority associations have urged authorities always to respond positively and speedily to Commissioners' findings.[4]

A Local Commissioner is precluded from investigating any of the following particular matters:

(a) any action in respect of which the complainant has or had a right of appeal to a statutory tribunal;

(b) any action in respect of which the complainant has or had a right of appeal to a Minister; or

(c) any action in respect of which the person aggrieved has or had a remedy in law.

But there is a proviso to this. A Commissioner may in fact conduct an investigation into these situations if he is satisfied that in the particular circumstances it was not reasonable to expect the complainant to have taken advantage of the remedies open to him.[5]

R. v. *Local Commissioner, ex p. Bradford Metropolitan City Council.*[6] A mother made various complaints concerning the actions of the local authority in taking her two children into care in March 1975, and in dealing with them thereafter:

(1) that the authority had failed in their duty under section 1 of the Children and Young Persons Act 1963 to use their resources to help the complainant look after the children herself;

(2) that a senior social worker said that she would strongly oppose the mother having the children back as the girl suffered from fits but later said that she did not so suffer;

(3) that the children were separated against the mother's wishes and assigned to different foster parents;

(4) that the senior social worker said that she would have the children adopted without the mother's consent and that they were placed with prospective adopters without consulting the mother.

The Court of Appeal *held* that the investigation of these complaints by the Commissioner was not barred by s. 26(6). The local authority had applied successfully to the juvenile court for a care order in August 1975, and there were to be adoption proceedings in relation to the children for them to be

---

[2] 1974 Act, s. 31(3), added by the Local Government Act 1978. A Local Commissioner's report is a necessary pre-condition to the exercise of this power.

[3] Annual Report of the English Commission for 1984–85, paras. 88–92.

[4] *Ibid.* Appendix 6.

[5] 1974 Act, s. 26(6).

[6] [1979] Q.B. 287.

adopted by their foster parents. Eveleigh L.J. stated[7] that the juvenile court and adoption proceedings did not provide a remedy for the complaints made in this case, as the issues whether the complainant had suffered injustice and whether there had been maladministration did not arise in those proceedings. Sir David Cairns agreed[8] that none of the remedies mentioned in subs. (6) were applicable to the actions of which complaint was made. Lord Denning M.R. stated[9] that there was no conflict at all in relation to complaints (2) and (4). In relation to complaints (1) and (3) there was no conflict as the Local Commissioner had decided to consider only matters which arose between March and August 1975.

4-69   There are some additional areas of investigation from which a Local Commissioner is excluded. He may not look into cases where the complainant claims to have suffered from a decision affecting the public at large, nor into any of the matters listed in Schedule 5. The list includes legal proceedings, investigation of crime, certain commercial transactions, and issues relating to appointments, pay, discipline and other personal matters.

4-70   Local Commissioners are required to submit an annual general report to the Commissions, and each year the Commissions are required to review the operation of these provisions and are empowered to convey to local authorities, through the appropriate local authority associations, or to government departments, any recommendations or conclusions reached in the course of their reviews. Major reviews were conducted in 1978, 1980 and 1984.[10] The Secretary of State has resisted proposals for the extension of the Commissioners' jurisdiction and for the abolition of the requirement that complaints be channelled through an authority member.

The local authority associations, in co–operation with the Commission for Local Administration in England, have issued a Code of Practice concerning the complaints procedures of local authorities. It is reproduced in Appendix 9 to the Report of the English Commission for 1977–78. Part 2 of this Code covers local action without involving a Local Commissioner. Part 3 concerns complaints to be referred to a Local Commissioner, and has been endorsed by the Representative Body and the Commission. A supplement was issued in 1982.[11]

---

[7] At p. 317.
[8] At p. 318.
[9] At pp. 310–311.
[10] Annual Reports of the English Commission for 1977–78, paras. 62–159, 1980–81, Appendices VII and VIII and 1984–85, Appendices 4 and 5. The Secretary of State's response to the first two reviews may be found in the Annual Reports for 1978–79. Appendix 9, and for 1983–84, paras. 91–98 and Appendix 4. See also the Justice report, *The Local Ombudsmen: A review of the first five years* (1982).
[11] See generally P. Birkinshaw, *Grievances, Remedies and the State* (Sweet and Maxwell, 1985), Chap. 2.

CHAPTER 5

ACQUISITION, APPROPRIATION, DISPOSAL AND DEVELOPMENT OF LAND

1. *ACQUISITION*

THIS topic falls under two heads: (A) powers and duties in relation to **5-01** acquisition and (B) procedure for compulsory acquisition.

A. POWERS AND DUTIES

The Local Government Act 1972 empowers a principal council to acquire **5-02** by agreement any land inside or outside its area (a) for the purposes of its functions under any enactment, or (b) for the benefit, improvement or development of its area, whether it is immediately required for any such purpose or not.[1] The Act also provides that a principal council may be authorised by the Minister concerned to purchase compulsorily any land, inside or outside its area, for any purpose for which it is authorised by any enactment to acquire land, with certain exceptions, namely, (i) the purposes mentioned in (b) above, (ii) purposes of the Local Authorities (Land) Act 1963 (see para. 5–47), or (iii) where the enactment in question specifically limits the power to acquisition by agreement.[2] The Act gives similar powers to parish and community councils, save that such councils cannot take compulsory purchase proceedings themselves.[3] These must be taken by the district council, where the district council thinks it appropriate, after inquiry, on the representation of the parish or community council.

Apart from these general provisions, Acts conferring specific functions on authorities normally confer specific powers of acquisition of land, and, where a specific power is given, it is usual for that power to be used rather than any more general power. Thus the powers in the Education Acts and the Highways Acts would be used for land acquisitions for education and highways purposes. A list of statutes giving specific powers of compulsory purchase appears in Appendix 3.

In one case an Act conferring specific functions contains wide powers **5-03** of acquisition. Sections 112[4] and 119 of the Town and Country Planning

---

[1] s. 120. A joint authority and the Inner London Education Authority are treated as principal councils for the purposes of s. 120 (except subs. (1)(*b*)) and ss. 121–123: s. 146 A (1)(*b*) inserted by the Local Government Act 1985, Sched. 14, para. 16.

[2] s. 121.

[3] ss. 124 and 125.

[4] As amended by the Local Government, Planning and Land Act 1980, s. 91.

Act 1971 empower certain authorities[5] to acquire compulsorily, or by agreement, any land in their areas which is suitable for, and is required in order to secure the carrying out of, development, redevelopment or improvement, or which is required for a purpose which it is necessary to achieve in the interests of the proper planning of an area in which the land is situated. Moreover, it is immaterial by whom the authority proposes that any activity or purpose mentioned should be undertaken or achieved, and, in particular, it need not propose to undertake the activity or achieve the purpose itself.

The 1971 Act as amended thus gives very wide powers to such an authority to acquire land for development by itself or to acquire and assemble it for disposal to private developers. In considering whether land is suitable for development, redevelopment or improvement, the authority must have regard to the development plan, to whether any planning permission for the development of the land is in force, and to any other considerations which would be material to determining an application for planning permission for development of the land. Accordingly, in exercising these wide powers, the authority is to be guided by planning considerations.

5-04   Where an authority may be authorised to purchase land compulsorily under any Act it may be authorised to acquire, instead of the land itself, new rights, *e.g.* a right of way, over the land.[6]

5-05   Apart from the powers of acquisition mentioned above, a principal council, or a parish or community council, may accept gifts of property for the purpose of any of its functions or for the benefit of the inhabitants of its area.[7]

A local authority may only acquire land for the purposes set out in the relevant enactment or enactments, and not for any ulterior purpose.[8]

5-06   Where land is acquired by compulsory purchase the compensation money, or purchase price, is payable on the basis described in paragraphs 5-22 to 5-36. Where, as happens in the majority of cases, the land is acquired by agreement although the authority has power to make a compulsory purchase order if it so desires, the compensation money will normally be negotiated and settled on the same basis. Where an authority acquires

---

[5] Councils of counties, districts and London boroughs (s. 112(5)); the Common Council of the City of London (definition of "London borough" in s. 290(1)); Planning Boards (Local Government, Planning and Land Act 1980, s. 119). Where the Secretary of State has power to authorise compulsory purchase by one of these authorities, he may, after the requisite consultation, authorise acquisition by another local authority (as defined in s. 290(1) to include, *inter alia*, drainage authorities and joint boards or committees) (s. 112(2)(3)).

[6] Local Authorities (Miscellaneous Provisions) Act 1976, s. 13.

[7] Local Government Act 1972, s. 139.

[8] See, *e.g. Gard* v. *Commissioners of Sewers of the City of London* (1885) 28 Ch.D. 486; *Marquess of Clanricarde* v. *Congested Districts Board* (1915) 79 J.P. 481; *Municipal Council of Sydney* v. *Campbell* [1925] A.C. 338; *Hanks* v. *Minister of Housing and Local Government* [1963] 1 Q.B. 999; *Meravale Builders Ltd.* v. *Secretary of State for the Environment* (1978) 77 L.G.R. 365; *Costello* v. *Dacorum District Council* (1982) 81 L.G.R. 1. See also § 5-17.

land for a purpose for which it has no power of compulsory purchase, and this is unusual, there is nothing to compel the owner to sell, so that the authority will have to pay him the price he wants if it is to have the land.

Where land is acquired by agreement in cases where the authority **5-07** could have made a compulsory purchase order, many of the provisions of the Compulsory Purchase Act 1965 apply as if it was a compulsory purchase, and restrictive covenants on the land acquired may be overridden.[9]

B. COMPULSORY PURCHASE PROCEDURE

Authorisation of the use of statutory powers

An authority cannot exercise a statutory power to acquire land **5-08** compulsorily in any particular case unless it receives a specific authorisation to do so. The Acquisition of Land Act 1981, replacing the earlier Acquisition of Land (Authorisation Procedure) Act 1946, sets out a uniform procedural code for the authorisation of compulsory purchase which applies to nearly all acquisitions under compulsory powers conferred on local authorities by statutes existing at the time when the 1981 Act was passed and to those under powers conferred by any subsequent statute which incorporates the code by reference. There is one important exception to this rule—the code does not apply to land acquired compulsorily under Part IX of the Housing Act 1985, which deals with clearance areas; a similar code contained Schedule 22 to the Act of 1985 applies instead. Apart from this and a few other exceptions, including acquisition under the New Towns Act 1981 and the Pipe-lines Act 1962, the code is in general use.

Compulsory purchase order

The authority must first make a compulsory purchase order in the **5-09** prescribed form,[10] describing by reference to a map the land to which it relates and citing the statute on which the authority relies for compulsory powers.[11] The order is submitted to the appropriate Minister for confirmation, *i.e.* to the Minister who, under the statute under which the land is acquired, is empowered to authorise the purchase; but before this is done the authority is required to publish in one or more local newspapers in two successive weeks a notice in the prescribed form[12] stating that the order is to be submitted for confirmation, giving details of the contents of the order, and specifying a time (to be not less than twenty-one days) within which objections may be made. A notice in

---

[9] *Ibid.* ss. 120 and 124 and see, *e.g.* Town and Country Planning Act 1971, s. 127.
[10] Compulsory Purchase of Land Regulations 1982 (S.I. 1982 No. 6).
[11] Part II of the Acquisition of Land Act 1981 sets out the procedure to be followed. And see DoE Circular 26/77.
[12] *Supra*, n. 10.

similar terms is sent to every owner,[13] lessee and occupier (except tenants for a month or a less period). If sent by post, it must be sent by registered letter or by recorded delivery service. A notice for an incorporated company or body is duly served if served on the secretary or clerk thereof. When it is not practicable to find the name and address of an owner, lessee or occupier the notice may be addressed to the "owner," "lessee," or "occupier" and delivered to someone on the premises or, if they are unoccupied, affixed to the premises.[14] If no objections are raised, or if objections are withdrawn, the Minister may confirm the order with or without modification. If objections remain (other than those which relate to matters of compensation only), then the Minister must hold a local public inquiry, or alternatively a private hearing, at which the objector and the acquiring authority may state their views.[15] However, where an order is made under section 112 of the Town and Country Planning Act 1971, the Secretary of State may disregard an objection which amounts in substance to an objection to the provisions of the development plan defining the proposed use of the land.[16]

5-10   The Minister then decides whether or not to confirm the order, and is under an obligation to give reasons for his decision.[17]

5-11   A notice to the effect that the order has been confirmed is published in one or more local newspapers and sent, with a copy of the confirmed order, to persons to whom notice was originally given or is addressed as mentioned in paragraph 5–09 and delivered to someone on the premises or affixed to the premises. The order becomes operative, subject to any challenge in the High Court, on the date of the first publication. A person aggrieved by the order may not challenge it except by the proceedings set out in Part IV of the 1981 Act. The grounds on which the order may be questioned are limited to two: that it is *ultra vires*, which would include failure to observe the principles laid down in the *Wednesbury* case described in paragraph 12–20, or that there has been a failure to comply with some statutory requirement. A person aggrieved on either of these grounds may, within six weeks from the date on which notice of confirmation was first published, apply to the High Court that the order be quashed. The court may quash the order on the second ground only if satisfied that the interests of the applicant have been substantially prejudiced by failure to observe formalities. If the order is not challenged within the six weeks'

---

[13] See hereon *Grimley* v. *Minister of Housing and Local Government* [1971] 2 Q.B. 96, in which it was held that an easement of support was not "land" so as to entitle the owner of the dominant tenement to notice.

[14] Acquisition of Land Act 1981, s. 6.

[15] Acquisition of Land Act 1981, s. 13. As to the procedure to be followed, see the Compulsory Purchase by Local Authorities (Inquiries Procedure) Rules 1976 (S.I. 1976 No. 746).

[16] Town and Country Planning Act 1971, s. 132(1).

[17] Tribunals and Inquiries Act 1971, s. 12, and rule 10.

period it cannot subsequently be questioned, even where fraud is alleged.[18]

Special parliamentary procedure

5-12 The Act prescribes a supplementary procedure[19] in the case of land which falls within the following groups:

(a) land held inalienably by the National Trust;
(b) land forming part of a common or open space;
(c) land comprising an ancient monument.

A compulsory purchase order in respect of land falling in group (a) is subject to special parliamentary procedure under the Statutory Orders (Special Procedure) Acts 1945 and 1965 if the National Trust have raised objections. A compulsory purchase order relating to land in group (b) is subject to special parliamentary procedure unless the appropriate Minister certifies that equivalent land will be given in exchange or that the land does not exceed 250 square yards, is required for road widening, and the giving of other land in exchange is unnecessary. Before issuing a certificate, the Minister must give an opportunity to interested persons to make representations to him.

A compulsory purchase order affecting land in group (c) is similarly subject to special parliamentary procedure unless the Secretary of State certifies that the acquiring authority has agreed to observe appropriate conditions as to the use of the land.

Housing Act 1985, Part IX

5-13 As has been noted, the provisions of the Acquisition of Land Act 1981 do not apply where land is acquired under the clearance provisions of Part IX of the Housing Act 1985. The procedure to be followed is found in the 22nd Schedule to that Act, but it is basically the same as the procedure which the 1981 Act prescribes and it is not therefore separately described.

Procedure following authorisation

5-14 After an order has been confirmed a number of further steps must be taken before the acquiring authority becomes the owner. The rules governing this subsequent procedure are now largely found in the Compulsory Purchase Act 1965, which replaced the Lands Clauses Consolidation Act 1845 so far as acquisitions under the code in the Acquisition of Land (Authorisation Procedure) Act 1946, and now the

---

[18] *Smith* v. *East Elloe Rural District Council* [1956] A.C. 736, followed in *R.* v. *Secretary of State for the Environment, ex p. Ostler* [1977] Q.B. 122. As to the right of challenge, see also *Webb* v. *Minister of Housing and Local Government* [1965] 1 W.L.R. 755 and *Ashbridge Investments Ltd.* v. *Minister of Housing and Local Government* [1965] 1 W.L.R. 1320 (see § 12–42), a case arising under a similar provision in the Housing Act 1957.
[19] This is found in Part III of the Acquisition of Land Act 1981.

1981 Act, are concerned. The 1845 Act, however, has not been wholly repealed and can still operate in a few special cases. The provisions in the 1965 Act deal with such matters as the notice to treat, entry before completion, and completion.

Notice to treat

5-15   When the order has been confirmed, the authority is required by section 5 of the 1965 Act to serve notice on all parties interested in the land, stating that the authority has been authorised to acquire the land and is willing to treat for its purchase. The notice asks the parties concerned for details of their interests and claims. The persons on whom notice is served are those who will be required to convey or join in conveying an estate or interest, and all persons who have an interest in the land by reason of which they could interfere with the authority's possession.[20] The method of service is prescribed in section 6 of the 1981 Act as applied by section 30 of the 1965 Act, now substituted by the 1981 Act; see paragraph 5–09.

5-16   The service of a notice to treat does not create a contract of sale, although establishment of the agreed price pursuant to the notice creates an obligation to convey—the point is discussed in *Birmingham Corporation* v. *West Midlands Baptist (Trust) Association (Inc.).*[21] Salmon L.J. said[22]:

> "It is not until compensation is agreed or assessed that the equitable title in the land passes to the party who has served the notice to treat. Either party can then—but only then—obtain specific performance, the one to have the legal title conveyed to him on payment of the price, the other to have the price paid on conveying the legal title."

5-17   Notice to treat may not be withdrawn except by consent unless pursuant to some statutory power. An authority is enabled by the Land Compensation Act 1961 to withdraw the notice within six weeks of receiving a claim for compensation, or to withdraw it within six weeks of the determination of the purchase price by the Lands Tribunal if the owner fails to put in a claim.[23] Further, under section 8 of the Compulsory Purchase Act 1965, where the authority requires part only of any house, building or manufactory, or park or garden belonging to a house, and the owner is willing to sell the whole, he may require the authority to purchase the whole, and the authority in these circumstances may abandon the notice to treat.[24] But although a notice to treat may not be withdrawn except in the circumstances mentioned, the court may infer an abandonment of rights conferred by the notice. The Court of Appeal in

---

[20] But it need not be served on tenants from year to year or for a year or less period; they are dealt with by notice of entry and s. 20 of the Act.
[21] [1970] A.C. 874.
[22] In the Court of Appeal [1968] 2 Q.B. 188 at p. 215.
[23] s. 31.
[24] *King* v. *The Wycombe Railway Company* (1860) 29 L.J. Ch. 462.

Simpsons Motor Sales (London) Ltd. v. *Hendon Corporation*[25] reviewed the law on this topic generally and stated the following propositions.

(1) The acquiring authority is under a duty to proceed to acquire the land within a reasonable time and if this is not done the authority may lose its right to enforce the notice to treat.

(2) The authority may evince an intention to abandon the notice to treat in which case the owner may regard it as abandoned, or may refuse to accept abandonment and enforce the notice—but he must make his position clear and proceed within a reasonable time.

(3) If the authority shows a continuing intention to acquire the land but for a purpose not authorised by the compulsory purchase order, the notice may be restrained as *ultra vires*.[26]

(4) Apart from delay or abandonment, a party may so have conducted or misconducted himself in relation to the other party as to lose, against him, the right to enforce the notice to treat.

The decision of the Court of Appeal was upheld by the House of Lords, where the particular point was made that the court may interfere in its equitable jurisdiction to prevent an acquiring authority from enforcing its legal rights under a notice to treat, but only if to do so would be against good conscience because of bad faith or abuse of power by the authority, or an alteration in his position by the owner making it unfair in the particular circumstances.

If notice to treat is not served within three years of the coming into **5-18** operation of the compulsory purchase order, the order lapses.[27]

Notice of entry and interest

In the ordinary course of events a purchaser enters the land on **5-19** completion, but under the Compulsory Purchase Act 1965 the acquiring authority may at any time after notice to treat has been served give notice of entry, to take effect not less than fourteen days after service.[28] Interest is payable at the prescribed rate on the purchase price as finally assessed from the date of entry to the date of payment. When possession has been taken the claimant has a right upon request to an advance payment of 90 per cent. of the agreed or estimated compensation.[29]

Conveyance

When notice to treat has been served and the amount of compensation **5-20** has been settled the land is conveyed in accordance with normal conveyancing practice. The Compulsory Purchase Act 1965 provides for

---

[25] [1963] Ch. 57, C.A.; [1964] A.C. 1088, H.L.
[26] See hereon *Grice* v. *Dudley Corporation* [1958] Ch. 329.
[27] Compulsory Purchase Act 1965, s. 4.
[28] s. 11; Land Compensation Act 1961, s. 32. For special powers of entry when a general vesting declaration has been made, see ss. 8 and 9 of the Compulsory Purchase (Vesting Declarations) Act 1981: see § 5–21.
[29] Land Compensation Act 1973, s. 52.

the vesting of the land in the acquiring authority where the parties refuse to take compensation or to convey, or do not show title, or cannot be found: the purchase-money is lodged in court and a deed poll is executed by which the land vests in the authority.[30] The costs of all conveyances, including all incidental expenses, are to be borne by the acquiring authority.[31] The Act of 1965 also contains provisions relating to conveyance by persons under disability, but these provisions are now rarely invoked, for under modern law the power of sale has been greatly extended.[32]

General vesting declarations

5-21   The Compulsory Purchase (Vesting Declarations) Act 1981, replacing powers which earlier appeared in the Town and Country Planning Act 1968, makes possible a speedier vesting process by means of general vesting declarations. Where this procedure is followed, legal title to the land which is the subject of a confirmed compulsory purchase order passes to the acquiring authority on the date on which the declaration takes effect, and thereafter the authority is able to deal with the land as it chooses, and may resell the land, without having to await the investigation of title and without having to wait for completion in the conveyancing sense. Compensation in respect of the acquisition can be claimed by the former owner as if notice to treat had been served, and he would then be required to establish his title to the land acquired.[33]

This procedure is available to all authorities possessing compulsory powers under whatever legislation those powers are conferred.

Principles of compensation

5-22   The acquiring authority will have served notice to treat on interested parties, requiring them, *inter alia*, to submit particulars of their claims. Their claims may, of course, be settled by agreement, and in practice generally are, but if the parties fail to agree (or if no claim is made) the matter will be determined by the Lands Tribunal in accordance with the principles laid down in the Land Compensation Acts 1961 and 1973.[34] In the case of tenants from year to year or for a year, or lesser period, who are not entitled to notice to treat, provision for compensation is made by section 20 of the Compulsory Purchase Act 1965.

5-23   Compensation on compulsory purchase is made up of three principal elements—(a) the value of the land taken; (b) if only part of the owner's land is taken, compensation for severance and/or injurious affection in respect of the land retained; and (c) compensation for disturbance or any other matter not directly based on the value of the land.

---

[30] ss. 5(3), 9 and Sched. 2.
[31] Compulsory Purchase Act 1965, s. 23.
[32] ss. 2, 3 and Sched. 1.
[33] See hereon the Compulsory Purchase of Land Regulations 1982 (S.I. 1982 No. 6) form 9.
[34] Compulsory Purchase Act 1965, s. 6.

The fundamental principle underlying this basis of compensation was stated in the often repeated words of Lord Justice Scott in *Horn* v. *Sunderland Corporation*,[35] when he said that the owner:

"has the right to be put, so far as money can do it, in the same position as if his land had not been taken from him. In other words, he gains the right to receive a money payment not less than the loss imposed on him in the public interest, but, on the other hand, no greater."

The totality of the compensation should recompense the owner accordingly.[36]

The Land Compensation Act 1961 lays down (a) certain general rules **5-24** for assessing compensation; (b) certain special rules concerning the appreciation or depreciation in the value of land resulting from the compulsory purchase scheme; and (c) what assumptions may be made in valuing the land as to the grant of planning permission for its future development.

The general rules

The Lands Tribunal in fixing the *total* amount of compensation must **5-25** have regard to the rules in section 5 of the Land Compensation Act 1961. These are as follows:

(1) No allowance shall be made on account of the acquisition being compulsory.

(2) The value of land shall be taken to be the amount which the land if sold in the open market by a willing seller might be expected to realise.

(3) The special suitability or adaptability of the land for any purpose shall not be taken into account if that purpose is a purpose to which it could be applied only in pursuance of statutory powers, or for which there is no market apart from the special needs of a particular purchaser or the requirements of any authority possessing compulsory purchase powers.

(4) Where the value of the land is increased by reason of the use thereof or of any premises thereon in a manner which could be restrained by any court, or is contrary to law, or is detrimental to the health of the occupants of the premises or to the public health, the amount of that increase shall not be taken into account.

(5) Where land is, and but for the compulsory acquisition would continue to be, devoted to a purpose of such a nature that there is no general demand or market for land for that purpose, the compensation may, if the Lands Tribunal is satisfied that reinstatement in some other place is bona fide intended, be

---

[35] [1941] 2 K.B. 26 at p. 42.
[36] In *Wimpey & Co. Ltd.* v. *Middlesex County Council* [1938] 3 All E.R. 781 a claim for prospective profits of a building developer was disallowed.

assessed on the basis of the reasonable cost of equivalent reinstatement.

(6) The provisions of rule 2 shall not affect the assessment of compensation for disturbance or any other matter not directly based on the value of land.

The special rules

5-26   In applying the rules contained in section 5 the Tribunal must leave certain matters out of account and must take certain matters into account. They are contained in sections 6–9 of the 1961 Act and may be summarised as follows:

(a) No account shall be taken of any increase or decrease in the value of the land which is attributable to development, or the prospect of development, under the kinds of scheme of development specified in Schedule 1 to the Act for which the land is being acquired.

(b) Where the owner of the land acquired retains ownership of contiguous or adjacent land and the value of the land he retains is enhanced by the general scheme, the amount by which the value is increased is to be deducted.

(c) No account shall be taken of any depreciation in the value of the land attributable to the fact that an indication has been given that the land was to be acquired by a public authority.

It was decided in *Pointe Gourde Quarrying and Transport Co. Ltd.* v. *Sub-intendent of Crown Lands*[37] that compensation should not be increased by reason of the acquiring authority's scheme[38] and this common law principle still applies in addition to the statutory provisions.[39]

The planning assumptions

5-27   The grant of planning permission can substantially increase the value of the land taken, and the Lands Tribunal must take into account any planning permission in force at the date of the notice to treat. But section 14 of the Land Compensation Act 1961 provides that various assumptions as to the grant of other planning permissions may be made in addition. These are divided into two kinds:

(a) assumptions not derived from development plans and
(b) assumptions derived from development plans.

---

[37] [1947] A.C. 565.

[38] As to the meaning of "scheme," see *Wilson* v. *Liverpool City Council* [1971] 1 W.L.R. 302. "Scheme" in this context is not confined to the kinds of scheme in the 1961 Act as at (a) above.

[39] See also *Melwood Units Pty. Ltd.* v. *Commissioner of Main Roads* [1979] A.C. 426. The principle also requires a decrease in value entirely due to the scheme underlying the development to be disregarded: *Jelson Ltd.* v. *Blaby District Council* [1977] 1 W.L.R. 1020; *cf. Birmingham District Council* v. *Morris and Jacombs* (1976) 33 P. & C.R. 27.

Assumptions not derived from development plans[40]

(1) That planning permission would be given for the development **5-28** envisaged in the proposals of the acquiring authority in relation to the land.[41]

(2) That planning permission would be given for development of any class specified in Schedule 8 to the Town and Country Planning Act 1971 (which relates to development included in the existing or current use of land (see para. 19–52)). But there are two exceptions to this rule. First, if permission for Eighth Schedule development has been refused, or granted conditionally, and compensation has become payable, permission will not be assumed, or will be assumed subject to the conditions. Secondly, if compensation has become payable in respect of an order under section 51 of the 1971 Act, requiring the removal of a building or the discontinuance of a use, it will not be assumed that permission would be granted for rebuilding or for the resumption of the use.

(3) That planning permission would be given for development in respect of which a certificate of appropriate alternative development has been issued by the local planning authority under Part III of the Land Compensation Act 1961.

Under this procedure either the owner of the interest to be acquired or the acquiring authority may apply to the local planning authority, under section 17 of the Land Compensation Act 1961,[42] for a certificate, known as a certificate of appropriate alternative development, stating the classes of development, if any, for which planning permission would have been granted if the land were not to be acquired by a public authority. It is for the applicant to specify the class or classes of development which he thinks appropriate. The local planning authority may issue a certificate for all or any of the specified classes or some other class or classes. Regard may properly be paid to the possibility of development on a site comprising both the applicant's site and other land not under his ownership or control and to the possibility of a particular development of an exceptional nature.[43] This procedure is not available if the land is in an action area or in an area allocated primarily for residential, commercial or industrial purposes, in which cases the assumptions to be made are dealt with under (2) below. An appeal lies to the Secretary of State by the owner or the acquiring authority.

[40] Land Compensation Act 1961, s. 15.
[41] See *Myers* v. *Milton Keynes Development Corporation* [1974] 1 W.L.R. 696.
[42] s. 17; as amended by s. 121 of the Local Government, Planning and Land Act 1980 and now reproduced as amended in Sched. 24 to the 1980 Act; and Land Compensation Development Order 1974 (S.I. 1974 No. 539). See also *Grampian Regional Council* v. *Secretary of State for Scotland* [1983] 1 W.L.R. 1340.
[43] *Sutton* v. *Secretary of State for the Environment* (1984) 50 P. & C.R. 147.

Assumptions derived from development plans [44]

5-29   (1) Where land is included in a development plan (see paras. 19–06 to 19–13), and is shown in the plan as intended for *specified development*, then it will be assumed that planning permission would be given for that development.

(2) Where the land is shown in the development plan as an area allocated primarily for a specified use (for example, residential) or a range of two or more primary uses (for example, commercial and industrial) it will be assumed that permission would be granted for any development, falling within the specified primary use or range of uses, for which permission might reasonably have been expected if none of the land in question had been proposed to be acquired.

(3) Where land is to be comprehensively developed, and this is to be construed as an action area for which a local or unitary plan is in force (see paras. 19–11 and 19–13), it will be assumed that planning permission would be given for any development falling within the range of uses allowed for the area. This is subject to it being development for which planning permission might reasonably have been granted on the assumptions:

(a) that the area had not been defined as an area of comprehensive development and no particulars or proposals relating to any land in the area had been comprised in the current plan, and

(b) that no development or redevelopment already carried out in accordance with the plan had taken place, and

(c) that no part of the land was proposed to be acquired by a public authority.

All the assumptions derived from the development plan are on the basis that they are subject to any conditions which might reasonably have been imposed and any indication in the current development plan that the development might only be allowed to take place at some future date.

Where in any area structure and local plans are in force, these together will provide the planning assumptions: where, in the transitional period, the structure plan but not a local plan is in force either the structure plan or the former development plan will be taken to be the development plan, whichever gives rise to those assumptions as to the grant of planning permission which are more favourable to the owner.

Where a unitary development plan is in force (see para. 19–13), this plan will provide the planning assumptions.

5-30   Having set out these various rules and assumptions for the assessment of compensation, consideration is now given to the three elements of compensation mentioned in paragraph 5–23.

---

[44] Land Compensation Act 1961, s. 16. And see *Re Croydon Development Plans 1954 and 1959; Harrison* v. *London Borough of Croydon* [1968] Ch. 479; *Margate Corporation* v. *Devotwill Investments Ltd.* [1970] 3 All E.R. 864; and *Provincial Properties (London) Ltd.* v. *Caterham and Warlingham Urban District Council* [1972] 1 Q.B. 453.

Value of the land taken

Compensation for the value of the land taken will be assessed at either **5-31** (a) the open market value provided for by rule 2 of section 5 of the 1961 Act or (b) the equivalent reinstatement basis in rule 5. It is only in rare cases that the rule 5 basis is applicable.

Compensation for a church or mission would generally fall to be assessed on the basis of the cost of equivalent reinstatement under rule 5,[45] but where this rule is applied there must be a bona fide intention on the part of the claimant to rebuild in some other place.

> *Edgehill Light Ry.* v. *Secretary of State for War.*[46] The company, whose land had been acquired compulsorily, claimed that in calculating the amount of compensation the principle of equivalent reinstatement applied, since the land acquired was devoted to a purpose for which no general demand or market existed. But the company failed to establish its claim for compensation based on rule 5 on the ground that it had no intention to rebuild the railway in some other place.

In the expression "no general demand or market for land for that purpose" in rule 5, the term "general" qualifies only "demand" and not "market" as well.

> *Harrison & Hetherington Ltd.* v. *Cumbria County Council.*[47] The House of Lords *held* on the facts that rule 5 applied in respect of the compulsory purchase of land used for a livestock auction market. "General demand" did not include a special demand which might only arise in particular circumstances, such as when an existing market was offered for sale. The evidence was that in the north of England, a state of equilibrium had been reached and that there had been no sale of virgin land for such a market which was not a replacement of an existing market.

Furthermore, the application of rule 5 is in any case in the discretion of the Lands Tribunal so that, *e.g.* if the cost or reinstatement would be out of all proportion to the benefits resulting from reinstatement the Tribunal could reject the basis.[48]

The Land Compensation Act 1973 specifically provides for the application of rule 5 to the acquisition of any dwelling substantially modified for a disabled person.[49]

The date for valuation will in a rule 2 case be the date on which the **5-32** authority take possession or on which the compensation is settled,

---

[45] *Zoar Independent Church Trustees* v. *Rochester Corporation* [1975] Q.B. 246. See also *Nonentities Society* v. *Kidderminster Borough Council* (1971) 22 P. & C.R. 224 and *Manchester Homeopathic Clinic* v. *Manchester Corporation, ibid.* at p. 243 (theatre and clinic respectively within rule 5).

[46] (1956) 6 P. & C.R. 211.

[47] (1985) 275 E.G. 457.

[48] See *Festiniog Rly.* v. *Central Electricity Generating Board* (1962) 13 P. & C.R. 248—here the cost of reinstatement was found to be disproportionately high; *cf. Sparks* v. *Leeds City Council* (1977) 34 P. & C.R. 248.

[49] s. 45.

whichever is the earlier, and in a rule 5 case the earliest date at which reinstatement could reasonably have been carried out.[50]

There may, of course, be more than one interest in the land to be valued, *e.g.* a freehold interest and a leasehold interest, and there may also be a lesser interest to be compensated under section 20 of the 1965 Act.

Compensation for severance and injurious affection

5-33   Compensation under this head stems from section 7 of the Compulsory Purchase Act 1965. It applies where the owner holds other land with the land taken and that other land, called the retained land, is depreciated in value, *e.g.* where the value of the retained land plus the compensation for the value of the land taken is worth less than the value of the whole before the compulsory acquisition; indeed, the depreciation would usually be valued by taking a before and after valuation of the rule 2 open market value.[51] Thus, if most of the front garden of a house is acquired for a road widening scheme, the value of the land taken may be small and the retained house may be depreciated much more because it now has practically no front garden, and the noise, dust and lights of traffic are brought nearer to it. The retained land need not be contiguous to the acquired land for compensation to be claimed under this head, provided that the owner's possession and control of each of the relevant pieces of land gives an enhanced value to all of them.[52]

Under section 44 of the Land Compensation Act 1973, where damage is caused by works constructed partly on land taken and partly on other land, a claim for injurious affection may include the effect of the works as a whole. If injury or depreciation arises from a wrongful use of statutory powers, the appropriate remedy would be by way of an action for damages or for an injunction or both.

Compensation for disturbance or any other matter not directly based on the value of the land taken

5-34   This compensation derives from case law and is expressly preserved by rule 6 of section 5 of the Land Compensation Act 1961. Broadly, it covers all the expenditure or loss which an owner may incur in having to uproot himself from the land taken and re-establish himself elsewhere. The Court of Appeal considered the principles in the following case:

---

[50] *Birmingham Corporation* v. *West Midlands Baptist (Trust) Association (Inc.)* [1970] A.C. 874. This rule 2 principle will also apply where the purchase is by agreement leaving the price to be fixed as if a notice to treat had been served; *Washington Development Corporation* v. *Bamblings (Washington) Ltd.* (1985) 129 S.J. 100.

[51] *Exors. of J. R. Bullock, deceased* v. *Ministry of Transport* (1969) 211 E.G. 235. See, generally, *Duke of Buccleuch* v. *Metropolitan Board of Works* (1872) L.R. 5 H.L. 418; (injurious affection); *Holt* v. *Gas Light and Coke Co.* (1872) L.R. 7 Q.B. 728 (severance).

[52] *Cowper Essex* v. *Acton Local Board* (1889) 14 App. Cas. 153; *Sisters of Charity of Rockingham* v. *R.* [1922] 2 A.C. 315.

Harvey v. *Crawley Development Corporation.*[53] This was an appeal on case stated by the Lands Tribunal. Mrs. Harvey agreed with the Crawley Development Corporation to sell her house at an agreed price. She claimed in addition as "compensation for disturbance" (1) the expenses of moving her furniture and having curtains and carpets adjusted to fit a new house, and (2) surveyor's fees, legal costs and travelling expenses incurred by her, first, in an abortive proposed purchase of a new home, and secondly, in the purchase of a new home. The corporation admitted that the items at (1) were so claimable, but disputed those at (2). *Held,* Mrs. Harvey was entitled to the costs claimed, for any loss sustained by a dispossessed owner-occupier of a house which flowed from the compulsory acquisition could properly be the subject of compensation for disturbance, provided (a) that it was not too remote, and (b) that it was the natural, direct and reasonable consequence of dispossession.

Compensation for disturbance may cover many items, especially in commercial cases, such as the cost of transferring plant and equipment to new premises, loss of goodwill attached to the premises taken, loss of profits while re-establishing a business, and, in a case where it is not reasonably possible to re-establish the business, loss from the extinction of the business. By section 60 of the 1973 Act where a person occupying business premises is over 60 and does not wish to relocate the business, it may be assumed that it is not reasonably practicable to re-establish the business provided that he undertakes that he will not dispose of the goodwill or re-engage in a similar business elsewhere within an area and for a time laid down by the acquiring authority. Compensation under this head may also be payable where only part of the land is taken, *e.g.* where part of a farm is taken and the farmer suffers a loss by having to make a forced sale of part of his stock. It is usual to leave the quantification of a disturbance claim until the loss or expenditure concerned has materialised.[54] But, if this is not done, the Lands Tribunal will have to make the best estimate they can on the available evidence. Costs incurred prior to acquisition but in reasonable anticipation of it may be recoverable.[55]

The costs of preparing and negotiating the claim may be claimed as a matter not directly based on the value of the land under rule 6,[56] but this rule does not include either the costs of opposing a compulsory purchase order or the costs incurred in obtaining, on appeal to the Secretary of State, a certificate of appropriate alternative development to enable the value of the land to be assessed on higher basis.[57] The costs of any reference to the Lands Tribunal are not a subject of claim but will be awarded by the Tribunal according to the outcome of the case.[58] The costs

[53] [1957] 1 Q.B. 485. See also *Horn* v. *Sunderland Corporation* [1941] 2 K.B. 26; *Woolfson* v. *Strathclyde Regional Council* (1978) 38 P. & C.R. 521.
[54] *Birmingham Corporation* v. *West Midlands Baptist (Trust) Association (Inc.)* [1970] A.C. 874 at p. 896.
[55] *Prasad* v. *Wolverhampton Borough Council* [1983] Ch. 333 (a case concerning a disturbance payment claimed under the Land Compensation Act 1973, s. 37 (see § 5–40)).
[56] *London County Council* v. *Tobin* [1959] 1 W.L.R. 354; *Radnor Trust Ltd.* v. *Central Electricity Generating Board* (1960) 12 P. & C.R. 111.
[57] *Hull and Humber Investment Co. Ltd.* v. *Hull Corporation* [1965] 2 Q.B. 145.
[58] Land Compensation Act 1961, s. 4.

of the conveyance to the authority will be payable by them under section 23 of the 1965 Act.

5-35   As mentioned in paragraph 5–22, a tenant from year to year or for a year or less period is separately provided for by section 20 of the Compulsory Purchase Act 1965. This provides that such a person shall be entitled to compensation for the value of his unexpired term or interest in the land, for damage from severance and injurious affection if only part of his land is taken, for any just allowance which ought to be made to him by an incoming tenant, and for any loss or injury he may sustain. In short, it puts him in very much the same position as any other claimant. Where he is a business tenant his right to apply for a new tenancy will be taken into account,[59] and where he is a tenant farmer his security of tenure under the Agricultural Holdings Act 1948 may be taken into account.[60]

5-36   Apart from the settlement of the compensation under the foregoing provisions the Land Compensation Act 1973 contains a number of special provisions in relation to persons displaced from land by compulsory purchase, or, in some cases, by other means also.

Special statutory payments and benefits

5-37   The provisions of the 1973 Act apply to those displaced from land whether or not, in cases (a), (c) and (d) below, they have sufficient interest in the land to entitle them to compensation under the rules appearing in the preceding paragraphs. These provisions relate to home loss payments, farm loss payments, disturbance payments, and the right to rehousing. In some cases a claimant is entitled as of right; in others a discretion lies with the authority.

5-38   (a) *Home loss payments.*[61] This payment is due to a person displaced from his home in consequence of a compulsory acquisition of the premises, or on account of redevelopment by the authority, or because of the making of certain orders under the Housing Acts, the more common being a closing order or a demolition order. He must have occupied the dwelling as his main residence throughout the previous five years. A displaced caravan dweller may also be qualified unless he is given an alternative site on which to place his caravan. Where the acquisition results from a blight notice (see para. 19–14) a home loss payment may not be made to the one who served the notice. This payment is mandatory. Payment to the vendor is discretionary where the authority acquires by agreement though having compulsory powers, but any person other than the vendor who is displaced in such a case is entitled to a payment.

The amount of the home loss payment is three times the rateable value of the premises, with a maximum of £1,500 and a minimum of £150.

---

[59] Land Compensation Act 1973, s. 47.
[60] *Ibid.* s. 48.
[61] *Ibid.* ss. 29–33.

(b) *Farm loss payment.*[62] This is due to a farmer displaced from the **5-39**
whole of his land because of the compulsory acquisition of his interest in
it, provided that he is the owner of the farm or is a tenant with a term of
years certain with not less than three years to run, and provided that he
begins to farm elsewhere within three years of displacement. In general
terms the amount due is a sum equal to the average annual profit from the
land acquired for a three-year period after deducting a notional rent. It is
not payable where the compensation paid for the interest of the farmer
includes development value and exceeds the existing use value plus the
farm loss payment.

An authority has a discretionary power to make a farm loss payment
where the acquisition is by agreement under the shadow of compulsory
powers.

(c) *Disturbance payment.*[63] A person who is displaced from land for any **5-40**
of the reasons mentioned in (a) above and who has no compensatable
interest (he may, for example, be a lodger who occupies under a licence)
is entitled to a disturbance payment. Where there is no legal entitlement
under this provision an authority is empowered to make a discretionary
payment. The disturbance payment consists of removal expenses, and, in
appropriate cases, the loss sustained by reason of the disturbance of trade
or business consequent upon the claimant having to quit his land.
Particular provision is made for the disabled.

(d) *Rehousing.*[64] A housing authority is under a duty to secure the **5-41**
provision of suitable alternative accommodation, where this is not
otherwise available on reasonable terms, for any person displaced from
residential accommodation for any of the reasons mentioned under (a)
above, unless the displacement results from his serving a blight notice (see
para. 19–14). The provision also applies to a caravan dweller displaced
from a site with no suitable alternative site. Power is given to offer an
owner-occupier or lessee with more than three years of his lease to run a
mortgage advance repayable on maturity. In the case of a short term
tenant the displacing authority may pay any reasonable expenses he
incurs, other than the purchase price, in connection with the acquisition
of an alternative dwelling.

Compensation to adjoining owners

So far in this Chapter we have been considering compensation to **5-42**
persons whose land is taken for some public project. But often the
property of neighbouring owners, none of whose land is taken, may be

---

[62] Land Compensation Act 1973, ss. 34–36.
[63] *Ibid.* ss. 37 and 38. In *R.* v. *Islington London Borough Council, ex p. Knight* [1984] 1 W.L.R.
205, a council tenant rehoused by agreement was held not to be entitled to claim a
disturbance payment, as the relinquishment of the tenancy did not amount to the
acquisition of land by the council.
[64] *Ibid.* ss. 39–43. See *R.* v. *Bristol Corporation, ex p. Hendy* [1974] 1 W.L.R. 498.

depreciated by the construction of the works or the use of them. Such owners may be entitled to claim under section 10 of the Compulsory Purchase Act 1965, which confers a right to compensation on an adjoining owner whose lands are injuriously affected by the *works* which the acquiring authority carries out in lawfully exercising statutory powers: compensation, it is to be observed, is payable only when lands have been injuriously affected by the execution of works and not, under this section, by the subsequent user of those works.[65] An action in tort might, of course, lie if there were a negligent or otherwise wrongful use of a statutory power. Not every injurious act entitles an adjoining owner to compensation—the act complained of must be one which, if it had been committed by someone other than an authority acting under statutory powers, would have been actionable at common law. The compensation will be the amount by which the claimant's land is depreciated by the construction of the works.

If there are easements, *e.g.* a right of way over, or restrictive covenants affecting the land compulsorily acquired in favour of an adjoining owner's land, he cannot maintain an action against the acquiring authority for obstruction of the easement or breach of the covenants[66]; his remedy is compensation under section 10 of the Act of 1965.[67] Section 14 of the Local Government (Miscellaneous Provisions) Act 1976 extends section 10 to cases where the land on which the works are constructed was acquired by agreement.

5-43   A right to compensation for depreciation caused by the *use* of public works is given by the provisions in Part I of the Land Compensation Act 1973.[68] A right to compensation is given where the value of an interest in land is depreciated by certain physical factors caused by the *use* of highways, aerodromes and other works on land provided or used in the exercise of a statutory power. The physical factors are noise, vibration, smell, fumes, smoke and artificial lighting, and the discharge onto the land of any solid or liquid substance. The right to claim is available only in cases where the persons concerned are debarred by statute from bringing an action for nuisance at common law. Generally speaking the property owner has no redress at common law since the use is immune, expressly or by implication, from an action in nuisance.

This right to compensation is available to resident owner-occupiers of residential property, owner-occupiers of agricultural units, and owner-occupiers of other premises where the rateable value does not exceed £2,250. The owner must have a freehold interest or a tenancy with not less than three years to run.

---

[65] *Metropolitan Board of Works* v. *McCarthy* (1874) L.R. 7 H.L. 243.
[66] *Kirby* v. *Harrogate School Board* [1896] 1 Ch. 437; Town and Country Planning Act 1971, s. 127; Local Government Act 1972, s. 120(3); and Local Government (Miscellaneous Provisions) Act 1976, s. 14.
[67] *Long Eaton Recreation Grounds Co.* v. *Midland Railway* [1902] 2 K.B. 574; *Re Simeon and Isle of Wight Rural District Council* [1937] Ch. 525.
[68] See also the Noise Insulation Regulations 1975 (S.I. 1975 No. 1763).

2. *APPROPRIATION, DISPOSAL AND DEVELOPMENT*

Appropriation

A local authority may appropriate land held for one statutory purpose, **5–44** and which is no longer required for that purpose, to some other statutory purpose.[69] Common land may not be appropriated under this provision if it exceeds an area of 250 square yards; if it does an appropriation may be undertaken under section 121 of the Town and Country Planning Act 1971. This involves special parliamentary procedure unless equally advantageous land is provided in exchange, or the land is required for the widening or drainage of a highway and the Secretary of State is satisfied that exchange land is not necessary. Common land having an area of 250 square yards or less, or land forming part of an open space, may not be appropriated until after public notice has been given and any objection considered by the authority.

Under section 122 of the Town and Country Planning Act 1971, as amended by the Local Government, Planning and Land Act 1980, Sched. 23, land held for planning purposes may be appropriated to other purposes.

Disposal

Section 123 of the Local Government Act 1972, as amended by the **5–45** Local Government, Planning and Land Act 1980, Sched. 23, enables a principal council, and section 127, as so amended, enables a parish or community council to dispose of any of its land as it chooses. But an authority may not dispose of open space land under either section until after public notice has been given and any objections considered. Except in the case of a short tenancy, the consent of the appropriate minister is required if it is intended to dispose of the land at less than the best consideration that can reasonably be obtained. Section 123 of the Town and Country Planning Act 1971, as amended by the 1980 Act, Sched. 23, contains a wide power for the disposal of land held for planning purposes.

The Secretary of State may by order apply Part X of the Local Government. Planning and Land Act 1980 to the area of any district or London borough council, and he has so applied it to all areas in England and Wales. He may then for any area to which the Part is so applied maintain a public register of land owned by certain public bodies in the area, including local authorities other than parish or community councils, which in his opinion is not being used, or sufficiently used, for the

---

[69] Local Government Act 1972, ss. 122 and 126, as amended by the Local Government, Planning and Land Act 1980, Sched. 23. The question whether land is no longer required for its existing purpose is for the local authority to decide and not the court: *Att. Gen.* v. *Manchester Corporation* [1931] 1 Ch. 254; *Dowty Boulton Paul Ltd.* v. *Wolverhampton Corporation (No. 2)* [1976] Ch. 13. Joint authorities and the Inner London Education Authority are treated as principal councils for the purposes of s. 122: s. 146A(1)(*b*), inserted by the Local Government Act 1985, Sched. 14, para. 16.

functions of the body concerned. He may, subject to certain conditions, direct the disposal of any land on the register.

5-46   Capital money received by a local authority on a disposal of land under section 153 of the Local Government Act 1972 must be applied towards the redemption of debt or to a new capital purpose, and as a broad rule the consent of the Secretary of State is required to the application of capital money in this way. This general rule is, however, modified by section 27 of the Town and Country Planning Act 1959, by virtue of which consent may not be required in certain cases. These provisions are subject to provisions relating to the capital expenditure of local authorities contained in the Local Government, Planning and Land Act 1980, referred to at paragraphs 7–29 to 7–34.

Development

5-47   Section 124 of the Town and Country Planning Act 1971 enables an authority to construct any building or carry out any work on land acquired or appropriated for planning purposes—this power may not, however, be relied on for carrying out work or building for which express statutory power already exists under some other enactment.

The Local Authorities (Land) Act 1963[70] gives certain development powers to local authorities. For the benefit or improvement of its area, an authority may erect buildings and construct and carry out works on land. For such benefit or improvement it may lend money to any person, to enable him to acquire land or to erect buildings on land. Money may be loaned in pursuance of building agreements. Garages may be erected and buildings converted into garages.

---

[70] ss. 2 to 5, as amended, in particular in the case of s. 3, by the Local Government (Miscellaneous Provisions) Act 1982, s. 43.

CHAPTER 6

BY-LAWS

A LOCAL authority by-law may be defined in simple terms as a law which   **6-01**
operates over the area of the authority, having been made by the
authority under a power conferred by statute and confirmed by the
Secretary of State for the Home Department or other appropriate
Minister. Lord Russell C.J. said in *Kruse* v. *Johnson*[1]:

> "A by-law, of the class we are here considering, I take to be an ordinance
> affecting the public, or some portion of the public, imposed by some authority
> clothed with statutory powers ordering something to be done or not to be done,
> and accompanied by some sanction or penalty for its non-observance. It
> necessarily involves restriction of liberty of action by persons who come under
> its operation as to acts which, but for the by-law, they would be free to do or not
> do as they please. Further, it involves this consequence—that, if validly made, it
> has the force of law within the sphere of its legitimate operation."

The law on this topic is considered under the following headings: the
source of by-law making powers; the procedure to be followed in the
making of by-laws; judicial tests as to the validity of by-laws; penalties
and enforcement; waiver, relaxation and repeal.

A. BY-LAW MAKING POWERS

All local authority by-laws derive from statute. There is a doctrine that   **6-02**
corporate bodies have an inherent power—that is to say, apart from
statute—to make by-laws regulating any matter connected with the
purposes for which they are established, but it is doubtful if this doctrine
has had any significance in modern times so far as local authorities are
concerned. It is in any case certain that local authorities do not rely on a
common law right.

There are a number of statutes which authorise the making of by-laws,
and these are listed in Appendix 5. One general power is mentioned here,
namely that conferred by section 235 of the Local Government Act 1972,
enabling the councils of districts and London boroughs to make by-laws
for good rule and government and for the suppression of nuisances. This
provision makes possible a wide range of by-laws—indeed the section is
so widely drawn that there would appear to be no limit to the number of
offences which could be created. There are, however, two restrictive
factors. First, a by-law is not effective unless confirmed by the Secretary
of State for the Home Department or other Minister, and, secondly, the

---

[1] [1898] 2 Q.B. 91 at p. 96.

courts apply certain stringent tests when the validity of a by-law is challenged; so that in practice the form and substance of by-laws made under this section follow a fairly constant pattern. These matters are referred to in succeeding paragraphs.

6-03   By-laws for good rule and government and for the suppression of nuisances do in practice cover a wide variety of topics, as may be seen from the model code which the Secretary of State for the Home Department has issued, notwithstanding the limiting factors referred to above. The model contains clauses on the following topics: music near houses, churches, hospitals; noisy hawking; touting; wireless loudspeakers, gramophones and organs; shooting galleries; indecent language; violent behaviour on school premises; fighting; indecent bathing; indecent shows; nuisances contrary to public decency; wilful jostling; loitering at church doors; advertising vehicles; flags; defacing pavements; advertising bills; broken glass; carrying soot; carrying carcasses; dangerous games near streets; spitting; bulls; cycling on footpaths; the fouling of footpaths by dogs; and noisy animals.

B. PROCEDURE FOR THE MAKING OF BY-LAWS

6-04   A common procedure is contained in section 236 of the Local Government Act 1972.[2] It applies to all by-laws made by a local authority under the 1972 Act or made by a local authority, a metropolitan county passenger transport authority or the Inner London Education Authority under any other enactment, unless specific statutory provision is otherwise made or unless the procedure is specifically excluded: by-laws made by statutory water undertakers for preventing waste, misuse or contamination of water come in the second class.[3] This common code requires a by-law to be made under the seal of the council, or under the hands and seals of two members in the case of a parish or community council not having a seal. The next step is a submission to the confirming authority named in the statute under which the by-law is made. The confirming authority in the case of by-laws for good rule and government and for the suppression of nuisances is the Secretary of State for the Home Department. The council is required to publish in one or more local newspapers notice of its intention, after the expiration of one month, to submit the by-law for confirmation, and during this period it is open to anyone to inspect the by-law and to purchase copies. The confirming authority as a matter of practice examines the by-law to see, first, whether it is *intra vires* in the narrow sense, secondly, whether it is likely to satisfy the other judicial tests as to validity if it is challenged in the courts, and, thirdly, whether in any case the by-law is necessary.

6-05   It is common practice for the confirming authority to issue model by-

---

[2] As amended by the Local Government Act 1985, Sched. 14, para. 31(1).
[3] See the Water Act 1945, s. 19, and Part I of Sched. 1; Water Act 1973, Sched. 7.

laws, and it is often difficult to secure the confirmation of a by-law which is outside the model or which departs from it in some important respect. In many cases the models have been built up out of practical experience over the years, which means that a by-law in the form of the model is unlikely to be upset in the courts. Moreover, the use of the model makes for some measure of uniformity, a generally desirable feature.

The confirming authority may confirm or reject the by-laws, and if they are confirmed may fix a time when they are to take effect. A copy of the by-laws when confirmed is to be made available for public inspection at the offices of the council, and must be available for sale at a cost not exceeding 20p. Copies are sent to other related authorities.

C. JUDICIAL TESTS AS TO VALIDITY

It has been said that by-laws have the force and effect of law. There is, **6-06** however, an important respect in which by-laws differ from statute law—in the case of statutes the courts have no alternative but to enforce them as they stand, whatever the consequences and howsoever they are framed. By-laws, on the other hand, are subject to scrutiny by the courts and certain rules as to validity have emerged from a long line of cases. The jurisdiction of the courts in such matters dates from earliest times. Lord Hobhouse said in *Slattery* v. *Naylor*[4]:

> "The jurisdiction of testing by-laws by their reasonableness was originally applied in such cases as those of manorial bodies, towns, or corporations having inherent powers or general powers conferred by charter of making such laws. As new corporations or local administrative bodies have arisen, the same jurisdiction has been exercised over them."

The rules which the courts have applied when the validity of a by-law has been challenged may be stated as follows: the by-law must be reasonable, certain in its terms, consistent with the general law, and *intra vires* the authority which made it. It should be noted that all these rules may be regarded as aspects of the *ultra vires* doctrine.[5]

(1) Reasonableness

The principle of reasonableness is dealt with fully in the first of the **6-07** following two cases:

> *Kruse* v. *Johnson*.[6] The Kent County Council made a by-law prohibiting any person from playing music or singing in any place within fifty yards of any dwelling-house after being requested to desist. A person convicted under this by-law appealed to the Divisional Court, contending that the by-law was bad because it was unreasonable. *Held* (one member of the court dissenting) that

---

[4] (1888) 13 App. Cas. 446 at p. 452.
[5] *Per* Diplock L.J. in *Mixnam's Properties Ltd.* v. *Chertsey Urban District Council* [1964] 1 Q.B. 214 at pp. 237–238.
[6] [1898] 2 Q.B. 91. See also *Cinnamond* v. *British Airports Authority* [1980] 1 W.L.R. 582; *Staden* v. *Tarjanyi* (1980) 78 L.G.R. 614.

the by-law was valid. Lord Russell C.J. expressed the view that by-laws made by local authorities, being bodies of a public representative character entrusted by Parliament with delegated authority, should be supported if possible. On the other hand this did not mean that the courts ought to be slow to condemn as invalid any by-law on the grounds of supposed unreasonableness. He said: "But unreasonable in what sense? If, for instance, they were found to be partial and unequal in their operation as between classes; if they were manifestly unjust; if they disclosed bad faith; if they involved such oppressive or gratuitous interference with the rights of those subject to them as could find no justification in the minds of reasonable men, the court might well say, 'Parliament never intended to give authority to make such rules; they are unreasonable and *ultra vires*.' But it is in this sense, and in this sense only, as I conceive, that the question of unreasonableness can properly be regarded. A by-law is not unreasonable merely because particular judges may think that it goes further than is prudent or necessary or convenient, or because it is not accompanied by a qualification or an exception which some judges may think ought to be there."

Arlidge v. *Islington Corporation*.[7] A by-law under the Public Health (London) Act 1891 required the landlord of a lodging-house to cause every part of the premises to be cleansed in April, May or June every year. The by-law applied even to landlords who had no right of entry, and who would commit a trespass or be in breach of contract if they complied with it. *Held*, the by-law was unreasonable and bad.

6-08 **(2) Certainty of terms**

In *Kruse* v. *Johnson*[8] Mathew J. said:

"From the many decisions on the subject it would seem clear that a by-law to be valid must, among other conditions, have two properties—it must be certain, that is, it must contain adequate information as to the duties of those who are to obey, and it must be reasonable."

Certainty includes positiveness and an absence of ambiguity.

Scott v. *Pilliner*.[9] A by-law made by the Staffordshire County Council imposed a penalty on any person frequenting and using any street or public place "for the purpose of selling or distributing any paper or written or printed matter devoted wholly or mainly to giving information as to the probable result of races, steeplechases, or other competitions." *Held* (by a majority of the court), that the by-law was bad. Kennedy J. based his decision on the grounds of unreasonableness. Lord Alverstone C.J. relied on the principle of certainty. He said[10]: "I think that this court ought not to interfere with a by-law made by a local authority if it can be supported on reasonable grounds: but I also think that it is desirable for the good government of a locality that by-laws should be clear and definite and free from ambiguity, and also that such by-laws should not make unlawful things which are otherwise innocent. . . . It seems to me that the main objection to this by-law is that it is too wide, and that it would include cases where the sale of the paper was not in aid of street betting or of any betting at all. . . . There may be perfectly innocent sales of such papers, and their publication and distribution might not conduce to any betting offence at all, and yet they would fall within this by-law. . . . Therefore, both on the

---

[7] [1909] 2 K.B. 127.
[8] [1898] 2 Q.B. 91 at p. 108.
[9] [1904] 2 K.B. 855.
[10] At p. 858.

ground of uncertainty, and mainly on the ground that it may strike at perfectly innocent sales of papers, I think that this by-law is bad and cannot be supported."

United Bill Posting Co. Ltd. v. *Somerset County Council.*[11] The Divisional Court upheld a by-law (under the Advertisements Regulation Act 1907, s. 2(2)), which provided that "No advertisements shall be exhibited on any hoarding, stand or other similar erection so as to be visible from any public highway, . . . public waterway . . . or . . . any railway, and to disfigure the natural beauty of the landscape." Lord Hewart C.J. said[12]: "The degree of certainty required must obviously be related to the subject matter, and in my opinion this by-law dealing with a necessarily somewhat ambiguous matter cannot be said to be invalid on the ground of uncertainty." Shearman J. said[13]: " 'Natural beauty' is a thing which cannot be defined by specific instances, and the only complaint of the appellants really is that the county council have not attempted to define the indefinable."

Nash v. *Finlay.*[14] A by-law in terms that "no person shall wilfully annoy passengers in the street" was held to be void on account of uncertainty.

Staden v. *Tarjanyi.*[15] Adur District Council made a by-law under section 164 of the Public Health Act 1875, in respect of a pleasure ground, which provided: "A person shall not in the pleasure ground . . . (ii) take off, fly or land any glider, manned or unmanned, weighing in total more than four kilogrammes. . . . " The respondent flew a hang glider over the pleasure ground and was prosecuted under the by-law. It was conceded that "in" meant "in or over." The Divisional Court held that the by-law was invalid for uncertainty. *Per* Lord Lane C.J.[16]:

" . . . [To] be valid, a by-law . . . must be certain and clear in the sense that anyone engaged upon the otherwise lawful pursuit of hang gliding must know with reasonable certainty when he is breaking the law and when he is not breaking the law . . . [T]o be valid the by-law must set some lower level below which the glider must not fly."

Woolf J. agreed, although he stated that this was an "exceptional case," which in relation to uncertainty should not be regarded as having a wide application.

(3) Consistency with the general law

A by-law is invalid if it is inconsistent with or repugnant to the general **6-09** law or if it deals with a matter already precisely covered by statute law. It cannot permit what a statute expressly forbids (this point is added merely for completeness, for by-laws would rarely attempt this); nor can it forbid what is expressly or impliedly permitted by statute. It is not often that a statute expressly permits an act—the law is generally negative in form. But there are occasions where a group of acts are forbidden, with certain exceptions, or are forbidden unless certain conditions are fulfilled. In such cases it can be said that the law expressly or by necessary implication permits the excepted acts and permits the other acts if the specified conditions are fulfilled. A by-law making unlawful one of these acts

---

[11] (1926) 42 T.L.R. 537.
[12] At p. 538.
[13] *Ibid.*
[14] (1901) 85 L.T. 682. See also *Leyton Urban District Council* v. *Chew* [1907] 2 K.B. 283.
[15] (1980) 78 L.G.R. 614.
[16] At p. 623.

expressly or impliedly approved by the law would be invalid as being in conflict with the general law.

> *Powell* v. *May.*[17] A by-law made by the Glamorgan County Council prohibited betting in a public place, although both the Street Betting Act 1906, and the Betting and Lotteries Act 1934, allowed betting in a public place provided that certain requirements were complied with. *Held*, the by-law was bad, for it prohibited the doing of an act which the law expressly or impliedly allowed.

Similarly, a by-law may be invalidated by the courts if repugnant to some basic principle of the common law.

> *London Passenger Transport Board* v. *Sumner.*[18] A by-law of the Board provided that "each passenger shall, immediately upon demand, or, in case no demand shall have been made, before leaving the carriage, pay to the conductor the fare legally demandable for his journey and accept a ticket therefor." An information was preferred against a passenger who paid her fare to a certain point but went beyond it without tendering or being asked for the extra fare. She offered to pay when challenged by an inspector, but payment was refused. The Chief Magistrate at Bow Street who heard the case dismissed it on the ground that the by-law was bad, being repugnant to the laws of England for "no act or omission can be a crime unless *mens rea* is present, or there is express statutory provision that the act or omission is a crime without any criminal intent, or it can be clearly inferred from the terms of the statute that the mere act or omission is in itself an offence." The Divisional Court upheld the decision on appeal, adopting the reasoning of the Chief Magistrate.
>
> *Staden* v. *Tarjanyi.*[19] The by-law in this case[20] was held not to be repugnant to the Civil Aviation Rules of the Air and Air Traffic Control Regulations 1976, which exempted "any glider while it is hill-soaring," from the rules prohibiting low flying. The circumstances envisaged by the regulations and those envisaged by the by-law were "entirely different."[21]

A by-law may, of course, add to the law, making an offence where none existed—indeed, this is the effect of most by-laws. Such an addition, if rightly made, is in the nature of an extension to the law, a supplement to the law in keeping with it.

> *Morrissey* v. *Galer.*[22] Justices convicted a man for an offence against a local authority by-law prohibiting the keeping on any premises of "any noisy animal which shall be or cause a serious nuisance to residents in the neighbourhood." It was argued that this by-law was *ultra vires* as it dealt with the same subject matter as section 92 of the Public Health Act 1936, under which "any animal kept in such a place or manner as to be prejudicial to health or a nuisance" was a statutory nuisance: *Held*, the by-law was valid. Section 92 did not cover noisy animals, but only nuisance arising from the conditions under which animals were kept. Lord Goddard C.J. stated[23]: "No one doubts, that if the statute deals with precisely the same matter, the by-law would be *ultra vires* because if it

---

[17] [1946] K.B. 330.
[18] (1935) 99 J.P. 387. See also *Nicholls* v. *Tavistock Urban District Council* [1923] 2 Ch. 18.
[19] (1980) 78 L.G.R. 614.
[20] See § 6–08.
[21] *Per* Lord Lane C.J. at p. 619.
[22] [1955] 1 W.L.R. 110.
[23] At p. 112.

deals with precisely the same matter as the statute there is no necessity for it, and if it tries to go beyond the statute it is bad."

It is submitted, however, that not every by-law which "tries to go beyond the statute" is bad. In *Thomas* v. *Sutters*[24] Sir F. H. Jeune said[25]:

"An Act of Parliament for the whole country renders certain things illegal. It does not at all follow that a by-law speaking for a particular locality may not make some more stringent regulations with the same object. . . . When an Act of Parliament has forbidden certain things to be done in certain places, it seems to me perfectly consistent with that that a municipality, with regard to their particular locality, should go somewhat beyond the Act, not contravening its spirit, but carrying it out, and making regulations somewhat wider than those to be found in the Act."

In relation to the power of councils to make by-laws for good rule and government and suppression of nuisances, section 235(3) of the Local Government Act 1972 now expressly provides that: "By-laws shall not be made under this section for any purpose as respects any area if provision for that purpose as respects that area is made by, or is or may be made under, any other enactment."

(4) Intra vires

Reference was made in the opening paragraphs of this Chapter to the fact that the by-laws of local authorities must stem from statute law. They must have their source there, and in addition, must be wholly within the scope of the statutory provision, going no further than the precise wording of the statute allows. **6-10**

> *R.* v. *Wood.*[26] The Public Health Act 1848 enabled a local board of health to make by-laws with respect to the removal by the occupier of dust, ashes, rubbish, filth, manure, dung and soil. A board made a by-law under this provision directing all occupiers to remove all snow from the footpath opposite to their premises. *Held*, the by-law was *ultra vires*, for it went beyond the enabling powers.[27]

A power to "regulate" an activity by a by-law would not authorise the complete prohibition of that activity: "a power to regulate and govern seems to imply the continued existence of that which is to be regulated or governed."[28] However, a power to make by-laws for regulating the use and operation of an aerodrome was held sufficient to authorise the prohibition of the use of the aerodrome by certain persons for certain specified purposes, *viz.* taxi drivers plying for hire without permission.[29]

---

[24] [1900] 1 Ch. 10.

[25] At p. 16.

[26] (1855) 5 E. & B. 49.

[27] Powers to make by-laws in regard to the clearance of snow are now available under s. 81 of the Public Health Act 1936.

[28] *Per* Lord Davey in *City of Toronto Municipal Corporation* v. *Virgo* [1896] A.C. 88 at p. 93.

[29] *R.* v. *British Airports Authority, ex p. Wheatley* [1983] R.T.R. 147, 466.

D. PENALTIES AND ENFORCEMENT

6-11   By-laws made under the procedure contained in the Local Government
Act 1972 may provide for the imposition of fines, recoverable on
summary conviction, not exceeding such sum as may be fixed by the
enabling statute, or if no sum is fixed, level 2 on the standard scale.[30] The
new figure is applicable to existing as well as to future by-laws. By-laws
under section 235 of the Local Government Act 1972 relating to the
burning of straw or stubble may provide for the imposition of a fine not
exceeding level 5 on the standard scale, or not exceeding a lesser
amount.[31] Where the offence is a continuing one, a by-law may provide
for a further fine for each day during which the offence continues. The
maximum continuing penalty is that fixed by the enabling statute, or £5 if
no sum is prescribed.[32] Where by-laws have been made under some other
code then the rules contained in that code as to penalties apply. For
example, by-laws made under section 19 of the Water Act 1945,[33] may
include a maximum penalty not exceeding level 5 on the standard scale,
and a maximum penalty of £50 each day for continuing offences. By-laws
as to pleasure fairs, roller skating rinks and seaside pleasure boats, under
sections 75 and 76 of the Public Health Act 1961, may provide for a
maximum fine not exceeding level 3 on the standard scale or not
exceeding a lesser amount.[34]

It is open to any person to institute proceedings for a breach of a by-law
unless the statute under which the by-law is made restricts the right to
prosecute.

> *R. v. Stewart.*[35] The Secretary of the Royal Society for the Prevention of
> Cruelty to Animals preferred an information against the master of a steamship
> for offences against an order under the Diseases of Animals Act 1894. The
> stipendiary magistrate upheld an objection that under the Act only the borough
> council could institute proceedings. *Held*, the objection was ill-founded. Kay
> L.J. said[36]: "Prima facie there is no doubt that anybody may take proceedings to
> recover a penalty. That is an old rule and is well established. The Act now
> under consideration in terms provides that penalties shall be imposed for
> certain acts, and that those penalties shall be regarded as though they were
> penalties incurred under the Summary Jurisdiction Acts. In order to prevent
> the application of the general rule, it must be shown that the Act in plain terms
> prevents anyone, except certain specified persons, from prosecuting for offences
> under the Act."

6-12   An example of a statutory restriction on the right to institute proceedings
appears in section 298 of the Public Health Act 1936. Only an aggrieved

---

[30] Local Government Act 1972, s. 237, as amended by the Criminal Justice Act 1982, s. 46.
[31] Criminal Justice Act 1982, ss. 43, 46(1), (2). The maximum penalty for a by-law in force on
April 11, 1983, is £1,000: s. 43.
[32] Local Government Act 1972, s. 237.
[33] As amended by the Control of Pollution Act 1974, Sched. 2, para. 15.
[34] Criminal Law Act 1977, s. 31(4)(*a*) and (*b*); Criminal Justice Act 1982, s. 46(1)(2).
[35] [1896] 1 Q.B. 300.
[36] At p. 303.

party or the council or other body whose function is to enforce the by-law in question may prosecute without the written consent of the Attorney General. Notwithstanding this or any similar provision, a constable may take proceedings in respect of an offence against a by-law, made by a local authority under any enactment, without the consent of the Attorney General.[37] It has been held in an Irish case[38] that the general right to prosecute might apply only where the by-laws concern the public interest.

A breach of a by-law may be insufficient to sustain an action in **6-13** damages. This depends on the application of the principles relevant to determine whether breach of a statute gives rise to civil liability.[39]

> *Newman* v. *Francis*.[40] A London County Council by-law forbade a person to allow his dog to annoy or injure anyone in any open space. The plaintiff was knocked down by the defendant's dog. He claimed damages alleging, first, negligence and, secondly, a breach of the by-law. *Held*, the by-law was intended for enforcement by the council; it was not intended to give a cause of action to members of the public, either one against the other, or, for breach of them, against the county council.

There are dicta in this case in support of the view that only the London County Council could have proceeded under the by-law.

In *Anns* v. *Merton London Borough Council*,[41] the House of Lords held that the council owed the plaintiff a duty to take reasonable care to ensure that builders complied with building by-laws. In addition, Lord Wilberforce stated[41a] that "since it is the duty of the builder . . . to comply with the byelaws, I would be of opinion that an action could be brought against him, in effect, for breach of statutory duty by any person for whose benefit or protection the byelaw was made."

The threatened breach of a by-law may be restrained by an injunction.

> *Burnley Borough Council* v. *England and others*.[42] The defendants objected to a new by-law which made it an offence for a person to cause a dog belonging to him or in his charge to enter or remain in any of a number of pleasure grounds, other than a guide-dog in the charge of a blind person. They organised a protest walk in the grounds by a large number of people with their dogs. This also involved breaches of a by-law which prohibited meetings or processions in the grounds without the council's prior consent. The walk took place, but no-one was prosecuted. However, when another protest was organised the council sought an interlocutory injunction to restrain the breaches of the two by-laws. *Held*, the injunction should be granted. The council had made out a prima facie case that the by-laws were valid, and if the defendants were not restrained by injunction until trial, serious damage to the public interest was likely. The defendants would continue to encourage members of the public to flout the by-laws, and this would place the park rangers and police in a most difficult and invidious position in any attempt to enforce the law. Had the defendants acted

---

[37] Local Government (Miscellaneous Provisions) Act 1982, s. 12.
[38] *Kenealey* v. *O'Keefe* [1901] 2 I.R. 39.
[39] See §§ 10–26 *et seq.*
[40] (1953) 51 L.G.R. 168.
[41] [1978] A.C. 728. See §§ 10–33 *et seq.*
[41a] At p. 759.
[42] (1977) 76 L.G.R. 393.

individually in breach of the by-laws, and not in concert, the judge would probably have left the council to their remedy under the criminal law.[43] The by-law relating to dogs was subsequently held to be reasonable,[44] and injunctions were granted against two of the defendants. The other defendants undertook not to break the by-law.

E. WAIVER, RELAXATION AND REPEAL

6-14   An authority has no power to waive its by-laws or to relax them in any respect unless the by-laws themselves contain provisions enabling this to be done (it is highly improbable that by-laws containing a dispensing power would be confirmed) or else there is specific statutory provision for waiver or relaxation.

> *Yabbicom* v. *King*.[45] An urban district council "approved" a plan though in fact it was contrary to the by-laws. Before the building was erected the area was transferred to the City of Bristol, the council of which instituted proceedings against the respondent for unlawfully erecting the house. *Held*, an "approved" plan is one which is lawfully approved by a local authority and not one which is merely approved in fact. The urban district council had no power to sanction plans for a building which would contravene the by-laws. Day J. said[46]: "The district council could not control the law, and by-laws properly made have the effect of laws; a public body cannot any more than private persons dispense with laws that have to be administered; they have no dispensing power whatever."

6-15   The Highways Act 1980, and the Water Act 1945, respectively contain provisions for the relaxation of new streets by-laws and by-laws preventing waste. Section 190 of the Act of 1980 enables an authority, with the consent of the Secretary of State for the Environment, to relax the requirements of a by-law as to new streets or to dispense with its compliance if it considers its operation to be unreasonable in any particular case. The authority must give notice of its intention to apply for the Secretary of State's consent, and, in reaching his decision, he must have regard to any objection which may have been raised. A similarly worded provision appears in section 19 of the Water Act 1945.

It is open to an authority to repeal its by-laws with the consent of the appropriate confirming authority. Section 4 of the Interpretation Act 1978 reads:

> "Where an Act ... confers power to make ... by-laws, the power shall, unless the contrary intention appears, be construed as including a power, exercisable in the like manner and subject to the like consent and conditions, if any, to rescind, revoke, amend, or vary ... by-laws."

In practice a by-law made in substitution of another would itself contain a clause repealing the one it replaces. In certain cases, by-laws

---

[43] Slade J. at p. 400.
[44] *Burnley Borough Council* v. *England* (1978) 77 L.G.R. 227.
[45] [1899] 1 Q.B. 444.
[46] At p. 448.

cease to be valid after the expiration of a prescribed period unless a Secretary of State by order extends their life. By-laws made under the Water Act 1945 fall in this category—they are effective for a period of ten years from the date on which they are made, unless the Secretary of State for the Environment extends them.[47] In a few instances, by-laws have been wholly repealed by statute.

[47] Water Act 1945, s. 19(6)(*a*).

CHAPTER 7

LOCAL AUTHORITY FINANCE

7-01   MOST of the law relating to local authority finance is contained in Part VIII of the Local Government Act 1972 and Schedule 13 to that Act, the Local Government Act 1974, the Local Government (Miscellaneous Provisions) Act 1976, the Local Government, Planning and Land Act 1980, the Local Government Finance Act 1982, the General Rate Act 1967, the Rates Act 1984 and the Local Government Act 1985. It is considered here in six parts: expenses and receipts; audit; control of capital expenditure; borrowing; special funds; investments.

A. EXPENSES AND RECEIPTS

Expenses of principal councils

7-02   Except as follows, the expenses of principal councils are general expenses, chargeable on the whole of the area.[1] The following are special expenses, chargeable against only a part of the area. First, where under any legislation particular expenses are declared to be special expenses. Secondly, in the case of a county council, expenses incurred under any enactment passed before June 1, 1934 (the date on which the Local Government Act 1933 came into operation) and not declared to be general expenses. Thirdly, where a district council has by resolution declared particular expenses to be special expenses; a resolution of this kind may be varied or revoked by the council.[2] Fourthly, where the expenses of a district council arise from the possession of property (often in the form of investments) held by the council in trust for a rating district—any net expenditure to be met from the rates is a special expense for the rating district. Lastly, an order made before April 1, 1974, declaring any expenses to be special expenses continues in force until varied or revoked by the district council. The original order is deemed to be the equivalent of a resolution of the district council.

A principal council may meet all or part of any special expenses by a contribution from its general expenses.[3]

---

[1] Local Government Act 1972, s. 147.
[2] Expenses can be declared special only if incurred by the council acting as local authority for the district; not if alleged to be due for work done under contract for a parish: *Randall v. D.A. for Tendring D.C.* (1980) 79 L.G.R. 207.
[3] Local Government Act 1972, s. 147(5).

Expenses of parish and community councils

There are several situations here.[4] First, the expenses of a separate **7-03** parish or community council and a separate parish or community meeting are chargeable on the parish or community. Secondly, the expenses of parish or community councils of grouped parishes or communities are chargeable on the group. Thirdly, expenses of parish or community meetings within a group are chargeable on the separate parish or community.

The expenses of these bodies are generally paid by the bodies themselves or, in the case of meetings, by the corresponding council, and an appropriate precept is made on the district council concerned for the sums required.[5] However, the expenses of a community meeting where there is no community council are paid by the district council.[6] This exception derives from the fact that the community meeting does not necessarily have continuity of existence and no one is charged by law to keep its accounts.[7] Expenses relating to the election of parish and community councils are met by the district council and charged against the accounts of the parish or community council.[8] Cheques and orders for payment by parish and community councils are required to be signed by two council members.[9]

A parish or community council or a parish meeting may declare expenses incurred under section 1 of the Parish Councils Act 1957 (street lighting) to be chargeable on part only of its area.[10]

Funds and accounts

The councils of districts and London boroughs are required to keep a **7-04** general rate fund and county councils a county fund.[11] All their receipts are carried to these funds and all their liabilities are met therefrom.[12] There is a particular provision about income received for the relief of rates by an authority which is not a rating authority. Any net income received from this source is paid to the rating authority and the rating authority is required to credit the amount to the part of its area to which the income relates.[13]

Accounts must be kept of receipts into and payments from the appropriate fund, and separate accounts must be kept for general expenses and any class of special expenses.[14]

[4] Local Government Act 1972, s. 150.
[5] *Ibid.* s. 150(2), (4), (7).
[6] *Ibid.* s. 150(3).
[7] *Ibid.* s. 27(1); *cf.* ss. 9(1), 150(6); *ibid. re* parish meetings.
[8] *Ibid.* s. 42(6).
[9] *Ibid.* s. 150(5).
[10] *Ibid.* Sched. 13, para. 25.
[11] *Ibid.* s. 148(1), (2).
[12] *Ibid.* s. 148(4).
[13] *Ibid.* s. 148(3).
[14] *Ibid.* s. 148(5).

Each new authority established under the Local Government Act 1985 must maintain a general fund to and from which all receipts are carried and all liabilities discharged, account being kept thereof.[15] Proper accounts and records must be kept for the residuary bodies set up by the 1985 Act, and statements of accounts prepared. The accounts, records and statements must comply with any directions given by the Secretary of State.[16]

Financial administration

7-05   Every local authority is required to make arrangements for the proper administration of its financial affairs and to secure that one of its officers has responsibility for the administration of those affairs.[17] Under earlier law, payment out of the county fund or borough fund could only be made by the treasurer and his duties in that respect were the subject of case law.

> *Att.-Gen.* v. *De Winton.*[18] The facts in this case are not important. But of the borough treasurer, Farwell J. said: "[he] is not a mere servant of the council: he owes a duty and stands in a fiduciary relation to the burgesses as a body; he is the treasurer of the borough; all payments to and out of the borough fund must be paid to and by him; . . . although he holds office during the pleasure of the council only, this does not enable him to plead the orders of the council as an excuse for an unlawful act. In my opinion the observations of Erle J. in *R.* v. *Saunders* ((1855) 24 L.J.M.C. 45) with relation to a county treasurer, apply with equal force to a treasurer under the Municipal Corporations Act: 'If an order be made on a county treasurer to pay expenses wholly disconnected with county matters, such an order is without jurisdiction, and one which the county treasurer would be bound to disobey.' "

It is submitted that the legal status of the responsible officer is not materially affected by the change in the law. Quite apart from the *De Winton* case an officer cannot plead a council's order to excuse an illegality.[19]

Revenues from undertakings

7-06   Statutes which authorise the operation of trading undertakings generally deal with the application of surplus moneys. Any such provision is not overridden by the rules referred to above.[20]

Application of capital money on disposal of land

7-07   In general, capital receipts from the sale of land and buildings by a local authority are to be applied, with the consent of the Secretary of State, in discharge of debt or otherwise for any purpose for which capital

---

[15] Local Government Act 1985, s. 72(1), (2).
[16] *Ibid.* s. 78.
[17] Local Government Act 1972, s. 151. This requirement falls to the new authorities appointed under the Local Government Act 1985: see *ibid.* s. 73.
[18] [1906] 2 Ch. 106.
[19] See § 7-22.
[20] Local Government Act 1972, s. 152 and Local Government Act 1985, s. 72(4).

money may properly be applied.[21] Proceeds of sale of charity land must be applied in accordance with any directions given under the Charities Act 1960.[22]

Under section 27 of the Town and Country Planning Act 1959,[23] ministerial consent is not required where a capital receipt of principal councils and other specified bodies:

(a) does not exceed the limits prescribed by the section, generally the lesser of £1,000 or the product of a rate of 0.4p. in the £;

(b) is applied in reduction of the debt incurred to acquire the asset;

(c) is applied in repaying any loan having 15 years or more outstanding to final repayment;

(d) is used to meet expenditure on any purpose for which borrowing has been authorised; or

(e) is transferred to a capital fund, except that consent is required if the capital receipt arises from the disposal of property for which income and expenditure was included in the housing revenue account.[24]

Department of the Environment Circular 9/83 conveys a general consent to the application of capital money from sales of land under the 1972 Act or the Town and Country Planning Act 1971 in or toward the repayment of debt or any other capital purpose. Such adjustment of the authority's accounts as is requisite must be made on the utilisation of moneys received from the sale of land, and a ministerial direction is required where a grant-aided service is involved and the application is to a purpose other than that for which the land was held.[25]

Expenditure and the ultra vires rule

No expenditure may be incurred unless there is specific statutory **7-08** authority for the particular purpose.[26] There is an exception to this rule—a local authority may incur expenditure which in its opinion is in the interests of its area or any part of it or all or some of its inhabitants, provided that the object of the expenditure is not the subject of other statutory provision.[27]

In *Manchester City Council* v. *Greater Manchester Metropolitan County*

---

[21] Local Government Act 1972, s. 153. This provision applies to a new authority under the Local Government Act 1985: see Sched. 17, para. 14.

[22] *Ibid.* ss. 123(6) and 127(4). See also s. 131 as to savings for provisions in other Acts, including those relating to housing.

[23] As amended by the Local Government Act 1972, Sched. 13, para. 26.

[24] See Local Government (Miscellaneous Provisions) Act 1976, s. 28.

[25] Town and Country Planning Act 1959, s. 27(4), (5); DoE Circular 9/83, para. 34.

[26] See § 1-07.

[27] Local Government Act 1972, s. 137 and the Local Authorities (Expenditure Powers) Act 1983.

Council,[28] the House of Lords upheld the validity of payments by the county council under section 137 to a trust established by that council for the provision of free or assisted places at independent schools for children of parents in the area. Education was not one of the functions of the county council, and the challenge was made by the Manchester City Council as the local education authority claiming that the county council had acted *ultra vires.*

It was argued, *inter alia,* that the trust fund payment, which was made in one year to cover a period of seven years, infringed the principle that local government finance should be conducted on an annual basis. It was held that, provided the expenditure was properly incurred within the section 137 budget in one year, it did not matter that the greater part of the money was to be held by the trustees for expenditure in future years. Nor did the fact that the commitment could not be revoked by a succeeding authority infringe any established principle. The creation of the trust was upheld as incidental to the exercise of the power to incur expenditure under section 137(1). It did not represent an unlawful surrender or delegation of the council's powers to trustees. Through the medium of trust objects the trustees had been effectively directed as to the manner in which money was to be spent. Thereafter, the trustees were obliged under the general law to administer the fund in accordance with those purposes. In *Lobenstein* v. *Hackney L.B.C.*[29] Pain J., upholding a grant under section 137 to expenses in connection with the Moscow Olympics, indicated that the word "interests" should not be given too restricted a meaning, and that review by the court of the council's opinion was governed by *Wednesbury* principles.[30] The limit of expenditure under this provision in any financial year is the product of a rate of 2p in the pound or a higher or lower amount fixed by the Secretary of State. An authority may also, under this provision, contribute to charitable funds and the like.

There are, additionally, certain fairly widely expressed powers.[31] An authority may spend money on gifts of real or personal property donated for the benefit of the inhabitants of the area. The gift may be related, or unrelated, to a statutory purpose. In the latter case expenditure relating to such gifts counts against the 2p limit referred to above.

A principal council may spend money or grant loans in connection with emergencies and disasters affecting a part or the whole of its area. The Secretary of State for the Environment is to be notified of the action taken and he himself may give directions.

---

[28] (1980) 78 L.G.R. 560. *Cf. R.* v. *District Auditor, ex p. West Yorkshire M.C.C., The Times,* July 25, 1985.
[29] (1980), unreported.
[30] See § 12–20.
[31] Local Government Act 1972, ss. 138, 139.

B. AUDIT

The audit of local authority accounts for periods commencing on or **7-09** after April 1, 1983, is governed by Part III of the Local Government Finance Act 1982, which also extends to other bodies and to accounts of officers, and to new authorities under the Local Government Act 1985.[32]

The Audit Commission

The Local Government Finance Act 1982 established the Audit Commission for Local Authorities in England and Wales to take responsibility for audit arrangements. The Commission is appointed by the Secretary of State, after consultation with local authority associations and professional accountancy bodies.[33] Detailed provisions as to the Commission appear in Schedule 3. The Secretary of State may give the Commission directions on the discharge of its functions.[34] The Commission must appoint a chief officer, known as the Controller of Audit, and such other officers as it considers necessary. The first Controller was appointed by the Secretary of State and subsequent appointments to the office will require his approval.[35]

Appointment of auditors

The auditor for each body covered by Part III of the Local **7-10** Government Finance Act 1982 is appointed by the Commission after consultation with the body.[36] The auditor may be an officer of the Commission or a private accountant or firm of accountants. He must be a member of one of the specified accountancy bodies or have such other qualification as may be approved by the Secretary of State. The Commission may arrange for joint audits, in which the auditors may act jointly or separately for different parts of the accounts or in discharge of different functions. The Commission may also approve arrangements for persons assisting an auditor to carry out such of the auditor's statutory functions as may be specified.

These arrangements differ substantially from the former provisions for the appointment of auditors in Part VIII of the Local Government Act 1972. Bodies subject to audit under that Act were empowered to choose whether their accounts should be audited by a district auditor, appointed by the Secretary of State with the consent of the Minister for the Civil Service, or an "approved auditor," that is, a private accountant appointed by the body and approved by the Secretary of State. The 1982 Act does not use the title "district auditor," but the Commission has retained the title for its own officers appointed as auditors under section 13 of the Act.

---

[32] Local Government Finance Act 1982, ss. 12, 25, 31; Local Government Act 1985, s. 72.
[33] Local Government Finance Act 1982, s. 11.
[34] *Ibid.* Sched. 3, para. 3(1).
[35] *Ibid.* para. 7.
[36] ss. 12(1), 13(3).

Code of audit practice

7-11   Section 14 of the Local Government Finance Act 1982 provides for a code of audit practice to be prepared, kept under review and published by the Commission and to be approved by each House of Parliament at intervals of not more than five years. Local authority associations and accountancy bodies must be consulted before the preparation and alteration of the code which must embody what appears to the Commission to be the best professional practice with respect to the standards, procedures and techniques to be adopted by auditors. The auditor is under a duty to comply with the code.

The statutory Code of Local Government Audit Practice for England and Wales, prepared by the Commission and approved by Parliament in accordance with section 14 of the 1982 Act, came into force on November 7, 1983. The main provisions of the Code are in two parts. The first part sets out the general duties of auditors under the 1982 Act and refers to requirements placed on the auditor in accordance with the basic philosophy of the Commission and considerations of independence, due professional care, and a recognition of the public interest. The second part relates to the detailed conduct of the audit and summarises the auditor's particular responsibilities with respect to fraud, corruption and value for money. It is made clear in the Introduction to the Code that it does not detract from the auditor's independence (both of the Commission and audited authority) in the discharge of his professional responsibilities.

General duties of auditors

7-12   Section 15(1) of the 1982 Act requires the auditor to satisfy himself:

(a)   that the accounts are prepared in accordance with regulations made under section 23 of the Act and otherwise comply with statutory provisions;

(b)   that proper practices have been observed in the compilation of the accounts;

(c)   that the body has made proper arrangements for securing economy, efficiency and effectiveness in its use of resources.

The traditional view taken by the courts of the responsibility of the district auditor was restated by Lord Denning M.R. in *Asher* v. *Secretary of State for the Environment*[37] in the following terms:

> "The district auditor holds a position of much responsibility. In some respects he is like a company auditor. He is a watchdog to see that the accounts are properly kept and that no one is making off with the funds. He is not bound to be of a suspicious turn of mind: seee *In re Kingston Cotton Mill Co. (No. 2)* [1896] 2 Ch. 279; but, if anything suspicious does turn up, it is his duty to take care to follow it up: see *In re Thomas Gerrard & Son Ltd.* [1968] Ch. 455. In

---

[37] [1974] Ch. 208 at p. 219. The auditor no longer has direct power to surcharge.

other respects, however, the duties of a district auditor go far beyond those of a company auditor. He must see whether, on the financial side, the councillors and their officers have discharged their duties according to law. He must listen to any elector who makes objection to the accounts. He must make his own investigation also. If he finds that the councillors or the officers, or any of them, have expended money improperly, or unreasonably, or allowed it to be so expended, it is his duty to surcharge them: see *Roberts* v. *Hopwood* [1925] A.C. 578 and *Pooley* v. *District Auditor No. 8 Audit District* (1964) 63 L.G.R. 60 and in the Court of Appeal, (1965) 63 L.G.R. 236."

The auditor's report

Section 15(3) of the 1982 Act provides that the auditor is to consider 7-13 whether in the public interest he should make a report on any matter coming to his notice in the course of the audit in order that it may be considered by the body concerned or brought to the attention of the public. He is also to consider whether the public interest requires an immediate report rather than a report at the conclusion of the audit. A report (other than an immediate report) is to be sent to the body under audit not later than 14 days after the conclusion of the audit; all reports must be considered by the body under audit as soon as practicable after receipt.[38] The agenda for the meeting of the authority to which the report is submitted must be accompanied by the report, which must not be excluded from the documents to be made available to the Press and public under the Public Bodies (Admission to Meetings) Act 1960 and Part VA of the Local Government Act 1972.[39] Local government electors may inspect and copy, or pay for copies of, auditors' reports and statements of accounts.[40]

Paragraphs 24–29 of the Code of Audit Practice contain sundry comments and examples concerning audit reports. Paragraph 26 points out that it is not the function of the auditor to express his opinion as to the the wisdom of particular decisions taken by councils in the lawful exercise of their discretion, and that reports relating to such decisions should only refer to facts which have not previously been brought to the attention of the authority or which ought to be brought to the attention of the public. Paragraph 43 states that it is not the auditor's function to question policy, but makes it clear that it is his responsibility to consider the effects of policy and to examine the arrangements by which policy decisions are reached, and gives examples of aspects of policy decisions into which he should enquire. A cross-reference to paragraph 26 appears to indicate that the bar on "questioning" policy relates rather to the limitation that the auditor should not express his own opinion on the wisdom of council decisions in the lawful exercise of discretion.

Decisions of the courts are also relevant to the question of the auditor's

---

[38] s. 18(3).
[39] s. 18(5) of the Local Government Finance Act 1982 as amended by the Local Government (Access to Information) Act 1985, Sched. 2.
[40] Local Government Finance Act 1982, s. 24(1).

function in respect of policy decisions. In *Anns* v. *Merton London Borough Council*,[41] Lord Wilberforce indicated that policy was to be equated with discretion, and it is well established that it is the auditor's function, under section 19 of the 1982 Act and its predecessors, to consider whether discretion has been exercised lawfully. If discretion has been exercised lawfully, the Irish case of *R. (Drury)* v. *Dublin Corporation*,[42] referring to audit legislation not significantly different, indicates that the auditor nevertheless has power to report on (and hence to enquire into) matters within the discretion of the authority (*i.e.* policy matters) in order that the public might be informed and the authority give further consideration to those matters, the ultimate discretion of the authority being unimpaired. To the same effect is a dictum in *R.* v. *Roberts*.[43]

The auditor's certificate and opinion on the accounts

7-14   Section 18(1) of the Local Government Finance Act 1982 requires the auditor, at the conclusion of the audit, to enter on the statement of accounts prepared pursuant to regulations: (a) a certificate that he has completed the audit in accordance with the Act, and (b) his opinion on the statement of accounts.

The Code of Audit Practice requires the auditor to refer expressly in his opinion (a) to whether the audit has been completed in accordance with the Code and (b) to whether the statement of accounts presents fairly the financial position of the authority. Where the auditor is unable to give an affirmative opinion on these matters, he is to qualify his opinion by referring to all material matters about which he has reservations.

Miscellaneous duties and powers of the Commission

7-15   Apart from the duties of the Audit Commission in relation to audits and auditors, the Local Government Finance Act 1982 imposes directly on the Commission itself certain duties in relation to bodies audited under the Act. Section 26(1), for example, requires the Commission, after consultation with relevant associations, to undertake or promote comparative across-the-board studies concerning economy, efficiency, effectiveness and financial or other management of bodies subject to audit. Section 29(2) enables the Commission to promote or undertake value-for-money studies into transactions of a body if the body, after consulting employees' associations, so requests.

Access to documents, etc.

7-16   An auditor has a right of access at all reasonable times to all documents relating to an audited body which appear to him to be necessary for the

---

[41] [1978] A.C. 728 at p. 754.
[42] (1907) 41 I.L.T.R. 97.
[43] [1908] 1 K.B. 407 at p. 434.

purposes of the audit.[44] The phrase "at all reasonable times" gives statutory authority to current auditing. The auditor may also require any person holding or accountable for such a document, and any member or officer of the body, to give information or explanation which he thinks necessary for the purposes of the audit, and to attend before him for that purpose or to produce the document.

A person who without reasonable excuse fails to comply with an auditor's lawful requirement, or that of the Commission, is liable on summary conviction to a fine of up to level 3 on the standard scale under the Criminal Justice Act 1982 and to an additional fine of £20 for each day on which the offence continues after conviction.[45] The defence of "reasonable excuse" does not extend to ignorance or mistake as to the law, even if this is in doubt at the time of the offence.[46]

It is well established by case law under earlier similar provisions that the auditor's powers are not restricted to officers or documents of the authority; they apply, for example, to contractors and their documents.[47]

Public rights

Section 17(1) of the Local Government Finance Act 1982 provides that   **7-17**
all persons interested may inspect the accounts to be audited and all books, deeds, contracts, bills, vouchers[48] and receipts, and they may make copies of them. The right is "to all persons interested," a term which is wider than "ratepayer" or "local government elector."[49] An interested person would appear entitled to depute an agent to make an inspection on his behalf.

> *R.* v. *Bedwellty Urban District Council*[50]. A ratepayer, the secretary of the local ratepayers' association, appointed an accountant, who was not a ratepayer, to inspect with him the books of account and to report to the association thereon. The accountant was refused permission to see the books of account on the ground that he was not a "person interested." *Held*, that a person interested was entitled to inspect by an agent. Charles J. said (at p. 341): "the whole purpose of the section would be defeated if only the ratepayer were allowed to inspect, without a skilled person at his elbow to act as his agent for the inspection."

A local government elector for any area to which the accounts under audit relate, or his representative, may question the auditor about the accounts, and may attend before the auditor and make objections—(a) as to matters on which the auditor could take action under section 19 or 20 of the 1982 Act; or (b) as to any other matter on which he could make a

---

[44] Local Government Finance Act 1982, s. 16(1).
[45] *Ibid.* ss. 16(4), 28(3).
[46] *R.* v. *Reid* [1973] 3 All E.R. 1020.
[47] *Re Hurle-Hobbs* [1944] 2 All E.R. 261; *R.* v. *Hurle-Hobbs, ex p. Simmons* [1945] K.B. 165.
[48] As to the meaning of the term voucher, see *R.* v. *Monmouthshire County Council* (1935) 33 L.G.R. 279.
[49] *Marginson* v. *Tildsley* (1903) 1 L.G.R. 333.
[50] [1934] 1 K.B. 333.

report under section 15(3).[51] The objector must give written notice of a proposed objection, stating its grounds, the facts relied on, and particulars of the action which it is proposed the auditor should take.[52]

Accounts and other documents must be made available for inspection for 15 full working days before the date appointed by the auditor for questioning and objections. At least 14 days public notice must be given of the rights available under section 17, by advertisement in local newspapers or, in the case of parish councils and the like, by displaying notices in public places.

Unlawful items of account

7-18   Where it appears to the auditor that an item of account is contrary to law he may apply to the court for a declaration to that effect.[53] The phrase "contrary to law" has been the subject of much litigation under earlier law which gave the district auditor power to surcharge illegal expenditure on the members or officers responsible for incurring it. Expenditure has been held to be contrary to law if it is unreasonable in its extent or excessive and incurred by abuse of discretion.

> *Roberts* v. *Hopwood*.[54] Under the Metropolis Management Act 1855, the Poplar Council had authority to employ such servants as might be necessary and to pay such servants such wages as the council thought fit. The council resolved to pay a minimum wage of £4 per week to its employees, a figure higher than that paid to persons doing similar work in the district. In an affidavit the council stated that "a public authority should be a model employer and that a minimum rate of £4 is the least wage which ought to be paid to an adult." The district auditor disallowed what he considered to be excess wages and surcharged the members of the council. The members of the council appealed to the Divisional Court, which upheld the auditor's action. The Court of Appeal reversed the decision of the Divisional Court; on further appeal the House of Lords reversed the decision of the Court of Appeal. The headnote to the report, which has been much quoted, records it to have been held "(1) that the discretion conferred upon the council must be exercised reasonably, and that the fixing by the council of an arbitrary sum for wages without regard to existing labour conditions was not an exercise of that discretion; (2) that an expenditure upon a lawful object might be so excessive as to be unlawful, and that to the extent by which the amount exceeded legality the auditor was bound to disallow it and surcharge the excess upon the persons responsible," and that the disallowance and surcharge were therefore rightly made.

The *ratio decidendi* of *Roberts* v. *Hopwood* has been the subject of comment and interpretation in subsequent cases, however, and in *Pickwell* v. *Camden London Borough Council* (below) Ormrod L.J. expressed the view that the headnote of *Roberts* v. *Hopwood* did not accurately reflect the *ratio decidendi* of the case.

---

[51] s. 17(2), (3).
[52] s. 17(4), (5); Accounts and Audit Regulations 1983 (S.I. 1983 No. 1761), reg. 12.
[53] Local Government Finance Act 1982, s. 19(1).
[54] [1925] A.C. 578.

Associated Provincial Picture Houses Ltd. v. *Wednesbury Corporation.*[55] Lord Greene M.R. said, at p. 232, "When the case [*Roberts* v. *Hopwood*] is examined, the word 'unreasonable' is found to be used rather in the sense I mentioned a short while ago, namely, that in fixing £4, they had fixed it by reference to a matter which they ought not to have taken into account and to the exclusion of those elements which they ought to have taken into consideration in fixing a sum which could fairly be called a wage. That is no authority whatsoever to support the proposition that the court has power, a sort of overriding power, to decide what is reasonable and what is unreasonable."

Giddens v. *Harlow District Auditor.*[56] The appellant had objected at the audit, alleging that a loss had been incurred by negligence or misconduct because of the council's failure to charge reasonable rents. She also objected to the expenditure of some £5,000 on the purchase of a wood as a nature reserve, claiming that the wood would benefit only a privileged minority of ratepayers. The district auditor considered the evidence and, applying the principle in *Associated Provincial Picture Houses Ltd.* v. *Wednesbury Corporation,*[57] decided that none of the conditions required to establish unreasonable and unlawful exercise of discretion was satisfied. He accordingly dismissed the objection. The applicant appealed against the auditor's decision. *Held,* dismissing the appeal, that whether or not the authority's conduct was politically motivated, the auditor had applied the correct principles in deciding that it had acted lawfully, and nothing justified the contention that he had erred in law in reaching his decision. Ashworth J. said at p. 487, "It is perhaps worth just citing the three reasons on which, as he says rightly, he could and should interfere: (a) the council have taken into account matters which it ought not to have taken into account; or (b) it had refused or neglected to take into account matters which it ought to take into account; or (c) it had come to a conclusion so unreasonable that no reasonable authority could ever have come to it."

Pickwell v. *Camden London Borough Council.*[58] The council made a local settlement with its manual workers who, in common with other local government workers, were striking for higher pay and reduced working hours. The local settlement was substantially higher than the national settlement reached shortly afterwards. The district auditor applied to the court, under section 161 of the Local Government Act 1972, for a declaration that the payments under the Camden settlement were in part contrary to law. He relied on *Roberts* v. *Hopwood* and also on the *Wednesbury* case, on the basis that the respondents must have taken irrelevant matters into account or failed to take account of matters which they ought to have considered, or alternatively that the decision was one which no reasonable authority could have reached. Ormrod L.J. said that the headnote to *Roberts* v. *Hopwood* did not accurately reflect the *ratio decidendi.* The true reason for that decision, he said, was that the local authority had purported to exercise their power to pay wages in order to make gifts to their staff rather than pay wages; the payments were accordingly *ultra vires* and contrary to law. As to the *Wednesbury* case, Ormrod L.J. said that a failure to take into account relevant matters, or the taking into account of irrelevant matters (and also excessive expenditure) were in effect only evidence that the authority may have acted *ultra vires* and therefore contrary to law. That did not, however, amount to illegality in itself. Attention was to be paid to the quality of the decision rather than to the method by which it was reached. For the district auditor to succeed, he must establish that the council had acted

[55] [1948] 1 K.B. 223.
[56] (1972) 70 L.G.R. 485.
[57] *Supra.*
[58] [1983] 1 Q.B. 962.

outside its powers, either by showing that the decision was not a real exercise of the power to pay wages but was made for an ulterior purpose, or by satisfying the court that no reasonable authority could have made such a decision. The first of these alternatives had not been put forward. The second would require clear and compelling evidence, leading almost to a finding that the council had acted in bad faith; the evidence before the court was quite insufficient to permit the court to make any such finding of fact. The application therefore failed. The judgment of Forbes J. was based more closely on *Wednesbury* principles. He said that there was no direct evidence of breach of those principles and that it could not be inferred from the amount of the payments that the council ignored relevant material, were guided by improper motives or acted in such a way that no reasonable council could act.

It is arguable that the judgment of Forbes J. was based on a narrow ground confined to the necessities of the decisions, that the wider propositions of Ormrod L.J. went beyond those necessities, and that the reasoning of Forbes J. should therefore be taken as the true *ratio decidendi*. However, the words of Ormrod L.J. must carry great weight any may be taken as precluding audit action on alleged excessive expenditure unless there is evidence to show an ulterior purpose or that no reasonable authority could have made such a decision.

In the next case the authority had a discretion to recover certain sums but chose not to do so. In the circumstances of this case it was held by the High Court that the district auditor was right in making a surcharge against members of the authority for having acted contrary to law.

> *Taylor* v. *Munrow*.[59] The facts of this case are somewhat involved but, stated shortly, the authority was obliged to pay to the landlords of requisitioned property the full standard rent under the Rent Acts, the difference between that and the actual rent paid by the occupier being borne by the general rate fund unless the authority should "otherwise determine," by revising the rent. The authority failed to make a determination, paying the whole of the difference, arguing, *inter alia*, that a means test would be involved and was undesirable. The auditor surcharged the councillors with the sums falling to the general rate fund and in addition he found the members of the council to have been guilty of negligence. The court on appeal upheld the district auditor in his view that the discretion given to the council under the Requisitioned Houses and Housing (Amendment) Act 1955 was a discretion which the council was bound to exercise and was bound to exercise reasonably, for the council had always a duty to preserve a balance between a duty owed to the general body of ratepayers and a duty owed to particular tenants.

7-19   *Roberts* v. *Hopwood* (read in light of the *Giddens* and *Camden* decisions)[60] is an authority for the view that excessive expenditure may be held contrary to law if it is shown to have stemmed from an abuse of discretion. *Taylor* v. *Munrow* may be taken as an authority for the view that an improper failure to exercise a discretion at all may be equally regarded as contrary to law.

If unlawful exercise of discretion produces expenditure which is

[59] [1960] 1 All E.R. 455.
[60] All *supra*.

objectively reasonable, it cannot be held contrary to law. In *Re Walker's Decision*,[61] the district auditor disallowed payments of children's allowances to employees on the grounds that an employee's living expenses (and therefore family size) were irrelevant considerations in fixing remuneration. The court held that the amounts paid were not contrary to law because they were not in themselves unreasonable. Goddard L.J. said "If the result is a reasonable sum, that is enough to justify the payment," and referred with approval to a dictum of Lord Sumner at p. 604 in *Roberts* v. *Hopwood*, above, in which he said that even in case of bad faith, if "the councillors' evil minds had missed their mark and the expenditure itself was right, then the expenditure would not be contrary to law."

The meaning of the phrase "contrary to law" was considered in *Beecham* v. *Metropolitan District Auditor*[62] in a somewhat different context from *Roberts* v. *Hopwood*, *Giddens* and *Camden*. The appellant objected at district audit to expenditure on demolition of property on the grounds that planning permission for the demolition was required and had not been obtained. He argued that the demolition was contrary to law and that accordingly the expenditure incurred was contrary to law. The district auditor disallowed the objection. The objector appealed, and failed. Boreham J. said, at p. 83:

> "...the council in the present case has power to demolish their houses and to expend money in so doing. They were therefore in that regard acting *intra vires*. Secondly, the failure to obtain planning permission or consent, assuming that such permission was required, does not in my view render *ultra vires* what was otherwise *intra vires*. It follows, therefore, that the item to which the appellant was objecting was not contrary to law.... Of course, if planning permission was required in this case, and if the council's failure to obtain it were in the future to lead to loss, then it would be incumbent no doubt upon the district auditor to consider whether such loss ought to be surcharged upon the person responsible...."

The auditor may not make application to the court in respect of an item of account sanctioned by the Secretary of State.[63] This appears as a dispensing power in the hands of the Secretary of State, for an auditor cannot in effect look at an account where payment has been approved in this way notwithstanding the fact that it is *ultra vires* or otherwise illegal; but the sanction does not legalise a payment, and an elector who objects to any account may exercise the other (though more expensive) remedies available.

The policy originally adopted by the Local Government Board in issuing sanctions still appears substantially to be followed by the Secretary of State. The Board said in its Annual Report for 1887–88:

[61] [1944] 1 K.B. 644.
[62] (1976) 75 L.G.R. 79.
[63] Local Government Finance Act 1982, s. 19(1). See hereon *R.* v. *Grain, ex p. Wandsworth Guardians* [1927] 2 K.B. 205 and *Att.-Gen.* v. *East Barnet Urban District Council* (1911) 9 L.G.R. 913.

"The power of sanction is intended to be used in those cases where the expenditure is incurred bona fide but in ignorance of the strict letter of the law, or inadvertently without the observance of requisite formalities, or under such circumstances as make it fair and equitable that the expenditure should not be disallowed by the auditor. . . . We do not regard the Act as intended to supply the want of legislative or other authority for particular expenditure or classes of expenditure, and as justifying us in giving prospective sanction to recurring expenses."

7-20   Where the court makes the declaration asked for, it may order repayment by the person concerned and may order the rectification of accounts. Where the person concerned is a member and the expenditure exceeds £2,000 he may be disqualified from membership for a specified period. The court in making an order must have regard to the person's ability to pay and is precluded from making one if satisfied that he acted reasonably or in the belief that the expenditure was authorised by law.[64]

A person answerable under these provisions is one responsible for incurring or authorising expenditure declared unlawful. He is responsible if he voted in favour and he may be responsible if he abstained from voting, or even if he does not attend the meeting.[65]

The court before which these matters are brought is the High Court but where the sum involved does not exceed the amount over which the county courts have jurisdiction in actions founded on contract, the county court has concurrent jurisdiction with the High Court.[66]

Misconduct and failure to account

7-21   Where a person has failed to bring into account a sum which ought to have been included, or where there is loss or deficiency due to wilful misconduct, the auditor may certify a sum due from the person responsible, which, subject to rights of appeal, is then recoverable either by the auditor or the body.[67] The auditor's expenses in enforcing recovery are recoverable from the body unless the court otherwise directs. If that person is a member and the amount exceeds £2,000 he will, subject to appeal, be disqualified for a period of five years. The phrase under earlier law was "negligence or misconduct."[68] In *Asher* v. *Lacey* [69] the failure of the councillors of the Clay Cross Urban District Council to increase council house rents as required by the Housing Finance Act 1972 was held to be negligence or misconduct. Members were surcharged for the resulting "loss or deficiency." There had been a breach of duty.

[64] Local Government Finance Act 1982, s. 19(2), (3).
[65] See hereon generally *Roberts* v. *Hopwood* [1925] A.C. 578; *R.* v. *Browne* [1907] 2 I.R. 505; *R.* v. *Hendon Rural District Council, ex p. Chorley* [1933] 2 K.B. 696 at p. 703; *Att.-Gen.* v. *Tottenham Local Board* (1872) 27 L.T. (N.S.) 440 and *Rothnie* v. *Dearne Urban District Council* (1951) 50 L.G.R. 123.
[66] Local Government Finance Act 1982, s. 19(6).
[67] *Ibid.* s. 20.
[68] The word "misconduct" was considered in this context in *R.* v. *Roberts* [1908] 1 K.B. 407; *Roberts* v. *Hopwood* [1925] A.C. 578; *R.* v. *Browne* [1907] 2 I.R. 505.
[69] [1973] 1 W.L.R. 1412.

Graham v. *Teesdale*.[70] A sum was certified due from the former chairman of a parish council in respect of payments made to him in purported reimbursement of out-of-pocket expenses and to others for his benefit (car repairs and insurance) during a period when he had taken on the responsibility of the council's financial and general administration. No detailed accounts or vouchers were produced for the alleged out-of-pocket expenses; the appellant alleged that such accounts and vouchers had been passed to another member of the council, who did not admit their receipt. The majority of the payments were not authorised by the council; as to the remainder the district auditor found that the council's approval had been obtained by misrepresentation. The appeal was on the grounds, *inter alia*, (1) that the district auditor had misdirected himself in law as to the meaning of "wilful misconduct" and (2) that he had failed to observe the requirements of natural justice in that (*a*) he failed to permit the appellant to question witnesses; (*b*) he heard evidence adverse to the appellant in his absence. *Held*: (i) that "wilful misconduct" in section 161(4) of the 1972 Act meant "deliberately doing something which is wrong knowing it to be wrong or with reckless indifference whether it is wrong or not"; (ii) that the requirements of fairness by a district auditor were (*a*) that any material adverse to a person must be put to him and he must be allowed to deal with it by adducing evidence and otherwise; (*b*) that if there is a hearing (though no hearing is statutorily required) he must be allowed to question witnesses who give evidence at the hearing, through his legal representative, if any, or otherwise through the district auditor; (iii) that the district auditor had correctly directed himself under (i) and had met the requirements of fairness under (ii); (iv) that the appeal should be dismissed.

In defining misconduct the judgment refers only to "doing something" and does not specifically cover wrongful omission to act, as do other cases cited in the judgment, *e.g. Forder* v. *G.W.R. Co.*[71] *Horabin* v. *B.O.A.C.*.[72] However, the judgment later refers to "acts or omissions" which the district auditor had found to constitute misconduct, and does not distinguish between acts and omissions in upholding the auditor's decision. It is not therefore in conflict with the clear authority of such cases as *Forder* and *Horabin* that wilful misconduct includes wrongful omission to act where the omission is known to be wrongful or there is reckless indifference whether it is wrongful or not.

Responsibilities of officers

In cases of illegality or misconduct where the primary responsibility is 7-22 that of the members of the council or other body some responsibility may also be borne by officers. In *R.* v. *Saunders*[73] it was held that a county treasurer who was ordered to make an illegal payment should disobey the order. In *Att.-Gen.* v. *De Winton*[74] it was similarly held that a borough treasurer stood in a fiduciary relationship to the burgesses and could not plead the orders of the council for an unlawful act. In *Re Hurle-Hobbs, ex*

---

[70] (1981) 81 L.G.R. 117.
[71] [1905] 2 K.B. 532.
[72] [1952] 2 All E.R. 1016.
[73] (1854) 3 E. & B. 763.
[74] [1906] 2 Ch. 106.

p. Riley,[75] the court upheld a surcharge on the Town Clerk of Finsbury on the ground that loss had been caused by his misconduct in withholding information from the council on the instructions of the leader of the majority group (who was also surcharged). The court rejected the clerk's defence that he acted under threat of dismissal.

7-23   While the offices of county and borough treasurer and town clerk are no longer statutory, the officer responsible for administration of a body's affairs under section 151 of the Local Government Act 1972 has duties which effectively include those of treasurers under earlier legislation and the chief executive officer and chief legal adviser of a body (under whatever title or titles) is or are as much "an important part of the machinery of local government" as the town clerk who was so described in *Riley's* case. It would therefore appear that these officers would be under a duty, first to advise the council against any unlawful action or misconduct to the detriment of ratepayers, and in the last resort to refuse to implement instructions which are manifestly illegal, such as for the making of illegal payments. Similar considerations would presumably apply to other chief officers and are consistent with the general rule of law, applicable to all officers, that an order of a superior or other duress is not recognised as an excuse for an act which is known to be unlawful. In *Riley's* case Viscount Caldecote C.J. said that "the integrity of the administration of public affairs is such that publicity may be safely relied on to secure protection for anyone in the position in which the Town Clerk was said to have been placed." It would seem that surer protection is now provided by statute, on the assumption that dismissal for refusal to obey unlawful instructions would be held to be unfair within the meaning of the Employment Protection (Consolidation) Act 1978 and would therefore result, on complaint to an industrial tribunal, in an order of reinstatement or compensation under that Act.

Appeals

7-24   A person who has made an objection at audit and is aggrieved by the auditor's decision, and a person from whom the auditor has certified a sum due, may require the auditor, not later than six weeks after the decision has been notified, to state in writing the reasons for his decision, and may appeal against the decision to the High Court, or if the amount at issue is not more than £5000 to the county court.[76]

Fees for audit

7-25   Section 21 of the Local Government Finance Act 1982 provides for the Audit Commission, after consultation with local authority associations

---

[75] (1944), unreported. A full report of the judgments, however, appears in Hurle-Hobbs, *The Law Relating to District Audit* (1955), now out of print, and a summarised note, with extracts of judgments, in R. Jones, *Local Government Audit Law* (2nd ed., 1985).
[76] Local Government Finance Act 1982, ss. 19(4), (6), 20(2), (3), (9).

and accountancy bodies, to fix scales of fees payable to the Commission which may be varied according to the work involved in a particular audit. The fee must be the same whether the auditor is an officer of the Commission or not. The Secretary of State is given a reserve power to set fee scales, after consultation, in place of those prescribed by the Commission.

Extraordinary audit

The Audit Commission may direct an auditor to hold an extraordinary **7-26** audit of accounts of any body subject to audit if it appears to them desirable, either on application by a local government elector or otherwise, and the Secretary of State may require the Commission to do so. Three days' notice must be given to the body. All the normal audit provisions apply, except the public rights of inspection of accounts and questioning the auditor. Public notice must be given of the right to make objection.[77]

Accounts and returns

All accounts are required to be made up to March 31, or such other **7-27** date as the Secretary of State may generally or in any special case direct.[78] The Accounts and Audit Regulations 1983 (S.I. 1983 No. 1761) made under section 23 of the Local Government Finance Act 1982, make provision for various matters concerning the accounts and public rights relating thereto, including the publication of a statement of accounts with the auditor's opinion thereon. At the time of going to press further draft regulations had been issued prescribing in detail the form and content of such statements of accounts. Local authorities and rating authorities are required to make annual returns to the Secretary of State of the income and expenditure of the former and of the rates levied and precepts paid by the latter.[79]

Local Government Act 1985—new authorities and residuary bodies

All the audit provisions of Part III of the Local Government Finance **7-28** Act 1982 are applied to the Inner London Education Authority and the joint authorities established by the Local Government Act 1985.[80]

For the residuary bodies set up by the 1985 Act, section 79 of this Act applies the 1982 Act audit provisions, with the exception of sections 15(1)(a) (auditor's duty as to compliance with statutory provisions), 17 (public inspection of accounts and right of challenge), 19 (unlawful items of account), 20 (failure to account and wilful misconduct), 22 (extraordinary audit), 23 (regulations) and 24 (right to inspect statement of accounts

---

[77] Accounts and Audit Regulations 1983 (S.I. 1983 No. 1761), reg. 16.
[78] Local Government Finance Act 1982, s. 12.
[79] Local Government Act 1972, s. 168.
[80] Local Government Act 1985, s. 72(3).

and auditor's report). However, section 79 of the 1985 Act itself confers similar rights on local government electors in respect of inspection and copies of accounts and documents (subs. (3)) and of statements of accounts and auditors' reports (subs. (6)). No sanctions are provided against obstruction of these rights. Electors may also question the auditor and draw his attention to any matter on which he could make a report. At the conclusion of an audit copies of the statement of accounts and auditor's report must be sent to the Secretary of State and laid by him before Parliament.

The residuary bodies are responsible for discharging outstanding functions in respect of the accounts of the Greater London Council and the metropolitan county councils, including the preparation of their final accounts.[81] Part III of the Local Government Finance Act 1982 applies in full to these accounts.[82]

C. CONTROL OF CAPITAL EXPENDITURE

7-29 Part VIII of the Local Government, Planning and Land Act 1980 enables the Secretary of State by order to control expenditure for capital purposes, whatever the source of the finance. Part VIII applies to county councils, district councils, London borough councils, the Common Council of the City of London, the Inner London Education Authority, the joint authorities established by the Local Government Act 1985 and certain other authorities.[83]

The direct control of capital expenditure under Part VIII replaced, from April 1, 1981, the previous system under which borrowing controls were used as a means of controlling expenditure.

Prescribed expenditure

7-30 A duty falls to the appropriate minister to specify in relation to any authority an amount of prescribed expenditure for each year before the beginning of the year.[84] Additional allocations may be made at a later stage. A specification may at any time be withdrawn by a minister so far as it relates to any payments not made, but not in respect of liabilities under a binding contract entered into by the authority.[85] Prescribed expenditure is defined in Schedule 12 to the Act of 1980. It consists of expenditure in connection with the acquisition of land (including buildings), the construction of buildings, and various other items generally recognised as of a capital nature.

The Local Government (Prescribed Expenditure) Regulations 1983, as

---

[81] Local Government Act, 1985, s. 63.
[82] *Ibid.* s. 79(8).
[83] Local Government, Planning and Land Act 1980, s. 71 as amended by the Local Government Act 1985, Sched. 14, para. 59.
[84] Local Government, Planning and Land Act 1980, ss. 72(1), 76.
[85] *Ibid.* s. 74.

amended and the Local Government (Prescribed Expenditure) (Wales) Regulations 1983[86] provide that certain types of expenditure shall not be prescribed expenditure. The exemptions include expenditure on the police, probation and magistrates' court services; capital expenditure on these services is subject to separate control by the Home Office, from whom loan sanctions must be sought.

For other services, local authorities are given an expenditure allocation each year in six service blocks—housing, education, transport, personal social services, urban aid and other services. These allocations may be aggregated and used for such purposes as the authority thinks fit and for which they have power to make payments.[87] However, the appropriate minister may direct, in relation to projects of national or regional importance, that a specified part of an authority's aggregate allocation may be spent only on a specified project.[88]

An authority may add to its allocation in any year:

(a) a maximum of 10 per cent. of its allocation for that year.
(b) any additional allocation which may be given in the course of the year.
(c) any allocation switched from another local authority.[89]
(d) certain amounts in respect of capital receipts from that or any preceding year.
(e) an amount for the year equal to the authority's entitlement of the profits of a trading undertaking owned by the authority individually or as a member of a joint committee of local authorities.

If actual expenditure exceeds the initial allocation plus the adjustments at (b) and (d), above, the excess will be deducted from the following year's allocation. But if in the previous year the authority had not spent its basic allocations, the deduction from the following year's allocation will be reduced by that underspending, subject to the limitation of the 10 per cent. tolerance under (a) above.[90] It may be noted that this deduction does not on the face of it make allowance for the adjustments referred to at (c) and (e) above. However, these adjustments take effect as additional allocations by the Secretary of State and therefore fall under adjustment (b) for this purpose.[91]

Capital receipts

Capital receipts are defined differently, for the purposes of Part VIII of **7-31** the 1980 Act, according to whether they were received before or after

---

[86] S.I. 1983 No. 296; S.I. 1984 No. 223; S.I. 1985 No. 259; S.I. 1983 No. 1191.
[87] DoE Circulars 9/83, para. 5 and 6/84, para. 5.
[88] DoE Circular 9/83, para. 46.
[89] Local Government, Planning and Land Act 1980, s. 77.
[90] *Ibid.* s. 72(8), (10). DoE Circular 6/84, paras. 7 and 8.
[91] *Ibid.* s. 77. DoE Circular 9/83, para. 37.

April 1, 1981.[92] Sums received before that date in respect of disposals of land, buildings, vehicles, vessels, plant and machinery, and in respect of repayments to the authority of grants and advances of a capital nature, are counted as capital receipts, subject to deduction of amounts spent out of such receipts before that date, for whatever purpose. Similar receipts after April 1, 1981, are counted as capital receipts without any such deduction. The Local Government (Prescribed Expenditure) Regulations 1983 also specify a number of items of income which are to be treated as capital receipts, including gifts and bequests, local lottery proceeds, and various payments arising from highways and planning statutes.

An authority's allocation of prescribed expenditure may be increased by its "net capital receipts" or such proportion of those receipts as may be prescribed.[93] "Net capital receipts" means capital receipts as defined,[94] reduced by any payment in a previous year authorised by section 72(3)(d); the effect is that once capital receipts have been used to justify an increase of prescribed expenditure over the basic allocation they cannot be used again for that purpose.

The Local Government (Prescribed Expenditure) Regulations 1983, as amended,[95] limit the proportion of net capital receipts which may be added to prescribed expenditure allocations. The figure of "net capital receipts," to which these proportions are applied, is recalculated annually, and in each year an authority may therefore add to expenditure allocations the prescribed proportion of unused sums from previous years.[96]

Capital receipts of residuary bodies established by the Local Government Act 1985 may be the subject of an order by the Secretary of State, providing for the distribution of such receipts to rating authorities or to new authorities established by the Act and for their treatment as capital receipts of those authorities for the purposes of Part VIII of the 1980 Act.[97]

Profits of trading undertakings

7-32   Guidelines to the assessment of the profits of an undertaking (which may be used to increase capital expenditure allocations, appear in Circular 9/83. Briefly, assessment of profits is to be based on commercial accounting practice on a current cost accounting basis.

Leasing

7-33   Where an authority acquire a leasehold interest in property, section 80 provides, broadly, that the authority will be regarded for the purpose of

---

[92] *Ibid.* s. 75(1).
[93] s. 72(3)(d).
[94] See s. 75(1).
[95] S.I. 1983 No. 296; S.I. 1984 No. 223; S.I. 1985 No. 259; S.I. 1983 No. 1191.
[96] DoE Circular 9/83, para. 32.
[97] Local Government Act 1985, s. 77.

Part VIII as having paid the freehold or market value of the land or goods. But this does not apply to non-building leases of less than twenty years or to leases of plant and equipment, including vehicles.[98]

Ultra vires control

If the Secretary of State is of the opinion that an authority has failed or 7-34 is likely to fail to conform to the rules as to payments in respect of prescribed expenditure he may issue a direction prohibiting the authority from making any payments in excess of the aggregate amount of prescribed expenditure for that year and limiting the powers of the authority to enter into contracts for carrying out works without the consent of the appropriate Minister.[99]

An authority does not act beyond its powers if it makes a payment or enters into a contract which entails making payment in excess of its allocation. It is, however, *ultra vires* an authority to make a payment or enter into a contract in contravention of a direction given by a Minister under section 73 in relation to projects of national or regional importance or a direction from the Secretary of State under section 78. But a transaction between a person and an authority shall not be void by reason only that it was carried out in contravention of a direction, and that person is not concerned to see or inquire whether a direction has been given or complied with.[1]

D. BORROWING

The principal statutory provisions relating to borrowing by local 7-35 authorities are contained in Schedule 13 to the Local Government Act 1972. A principal council may borrow money for lending to another authority, and a local authority may, subject to certain exemptions, borrow money for any purpose or class of purpose approved by the Secretary of State.[2]

Department of the Environment Circular No. 9/85, Annex A, conveys general consent for each local authority to which Part VIII of the Act applies to borrow up to an amount equal to the aggregate of the following items referred to in paragraph 7-30, above, namely, the aggregate of the annual expenditure allocations, any additional allocation, any allocation transferred from another authority, and any amounts switched, within the permissible limits, from the preceding or following year, *less* the aggregate of the following, namely, any allocations transferred to another authority, any amounts switched to the preceding or following year, any

[98] Local Government (Prescribed Expenditure) Regulations 1983, Sched. 3; DoE Circular 9/83, para. 41. As to the effect of a disposal of a leasehold interest, see the Local Government, Planning and Land Act 1980, s. 80.
[99] Local Government, Planning and Land Act 1980, s. 78.
[1] *Ibid.* s. 79.
[2] Local Government Act 1972, Sched. 13, paras. 1, 13, 14.

capital grant received in the year from central government or from the European Regional Development Fund, and borrowing under local Acts or powers to borrow without ministerial consent. Adjustment is made for contributions by county councils to works of coast protection by district councils. There are additional borrowing controls for housing schemes. No additional borrowing approval will be given to match capital receipts available to augment expenditure allocations.

Subject to some modifications, the new authorities and residuary bodies established by the Local Government Act 1985 are treated as local authorities for the purposes of the above provisions.[3]

Methods of raising loans

7-36   Local authority loans may be raised in a variety of ways, by mortgage, by the issue of stock, by the issue of debentures or annuity certificates under the Local Loans Act 1875, by the issue of bonds, by the issue of bills, by an agreement entered into with the Public Works Loan Commissioners under section 2 of the Public Works Loans Act 1965, or by any other means approved by the Secretary of State with the consent of the Treasury.[4] As noted in paragraph 7-44, the balances of internal funds may also be used.

Borrowing by local authorities is subject to regulations made by the Secretary of State.[5] The regulations concern:

(a)   the form of mortgage deeds;

(b)   the issue of stocks and bonds;

(c)   the transfer dealing and redemption of mortgages, stocks and bonds, and

(d)   public inspection of the relevant documents.

Stock and bonds may bear interest at variable rates.[6]

There are particular rules about the issue of bills. First, an authority whose estimated gross rate income is less than £3 million, or such other sum as the Treasury may prescribe, may not use this method. Where so allowed, bills may be issued, payable within 12 months from the date of issue, for capital or for revenue purposes. The total amount of bills on issue may not exceed one-fifth of the estimated gross rate income for the year in the case of a county council. In the case of any other authority the proportion is one-fifth of the proportion of the estimated gross income retained by the council for its own purposes. These limits may be varied by the Treasury.[7] A local authority may, with the consent of the Treasury,

---

[3] Local Government Act 1985, ss. 70, 75.

[4] Local Government Act 1972, Sched. 13, para. 2.

[5] Local Government Act 1972, Sched. 13, para. 4 and the Local Authority (Mortgages) Regulations 1974 (S.I. 1974 No. 518) and the Local Authority (Stocks and Bonds) Regulations 1974 (S.I. 1974 No. 519).

[6] S.I. 1974 No. 519, regs. 2, 3, 6, as amended by S.I. 1983 No. 529.

[7] Local Government Act 1972, Sched. 13, para. 5.

issue bearer bonds and other bearer securities.[8] All money borrowed, and the interest payable thereon, is charged indifferently on all the revenues of the authority and all securities rank equally without priorities.[9]

A person lending money to a local authority is not bound to inquire whether the borrowing of the money is legal or regular or whether the money raised was properly applied. He is not prejudiced by any illegality or irregularity, or by the misapplication or non-application of any of that money.[10]

Treasury controls

The Control of Borrowing Order 1958,[11] made under the Borrowing 7-37 (Control and Guarantees) Act 1946, in its application to local authorities, requires Treasury consent to the borrowing of money in excess of £50,000 in any period of 12 months, but a General Consent dated October 19, 1983 has been given which permits borrowing for the purposes of the Order without restriction, subject to certain exceptions.

These are:

(a) the issue of any stock, or of any bonds in respect of which application has been or is to be made to the Council of the Stock Exchange for admission to the Official List or which are issued in whole or in part to a bank, discount house, issuing house or broker in the City of London, unless the times and terms of issue have secured the prior approval of the Bank of England on behalf of H.M. Treasury;

(b) the issue of any bonds at a discount exceeding one-half of one per cent. for each year of the period within which the money borrowed is to be repaid, or fifteen per cent., whichever rate is the lower;

(c) the borrowing of any money for any purposes authorised by a local Act (unless the transaction has been sanctioned by a government department);

(d) the issue of money bills, except in anticipation of the proceeds of an approved stock issue;

(e) borrowings for capital purposes of any money repayable in less than 12 calendar months in excess of prescribed maxima.

Treasury consent is not required to borrowing by a local authority for the sole purpose of defraying expenditure (including the payment of sums due by them to meet the expenses of other authorities) pending the receipt of revenues receivable by them in respect of the period of account in which that expenditure is chargeable, so long as (i) the expenditure is not capital expenditure; and (ii) the money is repayable not later than one

---

[8] Local Government Act 1972, Sched. 13, para. 6.
[9] *Ibid.* para. 11.
[10] *Ibid.* para. 20.
[11] S.I. 1958 No. 1208, as amended by Control of Borrowing (Amendment) Orders (S.I. 1967 No. 69, S.I. 1970 No. 708, S.I. 1975 No. 12, S.I. 1977 No. 1602 and S.I. 1979 No. 794).

month after the termination of that period of account; and (iii) the amount outstanding at any one time does not exceed one-half of the total revenues received or receivable in respect of that period of account.[12]

Powers of trustees to invest with local authorities

7-38　　The Trustee Investments Act 1961 (a note of which appears at para. 7-43, below) enables trustees to make loans to local authorities, to purchase local authority securities, and to make temporary deposits with local authorities.[13] Investments in this field are described as narrower-range investments.

Provision for repayment of loans

7-39　　A local authority which borrows must in each year make provision for loan repayment by debiting the account from which the expenditure would otherwise fall to be defrayed with a sum equivalent to an instalment of principal and interest combined such that if it were paid annually the debt would be cleared by the end of the "fixed period" of loan consent—this is the period within which the money is to be repaid as determined by the local authority with the consent of the Secretary of State.[14] Maximum "fixed periods" are prescribed in Department of the Environment Circular 9/85.

The annual amount of provision may be varied where money is borrowed to advance to others.[15] In certain circumstances there may be a postponement of provision—where money is borrowed (a) for capital works for a revenue-producing undertaking; (b) for carrying out on land any other operations specified by the Secretary of State; (c) for acquiring land for (a) or (b); or (d) for acquiring any other land specified by the Secretary of State. The authority may, during the permitted period of suspension, borrow to pay interest.[16]

Borrowing without consent

7-40　　An authority may borrow without consent to repay existing loans within the fixed period of the loan consent,[17] and may borrow without consent by way of temporary loan, bank overdraft or otherwise, (a) for the purpose of defraying expenses pending the receipt of revenues, and (b) for the purpose of defraying, pending the raising of an authorised loan, expenses intended to be defrayed by means of that loan. Borrowing under (b) is treated as dating back to the raising of the temporary loan: paragraph 10.

[12] S.I. 1958 No. 1208, art. 1(2)(c).
[13] s. 1 and Sched. 1, Pt. II.
[14] Local Government Act 1972, Sched. 13, paras. 7, 22.
[15] Sched. 13, para. 7(3).
[16] Ibid. para. 9.
[17] Ibid. para. 8.

E. Special Funds

In accordance with a scheme which it is authorised to make, a local **7–41** authority may (and must if it borrows by the issue of stocks or bonds) establish and operate a loans fund for defraying any expenditure which the authority is authorised to meet out of monies borrowed by the authority and for the repayment or redemption of debt.[18]

Apart from setting up and operating a loans fund (or loans pool—for that is what is is), a local authority may establish such other funds as it considers appropriate for the purpose of meeting any expenses in connection with its functions and may make into such other funds whatever payments it thinks fit.[19] This provision empowers the authority to maintain capital funds, repairs and renewal funds, insurance funds and the like. Some limitations on the operation of such funds are imposed by paragraphs 17 and 18, relating to trading undertakings, insurance funds, and housing receipts.

The new authorities established by the Local Government Act 1985 are local authorities for the purposes of the above provisions.[20]

F. Investments

Superannuation Funds

The Local Government Superannuation (Amendment) (No. 2) Regu- **7–42** lations 1983[21] substituted a new regulation governing use and investment of superannuation fund moneys for regulation B6 of the Local Government Superannuation Regulations 1974[22] under which investment was governed by the Trustee Investments Act 1961 with some modifications. The changes made by the 1983 Regulations are explained in Department of the Environment Circular 24/83.

Under the substituted regulation B6, administering authorities are required to invest superannuation fund moneys not for the time being required for the payment of benefits. Circular 24/83 suggests that "invest" includes any employment of capital to obtain income, including bank deposits, loans, property, etc.[23] Limitations are imposed by regulation B6(4), (5), however, to restrict the proportion of the fund's investments which may be placed in four categories, namely (a) securities not listed on a reputable stock exchange (maximum 10 per cent. of total value of investments); (b) single holdings, except for gilts, bank deposits

---

[18] Local Government Act 1972, Sched. 13, para. 15. Local Authorities (Stocks and Bonds) Regulations 1974 (S.I. 1974 No. 519), para. 15.

[19] *Ibid.* para. 16, as substituted by the Local Government (Miscellaneous Provisions) Act 1976, s. 28.

[20] Local Government Act 1985, s. 70.

[21] S.I. 1983 No. 1270.

[22] S.I. 1974 No. 520.

[23] App. B, para. 3.

and the Local Authorities Mutual Investment Trust (5 per cent.); (c) deposits with a single bank, institution or person other than the National Savings Bank (10 per cent.); (d) loans to persons or bodies (including local authorities), other than the Government or bankers and the like (as defined), *plus* use by the authority itself under borrowing powers—see paragraph 7–44, below (10 per cent. in aggregate).

An administering authority must have regard to the need for diversification and the suitability of investments, and to advice from an officer or other person reasonably believed to be qualified by financial ability and experience.[24]

Other funds

7-43　Money in funds established for the purposes of paragraph 16 of Schedule 13 to the Local Government Act 1972[25] must, until needed, be invested in securities in which superannuation funds may be invested. The investment of funds held on charitable or other trusts is subject to the provisions of the Trustee Investments Act 1961. The 1961 Act enables trustees to invest a part of their funds in equities, subject to certain safeguards and to a number of conditions.

Internal investment

7-44　The Local Government Act 1972[26] enables a local authority[27] to use, for any purpose for which it has a statutory borrowing power, surplus moneys of a fund established for debt repayment, a superannuation fund, or a fund established under Sched. 13, para. 16.[28] The money so used must be repaid within the period and by the method applicable to an external borrowing, or earlier if required by the fund. Interest on use of superannuation fund moneys must be calculated on a daily basis at a rate no lower than the lowest rate at which the same amount could be borrowed at seven days' notice.[29] For other funds interest is chargeable at a rate determined by the authority as that payable on a mortgage loan raised under the borrowing power: Local Government Act 1972.[30]

---

[24] reg. B6(6).
[25] See § 7–41.
[26] Sched. 13, para. 19.
[27] Including a new authority established by the Local Government Act 1985, s. 70.
[28] See § 7–41.
[29] Local Government Superannuation Regulations 1974, as amended, reg. B6(3).
[30] Sched. 13, para. 19(3) and (5).

CHAPTER 8

RATES AND RATING

THE income of local authorities is largely obtained from the levying of **8-01** rates and the issuing of precepts and from grants from the Central Government. Rates and rating and the issuing of precepts are considered in this Chapter and grants in the next.

The system of rating in England and Wales has grown out of, and is not fundamentally different from, the system imposed by the Poor Relief Act 1601—commonly referred to as the Statute of Elizabeth. Section 1 of that Act required the overseers of the poor to raise sums from inhabitants and occupiers of land in the parish to provide materials to enable the poor to be set to work and to maintain the lame, impotent, halt and blind. Liability fell on residents and on occupiers of property within the parish, and in an early case[1] it was held that assessments should be made according to the visible estate, both real and personal, of those living within the parish. Statutory recognition was given in the Parochial Assessments Act 1836 to the principle of ability to pay as disclosed by the estimated annual letting value of occupied property, and the liability of residents, as opposed to occupiers of property, was removed by the Poor Rate Exemption Act 1840. The Act of 1836 has been repealed, but the principle which it established is substantially valid today. Section 1 provided that no rate for the relief of the poor should be allowed unless it was made on an estimate of the net annual value of the property rated, *i.e.* on an estimate of the rent at which the property might reasonably be expected to be let from year to year, free of all tenant's rates and taxes and deducting therefrom the probable annual average cost of repairs, insurance and other expenses necessary to maintain the property in a state fit to command such rent. It was at that time thought that the wording of the section was such that only real property could be the subject of rating, but a decision to the contrary[2] led to the passing of the Poor Rate Exemption Act 1840, which removed all doubt on this point.

It is convenient to consider the subject-matter of this Chapter under the following headings: (a) the basis of rateability, (b) the measure of liability, (c) exemptions, special cases and personal reliefs, (d) valuation for rating, (e) the making of rates and the issuing of precepts, (f) the recovery of rates and appeals against the rate.

---

[1] *Sir Anthony Earby's Case* (1633) 2 Bulst. 354.
[2] *R.* v. *Lumsdaine* (1839) 10 A. & E. 157.

A. The Basis of Rating

8-02 Rates are levied on the occupiers of real property, and occupation is the general basis of rateability. There is no statutory definition of occupation—its meaning in rating has developed through a mass of complicated case law, from which certain fairly clear principles have emerged. Occupation to be rateable involves first possession, a *de facto* possession which embraces some form of use or enjoyment; secondly, there must be at least some element of permanence; thirdly, the occupation must be beneficial. The first two points are referred to in *R. v. St. Pancras Assessment Committee*[3]; the third in *Jones v. Mersey Docks.*[4] A definition mentioned in *John Laing and Son Limited v. Assessment Committee for Kingswood Assessment Area*[5] identifies a fourth ingredient—the occupation must be exclusive as well as actual.

>   *R. v. St. Pancras Assessment Committee.*[5a] The facts in this case are not of particular importance but the speech of Lush J. is continually referred to in rating law. He said[6]: "It is not easy to give an accurate and exhaustive definition of the word 'occupier.' Occupation includes possession as its primary element, but it also includes something more. Legal possession does not of itself constitute an occupation. The owner of a vacant house is in possession, and may maintain trespass against anyone who invades it, but as long as he leaves it vacant he is not rateable for it as an occupier. If, however, he furnishes it, and keeps it ready for habitation whenever he pleases to go to it, he is an occupier, though he may not reside in it one day in a year. On the other hand, a person who, without having any title, takes actual possession of a house or piece of land, whether by leave of the owner or against his will, is the occupier of it. Another element, however, besides actual possession of the land, is necessary to constitute the kind of occupation which the Act contemplates, and that is permanence. An itinerant showman who erects a temporary structure for his performances, may be in exclusive actual possession, and may, with strict grammatical propriety, be said to occupy the ground on which his structure is placed, but it is clear that he is not such an occupier as the statute intends. ... A transient, temporary holding of land is not enough to make the holding rateable. It must be an occupation which has in it the character of permanence; a holding as a settler not as a wayfarer."
>   *Jones v. Mersey Docks.*[7] The Board claimed that it was not rateable for the docks for it was required by statute to apply moneys received in defraying conservancy and pilotage expenditure and other expenditure prescribed by statute. No member of the Board derived a benefit from the execution of the trusts. *Held*, the Board was liable. In the course of his judgment Lord Cranworth discussed the term "beneficial occupation." He said[8]: "If by beneficial occupation is meant any occupation of something valuable, something in its own nature beneficial to someone, I think it is fair to consider that word as impliedly included in the statute. It was not meant to impose the

---

[3] (1877) 2 Q.B.D. 581.
[4] (1865) 11 H.L.C. 443.
[5] [1949] 1 K.B. 344.
[5a] *Supra*, n. 3.
[6] At p. 588.
[7] (1865) 11 H.L.C. 443.
[8] At p. 507.

duty of contributing to the relief of the poor or anyone merely because he might be the occupier of a barren rock, neither yielding, nor capable of yielding, any profit from its occupation. But I can discover nothing either in the words or in the spirit of the Act exempting from liability the occupier of valuable property, merely because the profits of the occupation are not to be enjoyed by him or by anyone on whose behoof he is occupying, but are to be devoted to the benefit of the public."

John Laing and Son Ltd. v. *Assessment Committee for Kingswood Assessment Area*.[9] The plaintiffs erected contractors' offices, canteens and other structures on land belonging to the Air Ministry. The site was handed over to the plaintiffs but under the terms of the contract the work was subject to the Ministry's officers. It was argued for the plaintiffs that occupation to be rateable must be something more than occupation by subordinates for the purposes of the predominant occupier. *Held*, the control exercised under the contract had relation only to the performance of the contract and was not such as to interfere with the exclusive occupation of the hereditament by the contractors for the purposes of their business. Jenkins J. said[10]: "It seems to me that their possession was nonetheless exclusive because they were subject to the general controlling authority of the superintending officers." Tucker L.J., in the course of his judgment, referred to the general principles of law relating to rateable occupation. He said[11]: "First, there must be actual occupation; secondly, that it must be exclusive for the particular purposes of the possessor; thirdly, that the possession must be of some value or benefit to the possessor; and fourthly, the possession must not be for too transient a period."

On the principles settled by these cases the owner of an empty house **8-03** would not be rateable, since there is possession but no use or enjoyment.[12] Lord Russell of Killowen stated this as a broad rule in *Westminster City Council* v. *Southern Ry*.[13] He said: "The owner of an empty house has the legal possession, but he is not in rateable occupation." But it was held in *Bayliss* v. *Chatters*[14] that the owner of empty bungalows advertised as being available for letting was in beneficial occupation—in this case four bungalows formed part of a group of six, let when tenants could be found. During the winter the furniture was taken out of the four bungalows and stored in a fifth. The Divisional Court held that there was evidence on which the justices were entitled to find that the owner was in beneficial occupation of all the bungalows. By contrast, in *Wirral Borough Council* v. *Lane*[15] the Divisional Court decided that, where an owner did not sleep in his house but had some furniture there, kept the property heated and used the telephone for private and business calls, the magistrates'

---

[9] [1949] 1 K.B. 344. *cf. Forces Help Society and Lord Roberts Workshops* v. *Canterbury City Council* (1978) 77 L.G.R. 541, where it was held that, in the case of property occupied by a licensee, the question of who was in rateable occupation must be determined having regard to the degree of control exercised by the owner and the purpose for which the licensee was allowed to occupy the property.

[10] At p. 357.

[11] At p. 350.

[12] *R.* v. *St. Pancras Assessment Committee* (1877) 2 Q.B.D. 581. As to the rating of empty property, see § 8–33.

[13] [1936] A.C. 511 at p. 529.

[14] [1940] 1 All E.R. 620.

[15] (1979) 251 E.G. 61.

conclusion that he was not in rateable occupation would not be set aside. The magistrates might well have come to the opposite conclusion but the question for the Divisional Court was not whether they had reached a wrong decision but whether it was one which they could not reasonably have reached. In *R.* v. *Melladew*[16] it was held that an empty warehouse would be beneficially occupied if it were ready to receive goods and advertised as such, for a warehouse is full, half-full or empty from time to time according to the fluctuations of trade, and warehousemen must contemplate the use for considerable periods of parts of the premises as spare room. This case was distinguished in *Associated Cinema Properties Ltd.* v. *Hampstead Borough Council.*[17] Here a company acquired a lease of premises intending to use them as offices if their existing accommodation became unusable through enemy action. They left the premises vacant, did not use them in any way, and did not install any furniture or other goods. It was held that there was no rateable occupation, du Parcq L.J. said[18]:

> "It is significant that no case could be cited in which occupation has been held to be established without proof of some overt act amounting to evidence of user. In *R.* v. *Melladew* the owner had advertised the premises as a warehouse. In most cases user has been proved by showing that the house had been furnished, or equipped for some business purpose ... in our judgment, a mere intention to occupy premises on the happening of a future uncertain event, cannot, without more, be regarded as evidence of occupation."

The *Hampstead* case was followed in *Bexley Congregational Church Treasurer* v. *London Borough of Bexley.*[19] A manse had been vacant for eleven months and during that time was held available for the next minister. The Divisional Court held that it was "occupied," relying on *Gage* v. *Wren*[20] and *R.* v. *Melladew.*[21] The Court of Appeal reversed this decision, holding that a mere intention to occupy the premises did not constitute occupation. In *British Telecommunications* v. *Kennet District Council*[22] the House of Lords held that a telephone exchange was in rateable occupation during the installation of telephone equipment. Lord Keith said that the question at issue was "whether that hereditament was during the relevant period serving the business purpose of the respondents, in the sense that they were enjoying the accommodation which it afforded."

The nature of occupation was also considered in *Re Briant Colour Printing Co. Ltd.*[23] where it was held that an owner of a factory who is totally excluded therefrom by a "work-in" by former employees is not to

---

[16] [1907] 1 K.B. 192.
[17] [1944] 1 K.B. 412.
[18] At p. 416.
[19] [1972] 2 Q.B. 222.
[20] (1902) 87 L.T. 271.
[21] [1907] 1 K.B. 192.
[22] [1983] R.A. 43.
[23] [1977] 1 W.L.R. 942.

be regarded as being in rateable occupation of the premises during the period of such exclusion. In *Routhan* v. *Arun District Council* [24] and *R.* v. *Harrow Magistrates' Court, ex p. Harrow London Borough Council and Thicken* [25] the courts have considered the issue of occupation as between husband and wife. In *Verrall* v. *Hackney London Borough Council* [26] it was held that occupation by an unincorporated association is impossible in law.

B. The Measure of Liability

The amount which falls to be paid in respect of any hereditament **8-04** depends primarily on its rateable value. The value is ascertained on the basis of principles set out in the General Rate Act 1967, which consolidated much of the rating legislation. Hereditaments are divided by section 19 of the 1967 Act into two groups. Group (a) consists broadly speaking of houses and other non-industrial buildings without land other than a garden, yard, court or forecourt [27]; group (b) consists of all other hereditaments. In the case of hereditaments in group (a) the *gross* value is first ascertained. This is defined by section 19(6) of the Act of 1967 as:

> the rent at which a hereditament might reasonably be expected to let from year to year if the tenant undertook to pay all usual tenant's rates and taxes and the landlord undertook to bear the cost of the repairs and insurance, and the other expenses, if any, necessary to maintain the hereditament in a state to command that rent.

When gross value has been ascertained certain deductions are then made from it in accordance with an order made by the Secretary of State [28] and the resulting figure is the rateable value. The statutory deductions contained in the order represent a fixed allowance for repairs, insurance and other expenses necessary to maintain the hereditament. It is assumed that rental values of properties in group (a) cover these items.

In the case of properties falling within group (b), the net annual value **8-05** is arrived at directly. It is defined in section 19 of the Act of 1967 as:

> an amount equal to the rent at which it is estimated the hereditament might reasonably be expected to let from year to year if the tenant undertook to pay all usual tenant's rates and taxes and to bear the cost of the repairs and

---

[24] [1982] Q.B. 502.

[25] [1983] R.V.R. 53.

[26] [1983] Q.B. 445.

[27] From the coming into force of the first new valuation list after the Local Government, Planning and Land Act 1980, this group will consist only of a hereditament consisting of a dwelling-house, private garage with a floor area not exceeding 25 square metres, or private storage premises for articles of domestic use. All other hereditaments in this group which formerly were valued on gross value basis will be valued on net annual value and will fall within group (b). See s. 29 of the 1980 Act. For other changes in the valuation system effected by the 1980 Act, see § 8-23.

[28] Local Government Act 1974, s. 17; Valuation (Statutory Deductions) Order 1962 (S.I. 1962 No. 940) as amended by S.I. 1973 No. 2139.

insurance and the other expenses, if any, necessary to maintain the hereditament in a state to command that rent.

The annual values taken for rating purposes, under both (a) and (b), are the estimated rental values on year-to-year lettings. Lord Herschell L.C. said in *London County Council* v. *Erith Parish (Churchwardens, etc.)*[29]:

> "Whether the premises are in the occupation of the owner or not, the question to be answered is: Supposing they were vacant and to let, what rent might reasonably be expected to be obtained for them?"

Scott L.J. said in *Robinson Bros. (Brewers) Ltd.* v. *Houghton and Chester-le-Street Assessment Committee*[30]:

> "The rent to be ascertained is the figure at which the hypothetical landlord and tenant would, in the opinion of the valuer or the tribunal, come to terms as a result of bargaining for that hereditament, in the light of competition or its absence in both demand and supply, as a result of 'the higgling of the market.' I call this the true rent because it corresponds to real value."

In *Garton* v. *Hunter (Valuation Officer)*[31] it was held that in arriving at the rent which a hypothetical tenant would pay for the particular hereditament, its actual rent and those of truly comparable hereditaments might be useful but were not necessarily decisive. In a proper case, other relevant evidence, such as evidence on the profits or contractor's basis, should also be admitted. Such a case would be a caravan site or premises in respect of which there were only rarely true comparables. All relevant evidence was admissible. The goodness or badness of it would go only to weight, and not to admissibility.

In *Black* v. *Oliver*[32] it was held that harassment by neighbours might affect the rateable value of a dwelling and the value might be reduced by that and other factors to nil, even if there were a tenant in occupation. In *Saunders* v. *Maltby*[33] it was decided that, when a house was in a very bad condition but capable of repair, it should not necessarily be assessed on the test of the hypothetical landlord and tenant in section 19(6) of the General Rate Act 1967 as if it had been repaired. One had to look at the condition of the premises and see whether it would be reasonable to do repairs because if the cost of repair was out of all proportion, the landlord would let it at the rent which he could get.

The General Rate Act 1970 renders admissible as evidence of rental values the rents of other dwelling-houses of the same or of a different description.

The Secretary of State may by order exclude certain items of plant or

[29] [1893] A.C. 562 at p. 588.
[30] [1937] 2 K.B. 445 at p. 470.
[31] [1969] 2 Q.B. 37.
[32] [1978] Q.B. 870.
[33] (1976) 239 E.G. 205, C.A.

machinery from being treated as part of a hereditament for the purposes of valuation.[34]

By section 20 of the 1967 Act any new or altered values are to be in accordance with the "tone of the list," *i.e.* they must not be more than would have applied if the property had existed in the circumstances obtaining during the year before the list came into force.

By section 21 of the Local Government Act 1974 valuation lists are not to be altered as a result of (a) the installation of a central heating system, or (b) making minor structural alterations to a dwelling-house or mixed hereditament where the increase in the gross value would not exceed a prescribed amount.[35]

C. EXEMPTIONS, SPECIAL CASES AND PERSONAL RELIEFS

Certain classes of hereditament are exempt from rating, and in certain **8-06** cases the measure of liability is calculated on a basis different from that discussed above. There are several cases where relief, in whole or part, may be claimed by bodies or individuals.

Crown property

It is a general principle of law that the Crown is not bound by statute unless expressly named. The Crown was not mentioned in the Statute of Elizabeth and therefore Crown properties were not rateable. The position is now governed by section 37 of the General Rate Act 1967, which provides that where any hereditament is occupied by or on behalf of the Crown for public purposes no gross value shall be determined or entered in the valuation list in respect of that hereditament. Premises occupied by the departments of state and the fighting services clearly come within this category—government offices, army barracks, prisons and hospitals under the control of area health authorities. Post Office property ceased to be exempt when the Post Office became a public corporation on October 1, 1970.[36] The Crown exemption is extended to properties occupied for the purposes of the Crown in the carrying out of functions of the Central Government, even though the occupants are not strictly the servants of the Crown. Perhaps the best example of properties falling within this

---

[34] General Rate Act 1967, s. 21; Local Government Act 1974, s. 18; Plant and Machinery (Rating) Order 1960 (S.I. 1960 No. 122) as amended by S.I. 1974 No. 413. The presence of plant is to be ignored even if it tends to depress the value of the heraditament: *Edmondson* v. *Teeside Textiles* (1984) 83 L.G.R. 317.

[35] The Rating of Minor Structural Alterations to Dwellings (Specified Amount) Order 1974 (S.I. 1974 No. 629) specified an amount of £30.

[36] Post Office Act 1969, s. 6(5). For rating assessment of the post office railway and the telecommunications network see the Post Office (Rateable Values) Orders 1972 (S.I. 1972 No. 1794) and 1976 (S.I.s 1976 Nos. 206, 207) and the British Telecommunications Act 1981, s. 35.

class are police stations. Lord Blackburn said in *Coomber* v. *Berkshire JJ.*[37]:

> "I do not think it can be disputed that the administration of justice, both criminal and civil, and the preservation of order and prevention of crime by means of what is now called police, are among the most important functions of government, nor that by the constitution of this country these functions do, of common right, belong to the Crown."

This case was concerned with a tax payment, but the rule it establishes applies equally to the law of rating and is now embodied in statute.[38] The exemption of Crown property does not significantly affect the income of rating authorities. The Treasury makes a contribution in lieu of rates in respect of Crown properties on the basis of a valuation made by the Treasury Valuer, ascertained by reference to the principles applicable to the valuation of other hereditaments.

Where a contribution is made by the Crown in aid of rates in respect of a hereditament, the value on which it is based is entered in the valuation list as representing its rateable value. This enables the amount of the contribution to be taken into account for the purpose of ascertaining totals or the proceeds of any rate.

Places of public worship

8-07   Section 39 of the General Rate Act 1967 exempts from rating places of public religious worship. The exemption extends to church and chapel halls and similar buildings used in connection with any such place of public worship and "so used for the purposes of the organisation responsible for the conduct of public religious worship in that place." If, however, they are not used or not solely used in this way (*i.e.* for public worship or for the purposes of the church or chapel) but are let at any time for payment, then if the average amount of the payments received is no more than the average annual amount of the expenses attributable to the lettings a "nil" assessment results; if there is an excess, then the assessment is calculated by reference to the amount of the excess.

Agricultural land and buildings

8-08   Section 26 of the General Rate Act 1967 gives total exemption from rates to agricultural land and buildings. Agricultural land includes any land "used as arable, meadow or pasture ground only." This is the most important part of the definition. Certain other lands are included in the term, such as nursery grounds, market gardens and land exceeding 0.10 hectare used for poultry farming. Land used for sport or recreation and land used as a racecourse is specifically excluded, and land used as such

---

[37] (1882) 2 App. Cas. 61 at p. 67.
[38] s. 38 of the General Rate Act 1967, as amended by the Local Government Act 1972, Sched. 13, para. 28, enables a police authority to make contributions in aid of rates in respect of court buildings and police stations.

for only one day a year may be so excluded unless the facts are such that the maxim *de minimis non curat lex* applies.[39] Agricultural buildings consist of buildings (other than dwelling-houses) occupied with agricultural land or forming part of a market garden and in either case used solely in connection with agricultural operations thereon. The words "only" and "solely" in the definition are of particular significance. One example of the restrictive effect of these words is given.

> *Meriden and Solihull Rating Authority* v. *Tyacke*.[40] A farmer sold turf from one of his fields primarily to rid the land of parasites which injured his young cattle. Adult cattle grazed in the field whilst the turf was being removed. *Held*, during the removal of the turf the land was being used for pasture, but not for pasture only. The land did not therefore come within the derating provisions.

Part I of the Rating Act 1971 extends the exemption of buildings to include those used for the keeping or breeding of livestock and certain buildings occupied by incorporated agricultural co-operatives. Section 26A of the General Rate Act 1967 (added by section 31 of the Local Government, Land and Planning Act 1980) gives exemption to land and buildings (other than dwellings) used solely for or in connection with fish farming.

Transport, electricity and gas undertakings

The General Rate Act 1967 sets out the rules with respect to the **8–09** rateability of transport, electricity and gas undertakings but the Secretary of State was enabled under section 19 of and Schedule 3 to the Local Government Act 1974 to prescribe other methods for determining the rateable value of these undertakings and to amend the relevant statutory provisions as appropriate.

Section 32 of the General Rate Act 1967 provides that railway and canal hereditaments shall not be liable for rating. Premises occupied as a dwelling-house, hotel or place of public refreshment, or so let out as to be capable of separate assessment, are excluded from this exemption and are rated in the ordinary way. In lieu of rates, payments are made for the benefit of local authorities by the railway and canal authorities in accordance with calculations prescribed by and under Schedule 5 to the 1967 Act. The Rates Act 1984[41] makes provision to replace these arrangements, from a day to be appointed, by a procedure under which those authorities will be treated as occupying hereditaments in each rating area of rateable values prescribed (as for other public utilities) by order under the Local Government Act 1974, section 19.

The law with respect to the rating of property occupied by electricity **8–10** boards is contained in section 34 of and Schedule 7 to the General Rate

---

[39] s. 26(3); *Hayes* v. *Loyd* [1985] 1 W.L.R. 714.
[40] [1950] 1 All E.R. 939.
[41] Sched. 1, paras. 5–6, substituting General Rate Act 1967, s. 32, and inserting new ss. 32A and 32B.

1967 and the Electricity Boards (Rateable Values) Order 1976[42] made under section 19 of the Local Government Act 1974. The Central Electricity Generating Board is deemed to occupy in each rating area a notional hereditament the rateable value of which is calculated in accordance with Schedule 7; each area board is deemed to occupy in each rating area which lies wholly or partly within the particular board's area a hereditament calculated in accordance with the formula contained in the same Schedule. The formula is a complex one. Stated shortly, the Secretary of State prescribes a "basic electricity rateable value"; this is allocated to rating authorities and is treated as a basic sum, to be varied from year to year in accordance with variations in the output of the board and divided between generation and distribution activities. Certain properties are rated in the ordinary way, namely, premises used as a dwelling-house, showrooms and premises occupied by the Electricity Council but when unoccupied they are exempt from rating and are not subject to rates as unoccupied premises under section 17 of the General Rate Act 1967 (see para. 8–33, below).[43]

8-11   Section 33 of and Schedule 6 to the General Rate Act 1967[44] set out the method by which the British Gas Corporation is rated. The assessment is not calculated on the actual hereditaments occupied by the Corporation in a rating authority's area, but on a notional hereditament. The formula by which the basic rateable value of this notional hereditament is calculated appears in Schedule 6.[45] This total basic rateable value is adjusted upwards or downwards according to differences in the number of therms supplied and is apportioned among rating areas by reference to the quantities produced and supplied in those areas. Dwellings, showrooms and office premises occupied by the Corporation are rateable in the ordinary way. When such premises are unoccupied the position would presumably be the same as in the case of Electricity Boards referred to in the previous paragraph.

Other public utility undertakings

8-12   Valuation of certain hereditaments (hereditaments of the National Coal Board, mines and quarries, docks and harbours) is determined by orders made by the Secretary of State under section 19 of the Local Government Act 1974. Under the National Coal Board (Rateable Values) Order 1977[46] a national basic rateable value is ascertained for mine properties on the basis of a complex formula; associated properties, such as offices and sales depots, are valued in accordance with section 19

---

[42] S.I. 1976 No. 489.

[43] *Tower Hamlets London Borough Council* v. *London Electricity Board* (1977) 75 L.G.R. 810.

[44] As substituted by the Gas Act 1972, s. 34 and Sched. 5 and amended by the Gas Hereditaments (Rateable Values) Order 1976 (S.I. 1976 No. 490).

[45] As substituted by Sched. 5 to the Gas Act 1972.

[46] S.I. 1977 No. 2083.

of the General Rate Act 1967 (see para. 8–04). Mines and quarries, other than National Coal Board properties, are dealt with in the Mines and Quarries (Valuation) Order 1983.[47] The valuation of docks and harbours is based on a percentage of receipts in accordance with the Docks and Harbours (Rateable Values) Order 1976.[48]

Water undertakings were formerly valued on a "profits" basis, the **8-13** relevant principal factors being gross receipts and expenses. From April 1, 1963, a new principle was adopted. The "cumulo value" (this is the net annual value of the undertaking as a whole) of any particular water undertaking is adjusted from time to time, taking into account, as a principal factor, changes in the volume of water supplied. The cumulo is then shared out in accordance with a statutory formula between authorities in which the undertaker's premises and apparatus are situated.[49] The power of the Secretary of State by order to determine methods of valuation, referred to above, applies equally to water undertakings.[50]

Charitable and other organisations

Charitable organisations and certain other bodies which exist for **8-14** public benefit are eligible for rating relief under section 40 of the General Rate Act 1967.

Under this provision a hereditament occupied by a charity (or by trustees for charities) and wholly or mainly used for charitable purposes, or an almshouse, or a house of a full-time minister of religion, can be charged no more than half the rate which would have been payable apart from this provision. This is mandatory.

But a rating authority has a discretionary power further to reduce or remit the payment of rates in respect of such properties beyond what the law requires and also to remit or reduce rates in respect of other properties, namely,

(a) hereditaments which are occupied for the purposes of organisations which are not established or conducted for profit and whose main objects are charitable or are otherwise philanthropic or religious or concerned with education, social welfare, science, literature, or the fine arts;

(b) other hereditaments which are occupied for the purposes of a club, society or other organisation not established or conducted for profit and wholly or mainly used for the purposes of recreation.

The reductions or remissions may be granted for one year, up to five years, or for an indefinite period.

---

[47] S.I. 1983 No. 547.
[48] S.I. 1976 No. 535.
[49] General Rate Act 1967, s. 31 and Sched. 4.
[50] See the Rating (Water Hereditaments) Order 1975 (S.I. 1975 No. 540) continuing the same method with certain amendments.

In the cases which follow the issue was whether the occupation of a house by employees of a charity was occupation by the charity.

> *Glasgow City Corpn.* v. *Johnstone.*[51] A house and church were parts of a single building, and the only access to the house was through the church premises. Under the terms of his contract of service the church officer was required to live in the house. The House of Lords held that his employers "occupied" the house for the purposes of a Scottish provision similar to section 40 of the 1967 Act.
>
> *Commissioner of Valuation for Northern Ireland* v. *Fermanagh Protestant Board of Education.*[52] Six assistant masters at a school were allowed to reside with their families rent-free in a number of adjacent houses. Their occupation was held not to be an occupation by the charity. Lord Upjohn said[53]: "First, if it is essential to the performance of the duties of the occupying servant that he should occupy the particular house, or it may be a house within a closely defined perimeter, then, it being established that this is the mutual understanding of the master and the servant, the occupation for rating and other ancillary purposes is that of the master and not of the servant.... Secondly, there is the case where it is not essential for the servant to occupy a particular house or to live within a particular perimeter, but by doing so he can better perform his duties as servant to a material degree: then, in such case, if there is an express term in the contract between master and servant that he shall so reside, the occupation for rating and ancillary purposes is treated as the occupation of the master and not of the servant."

In the *Glasgow City Corpn.* case the phrase "wholly or mainly used for charitable purposes" was considered. Of this Lord Reid said[54]: "If the use which the charity makes of premises is directly to facilitate the carrying out of its main charitable purposes that is, in my view, sufficient to satisfy the requirements that the premises are used for charitable purposes."

In *Oxfam* v. *Birmingham City Council*[55] it was decided that shops occupied by charitable organisations did not qualify for rating relief under section 40 of the General Rate Act 1967 but the effect of this decision was reversed by the Rating (Charity Shops) Act 1976 in respect of shops used wholly or mainly for the sale of goods donated to a charity.

Other exemptions and special cases

Voluntary schools and county schools

8–15   Under section 30 of the General Rate Act 1967, the Secretary of State for the Environment and the Secretary of State for Education and Science are authorised to make regulations with respect to the valuation of county and voluntary schools. Broadly speaking, valuation will be linked to the

---

[51] [1965] A.C. 609.

[52] [1969] 3 All E.R. 352. Rating relief is not available where property is let on normal commercial terms; see *Polish Historical Institution* v. *Hove Corporation* (1963) 61 L.G.R. 438. See also *Soldiers', Sailors' and Airmen's Families' Association* v. *Merton Corporation* [1966] 3 All E.R. 780 where property was let to widows of commissioned officers in fulfilment of a charitable purpose.

[53] At p. 359.

[54] At p. 735.

[55] [1976] A.C. 126.

cost of providing a place in such a school. No regulations have been made—the practice is to value schools in accordance with a formula agreed between government departments and the local authority associations. If, as is generally the case, a voluntary school is for the purposes of the Act a charitable organisation, then the local authority must give a 50 per cent. remission of rates and may increase this remission if it chooses. The relevant provisions are considered above.

Miscellaneous exemptions

The General Rate Act 1967 gives exemption in the case of sewers[56] and **8-16** land occupied for specified purposes by drainage authorities.[57]

The Local Government, Planning and Land Act 1980, Schedule 32, Part IV, relieves from rating liability certain hereditaments in enterprise zones, mainly commercial and industrial. Reference is made to enterprise zones in paragraph 19–71.

There are a number of other classes of occupation which are exempt from rating—some are mentioned briefly here without reference to limiting or other factors: property occupied by diplomats,[58] public parks,[59] rooms in an unoccupied house used for election purposes,[60] non-domestic hereditaments used only for keeping plant, etc., formerly used or intended for future use in the hereditaments.[61]

Disabled persons

The Rating (Disabled Persons) Act 1978, which came into operation on **8-17** April 1, 1979, replaced earlier provisions for rating relief for disabled persons which had caused some difficulty.[62] Section 1 and Schedule 1 provide for rebates on the rates chargeable on a hereditament having special facilities for a disabled person who resides or is usually resident there. Section 2[63] requires rebates to be made in respect of institutions used wholly or predominantly for residential accommodation, welfare services or employment for disabled persons. There is an appeal to the county court against a refusal to grant a rebate. Under section 69 of the Local Government, Planning and Land Act 1980, 90 per cent. of the cost of providing rebates is met by the Exchequer.

---

[56] General Rate Act 1967, s. 42.

[57] *Ibid.* s. 43.

[58] This stemmed from the Diplomatic Privileges Act 1708: see now International Organisations (Immunities and Privileges) Act 1950: Diplomatic Immunities (Commonwealth Countries and Republic of Ireland) Act 1952; Diplomatic Privileges Act 1964.

[59] General Rate Act 1967, s. 44. As to parks dedicated by statute to public use, see *Lambeth Overseers* v. *London County Council* [1897] A.C. 625.

[60] Local Election (Principal Areas) Rules 1973 (S.I. 1973 No. 79), r. 18(3).

[61] Rates Act 1984, Sched. 1, para. 9, inserting new s. 46A in the General Rate Act 1967.

[62] These were contained in the General Rate Act 1967, s. 45, and the Local Government Act 1974, s. 20.

[63] As amended by the Rates Act 1984, Sched. 1, para. 22.

Moorings

8-18   Moorings fixed to the bed or bank of a waterway were held to be rateable in *Cory* v. *Bristow*. [63a] Part I of Schedule 2 to the Rates Act 1984 establishes that moorings held only by a weight on the waterway bed are not rateable. Part II of the Schedule allows moorings which are separately occupied to be rated as a single hereditament in the deemed occupation of the owner.

Hereditaments partly occupied

8-19   Where part of a hereditament is unoccupied but will remain so for a short time only, the authority may request the valuation officer to apportion the rateable value. If the apportionment is agreed by the authority and the occupier, rates will be payable only on the occupied part for the rate period in which the request was made, and for subsequent periods if the authority so determines. [64]

Compulsory Purchase Act 1965

Where land is acquired under this Act, the acquiring authority is required to make good one half of any consequent loss of rates during the construction of works: section 27. This section does not apply to an acquisition of land under the Housing Act 1985 or to any case where the compulsory purchase order so provides.

Refund of overpayments

8-20   Section 9 of the General Rate Act 1967 empowers rating authorities to refund rates on the ground that (a) the entry in the valuation list was excessive; (b) the rate levied did not accord with the valuation list; (c) exemption or relief was not allowed; (d) the hereditament was unoccupied; or (e) rates were paid by a person not liable. A certificate of the valuation officer is required for a refund under (a), or under (c) where the exemption or relief should have appeared in the valuation list. In *R.* v. *Rochdale M.B.C., ex p. Cromer Ring Mill Ltd.*[65] a decision not to make a refund was quashed on judicial review, on the ground that the authority had been misdirected in the exercise of their discretion by their treasurer's advice that Parliament intended the discretion to be used only to alleviate gross unfairness.

Personal reliefs

Rate rebates

8-21   The General Rate Act 1967[66] granted widespread rate relief to domestic ratepayers with low incomes. The Social Security and Housing Benefits

---

[63a] [1877] 2 A.C. 262.
[64] General Rate Act 1967, s. 25, as amended by Rates Act 1984, Sched. 1, para. 4.
[65] [1982] 3 All E.R. 761.
[66] s. 49.

Act 1982[67] continues such relief. The Secretary of State may by regulation prescribe the terms of a statutory rate rebate scheme.[68] Claimants establish entitlement to rate rebates either by application to the authority for assessment ("standard cases") or by a successful claim to the Department of Health and Social Security for ordinary supplementary benefit, which carries with it entitlement to 100 per cent. rate rebate, subject to deduction for any non-dependent residents ("certificated cases").

A rating authority may by resolution modify the statutory scheme so as to make a local rate rebate scheme for its area. The local scheme must be so drawn that no ratepayer receives a rebate which would be less than that to which he would have been entitled under the statutory scheme and that the estimated total of rebates granted under the local scheme does not exceed the total which could have been granted under the statutory scheme by more than 10 per cent. of the statutory rebates for standard cases.[69]

Exchequer subsidy is payable at 90 per cent. of the cost of rebates in **8-22** "standard cases" and at 100.6 per cent. in "certificated cases"; also at 60 per cent. (70 per cent. in Wales) of the cost of administration. The extra cost of rebates arising from local modifications to the statutory scheme does not qualify for subsidy.[70]

Other relief

A rating authority has, under section 53 of the General Rate Act 1967, a general power to reduce or remit the payment of any rate on account of the poverty of the person liable to pay it.

D. RATING VALUATION

The Local Government Act 1948 relieved rating authorities of their **8-23** valuation functions and abolished those bodies having statutory duties in relation to the valuation lists—the assessment committees, county valuation committees and the central valuation committee. Part III of the Act transferred this work to the valuation officers of the Commissioners of Inland Revenue. The first list prepared under this system came into force on April 1, 1956. Fresh lists were required to be made at five-yearly intervals, from April 1, 1973[71] but the General Rate Act 1975 postponed the 1978 review to April 1, 1980, and after a further postponement by order of the Secretary of State,[72] the statutory requirement for quinquen-

---

[67] s. 28.
[68] See the Housing Benefit Regulations 1985 (S.I. 1985 No. 677).
[69] Social Security and Housing Benefits Act 1982, s. 30; Housing Benefits (Permitted Totals for Local Schemes) Regulations 1982 (S.I. 1982 No. 1129).
[70] Housing Benefits (Subsidy) Order 1985 (S.I. 1985 No. 440).
[71] s. 68. As to the form of the lists, see Valuation Lists Rules 1972 (S.I. 1972 No. 1612).
[72] See the Valuation Lists (Postponement) Order 1978 (S.I. 1978 No. 993).

nial revisions of the valuation lists was abolished by section 28 of the Local Government, Planning and Land Act 1980. This section amended section 68 of the General Rate Act 1967 to authorise the preparation of new valuation lists for each rating area so as to come into force on April 1 in such a year as the Secretary of State may specify by order. Section 30 adds new sections 19A and 19B to the General Rate Act 1967. When a new valuation list is to come in force the Secretary of State is empowered to specify which classes of hereditament are to be the subject of the valuation, and to specify a date, earlier than the date when the new list comes into force, as the date for valuation purposes. Where this earlier date is specified certain assumptions are to be made—they relate to the physical state of the property, the locality and other relevant factors. In the case of any classes of hereditaments not so specified, the net annual value in the new valuation lists of those hereditaments will be the same as in the valuation list in force immediately preceding the new list. Under section 19B the Secretary of State may by order prescribe a method of adjusted rateable values. The purpose of this provision is to preserve the ratio immediately before the coming into force of the new valuation lists between rateable values of specified hereditaments as a whole and the rateable values of unspecified hereditaments as a whole.

8-24   Proposals to alter the lists may be made by the valuation officer, and by any person (including a rating authority) who is aggrieved by the inclusion of a hereditament in the list, or by any value in the list, or by the valuation as a single hereditament of a building occupied in parts.[73] The valuation officer must give notice of the proposal to the rating authority and to the occupier (if he is not the proposer) and these parties may object to it.[74] In *Arsenal Football Club Ltd.* v. *Smith*[75] it was held by the House of Lords that a person who as agent for the owner receives the rents of a hereditament in a rating area is a "person aggrieved" so as to enable him to complain that another hereditament in the same area is under-assessed for rating purposes even though he might not thereby suffer detriment.

Section 85 of the 1967 Act places a duty on all local authorities[75a] to inform the valuation officer of any information coming to their notice which leads them to suppose that a valuation list requires alteration. For this purpose valuation officers provide rating authorities with Forms CV/R/7, on the submission of which the completeness of the valuation list largely depends.

The valuation officer may accept a proposal, but if he or any other

---

[73] General Rate Act 1967, s. 69; Valuation Lists (Proposals for Alteration) Regulations 1974 (S.I. 1974 No. 2213).

[74] The rating authority's right to object is subject to the pre-condition that it serves notice on the valuation officer that it wishes to have that right in relation to specified classes of hereditament: General Rate Act 1967, s. 70(2), as substituted by Rates Act 1984, Sched. 1, para. 12.

[75] [1979] A.C. 1.

[75a] Including the Inner London Education Authority and joint authorities: s. 85(2), as amended by the Local Government Act 1985, Sched. 14, para. 42 (*a*).

party is not in agreement then the matter must be referred by him to a local valuation court. The valuation list may then only be altered by a direction of the valuation court or following agreement between the persons entitled to be heard by the court, *i.e.* the appellant, the valuation officer, the owner or occupier of the hereditament, the rating authority and the objector (who will in most cases be one of the parties previously named).

Under section 79 of the General Rate Act 1967, an alteration of the **8-25** valuation list has effect from the commencement of the rate current when the proposal was served, except that where the alteration relates to a new or altered hereditament or to other specified events, it takes effect only from the date of occupation of the new or altered hereditament or from the happening of the event giving rise to the alteration.

In certain cases the amount recoverable pending settlement of a proposal to alter a new list may not exceed the amount last levied increased by half the difference between that amount and the amount of the new charge. The Secretary of State has, however, power to make orders varying the percentage of rates which rate-payers may retain until determination of proposals made by them arising out of a new valuation list.[76]

Matters relating to the determination of rateable value are considered in paragraphs 8–04, 8–05, above.

Local valuation courts to hear and determine appeals against rating assessments are constituted under the General Rate Act 1967.[77] Each court is drawn from a panel of members appointed under a scheme prepared by non-metropolitan county, metropolitan district and London borough councils for their areas or by such councils acting jointly. These schemes become operative after approval by the Secretary of State and provide for the appointment of the panels and for the constitution of the courts from panel members. Section 77 of the 1967 Act gives to a person attending the valuation court who is aggrieved by its decision a right of appeal to the Lands Tribunal. There is a right of appeal, on a point of law, to the Court of Appeal and, by leave, to the House of Lords.

E. The Making of Rates and the Issuing of Precepts

Rating and precepting authorities

The councils of districts and London boroughs, the Common Council **8-26** of the City of London, the Sub-Treasurer of the Inner Temple and the Under-Treasurer of the Middle Temple are rating authorities.[78] Rates are levied over the whole of the rating authority's area in respect of general

---

[76] General Rate Act 1967, s. 8 and the Local Government, Land and Planning Act 1980, s. 35. This latter provision comes into force by order of the Secretary of State.

[77] s. 88–91, as amended by the Local Government Act 1985, s. 14. See also Local Government Act 1972, Sched. 13, para. 29 for supplementary provisions.

[78] General Rate Act 1967, s. 1; Local Government Act 1972, s. 149.

expenses and over a part of the area in respect of special expenses (see para. 7–02, above). County councils issue precepts to the rating authorities for areas within the county. Precepts are issued so as to require a levy of the rate over the whole of the precepting authority's area in the case of general expenses and over the appropriate part of the area in respect of special expenses. Parish and community councils and parish meetings not having a parish council may issue a precept on the district council concerned.[79] Other precepting authorities are the Inner London Education Authority and the joint authorities established by the Local Government Act 1985,[80] the Receiver for the Metropolitan Police,[81] water authorities (for land drainage),[82] joint boards and port health authorities.[83] The residuary bodies established by the 1985 Act may make levies on rating authorities in a manner similar to precepts, but in proportion to population. Revenue receipts of residuary bodies may be distributed to rating authorities in the same proportions as would apply to a levy made in the year.[84]

The Secretary of State is empowered to make an equalisation scheme to reduce disparities in rates in different rating areas in Greater London.[85]

Duty to make sufficient rates and precepts

8-27 Rating authorities are required by section 2 of the General Rate Act 1967 to make from time to time a general rate sufficient to provide for their estimated net expenditure during the rate period (including amounts payable under precept), together with amounts to cover previous expenditure not provided for, contingencies, and expenditure to be incurred before income from the subsequent rate is available. Precepting authorities are similarly required by section 11 of the 1967 Act to issue sufficient precepts for the like purposes.

The Rates Act 1984, section 13, requires rating and major precepting authorities, before determining their estimated expenditure for a financial year, to consult representatives of industrial and commercial ratepayers. Information is to be supplied as prescribed by the Industrial and Commercial Ratepayers (Consultation) Regulations 1984 (S.I. 1984 No. 1355) and regard must be had to a Code of Guidance issued by the Secretary of State.

Authorities may not budget deliberately for a surplus to be carried forward to the following period, except to the extent of a reasonable

---

[79] Such a precept is chargeable on the parish and met from an additional item of the general rate: Local Government Act 1972, s. 150; General Rate Act 1967, s. 2(4).
[80] s. 68.
[81] Local Government Act 1948, s. 121.
[82] Land Drainage Act 1976, ss. 45–47.
[83] Under the provisions of the order constituting the board or authority.
[84] Local Government Act 1985, ss. 74, 77(4).
[85] London Government Act 1963, s. 66; Local Government Act 1985, s. 83.

working balance.[86] A rate or precept may be quashed on judicial review if it is made in part for financing expenditure which the authority could not lawfully incur.[87] This is now the only method of questioning the validity of a rate or precept on general grounds not relating to particular persons or hereditaments only.[88]

Before the Local Government Finance Act 1982 the length of the rate   **8-28** or precept period was left to the discretion of the authority, who could also levy a supplementary rate or precept at any time. Sections 1 and 2 of the 1982 Act abolished these powers, so that authorities are now limited to making only one rate or precept for each financial year. Section 3 of the 1982 Act authorised the making of rates and precepts in substitution for those previously made for the year, whether valid or invalid, but with the limitation that the substituted rate or precept could not be higher than the one for which it was substituted. This limitation was modified by the Rates Act 1984. Where the original rate or precept has been quashed as insufficient to meet the expenditure required to be taken into account, a substituted rate or precept sufficient to meet that expenditure is permitted. A higher substituted rate is also allowed where necessary to meet a precept received after the original rate was made.[89]

There is no express provision stating by what date an authority should make a rate, but in *R. v. London Borough of Hackney, ex p. Fleming*,[90] Woolf J. held that in accordance with general principles the discretion as to when to fix a rate must be exercised reasonably and that failure to make a rate within a reasonable time—weeks rather than months—after the beginning of the financial year would, in the absence of a reasonable explanation, be *prima facie* unreasonable and therefore in breach of duty. Precepts must be issued, or information given as to the amount of the levy, to each rating authority, not less than 21 days before the beginning of the financial year.[91]

Rate limitation

The Rates Act 1984 introduced schemes of rate limitation, commonly   **8-29** known as rate capping. Part I established a scheme of selective limitation, by which the Secretary of State was empowered to prescribe maximum rates and precepts for designated authorities. Authorities may be designated only if their expenditure is likely (a) to exceed £10 million, or

---

[86] *Att.-Gen.* v. *Newcastle upon Tyne Corporation* [1892] A.C. 568; see also *Pearl Dance Ltd.* v. *Newcastle upon Tyne City Council* [1982] R.V.R. 97.

[87] *Bromley London Borough Council* v. *Greater London Council* [1983] 1 A.C. 768.

[88] Local Government Finance Act 1982, s. 4.

[89] Local Government Finance Act 1982, s. 3(9), (10), inserted by the Rates Act 1984, s. 16, Sched. 1, para. 24. See also ss. 5(4), 11(3) of the 1984 Act (variations in maximum rates).

[90] April 16, 1985 (unreported). At the time of going to press the Government had introduced a Bill which, *inter alia* would impose a duty on rating authorities to make a rate on or before April 1 of the financial year.

[91] General Rate Act 1967, s. 12(6).

such greater sum as may be prescribed[92] (this will exclude most non-metropolitan district councils); (b) to exceed their grant-related expenditure as determined under the Local Government, Planning and Land Act 1980; and (c) to be excessive having regard to economic conditions.[93] The Secretary of State is to determine expenditure levels, and hence maximum rates or precepts, for designated authorities on uniform principles for each class of authority, but there is provision for authorities to seek re-determination, when individual circumstances may be taken into account.[94] Rates and precepts which exceed the maxima so determined are invalid.[95]

Part II of the 1984 Act makes provision for a scheme of general limitation which is intended to be held in reserve, and may only be brought into operation by order following consultation with local authority associations and an affirmative resolution of each House of Parliament.[96] If the general scheme is brought into operation, Part I will apply to all rating authorities and major precepting authorities unless they are individually exempted. Exemption may be on the ground that the authority has for three years kept within its grant-related expenditure or its expenditure guidance target under section 59(6)(*cc*) of the Local Government, Planning and Land Act 1980 and is likely to do so in the current year; or on the ground that its total expenditure is not likely to exceed a prescribed sum.[97]

The new authorities established by the Local Government Act 1985 are made subject to rate limitation under Part I of the Rates Act 1984 and will be deemed to have been designated under that Act in respect of the three years following the abolition date.[98]

Procedure for the making of a rate

8-30   The General Rate Act 1967[99] prescribes in detail the procedure to be followed in relation to the making of a rate and the issue of a precept. Every general rate is to be made and levied as a single consolidated rate at a uniform amount per pound on the rateable value of each hereditament in the rating area, except where, by virtue of a precept or otherwise, there are separate charges on particular parts of a rating area, when an

---

[92] The exemption limit was increased to £10.5 million in Wales and £10.6 million in England by the Rate Limitation (Designation of Authorities) (Exemption) (Wales) Order 1985 (S.I. 1985 No. 823) and the Rate Limitation (Designation of Authorities) (Exemption) Order 1985 (S.I. 1985 No. 863).

[93] s. 2.

[94] ss. 3 and 4.

[95] s. 6. Maximum rates and precepts for certain authorities for the year 1985/6 were prescribed by the Rate Limitation (Prescribed Maximum) (Rates) Order 1985 (S.I. 1985 No. 256) and the Rate Limitation (Prescribed Maximum) (Precepts) Order 1985 (S.I. 1985 No. 147).

[96] s. 9.

[97] s. 10.

[98] Local Government Act 1985, s. 68(4)–(6).

[99] s. 4, as amended by s. 44 of the Local Government, Planning and Land Act 1980.

additional item of the rate is leviable. Notice of a rate must be given by the authority within 21 days beginning with the day on which it is made. The rating authority may affix a notice on or near the doors of churches and chapels or in some public or conspicuous place, or may publish the notice in one or more newspapers circulating within the area of the authority. A demand for payment is a condition precedent to the recovery of the rate by distress, and the demand note is required by section 5 of the 1967 Act to contain certain specific information such as the description and situation of the hereditament in question, its rateable value, the amount in the pound on which the rate is charged, the amounts in the pound which are being levied for the purposes respectively of the rating authority and any precepting authorities, and the amounts in the pound which are being levied for each of the principal services administered respectively by the rating authority and precepting authorities.

Further requirements as to the contents of demand notes are prescribed by the Demands and Notice of Rates and Precepts Rules 1985.[1]

Section 14 of the Rates Act 1984 provides that rules may require rating and precepting authorities to serve on ratepayers notice containing information about changes in rates or precepts and past or proposed expenditure. Section 15 requires rating authorities to serve notice containing prescribed rating information on occupiers of dwelling-houses who do not receive a rate demand.[2]

Amendment of rate

The rating authority is empowered by section 6 of the 1967 Act to make **8-31** amendments in a rate (being either the current or the last preceding rate) in order to make it conform with the enactments relating thereto. In particular, the authority may (a) correct clerical or arithmetical errors, (b) correct erroneous insertions, omissions or misdescriptions, and (c) make additions or corrections necessary by reason of new or unoccupied hereditaments coming into occupation, changes of occupation or the splitting of assessments. Alterations of rateable value or inclusion of new hereditaments can only be effected either to bring the rate into conformity with the valuation list or if a proposal for a corresponding alteration of the valuation list has been made by the valuation officer.[3]

In *B. Kettle Ltd.* v. *Newcastle-under-Lyme B.C.*,[4] it was held that a resolution making the rate was sufficient authority to enable officers to make amendments under this section. But in *Debenhams Ltd.* v. *Ealing L.B.C.*[5] it was held that the rate-making resolution was not framed widely enough to enable an officer to amend the rate on the basis of a valuation officer's proposal.

---

[1] S.I. 1985 No. 1486.
[2] *Ibid.*.
[3] s. 6(2).
[4] (1979) 77 L.G.R. 700.
[5] [1981] R.A. 194.

Rating of owners: compounding

8-32   In general it is the occupier upon whom falls the liability to pay rates. Under section 55 of the General Rate Act 1967, however, (as amended by section 36 of the Local Government, Planning and Land Act 1980), a rating authority may direct that in the case of certain hereditaments the owner shall be rated instead of the occupier. Such hereditaments may fall into one of two classes: (a) hereditaments of a class defined by resolution by reference to rateable value, (b) hereditaments defined also by reference to the interval at which rent becomes payable or is collected. This is known as "compounding." The upper limit of rateable value is £200.[6]

The 1967 Act requires the rating authority to make an allowance of such proportion as the authority determines to the owners of compounded properties if they pay the amounts due before the expiration of one-half of the rating period, or, if the rate is paid by instalments, one-half of the instalment period. The authority may, however, by resolution specify later dates than these.

By section 56 of the 1967 Act, as amended by section 36 of the Local Government, Planning and Land Act 1980, the authority may also enter into agreements with the owners of hereditaments of any rateable value, the rents of which become payable or are collected at shorter than quarterly intervals, for the payment or collection by the owners of the rates, and where this is done the authority may make an allowance of a proportion of the amounts payable, subject to the payment being made by a specified date.

Provision is made in section 37 of the Local Government, Planning and Land Act 1980 for the recovery of rates from owners who charge rents inclusive of rates. The authority may recover an appropriate proportion of the sums received by the owners in the same way and subject to the same conditions as sums due from occupiers in respect of rates.[7]

Under the Rating (Caravan Sites) Act 1976, certain sites used for static leisure caravans are to be treated for rate purposes as a single unit and the operator is to be responsible for the payment of the rates with the right to recover a contribution from the occupiers of the individual caravans.[8]

Unoccupied property rate

8-33   A rating authority may resolve to rate properties, other than those in exempt categories, which are unoccupied for a continuous period exceeding three months (six months for new properties).[9] Under section 42

---

[6] Rating of Owners Order 1972 (S.I. 1972 No. 1983).
[7] See also § 8–40, below, n. 32.
[8] As to the rating of owners of moorings, see § 8–18, above.
[9] General Rate Act 1967, s. 17, and Sched. 1 as amended by the Local Government Act, 1974, s. 15, and the Local Government, Planning and Land Act 1980, s. 42; Rating (Exemption of Unoccupied Property) Regulations 1967 (S.I. 1967 No. 954); Rating (Exemption of Unoccupied Industrial Hereditaments) Regulations 1984 (S.I. 1984 No. 221). See hereon *Camden London Borough Council* v. *Bromley Park Gardens Estates Limited, The Times,* October 7, 1985.

of the Local Government, Planning and Land Act 1980, these periods are renamed "the standard period" and "the new house period" respectively and the Secretary of State is authorised to specify by order different periods, either generally, or different periods in respect of different classes of hereditament. No order has yet been made under this provision. Where such a resolution is in operation, the owner of unoccupied property is deemed to be in occupation during the relevant period of vacancy (which begins at the end of the standard or new house period) and he is liable to pay such proportion of the rates which would have been due for that period as is specified in the resolution, subject to a maximum of one half for hereditaments other than houses.[10] No domestic relief is allowable under the provisions referred to in paragraph 8–34, below. An authority may resolve to levy rates on unoccupied property selectively on different classes of property and in different parts of the authority's area and in different proportions. Section 17(1) of the General Rate Act 1967 provides that the resolution to apply the provisions of the Act respecting the rating of unoccupied property shall specify the date on which it is to come into operation. In *Sheffield City Council* v. *Graingers Wine Ltd.*[11] it was held that on the true construction of the section, the word "specified" meant "made clear" and that where the operative date was evident from the surrounding circumstances the resolution was valid notwithstanding the fact that the date was not specified in it. Remission is possible in hardship cases.[12]

Sections 17A and 17B of the General Rate Act 1967[13] provided that where a commercial building had been unused continuously for more than six months for the purpose for which it was constructed the owner, if he had not tried his best to let it, should be required to pay, for the period of non-use, a surcharge additional to the rates (if any) payable apart from these provisions. Section 41 of the Local Government, Planning and Land Act 1980 empowered the Secretary of State to suspend these provisions, and they were so suspended from April 1, 1981.[14]

Reduction for domestic element grant

The rate support grant described in Chapter 9 includes a domestic **8–34** element to assist the domestic ratepayer. By section 48 of the General Rate Act 1967, as amended by section 33 of the Local Government, Planning and Land Act 1980, each rating authority must reduce the amount of the rate levied on domestic or mixed hereditaments by a prescribed rate poundage, known as the standard amount. The reduc-

---

[10] Unoccupied Property Rate (Valuation of Current Ceiling) Order 1980 (S.I. 1980 No. 2012).

[11] [1977] 1 W.L.R. 1119.

[12] General Rate Act 1967, Sched. 1, para. 3A, inserted by Local Government Act 1974, s. 15(5). As to appeal, see § 8–37, below.

[13] Inserted by Local Government Act 1974, s. 16.

[14] Rating Surcharge (Suspension) Order 1980 (S.I. 1980 No. 2015).

tion for mixed hereditaments is one-half, one-quarter or one-eighth depending upon the private dwelling proportion of the hereditament. In *Skittrall* v. *South Hams District Council*[15] the court refused an application for domestic relief under section 48 of the properties let out as holiday flats on the ground that the applicant was carrying on a business. The test was the use which the rateable occupier made of the premises. Under section 33 domestic rate relief is given to "domestic hereditaments"—this term is so defined to include not only a dwelling-house but a garage not exceeding 25 square metres and private storage premises.

Discount and instalments

8-35 An authority may give a uniform discount generally or limit it to occupiers of domestic properties only.[16] In order to qualify, payments must be made before such dates as the authority prescribes. An owner receiving an allowance under sections 55 or 56 of the 1967 Act cannot in addition be granted a discount.

Under section 50 of the 1967 Act, as amended by section 34 of the Local Government, Planning and Land Act 1980 and paragraph 11 of Schedule 1 to the Rates Act 1984, ratepayers may choose to pay their rates by instalments (not less than 10 in respect of a full year's rates) unless they already in effect pay rates by instalments under a compounding arrangement. A general power to accept instalments appears in section 3 of the 1967 Act. A discount may not be allowed where rates are paid by instalments under section 50.

Precepts

8-36 A code of rules as to the issuing of precepts is contained in sections 11 to 15 of the 1967 Act. Precepts issued by county councils, the Receiver for the Metropolitan Police and the new authorities established by the Local Government Act 1985 are levied on a poundage basis.[17] The amount due under the precept is the amount produced by a rate levy of the amount in the pound specified in the precept, and is ascertained according to prescribed rules.[18] Interest is payable on any amounts not paid at the dates specified in the precept.[19]

Right of appeal

8-37 The Poor Relief Acts of 1601 and 1743 gave to ratepayers aggrieved by the rate a right of appeal to quarter sessions, and until the coming into force of the Rating and Valuation Act 1925, this was the normal method

---

[15] [1976] 3 All E.R. 1.
[16] General Rate Act 1967, ss. 51 and 54; Local Government Act 1974, Sched. 8.
[17] General Rate Act 1967, s. 12; Local Government Act 1985, s. 68.
[18] General Rate Act 1967, s. 12(7); Rate Product Rules 1981 (S.I. 1981 No. 327), amended by S.I. 1983 No. 268.
[19] *Ibid.* s. 12(8), (9); Precepts (Rate of Interest) Rules 1982 (S.I. 1982 No. 1224).

by which rating disputes were determined. That Act, however, materially curtailed this remedy, supplying an alternative where issues of *valuation* were concerned. The position is now dealt with in section 7 of the 1967 Act,[20] which provides that there is no appeal to the Crown Court in respect of matters capable of being dealt with under the machinery introduced by the Act for the alteration of the valuation lists, referred to above at paragraphs 8-23 to 8-25. The Local Government Finance Act 1982 further restricted the right of appeal to the Crown Court to questions relating to the rating of particular hereditaments.[21] The validity of precepts, and the validity of rates as a whole on general grounds, may only be questioned by application for judicial review by the High Court.[22]

Rate accounts and records

Rating authorities were freed by the Rating and Valuation Act 1961,[23]   **8-38** from an obligation to keep rate books, a change which enabled them to use machine accounting. A ratepayer has a right to be given a statement of rates payable and paid in connection with any hereditament in respect of which he has or has had liability, and he has the right to inspect the valuation list and certain other documents.[24]

F. THE RECOVERY OF RATES

The law with respect to the recovery of rates is contained in Part VI of the   **8-39** General Rate Act 1967.[25] If a person fails to pay his rates within seven days of demand, the rating authority may apply to a justice of the peace for a summons requiring the defaulting ratepayer to appear before the magistrates' court to show why he should not pay. Unless the ratepayer proves a good defence the magistrates' court must issue a warrant of distress.[26] There are several valid defences open to a ratepayer in proceedings for the issue of a distress warrant, *e.g.* that the rate is a nullity because of some informality in the making of the rate or its publication, or that there is some defect on the face of the rate. A distress warrant can only be issued where the person rated occupies premises which fulfil the description in the valuation list.[27]

---

[20] As amended by the Courts Act 1971, Sched. 9.
[21] In *Norwich City Council* v. *Investors in Industry Commercial Properties Ltd.* [1985] 3 W.L.R. 711, the Court of Appeal held that the Crown Court had jurisdiction to hear an appeal against a refusal by the rating authority to remit or reduce payment of rates on unoccupied property on grounds of hardship (see § 8-33, above).
[22] s. 4.
[23] s. 14 and the Rate Books Order 1962 (S.I. 1962 No. 1).
[24] General Rate Act 1967, ss. 10 and 108 (as substituted by Rates Act 1984, Sched. 1, para. 20).
[25] As amended by the Local Government, Planning and Land Act 1980, s. 38.
[26] The court may include in the warrant a reasonable sum for the costs of obtaining it; charges for levying distress are fixed by order: General Rate Act 1967, ss. 100, 101; Distress for Rates Orders 1979, 1980 (S.I. s. 1979 No. 1038, 1980 No. 2013).
[27] *Camden London Borough Council* v. *Herwald* [1978] Q.B. 626.

A person aggrieved by distress has a right of appeal to the Crown Court. This appeal is against the distress and may not be exercised until it has been levied unless the ratepayer has been prejudiced by having to pay distress fees.[28] The justices may state a case for the opinion of the High Court, under the Magistrates' Courts Act 1980, when called upon to issue a distress warrant for a rate. A further appeal lies to the Court of Appeal.[29]

8-40 If a distress warrant cannot be executed because there is an insufficiency of goods or chattels to meet the amount due and the costs incurred, the justices have a discretion to issue a warrant of commitment. But a warrant of commitment may not be issued if the court are of opinion that failure to pay has not been due either to wilful refusal or culpable neglect. Under section 39 of the Local Government, Planning and Land Act 1980, a warrant of commitment may be postponed for such period and on such conditions as the court thinks just. Before issuing or postponing a warrant of commitment the justices must inquire into the defendant's means. If they consider that his failure to pay is not due to his wilful refusal or culpable neglect, they may not issue or postpone the warrant. If they do not issue or postpone the warrant they may remit the rates in whole or part. A warrant of commitment will specify a period of imprisonment of not more than three months unless the sums due are sooner paid. On part payment the period of imprisonment will be reduced proportionately.[30]

Unpaid rates cannot be recovered by action[31] but if an owner requests the rating authority to send demand notes to him and fails to make payment the rating authority may be entitled to recover on the agreement.[32] Where rates are due on a domestic hereditament a person who has an interest in the property and the rating authority may agree that his interest shall be charged as security for payment of rates and interest thereon and that the authority shall not exercise its powers of recovery by distress or otherwise.[33] Rates due on unoccupied property (referred to in para. 8-33, above) may be recovered as a civil debt. Unpaid rates may form a sufficient basis for a petition in bankruptcy by the rating authority against the ratepayer,[34] or for a petition to wind up a limited company.[35] Where rates are in arrears, the authority may give notice to the ratepayer's tenants and lodgers in the hereditament, requiring them to make future payments of rent direct to the authority until the arrears are cleared. The notice operates to transfer to the authority the right to recover the rent.[36]

---

[28] *R.* v. *London JJ.* [1899] 1 Q.B. 532; *Greaves* v. *Liverpool City Council* (1979) 77 L.G.R. 440.
[29] *Camden London Borough Council* v. *Herwald, supra.*
[30] General Rate Act 1967, ss. 102–104.
[31] *Liverpool Corporation* v. *Hope* [1938] 1 K.B. 751.
[32] *Reigate Corporation* v. *Wilkinson* (1919) 18 L.G.R. 353. See also § 8-32, above.
[33] Local Government, Planning and Land Act 1980, s. 40.
[34] *Re McGreavy* [1950] Ch. 150; Bankruptcy Act 1914, ss. 4 and 33.
[35] *Re North Bucks Furniture Depositories Ltd.* [1939] 2 All E.R. 549.
[36] General Rate Act 1967, s. 61.

CHAPTER 9

THE GRANT SYSTEM

EXCHEQUER grants in aid of local authority services fall into two groups, **9-01**
the rate support grant and specific grants. The rate support grant is
considered in this Chapter. A list of specific grants appears in Appendix 6.

The rate support grant was introduced by the Local Government **9-02**
Act 1966 and continued in altered form, first, under Part I of the Local
Government Act 1974 and, from April 1, 1981, under Part VI of the
Local Government, Planning and Land Act 1980 as amended by Part
II of the Local Government Finance Act 1982. Local authorities for
the purposes of Part VI of the Act of 1980 are county and district
councils, the Inner London Education Authority, London borough
councils, the Common Council of the City of London, the Council of
the Isles of Scilly and the joint authorities established by the Local
Government Act 1985.[1] Block grant is also payable to the Receiver for
the Metropolitan Police District.[2] Different provisions may be made for
England and Wales.[3]

This form of grant provides general financial aid to local authorities, it
affords the Government a means by which to exert control over the total
level of local authority spending, and it enables a degree of equalisation
to be achieved. It is the aim of equalisation to allow authorities to provide
a comparable level of service for a similar rate in the pound disregarding
their spending needs and their rateable resources.

For the purpose of fixing the aggregate amount of the rate support **9-03**
grants for any year, the Secretary of State first determines the amount
which he estimates is to be made available for the payment of grants to
local authorities in respect of their "relevant expenditure" for that year.[4]
Housing subsidies and mandatory awards to students are the main items
outside this aggregate amount.[5]

The Secretary of State then deducts from the amount so determined (a) **9-04**
the amounts which he estimates will be paid out in specific grants towards
revenue expenditure and (b) supplementary grants for transport purposes
and for National Parks under sections 6 and 7 respectively of the 1974

---

[1] Local Government, Planning and Land Act 1980, s. 53(5), as amended by the Local
Government Act 1985, s. 69.
[2] Local Government Finance Act 1982, s. 10 and Sched. 2.
[3] Local Government, Planning and Land Act 1980, s. 53(4).
[4] "Relevant expenditure" is defined in s. 54(5) of the 1980 Act as expenditure to be defrayed
out of local authority rate funds, subject to adjustments detailed in the section and
reduction by rate fund income as specified by the Secretary of State.
[5] *Ibid.* s. 54 (1).

9-04   Act.[6] The amount remaining after making these deductions is the aggregate amount of rate support grants for the year.[7]

9-05   Before determining the amount available for grants and the estimates of amounts to be deducted, the Secretary of State is required to consult the local authority associations and any local authority with whom consultation appears to him to be desirable and he must take into account probable general changes in demand for services and in levels of pay and prices.[8]

    The rate support grants consist of the domestic rate relief grant and the block grant.

Domestic rate relief grant

9-06   The amount of this grant is determined by the Secretary of State in accordance with Schedule 9 to the Local Government, Planning and Land Act 1980 and is payable to rating authorities to compensate for the reduction in the rate levied on dwelling-houses and mixed hereditaments under section 48 of the General Rate Act 1967, as amended by section 33 of the 1980 Act. The amount of the domestic rate relief grant is specified in the rate support grant report as an amount in the pound. Different amounts may be specified for different rating areas, but the Secretary of State must seek to secure that the total amount of the reduction under section 48 of the General Rate Act 1967 for all rating areas will correspond to the aggregate amount of the domestic rate relief grant for England or for Wales as the case may be.[9]

The block grant

9-07   The aim of this grant is to compensate for differences in resources as well as to provide help for needs. It provides grant aid to local authority expenditure to enable authorities to provide a similar standard of service for a similar rate poundage, and limits the extent to which an authority which provides a higher standard can finance its higher spending by an automatic increase in the grant. The aggregate amount of the grant for a year is the balance left after deducting the amount of the domestic rate relief grant from the aggregate amount of the rate support grants.[10] A county council may by notice inform the Secretary of State that it does not wish to be paid block grant for any year and, if he consents, the amount which would have been payable will be distributed directly to the constituent district councils instead in proportion to their share of the gross rateable value of the county.[11]

9-08   The amount of block grant payable to any particular local authority is

---

[6] *Ibid.* s. 54(2), (7).
[7] *Ibid.* s. 54(3).
[8] *Ibid.* s. 54(4).
[9] *Ibid.* s. 55 and Sched. 9.
[10] *Ibid.* s. 56(1).
[11] *Ibid.* s. 56(2)—(5).

calculated by deducting from the total expenditure (TE) to be incurred by the authority during the year an assumed rate contribution which is basically the product of the grant-related poundage (GRP) multiplied by the gross rateable value of its area (GRV).[12] The terms "total expenditure" and "grant related poundage" are now considered.

The total expenditure of a local authority is the relevant expenditure reduced by the amount of certain grants and adjusted by the addition or subtraction of such descriptions of expenditure or receipts as the Secretary of State may direct after consulting such local authority associations and any local authority with whom consultation appears to him to be desirable.[13]

Grant-related poundage, the second element referred to above, must be considered by reference to grant-related expenditure (GRE). The latter is a notional figure for each local authority, representing an assessment of how much it would cost that authority to provide a typical standard of service, having regard to its general circumstances and responsibilities. The grant-related poundage of an authority means a poundage related (a) to a given ratio between its total expenditure and its grant-related expenditure, or (b) to a given difference between its total expenditure divided by its population and its grant-related expenditure so divided.[14] The grant-related poundage and the grant-related expenditure for a local authority are determined by the Secretary of State in accordance with principles to be applied to all local authorities.[15] Certain principles to be applied are set out in section 58; otherwise the principles must be specified in the rate support grant report referred to below.[16]

For each financial year, different grant-related poundages are prescribed for different levels of spending in a "schedule of grant-related poundages" annexed to the rate support grant report for that year; amended poundages may be fixed in a supplementary report. The schedule fixes a national grant-related poundage for spending equal to grant-related expenditure, and splits it between classes of authority in proportion to their overall share of grant-related expenditure in the type of area in which they are located (*i.e.* the non-metropolitan areas, the metropolitan areas and London). Thus the basic grant-related poundage (GRP*), for expenditure equal to an authority's assessed grant-related expenditure, is the same for all authorities of the same class (*e.g.* non-metropolitan districts). This basic poundage is then adjusted for levels of spending. For each £1 increase or decrease of an authority's expenditure per head of population over its grant-related expenditure per head, the grant-related poundage is increased or decreased by a sum, the "marginal poundage cost" (MPC), which is specified in the poundage

---

[12] *Ibid.* s. 56(6).
[13] *Ibid.* s. 56(8).
[14] *Ibid.* s. 56(8).
[15] *Ibid.* s. 57(1).
[16] *Ibid.* s. 57(2).

schedule, and which applies to all authorities. If excess expenditure per head is greater than a prescribed "threshold," each extra £1 of expenditure per head above that threshold will require a higher prescribed increase in grant-related poundage. The result is that the higher the expenditure per head, the higher is the proportion of the assumed rate contribution and the lower the grant percentage.

The basic calculation of block grant may be summarised by the following formulae, using initials as identified above:

$$\text{Grant} = \text{TE} - \text{GRP} \times \text{GRV}$$

$$\text{GRP} = \text{GRP*} + \frac{\text{MPC} \times (\text{TE} - \text{GRE})}{\text{Population}}$$

Where expenditure per head exceeds the threshold, a higher MPC applies to the excess.

The overall effect of the calculation is that, subject to adjustments referred to below, an authority which spends at a level equal to its GRE receives an amount of grant such that the rate poundage required to meet its total expenditure equals the grant-related poundage for that class of authority, as fixed for the year by the rate support grant report. An authority which spends more than its GRE receives a lower rate of grant, and vice versa: hence the effect on ratepayers of expenditure variation from GRE is magnified. For expenditure over the threshold, the rate of grant decreases more rapidly, with consequent enhanced effect on the rates.

9-09   The Secretary of State has power to make adjustments in the distribution of the block grant by providing in a rate support grant report for the amount payable to a local authority to be calculated by deducting from its total expenditure the product of its grant-related poundage and gross rateable value multiplied by a multiplier determined by him.[17] The power may be exercised for specified purposes. These include the provision of a cushion against excessive changes in grant from one year to the next[18] and the adjustment of grant according to the extent to which an authority complies with expenditure guidance targets issued by the Secretary of State.[19] Different multipliers may be applied to different authorities but only in accordance with principles applicable to all local authorities or to all local authorities of a particular class.[20] The principles

---

[17] *Ibid.* s. 59(1).

[18] *Ibid.* s. 59(6)(*a*).

[19] *Ibid.* s. 59(6)(*cc*), as substituted by the Local Government Finance Act 1982, s. 8. From 1981/2 to 1985/6 expenditure guidance "targets" were set for each authority by reference to its spending in previous years. Authorities which did not meet their targets were subject to "penalties," or "holdback," reducing their grant by the application of multipliers greater than one. The Secretary of State has announced that targets and the related penalties/holdback will not apply in 1986/7.

[20] *Ibid.* s. 59(5)(*a*) of the 1980 Act, s. 8(6) of the 1982 Act. See hereon *R.* v. *Secretary of State for the Environment, ex p. Nottinghamshire C.C.* [1986] 2 W.L.R. 1.

on which the power is exercised must be specified in the statutory rate support grant report.[21]

R. v. Secretary of State for the Environment, ex p. Hackney L.B.C.[22] The council **9-10** applied for judicial review of the expenditure guidance for 1984/5 issued to it by the Secretary of State for rate support grant purposes under section 59(6)(*cc*) of the 1980 Act. It was argued that the guidance was not lawful since it was impossible for the council to comply with it without precluding the reasonable discharge of its statutory duties; and that the guidance had not been "framed by reference to principles applicable to all local authorities," as required by section 59(11A).

Forbes J. held, dismissing the application: (1) that it would be open to the Secretary of State, under section 59(6)(*cc*), to issue guidance indicating a level of expenditure which he knew was impossible to achieve and thus force an increase in the rates if he believed that was necessary in order to reduce the level of local authority expenditure; (2) if that was wrong, it could not on the evidence before the court be said that the Secretary of State had not been reasonably satisfied that the council could comply with the guidance without being in breach of statutory duty; (3) that "principle" in section 59(11A) meant a "self-sufficient proposition intended to be applied to sets of circumstances" and that in that sense the guidance followed principles applicable to all authorities. The council's appeal against this decision was dismissed by the Court of Appeal.[23]

The Secretary of State may defray any expenditure incurred in any **9-11** year in the provision of services for local authorities by any body specified in regulations made by him and deduct from the aggregate amount of the block grant for that year all or part of the amount so defrayed.[24]

Rate support grant reports

The Secretary of State is required to make for each year a rate support **9-12** grant report relating to relevant grants. The report, which requires the consent of the Treasury, must specify all the determinations required to be made in relation to rate support grants payable under the 1980 Act and under sections 6 and 7 of the Local Government Act 1974 (supplementary grants for transport and National Parks) together with the considerations leading to those determinations.[25] Before making a report the Secretary of State must consult the local authority associations.[26]

The report must be laid before the House of Commons and no payments may be made until the report is approved by resolution of the House and any payment may then only be made in accordance with the report or any supplementary report.

The Secretary of State may at any time when he thinks fit make supplementary reports for any year specifying fresh determinations in place of any of those in the rate support grant report except in relation to

---

[21] *Ibid.* s. 59(8) of the 1980 Act, s. 8(4), (7) and (9) of the 1982 Act.

[22] *The Times,* March 26, 1984.

[23] *The Times,* May 11, 1985.

[24] Local Government, Planning and Land Act 1980, s. 56(9).

[25] *Ibid.* s. 60.

[26] *Ibid.* s. 60(5).

the domestic rate relief grant. The supplementary reports are subject to the same provisions as to consultation and House of Commons approval as the main report.[27]

Adjustment of block grant total

9-13   In order to ensure that the total amount paid in respect of block grant in any year is the same as the aggregate amount available for that grant, the Secretary of State may make adjustments by increasing or decreasing the amount payable to each local authority. The adjustments must be in the same ratio for all authorities. Under this power the Secretary of State may make a fresh calculation of the entitlement of each authority to block grant, substituting the total expenditure actually incurred for the amount on which the original grant was based.[28] The block grant is also subject to adjustments in respect of the pooling and apportionment between local education authorities of expenditure on advanced further education and certain other education services.[29]

Each local authority is required to submit to the Secretary of State such information as he may from time to time require in connection with the total expenditure to be incurred by the authority during the year and, where he is not satisfied that the information accurately reflects the amount used in calculating the general rate or precept for the year, he may make such adjustments as he considers appropriate after giving the authority a chance to submit representations on the matter.[30]

Estimates and calculations

9-14   The Secretary of State must estimate and notify to each local authority the amounts of domestic rate relief grant and block grant which will become payable to the authority for a year. As soon as practicable after receiving what appears to be sufficient information for the purpose, the Secretary of State must make a conclusive calculation of the amounts and notify the local authority. Where it appears that a sum in excess of the estimate or calculation has already been paid in respect of rate support grants, the Secretary of State may recover such sum from any amount due in respect of such grants for the current or any subsequent year, or by issuing a demand for repayment.[31]

After the block grant payable to a local authority has been determined, the authority may request the Secretary of State to recalculate it if the gross rateable value for the area has been reduced by a percentage to be specified by the Secretary of State in regulations made after consultation with any local authority association concerned.[32]

[27] *Ibid.* s. 61.
[28] *Ibid.* s. 62.
[29] *Ibid.* s. 63 and Sched. 10.
[30] *Ibid.* s. 65.
[31] *Ibid.* s. 66.
[32] *Ibid.* s. 67.

CHAPTER 10

CONTRACT, TORT AND CRIMINAL LIABILITY

1. *CONTRACT*

THE contracts of local authorities are governed by the general principles   **10-01**
of the law of contract, supplemented in some respects by special rules.
This topic falls into three parts—the powers of local authorities to enter
into contracts and to be bound by them, the rules which apply when these
powers are exercised, and the exclusion of liability.

A. POWERS TO CONTRACT

A local authority is enabled, by section 111 of the Local Government Act   **10-02**
1972,[1] to do anything which is calculated to facilitate, or is conducive or
incidental to, the discharge of any of its functions. It has therefore a
general power to enter into contracts for the discharge of any of its
functions. In a number of statutes a *specific* power to contract is conferred.
For example, section 9 of the Agriculture (Miscellaneous Provisions) Act
1954 enables an authority to enter into an agreement as to payment for
kitchen waste. An authority has specific power to enter into agreements
for the supply of electricity (to an electricity board), or heat,[2] and for the
use by others of spare capacity on a local authority computer.[3] The Local
Authorities (Goods and Services) Act 1970 enables a local authority[4] to
make an agreement on appropriate terms with another local authority
and, subject to the Secretary of State for the Environment making
appropriate regulations,[5] with other public bodies, for that authority or
body to supply to the other goods, materials, services, transport and
equipment and to carry out maintenance works. But a specific power is
not simply a duplication of general power; a statute enabling authorities
to enter into agreements in respect of specified matters in effect confers a
power to do whatever is involved—in the first example given, to pay for
kitchen waste. In a few instances there is an express statutory prohibition

---

[1] This power applies also to joint authorities and the Inner London Education Authority
(s. 146A, inserted by the Local Government Act 1985, Sched. 14, para. 16) and to
residuary bodies (1985 Act, Sched. 13, para. 12(*a*)).

[2] Local Government (Miscellaneous Provisions) Act 1976, s. 11.

[3] *Ibid.* s. 38. This power applies also to joint authorities and the Inner London Education
Authority (s. 44(1), as amended by the Local Government Act 1985, Sched. 14,
para. 53(*b*)) and to residuary bodies (1985 Act, Sched. 13, para. 13(*g*)).

[4] The Act applies also to joint authorities, the Inner London Education Authority and
residuary bodies: § 4–59, n. 74.

[5] See the Local Authorities (Goods and Services) (Public Bodies) Orders 1972 and 1975 (S.I.
1972 No. 853 and S.I. 1975 No. 193).

against entering into certain agreements—a fire authority, for example, is precluded by section 3(4) of the Fire Services Act 1947 from making a charge for services except as provided for in the Act.

A special power of increasing significance is the power to enter agreements with owners regulating or restricting the development or the use of land[6] or "for the purpose of securing the carrying out of works on or facilitating the development of . . . land."[7] Such agreements are enforceable against successors in title.[8] An analogous agreement under a local Act was enforced as a matter of contract in *Beaconsfield District Council* v. *Gams*[9] and an injunction was obtained by a local authority to enforce a section 52 agreement in *Avon County Council* v. *Millard.*[10] A council may not, however, by entering a section 52 agreement fetter its exercise of other statutory powers.[11]

10-03   The power to contract (whether given generally or specifically) is a limited power: it may be exercised only in the discharge of an authority's functions. If an authority enters into a contract in regard to some matter which is *ultra vires* the authority, then the contract is null and void and neither party can sue on it: it is as if no contract has been made. Moreover it is no avail to the party who thinks he has entered into a contract to establish that he was not aware of the limits to the authority's statutory powers.

> *Ashbury Railway Carriage and Iron Co.* v. *Riche.*[12] The company entered into a contract the purpose of which was beyond the objects expressed or implied in the memorandum of association. The contract was therefore *ultra vires* the company. The company repudiated the contract as being *ultra vires* and the respondent brought an action to recover damages for its non-fulfilment. *Held,* the contract, being *ultra vires* the company, was wholly void (though not necessarily illegal). It could not, therefore, be enforced against the company. (It may be noted that the *ultra vires* rule has been modified in respect of companies registered under the Companies Acts by section 9(1) of the European Communities Act 1972 (now section 35(1) of the Companies Act 1985).)

An authority cannot by its own acts enlarge the powers given by statute.

> *Rhyl Urban District Council* v. *Rhyl Amusements Ltd.*[13] The council had granted a lease relying on certain private Act powers. These powers did not in fact cover the particular transaction, so that, if the lease were to be *intra vires,* the council would have to rely on the general law. Section 177 of the Public Health Act 1875 (the relevant provision in the general law) required the consent of the Local Government Board (the predecessor of the Ministry of Health) to

---

[6] Town and Country Planning Act 1971, s. 52.
[7] Local Government (Miscellaneous Provisions) Act 1982, s. 33.
[8] *Ibid.* ss. 52(2) and 126(2).
[9] (1974) 234 E.G. 749.
[10] (1985) 274 E.G. 1025.
[11] *Windsor and Maidenhead Royal Borough* v. *Brandrose Investments Ltd.* [1983] 1 W.L.R. 509.
[12] (1875) L.R. 7 H.L. 653.
[13] [1959] 1 W.L.R. 465.

the lease of land, but such consent was not obtained. *Held*, that the lease was null and void, for the council in granting it had acted *ultra vires*. It was further held that the council, having acted *ultra vires* in granting the lease, could not be estopped for denying its validity. On this point Harman J. said[14]: "If the plaintiffs were private people this would be a strong plea, but in my judgment a plea of estoppel cannot prevail as an answer to a claim that something done by a statutory body is *ultra vires.*"

The application of this rule presents no difficulty where there is a **10-04** complete absence of a statutory power or an expressed prohibition. But problems of construction and interpretation arise where a prohibition is to be implied from the terms of the statute[15] and where an otherwise lawful act becomes *ultra vires* because a power has been unreasonably exercised.[16]

There is one further limitation on the power to contract—an authority may not enter into a contract incompatible with the due exercise of its powers or the discharge of its duties or which divests the authority of its statutory powers or which obliges the authority not to exercise its powers.[17]

B. The Exercise of Contractual Powers

Compliance with standing orders

The Local Government Act 1972, s. 135,[18] provides that a local **10-05** authority (1) may make standing orders with respect to the making of contracts, and (2) must make such orders with respect to contracts for the supply of goods or materials or for the execution of works. In relation to the latter, the standing orders must include provisions for securing competition and for regulating the manner in which tenders are invited. But they may exempt contracts for a price below that specified in the standing orders and may authorise the authority to exempt any contract from the relevant standing order when the authority is satisfied that the exemption is justified by special circumstances. A person contracting with a local authority is not bound to inquire whether standing orders have been complied with, and non-compliance with such orders does not invalidate any contract entered into by or on behalf of the authority. This provision will not, however validate a contract which is otherwise invalid, for example, by being *ultra vires*.[19]

---

[14] At p. 474.
[15] *Melliss* v. *Shirley Local Board* (1885) 16 Q.B.D. 446.
[16] *Municipal Mutual Insurance Ltd.* v. *Pontefract Corporation* (1917) 116 L.T. 671.
[17] *York Corporation* v. *Henry Leetham & Sons Ltd.* [1924] 1 Ch. 557; *Birkdale District Electric Supply Co.* v. *Southport Corporation* [1926] A.C. 355, *per* Lord Birkenhead at p. 364; *Wm. Cory & Son Ltd.* v. *London Corporation* [1951] 2 K.B. 476; *Stringer* v. *Minister of Housing and Local Government* [1970] 1 W.L.R. 1281, *per* Cooke J. at p. 1289; *Re Staines Urban District Council's Agreement, Triggs* v. *Staines Urban District Council* [1969] 1 Ch. 10, *per* Cross J. at p. 18; *cf. Dowty Boulton Paul Ltd.* v. *Wolverhampton Corporation* [1971] 1 W.L.R. 204. See §§ 12–09—12–11.
[18] This section applies also to joint authorities and the Inner London Education Authority: s. 146A, inserted by the Local Government Act 1985, Sched. 14, para. 16.
[19] *North West Leicestershire District Council* v. *East Midlands Housing Association Ltd.* [1981] 1 W.L.R. 1396.

Model standing orders for local authority contracts have been issued by the Department of the Environment after consultation with the local authority associations, government departments and other bodies.[20]

It would appear that there is no immediate sanction against an authority which acts in breach of these rules, though mandamus might issue to compel compliance.

> *R. v. Hereford Corporation, ex p. Harrower.*[21] The council invited the local gas and electricity boards and the National Coal Board to submit schemes and prices for the installation of central heating apparatus in council houses, and one submission was accepted. Several electrical contractors on the council's approved list applied to the Court for an order of mandamus directing the authority to comply with standing orders relating to public advertisement and public tender. The standing orders provided that there should be no exceptions to the rules contained in them otherwise than by a direction of the council. It was held that an order of mandamus would issue, for there was a clear statutory duty on the authority to comply with standing orders. But since the council had a right to suspend standing orders, the order would not issue immediately so that the council might have an opportunity to suspend them. It was further held that the applicants, as ratepayers, but not as electrical contractors, had a sufficient legal right to apply for the order.

In practice, an auditor might well comment on any breach in his statutory report.

The Model Standing Orders expressly require compliance with the EEC Treaty and any relevant EEC Directives, in addition to compliance with standing orders.[22] The Notes to the Model draw attention to Article 30 of the Treaty, which prohibits quantitive restrictions on imports between member states and measures having equivalent effect to such restrictions. The relevant directives require the abolition of any restrictive or discriminatory practices which might prevent contractors from other member states from participating in public contracts on equal terms with national contractors,[23] and lay down common advertising procedures and award criteria for public contracts with an estimated value above the prevailing threshold.[24] Contracts must be advertised in the Official Journal of the European Communities. The Department of the Environment has given guidance on the application of these Directives.[25]

Special rules apply where work is to be undertaken by direct labour departments.[26]

---

[20] *Model Standing Orders: Contracts* (3rd ed., 1983); see DoE Circular 15/83.
[21] [1970] 1 W.L.R. 1424. See also *McKee* v. *Belfast Corporation* [1954] N.I. 122.
[22] S.O.1.
[23] Directive 71/304 (public sector construction contracts); Directive 70/32 (public sector supplies contracts).
[24] Directives 71/305 and 72/277 (public sector construction contracts); Directive 77/62 (public sector supplies contracts). The current "prevailing thresholds" are 1,000,000 European Currency Units for construction contracts and 200,000 European Currency Units for supply contracts.
[25] DoE Circulars 4/73 and 59/73 (as amended by Circulars 102/76 and 67/78) (construction contracts) and DoE Circulars 4/73, 46/78 and 27/81 (supplies contracts).
[26] See §§ 27–29 — 27–32.

Disclosure of interest

When matters relating to contracts are discussed in council or **10-06** committee, there is a duty on members and officers having an interest to declare it.[27]

Sealing of contracts

The Corporate Bodies' Contracts Act 1960 brought order and certainty **10-07** to the law with respect to the sealing of local authority contracts and greatly simplified administrative practice. It was formerly a rule of the common law that a corporation (other than a trading corporation) could not bind itself in contract except by seal,[28] a rule sensible enough where large sums were involved but administratively impossible in trifling matters. The effect of the Act of 1960 is as follows. If a contract is one which, if made between private persons would be required by law to be in writing, then it may be made by a local authority in writing, signed by a person acting under its authority, express or implied: if a contract made between private persons would by law be valid although made verbally, then such a contract can be made verbally on behalf of a local authority by any person acting under its authority express or implied. A local authority is, therefore, in substantially the same position in respect to the *formalities* attaching to contracts as is a private person. But an authority may continue to seal contracts which now need not be sealed, if only to preserve the safeguards which the formalities of sealing might be considered to give. Local authorities generally systematise the position through standing orders, frequently authorising the appropriate officers to sign all contracts below a certain amount and requiring all others to be sealed. Or the authority may authorise several officers to sign contracts of particular kinds and below specified sums.

Formalities

The formalities to be observed in the making of contracts (applicable as **10-08** well to local authorities as to private persons) are to be found in common law and statute. It is a general rule of the common law that a contract is binding upon the parties to it if it is made *verbally*: there is no need in common law to have a contract reduced to writing for oral evidence can be given of its terms. But statute has provided exceptions to this broad rule. Certain contracts are *void* unless they are reduced to writing, and certain contracts although not void are nevertheless unenforceable if not evidenced in writing. In the first class, the absence of a document is fatal; in the second, one of the parties can plead the absence of writing, and if this is done the contract becomes unenforceable. In the first group are, for example, assignments of copyright,[29] agreements between employer and

---

[27] ss. 94 to 98 of the Local Government Act 1972 and §§ 4–26—4–33.
[28] *Austin* v. *Bethnal Green Guardians* (1874) L.R. 9 C.P. 91, *per* Lord Coleridge C.J. at p. 94.
[29] Copyright Act 1956, s. 36.

workmen for certain deductions of wages,[30] and agreements to submit differences to arbitration.[31] In the second group are contracts for the sale or other disposition of an interest in land.[32] There are certain contracts which still require to be under seal—generally speaking all conveyances of land or interests therein,[33] and contracts made without consideration.

Authority to enter contracts

10-09   It will be seen, therefore, that most local authority contracts can be made under hand and indeed verbally. They may be signed by a person acting under the authority of the corporation, and that authority may be express or implied. The rules as to implied authority are found in the common law and in their application to local authorities two of them are of particular importance. In the first place, if a contracting party has good reason to suppose, in all the circumstances, that an officer or servant has power to bind his corporation, then the corporation may be bound in contract by the act of that officer or servant.[34] Secondly, where an officer or servant has express authority, then that authority extends by implication to all acts which are incidental to the main purpose.[35]

10-10   A contracting party is not bound to satisfy himself as to the authority which the officer holds. A public works contractor would have good reason to suppose that an engineer has power to enter into a contract on behalf of his authority for the supply of tarmacadam: a supplier of textbooks could reasonably suppose that a chief education officer had power to order books for the schools in his area. Authority in such circumstances would generally be express, but if this were not so it could well be implied. Where a corporation is committed by the acts of its officers to whom express or implied authority is given it will be no defence to the corporation to say that a particular act was unauthorised. Conversely, a clause in a contract agreed to by a council officer will not bind the council if the officer has no authority, whether actual, implied or usual, to assent to that clause.[36]

C. The Exclusion of Liability

10-11   The Unfair Contract Terms Act 1977 limits the extent to which civil liability for breach of contract or negligence can be avoided by contract terms or other notices. The main limitations are applied only to "business

---

[30] Truck Acts 1831 and 1896.
[31] Arbitration Act 1950, s. 32.
[32] Law of Property Act 1925, s. 40.
[33] *Ibid.* s. 52.
[34] *Brady* v. *Todd* (1861) 9 C.B. (N.S.) 592. But see §§ 12–12—12–14.
[35] *Bayley* v. *Wilkins* (1849) 7 C.B. 886.
[36] *North West Leicestershire District Council* v. *East Midlands Housing Association Ltd.* [1981] 1 W.L.R. 1396.

liability," but "business" is defined so as to include the activities of any local or public authority.[37] An authority is unable to exclude or restrict by reference to any contract term, or to a notice given to persons generally or to particular persons, liability for death or personal injury resulting from negligence.[38] Similar exclusions or limitations relating to other loss or damage resulting from negligence are subject to the test of reasonableness.[39] Clauses of various kinds (including exemption clauses) affecting contractual liability are also subject on the test of reasonableness, where one party "deals as consumer or on the other's written standard terms of business."[40] A party "deals as consumer" if "(a) he neither makes the contract in the course of a business nor holds himself out as doing so; and (b) the other party does make the contract in the course of a business; and (c) in the case of a contact governed by the law of sale of goods or hire purchase, or by section 7 of this Act, the goods passing under or in pursuance of the contract are of a type ordinarily supplied for private use and consumption."[41] A contract with a member of the public acting in an individual capacity (e.g. one arising out of enquiries made of local authorities in the course of conveyancing) will be subject to section 3 where the other party "deals as consumer." Contract terms authorised or required by an enactment are unaffected; and terms approved by a competent authority "acting in pursuance of a statutory jurisdiction or function" are taken to be "reasonable."[42] An example of the latter is the power of the Secretary of State under the Water Act 1945,[43] relating to terms and conditions for the supply of water for non-domestic purposes. Any contract is unaffected by section 2 to 4 in so far as it relates to the creation or transfer of an interest in land.[44]

2. TORT

A tort is a civil wrong (which is not exclusively a breach of contract or a **10–12** breach of trust), the remedy for which is a common law action for damages and, where necessary, a decree of the court such as an injunction. The law of tort is therefore concerned with such matters as trespass to persons, lands and goods, nuisance, negligence, defamation, deceit. A tort is to be distinguished from a crime, which is an offence for which punishment is meted out by the State as a result of criminal proceedings. The same facts may, of course, form a basis for a criminal

[37] ss. 1(1) and (3) and s. 14.
[38] s. 2(1).
[39] ss. 2(2) and (11).
[40] ss. 3, 11 and 13.
[41] s. 12(1).
[42] s. 29.
[43] s. 27.
[44] Sched. 1, para. 1(b).

charge and for an action in tort, *e.g.* manslaughter and negligence arising from an act of careless driving.

A local authority, as corporate body, may itself sue in tort. Section 222 of the Local Government Act 1972 gives a general power to prosecute and defend legal proceedings.[45] Examples of such proceedings are *Ilford Urban District Council* v. *Beal*[46] (nuisance), *Esso Petroleum Co. Ltd.* v. *Southport Corporation*[47] (trespass, nuisance and negligence), *Shoreham-by-Sea Urban District Council* v. *Dolphin Canadian Proteins Ltd.*[48] (public nuisance), and *Bognor Regis Urban District Council* v. *Campion*[49] (defamation). Naturally, an authority may sue to recover possession of its land.[50]

The general rules of tortious liability apply both to corporate bodies and natural persons: they are not therefore examined here except in so far as they are of particular importance in local administration.[51] The following matters are considered to fall in this category: the general liability of corporate bodies for tortious acts; the construction of statutory powers, *i.e.* whether a defence can be raised that an act is committed in order to comply with a statutory requirement; negligence in the performance of statutory functions; failure to perform duties; failure to exercise powers; the liability of local authorities as occupiers of premises; the application of the rule in *Rylands* v. *Fletcher* to local authorities; negligent misstatement; misfeasance in a public office; and the personal liability of individual members of local authorities and their officers. The payment of compensation following a finding of maladministration by a Local Commissioner is also considered.

In *Rookes* v. *Barnard*,[52] the House of Lords held that the award of "exemplary" or "punitive" damages should be confined to three situations. The first of these, of relevance here, is where there is "oppressive, arbitrary or unconstitutional action by the servants of the government."[53] These limitations were endorsed by the House in *Broome* v. *Cassell & Co.*[54] Here it was stated *obiter* that Lord Devlin's first category was not confined to Crown servants, but extended to all those exercising governmental functions, including local authorities.[55]

A claim for damages may now be made on an application for judicial

---

[45] See also § 12–47—12–48.
[46] [1925] 1 K.B. 671.
[47] [1956] A.C. 218.
[48] (1972) 71 L.G.R. 261.
[49] [1972] 2 Q.B. 169.
[50] *Manchester Corporation* v. *Connolly* [1970] 1 Ch. 420; *Bristol Corporation* v. *Persons Unknown* [1974] 1 W.L.R. 365; *Greater London Council* v. *Jenkins* [1975] 1 W.L.R. 155; R.S.C. Ord. 45, r. 13 and Ord. 113.
[51] See *Clerk and Lindsell on Torts* (15th ed.) for general principles.
[52] [1964] A.C. 1129.
[53] *Per* Lord Devlin at p. 1226.
[54] [1972] A.C. 1027.
[55] See Lord Reid at pp. 1087–1088, and Lord Diplock at p. 1130; *cf.* Lord Hailsham at p. 1077–1078, and Lord Kilbrandon at p. 1134.

review, in combination with a claim for mandamus, certiorari, prohibition, an injunction or a declaration.[56] Prior to 1978 an application for one of the prerogative orders could not be coupled with a claim for damages. This development is purely procedural; it confers no new right to damages, and leaves unaffected the power of a plaintiff to choose to commence an action in the ordinary way.

A. GENERAL PRINCIPLES OF TORTIOUS LIABILITY

It was at one time doubted whether a statutory corporation could commit **10-13** a tort, since it can do only those things for which it has specific authority in law, and clearly it has no authority to commit a wrong. The position was clarified in *Mersey Docks and Harbour Board Trustees* v. *Gibbs*[57] which laid down the general rule that a corporate body may be liable in tort in the same way as a natural person. This is obviously so when the function in which the act occurs is *intra vires*, and it appears that an authority cannot escape liability by pleading that the function in which the wrongful act occurs is *ultra vires*, notwithstanding the doubts which have been expressed on this point.[58]

> *Campbell* v. *Paddington Corporation*.[59] In this case the act complained of was specifically authorised by the council. A resolution was passed instructing the council's servants to erect a stand in the highway from which councillors and their friends could watch the funeral procession of Edward VII. The act was held to constitute a nuisance for which the council was made liable. The council put as one defence that, being a corporation, it could not be sued in tort because it had no authority in law to authorise the erection of the stand. On this Avory J. said[60]: "To say that because the borough council had no legal right to erect it [the stand], therefore the corporation cannot be sued, is to say that no corporation can ever be sued for any tort or wrong.... That would be absurd."

The liability of a local authority for tortious acts is normally a vicarious liability: it acts through its servants, agents or contractors. Since somewhat different principles apply to each of these categories it is important, in any particular case, to establish the relationship of the local authority to the tortfeasors, whether it be that of master and servant, principal and independent contractor, or principal and agent.

Servants

Generally speaking, a local authority is vicariously liable for a tort **10-14** committed by its servant whilst engaged on the work of the authority and during the course of his employment. The term "during the course of

---

[56] R.S.C. Ord. 53, r. 7, substituted by S.I. 1977 No. 1955.
[57] (1866) L.R. 1 H.L. 93.
[58] e.g. by P. S. Atiyah, *Vicarious Liability in the Law of Torts*, pp. 383–387; cf. *Salmond on the Law of Torts* (18th ed.), pp. 404–405.
[59] [1911] 1 K.B. 869.
[60] At p. 875.

employment" has been the subject of much litigation and the courts have tended to give it an extended meaning.

> *Smith* v. *Martin and Hull Corporation.*[61] A school teacher directed a child to attend to the fire in the teachers' common room in preparation for the teachers' lunch, and the child was injured in so doing. *Held,* that the relation of master and servant existed between the local education authority and the teachers employed by them, and that the act of the teacher was within the scope of her employment, which was not strictly confined to teaching alone. The corporation was accordingly held liable for the act of the teacher.

A servant employed by a local authority may not in fact be carrying out the work of the authority but duties imposed by law on government departments. The employing authority may not be liable for the torts of such employees.

> *Stanbury* v. *Exeter Corporation.*[62] An inspector appointed by the council under the Diseases of Animals Act 1894 negligently carried out a duty imposed upon him by an Order of the Board of Agriculture. *Held,* the corporation could not be made liable, for the inspector was not acting in performance of a duty imposed by statute on the local authority.[63]

10-15   A servant is commonly defined for the purposes of liability in tort as a person subject to the control and direction of his employer as to the manner in which he shall do his work.[64] The question has been raised as to whether professional persons in the employment of an authority come under this definition so far as tortious liability is concerned. The issue was of particular importance prior to the National Health Service Act 1946, when many local authorities maintained public hospitals. There was then some doubt as to whether medical practitioners and other skilled employees were "servants" of a hospital authority so as to make the authority liable for negligence, but this was resolved in the two cases which follow. In view of these decisions it is doubtful whether professional staff of a local authority are ever excluded from the term "servant" so as to excuse the local authority from liability for tortious acts committed during the course of their employment and in the work of the authority.

> *Gold* v. *Essex County Council.*[65] A visiting doctor ordered ray treatment for a child patient suffering from warts, and a qualified radiographer employed by the county council administered the treatment negligently so that the child was permanently disfigured. *Held,* one who employs a servant is liable to another person if the servant does an act within the scope of his employment so negligently as to injure that other. That principle applies even though the work which the servant is employed to do is of a skilful or technical character as to the method of performing which the employer is himself ignorant.

---

[61] [1911] 2 K.B. 775.
[62] [1905] 2 K.B. 838.
[63] *cf. Ministry of Housing and Local Government* v. *Sharp* [1970] 2 Q.B. 223; local authority not vicariously liable for the clerk to the council when acting in the capacity of Registrar of Local Land Charges.
[64] *Yewens* v. *Noakes* [1880] 6 Q.B.D. 530, *per* Bramwell L.J. at p. 532.
[65] [1942] 2 K.B. 293.

Cassidy v. *Ministry of Health*.[66] The plaintiff entered hospital for an operation on his hand which necessitated post-operational treatment. Whilst undertaking that treatment he was under the care of the surgeon who performed the operation, the house surgeon and members of the nursing staff, all of whom were employed under contracts of service. At the end of his treatment the plaintiff's hand became useless. *Held*, a hospital authority is liable for the negligence of doctors and surgeons employed by the authority under a contract of service arising in the course of the performance of their professional duties. It was no answer for them to say that their staff were professional men and women who do not tolerate any interference by their lay masters in the way they do their work. The reason why employers are liable in such cases is not that they can control the way in which the work is done but that they employ the staff and have chosen them for the task and have in their hands the ultimate sanction for good conduct, the power of dismissal.

It will be observed that the medical and nursing staff in the *Cassidy case* **10-16** were under contracts of service, that it is say, they were employees in the sense in which this term is commonly understood, giving all their time to the hospital authority. Denning L.J. would have taken the matter further and would have imputed liability to the hospital authority even though the medical staff were under *contracts for services*, being employed, for example, on a sessional basis of work of a highly specialised nature. The point is mentioned here to illustrate a tendency of the courts to widen the scope of vicarious liability of public authorities arising from acts of all who are employed by them, whether servants whose work they can "control" or specialists about whose techniques they are wholly ignorant. There is a tendency, too, to take all the factors in the relationship into account—the terms of the contract, the degree of control, the economic risk.[67]

There are particular rules with respect to liability for tortious acts committed by police constables.[68]

Independent contractors

There is a distinction between a servant as considered above and an **10-17** independent contractor—a person engaged to give some service or to undertake a particular piece of work in the carrying out of which the council exercises no detailed control. A firm engaged in the building of houses or the construction of a road under a contract with the authority is an independent contractor. The firm will work to a specification provided by the authority and the authority will satisfy itself that the work done conforms to the requirements of the contract. But there will be no supervision of workmen, and orders will not be given to employees, as would be the case in a direct works scheme, *i.e.* where the work itself is entrusted to one of the council's departments.

---

[66] [1951] 2 K.B. 343.
[67] See *Market Investigations Ltd.* v. *Minister of Social Security* [1969] 2 Q.B. 173. For a further discussion on this issue, see *Stevenson, Jordan and Harrison Ltd.* v. *Macdonald and Evans* [1952] 1 T.L.R. 101 and *Ready Mixed Concrete (South East) Ltd.* v. *Minister of Pensions and National Insurance* [1968] 2 Q.B. 497.
[68] See Police Act 1964, s. 48 and Chap. 21.

10–18   A local authority is not liable for the torts of an independent contractor except in the following circumstances: (a) where the independent contractor is carrying out a duty imposed by law upon the local authority,[69] (b) where the authority interferes to prescribe how the work shall be undertaken,[70] (c) where the authority specifically authorises the tortious act (*qui facit per alium facit per se*), or (d) where the work required to be undertaken is particularly hazardous.[71] But an authority is not liable for the collateral negligence of a contractor. Lord Blackburn stated the law in *Dalton* v. *Angus*.[72] He said:

> "Ever since *Quarman* v. *Burnett* (1840) 6 M. & W. 499 it has been considered settled law that one employing another is not liable for his collateral negligence unless the relation of master and servant existed between them. So that a person employing a contractor to do work is not liable for the negligence of that contractor or his servants. On the other hand, a person causing something to be done, the doing of which casts on him a duty, cannot escape from the responsibility attaching on him of seeing that duty performed by delegating it to a contractor. He may bargain with the contractor that he shall perform the duty and stipulate for an indemnity from him if it is not performed, but he cannot thereby relieve himself from liability to those injured by the failure to perform it."

Lord Blackburn here contrasts a contractor's negligence, which he calls "collateral," with failure on the part of a contractor to perform the duty falling by law to his employer. For the first the employer is not liable; for the second he is, whether the failure is attributable to negligence or not.

> *Hardaker* v. *Idle District Council*.[73] A district council, being about to construct a sewer under their statutory powers, employed a contractor to construct it for them. In consequence of his negligence in carrying out the work a gas-main was broken, and the gas escaped from it into a house in which the plaintiffs (a husband and wife) resided, and an explosion took place, by which the wife was injured, and the husband's furniture was damaged. In an action by the plaintiffs against the district council and the contractor: *Held*, that the district council owed a duty to the public (including the plaintiffs) so to construct the sewer as not to injure the gas-main; that they had been guilty of a breach of this duty; notwithstanding that they had delegated the performance of the duty to the contractor, they were responsible to the plaintiffs for the breach.

In the course of his judgment Lindley L.J. said[74]:

> "I pass now to consider the duty of the district council in the present case. Their duty in sewering the street was not performed by constructing a proper sewer. Their duty was, not only to do that, but also to take care not to break any gas-pipes which they cut under: this involved properly supporting them. This duty was not performed. They employed a contractor to perform their duty for

[69] See *Penny* v. *Wimbledon Urban District Council* [1899] 2 Q.B. 72; *Hardaker* v. *Idle District Council* [1896] 1 Q.B. 335; Highways Act 1980, s. 41.
[70] *McLaughlin* v. *Pryor* (1842) 4 M. & G. 48.
[71] *Honeywill and Stein Ltd.* v. *Larkin Bros. Ltd.* [1934] 1 K.B. 191.
[72] (1881) 6 App. Cas. 740 at p. 829.
[73] [1896] 1 Q.B. 335.
[74] At p. 342.

them, but he failed to perform it. It is impossible, I think, to regard this as a case of collateral negligence. The case is not one in which the contractor performed the district council's duty for them, but did so carelessly; the case is one in which the duty of the district council, so far as the gas-pipes were concerned, was not performed at all."

These general principles were reaffirmed in *Cassidy* v. *Ministry of Health*.[75] Denning L.J. said[76]:

"The truth is that, in cases of negligence, the distinction between a contract of service and a contract for services only becomes of importance when it is sought to make the employer liable, not for a breach of his own duty of care, but for some collateral act of negligence of those whom he employs. He cannot escape the consequences of a breach of his own duty but he can escape responsibility for collateral or casual acts of negligence if he can show that the negligent person was employed, not under a contract of service but only under a contract for services.... Take now an instance where an employer is under a duty himself. Suppose an employer has a lamp which overhangs his shop door; he is himself under a duty to his customers to use reasonable care to see that it is safe and he cannot escape that duty by employing an independent contractor to do it. He is liable, therefore, if the independent contractor fails to discover a patent defect which any careful man should have discovered, and in consequence the lamp falls on a customer; but he is not liable if the independent contractor drops a hammer on the head of a customer, because that is not negligence in the employer's department of duty. It is collateral or casual negligence by one employed under a contract for services."

Agents

A local authority is in general answerable for the acts of its agents where   **10-19**
it has expressly authorised them or subsequently ratifies them. The agent also may be liable, for a person cannot excuse himself by saying that he was acting as the agent of another. In applying this principle to particular cases regard must be had to the extent to which the authority controls the conduct of the agent in the discharge of the work entrusted to him. The agent may in this regard be nearer either to a servant or to an independent contractor, and the appropriate rules apply whichever might be the case.

B. CONSTRUCTION OF STATUTORY POWERS

Whether an authority is liable for a wrongful act depends, amongst other   **10-20**
things, on the construction of the authorising statute. The statute itself may specifically require or authorise the doing of things which would otherwise be tortious. It may require or authorise something to be done which is necessarily an infringement of a legal right. In such a case the authority is absolved from liability, provided there is no negligence on the part of the authority in what it does.

In deciding whether a defence of statutory authority can be raised, a number of factors may be relevant.

---

[75] [1951] 2 K.B. 343.
[76] At p. 364.

The precision of the statutory authorisation

10-21   The more precisely defined are the acts authorised by the statute, so it is more easily established that the legislature intended to authorise the performance of acts otherwise tortious.

> *Metropolitan Asylum District* v. *Hill*.[77] Section 5 of the Metropolitan Poor Act 1867 enacted that "asylums . . . may be provided under this Act for reception or relief of the sick, insane, or infirm, or other class or classes of the poor. . . ." The managers of the Metropolitan Asylum District, in accordance with the Board's directions, built a smallpox hospital in a residential area of Hampstead. It was alleged by the residents to be a nuisance. *Held*, that the statutory authority by which the managers acted was no defence. Lord Selborne L.C. said[78]: "The result is: (1) that this Act does not necessarily require anything to be done under it which might not be done without causing a nuisance; (2) that as to those things which may or may not be done under it, there is no evidence on the face of the Act that the legislature supposed it to be impossible for any of them to be done (if they were done at all) somewhere and under some circumstances, without creating a nuisance; and (3) that the legislature has manifested no intention that any of these optional powers, as to asylums, should be exercised at the expense of . . . private rights . . . [N]o place, or limit of space, is defined within which the establishment of such an asylum is made lawful." Lord Watson said[79]: "The respondents did not dispute that if the appellants . . . had been . . . expressly empowered to build the identical hospital which they have erected at Hampstead, upon the very site which it now occupies, and that with a view to its being used for the treatment of patients suffering from smallpox, the respondents would not be entitled to the judgment which they have obtained."
>
> *Allen* v. *Gulf Oil Refining Ltd*.[80] Gulf were authorised by a private Act of Parliament to construct an oil refinery on certain land. The House of Lords held that this was sufficient to confer on Gulf immunity from proceedings for any nuisance which might be the inevitable result of constructing a refinery on the land, however carefully sited, constructed and operated. Unlike the situation in *Metropolitan Asylum District* v. *Hill, supra*, the statute in question here specified the land on which the works were to be constructed.[81]

Whether functions are "imperative" or "permissive"

In *Metropolitan Asylum District* v. *Hill, supra*, Lord Watson stated[82]:

> "If the order of the legislature can be implemented without nuisance, they cannot, in my opinion, plead the protection of the statute; and, on the other hand, it is insufficient for their protection that what is contemplated by the statute cannot be done without nuisance, unless they are also able to show that the legislature has directed it to be done. Where the terms of the statute are not imperative, but permissive, when it is left to the discretion of the persons empowered to determine whether the general powers committed to them shall be put into execution or not, I think the fair inference is that the legislature

---

[77] (1881) 6 App. Cas. 193.
[78] At p. 201.
[79] At p. 212.
[80] [1981] A.C. 1001. See also *Tate & Lyle Food and Distribution Ltd*. v. *Greater London Council* [1983] 2 A.C. 509.
[81] See Lord Diplock at p. 1014.
[82] At p. 213.

intended that discretion to be exercised in strict conformity with private rights . . . ."

This statement has been influential, but is not a strict rule. Certainly, the presence of a discretion as to the execution of powers makes it more difficult to establish a defence of statutory authority, but it does not make it impossible.[83]

The presence of a "compensation clause"

Many statutes contain express provision for the payment of compensa- **10-22**
tion to persons who are affected by authorised works. The presence of a "compensation clause" will normally indicate that the legislature did authorise the performance of acts which would otherwise be tortious, but that the only remedy in respect of such acts is that provided by the clause. Hence, an injunction would not be available; compensation would not be obtainable in an action for damages at common law, but only under the statutory procedure. The absence of a compensation clause makes it more difficult to establish a defence of statutory authority, given that the plaintiff in such a case would be without a remedy of any description.

Marriage v. *East Norfolk Rivers Catchment Board.*[84] The Board had dredged the River Waveney in the exercise of a statutory power and had deposited the spoil on the south bank, raising the level of the bank. This prevented the water at a time of flood from escaping over the south bank as had happened before, and as a consequence a by-pass channel on the north side received an abnormal spate, which swept away the plaintiff's bridge. The plaintiff claimed an injunction and damages for nuisance, alternatively for negligence. *Held*, the injury was of the kind contemplated by the Act, and the plaintiff's sole remedy was therefore a claim for compensation under section 34(3) of the Land Drainage Act 1930. Singleton L.J. said[85]: "Wide powers are given to the board, and it is clear that they have a discretion as to what work they shall undertake, and when; and, speaking generally, the way or manner in which they shall perform the work is left to them. It is equally clear from the nature of the work that the doing of it may cause nuisance and damage to a number of people. One cannot interfere with the course of a river . . . without causing upset: the operation of dredging or cleansing a river or a ditch results in soil which has to be put somewhere, and that may create a nuisance. This was recognised by Parliament and s. 34 subsection 3 provides [the remedy]."
    Jenkins L.J.[86] drew a distinction "between (a) statutory powers to execute some particular work or carry on some particular undertaking (for example, the construction and operation of the reservoir, in *Geddis* v. *Proprietors of Bann Reservoir*,[87] the provision of hospitals, in *Metropolitan Asylum District Managers* v. *Hill*,[88] and the construction and operation of the generating station in *Manchester Corporation* v. *Farnworth*[89]) and (b) statutory powers to execute a

---

[83] See, *e.g. Dormer* v. *Newcastle-upon-Tyne Corporation* [1940] 2 K.B. 204 and *Marriage* v. *East Norfolkk Rivers Catchment Board, infra.*
[84] [1950] 1 K.B. 284. See also § 23–23.
[85] At p. 297.
[86] At pp. 307–309.
[87] (1878) 3 App. Cas. 430.
[88] (1881) 6 App. Cas. 193.
[89] [1930] A.C. 171.

variety of works of specified descriptions in a given area (the works in question being of such a kind as necessarily to involve some degree of interference with the rights of others) and as when the body invested with the powers deem it necessary or expedient to do so in furtherance of a general duty imposed on it by the Act (for example, the powers conferred on the board in the present case ...) ... In cases of the former class, the powers are, in the absence of clear provision to the contrary in the Act, limited to the doing of the particular things authorised without infringement of the rights of others, except in so far as any such infringement may be a demonstrably necessary consequence of doing what is authorised to be done.... In cases of the latter class, such as the present, it is obvious that, if the powers are subjected to an implied limitation to the effect that they are not to be exercised so as to cause any avoidable infringement of the rights of others, the powers will in great measure be nullified and the manifest object of the Act will be largely frustrated.... The Act including, as it does, a provision for compensation ... the considerations stated seem to me to lead irresistibly to the conclusion that the intention of the Act was to make the board, acting in good faith and within their powers, the sole judge of what was necessary or proper to be done in the way of drainage operations.... "

Jenkins L.J. left open the question whether this distinction should be applied where there is no "compensation clause."

The absence of a compensation clause is not, however, conclusive.[90]

The presence of a "nuisance clause"

10-23   Several statutes contain express provisions retaining liability for nuisance. These will negative any defence of statutory authority, but have also been interpreted as requiring a plaintiff to prove fault, thus excluding any liability under the rule in *Rylands* v. *Fletcher*[91] or any strict liability in nuisance, although in either case perhaps only where the liability relates to the performance of a statutory duty as distinct from the exercise of a statutory power.[92] Two cases where, as a matter of interpretation, "nuisance clauses" have been held not to relate to the acts in question are *Manchester Corporation* v. *Farnworth*,[93] and *Dormer* v. *Newcastle-upon-Tyne Corporation*.[94]

The onus of proof

10-24   It is clear that the onus of establishing a defence of statutory authority lies on the public body concerned.

> *Manchester Corporation* v. *Farnworth*.[95] A private Act empowered the corporation to establish an electricity generating station on a certain site. The

---

[90] *Edgington* v. *Swindon Corporation* [1939] 1 K.B. 86; *Allen* v. *Gulf Oil Refining Ltd.* [1981] A.C. 1001 at p. 1016.

[91] (1869) L.R. 3 H.L. 330. See, *e.g. Smeaton* v. *Ilford Corporation* [1954] Ch. 450 at p. 477 (see also § 16–11) and *Dunne* v. *North Western Gas Board* [1964] 2 Q.B. 806.

[92] *Per* Webster J. in *Department of Transport* v. *North West Water Authority* [1984] A.C. 336 at p. 344, approved by the House of Lords: [1984] A.C. 336 at pp. 359–360. See also § 10–24.

[93] [1930] A.C. 171.

[94] [1940] 2 K.B. 204.

[95] [1930] A.C. 171.

plaintiff, a farmer, sought an injunction and damages in respect of the damage to his property from sulphur fumes emitted by the station. *Held,* damages were to be awarded, and an injunction granted (after a one year suspension). The injunction would be dissolved, and damages would cease to be payable when the corporation established that they had exhausted all reasonable modes of preventing mischief to the plaintiff, and undertook to adopt "the most effective of these modes until they have replaced them by other reasonable but more effective modes of prevention which may thereafter be discovered. . . ." Viscount Dunedin said[96]: "When Parliament has authorised a certain thing to be made or done at a certain place, there can be no action for nuisance caused by the making or doing of that thing if the nuisance is the inevitable result of the making or doing so authorised. The onus of proving that the result is inevitable is on those who wish to escape liability for nuisance, but the criterion for inevitability is not what is theoretically possible but what is possible according to the state of scientific knowledge at the time, having also in view a certain commonsense appreciation, which cannot be rigidly defined, of practical feasibility in view of the situation and of expense. It is true that in this case we can hold so far that by their callous indifference in planning the construction of the station to all but its own efficiency, the defendants have not discharged the onus incumbent on them." Viscount Sumner concluded: "that the defendants have not shown that a generating station . . . could not have been erected then and cannot be used now without causing a nuisance, but that they have failed to show that they have used all reasonable diligence and taken all reasonable steps and precautions to prevent their operations from being a nuisance. . . . "

The overall position was summarised as follows by Webster J. in *Department of Transport* v. *North West Water Authority*[97]:

"1. In the absence of negligence, a body is not liable for a nuisance which is attributable to the exercise by it of a duty imposed upon it by statute.[98] 2. It is not liable in those circumstances even if by statute it is expressly made liable, or not exempted from liability, for nuisance.[99] 3. In the absence of negligence, a body is not liable for a nuisance which is attributable to the exercise by it of a power conferred by statute if, by statute, it is not expressly either made liable, or not exempted from liability, for nuisance.[1] 4. A body is liable for a nuisance attributable by it to the exercise of a power conferred by statute, even without negligence, if by statute it is expressly either made liable, or not exempted from liability, for nuisance.[2]

In these rules, references to absence of negligence are references to: 'the qualification, or condition, that the statutory powers are exercised without 'negligence'—that word here being used in a special sense so as to require the undertaker, as a condition of obtaining immunity from action, to carry out the work and conduct the operation with all reasonable regard and care for the interest of other persons . . .': see *Allen* v. *Gulf Oil Refining Ltd.*[3]

---

[96] At p. 183.
[97] [1984] A.C. 336 at p. 344.
[98] *Hammond* v. *Vestry of St. Pancras* (1874) L.R. 9 C.P. 316.
[99] *Stretton's Derby Brewery Co.* v. *Mayor of Derby* [1894] 1 Ch. 431; *Smeaton* v. *Ilford Corporation* [1954] Ch. 450.
[1] *Midwood & Co. Ltd.* v. *Manchester Corporation* [1905] 2 K.B. 597; *Longhurst* v. *Metropolitan Water Board* [1948] 2 All E.R. 834; *Dunne* v. *North Western Gas Board* [1964] 2 Q.B. 806.
[2] *Charing Cross Electricity Supply Co.* v. *Hydraulic Power Co.* [1914] 3 K.B. 772.
[3] [1981] A.C. 1001, *per* Lord Wilberforce, at p. 1011.

References to nuisance are to be taken as references either to liability in nuisance simpliciter, or to liability under the rule in *Rylands* v. *Fletcher*.'[4]

These propositions were expressly approved by the House of Lords.[5] It should be noted, however, that as the House held the nuisance in question to be attributable to the performance of a statutory duty, the principles stated to be applicable in cases of statutory powers are *obiter*.

C. NEGLIGENCE IN THE PERFORMANCE OF STATUTORY FUNCTIONS

10-25 In situations where a private citizen or corporation would be liable in negligence, the mere fact that the defendant is a local authority of itself makes no difference to liability. The defence of statutory authority will rarely if ever be available.

> *Geddis* v. *Proprietors of the Bann Reservoir*.[6] The defendants, acting under statutory authority, constructed a reservoir. They neglected to cleanse a channel leading from the reservoir, although they had statutory power to do so, with the result that the plaintiff's land was flooded. *Held*, the defendants were liable. Lord Blackburn stated[7]: "It is now thoroughly well established that no action will lie for doing that which the legislature has authorised, if it be done without negligence, although it does occasion damage to anyone; but an action does lie for doing that which the legislature has authorised if it be done negligently. And I think that if by a reasonable exercise of the powers, either given by statute to the promoters, or which they have at common law, the damage could be prevented, it is, within this rule, 'negligence' not to make such reasonable exercise of their powers."

Many well-known cases in the law of negligence in fact involve local authorities as defendants. In *Fisher* v. *Ruislip-Northwood Urban District Council*,[8] the council was held liable where it built an air raid shelter in the road but left it unlit at night so that a motorist collided with it. In *Carmarthenshire County Council* v. *Lewis*,[9] the council was held liable where precautions were not taken to prevent a four-year-old child straying from school into the highway, with the result that a lorry driver was killed when he swerved to avoid him. In *Rimmer* v. *Liverpool City Council*[10] the council was held liable for constructing a flat with an interior glass panel of insufficient thickness. Other examples include cases on occupiers' liability[11] and negligent misstatement.[12]

The position is more complex where a public authority is performing functions not generally undertaken by private citizens. Here it may be difficult to establish that the authority owes a duty of care. In recent cases,

---

[4] (1868) L.R. 3 H.L. 330.
[5] [1984] A.C. 336 at pp. 359–360.
[6] (1878) 3 H.L. 430.
[7] At pp. 455, 456.
[8] [1945] K.B. 584.
[9] [1955] A.C. 549.
[10] [1985] Q.B. 1.
[11] §§ 10–36, *et seq.*
[12] § 10–41.

the courts have shown a greater willingness to hold that such duties are owed, taking into account the nature of the statutory responsibilities of the authority, and questions of policy.[13] However, this may to an extent be balanced by a tendency to restrict liability for allegedly negligent discretionary decisions to situations where the exercise of discretion is *ultra vires*.[14]

D. Failure to Perform Statutory Duties

It is not possible to state concisely the principle on which an action for **10-26** damages can be sustained against a local authority for a breach of a statutory duty, or a failure to exercise a statutory power. The cases on this subject indicate clearly the circumstances in which an action will *not* lie—indeed the grounds for excluding such an action are so comprehensive that it is frequently said that an action for damages will not lie against an authority for nonfeasance, *i.e.* for failure to do an act which ought to have been done. This, it is submitted, goes too far. Vaughan Williams L.J. said in *Groves* v. *Wimborne*[15] (an action to recover damages for an alleged breach of a statutory duty to fence machinery):

> " ... it cannot be doubted that, where a statute provides for the performance by certain persons of a particular duty, and someone belonging to a class of persons for whose benefit and protection the statute imposes the duty is injured by failure to perform it, prima facie, and if there be nothing to the contrary, an action by the person so injured will lie against the person who has so failed to perform the duty."

It is clear from the cases, however, that certain stringent tests must be applied. It must first be ascertained whether the relevant statute confers a power or imposes a duty—whether the function is one which the council may undertake or not, as it chooses, or one which the authority has an absolute duty in law to carry out.

Secondly, the relevant statute as a whole must be examined to see whether a remedy for the injury complained of is prescribed. It may be taken as a general rule that the provision of a specific remedy excludes a common law action in tort. Two cases are cited: in the first it was held that the prescribed remedy excluded all others; in the second that, *taking the statute as a whole*, the common law remedy (*i.e.* an action for damages) was available.

---

[13] See *Home Office* v. *Dorset Yacht Co.* [1970] A.C. 1004; *Ministry of Housing and Local Government* v. *Sharp* [1970] 2 Q.B. 223; *Dutton* v. *Bognor Regis Urban District Council* [1972] 1 Q.B. 373; *Anns* v. *Merton London Borough Council* [1978] A.C. 728 and *Page Motors Limited* v. *Epsom and Ewell Borough Council* (1981) 80 L.G.R. 337.

[14] *Home Office* v. *Dorset Yacht Co., supra, per* Lords Reid and Diplock; *Anns* v. *Merton London Borough Council, supra*; see §§ 10–33, *et seq.*

[15] [1898] 2 Q.B. 402 at p. 415.

Hesketh v. *Birmingham Corporation.*[16] The corporation owned a sewer which ran alongside a natural stream. A number of storm water outlets were made in the sewer to relieve pressure on it in times of heavy rain by discharging the surplus water into the stream. At the time the outlets were made the stream was of sufficient capacity to carry off all the water that was discharged into it, but in course of time, owing to the neighbouring land having been almost entirely built over, it had become insufficient. After a heavy storm so much surplus water was discharged from the sewer into the stream that adjoining land was flooded and certain houses of the plaintiff were damaged. *Held*, the defendant's neglect to enlarge the capacity of the stream or otherwise improve their drainage system to meet the requirements of the increased population was not negligence for which an action would lie; it was nonfeasance, the remedy, if any, for which was by an application to the Local Government Board under section 299 of the Public Health Act 1874, and assessment of compensation by arbitration under section 308.

Read v. *Croydon Corporation.*[17] The corporation was under a statutory duty to maintain a supply of pure and wholesome water, but it failed in this and the water supply became contaminated with typhoid bacilli. A ratepayer's daughter, who lived in his house, contracted typhoid fever. The ratepayer claimed damages for expenses to which he had been put by his daughter's illness, and his daughter claimed damages for pain and suffering. *Held*, that on a proper construction of the Act, an action lay for damages, founded on a breach of statutory duty, *at the suit of the ratepayer*. Stable J. said[18]: "While there is no doubt that, for breaches of some of the statutory duties imposed by the Waterworks Clauses Act, the penalty (provided in the Act) is exclusive, it is difficult to believe that the legislature intended that it should be exclusive in the case of each breach of every duty under the Act. I find it impossible to hold, unless compelled by authority so to do, that the legislature intended that there should be one remedy, and one remedy only, equally applicable to so trivial a breach as the failure to maintain a certain pressure of water behind a fire plug and to a deliberate dereliction of duty resulting in the destruction of a large community by the supply of poisonous water."

10-27   It will be noted that the court in the *Croydon* case held that the action would lie *on the proper construction of the Act*. The court will look at the general scope of the Act, the nature of the statutory duty, the nature of the injuries likely to arise from a breach of that duty, and the amount of the penalty imposed.[19]

In some cases it has been suggested that the existence of a statutory remedy excludes any private right of action for breach of the statutory duty in question *only* where there is *nonfeasance*, and not where there is *misfeasance*. It is submitted that this is clearly correct where the allegations of misfeasance amounts to an allegation that the defendant

---

[16] [1924] 1 K.B. 260. For other examples of cases where the existence of a statutory remedy has been held to exclude a private right of action, see *Pasmore* v. *Oswaldtwistle Urban District Council* [1898] A.C. 387; *Watt* v. *Kesteven County Council* [1955] 1 Q.B. 408; *Bradbury* v. *Enfield London Borough Council* [1967] 1 W.L.R. 1311 at p. 1324; *Wyatt* v. *Hillingdon London Borough Council* (1978) 76 L.G.R. 727; *Strable* v. *Borough Council of Dartford* [1984] J.P.L. 329.

[17] [1938] 4 All E.R. 631.

[18] At p. 652.

[19] *Per* Lord Cairns in *Atkinson* v. *Newcastle Co.* (1877) 2 Ex. D. 441. See also *Cutler* v. *Wandsworth Stadium Ltd.* [1949] A.C. 398, *per* Lord Normand at p. 413.

authority has tortiously infringed the legal rights of the plaintiff apart from any consideration of the statutory provisions,[20] or where the alleged misfeasance comprises a positive act *ultra vires* the authority (and *a fortiori* a positive act expressly prohibited by the statute).[21] However, where there is merely an incompetent attempt to perform the statutory duty, the case is on proper analysis one of nonfeasance: the essence of the plaintiff's complaint is still that he has not received the benefit of performance of the duty in question.

The alternative remedies discussed in these cases were expressly given in the relevant statute. The possibility of seeking judicial review will not exclude an action for damages.[22]

Thirdly, if the duty is an imperative one and no special remedy is provided then a further test must be applied. It must be ascertained whether a duty to give the service is owed to the community at large or to persons of whom the plaintiff is one. If an action is to lie the duty must be to individuals of whom the plaintiff is one. This principle is illustrated in *Read* v. *Croydon Corporation*. It will be observed from the words in italics in the note of the case above that, in so far as the action was founded on a breach of statutory duty, only the ratepayer could sue, for on the construction of the Act the statutory duty was owed to a class of persons of whom the ratepayer was one, but the daughter was not.

If these tests are satisfied—if injury is sustained through a failure of a **10-28** local authority to exercise a *duty*, an imperative duty that is, and if that duty is owed to the aggrieved person, as opposed to the community at large, and if the statute itself provides no adequate remedy for such default, then an action for damages may lie at the suit of the injured party.

> *Reffell* v. *Surrey County Council.*[23] A girl hurrying along a corridor in a controlled school put out her hand to stop a swing door that was swinging towards her, and she was injured. The plaintiff succeeded in a claim for damages for breach of statutory duty under section 10 of the Education Act 1944, and regulation 51 of the Standards for School Premises Regulations 1959. Veale J. asked, at pp. 362, 363, three questions (drawn from *Charlesworth on Negligence*, 4th ed., at p. 454) in relation to the facts of the case. First, was the action brought in respect of the kind of harm which the statute was intended to prevent? Secondly, was the person bringing the action one of the class which the statute desired to protect? Thirdly, was the special remedy by the statute adequate for the protection of the person injured? He found that the first two

---

[20] The *Pride of Derby* case (§ 10–29) may be an example of this.
[21] *Gateshead Union* v. *Durham County Council* [1918] 1 Ch. 146; *Wood* v. *Ealing London Borough Council* [1967] Ch. 364, 386; *Bradbury* v. *Enfield London Borough Council* [1967] 1 W.L.R. 1311 at p. 1326; *Meade* v. *Haringey Council* [1979] 1 W.L.R. 637; *R* v. *Secretary of State for the Environment, ex p. Ward* [1984] 1 W.L.R. 834.
[22] *Thornton* v. *Kirklees Metropolitan Borough Council* [1979] Q.B. 626.
[23] [1964] 1 W.L.R. 358. It was held in *Thornton* v. *Kirklees Metropolitan Borough Council* [1979] Q.B. 626 that since the Housing (Homeless Persons) Act 1977 imposed a duty on a housing authority for the benefit of a specified category of persons and provided no special remedy, an action in damages would lie against an authority which failed to provide accommodation in an appropriate case.

questions were answered in the affirmative, and the third in the negative. The provisions imposed an absolute duty, the test of breach was an objective test, *viz.*, that there would be a breach of duty if safety were not reasonably assured, and, on the facts, safety had not been reasonably assured. The authority was also liable in negligence at common law, since it knew that the door was a real danger and was a reasonably foreseeable risk.

10-29   In each of the cases so far considered, the plaintiff either based his action on negligence, alleging that a failure on the part of an authority to perform its statutory duty amounted in itself to negligence; or claimed damages for breach of statutory duty as a cause of action distinct from negligence. But different considerations may well arise if an action is based on nuisance, for a plaintiff may have a right of action notwithstanding the presence of a remedy in the relevant statute if he suffers injury through nuisance, even though it is brought about through an authority's inactivity. This proposition emerges from *Pride of Derby and Derbyshire Angling Association* v. *British Celanese*,[24] a case dealing with sewers and sewerage systems. The rule clearly applies where a system has been constructed by an authority or "adopted" by an authority within the principles laid down in *Sedleigh-Denfield* v. *O'Callaghan*[25]; its application is doubtful where an authority has "inherited" drains and sewers, and those drains and sewers constitute a nuisance by reason only that they have ceased to deal adequately with the sewage of the authority's area, the local authority not having itself been at fault except that it has not used its statutory powers to enlarge the sewerage system.

> *Pride of Derby and Derbyshire Angling Association* v. *British Celanese*. [25a] One of the defendants, the Derby Corporation, had polluted the River Derwent by discharging insufficiently treated sewage into the river. It was argued on behalf of the corporation that the sewerage system, which had been constructed in accordance with the statutory powers, did not cause pollution at the time it was completed. The present pollution had resulted from the increase in the population of Derby which had caused the system to become inadequate. The council, it was contended, could not be made liable since the injury was the result of nonfeasance. *Held*, as regards sewers and drains it was necessary to keep in mind the possibility of two distinct causes of action, namely, nuisance and negligence. As regards negligence, it may be that nonfeasance, in the sense of failing to perform some positive statutory duty, did not give rise to a cause of action for negligence against the local authority in respect of its sewerage system. In regard to nuisance, however, the question of nonfeasance as distinct from misfeasance had no real relevance. Evershed M.R. said[26]: "Now it is clear that if a public authority so exercises any of its functions as to cause a private nuisance to any person, the authority is liable . . . to be sued in these courts, . . . unless it can rely upon some statute as providing, by express language or necessary or proper inference, a defence to such an action. So much appears, for example, from *Metropolitan Asylum District* v. *Hill*."[27]

---

[24] [1953] Ch. 149, see also *Page Motors Limited* v. *Epsom and Ewell Borough Council, supra.*
[25] [1940] A.C. 880.
[25a] *Supra*, n.24.
[26] At p. 163.
[27] (1881) 6 App. Cas. 193.

It appears, however, that there was an element of *misfeasance* in this case, an active dealing with the sewage which came into the council's works. Denning L.J.[28] based his decision on the fact that

"When the increased sewage came into their sewage disposal works . . . they took it under their charge, treated it in their works, and poured the effluent into the River Derwent. . . . Their act in pouring a polluting effluent into the river makes them guilty of nuisance."

A plaintiff claiming damages from a local authority for *failure to carry out a statutory duty*, if he relies solely on the *Derby* case, may well be faced with the substantial point that, on the facts, this case was not wholly one of nonfeasance. The law on this topic is by no means settled.

A statutory duty may be held not to be absolute, but to be a duty to exercise care.[29]

Until the coming into force of section 1 of the Highways (Miscellane-   **10-30** ous Provisions) Act 1961, the failure of a highway authority to perform the duties of repair and maintenance imposed by the common law or by statute was held not to give rise to a liability to pay damages to persons injured as a result. This much-criticised immunity was not extended to other authorities,[30] and was subsequently abrogated by section 1(1) of the 1961 Act. Section 1(2) provided that in an action against a public authority for damage resulting from their failure to maintain a highway it shall be a defence to prove that the authority has taken such care as is reasonable in the circumstances to secure that the part of the highway to which the action relates was not dangerous for traffic. The test of whether a highway is "dangerous" for these purposes is whether the condition of the road is foreseeably dangerous "to traffic being driven in the way normally expected on that highway."[31]

Parliament is frequently exhorted to indicate expressly whether failure to perform a statutory duty may lead to liability in damages. Occasionally this is done. Section 1(5) of the Refuse Disposal (Amenity) Act 1978 reads:

"No action shall lie against a local authority in respect of damage resulting from their failure to carry out their duty under this section [to provide places where the public may dispose of refuse]; but if the Secretary of State is satisfied, after holding a local inquiry, that a local authority have failed to carry out that duty he may by order require the authority to take such steps for carrying it out as are specified in the order."

---

[28] At p. 191.
[29] See *Sephton* v. *Lancashire River Board* [1962] 1 W.L.R. 623; *Rippingale Farms* v. *Black Sluice Internal Drainage Board* [1963] 1 W.L.R. 1347; *Ministry of Housing and Local Government* v. *Sharp* [1970] 2 Q.B. 223.
[30] See, *e.g. Att.-Gen.* v. *St. Ives Rural District Council* [1960] 1 Q.B. 312.
[31] *Per* Sachs L.J. in *Rider* v. *Rider* [1973] 1 All E.R. 294 at p. 300. See also *Griffiths* v. *Liverpool Corporation* [1967] 1 Q.B. 374; *Meggs* v. *Liverpool Corporation* [1968] 1 W.L.R. 689; *Littler* v. *Liverpool Corporation* [1968] 2 All E.R. 343; *Burnside* v. *Emerson* [1968] 1 W.L.R. 1490; *Haydon* v. *Kent County Council* [1978] Q.B. 343; *Bird* v. *Pearce and Another, Somerset County Council* [1979] R.T.R. 369; and *Tarrant* v. *Rowland* [1979] R.T.R. 144. See also § 14–31.

E. FAILURE TO EXERCISE DISCRETIONARY POWERS

10-31   Where the legislature has given a local authority a power to act for the benefit of individual citizens, or for the community at large, but has not imposed a duty so to act, it follows logically that the authority should not normally be liable in damages where it chooses not to exercise that power in a particular case. The fact that it has a discretion whether to exercise the power means that it is legally entitled not to do so if it so wishes.

> *Sheppard* v. *Glossop Corporation.*[32] The council resolved that street lamps be extinguished at about 9 p.m. each night in the interests of economy. Because a lamp was unlit the plaintiff strayed onto private land and then fell onto the highway from the private land over a retaining wall at a point where the level of the street was lower than the private land. The plaintiff sued the council for damages. *Held*, that section 161 of the Public Health Act 1875 conferred on urban authorities a discretion, but imposed on them no obligation, to light the streets in their districts; consequently that the defendants, who had begun, were not bound to continue to light the street; and that having done nothing to make the street dangerous they were under no obligation, whether by lighting or otherwise, to give warning of danger. The defendants were not, therefore, liable.

Similarly, there should normally be no liability where there is a delay before the power is exercised.

10-32   There is a House of Lords authority to the effect that where a power to confer a benefit is incompetently exercised, an authority will be liable for "fresh damage" which would not have occurred had the power not been exercised at all, but not merely for failure to confer the benefit in question. The authority's intervention must in some respect make the situation worse, and damages will only be payable in respect of the "worsening."

> *East Suffolk Rivers Catchment Board* v. *Kent.*[33] An exceptionally high spring tide caused the River Deben to overflow its banks and many pastures were flooded. The trial judge found that the Board's staff had so inefficiently carried out repair works that it took them 178 days, whereas with reasonable skill the gap should have been closed in 14 days. The Board had no statutory *duty* to repair the breach but had a statutory power to do this. *Held*, the Board could not be made liable in damages. Lord Romer said[34]: "Where a statutory authority is entrusted with a mere power it cannot be made liable for any damage sustained by a member of the public by reason of a failure to exercise that power. If in the exercise of their discretion they embark upon an execution of that power, the only duty they owe to any member of the public is not thereby to add to the damages that he would have suffered had they done nothing. So long as they exercise their discretion honestly, it is for them to determine the method by which and the time within which and the time during which the power shall be exercised; and they cannot be made liable, except to the extent that I have just mentioned, for any damage that would have been avoided had they exercised their discretion in a more reasonable way." Given

[32] [1921] 3 K.B. 132.
[33] [1941] A.C. 74.
[34] At p. 102.

that the duty was limited to the avoidance of extra damage there was no causal link between any breach of that duty and the damage of which the plaintiff complained, namely the continuance of the inundation for 164 extra days.

The principles applied in the *East Suffolk* case are illustrations of the general reluctance of the courts to impose duties of affirmative action within the framework of the law of negligence. There are, however, certain situations where such duties are well established, and a local authority will be liable here just as other defendants would be. For example, the law requires persons who exercise control over others to exercise care (1) to protect them from harm, and (2) to prevent them from causing harm to third parties. Thus, a local authority will owe a duty to take reasonable affirmative steps to protect children in its care or attending its schools,[35] and to prevent such children causing harm to others.[36] The law also requires the occupiers of premises to take reasonable affirmative action to prevent visitors suffering harm from defects in the premises (see also below, paras. 10–36 *et seq.*), Even where there is no special relationship of this sort, someone in the position of the plaintiff in the *East Suffolk* case might be able to recover damages if he had acted to his detriment, reasonably expecting that the authority would perform its task competently. In the *East Suffolk* case itself, Slesser L.J. in the Court of Appeal found for the plaintiff on this basis.[37] However, it was held in the House of Lords that detrimental reliance had not been established on the facts as pleaded.[38]

The decision of the House of Lords in *Anns* v. *Merton London Borough* **10-33** *Council*[39] introduces qualifications to the two propositions: (1) that a failure to exercise a power to confer a benefit will not lead to liability in damages, and (2) that a careless exercise of such a power will lead to liability in damages only in respect of extra damage. A step in that direction had previously been taken by the Court of Appeal in *Dutton* v. *Bognor Regis Urban District Council.*[40] Both cases concern the powers of local authorities in the inspection of building work in progress to ensure compliance with building by-laws made under the Public Health Acts. The relevant requirements are now contained in building regulations made by the Secretary of State under section 1 of the Building Act 1984.

Anns v. *Merton London Borough Council.*[41] The Public Health Act 1936 gave powers to local authorities to make building by-laws under which they had power to supervise the construction of buildings in their area to ensure compliance with standards laid down by the by-laws. In 1962 the predecessor council of the defendants approved plans under the by-laws for a block of

---

[35] *e.g. Carmarthenshire County Council* v. *Lewis* [1955] A.C. 549; *Shepherd* v. *Essex County Council* (1913) 29 T.L.R. 303; *Fryer* v. *Salford Corporation* [1937] 1 All E.R. 617.
[36] *e.g. Ricketts* v. *Erith Borough Council* [1943] 2 All E.R. 629.
[37] See [1940] 1 K.B. at pp. 327–328 and *cf.* MacKinnon L.J. at p. 333.
[38] [1941] A.C. 74, *per* Lord Porter at p. 107; *cf.* Lord Romer at p. 97.
[39] [1978] A.C. 728.
[40] [1972] 1 Q.B. 373.
[41] *Supra*, n. 39.

maisonettes, which plans showed foundations of 3 feet or deeper. The block was completed in 1962. Cracks and other defects appeared in 1970. The foundations proved to be only 2 feet 6 inches deep. The plaintiffs claimed that the defects were attributable to inadequate foundations, and claimed damages against the defendants alleging negligence in approving the foundations and/or in failing to inspect under the by-laws. The House of Lords determined a preliminary issue as to whether a duty of care was owed by the council in law. Lord Wilberforce summarised his main conclusions as follows[42] (with the concurrence of three of the other four members of the House of Lords). He said "I would hold:

1. that *Dutton* v. *Bognor Regis Urban District Council*[43] was in the result rightly decided. The correct legal basis for the decision must be taken to be that established by your Lordships in this appeal;
2. that the question whether the defendant council by itself or its officers came under a duty of care toward the plaintiffs must be considered in relation to the powers, duties and discretions arising under the Public Health Act 1936;
3. that the defendant council would not be guilty of a breach of duty in not carrying out inspection of the foundations of the block unless it were shown (*a*) not properly to have exercised its discretion as to the making of inspections, and (*b*) to have failed to exercise reasonable care in its acts or omissions to secure that the by-laws applicable to the foundations of the block were complied with;
4. that the defendant council would be liable to the respondents for breach of duty if it were proved that its inspector, having assumed the duty of inspecting the foundations, and acting otherwise than in the bona fide exercise of any discretion under the statute, did not exercise reasonable care to ensure that the by-laws applicable to the foundations were complied with. . . . "

Lord Wilberforce held that a prima facie duty of care arose where "as between the alleged wrongdoer and the person who has suffered damage there is a sufficient relationship of proximity or neighbourhood such that, in the reasonable contemplation of the former, carelessness on his part may be likely to cause damage to the latter." However, it was also necessary to examine the public powers and duties of the authority to see whether there were considerations which ought to negative, or limit the scope of the duty. In a passage of great significance his Lordship stated[44]:

"Most, indeed probably all, statutes relating to public authorities or public bodies, contain in them a large area of policy. The courts call this 'discretion' meaning that the decision is one for the authority or body to make, and not for the courts. Many statutes also prescribe or at least presuppose the practical execution of policy decisions: a convenient description of this is to say that in addition to the area of policy or discretion, there is an operational area. Although this distinction between the policy area and the operational area is convenient, and illuminating, it is probably a distinction of degree; many 'operational' powers or duties have in them some element of 'discretion.' It can safely be said that the more 'operational' a power or duty may be, the easier it is to superimpose upon it a common law duty of care.

I do not think that it is right to limit this to a duty to avoid causing extra or additional damage beyond what must be expected to arise from the exercise of

---

[42] At p. 760.
[43] *Supra*, n. 40.
[44] At p. 754.

the power or duty. That may be correct when the act done under the statute *inherently* must adversely *affect* the interest of individuals. But many other acts can be done without causing any harm to anyone—indeed may be directed to preventing harm from occurring. In these cases the duty is the normal one of taking care to avoid harm to those likely to be affected."

The decision in *Anns* v. *Merton London Borough Council*[45] is important in   **10-34** a number of respects. Two are of significance here. First, it established that local authorities owe a duty to protect the owners or occupiers of buildings from losses inflicted on them by builders as a result of defective building work: reasonable care must be taken to exercise the powers of control over building work in order to ensure that buildings are constructed in accordance with the relevant regulations and plans. There may, accordingly, be liability both where there is no inspection and where an inspection is carelessly carried out. Secondly, this duty is subject to the qualification that where the impugned decision to exercise or not to exercise the powers, or decision as to the method of exercise, falls within the "policy" or "discretionary" area, the plaintiff must show not merely that there was a failure to take reasonable care but also that the decision was *ultra vires*.[46] The underlying principles were explained as follows by Robert Goff L.J. in *Fellowes* v. *Rother District Council*[47]:

"The underlying basis appears to be that citizens are entitled to expect that powers conferred on public authorities will be exercised, and entitled therefore to expect that such powers will be exercised with due care, subject to being unable to found a cause of action on an act done within the limit of a discretion bona fide exercised and to the ordinary criteria of an action in negligence being fulfilled. Such powers cannot be regarded as mere liberties, or as mere authority to invade the proprietary interests of another, as under private Acts of Parliament. So, although a mere omission by a public authority to exercise a statutory power will not ordinarily be actionable by a private citizen as such (being within the area of discretion), nevertheless the local authority may be responsible for the consequences of a negligent act done in a purported exercise of the power (but not in fact within the limits of a discretion bona fide exercised) even though no fresh or additional damage is caused."

Furthermore, the courts appear to regard this qualification as relevant   **10-35** not only in cases of the *Kent, Dutton* and *Anns* type, where the complaint is of an authority's omission to confer a benefit upon or protect the plaintiff, but in all cases where the plaintiff alleges that there has been a negligent exercise or non-exercise of a statutory discretion.[48]

The distinction between the "policy" and "operational" areas can be difficult to draw. Recent judgments have provided some indication of

---

[45] *Supra.*
[46] The principles under which an exercise or non-exercise of discretion will be held to be *ultra vires* are set out at §§ 12–05—12–26.
[47] [1983] 1 All E.R. 513 at p. 522.
[48] See, *e.g. Department of Health and Social Security* v. *Kinnear* (1984) 134 New L.J. 886 where actions in negligence against the Department in respect of the policy of promoting immunisation against whooping cough were struck out as the policy could not be shown to be *ultra vires*.

how the distinction will be applied to the facts of particular cases. In the *Anns* case itself, Lord Wilberforce stated[49] that the duty of a building inspector was "heavily operational" although "there may be a discretionary element in its exercise, discretionary as to the time and manner of inspection, and the techniques to be used." His Lordship regarded the *Kent* case "as an example ... where operational activity —at the breach of the wall—was still well within a discretionary area, so that the plaintiff's task in contending for a duty of care was a difficult one."[50] In *Bird v. Pearce, Somerset County Council (Third Party)*[51] the obliteration of road markings and the failure to put up temporary warnings after resurfacing were held to be operational matters. By contrast, the decision of a highway authority to concentrate on the maintenance of roads rather than footpaths in icy conditions was held to be a policy decision in *Haydon v. Kent County Council*.[52] Indeed, it was suggested in the *Haydon* case that the "policy"/"operational" distinction had no relevance in cases of breach of statutory duty.[53]

F. Liability of Local Authorities as Occupiers of Premises in Relation to Visitors and Trespassers

10-36 The rules which regulate the duty which an occupier of premises owes to his visitors in respect of dangers due to the state of the premises are contained in the Occupiers' Liability Act 1957. These rules replace the common law rules as to the nature and extent of this duty, but the common law rules as to who is the occupier and who are the visitors remain. Stated shortly, the duty prescribed in the Act is owed to those known to the common law as invitees and licensees and the duty is the same whether a visitor falls in the first or the second of these classes. An invitee is a person who is "invited into the premises by the owner or occupier for some purpose of business or of material interest"[54]; a licensee is "a person whom the proprietor has not in any way invited—he has no interest in his being there—but he has either expressly permitted him to use his lands or, knowledge of his presence ... having been brought home to him, he has then either accorded permission or shown no practical anxiety to stop his further frequenting the lands."[55]

---

[49] At p. 755.
[50] At p. 757.
[51] [1978] R.T.R. 290. The point was not taken on appeal: [1979] R.T.R. 369.
[52] [1978] Q.B. 343 at pp. 361, 363–364. See also the *Vicar of Writtle* v. *Essex County Council* (1979) 77 L.G.R. 656; *Hallett* v. *Nicholson* 1979 S.C. 1; *Fellowes* v. *Rother District Council* [1983] 1 All E.R. 513; *West* v. *Buckinghamshire County Council* (1984) 83 L.G.R. 449.
[53] *Ibid.* per Lord Denning M.R. at p. 361. See generally, W. V. H. Rogers, *Winfield and Jolowicz on Tort* (12th ed.), pp. 83–88.
[54] *Latham* v. *Johnson* [1913] 1 K.B. 398, *per* Hamilton L.J. at p. 410.
[55] *Addie & Sons* v. *Dumbreck* [1929] A.C. 358, *per* Lord Dunedin at p. 371.

Section 2 describes the occupier's duty. **10–37**

(1) An occupier of premises owes the same duty, the "common duty of care," to all his visitors, except in so far as he is free to and does extend, restrict, modify or exclude his duty to any visitor or visitors by agreement or otherwise.

(2) The common duty of care is a duty to take such care as in all the circumstances of the case is reasonable to see that the visitor will be reasonably safe in using the premises for the purposes for which he is invited or permitted by the occupier to be there.

(3) The circumstances relevant for the present purpose include the degree of care, and want of care, which would ordinarily be looked for in such a visitor, so that (for example) in proper cases—

    (*a*)   an occupier must be prepared for children to be less careful than adults; and

    (*b*)   an occupier may expect that a person, in the exercise of his calling, will appreciate and guard against any special risks ordinarily incident to it, so far as the occupier leaves him free to do so.

(4) In determining whether the occupier of premises has discharged the common duty of care to a visitor, regard is to be had to all the circumstances, so that (for example)—

    (*a*)   where damage is caused to a visitor by a danger of which he had been warned by the occupier, the warning is not to be treated without more as absolving the occupier from liability, unless in all the circumstances it was enough to enable the visitor to be reasonably safe; and

    (*b*)   where damage is caused to a visitor by a danger due to the faulty execution of any work of construction, maintenance or repair by an independent contractor employed by the occupier, the occupier is not to be treated without more as answerable for the danger if in all the circumstances he had acted reasonably in entrusting the work to an independent contractor and had taken such steps (if any) as he reasonably ought in order to satisfy himself that the contractor was competent and that the work had been properly done.

(5) The common duty of care does not impose on an occupier any obligation to a visitor in respect of risks willingly accepted as his by the visitor (the question whether a risk was so accepted to be decided on the same principles as in other cases in which one person owes a duty of care to another).

(6) For the purposes of this section, persons who enter premises for any purpose in the exercise of a right conferred by law are to be treated as permitted by the occupier to be there for that purpose, whether they in fact have his permission or not.

These rules apply to local authorities as they apply to other occupiers of property: they would apply, for example, in the case of persons who enter public offices to transact business. Most of the cases against local authorities in this context have concerned visitors to public parks[56]; children and visitors on school premises[57]; and persons injured in council

---

[56] *e.g. Glasgow Corporation* v. *Taylor* [1922] 1 A.C. 44; *Ellis* v. *Fulham Corporation* [1938] 1 K.B. 212; *Dyer* v. *Ilfracombe Urban District Council* [1956] 1 W.L.R. 218; *Simkiss* v. *Rhondda Borough Council* (1983) 81 L.G.R. 460.

[57] *e.g. Fryer* v. *Salford Corporation* [1937] 1 All E.R. 617; *Lyes* v. *Middlesex County Council* (1962) 61 L.G.R. 443; *Reffell* v. *Surrey County Council* [1964] 1 W.L.R. 358.

houses and flats.[58] Cases decided under the common law in relation to invitees may be of some relevance as illustrations of the standard of care appropriate in particular situations.

10-38   Officers of a local authority who enter premises under a statutory power (for the purpose of inspection or to carry out works) and police officers acting on a search warrant are "visitors" and the occupier owes them the "common duty of care" as regards his premises.[59] They are to be treated as permitted by the occupier to be there for that purpose, whether they in fact have his permission or not.[60]

The attempted exclusion or restriction of liability for negligence by the use of a notice, operating either as a contractual exclusion clause[61] or as a condition attached to a licence to enter the property[62]; is now subject to the Unfair Contract Terms Act 1977 (see para. 10–11). An appropriately worded notice may, however, enable the authority to discharge the common duty of care under section 2(4)(a) of the Occupiers' Liability Act 1957, *supra*. This kind of notice is unaffected by the 1977 Act. Moreover, a notice drawing a visitor's attention to dangers may be relevant to the establishment of the defence of *volenti non fit injuria*, which is expressly preserved by section 2(5) of the 1957 Act.[63] This is to be distinguished from a notice which merely purports to "exclude or restrict liability for negligence." A person's agreement to or awareness of such a notice "is not of itself to be taken as indicating his voluntary acceptance of any risk."[64]

An occupier of property does not owe the "common duty of care" towards a trespasser—one who comes to the land without right or permission—but it has long been established that he must not set a trap deliberately to injure a trespasser, and if he does he may be liable to the trespasser in tort.[65]

10-39   The common law liability of an occupier towards a trespasser was extended by the House of Lords in *British Railways Board* v. *Herrington*,[66] where the House of Lords unanimously held the Board liable to a child who was injured when he strayed on to an electrified line through a broken fence: the stationmaster knew that children had been seen on the line and that the fence had not been repaired. Their Lordships used varying terms in formulating both (1) the circumstances in which a duty to a trespasser, commonly termed a duty of common humanity, would

---

[58] *Hawkins* v. *Coulsdon and Purley Urban District Council* [1954] 1 Q.B. 319; *Greene* v. *Chelsea Borough Council* [1954] 2 Q.B. 127; *Moloney* v. *Lambeth London Borough Council* (1966) 64 L.G.R. 440.
[59] *Salmond on the Law of Torts* (18th ed.), pp. 258–260.
[60] Occupiers' Liability Act 1957, s. 2(6).
[61] See *White* v. *Blackmore* [1972] 2 Q.B. 651.
[62] *Ashdown* v. *Samuel Williams Ltd.* [1957] 1 Q.B. 409; *White* v. *Blackmore, supra.*
[63] *Supra.*
[64] Unfair Contract Terms Act 1977, s. 2(3).
[65] *Bird* v. *Holbrook* (1828) 4 Bing. 628; 6 L.J. (o.s.) C.P. 146.
[66] [1972] A.C. 877. See also *Pannett* v. *McGuiness & Co.* [1972] 2 Q.B. 599; *Melvin* v. *Franklins Builders and another* (1972) 71 L.G.R. 142; *Penny* v. *Northampton Borough Council* (1974) 72 L.G.R. 733; *Harris* v. *Birkenhead Corporation* [1976] 1 W.L.R. 279.

arise, and (2) the content of that duty. As a result it was difficult to ascertain the precise *ratio* of the case.[67] In respect of events occurring on or after May 13, 1984, the liability of an occupier to a trespasser is regulated by section 1 of the Occupiers' Liability Act 1984, and not by the law as stated in *Herrington's* case. This section provides that an occupier of premises owes a duty to another (not being his visitor) in respect of any risk of that person suffering injury on the premises by reason of any danger due to the state of the premises or to things done or omitted to be done on them if

"(a) he is aware of the danger or has reasonable grounds to believe that it exists;
 (b) he knows or has reasonable grounds to believe that the other is in the vicinity of the danger concerned or that he may come into the vicinity of the danger (in either case, whether the other has lawful authority for being in that vicinity or not); and
 (c) the risk is one against which, in all the circumstances of the case, he may reasonably be expected to offer the other some protection."

If a duty is owed,

"the duty is to take such care as is reasonable in all the circumstances of the case to see that he does not suffer injury on the premises by reason of the danger concerned."

The duty may in an appropriate case be discharged by taking reasonable steps to warn of the danger or to discourage persons from incurring the risk. No duty is owed by virtue of these provisions to any person in respect of risks willingly accepted and a person does not by reason of any breach of the duty incur any liability in respect of any loss of or damage to property. Furthermore, no duty is owed by virtue of this section to persons using the highway and the section does not affect any duty owed to such persons. The terms "occupier" and "visitor" in this section carry the same meanings as in the Occupiers' Liability Act 1957.

Under the *Herrington* principle, it was held that it was proper to take into account the defendant's skill and resources in deciding what it was reasonable to expect of *him*,[68] unless perhaps he had created the danger himself.[69] It is not clear whether resources can be taken into account under the Occupiers' Liability Act 1984.

---

[67] See Law Commission Report No. 75, Cmnd. 6428, paras. 5–7.
[68] *British Railways Board* v. *Herrington* [1972] A.C. 877 at pp. 899, 920, 942. A similar principle applies in respect of liability in nuisance for hazards occurring on land: *Goldman* v. *Hargrave* [1967] 1 A.C. 645; *Leakey* v. *National Trust* [1980] Q.B. 485; *Page Motors Ltd.* v. *Epsom & Ewell Borough Council* (1981) 80 L.G.R. 337. In the *Page Motors* case, the Court of Appeal held that the court was not limited to considering the council's physical and financial resources only, but was entitled to take into account matters arising from their public responsibilities, such as the need to engage in a democratic process of dialogue with interested parties.
[69] *Southern Portland Cement* v. *Cooper* [1974] A.C. 623 at p. 644.

G. The Application of the Rule in Rylands v. Fletcher

10-40 It is uncertain whether the doctrine of *Rylands* v. *Fletcher*[70] is applicable to the exercise of functions by public authorities. The rule was stated by Blackburn J., in the Court of Exchequer Chamber, as "that the person who for his own purposes brings on his lands and collects and keeps there anything likely to do mischief if it escapes, must keep it in at his peril, and if he does not do so is *prima facie* answerable for all the damage which is the natural consequence of its escape."[71] It has been held that there will be no liability unless the user of the land is "non-natural."[72] In *Rickards* v. *Lothian*, Lord Moulton[73] described "non-natural" user as "some special use bringing with it increased danger to others, and ... not merely ... the ordinary use of the land or such a use as is proper for the general benefit of the community." It has been argued that the collection by a public authority of such things as sewage, water and gas for public purposes is accordingly not within the Rule, as it is "for the general benefit of the community"[74] and not for the authority's "own purposes."[75] However, other judges have taken a different view. Evershed M.R. in the *Pride of Derby* case stated that he was "not satisfied" that local authorities have a special immunity from the Rule in *Rylands* v. *Fletcher*.[76] In *Smeaton* v. *Ilford Corporation*,[77] Upjohn J. held that the collection of sewage in sewers vested in the Corporation did amount to a "non-natural" user of land, and he rejected the arguments outlined above. Nevertheless, his Lordship held that the rule did not apply in this case in view of section 31 of the Public Health Act 1936, which provided: "A local authority shall so discharge their functions under the foregoing provisions of this Part of this Act as not to create a nuisance." "That section necessarily implies, in my judgment, that, provided the defendant corporation does not create a nuisance in carrying out its duties, it is to be absolved from liability." Accordingly, his Lordship did not have to express a "concluded view" on the difference of opinion between Denning L.J. and Evershed M.R. in the *Pride of Derby* case.[78]

---

[70] (1868) L.R. 3 H.L. 330.
[71] At p. 279.
[72] See Lord Cairns in *Rylands* v. *Fletcher* (1868) L.R. 3 H.L. 330 at p. 340; *Rickards* v. *Lothian* [1913] A.C. 263; *Read* v. *Lyons* [1947] A.C. 156.
[73] At p. 280. See n. 72.
[74] Denning L.J. in *Pride of Derby Angling Association* v. *British Celanese* [1953] Ch. 149 at p. 189.
[75] *Dunne* v. *North Western Gas Board* [1964] 2 Q.B. 806, 831.
[76] [1953] Ch. 149 at p. 176.
[77] [1954] Ch. 450.
[78] At p. 478.

H. Negligent Misstatement

In *Hedley Byrne & Co. Ltd.* v. *Heller and Partners Ltd.,*[79] the House of   **10-41**
Lords held that there may in some circumstances be liability in
negligence where a careless misstatement causes financial loss. The exact
scope of this liability is not clear. The principle was stated as follows by
Lord Morris of Borth-y-Gest in the *Hedley Byrne* case.[80]

> "If someone possessed of a special skill undertakes, quite irrespective of contract,
> to apply that skill for the assistance of another person who relies upon such skill,
> a duty of care will arise. The fact that the service is to be given by means of or by
> the instrumentality of words can make no difference. Furthermore, if in a sphere
> in which a person is so placed that others could reasonably rely upon his
> judgment or his skill or upon his ability to make careful inquiry, a person takes it
> upon himself to give information or advice to, or allows his information or advice
> to be passed on to, another person who, as he knows or should know, will place
> reliance upon it, then a duty of care will arise."

Lord Hodson agreed with this formulation.[81] Lord Reid stated[82] that a
duty would arise from:

> "all those relationships where it is plain that the party seeking the information
> or advice was trusting the other to exercise such a degree of care as the
> circumstances required, where it was reasonable for him to do that, and where
> the other gave the information or advice when he knew or ought to have known
> that the inquirer was relying on him."

Lord Pearce stated[83]:

> "If persons holding themselves out in a calling or situation or profession take
> on a task within that calling or situation or profession, they have a duty of skill
> and care. . . . To import [a duty of care,] the representation must normally, I
> think, concern a business or professional transaction whose nature makes clear
> the gravity of the inquiry and the importance and influence attached to the
> answer."

Lord Devlin was prepared to accept any of their Lordships' statements
as showing the general rule,[84] although he did suggest that liability would
attach to a "voluntary assumption of responsibility," and that "wherever
there is a relationship equivalent to contract (*i.e.* there would be a contract
but for the absence of formal consideration), there is a duty of care."

There will be no liability in respect of words spoken on a social or
informal occasion[85] or where there is an express disclaimer or liability (as in
the *Hedley Byrne* case itself), although express disclaimers are now subject
to the test of reasonableness under the Unfair Contract Terms Act 1977.

[79] [1964] A.C. 465.
[80] At pp. 502–503.
[81] At p. 514.
[82] At p. 486.
[83] At pp. 538 and 539.
[84] At p. 530.
[85] See Lord Pearce in *Hedley Byrne* at p. 539; Lords Reid and Morris in *Mutual Life and
Citizens' Assurance Co.* v. *Evatt* [1971] A.C. 793, 810–811.

A duty to take care may accordingly be imposed on a local authority which gives information or advice to members of the public. An action for damages might lie where a plaintiff is unable to establish that an authority is bound by a statement given by an officer (see paras. 12-12—12-14). Such a statement may be given in the course of the officer's employment, so as to render the authority vicariously liable in tort if it was negligently made.

10-42   The following is the only reported English case where a local authority has been held liable under the *Hedley Byrne* principle:

> *Coats Patons (Retails) Ltd.* v. *Birmingham Corporation.*[86] The plaintiff, in the course of searches before purchasing a shop, asked the council whether any proposals had been approved for the construction of a subway opposite the shop. A clerk entered the answer "No" on the search form without making the appropriate enquiries. In fact, the council had approved such a proposal two years previously, and the plaintiffs claimed that they had suffered financial loss when the subway was constructed. The search form included the following clause: "The replies below are furnished after appropriate enquiries, and in the belief that they are in accordance with the information at present available to the officers of the council, but on the distinct understanding that neither the council nor any officer of the council is legally responsible therefor." *Held*, that (1) as a result of the sending in of the enquiries form with the appropriate fees, and the giving of the answers, a contract was created; (2) the exclusion clause only operated to negative contractual liability, there being no clear words to exclude tortious liability; (3) the council was liable in tort under the *Hedley Byrne* principle; (4) alternatively, it was liable in contract as the making of appropriate enquiries by the council was a fundamental term of the contract, breach of such a term preventing reliance on the exemption clause.

As a consequence of the *Coats Patons* case, the exemption clause in the standard enquiries form (CON 29) was altered by the addition of the words "except for negligence." This does not seem to alter the authorities liability in tort in respect of incorrect answers.[87]

> *Ministry of Housing and Local Government* v. *Sharp.*[88] A landowner was refused permission to develop his land and obtained compensation from the Ministry under Part II of the Town and Country Planning Act 1954. Notice of compensation was registered in the local authority's register of local land charges as required by section 28(5) of the Act of 1954. Two years later, permission was granted, on a fresh application by the landowner. Prospective purchasers of the land, who as developers would be liable to repay the compensation, caused a search to be made in the register. The search was negligently carried out by a clerk of the second defendant (Hemel Hempstead Rural District Council), and a certificate signed by S., the registrar of local land charges, omitted any reference to the notice. The Court of Appeal *held* that (1) the omission entitled the developers to refuse to repay the compensation; (2) (*per* Salmon and Cross L.JJ., Lord Denning M.R. dissenting), the registrar was not liable, as section 17(2) of the Land Charges Act 1925 did not impose an

---

[86] (1971) 69 L.G.R. 356. See also *Co-operative Retail Services Ltd.* v. *Taff-Ely Borough Council* (1983) 133 New L.J. 577; *L. Shaddock & Associates Pty. Ltd.* v. *Parramatta City Council* (1981) 55 A.L.J.R. 713.
[87] See J. F. Garner, *Local Land Charges* (9th ed.), pp. 94–95.
[88] [1970] 2 Q.B. 223.

absolute obligation on him to make an effective search and issue a complete certificate, and negligence was not alleged against him; (3) (Cross L.J. *reservante*), the clerk who made the search was under a duty of care to anyone whom he knew or ought to have known might be injured if he made a mistake, and the local authority was vicariously liable for his negligence. Lord Denning stated[89] that his decision on the clerk's liability was based squarely on the *Hedley Byrne* principle, although he gave that principle a wide interpretation: "the duty to use due care in a statement arises, not from any voluntary assumption of responsibility, but from the fact that the person making it knows, or ought to know, that others, being his neighbours in this regard, would act on the faith of the statement being accurate." This duty was owed "to any person whom he knows, or ought to know, will be injuriously affected by a mistake. . . . " Salmon L.J. held that this case did not fit into any category of negligence yet considered by the courts: "The plaintiff has not been misled by any careless statement made to him by the defendant or made by the defendant to someone else who the defendant knew would be likely to pass it on to a third party, such as the plaintiff, in circumstances in which the third party might reasonably be expected to rely upon it . . . I am not, however, troubled by the fact that the case is, in many respects, unique."[90] His Lordship was much influenced by the fact that in some situations under the regulations, a clear certificate did not protect the purchaser, who would pay full value on the faith of the certificate and then discover that the land was encumbered. Such a purchaser would clearly be able to sue under the *Hedley Byrne* principle: "Our law would be greviously defective if the council did owe a duty of care to the purchaser in the one case but no duty to the incumbrancers in the other. The damage in each case is equally foreseeable."[91]

I. MISFEASANCE IN A PUBLIC OFFICE

Public authorities or officers may be held liable in damages if they are **10-43** responsible for an act which is *ultra vires*, which causes loss, and where there is either malice or (possibly) knowledge of the absence of *vires*.[92] Most of the authorities are from Commonwealth jurisdictions, but in *Dunlop* v. *Woollahra Municipal Council*[93] the Privy Council described the tort as "well-established." In *Smith* v. *East Elloe*[94] the House of Lords held that an action for damages could proceed against the council's clerk on the allegation that he had procured the compulsory purchase of the plaintiff's property wrongfully and in bad faith, even though the compulsory purchase order was rendered immune from challenge by the Acquisition of Land (Authorisation Procedure) Act 1946.[95] The action subsequently failed on the merits.[96] In *Dunlop* v. *Woollahra Municipal Council*,[97] the Council passed two resolutions which were subsequently

---

[89] At pp. 268–269.
[90] At p. 278.
[91] At p. 280. See now Local Land Charges Act 1975, s. 10.
[92] *Halsbury's Laws of England* (4th ed.), Vol. 1, para. 197; H. W. R. Wade, *Administrative Law* (5th ed.), pp. 669–674.
[93] [1982] A.C. 158 at p. 172.
[94] [1956] A.C. 736.
[95] Schedule 1, Part IV, para. 16.
[96] *Smith* v. *Pywell* (1959) 178 E.G. 1009.
[97] *Supra*, n. 93.

held to be void. The Privy Council held that, in the absence of malice, the passing of a void resolution without knowledge of its invalidity was not conduct capable of amounting to "misfeasance"; for the purpose of the tort. Furthermore, in *Bourgoin S.A.* v. *Ministry of Agriculture, Fisheries and Food*,[98] Mann J. held that in order to establish the tort it was not necessary to prove that an officer had been actuated by malice towards the plaintiff if it could be shown that the officer had known that his conduct was *ultra vires*, and would, or was foreseeably likely to, injure the plaintiff and that the plaintiff had been injured by it.

J. Personal Liability of Members and Servants

10–44 It is one of the incidents of incorporation that the corporate body is distinct from the members who compose it. Individual members of local authorities are not, therefore, personally liable for corporate acts. If, however, a corporation authorises a wrongful act and damages are awarded against the authority, the members who were parties to the authorisation may find themselves the subject of proceedings following audit.[99] The view is sometimes expressed that if a council expressly authorises an act which is *ultra vires* the authority and which proves to be tortious, the members who authorised it may themselves be sued, but the law on this point is not clearly settled. Members might well be liable if a wrongful act were wilful and malicious.[1] The position is somewhat different in the case of servants. The injured party may sue either the corporation or the servant (except where statutory protection is given to the servant as indicated below), but where the servant has acted outside the scope of his authority or not in the course of his employment, so that the council cannot be made liable, an action may lie only against the servant.

These common law rules as to immunity of individual members of corporations and as to actions against servants as well as employing authorities are affected by certain statutory provisions. Section 265 of the Public Health Act 1875 provides

> "No matter or thing done, and no contract entered into by any local authority ... and no matter or thing done by any member ... or by any officer of such authority or other person whomsoever acting under the direction of such authority shall if the matter or thing were done or the contract were entered into *bona fide* for the purposes of executing this Act, subject them or any of them personally to any action liability claim or demand whatsoever; and any expense incurred by any such authority member officer or other person acting as last aforesaid shall be borne and repaid out of the fund or rate applicable by such authority to the general purposes of this Act."

---

[98] [1985] 3 All E.R. 585. Mann J.'s decision on this point was approved by the Court of Appeal: *ibid.*
[99] See Local Government Finance Act 1982, Part III.
[1] *R.* v. *Watson* (1788) 2 T.R. 199.

This immunity does not extend to protect members from action by the auditor.[2] Section 265 was extended to cover other public health functions[3] and highways functions.[4] Officers enjoy specific protection under the Rag Flock and Other Filling Materials Act 1951[5] and the Food Act 1984.[6] The Local Government (Miscellaneous Provisions) Act 1976 extends section 265 to cover all local authorities including joint authorities, the Inner London Education Authority and parish and community councils[7] and the execution of any public general or local Act.[8] Other statutes extend section 265 to water authorities[9] and the various health authorities.[10]

K. COMPENSATION FOR MALADMINISTRATION

A Local Commissioner[11] has no power to order the award of compensa-   **10-45**
tion where he or she finds that maladministration has caused injustice. However, the payment of compensation has followed an adverse report by a Local Commissioner in a number of cases. It is not the practice for a Commissioner to propose remedies in his first report, although this may be done in a second report issued under section 31(2) of the Local Government Act 1974 where the Commissioner is not satisfied with the local authority's response to the finding of maladministration.[12] The Local Government Act 1978 added a new subsection (3) to section 31 of the 1974 Act, empowering a local authority to incur such expenditure as appears to them appropriate in making a payment to, or providing a benefit for, a person found by a Local Commissioner to have suffered injustice in consequence of maladministration. This met difficulties which arose where the Secretary of State refused to sanction such expenditure under section 161 of the Local Government Act 1972 (which removes the possibility of proceedings by the District Auditor, without rendering the expenditure lawful), and where there have been delays before sanction has been forthcoming.[13]

---

[2] Proviso to s. 265, as amended by the Local Government Finance Act 1982, Sched. 5, para. 1.
[3] Public Health Acts 1936, s. 305, and 1961, s. 1; Building Act 1984, s. 115; Public Health (Control of Disease) Act 1984, s. 69.
[4] Highways Act 1959, s. 261 and Highways (Miscellaneous Provisions) Act 1961, s. 16(3).
[5] s. 28.
[6] s. 116.
[7] See s. 44(1), definition of "local authority" as substituted by the Local Government Act 1985, Sched. 14, para. 53(*b*).
[8] s. 39.
[9] Control of Pollution Act 1974, s. 86.
[10] National Health Service Act 1977, s. 125.
[11] See §§ 4–64, *et seq.*
[12] Report of the Commission for Local Administration in England for 1975–76, paras. 61 and 74–79.
[13] See now Local Government Finance Act 1982, s. 19(1).

3. *CRIMINAL LIABILITY*

10-46   A body corporate may be convicted of criminal offences except those for which the only punishment is imprisonment or death and those which cannot be vicariously committed, *e.g.* bigamy. Similarly, a local authority may be convicted of offences under public health and similar statutes, *e.g.* for a statutory nuisance.[14]

---

[14] See *R.* v. *Epping Justices, ex p. Burlinson* [1948] K.B. 79. For a full discussion of criminal liability of incorporated bodies see *Tesco Supermarkets* v. *Nattrass* [1972] A.C. 153.

CHAPTER 11

CENTRAL CONTROL OF LOCAL AUTHORITIES

A. GENERAL POWERS OF CONTROL

IN one sense local authorities are wholly subject to central control, for **11–01**
Parliament is omnipotent. Parliament may allocate functions to local
bodies or take them away. It may prescribe how those functions shall be
carried out and may change the structure of local government as it
chooses. The control here considered is, however, the control exercised by
Ministers of the Crown and by the departments for which they are
responsible, and in this connection the point must first be made that
neither ministers nor departments have an overall control of the work of
local authorities. All formal control must be specifically authorised by
statute. Certain statutes, it is true, appear to vest supervisory powers in
Ministers of the Crown. It is the duty of the Secretary of State for
Education and Science, under section 1 of the Education Act 1944,

> "to promote the education of the people of England and Wales and the
> progressive development of institutions devoted to that purpose, and to *secure
> the effective execution by local authorities, under his control and direction,* of the
> national policy for providing a varied and comprehensive educational service
> in every area."

It is commonly held that the powers of control and direction referred to **11–02**
here are those specifically given in a number of sections in the Act, such
as the power to issue directions under section 68 to prevent the
unreasonable exercise of functions, and that these general words do not in
themselves give any direct supervisory authority. Section 7 of the Local
Authority Social Services Act 1970, confers a vaguer power on the
Secretary of State for Social Services. It reads:

> "Local authorities shall, in the exercise of their social services functions,
> including the exercise of any discretion conferred by any relevant enactment,
> act under *the general guidance* of the Secretary of State."

A similar provision appears in section 12 of the Housing (Homeless
Persons) Act 1977 (now section 71 of the Housing Act 1985):

> "(1) In relation to homeless persons and persons threatened with home-
> lessness, a relevant authority shall have regard in the exercise of their functions
> to such guidance as may from time to time be given by the Secretary of State.
> (2) The Secretary of State may give guidance either generally or to specified
> descriptions of authorities."

A Code of Guidance was issued by the Department of the Environment,
the Department of Health and Social Security and the Welsh Office
under this section.[1]

[1] See DoE Circular 90/77.

The legal significance of these provisions is not clear. Presumably an authority which fails to have regard to "guidance" from the Secretary of State in the exercise of the powers concerned may be said to have ignored a "relevant consideration" and thereby abused its discretion. On the other hand, a minister may not rely on a power to give "guidance" in order to give mandatory directions.[2]

11-03   Apart from these provisions, it is safe to say that central government departments have no legal control over the work of local authorities other than that directly conferred by statute. There is no doubt, however, that control is in fact exercised informally in the process of consultation between local authorities and officers of the various ministries and in the issue by the departments of circulars and memoranda. By these means the policy of a department works its way into the practice of local authorities, perhaps imperceptibly. It is referred to sometimes as "government by circular." An example of this was found in the building licensing work undertaken by the local authorities work from 1945 to 1954 on behalf of the Ministry of Works. There was no statutory authority which enabled the Ministry to delegate its function to local authorities[3] and there was no statutory authority empowering local authorities to undertake this work and to spend money on it. The precise form that the licensing should take and its limits and extent were prescribed in ministry circulars and followed by authorities.

11-04   No examination of the relationship between central and local government can therefore be satisfactory unless due regard is had to the conventions of control—the "pressures" of advice, consultations, practice codes, memoranda and circulars which explain or amplify a minister's policy. This acceptance of non-statutory control may rest on several factors. In spite of the criticisms by local authorities of the nature and extent of central control, there has to be a working partnership with a common purpose. A working partnership invariably involves some flexibility in the matter of rights and duties. There is, too, the very extensive practice of prior consultation between local authority associations and the central government departments under which the formulae of control are often jointly considered before they are imposed. This aspect of central control is considered further in the concluding paragraphs of this Chapter. The statutory forms of control are now examined.

B. Statutory Forms of Control

Control of borrowing, capital expenditure and revenue expenditure

11-05   The Local Government Act 1972, Sched. 13, para. 1, enables a local authority, with the consent of the Secretary of State, to borrow money for

---

[2] *Laker Airways Ltd.* v. *Department of Trade* [1977] Q.B. 643.
[3] *Jackson, Stansfield & Sons* v. *Butterworth* [1948] 2 All E.R. 558.

any purpose or class of purpose which he approves and subject to any conditions he lays down.

It was formerly the practice of ministers in exercising this power to **11-06** examine the merits of every capital scheme, ensuring that it was technically sound, adequate for its purpose, and within the resources of the authority seeking the sanction. From April 1, 1971, a procedure was adopted by the Secretary of State under which a general sanction to borrow in relation to specified kinds of schemes was given by Circular issued by the Department.[4]

This procedure was superseded by the Local Government, Planning and Land Act 1980 which changed the emphasis from control of individual *borrowings* to control over the level of each authority's capital *expenditure*.[5] The controls apply to county and district councils, London borough councils, the Common Council of the City of London, combined fire authorities, national park joint or special planning boards, the Inner London Education Authority and joint authorities.[6] The minister may prevent an authority from incurring "prescribed expenditure" above a limit set by a combination of an amount specified by the minister and *inter alia* the amount of the authority's net capital receipts. The term "prescribed expenditure" covers such matters as expenditure on the acquisition of land, vehicles, plant, machinery and apparatus, the construction of buildings and the making of capital grants other than to local authorities.[7] Specific approval may be necessary in respect of projects of national or regional importance.[8]

The Secretary of State is empowered by the Rates Act 1984 to prescribe a maximum for the rate made or precept issued by an individual local authority or local authorities generally.

These powers of control are considered in greater detail in Chapters 7 and 8.

Control through the system of grants

Exchequer grants fall broadly under two headings, specific grants in **11-07** aid of particular services and general grants. Fairly detailed control is a feature of specific grants. It is a general rule that a grant is not payable unless the appropriate minister is broadly satisfied with the service in respect of which the grant is claimed, and in most cases grant-earning expenditure must be "approved" expenditure; that is, approved, in one way or another, by the appropriate minister. The withholding of a grant is a rarity—in practice it is the power to withhold that enables the department to exercise an influence in the conduct of the service to which the grants relate.

---

[4] See DoE Circular 66/76, as amended by Circulars 18/77 and 63/77.
[5] Part VIII.
[6] Local Government, Planning and Land Act 1980, s. 71(1), as amended by the Local Government Act 1985, Sched. 14, para. 59(*a*).
[7] Local Government, Planning and Land Act 1980, s. 71(2) and Sched. 12.
[8] *Ibid.* s. 73.

11-08 The police grant is an example of a specific grant (it is a percentage grant, roughly one-half of the police authority's expenditure) and it illustrates the measure of control which accompanies the payment of such grants. Section 31 of the Police Act 1964 provides that the grants shall be:

> "of such amounts, be payable at such times, in such manner, and subject to such conditions, and be carried to such funds, as the Secretary of State may with the approval of the Treasury by order determine."

Payment is conditional upon the Secretary of State being satisfied that:

> "the police area in question is efficiently policed, that adequate co-operation is afforded by the police force to other police forces, that the police service is efficiently and properly maintained, equipped and administered, and that the rates of pay and allowances of the force are as prescribed or approved by him; and if he is not satisfied on any of these matters he may withhold the grant in whole or in part permanently or for such time as he may determine."[9]

11-09 A housing subsidy is payable to housing authorities under sections 421–427 of the Housing Act 1985 (see para. 15–24). Under section 427 of that Act where it appears to the Secretary of State that the purpose for which it was paid has not been fulfilled, or not completely or adequately, or not without unreasonable delay, he may recoup the whole or a part of the subsidy.

These are two examples of a minister's power of control through his ability to withhold or withdraw financial aid if schemes or activity are not of the kind or to the standards which he approves.

11-10 Part VI of the Local Government, Planning and Land Act 1980 and Part II of the Local Government Finance Act 1982 add new forms of control through the amount of rate support grant payable to individual local authorities. The system for calculating the grant is designed to discourage local authorities from raising their rates beyond levels thought appropriate by the Secretary of State.[10] The nature and extent of these controls is considered in Chapters 7 and 9.

Control through regulation

11-11 It is common for statutes conferring powers or duties on local authorities to authorise a minister to make regulations prescribing how the work shall be carried out or the standards to which the service shall conform or conditions subject to which a grant is payable. The statute lays down the broad principles on which a power or duty shall be undertaken and the detailed working rules are often left to a minister to prescribe.

11-12 The Town and Country Planning Act 1971 contains a number of examples which show how this form of control works out in practice. In many sections authority is given to the Secretary of State to make

---

[9] Police (Grant) Order 1966 (S.I. 1966 No. 223).
[10] See ss. 53–64.

regulations setting out the way in which the Act is to be administered. He may under section 18 make regulations with respect to the form and content of structure and local plans and with respect to the procedure to be followed in their preparation, submission, approval and amendment. The regulations made under this section[11] minutely prescribe the procedure which planning authorities must follow. The Secretary of State is empowered by section 24 to make general development orders which have the effect of granting permission to such classes of development as he specifies subject to such conditions or limitations as he may lay down. The Town and Country Planning General Development Order 1977[12] made under this provision specifies those classes of development which are permitted by the Order and which may be undertaken without the consent of the local planning authority. Section 22(2)(*f*) enables the Secretary of State by Order to specify "use classes" within which there can be made a change from one use to another without having to obtain the permission of the local planning authority.[13] By his powers under these two sections he can limit or extend the discretionary powers of local planning authorities in the granting or withholding of planning permission.

There are a number of similar provisions in planning legislation but the examples given indicate the significance of control by regulation. It is true that the rules must be laid before Parliament and that in most cases they may be annulled by a resolution of either House. But Parliament does not often use its right of challenge. The power to make regulations, illustrated by reference to planning legislation, is found in many statutes relating to local authority services.

Control through inspection

This form of control operates in a limited field: it is used principally in **11-13** the education, police and fire services. In section 77(2) of the Education Act 1944, a duty is put on the Secretary of State for Education and Science to cause an inspection to be made of every educational establishment at such intervals as he considers appropriate and to arrange a special inspection of any establishment whenever he thinks it desirable. The inspectorate exercises a considerable influence by way of advice, the interchange of ideas, the pooling of experience and the provision of a personal link between the administration in Whitehall and those who teach.

Inspectors of Constabulary are appointed under section 38 of the Police **11-14** Act 1964. They have a duty to inspect and to report to the Secretary of State for the Home Department on the efficiency of police forces, including the City of London force, and to carry out other duties for

[11] S.I.s 1974 No. 1481 and 1982 No. 555.
[12] S.I. 1977 No. 289, as amended.
[13] S.I. 1972 No. 1385, as amended.

furthering police efficiency as he may direct. The Report of the Royal Commission on the Police[14] said of the inspectorate:

"Thus the inspectors of constabulary will have four duties. They will continue, as now, to inspect each separate police force and report to the Secretary of State whether or not it is efficient, and in particular they will indicate any misgivings they may have about the competence of its chief constable, including the manner in which he deals with complaints against the police. Secondly, arising from their inspection of the force, they will form an opinion about the adequacy of the provision made by a police authority, and report any shortcomings in this respect to the Secretary of State. Thirdly, they will ensure that the results of central research are made available to the forces they inspect, and that new knowledge and up-to-date techniques are being applied, Fourthly, they will be responsible for advising upon arrangements for promoting collaboration between forces and the development of ancillary services. Although their duty will continue to be to the Secretaries of State, the inspectors should, in addition, keep in close touch with police authorities."

11-15   Section 24 of the Fire Service Act 1947 enables the Crown and the Secretary of State for the Home Department to appoint inspectors and assistant inspectors respectively, and precisely specifies what the inspectors are to do. They are to obtain information, first as to the manner in which fire authorities are carrying out their functions, and secondly as to technical matters relating to the fire service. In practice their second function is the one in which their influence is perhaps the more felt. In some ways like the school inspectorate the fire service inspectors can, by advice, encourage the acceptance of improved systems and techniques. They have a statutory duty to keep in touch with technical developments affecting the service and it is reasonable to suppose that the guidance they offer, based on their specialised knowledge, is carefully noted by fire authorities.

Powers in relation to authorities in default
11-16   In a number of cases, Parliament has given to Ministers of the Crown specific powers of control should authorities fail to carry out certain of their statutory functions. In several cases the minister concerned may issue directions or may transfer particular functions of a defaulting authority to himself or to another authority. These are legal powers which are very rarely used, but as they are available to the central government departments they must be noted. Two examples are given. Where the Secretary of State for the Environment is satisfied, after a local inquiry or hearing, that a planning authority has failed to carry out its functions in connection with the preparation and submission of a structure or local plan he may, under section 17 of the Town and Country Planning Act 1971, take over those functions himself or may transfer them to another planning authority with an interest in the proper planning of the area. The cost of carrying out the work involved falls to the defaulting authority.

[14] Cmnd. 1728 (1962).

The Secretary of State for Education and Science is given directive 11-17 powers under section 99 of the Education Act 1944, where he is satisfied, on complaint or otherwise, that a local education authority, or the or governors of any county or voluntary school, have failed to carry out any of their statutory duties. The Secretary of State may declare the authority or governors to be in default and may issue appropriate directions, enforceable by mandamus. He is not obliged to hold a local inquiry before exercising such powers. These default powers are available where there has been a failure to carry out statutory duties. But the powers of the Secretary of State under section 68 of the Act are wider still. The section provides that if he is satisfied on complaint or otherwise that a local education authority or the governors of a county or voluntary school have acted or are proposing to act unreasonably in exercising their functions, he may give such directions to them as he thinks expedient. The default here dealt with is not the failure to carry out a legal duty, but the failure to carry out statutory duties in a reasonable manner. However, the Secretary of State may only intervene where an authority is acting, or proposing to act, so unreasonably that no reasonable authority could act in that manner. He may not intervene merely because he disagrees with the authority's action.[15]

Control over officers

It is generally true to say that a local authority has control over the 11-18 appointment and dismissal of its officers and may stipulate what qualifications those officers shall hold. There are, however, a few exceptions to this general rule.[16] The extent of this control is relatively slight: its purpose, presumably, is to ensure minimum standards.

Section 18 of the Fire Services Act 1947, for example, enables the 11-19 Secretary of State for the Home Department, after consultation with the Central Fire Brigades Advisory Council, to make regulations prescribing the method of appointment of chief fire officers and the qualifications for appointment and promotion in all ranks.[17] It is illustrative of the preciseness of the regulations to note, for example, that a minimum chest measurement and expansion has been prescribed!

The confirmation of by-laws

As has been observed in Chapter 6, no local by-laws are effective until 11-20 confirmed by the appropriate minister. Central control is here absolute, as one might expect, for by-laws in the main create penal offences. The department concerned examines proposed by-laws first on the score of validity in law. As will have been noted, a local by-law is open to

---

[15] *Secretary of State for Education and Science* v. *Tameside Metropolitan Borough Council* [1977] A.C. 1014.
[16] See Local Government Act 1972, s. 112(4) and §§ 4–38 *et seq.*
[17] Fire Services (Appointment and Promotion) Regulations 1978 (S.I. 1978 No. 438), as amended.

challenge in the courts on one or more of the following grounds: that it is repugnant to or inconsistent with statute or common law, that it is unreasonable, that it is uncertain in its terms, that it is *ultra vires* the authority, and, in the case of good rule and government by-laws, that a summary remedy already exists for the prevention or suppression of the nuisance at which the by-law is aimed. The minister will not confirm a by-law which, in his opinion, will not satisfy the judicial tests as to validity. Additionally, the department is to be assured that the need exists in the particular locality for the by-law proposed, for it is clearly undesirable to have by-laws for their own sake. Some attempt is made, through the use of model codes, to secure a measure of uniformity in wording and substance.

Approval of schemes

11–21   In a limited number of cases statutes impose on local authorities a duty to prepare "schemes" or "proposals" or "plans," setting out how the authorities propose to carry out the duties which statute has put upon them. The broad lines on which they are to proceed appear in the statute and it is left to each authority to work out in some detail how the Act will be administered in its area, the nature and extent of the services proposed and the lines of future development which the council plans. By this means some elasticity is given to scheme making, the initiative coming from the authority itself. It then falls to the appropriate minister to approve or reject the scheme submitted or to approve it with his own modifications.

11–22   For example, sections 6 and 7 of the Town and Country Planning Act 1971, require every county planning authority to survey its area and to submit to the Secretary of State a report of its survey and a structure plan, formulating the authority's policy and general proposals in respect of the development and other use of the land in its area. The Secretary of State by regulation prescribes the form and content of structure plans.[18]

The powers of control over land use given by this Act to local planning authorities are very great, but it is clear that it is open to the Secretary of State, through the structure plan procedure, to exercise a considerable influence over the manner in which and the extent to which these powers may be employed. To take one important example, the local planning authority will have set out in its plan its policy and general proposals in respect of the development and other use of land in its area, including measures for the improvement of the physical environment and the management of traffic. The Secretary of State may vary this plan in any detail and at any point, and may amend partially or even substantially the basic ideas which the plan embodies, or he may reject it. In short, the wide powers conferred by the Act on local planning authorities are

---

[18] Town and Country Planning (Structure and Local Plans) Regulations 1982 (S.I. 1982 No. 55).

appreciably controlled by a minister, for the structure plan is of great importance in the exercise of planning powers.

In some cases an additional purpose is served in the use of the plan- 11-23 making device—departments are able to consider representations and objections made by interested parties. Before the Secretary of State approves a structure plan, for example, he is required to consider any objections or representations received by him and to hold an examination in public.

The issue of directions

The directions here considered are of a particular character, addressed 11-24 to an individual authority. If the power to issue directions of this kind were greatly extended then local autonomy would be severly jeopardised. The number of instances in which this power is conferred on Ministers is fairly substantial but except in the first example given the power is not widely used. Section 35 of the Town and Country Planning Act 1971, enables the Secretary of State for the Environment to give directions to any local planning authority (or to local planning authorities generally) requiring that any application for permission to develop land, or all applications of a specified class, shall be referred to him instead of being dealt with by the local planning authority. Reference has earlier been made to the powers of direction which vest in the Secretary of State for Education and Science under section 99 of the Education Act 1944, when he is satisfied that an authority is in default, and under section 68 of that Act where, in his opinion, an authority or the governors of any county or voluntary school have acted or are proposing to act unreasonably in carrying out their functions.

Section 8 of the Clean Air Act 1968 enables the Secretary of State for the Environment to require an authority to create a smoke control area and to carry out a smoke control programme. The Secretary of State may be concerned with a particular footpath—he has power under section 26 of the Highways Act 1980 to make a public path creation order. New powers of direction are contained in the Local Government, Planning and Land Act 1980: they include the powers of the Secretary of State to require a public body to dispose of land which in his opinion is not being used, or not being sufficiently used, for the authority's purpose,[19] to restrict capital expenditure[20] and to require an authority to make an assessment of land suitable for residential development.[21]

Appellate jurisdiction

In a number of statutes a right of appeal against a decision of a local 11-25 authority lies to a minister. An applicant for planning permission who is

[19] s. 98.
[20] s. 78.
[21] s. 116.

aggrieved by the decision of the local planning authority may appeal to the Secretary of State for the Environment under section 36 of the Town and Country Planning Act 1971. Section 233 of the Highways Act 1980 gives a right of appeal to the Secretary of State against certain decisions of local authorities when acting under the street works code.

Ministers have appellate jurisdiction in certain cases of dispute between authorities and between authorities and employees. It is the Secretary of State for the Social Services who settles a question between authorities as to a person's "ordinary residence" for the purposes of Part III of the National Assistance Act 1948.[22] The Superannuation Act 1972 and the regulations made thereunder provide that any question of rights or liabilities of an employee shall be decided in the first instance by the employing authority, and if the employee is dissatisfied with the decision reached he may appeal to the Secretary of State for the Environment, whose determination is final.[23]

Consent to individual acts

11-26　　There are a number of cases in which a local authority may act only with the consent of a Minister. For example, an authority may only use money accruing from a local lottery for a purpose other than that originally specified as the object of the lottery with the consent of the Secretary of State.[24]

The power to require information

11-27　　There are many examples of the power to hold inquiries and to require information from local authorities. There is an example of the former in section 46 of the Coast Protection Act 1949. The Secretary of State may cause a local inquiry to be held in any case where it appears to him to be advisable to do so in connection with any matter arising under that Act. As to the latter, section 168 of the Local Government Act 1972 requires the submission of financial returns to the Secretary of State in the form directed. The Department of Trade, under section 26 of the Trade Descriptions Act 1968, can require at any time a report from a weights and measures authority on the exercise of its functions under section 9 of the Hallmarking Act 1973 and the report must contain such particulars as the Department directs. Under section 97 of the Local Government, Planning and Land Act 1980, the Secretary of State may direct a public body to give him such information as he may specify about land being held by it. These are a few examples.

---

[22] s. 32(3).
[23] See Local Government Superannuation Regulations 1974, Part II (S.I. 1974 No. 520) as amended.
[24] Lotteries and Amusements Act 1976, s. 7(4).

Audit

Authorities were required by the Local Government Act 1972[25] **11-28** (applicable up to 1982/3) to submit their accounts to audit by the district auditor or by an auditor approved by the Secretary of State. It may sensibly be argued that audit, even under the 1972 Act, was not an instrument of central control. Approved auditors were approved by the Secretary of State on the test of professional skills, and district auditors, though appointed by him, were independent of him in decision making and were not answerable to him. He could not be questioned in Parliament as to their findings. But there may be something in the contrary view. District audit has been historically one of the more important ways in which Parliament secures the subordination of local authority to its will as expressed in statute. It had its origin in the Poor Law Act 1834 which provided that payments made contrary to the terms of the Act or the Orders of the Poor Law Commissioners should be illegal. The auditors appointed under the provisions of the Act had power to disallow illegal payments and to surcharge those responsible for making them.

With the changes to the audit system made by the Local Government Finance Act 1982 for 1983/4 onwards,[26] it may be considered that the independence of audit from central government is increased, since auditors are no longer employed or approved by the Secretary of State. The Audit Commission, which appoints the auditors, is itself appointed by the Secretary of State, however, and he is empowered to issue directions which the Commission must observe. But this does not detract from the independence of the auditors in carrying out their statutory functions. Their duties continue to be laid upon them directly by the statute and therefore neither the Commission nor the Secretary of State has any power to direct or influence them in the performance of those duties.

C. TRENDS IN CENTRAL CONTROL

An attempt was made in 1949 to simplify administrative procedures **11-29** involved in central control of local authority work. A committee, called the Local Government Manpower Committee, was set up to examine the problem generally. It consisted of representatives of government departments and local authority associations, and its terms of reference included a duty "to examine in particular the distribution of functions between central and local government and the possibility of relaxing departmental supervision of local authority activities and delegating more responsibility to local authorities." The Committee was concerned primarily with matters of procedure rather than with the forms of control prescribed by statute, though it did in fact make certain recommendations for an

[25] ss. 154–167.
[26] See § 7–09.

amendment of the law. It approached the problem with the view that "local authorities are responsible bodies competent to discharge their own functions and that ... they exercise their responsibilities in their own right," and accordingly "the objective should be to leave as much as possible of the detailed management of a scheme or service to the local authority and to concentrate the department's control at key points where it can most effectively discharge its responsibilities for government policy and financial administration."

11–30   The Committee made a number of recommendations for the loosening of central control by simplifying and shortening administrative procedures. The recommendations were accepted by the Government and were subsequently embodied in departmental circulars addressed to local authorities. It is doubtful whether a substantial or even measurable reduction of control stemmed from the acceptance of the recommendations of the Committee, but at least the problem was reviewed with some realism. This examination of the procedures involved and the reforms proposed indicated in an authoritative way how the statutory forms of control were exercised in practice.

11–31   The objectives of the Local Government Manpower Committee were noted with approval by the Committee on the Management of Local Government[27] which recommended that the Government, in consultation with the local authority associations, should examine existing legislation to see what provisions might be repealed with a view to leaving local authorities the maximum freedom in organising their affairs and carrying out their work.

These consultations did in fact take place and a great many items of control were removed by the Local Government Act 1972. Here are some examples. Though a chief education officer must be appointed, there is no longer a requirement to submit a short list to the Secretary of State for approval or veto.[28] The control exercised by the Secretary of State over charges in connection with ferry undertakings run by a local authority or passenger transport executive was removed.[29] The Act of 1972 cleared away many such minor and relatively unimportant forms of control.

Still more were removed or modified by the Local Government Act 1974. Schedule 8 contained a long list of repeals and amendments which had the effect of dispensing with the consent of ministers to particular acts, and the Secretary of State was empowered by regulation to make further amendments to statute to achieve this end.[30]

The process was taken a step further by the Local Government, Planning and Land Act 1980,[31] which removed many minor controls,

---

[27] Vol. I, para. 251.
[28] Local Government Act 1972, s. 112 and Sched. 30.
[29] *Ibid.* s. 186(6).
[30] s. 35.
[31] s. 1 and Scheds. 1–6, which give effect to proposals in the White Paper "Central Government Controls over Local Authorities" (Cmnd. 7634).

particularly over functions relating to clean air and pollution, amenity, weights and measures, and allotments, and controls over charges and rates of interest. However, as has been noted above, the Act also contained significant extensions of central control over levels of expenditure and, as will be seen in Chapter 27, introduced an appreciable degree of control over direct works organisations. Central controls over expenditure were reinforced by the Rates Act 1984 (see Chapter 8). Indeed, the practical effect of the removal of many detailed controls has been more than outweighed by the severe financial constraints set by central government under recent legislation.

D. CONSULTATIONS

An examination of these issues would be incomplete without some 11-32
reference to the processes, statutory and otherwise, involved in reaching decisions as to the controls to be imposed, and more particularly as to how they shall be exercised. In many cases a minister is required by statute first to consult some advisory body, generally one set up by statute and representative of all interested parties, before he makes regulations. An example of this is found in the Central Fire Brigades Advisory Council which the Secretary of State for the Home Department is required to establish under section 29 of the Fire Services Act 1947. This Council is composed of persons representing the interests of fire authorities, fire brigade members and such other persons as the Secretary of State chooses, being persons having special qualifications in this field. The Secretary of State is required to consult the Council before making certain regulations, those with respect to qualifications, for example, and the Council may offer advice on its own initiative. Section 54 of the Local Government, Planning and Land Act 1980, to take another example of statutory consultations, requires the Secretary of State for the Environment to consult with local authority associations before determining the amount of money available for grants payable under Part VI of the Act.

Perhaps of greater significance than the formal statutory consultations (made in the main with bodies appointed by the Minister who consults them) are the non-statutory discussions which invariably take place between government departments and the associations of local authorities on any major administrative change and on any new or amending legislation affecting local government.

The main local authority associations, as constituted following the reorganisation of local government under the Local Government Act 1972, are the Association of County Councils, the Association of Metropolitan Authorities, the Association of District Councils, the National Association of Local Councils (for parish and community councils) and the London Boroughs Association. There are also more specialised bodies, such as the Council of Local Education Authorities and the Water Authorities Association; and there are various associations of officers (*e.g.* the Society of Local Authority Chief Executives and the Society of Education Officers), and associations of members. These are not statutory bodies, but a local authority may pay reasonable subscriptions to

(a) any association of local authorities formed (inside or outside the United Kingdom) for the purpose of consultation as to the common interests of those authorities and discussion of matters relating to local government; or

(b) any association of officers or members formed for those purposes.[32]

The limits of these powers were considered in the following cases.

R. v. Greater London Council, ex p. Bromley London Borough Council.[33] In 1982, the London Boroughs Association, then with a Conservative majority, resolved to support the government policy of abolition of the G.L.C. In consequence, the Association of London Authorities was established, whose objects included retention of the G.L.C., the local accountability of the police in London and the establishment in London of a nuclear free zone. Although membership was open to all London borough councils, the G.L.C. and I.L.E.A., the objects were designed to attract only Labour controlled authorities. It was conceded that a local authority was not permitted to pay subscriptions under section 143 of the Local Government Act 1972 to bodies whose objects were to express party political views. *Held,* the A.L.A. was such a body and the subscriptions paid by the G.L.C. were *ultra vires* section 143. After this decision, all the defects of the original constitution of the A.L.A. which had caused Forbes J. to grant the declaration were removed by amendment, and in *R. v. Bromley London Borough Council, ex p. Lambeth London Borough Council,*[34] Hodgson J. held that a subscription to the association would now be *intra vires.*

11-33   A particular forum for consultation on financial matters is the Consultative Council on Local Government Finance (CCLGF), a non-statutory body first established in 1975. It is chaired by the Secretary of State for the Environment, and comprises ministers and civil servants from all departments concerned with local government and members selected by the local authority associations. Detailed, preliminary consideration is given to the Council's business by an Official Steering Group, comprising civil servants, the secretary of each local authority association, specialist professional staff of the associations and officer advisers. Among the consequences of the establishment of the Council havee been closer contacts among the main local authority associations, and the displacement of direct contacts on policy between individual local authorities and government departments.

Expectations that the council would be a forum for negotiation have not been fulfilled. Indeed, some have doubted its efficacy as a consultative body, viewing it rather as a forum for the announcement of

---

[32] Local Government Act 1972, s. 143. This power is also available to the Common Council (s. 143(2)) and to joint authorities and the Inner London Education Authority (s. 146A(1), inserted by the Local Government Act 1985, Sched. 14, para. 16).

[33] *The Times,* March 27, 1984.

[34] *The Times,* June 16, 1984.

decisions by central government.[35] It has certainly been in matters concerning the levels of expenditure that local authority influence has been weakest. There is a separate Council for Wales.

[35] See A. Alexander, *Local Government in Britain since Reorganisation* (1982), pp. 158–164.

CHAPTER 12

JUDICIAL CONTROL OF LOCAL AUTHORITIES AND LEGAL
PROCEEDINGS BY AND AGAINST LOCAL AUTHORITIES

1. *JUDICIAL CONTROL OF LOCAL AUTHORITIES*

12-01　LOCAL authorities are subject to the control of the courts in much the
same way as any other kind of corporate body or any natural person, in
the sense that if they infringe a private right or are in breach of contract,
they may be sued in tort or contract, and if they commit a criminal
offence, proceedings may be taken against them. The liability of local
authorities in these matters is considered in Chapter 10. But the term
"judicial control of local authorities" is commonly used in another sense.
The courts have a limited kind of supervisory jurisdiction over certain
acts of any executive agency, including local authorities, and in the
exercise of this jurisdiction may grant the orders of mandamus,
prohibition and certiorari where such orders run, may issue declarations
and injunctions in relation to acts or proposed acts which are *ultra vires,*
and may hear appeals against acts or decisions where a right of appeal is
conferred by statute. The courts will not take the initiative in any of these
matters; they will act only at the suit of a litigant with sufficient
"standing," a matter discussed at paragraphs 12–35, 12–36 and 12–40.

　The courts are rarely concerned with the *merits* of a particular decision.
They can only correct an *error of fact* where (1) Parliament has enacted
that an appeal shall lie on the merits, or (2) the error has caused the
authority to act *ultra vires.* These situations are exceptional. The normal
situations where a court may intervene are those where an authority has
made an *error of law.* Any error of law may be corrected (1) if there is a
statutory right of appeal, or (2) if an error of law appears on the face of
the record of proceedings, or (3) if it causes the authority to act *ultra vires.*

　The most straightforward examples of the application of the *ultra vires*
doctrine are discussed in Chapter 1. Here we consider the applications of
that doctrine in the context of "jurisdictional control."[1] We also consider
the issues that arise in connection with limits on the exercise of statutory
powers implied by the courts. The most significant of these limits relate to
the use of discretionary powers, and the application of the rules of natural
justice. Other matters considered are: statutory appeals; other remedies;
the exclusion of judicial review.

---

[1] The leading work on judicial review is J. M. Evans, *de Smith's Judicial Review of
Administrative Action* (4th ed.). Other works which deal with the principles at length
include H. W. R. Wade, *Administrative Law* (5th ed.); J. F. Garner and B. L. Jones,
Garner's Administrative Law (6th ed.); P. P. Craig, *Administrative Law.*

A. JURISDICTIONAL CONTROL

One of the most complex areas of administrative law is that concerning **12-02**
the distinction between those errors which cause a public authority to act
outside its jurisdiction (variously termed "jurisdictional" errors; errors on
"preliminary" or "collateral" questions) and those which do not ("errors
relating to the merits" or "errors with jurisdiction"). Many of the relevant
cases concern decisions by justices and tribunals rather than by local
authorities.[2]
The following points may be noted:

(1) "Preliminary" or "jurisdictional" questions may be questions of
law or fact: "a court with jurisdiction confined to the City of
London cannot extend such jurisdiction by finding as a fact that
Piccadilly Circus is in the ward of Chepe."[3] However, where the
determination of a question of fact depends on the conflicting
testimony of witnesses, a superior court will normally decline to
interfere with the decision of the tribunal which saw the witnesses.[4]

(2) The distinction between jurisdictional and non-jurisdictional
questions is of less practical significance today in the light of the
revival of the use of certiorari to quash for any error of law on the
face of the record (para. 12-32), and the broad interpretation given
to the powers of the court to quash compulsory purchase and other
orders on applications under statute (para. 12-42).

The following case illustrates the application of the principles of **12-03**
jurisdictional control to local authorities:

> *Re Ripon (Highfield) Housing 1938, White and Collins v. Minister of Health.*[5]
> Under the Housing Act 1936, a local authority had power to acquire land
> compulsorily, provided that it did not form "part of any park, garden or
> pleasure ground or is otherwise required for the amenity or convenience of any
> house" (s. 75). The Minister confirmed Ripon Borough Council's order for the
> purchase of 23 acres of land let for grazing which were part of the grounds of a
> house. The owners applied to the High Court for the order to be quashed.
> Affidavit evidence was given to the effect that the land was part of a park,
> which evidence was not before the Minister. Charles J. held that the Minister's
> decision that the land was not part of a park was a finding of fact with which he
> could not interfere. On appeal, the Court of Appeal *held* that the order should
> be quashed. Jurisdiction to make the order was dependent on this finding of
> fact, and the Minister's decision could be reviewed. There was no evidence to
> support the Minister's decision. Indeed, the court was satisfied on the evidence
> that the land was part of a park.[6]

---

[2] See *e.g. R.* v. *City of London etc., Rent Tribunal, ex p. Honig* [1951] 1 K.B. 641.
[3] *Per* Farwell L. J. in *R.* v. *Shoreditch Assessment Committee, ex p. Morgan* [1910] 2 K.B. 859
at p. 880.
[4] Devlin L.J. in *R.* v. *Fulham, etc., Rent Tribunal, ex p. Zerek* [1951] 2 K.B. 1, 11; Lord
Goddard C.J. in *ex p. Honig* [1951] 1 K.B. 641 at p. 646, *supra* n. 2.
[5] [1939] 2 K.B. 838.
[6] See also *Dowty Boulton Paul Ltd.* v. *Wolverhampton Corporation* [1976] Ch. 13 *per* Russell
L.J. at pp. 26, 27.

In *Anisminic Ltd.* v. *Foreign Compensation Commission,*[7] a leading modern case on jurisdictional control, Lord Pearce said[8]:

> "Lack of jurisdiction may arise in various ways. There may be an absence of those formalities or things which are conditions precedent to the tribunal having any jurisdiction to embark on an inquiry. Or the tribunal may at the end make an order that it has no jurisdiction to make. Or in the intervening stage, while engaged on a proper inquiry, the tribunal may depart from the rules of natural justice; or it may ask itself the wrong questions; or it may take into account matters which it was not directed to take into account. Thereby it would step outside its jurisdiction. It would turn its inquiry into something not directed by Parliament and fail to make the inquiry which Parliament did direct. Any of these things would cause its purported decision to be a nullity."

12-04   The *Anisminic* decision broadened significantly the range of errors that were to be regarded as causing a body to exceed its jurisdiction, but did not indicate the limits of that range with precision. *Pearlman* v. *Keepers and Governors of Harrow School*[9] raised the question whether an error by a county court judge on a rating matter was such as to cause him to exceed his jurisdiction. The members of the Court of Appeal were agreed that the judge had made an error of law. Lord Denning M.R. expressed the view that any error of *law* would cause a statutory body to exceed its jurisdiction.[10] Eveleigh L.J. was not prepared to go so far, but, applying *Anisminic*, agreed that the judge had exceeded his jurisdiction. Geoffrey Lane L.J. held that the error of law was not such as to cause an excess of jurisdiction.

As regards administrative tribunals and authorities, as distinct from courts of law, the wide approach in *Anisminic* has been endorsed *obiter* by Lord Diplock and Lord Keith in *In re Racal Communications Ltd.*[11] Per Lord Diplock[12]:

> "In *Anisminic* this House was concerned only with decisions of administrative tribunals. Nothing I say is intended to detract from the breadth of the scope of application to administrative tribunals of the principles laid down in that case. It is a legal landmark; it has made possible the rapid development in England of a rational and comprehensive system of administrative law on the foundation of the concept of ultra vires. It proceeds on the presumption that where Parliament confers on an administrative tribunal or authority, as distinct from a court of law, power to decide particular questions defined by the Act conferring the power, Parliament intends to confine that power to answering the question as it has been so defined, and if there has been any doubt as to what the question is this is a matter of courts of law to resolve in fulfilment of their constitutional role as interpreters of the written law and expounders of the common law and rules of equity. So, if the administrative tribunal or authority have asked themselves the wrong question and answered that, they have done something that the Act does not empower them to do and their decision is a

---

[7] [1969] 2 A.C. 147.
[8] At p. 195.
[9] [1979] Q.B. 56.
[10] At pp. 69–70.
[11] [1981] A.C. 374.
[12] At pp. 382–383.

nullity. Parliament can, of course, if it so desires, confer on administrative tribunals or authorities power to decide questions of law as well as questions of fact or of administrative policy; but this requires clear words, for the presumption is that where a decision-making power is conferred on a tribunal or authority that is not a court of law, Parliament did not intend to do so. The breakthrough made by *Anisminic* was that, as respects administrative tribunals and authorities, the old distinction between errors of law that went to jurisdiction and errors of law that did not was for practical purposes abolished. Any error of law that could be shown to have been made by them in the course of reaching their decision on matters of fact or of administrative policy would result in their having asked themselves the wrong question with the result that the decision they reached would be a nullity."

This view was not mentioned by the other members of the House of Lords. It has nevertheless been accepted (*obiter*) as representing the law by Lord Denning M.R. in the Court of Appeal and by the Divisional Court.[13] As regards courts of law, the dissenting judgment of Geoffrey Lane L.J. in *Pearlman* v. *Keepers and Governers of Harrow School*[14] was endorsed in *Racal* by Lords Diplock, Keith and Edmund-Davies[15] and by the Privy Council in *South East Asia Fire Bricks Sdn. Bhd.* v. *Non-Metallic Mineral Products Manufacturing Employees Union.*[16] Nevertheless, the Divisional Court has held that the *Anisminic* principle is applicable to a court of law (here, a coroner's inquest).[17]

B. Failure to Exercise Discretion

A local authority entrusted by Parliament with a statutory discretion will, **12-05** by definition, have some element of choice as to whether or how it will act. However, a power may be coupled with a duty to consider whether the power should be exercised in any particular case. An authority may not delegate the exercise of discretion without statutory authorisation, and must not act under the dictation of any other authority, unless that authority has statutory power to give directions. It may not improperly fetter its discretion by entering a contract or other undertaking, and it may not be estopped by its conduct from exercising its powers. It may be required to consider the exercise of discretion in each individual case and not by reference to an inflexible policy rule.

Unlawful delegation

A public authority may not delegate its decision-making functions **12-06** without express or implied statutory authority. A power to delegate is not

---

[13] R. v. *Chief Immigration Officer, Gatwick Airport, ex p. Kharrazi* [1980] 1 W.L.R. 1396 at p. 1403; R. v. *Surrey Coroner, ex p. Campbell* [1982] Q.B. 661.
[14] [1979] Q.B. 56.
[15] [1981] A.C. 374 at pp. 639, 645, 644.
[16] [1981] A.C. 363.
[17] R. v. *Greater Manchester Coroner, ex p. Tal* [1985] Q.B. 67; R. v. *Surrey Coroner, ex p. Campbell, supra,* not followed.

readily implied, particularly where the decision in question is judicial.[18] A local authority has wide powers under section 101 of the Local Government Act 1972 to arrange for the discharge of any of its functions by a committee, a sub-committee or officer of itself or any other local authority.[19] A local authority may lawfully place considerable reliance on the views of other persons or bodies, provided that the power of decision is in the last resort retained by the authority. This emerges from cases concerning the licensing of cinemas. In *Ellis* v. *Dubowski*,[20] the Divisional Court struck down a condition which provided that no film be shown which had not been certified for public exhibition by the British Board of Film Censors, a non-statutory body established by the film industry. However, a condition which provided that no film which had not been passed by the Board for universal exhibition should be shown to unaccompanied children under 16 *"without the express consent of the Council"* was upheld by the Divisional Court in *Mills* v. *London County Council*.[21] The licensing of cinemas can be regarded as an administrative function. Where judicial functions are concerned any other body involved in the decision-making process may normally only be used for gathering information—and this information must be fully summarised for the benefit of the authority which is to make the final decision.[22]

A lawful decision to delegate a function does not mean that the delegating authority may not continue to exercise that function concurrently with the delegate.[23] However, where the delegate makes a decision in the proper performance of the function delegated, that decision will be as binding as if it had been made by the delegating authority.[24]

12-07   The express powers of a local authority to delegate its functions under section 101 are so wide that it is difficult to see that there is room for the implication of any further powers to delegate. However, the following case suggests that this may be possible.

> *Provident Mutual Life Assurance Association* v. *Derby City Council*.[25] Schedule 1, para. 8, of the General Rate Act 1967 provides that where "a rating authority are of opinion" that a new building has been completed or can reasonably be expected to be completed within three months, a "completion notice" may be served on the owner. Rates thereafter become payable. Section 151 of the Local Government Act 1972 provides that "without prejudice to section 111 above, every local authority shall make arrangements for the proper

---

[18] See *Vine* v. *National Dock Labour Board* [1957] A.C. 488; *R.* v. *Gateshead JJ., ex p. Tesco Stores Ltd.* [1981] Q.B. 470.

[19] See §§ 4–48—4–59.

[20] [1921] 3 K.B. 621.

[21] [1925] 1 K.B. 213 (approved by the Court of Appeal in *R.* v. *Greater London Council, ex p. Blackburn* [1976] 1 W.L.R. 550).

[22] Compare *Osgood* v. *Nelson* (1872) L.R. 5 H.L. 636 with *Jeffs* v. *New Zealand Dairy Production and Marketing Board* [1967] 1 A.C. 551 and *R.* v. *Chester City Council and others, ex p. Quietlynn Ltd.* (1984) 83 L.G.R. 308, and see *Selvarajan* v. *Race Relations Board* [1976] 1 All E.R. 12, *per* Lord Denning M.R. at p. 20. See also § 4–49.

[23] See *Huth* v. *Clarke* (1890) 25 Q.B.D. 391, and s. 101(4) of the Local Government Act 1972.

[24] *Battelley* v. *Finsbury Borough Council* (1958) 56 L.G.R. 165. See § 4–50.

[25] (1981) 79 L.G.R. 297.

administration of their financial affairs and shall secure that one of their officers has responsibility for the administration of those affairs."

The council appointed their treasurer as the "proper officer" for rating purposes. The treasurer signed a typed form of completion notice. Copies were made, and were filled in where necessary by the principal rating assistant. The assistant decided when a notice should be served. Such decisions were not referred to the treasurer. There was no formal delegation of powers by the local authority to the assistant. The House of Lords *held* by four to one that this arrangement was *intra vires*. *Per* Lord Roskill[26]: "Parliament plainly contemplated that the actual machinery of enforcement and collection would not be operated personally by some senior local government official but would be so operated by the relevant senior official's staff." These were "administrative" matters, and what was done was "done as part of the proper administration of the respondents' financial affairs." Moreover, "the question is not whether the respondents' treasurer delegated power to Mr Wells [the assistant]. The question is whether what Mr Wells did was authorised by the respondents' treasurer so as to be the relevant opinion of the respondents. For the reasons I have given I think that it was. . . . ''

It is suggested that local authorities would be best advised to make formal arrangements for the delegation of functions rather than to rely upon the implication of powers to delegate, or to make "authorisations" of the kind contemplated by Lord Roskill (which seems, with respect, to amount to delegation by another name).

Acting under dictation

The converse of the situation described in the previous section is that a **12-08** local authority may not formally exercise its powers under the real or imagined dictation of another authority.

> *R. v. Stepney Corporation.*[27] A vestry clerk was entitled to compensation for the loss of his office which resulted from the transfer of the vestry's functions to a new local authority. The corporation had a discretion as to the amount, but mistakenly thought they were bound by the practice of the Treasury in relation to civil servants to deduct a quarter of the amount where an office was held part-time. *Held*, mandamus should be granted to compel the corporation to exercise its discretion in the light of the particular circumstances of the case.[28]

Parliament may, of course, expressly authorise a Minister to issue directions with which a local authority must comply.[29]

A power to give "guidance" may be distinguished from a power to give "directions."[30] On the other hand, Parliament may enable sanctions to be imposed for non-compliance with "guidance."[31]

---

[26] At pp. 306, 307.

[27] [1902] 1 K.B. 317.

[28] *Cf. Lavender* v. *Minister of Housing and Local Government* [1970] 1 W.L.R. 1231; *R. v. Manchester City Council, ex p. Fulford* (1982) 81 L.G.R. 292.

[29] See § 11-24.

[30] *Laker Airways Ltd.* v. *Department of Trade* [1977] Q.B. 643 at pp. 699-700, 714-717, 724-725.

[31] See *e.g.* s. 59(6)(*cc*) of the Local Government, Planning and Land Act 1980: above § 9-09.

Fettering discretion by contract or undertaking

12-09   A public authority may not enter into a contract or other agreement which is incompatible with the due exercise of its powers or the discharge of its duties or which divests the authority of its statutory powers or which obliges the authority not to exercise its powers. This principle has been invoked in a number of different situations. It has been relied on by local authorities to resist enforcement of an *express* contract,[32] covenant,[33] or non-contractual undertaking.[34] Terms can only be *implied* into existing agreements where they are compatible with the performance of statutory functions.[35] A plaintiff may challenge an exercise or non-exercise of discretion by a local authority on the ground that that discretion has been fettered by an agreement between the authority and a third party.[36]

12-10   It is of course clear that any contract by definition binds an authority to a course of action and this in turn limits its discretion in a particular field of activity. This is illustrated in *Dowty Boulton Paul Ltd.* v. *Wolverhampton Corporation.*[37] Here the corporation had sold land to the plaintiff company and had granted to it certain rights over an adjoining municipal airfield. During the currency of the lease the corporation decided to develop the airfield as a housing estate. Counsel for the corporation argued, *inter alia*, that under the general law regarding the exercise of statutory powers, the corporation was at any time entitled to override the licence it had granted to the company containing the rights referred to if the corporation required to use the airfield for any of its statutory purposes. Counsel based his contention on the principle that a body entrusted with statutory powers cannot by contract fetter the exercise of those powers. Pennycuick V.-C. said[38]:

> "I have said that the principle laid down . . . is established beyond doubt. That seems to me, however, a principle wholly inapplicable to the present case. What has happened here is that the corporation has made what is admittedly a valid disposition in respect of its land for a term of years. What is, in effect, contended . . . is that such a disposition—and, indeed, any other possible disposition of property by a corporation for a term of years, for example, an ordinary lease—must be read as subject to an implied condition enabling the corporation to determine it should it see fit to put the property to some other use in the exercise of any of its statutory powers. Nothing in the cases cited supports this startling proposition. The cases are concerned with attempts to fetter in advance the future exercise of statutory powers otherwise than by the valid exercise of a statutory power. The cases are not concerned with the position

---

[32] *Birkdale District Electric Supply Co.* v. *Southport Corporation* [1926] A.C. 355, at p. 364, per the Earl of Birkenhead.

[33] *Stourcliffe Estates Company* v. *Bournemouth Corporation* [1910] 2 Ch. 12.

[34] *R.* v. *Liverpool Corporation, ex p. Liverpool Taxi Fleet Operators' Association* [1972] 2 Q.B. 299: § 12–29.

[35] *William Cory & Son Ltd.* v. *London Corporation* [1951] 2 K.B. 476; *British Transport Commission* v. *Westmorland County Council* [1958] A.C. 126.

[36] *Stringer* v. *Minister of Housing and Local Government* [1970] 1 W.L.R. 1281.

[37] [1971] 1 W.L.R. 204. See also *Kirklees Metropolitan Borough Council* v. *Yorkshire Woollen Transport Company Limited* (1978) 77 L.G.R. 448.

[38] At p. 210.

which arises after a statutory power has been validly exercised. Obviously, where a power is exercised in such a manner as to create a right extending over a term of years, the existence of that right *pro tanto* excludes the exercise of other statutory powers in respect of the same subject matter, but there is no authority and I can see no principle upon which that sort of exercise could be held to be invalid as a fetter upon the future exercise of powers."

The court refused the remedy prayed for—a mandatory injunction **12-11** —on the technical ground that the court would not order what amounted, in this case, to specific performance of an obligation. The only remedy of the company lay in damages.[39]

An agreement will be invalid where it purports to divest the authority of a statutory power of primary importance, such as a power to make by-laws,[40] a power to purchase land,[41] or a discretion under the Town and Country Planning Acts to grant, refuse or revoke a planning permission.[42] In *Stringer* v. *Minister of Housing and Local Government*,[43] a county council and a rural district council entered into a formal agreement with Manchester University whereby they undertook to discourage development in the vicinity of Jodrell Bank radio telescope. Cooke J. held that the latter council's decision to refuse permission in a particular case, in accordance with this agreement, was void.

Failure to comply with a non-contractual undertaking may amount to a breach of the duty to act fairly.[44]

Estoppel
The powers of a local authority cannot be extended by the creation of **12-12** an estoppel.[45] Similarly, an authority cannot sanction the unlawful act of another,[46] and cannot be prevented by an estoppel from performing a statutory duty.

> *Maritime Electric Co. Ltd.* v. *General Dairies Ltd.*[47] The plaintiff electricity company was under a statutory duty to make certain charges. Through its own error, it undercharged the defendants over 28 months. The defendants relied on the accuracy of the sums charged to them in making their pricing decisions. *Held*, the plaintiff company was not estopped from recovering the full amount that should have been charged.

An example of a duty which cannot be hindered by the creation of an estoppel is the duty of an authority not to fetter or divest itself of its statutory discretions.

---

[39] *Cf. Blake* v. *Hendon Corporation* [1962] 1 Q.B. 283.
[40] *William Cory & Son Ltd.* v. *City of London Corporation* [1951] 2 K.B. 476.
[41] *Triggs* v. *Staines Urban District Council* [1969] 1 Ch. 10.
[42] *Ransom & Luck Ltd.* v. *Surbiton Borough Council* [1949] Ch. 180.
[43] [1970] 1 W.L.R. 1281.
[44] See §§ 12–28, 12–29, below.
[45] *Rhyl Urban District Council* v. *Rhyl Amusements Ltd.* [1959] 1 W.L.R. 465.
[46] *Yabbicom* v. *King* [1899] 1 Q.B. 444; *Redbridge London Borough Council* v. *Jacques* [1970] 1 W.L.R. 1604; *Cambridgeshire County Council* v. *Rust* [1972] 2 Q.B. 426.
[47] [1937] A.C. 610.

Southend-on-Sea Corporation v. *Hodgson (Wickford) Ltd.*[48] The borough engineer wrote to a builder to the effect that certain land had an existing use and that planning consent was not necessary for a builder's yard. Relying on this statement the builder purchased the land and used it as a builder's yard. The authority later took the opposite view and served an enforcement notice on the builder. He contended that the authority was estopped from saying that the premises had not been used throughout the period necessary to confer the right of an existing use. *Held*, estoppel cannot be raised to hinder the exercise of a statutory discretion conferred on a public authority.

Princes Investment Ltd. v. *Frimley and Camberley Urban District Council.*[49] The company was granted planning permission for housing development on condition that it would connect the houses to the public sewer to the satisfaction of the planning authority. The sewer was more than 100 feet from the nearest house. The company applied to the engineer for approval for the layout of the company's sewers and the engineer did in fact approve them. The company then claimed against the council for the cost of the excess of the sewers over 100 feet. The Divisional Court held that the authority had not "required" the connection of the public sewer and undertaken to bear a proportion of the cost under the Public Health Act since it could only act by resolution (and there had in fact been none) and the "requirements" could not be notified informally by the engineer.

12-13   The court in this case rejected the view that this matter fell within those recurring routine matters of day-to-day administration where no resolution was necessary and in doing so at least recognised the practice of informal delegation in routine matters.

The authority of the *Southend* case was somewhat diminished by *Lever (Finance) Ltd.* v. *Westminster (City) London Borough Council.*[50] A planning officer had informed a developer that a particular alteration to a plan was not a material alteration so as to require a fresh planning consent. The authority later called for a planning application and refused it. It was held that the planning officer's decision was a representation within the officer's ostensible authority, and having been acted on by the developers, it was binding on the planning authority. Lord Denning M. R. said[51]:

> "If the planning officer tells the developer that a proposed variation is not material, and the developer acts on it, the planning authority cannot go back on it. I know that there are authorities which say that a public authority cannot be estopped by any representations made by its officers. It cannot be estopped from doing its public duty. See, for instance, the recent decision of the Divisional Court in *Southend-on-Sea Corporation* v. *Hodgson (Wickford) Ltd.* But these statements must now be taken with considerable reserve.... If an officer, acting within the scope of his ostensible authority, makes a representation on which another acts, then a public authority must be bound by it, just as a private concern would be."

12-14   The following decision of the Court of Appeal restores somewhat the earlier principle.

[48] [1962] 1 Q.B. 416.
[49] [1962] 1 Q.B. 681.
[50] [1971] 1 Q.B. 222.
[51] At p. 230.

Western Fish Products Ltd. v. *Penwith District Council.*[52] The company claimed that there was an established user right to use a factory for a particular purpose. The matter was discussed between company representatives and the council's chief planning officer, the company supplying information as to the previous use. Subsequently, the officer wrote that the information had been checked and that "it is confirmed that the limits of the various component parts of the commercial undertaking as now existing appear to be established." The company's later applications for planning permission and for an established use certificate were refused. They sought a declaration, *inter alia*, that the representations made by the council estopped it from asserting that planning permission was necessary, from refusing planning permission and from taking enforcement action. The Court of Appeal *held* (1) that the representation in the letter related to the existing position and did not amount to confirmation of an existing user right in relation to the proposed project; (2) that the plaintiffs had not in fact changed their position in reliance on the representation as they would have gone ahead with their project anyway; (3) that even if the decision on the first two points had been otherwise, their claim would still have failed for the following reasons: (i) since "proprietary estoppel" was concerned only with the creation by estoppel of rights and interests in or over land; and (ii) since the council could not be estopped from performing its statutory duties under the Town and Country Planning Act 1971, or from exercising its statutory discretions. On the second point, an officer, even when acting within the apparent scope of his authority, could not do what the Act required the council to do. Although there was a power to delegate under section 101(1) of the 1972 Act, there had to be a formal act of delegation. By Standing Orders, designated officers had been authorised to perform specified functions including those arising under sections 53 (determinations as to whether planning permission was required) and 94 (applications for established use certificates). Those officers had no authority to make any other kinds of determination. The only exceptions to the principle that authorities cannot be estopped from performing statutory duties were (*a*) where a decision was made by a person acting within delegated powers, and (*b*) where an authority waived a procedural requirement (*Wells* v. *Minister of Housing and Local Government.*[53]) Exception (*a*) could be established either where there was a decision made by a person acting under powers formally delegated, or where there was "some evidence justifying the person dealing with the planning officer for thinking that what the officer said would bind the planning authority. Holding an office, however senior, cannot . . . be enough by itself" (*per* Megaw L. J.). The court disagreed with Lord Denning's view that a person is entitled to assume that all necessary resolutions have been passed.

On the facts of *Western Fish* (i) there was no formal delegation except in relation to section 53 and section 94 matters; (ii) there was no evidence justifying the belief that representations on other matters would bind the authority; (iii) the plaintiffs had not made the necessary formal applications for a section 53 determination (the *Wells* decision being confined to situations where an application for planning permission was to be regarded as impliedly containing an invitation to make a section 53 determination); (iv) there was no formal application under section 94; and (v) in any event, a certificate under section 94 would have to be a document complying with the prescribed formalities.

---

[52] [1981] 2 All E.R. 204. See also *Co-operative Retail Services Ltd.* v. *Taff-Ely Borough Council* (1979) 39 P. & C.R. 223; appeal dismissed (1982) 42 P. & C.R. 1.

[53] [1967] 1 W.L.R. 1000.

Rootkin v. *Kent County Council.*[54] The plaintiff's daughter was allocated a place at a school measured by the authority to be over three miles from her home. On that basis, the authority was under a duty either to provide transport or to reimburse travelling expenses, under section 39(2) of the Education Act 1944. It chose the latter course, and issued a bus pass, in the exercise of the discretionary power under section 55(2) of the 1944 Act. Shortly after, the authority made a more precise measurement and found the distance to be less than three miles. It then withdrew the bus pass. The plaintiff argued (1) that the authority was not entitled to rescind its determination that a bus pass should be issued, and (2) that the authority was estopped from revoking its decision. The Court of Appeal *held* that the authority was entitled to withdraw the pass. On the first point it was stated that "if a citizen is entitled to payment in certain circumstances and a local authority is given the duty of deciding whether the circumstances exist and if they do exist of making the payment, then there is a determination which the local authority cannot rescind. That was established in *Livingston* v. *Westminster Corpn.*[55] But that line of authority does not apply . . . to a case where the citizen has no right to a determination on certain facts being established, but only to the benefit of the exercise of a discretion by the local authority.[56] On the second point, it was held that an estoppel could not arise where that would prevent the exercise of a statutory discretion (*Southend-on-Sea Corporation* v. *Hodgson (Wickford) Ltd., supra*), that there was here no exceptional situation of a kind contemplated in the *Western Fish* case, and that in any event the plaintiff had not altered her position so as to entitle her to rely on the doctrine of estoppel.

Fettering discretion by self-created rules of policy

12-15　　A local authority may wish to ensure consistency in its decision making by establishing policy rules or guidelines. These must not (1) be based on considerations which are legally irrelevant,[57] nor (2) be applied so rigidly that an exercise of discretion in each individual case is precluded.

The latter principle was stated as follows by Bankes L.J. in *R.* v. *Port of London Authority, ex p. Kynoch Ltd.*[58]:

"There are on the one hand cases where a tribunal in the honest exercise of its discretion has adopted a policy, and, without refusing to hear an applicant, intimates to him what its policy is, and that after hearing him it will in accordance with its policy decide against him, unless there is something exceptional in his case. I think counsel for the applicants would admit that, if the policy has been adopted for reasons which the tribunal may legitimately entertain, no objection could be taken to such a course. On the other hand there are cases where a tribunal has passed a rule, or come to a determination not to hear any application of a particular character by whomsoever made. There is a wide distinction to be drawn between these two classes."

R. v. *London County Council, ex p. Corrie.*[59] The county council made by-laws prohibiting the selling of an article in the parks under its control except with the consent of the council. The council later resolved that no new permission should be granted and that the existing permissions should be

---

[54] [1981] 2 All E.R. 227.
[55] [1904] 2 K.B. 109.
[56] *Per* Lawton L.J. at p. 233; *cf.* Eveleigh L.J. at pp. 234–235 and Sir Stanley Rees at p. 237.
[57] See §§ 12–20, 12–25.
[58] [1919] 1 K.B. 176, at p. 184.
[59] [1918] 1 K.B. 68.

withdrawn. *Held*, the by-law conferred a discretion on the council. In passing the general resolution to grant no permissions it had failed to exercise its discretion at all. Mandamus accordingly lay to make the council hear an application and decide on its merits.[60]

In most cases which have arisen the issue has not been as clear-cut. **12-16** There are several areas of uncertainty. First, does an authority comply with the *Kynoch* principle if it *considers* all applications made to it, even though the operation of the policy will mean that each application will fail? In *British Oxygen Co. Ltd.* v. *Minister of Technology*,[61] Lord Reid cited the passage from the judgment of Bankes L.J. in *R.* v. *Port of London Authority, ex p. Kynoch Ltd., supra*, and continued[62]:

"I see nothing wrong with that. But the circumstances in which discretions are exercised vary enormously and that passage cannot be applied literally in every case. The general rule is that anyone who has to exercise a statutory discretion must not 'shut his ears to an application' (to adapt from Bankes L.J. on p. 183). I do not think there is any great difference between a policy and a rule. There may be cases where an officer or authority ought to listen to a substantial argument reasonably presented urging a change of policy. What the authority must not do is to refuse to listen at all. But a Ministry or large authority may have had to deal already with a multitude of similar applications and then they will almost certainly have evolved a policy so precise that it could well be called a rule. There can be no objection to that, provided the authority is always willing to listen to anyone with something new to say—of course I do not mean to say that there need be an oral hearing."

However, it may not be sufficient for an authority to listen to all that an **12-17** applicant has to say, if in fact it is not prepared to make any exception to its general policy.

Sagnata Investments Ltd. v. *Norwich Corporation*.[63] The corporation by a majority of 41 to 1 took a policy decision not to grant permits for amusements with prizes for any amusement arcade in Norwich. The plaintiffs applied for a permit. The committee to which the power to determine applications had been delegated afforded the plaintiffs a full hearing, but rejected the application. On appeal to quarter sessions, the recorder held that the committee had so fettered its discretion following the council's policy decision that no application could succeed, and that the committee had failed to exercise its discretion at all. The case ultimately came to the Court of Appeal, where Lord Denning M.R. (dissenting) held that the recorder had erred in law on these points, given that the committee had considered the application. However, the recorder's view was endorsed by Phillimore L.J.[64]: "[According to the recorder], the council had *not* exercised any form of discretion, they had simply dismissed this application after going through the necessary motions without regard to its individual merits or demerits. I take this to be a finding of fact with which this court is in

[60] See also *R.* v. *County Council of West Riding of Yorkshire* [1896] 2 Q.B. 386; *R.* v. *Flintshire County Council Licensing Stage Plays Committee, ex p. Barrett* [1957] 1 Q.B. 350; *Docherty* v. *South Tyneside Borough, The Times*, July 3, 1982; *R.* v. *Secretary of State for the Environment, ex p. Brent London Borough Council* [1982] Q.B. 593.
[61] [1971] A.C. 610.
[62] At p. 625.
[63] [1971] 2 Q.B. 614.
[64] At p. 630.

no position to interfere. Incidentally, I cannot see that the recorder could avoid this decision. . . . " Edmund Davies L.J. agreed with the recorder's view that it was "entirely proper" for the authority to adopt a general policy of refusing such application "provided that no inflexible, invarying attitude was adopted and that the local authority was prepared to depart from it where the justice of a particular case so required."[65]

12-18　　Secondly, the legality of reliance on a policy *may* depend on the number of applications to be processed. A court may be sympathetic to the adoption of fairly rigid guidelines where large numbers of applications are involved: see Lord Reid in the *British Oxygen* case (*supra*). Indeed, Viscount Dilhorne in the same case felt "some doubt whether the words used by Bankes L.J. . . . are really applicable to a case of this kind. It seems somewhat pointless and a waste of time that the Board should have to consider applications which are bound as a result of its policy decision to fail. Representations could of course be made that the policy should be changed."[66] This case concerned the discretion of the Board of Trade (subsequently the Ministry of Technology) to award investment grants in respect of new plant. They had a rule of practice not to make grants in respect of items which cost individually less than £25. This was held to be a lawful ground for rejecting an application, and as they had not declined to consider the application the plaintiffs had no cause for complaint. Where the case load is of more manageable proportions, the exercise of discretion on a more individualised basis may be called for.

12-19　　Thirdly, there is some authority for the proposition that reliance on a predetermined policy must not preclude the consideration of "all the issues which are relevant to each individual case as it comes up for decision."[67]

It is to be noted in this connection that Parliament may expressly authorise the adoption of inflexible policies of the kind not permitted by the common law. For example, the Lotteries and Amusements Act 1976 enables a local authority to pass a resolution that it will not grant, or will neither grant nor renew, any permits for the commercial provision of amusements with prizes in respect of premises of a class specified in the resolution.[68]

C. ABUSE OF DISCRETION

12-20　　Discretionary powers must not be abused in such a way that *express* or *implied* limits in the relevant statute are exceeded. The leading statement

---

[65] p. 632.
[66] [1971] A.C. 610 at p. 631.
[67] *Per* Cooke J. in *Stringer* v. *Minister of Housing and Local Government* [1970] 1 W.L.R. 1281 at p. 1298, and see *Lavender & Son Ltd.* v. *Minister of Housing and Local Government* [1970] 1 W.L.R. 1231; *Att.-Gen., ex rel. Tilley* v. *Wandsworth Borough Council* (1980) 78 L.G.R. 677; affirmed [1981] 1 W.L.R. 854.
[68] Sched. 3, para. 2: see *R.* v. *Herrod, ex p. Leeds City Council* [1978] A.C. 403.

of the relevant principles was made by Lord Greene M.R. in the
following case:

Associated Provincial Picture Houses Ltd. v. *Wednesbury Corporation.*[69] The
corporation granted the plaintiffs a licence to give cinema performances on a
Sunday on condition that no children under the age of 15 should be admitted.
The plaintiffs sought a declaration that the condition was *ultra vires. Held*, the
condition was valid. *Per* Lord Greene M.R.[70]: "It is not to be assumed prima
facie that responsible bodies like the local authority in this case will exceed
their powers; but the court, whenever it is alleged that the local authority have
contravened the law, must not substitute itself for that authority. . . . When an
executive discretion is entrusted by Parliament to a body such as the local
authority in this case, what appears to be an exercise of that discretion can only
be challenged in the courts in a strictly limited class of case. . . . It must always
be remembered that the court is not a court of appeal. When discretion of this
kind is granted the law recognises certain principles upon which that discretion
must be exercised, but within the four corners of those principles the discretion,
in my opinion, is an absolute one and cannot be questioned in any court of law.
What then are those principles? . . . The exercise of such a discretion must be a
real exercise of the discretion. If, in the statute conferring the discretion, there is
to be found expressly or by implication matters which the authority exercising
the discretion ought to have regard to, then in exercising the discretion it must
have regard to those matters. Conversely, if the nature of the subject-matter
and the general interpretation of the Act make it clear that certain matters
would not be germane to the matter in question, the authority must disregard
those irrelevant collateral matters. . . .

It is true the discretion must be exercised reasonably. Now what does that
mean? Lawyers familiar with the phraseology commonly used in relation to
exercise of statutory discretions often use the word 'unreasonable' in a rather
comprehensive sense. It has frequently been used and is frequently used as a
general description of the things that must not be done. For instance, a
person entrusted with a discretion must, so to speak, direct himself properly in
law. He must call his own attention to the matters which he is bound to
consider. He must exclude from his consideration matters which are irrelevant
to what he has to consider. If he does not obey those rules, he may truly be said,
and often is said, to be acting 'unreasonably.' Similarly, there may be
something so absurd that no sensible person could ever dream that it lay within
the powers of the authority. Warrington L.J. in *Short* v. *Poole Corporation*[71]
gave the example of the red-haired teacher, dismissed because she had red hair.
That is unreasonable in one sense. In another sense it is taking into
consideration extraneous matters. It is so unreasonable that it might almost be
described as being done in bad faith; and in fact, all these things run into one
another. . . . It is clear that the local authority are entrusted by Parliament with
the decision on a matter which the knowledge and experience of that authority
can best be trusted to deal with. The subject-matter with which the condition
deals is one relevant for its consideration. They have considered it and come to
a decision upon it. It is true to say that, if a decision on a competent matter is so
unreasonable that no reasonable authority could ever have come to it, then the
courts can interfere. That, I think, is quite right; but to prove a case of that kind
would require something overwhelming, and, in this case, the facts do not come
anywhere near anything of that kind."

[69] [1948] 1 K.B. 223.
[70] At pp. 228, 229, 230.
[71] [1926] Ch. 66 at pp. 90, 91.

The following points may be noted. First, the power of a court to control "abuses of discretion" is firmly rooted in the *ultra vires* doctrine. Indeed, a court can only intervene where express or implied limits in the relevant statute are exceeded, unless an error of law is apparent on the face of the record of proceedings, or there is a statutory right of appeal.

12-21 Secondly, the courts frequently affirm that they can only intervene where decisions are clearly unlawful. The views of the elected representatives of the people are entitled to considerable respect, both where it is alleged that an act of a local authority is *ultra vires*,[72] and where an appeal lies on the merits against a local authority's decision.[73]

12-22 Thirdly, the courts are no longer deterred by the enactment of powers in subjective form from exercising the usual measure of control in relation to discretionary powers. For example, powers to take action if *it appears* or if *the authority is satisfied* that it is *necessary* or *expedient* were interpreted literally in cases decided in wartime, or shortly thereafter.[74] The courts would defer to an authority's assertion that it was so "satisfied" or that it so "appeared," provided that they had acted in good faith. However, the courts have been unwilling to be as deferential in relation to the exercise of other statutory powers in peacetime.[75]

Fourthly, all the discretionary decision-making of local authorities is potentially reviewable in accordance with the *Wednesbury* principles, including decisions closely analogous to those taken by private citizens. Examples include the decision of a local authority as landlord to serve notice to quit on a council tenant,[76] as proprietor of a private as distinct from a statutory market,[77] or as owner of land.[78]

Fifthly, where items of account of expenditure of local authorities are challenged, a failure to take into account relevant matters or the taking into account of irrelevant matters does not amount to illegality in itself; it is merely evidence that the authority may have acted *ultra vires* or contrary to law. Attention must be directed to the quality of the decision, and to establish illegality it must be shown that the decision was not really made in exercise of the authority's powers but for some ulterior purpose, or that no reasonable authority could have reached such a decision.[79]

---

[72] Lord Russell of Killowen C.J. in *Kruse* v. *Johnson* [1898] 2 Q.B. 91 at p. 99.
[73] *Sagnata Investments Ltd.* v. *Norwich Corporation* [1971] 2 Q.B 614 at pp. 636–637 (Edmund Davies L.J.) and p. 640 (Phillimore L.J.).
[74] See e.g. *Point of Ayr Collieries Ltd.* v. *Lloyd George* [1943] 2 All E.R. 546; *Carltona Ltd.* v. *Commissioners of Works* [1943] 2 All E.R. 560; *Robinson* v. *Minister of Town and Country Planning* [1947] K.B. 702.
[75] See *Commissioners of Customs and Excise* v. *Cure and Deeley Ltd.* [1962] 1 Q.B. 340; *Secretary of State for Education and Science* v. *Tameside Metropolitan Borough Council* [1977] A.C. 1014 at pp. 1024–1025 (Lord Denning M.R.), 1030–1031 (Scarman L.J.), 1047 (Lord Wilberforce).
[76] *Cannock Chase District Council* v. *Kelly* [1978] 1 W.L.R. 1 (where the tenant's challenge failed on the merits).
[77] *R.* v. *Basildon District Council, ex p. Brown* (1981) 79 L.G.R. 655.
[78] *Cf. R.* v. *Wear Valley District Council, ex p. Binks* [1985] 2 All E.R. 699.
[79] *Per* Ormrod L.J. in *Pickwell* v. *Camden London Borough Council* [1983] Q.B. 962: see § 7–18.

In each of the following cases it was alleged that there had been a **12-23** wrongful use of a discretionary power.[80]

Westminster Corporation v. *London and North-Western Railway Co.*[81] The corporation had power to construct public lavatories underground but no power to construct a subway as such. They constructed lavatories under Parliament Street leading off an underground passage with entrances on each side of the street. There had been some reference in correspondence to the need for a subway at this point. The chairman of the works committee testified that "the primary object of the committee was to provide these conveniences." *Held*, the works were *intra vires*. *Per* Lord Macnaghten[82]: "In order to make out a case of bad faith it must be shewn that the corporation constructed this subway as a means of crossing the street under colour and pretence of providing public conveniences which were not really wanted at that particular place." On the evidence, the "primary object" was the construction of the conveniences.

Westminster Bank v. *Beverley Borough Council.*[83] The council refused planning permission for the extension of bank premises on the ground that "it might prejudice the future widening" of the street. Compensation was not payable. The council might have achieved the same result by prescribing an improvement line under the Highways Act 1959, but compensation would then have been payable. *Held*, the council was entitled to choose which of the powers to exercise. *Per* Lord Reid[84]:

"Parliament has chosen to set up two different ways of preventing development which would interfere with schemes for street widening. It must have been aware that one involved in paying compensation but the other did not. Nevertheless it expressed no preference, and imposed no limit on the use of either. No doubt there might be special circumstances which make it unreasonable or an abuse of power to use one of these methods but here there were none. Even if the appellants' view of the facts is right, the authority had to choose whether to leave the appellants without compensation or to impose a burden on its ratepayers. One may think that it would be most equitable that the burden should be shared. But the Minister of Transport had made it clear in a circular sent to local authorities in 1954 that there would be no grant if a local authority proceeded in such a way that compensation would be payable, and there is nothing to indicate any disapproval of this policy by Parliament and nothing in any of the legislation to indicate that Parliament disapproved by depriving the subject of compensation. I cannot in these circumstances find any abuse of power in the local authority deciding that the appellants and not its ratepayers should bear the burden."

Bromley London Borough Council v. *Greater London Council.*[85] Section 1 of the Transport (London) Act 1969 imposed on the G.L.C. the duty to develop policies and encourage measures which promote "the provision of integrated, efficient and economic transport facilities and services for Greater London." Those policies were to be implemented by the London Transport Executive. Section 5(1) required the L.T.E. to have due regard to "efficiency, economy and

---

[80] See also *Roberts* v. *Hopwood* [1925] A.C. 578, § 7–18.
[81] [1905] A.C. 426; *cf. Wheeler* v. *Leicester City Council* [1985] 3 W.L.R. 335, where the House of Lords held that the council could not lawfully ban a rugby club from using a public recreation ground in order to punish the club for failing to endorse in full the council's views in opposition to a tour by the Rugby Football Union to South Africa.
[82] At p. 132.
[83] [1971] A.C. 508.
[84] At p. 530.
[85] [1983] 1 A.C. 768.

safety of operation." Section 7(3)(*b*) provided that if at the end of an accounting period there was a deficit in the L.T.E.'s revenue account, the L.T.E. was required as far as practicable, to make up that deficit in the next accounting period. Under section 7(6) the G.L.C. could take action to enable the L.T.E. to comply with its duty under section 7(3)(*b*). In July 1981, the G.L.C. resolved to implement one of the election manifesto commitments of the controlling Labour group to cut fares on London Transport buses and tubes by an average of 25 per cent. A supplementary precept was issued to cover the deficit that the L.T.E. would incur as a result. The money would be paid by the G.L.C. to the L.T.E. in the exercise of the former's power to make grants to the L.T.E. "for any purpose" (1969 Act, s. 3(1)). The G.L.C. were aware that its fare reduction policy would result in the loss of approximately £50m of the rate support grant from the government. Bromley Council, one of the authorities to which the precept had been directed, sought certiorari to quash the supplementary rate on the grounds it was (1) *ultra vires* and (2) an invalid exercise of discretion. Lord Diplock and Lord Scarman regarded the separate arguments based on *ultra vires* and abuse of discretion as two ways of making the same point.[86] Lord Wilberforce and Lord Keith dealt with the case from the *ultra vires* standpoint. Lord Brandon dealt with both arguments.

The House of Lords held that certiorari should be granted, on a variety of grounds.

(1) The L.T.E. was required to run its transport undertaking on "ordinary business principles." This requirement was derived from the common law (*Prescott* v. *Birmingham Corporation*[87]) and (*per* Lords Wilberforce, Keith and Scarman), from the requirement that the L.T.E. have regard to "economy" (s. 5(1)). This did not require the L.T.E. to try to make a profit, but to ensure, so far as practicable, that outgoings were met by revenue.[88]

(2) Section 7(3) was to be interpreted as requiring the L.T.E. to operate, so far as possible, on a break-even basis. Grants could be made by the G.L.C. on the revenue account to make good unavoidable losses, actual or prospective, but not to achieve some object of social policy in total disregard of the L.T.E.'s obligations in (1) above and in section 7(3).[89]

(3) There was a breach of the fiduciary duty owed to the ratepayers. The G.L.C. had failed to balance their duty to the ratepayers against the duty to transport users.[90] Lord Diplock said[91] that the fiduciary duty owed to the ratepayers from whom it obtains moneys "includes a duty not to expend those moneys thriftlessly but to deploy the full financial resources available to it to the best advantage."

(4) The decision to implement this policy in the knowledge that the original contemplated cost to the ratepayers would be nearly doubled by the loss of rate support grant was not a decision which the council, directing themselves properly in law, could reasonably have made.[92]

(5) The majority group on the G.L.C. had misdirected itself by regarding the

---

[86] See pp. 820–821 and 836–837.
[87] [1955] Ch. 210.
[88] See Lord Wilberforce at pp. 815, 819; Lord Keith, *passim*; Lord Scarman at pp. 838–839, 841–842, 843; Lord Brandon at pp. 851, 852.
[89] See Lord Wilberforce at pp. 815–819; Lord Keith at pp. 833–834; Lord Scarman at pp. 844–846; Lord Diplock took a broader view of s. 7(3): see pp. 825–828.
[90] See Lord Wilberforce at pp. 815, 819–820; Lord Diplock at pp. 829–830; Lord Scarman at pp. 838–839, 842.
[91] At p. 829.
[92] See Lord Brandon at p. 853; *cf.* Lord Wilberforce at p. 820 and Lord Diplock at p. 830, who regarded this factor as an element in establishing a breach of the fiduciary duty.

G.L.C. as irrevocably committed by the election manifesto to carry out the policy.[93]

R. v. Merseyside County Council, ex p. Great Universal Stores Ltd.[94] In this **12-24** case, Woolf J. rejected a challenge to the validity of the council's policy of subsidising bus fares from the rates. The *Bromley* case, *supra*, was distinguished on a variety of grounds.

(1) The Council's powers were derived from the Transport Act 1968 and this was different in material respects from the Transport (London) Act 1969. Section 9(3) of the 1968 Act required the council to perform its functions "so . . . as to secure or promote the provision of a properly integrated and efficient system of public passenger transport to meet the needs of that area with due regard to the town planning and traffic and parking policies of the councils of constituent areas and to economy and safety of operation." The equivalent provision in the 1969 Act required the G.L.C. to promote the provision of "integrated, efficient *and economic* transport facilities." Moreover, under the 1968 Act the general duty of the executive was not made expressly subject to their financial duty. Woolf J. held that the council could require the executive to run a service which the executive considered would not be justified on ordinary business principles if the authority were prepared to undertake to meet the extra cost of running the service, although they were under a duty to balance the interests of the ratepayers against the advantage to the area of the proposed transport service.

(2) In the present case there was no question of the reduction in fares producing an automatic loss of rate support grant.

(3) The policies adopted by the council were in accord with the Merseyside Structure Plan.

(4) The members of the council here had not regarded themselves as committed to the implementation of their manifesto promise of a cheap fares policy. The proposal had been considered afresh on its merits after the elections.

(5) It could not be said that the new policy was manifestly inconsistent with the duty owed to the ratepayers.

In any event, relief would have been refused on the ground of delay, as the application for judicial review had been delayed pending the outcome of proceedings in the *Bromley* case. At the least the applicants should have warned the council of their intention to make the present application.

R. v. London Transport Executive, ex p. Greater London Council.[95] Following the decision in the *Bromley* case, fares were approximately doubled. Subsequently, the Divisional Court upheld the validity of a revised plan for London Transport fares, involving a reduction of about 25 per cent. in the new fares and an increase in the deficit on the L.T.E.'s revenue account of about 17 per cent., to be made good by a grant from the G.L.C. The G.L.C. was entitled to make grants to the L.T.E. to meet continuing losses, provided there was no breach of the principles laid down in the *Wednesbury* and *Prescott* cases. Kerr L.J. expressed broad agreement with the submission on behalf of the G.L.C. that

---

[93] See Lord Diplock at pp. 830–831 and Lord Brandon at p. 853; *cf.* Lord Wilberforce at p. 815. See also the analysis of the *ratio decidendi* of the *Bromley* case, derived from the speeches of Lords Wilberforce, Keith of Kinkel and Scarman, set out by Glidewell J. in *R. v. London Transport Executive, ex p. Greater London Council* [1983] Q.B. 484 at pp. 509–510.
[94] (1982) 80 L.G.R. 639.
[95] [1983] Q.B. 484.

the references in *Bromley* and *Prescott* to the requirement to conduct a transport system on business principles were primarily intended to exclude philanthropic considerations and to emphasize the need for proper and cost-effective use of resources; they did not mean that fare revenue had to be maximised on ordinary business principles of profit and loss.[96] The court granted declarations to the effect that the revised plan was within the powers of the G.L.C. and the L.T.E. on the true construction of the Transport Act 1969. It did not decide whether there was any breach of the *Wednesbury* and *Prescott* principles: both parties were agreed that there was no such breach and Kerr L.J. stated that "nothing has emerged in the evidence and argument presented to us which has led us to think the contrary,"[97] but the court expressly left the point open.[98]

12-25 The specific considerations that are relevant to an exercise of discretion may be set out in the statute. For example, section 604(1) of the Housing Act 1985 lists matters to which regard shall be had in determining whether a house is unfit for human habitation. Section 71 of the Race Relations Act 1976 requires local authorities to carry out their various functions with due regard to the need to eliminate unlawful racial discrimination and to promote equality of opportunity, and good relations, between persons of different racial groups.[99] Alternatively, the relevant considerations may be identified by the courts. There is, for example, much case law on the question of what are material planning considerations under the Planning Acts.[1] The Court of Appeal in *Bristol District Council* v. *Clark*[2] identified a number of factors which were relevant to decisions to evict council tenants.

12-26 Where the exercise of a power is expressly limited to occasions where there are "reasonable grounds" for its exercise, the courts normally require the authority to show that objectively reasonable grounds do exist.[3] However, in the context of the power of a local authority to charge "reasonable" rents under housing legislation, the court will only interfere where a rent is unreasonable in the narrower sense expounded by Lord Greene in the *Wednesbury* case.[4] Thus an increase of rent from £7 to £18,000 (a device to evade certain aspects of the Housing Finance Act 1972) was held to be unreasonable and *ultra vires* in *Backhouse* v. *Lambeth London Borough Council.*[5]

The term "bad faith" has in the past been employed as a synonym for

---

[96] See pp. 497, 499.
[97] At p. 497.
[98] See the form of the declarations set out at p. 502.
[99] See *Wheeler* v. *Leicester City Council* [1985] 3 W.L.R. 335 (*supra*, n. 81) where it was held that s. 71 did not justify the actions there held to be unlawful.
[1] See Chapter 19; see also *Encyclopedia of Planning Law and Practice*, paras. 2–875—2–877.
[2] [1975] 1 W.L.R. 1443. See also *Cannock Chase District Council* v. *Kelly* [1978] 1 W.L.R. 1 and *Sevenoaks District Council* v. *Emmott* (1979) 78 L.G.R. 346.
[3] See *Nakkuda Ali* v. *Jayaratne* [1951] A.C. 66, distinguishing *Liversidge* v. *Anderson* [1942] A.C. 206.
[4] See *Luby* v. *Newcastle-under-Lyme Corporation* [1964] 2 Q.B. 64; [1965] 1 Q.B. 214.
[5] (1972) 116 S.J. 802.

"abuse of discretion." The view has been expressed that it should only be used in respect of dishonest misuses of power.[6]

D. NATURAL JUSTICE

Local authorities may be required to observe natural justice in the course **12-27** of their decision-making. Traditionally, the rules of "natural justice" have been regarded as comprising the rules *audi alteram partem* and *nemo judex in causa sua*. Respectively, these apply to require the maker of a decision to give prior notice to persons affected by it and an opportunity for those persons to make representations, and to disqualify him from acting if he has a direct pecuniary or proprietary interest, or might otherwise be biased. These rules originated in relation to courts of law, but have been applied to judicial and quasi-judicial decision-making by administrative authorities. In *Ridge* v. *Baldwin*,[7] the House of Lords held that a duty to act judicially may arise wherever a decision "affects the rights of subjects," and not solely in situations where a decision is made as between two contending parties. In recent years, it has been suggested that a duty to observe natural justice, or at least an attenuated "duty to act fairly," may attach to all decision-making whether judicial or administrative.[8] Alternatively, it has been suggested that a duty to observe natural justice attaches to judicial or quasi-judicial decision-making, and a duty to act fairly to administrative decision-making.[9] This distinction is, however, difficult to draw satisfactorily, and it is submitted that the better view is that the courts should determine the appropriate content of the duty to observe natural justice or act fairly (however it is described) in the light of the particular circumstances of the case. In the case of decisions which are "purely" administrative, the content of the duty to act fairly may simply amount to an obligation to refrain from an *ultra vires* abuse of discretion.[10]

Audi alteram partem

The following are examples of situations where *procedural* standards **12-28** have been imposed:

(1) Where there is a *lis inter partes*, as when objections to a

---

[6] *Cannock Chase District Council* v. *Kelly* [1978] 1 W.L.R. 1 at p. 6 (Megaw L.J.) and p. 11 (Sir David Cairns).

[7] [1964] A.C. 40.

[8] See *Re H.K., an Infant* [1967] 2 Q.B. 617; *R.* v. *Birmingham City Justice, ex p. Chris Foreign Foods (Wholesalers)* [1970] 1 W.L.R. 1428; *Breen* v. *Amalgamated Engineering Union* [1971] 2 Q.B. 175; *R.* v. *Liverpool Corporation, ex p. Liverpool Taxi Fleet Operators' Association* [1972] 2 Q.B. 299; *R.* v. *Commission for Racial Equality, ex p. Cottrell & Rothon* [1980] 1 W.L.R. 1580 at pp. 1586–1587; *Bushell* v. *Secretary of State for the Environment* [1981] A.C. 75; *R.* v. *Commission for Racial Equality, ex p. Hillingdon London Borough Council* [1982] A.C. 779 at p. 787.

[9] See Lord Pearson in *Pearlberg* v. *Varty* [1972] 1 W.L.R. 534 at p. 547.

[10] See *Breen* v. *Amalgamated Engineering Union* [1971] 2 Q.B. 175 at pp. 195, 200.

compulsory purchase order made by a local authority are submitted to the minister,[11] or where a local authority has to determine whether a landlord or a tenant should receive compensation for a "well maintained" house;[12]

(2) Where a decision affects a person's livelihood;[13]

(3) Where a decision is taken to dismiss the holder from an office or employment terminable only for cause;[14]

(4) Where a decision infringes property rights;[15]

(5) Where a public authority has undertaken to afford a hearing: where an authority has promised to follow a certain procedure it is in the interests of good administration that it should act fairly and implement its promises so long as implementation does not interfere with its statutory duty.[16]

This list is by no means exhaustive. Lord Denning M.R. stated in *Breen* v. *Amalgamated Engineering Union*[17] that if a man "has some right or interest, or some legitimate expectation of which it would not be fair to deprive him without a hearing or reasons given, then these should be afforded him, according as the case may demand." The relevant provisions must be examined in each case.

Local Government Board v. *Arlidge*.[18] A local authority had made a closing order in respect of an unfit house. The Housing, Town Planning, etc., Act 1909 (now repealed), under which the order was made, gave the owner a right of appeal to the Local Government Board. The owner's appeal to the Board was dismissed. He then applied to the court for a writ of certiorari for the purpose of quashing the order on the ground that the appeal had not been determined in the manner provided by law, for he had been refused permission to be heard orally by the officer who decided the case and had been refused permission to see the report made by the Board's inspector upon the public local inquiry. He did not succeed. Lord Shaw said[19]: "The words 'natural justice' occur in arguments and sometimes in judicial pronouncements in such cases. My Lords, when a central administrative board deals with an appeal from a local authority

[11] *Errington* v. *Minister of Health* [1935] 1 K.B. 249.
[12] *Hoggard* v. *Worsborough Urban District Council* [1962] 2 Q.B. 93.
[13] *R.* v. *Liverpool Corporation, ex p. Liverpool Taxi Owners Association, infra; R.* v. *Barnsley Metropolitan Borough Council, ex p. Hook* [1976] 1 W.L.R. 1052.
[14] *Osgood* v. *Nelson* (1872) L.R. 5 H.L. 636; *Cooper* v. *Wilson* [1937] 2 K.B. 309; *Fullbrook* v. *Berkshire Magistrates' Courts Committee* (1971) 69 L.G.R. 75; *R.* v. *Kent Police Authority, ex p. Godden* [1971] 2 Q.B. 662; *Ridge* v. *Baldwin* [1964] A.C. 40; *Stevenson* v. *United Road Transport Union* [1977] I.C.R. 893; *R.* v. *British Broadcasting Corporation, ex p. Lavelle* [1983] 1 W.L.R. 23; *Chief Constable of the North Wales Police* v. *Evans* [1982] 1 W.L.R. 1155.
[15] *Cooper* v. *Wandsworth Board of Works* (1863) 14 C.B. (N.S.) 180 (board held liable in trespass where a house was demolished by the board's employees without prior notice to the owner).
[16] *R.* v. *Liverpool Corporation, ex p. Liverpool Taxi Fleet Operators' Association, infra; Att.-Gen. of Hong Kong* v. *Ng Yuen Shiu* [1983] 2 A.C.629.
[17] [1971] 2 Q.B. 175 at p. 191. This principle was endorsed by the House of Lords (*obiter*) in *O'Reilly* v. *Mackman* [1983] 2 A.C. 237 at p. 275 (Lord Diplock), and by the Privy Council in *Att.-Gen. of Hong Kong* v. *Ng Yuen Shiu* [1983] 2 A.C. 629.
[18] [1915] A.C. 120.
[19] At p. 138.

it must do its best to act justly, and to reach just ends by just means. If a statute prescribes the means it must employ them. If it is left without express guidance it must still act honestly and by honest means. In regard to these, certain ways and methods of judicial procedure may very likely be imitated: and lawyer-like methods may find especial favour from lawyers. But that the judiciary should presume to impose its own methods on administrative or executive officers is a usurpation."

Lord Parmoor said[20]: "The power of obtaining a writ of certiorari is not limited to judicial acts or orders in a strict sense, that is to say, acts or orders of a court of law sitting in a judicial capacity. It extends to the acts and orders of a competent authority which has power to impose a liability or to give a decision which determines the rights or property of the affected parties. Where, however, the question of the propriety of procedure is raised in a hearing before some tribunal other than a court of law there is no obligation to adopt the regular forms of legal procedure. It is sufficient that the case has been heard in a judicial spirit and in accordance with the principles of substantial justice."

Lord Moulton said[21]: "It is said, truthfully, that on such an appeal the Local Government Board must act judicially, but this, in my opinion, only means that it must preserve a judicial temper and perform its duties conscientiously, with a proper feeling of responsibility, in view of the fact that its acts affect the property and rights of individuals."

Ridge v. *Baldwin*.[22] A Watch Committee had power under section 191(4) of **12-29** the Municipal Corporations Act 1882 to dismiss any constable whom they thought negligent in or unfit for the discharge of his duty. R., the chief constable of Brighton, was acquitted on criminal charges of conspiracy, but his conduct was adversely criticised by the trial judge. R. was summarily dismissed by the committee without prior notice or an opportunity to make representations, and without compliance with regulations under the Police Act 1919, s. 4(1), establishing disciplinary procedures. The committee subsequently heard representations from R.'s solicitor, but gave no particulars of the case against him. R. appealed to the Home Secretary under the Police (Appeals) Act 1927, without prejudice to any right to contend that the purported dismissal was bad in law. He subsequently sought a declaration that the dismissal was *ultra vires*, and damages. The Court of Appeal held that natural justice did not have to be observed as the committee's action was "administrative" or "executive." R.'s appeal to the House of Lords was allowed. *Held*, the dismissal was void for breach of natural justice, and for non-compliance with the regulations. A duty to act judicially was to be inferred from the nature of the power, and this duty had not been observed. The defect was cured neither by the second meeting of the committee, as it did not amount to a full rehearing with disclosure of the case against R., nor by the appeal to the Secretary of State, as the committee's decision was a nullity and R. so maintained during the appeal.

R. v. *Liverpool Corporation ex p. Liverpool Taxi Owners' Association*.[23] The City Council had power under section 37 of the Town Police Clauses Act 1847 to license such number of hackney carriages as it thought fit. From 1948 onwards it limited the number to 300. In 1970 and 1971 the taxi cab operators' associations were assured by the town clerk that they would be consulted if any change in the numbers was contemplated. In 1971 a special sub-committee recommended increases for 1972 and 1973 and no restriction in numbers thereafter, and heard the applicants' case against the proposal. The chairman gave a public undertaking that the numbers would not be increased until

[20] At p. 140.
[21] At p. 150.
[22] [1964] A.C. 40.
[23] [1972] 2 Q.B. 299.

proposed legislation in the form of a private Bill had come into force. This undertaking was confirmed orally both by the chairman and by letter from the town clerk. In November the sub-committee resolved on an increase for 1972. The committee, and later the council, confirmed the resolution. The applicants applied *ex parte* to the Divisional Court for leave to apply for orders of prohibition, mandamus and certiorari. Leave was refused without reasons being given. The Court of Appeal allowed the appeal and held that though the determination as to the number of taxi cab licences was a policy decision and the court could not interfere with such a policy decision, the court could and should intervene to ensure that the council acted fairly in deciding that policy after due regard to conflicting interests. In view of the past history, and in particular the undertaking publicly given, the applicants were justifiably aggrieved by the council's subsequent unfair conduct. Accordingly the court should order prohibition to go to prohibit action upon the resolutions or the granting of further licences without first hearing representations. Lord Denning M.R. said[24]: " . . . when the corporation consider applications for licences under the Town Police Clauses Act 1847, they are under a duty to act fairly. This means that they should be ready to hear not only the particular applicant but also any other persons or bodies whose interests are affected. . . . It is perhaps putting it a little high to say they are exercising judicial functions. They may be said to be exercising an administrative function. But even so, in our modern approach, they must act fairly: and the court will see that they do so."

R. v. *Huntingdon District Council, ex p. Cowan.*[25] When dealing with an application for an entertainment licence under Part I of the Local Government (Miscellaneous Provisions) Act 1982 a local authority must (1) inform the applicant of the substance of any objection or representation in the nature of an objection (not necessarily the whole of it, nor to say necessarily who has made it); and (2) give the applicant an opportunity to make representations in reply.

12-30   These cases may be compared with a number of cases where procedural standards have not been imposed on the ground that the decision in question has been "administrative." Local authorities are not obliged to give anybody a hearing before passing a resolution declaring an area to be a clearance area.[26] The Minister is not obliged at common law to act judicially in relation to the process of compulsory purchase before objections to an order are made.[27] In *Essex County Council* v. *Minister of Housing and Local Government,*[28] Plowman J. held that the Minister was not obliged to observe the *audi alteram partem* rule when exercising his discretion under section 14 of the Town and Country Planning Act 1962 (now section 24 of the 1971 Act) to grant planning permission by means of a special development order. Accordingly, he was

---

[24] At pp. 307, 308.
[25] [1984] 1 W.L.R. 501. For other illustrations of the application of the duty to act fairly in licensing cases, see *R.* v. *Preston Borough Council and others, ex p. Quietlynn Ltd.* (1984) 83 L.G.R. 308; *R.* v. *Bristol City Council, ex p. Pearce,* (1984) 83 L.G.R. 711; *R.* v. *Wear Valley District Council, ex p. Binks* [1985] 2 All E.R. 699.
[26] *Fredman* v. *Minister of Health* (1935) 154 L.T. 240; Housing Act 1985, s. 289.
[27] *Frost* v. *Minister of Health* [1935] 1 K.B. 286; *Miller* v. *Minister of Health* [1946] K.B. 626; *Price* v. *Minister of Health* [1947] 1 All E.R. 47; *Summers* v. *Minister of Health* [1947] 1 All E.R. 184; *Johnson & Co.* v. *Minister of Health* [1947] 2 All E.R. 395. See also *Bushell* v. *Secretary of State for the Environment* [1981] A.C. 75.
[28] (1967) 66 L.G.R. 23.

not obliged to consider representations by the county council against the proposed development of the third London airport at Stansted. The principles of natural justice do not apply to legislative functions such as the making of a statutory instrument[29] or, presumably, a by-law. Similarly, a local authority need not give an opportunity for persons to be heard before making a decision which is universal in its application such as the fixing by the authority of the rates for the year or the scale upon which fees are to be charged.[30] The courts are disinclined to intervene unless there is at least a risk that someone has been prejudiced. They may decline, in the exercise of their discretion, to grant a remedy[31] or simply hold that there has been no "breach of natural justice."[32]

A breach of natural justice may in some circumstances be cured by an appellate hearing at which natural justice has been observed, provided that, overall, there has been a fair result reached by fair methods.[33]

Nemo judex in causa sua

It is not clear whether this rule applies in all situations to which the *audi* **12-31** *alteram partem* principle or the duty to act fairly now extends (see *supra*), or whether it is still relevant only to judicial or quasi-judicial decisions. In *Franklin* v. *Minister of Town and Country Planning*[34] the House of Lords held that the decision of the Minister to make an order designating Stevenage a new town under the New Towns Act 1946 was "purely administrative." The complaint that he had been biased was accordingly irrelevant. The only possible ground of challenge was that the Minister had not complied with his statutory duty to consider objections to the order, and the report of the local public inquiry. However, the *nemo judex* rule has been applied in a number of situations which are not strictly analogous to the decisions of a court of law.

    R. v. *London County Council, ex p. Akkersdyk.*[35] A committee decided by a majority to recommend to the Council that a music and dancing licence should not be renewed. Three members of the committee, who had voted with the majority, instructed counsel to oppose the renewal at the meeting of the Council. They attended the meeting, but did not vote. One of the three took an active part in the discussions. The Council refused renewal. The Divisional Court granted mandamus to compel the Council to hear and determine the

[29] *Bates* v. *Lord Hailsham of St. Marylebone* [1972] 1 W.L.R. 1373.
[30] *R.* v. *Greater London Council, ex p. The Rank Organisation, The Times,* February 19, 1982.
[31] *Glynn* v. *Keele University* [1971] 1 W.L.R. 487; *Malloch* v. *Aberdeen Corporation* [1971] 1 W.L.R. 1578 at p. 1595 (Lord Wilberforce).
[32] *Lake District Planning Board* v. *Secretary of State for the Environment* [1975] J.P.L. 20; *George* v. *Secretary of State for the Environment* (1979) 38 P. & C.R. 609; *Cinnamond* v. *British Airport Authority* [1980] 1 W.L.R. 582, *per* Brandon L.J. at p. 593 (but *cf. Annumunthodo* v. *Oilfield Workers' Trade Union* [1961] A.C. 945 at p. 956; *Kanda* v. *Government of Malaya* [1962] A.C. 322 at p. 337).
[33] *Calvin* v. *Carr* [1980] A.C. 574; *R.* v. *Oxfordshire Local Valuation Panel, ex p. Oxford City Council* (1981) 79 L.G.R. 432 at p. 446.
[34] [1948] A.C. 87.
[35] [1892] 1 Q.B. 190.

application according to law, on the ground that the councillors had "acted both as accusers and judges at the same time" contrary to natural justice.

This decision may be compared with *Royal Aquarium and Summer and Winter Garden Society* v. *Parkinson*,[36] where the Court of Appeal held that a similar meeting of the Council was not "judicial" for the purpose of being protected by absolute privilege in the law of defamation.

> *R.* v. *Hendon Rural District Council, ex p. Chorley*.[37] The council approved an application under the Town Planning Act 1925 by the potential purchaser of a certain site, for permission to build on that site. This permission safeguarded the applicants' right to compensation under section 10 of the Act, in the event of their property being injuriously affected by the making of a proposed town planning scheme. One of the councillors who voted for the grant of permission was an estate agent acting for the site owner. *Held*, (1) the councillor "was biased, or had such an interest in the matter as to disqualify him from taking part or voting"[38]; and (2) since the decision of the council to grant permission conferred a legal right to compensation and affected the rights of subjects, it was sufficiently near to a judicial decision to be the subject of certiorari. The decision was accordingly quashed.

High Court judges have differed on the question whether the *nemo judex* principle applies in any form to the decision of a local authority to grant or refuse planning permission under the Town and Country Planning Act 1971.[39]

At common law, an adjudicator is disqualified if he has a direct personal or pecuniary interest in the subject-matter of the adjudication.[40] He must not act both as "prosecutor" and "judge."[41] Moreover, he will be disqualified if there is a "real likelihood" or a "reasonable suspicion" of bias. In so far as there is any difference between these two tests, the current judicial opinion seems to favour the latter.[42]

E. ERROR OF LAW ON THE FACE OF THE RECORD

12-32   If a local authority, acting in a judicial or quasi-judicial capacity and within its jurisdiction, reaches a decision which discloses *on the face of the record* an error in law, then certiorari will lie to bring the decision into the High Court to be quashed.

---

[36] [1892] 1 Q.B. 431.
[37] [1933] 2 K.B. 696.
[38] *Per* Lord Hewart C.J. at p. 702 and Avory J. at p. 703.
[39] In favour: Webster J. in *Steeples* v. *Derbyshire County Council* [1985] 1 W.L.R. 256. Against: Glidewell J. in *R.* v. *Sevenoaks District Council, ex p. W.J. Terry* [1985] 3 All E.R. 234 and Stocker J. in *R.* v. *St. Edmundsbury Borough Council, ex p. Investors in Industry Commercial Properties Ltd.* [1985] 1 W.L.R. 1168.
[40] *Dimes* v. *Grand Junction Canal Proprietors* (1852) 3 H.L. Cas. 759.
[41] *R.* v. *London County Council, ex p. Akkersdyk, supra; R.* v. *Barnsley Metropolitan Borough Council, ex p. Hook* [1976] 1 W.L.R. 1052.
[42] *Metropolitan Properties Co. (F.G.C.) Ltd.* v. *Lannon* [1969] 1 Q.B. 577 at pp. 599, 604–606; *cf. Hannam* v. *Bradford Corporation* [1970] 1 W.L.R. 937 at pp. 941–942, 945–946, 949; *R.* v. *Liverpool City Justices, ex p. Topping* [1983] 1 W.L.R. 119; *Tracomin S.A.* v. *Gibbs Nathaniel (Canada) Ltd.* [1985] 1 Lloyd's Rep. 586.

R. v. *Northumberland Compensation Appeal Tribunal, ex p. Shaw.*[43] A decision of the tribunal was expressed in a "speaking order," *i.e.* one which contained the reasons which led the tribunal to its decision. These reasons disclosed that the tribunal had taken an erroneous view of the law. The tribunal admitted that its decision was wrong but argued that the court had no power to make an order of certiorari since the tribunal had not acted without jurisdiction. It was held that certiorari lay. Denning L.J. said[44]: "The answer to this argument, however (*i.e.* the contention of the tribunal), is that the Court of King's Bench has an inherent jurisdiction to control all inferior tribunals, not in an appellate capacity, but in a supervisory capacity. This control extends not only to seeing that the inferior tribunals keep within their jurisdiction, but also to seeing that they observe the law. The control is exercised by means of a power to quash any determination by the tribunal which, on the fact of it, offends against the law. The King's Bench does not substitute its own views for those of the tribunal, as a Court of Appeal would do. It leaves it to the tribunal to hear the case again, and in a proper case may command it to do so. . . . Of recent years the scope of certiorari seems to have been somewhat forgotten. It has been supposed to be confined to the correction of excess of jurisdiction, and not to extend to the correction of errors of law; and several learned judges have said as much. But the Lord Chief Justice has, in the present case, restored certiorari to its rightful position and shown that it can be used to correct errors of law which appear on the face of the record, even though they do not go to jurisdiction."

Courts have jurisdiction under this ground of challenge only where a tribunal is seen from the record to have acted in error of law. Decisions published without reasons would be difficult to challenge in this way, but section 12 of the Tribunals and Inquiries Act 1971 provides that tribunals listed in Schedule 1 to the Act and any Minister notifying a decision taken after a statutory inquiry must furnish a statement of reasons if requested by a person primarily concerned and may only refuse on grounds of national security. Any such statement is deemed to form part of the record.

F. Remedies

The legality of a decision of a local authority may be raised, directly or   **12-33** collaterally, in a number of ways: (1) on an "application for judicial review," where the court may award one or more of a number of remedies, namely, certiorari, mandamus, prohibition, an injunction, a declaration and damages; (2) in an action for an injunction, a declaration or damages; (3) on an appeal; (4) by way of defence to enforcement proceedings; (5) in proceedings before the district auditor[45]; and (6) by a request to a Minister to exercise a default power.

Application for judicial review

Order 53 of the Rules of the Supreme Court provides a common   **12-34** procedure for seeking remedies in administrative law, termed an

---

[43] [1952] 1 K.B. 338.
[44] At p. 346.
[45] See §§ 7–09—7–21.

"application for judicial review." The main features of Order 53 were enacted in section 31 of the Supreme Court Act 1981. An application for judicial review must be brought in the Queen's Bench Division.

An application for an order of mandamus, prohibition or certiorari, or for an injunction under section 30 of the Supreme Court Act 1981 restraining a person from acting in any office in which he is not entitled to act, *must* be made under Order 53.[46]

An application for a declaration or an injunction *may* be made by way of application for judicial review under Order 53. The court may grant the declaration or injunction claimed if it considers that it would be just and convenient so to do under Order 53, having regard to the nature of the matters in respect of which, and the persons and bodies against whom mandamus, prohibition or certiorari may be granted, and all the circumstances of the case.[47] Alternatively, a declaration or injunction may be obtained in an ordinary action. In *O'Reilly* v. *Mackman*[48] the House of Lords held that as a general rule it would be contrary to public policy and an abuse of the process of the court for a plaintiff complaining of a public authority's infringement of his public law rights to seek redress by ordinary action. However, this was a general rule to which there might be exceptions:

> "particularly where the invalidity of the decision arises as a collateral issue in a claim for infringement of a right of the plaintiff arising under private law, or where none of the parties objects to the adoption of the procedure by writ or originating summons. Whether there should be other exceptions should . . . be left to be decided on a case by case basis."[49]

Accordingly, in *Cocks* v. *Thanet District Council*,[50] the House of Lords held that challenges to determinations by a housing authority, under the Housing (Homeless Persons) Act 1977, whether a person (1) was homeless or threatened with homelessness; (2) had a priority need; and (3) was homeless intentionally, should be brought on an application for judicial review. This was so notwithstanding that determinations in favour of that person would give rise to rights in the field of private law. Similarly, in *Davy* v. *Spelthorne Borough Council*[51] the Court of Appeal struck out proceedings in the Chancery Division seeking an injunction restraining the council from implementing an enforcement notice and an order that the notice be set aside. On the other hand, the court refused to strike out an alternative claim for damages for negligent advice alleged to have been given by the council resulting in a failure to appeal against the notice, and this was affirmed by the House of Lords.[52] Furthermore, it has

---

[46] R.S.C., Ord. 53, r. 1(1); Supreme Court Act 1981, s. 31(1).
[47] *Ibid.* r. 1(2); *Ibid.* s. 31(2).
[48] [1983] 2 A.C. 237.
[49] *Per* Lord Diplock at p. 285.
[50] [1983] 2 A.C. 286. See also *Luxclose Ltd.* v. *London Borough of Hammersmith and Fulham* [1983] J.P.L. 662.
[51] (1983) 81 L.G.R. 580.
[52] [1984] A.C. 262.

been held that the principle of *O'Reilly* v. *Mackman*[53] does not prevent the defendant in a criminal case (here, a prosecution under the Town and Country Planning Act 1971 for breach of a stop notice) from relying on the *ultra vires* doctrine in his defence,[54] and that in a civil case a person may raise a matter of *vires* in defence of his private law rights, where those rights are not dependent on a public law decision.[55]

An applicant for judicial review must first obtain leave from a High **12-35** Court judge. Leave may not be granted unless the court "considers that the applicant has a sufficient interest in the matter to which the application relates." This is the only reference in the Rules to the problem of *locus standi*. The intention appears to be that there should be a uniform test for *locus standi* irrespective of the nature of the relief sought. Previously, the requirements for *locus standi* varied according to the remedy applied for.

The case law on the subject was complex and contradictory, the courts usually being less strict in applications for the prerogative orders than in actions for a private law remedy. Lord Denning M.R. formulated a general test as follows in *R.* v. *Greater London Council, ex p. Blackburn*,[56] where Mr. Blackburn was held to have *locus standi* to be granted an order of prohibition restraining the council from exercising their powers of film censorship according to the wrong legal test:

> "I would ask: Who then can bring proceedings when a public authority is guilty of a misuse of power? Mr. Blackburn is a citizen of London. His wife is a ratepayer. He has children who may be harmed by the exhibition of pornographic films. If he has no sufficient interest, no other citizen has. I think he comes within the principle which I stated in *McWhirter's* case[57] which I would recast today so as to read: I regard it as a matter of high constitutional principle that if there is good ground for supposing that a government department or a public authority is transgressing the law, or is about to transgress it, in a way which offends or injures thousands of Her Majesty's subjects, then any one of those offended or injured can draw it to the attention of the courts of law and seek to have the law enforced, and the courts in their discretion can grant whatever remedy is appropriate."

However, this broad approach was not adopted by the other judges. In *Gouriet* v. *Union of Post Office Workers*,[58] the House of Lords held that only the Attorney-General could sue on behalf of the public for the purpose of preventing public wrongs, such as breaches of the criminal law, and that a private individual could only take proceedings where he

---

[53] *Supra* n. 48.
[54] *R.* v. *Jenner* [1983] 1 W.L.R. 873. See also *Canterbury City Council* v. *Bern* (1981) 44 P. & C.R. 178 and *Scarborough Borough Council* v. *Adams* (1983) 47 P. & C.R. 133.
[55] *Wandsworth London Borough Council* v. *Winder* [1985] A.C. 461 (council tenant entitled to raise in defence to an action for arrears of rent that the authority's decision to increase the rent was an *ultra vires* abuse of discretion under the *Wednesbury* principles).
[56] [1976] 1 W.L.R. 550 at p. 558.
[57] *Att.-Gen., ex rel. McWhirter* v. *Independent Broadcasting Authority* [1973] Q.B. 629 at p. 649.
[58] [1978] A.C. 435.

would sustain injury as the result of the public wrong. The private law remedies of declaration and injunction were only available to persons whose legal rights were affected by unlawful action. *Per* Lord Wilberforce[59]:

> "There is no support in authority for the proposition that declaratory relief can be granted unless the plaintiff, in proper proceedings, in which there is a dispute between the plaintiff and the defendant concerning their legal respective rights or liabilities either asserts a legal right which is denied or threatened, or claims immunity from some claim of the defendant against him or claims that the defendant is infringing or threatens to infringe some public right so as to inflict special damage on the plaintiff. The present proceedings do not possess the required characteristics."

12-36   The question of *locus standi* under Order 53 was considered by the House of Lords in *R.* v. *Inland Revenue Commissioners, ex p. National Federation of Self Employed and Small Businesses Ltd.*[60] Here, the applicants sought a declaration that an "amnesty" in respect of tax evasion granted by the Inland Revenue to Fleet Street casual workers was unlawful and also sought mandamus requiring the Revenue to assess and collect income tax from those workers. The House of Lords held unanimously that the arrangement had been made by the Commissioners for reasons of good management and was not *ultra vires* or unlawful. The majority (Lords Wilberforce, Fraser and Roskill) held, further that the Federation did not have a sufficient interest in the matter, and that it would only be in a rare case that a taxpayer would have the standing to seek judicial review of decisions concerning other taxpayers.[61] Lords Diplock and Scarman held that the Federation would have had *locus standi* had the arrangement been shown to be *ultra vires*.[62] A number of points of general significance emerged:

(1) The question of *locus standi* cannot be considered in isolation from the legal and factual context of the application. A decision that an applicant has sufficient interest to be granted leave under Order 53, r. 3, does not preclude the issue of *locus standi* being raised at the full hearing, where the context of the application can be properly examined. Accordingly, it is inappropriate for the issue to be taken as a preliminary issue of law.[63]

(2) The question of *locus standi* is one of mixed law and fact which the court must decide on legal principles. It is not simply a matter for the court's discretion.[64]

[59] At p. 483.
[60] [1982] A.C. 617.
[61] See Lord Wilberforce at pp. 633, 635–636; Lord Fraser at pp. 644–645, 647; Lord Roskill at pp. 662–663, 664.
[62] See Lord Diplock at p. 644 and Lord Scarman at p. 654.
[63] See Lord Wilberforce at pp. 629–630; Lord Diplock at p. 636; Lord Fraser at p. 645; Lord Scarman at pp. 649, 653–654; and Lord Roskill at p. 656.
[64] See Lord Wilberforce at p. 631. Lords Fraser and Roskill expressly agreed with Lord Wilberforce's reasoning: pp. 644–645, 664.

(3) The courts should not take an unduly restrictive approach to questions of *locus standi*. The decision in *R. v. Lewisham Guardians*,[65] which had laid down a requirement for an applicant to show a specific legal right in the matter, was expressly disapproved.[66] Lord Fraser stated[67] that the new Order 53 had the effect of removing technical and procedural differences between the prerogative orders, although all the older law had not been overthrown. Lord Scarman cited[68] with approval a statement by Lord Wilberforce in respect of the prerogative orders to the effect that the courts have allowed individuals "liberal access under a generous conception of *locus standi*."[69] Lord Roskill regarded old decisions on the prerogative orders to be of little assistance, the former and stricter rules determining when they might issue having been greatly relaxed.[70] Lord Diplock went further,[71] approving Lord Denning M.R.'s statement in *R. v. Greater London Council, ex p. Blackburn.*[72] A "mere busybody", however, will not have *locus standi*.[73]

(4) A ratepayer has *locus standi* to challenge rating decisions concerning other ratepayers in the same area.[74]

(5) The decision in *Gouriet v. Union of Post Office Workers*[75] was distinguished on the ground that it was not concerned with government bodies or judicial review.[76]

Since this decision, *locus standi* under Order 53 has been accorded to persons and bodies such as amenity societies who oppose grants of planning permission,[77] but denied to a local authority which sought to

---

[65] [1897] 1 Q.B. 488.
[66] See Lord Diplock at p. 639, Lord Fraser at p. 646, Lord Scarman at p. 653. Lord Roskill expressly agreed with Lord Fraser's reasoning: p. 664.
[67] At pp. 645–646.
[68] At p. 653.
[69] *Gouriet v. Union of Post Office Workers* [1978] A.C. 435 at p. 482.
[70] [1982] A.C. 617 at pp. 656, 658.
[71] At p. 641.
[72] [1976] 1 W.L.R. 550, 559, *supra*. This view was, however, expressly disapproved by Lord Roskill (with whom Lord Fraser agreed) at [1982] A.C. 617 at pp. 660–661.
[73] See Lord Fraser at p. 646.
[74] See Lord Wilberforce at pp. 632–633; Lord Diplock at pp. 641–642; Lord Fraser at p. 646. These remarks are of course *obiter*. See also *Arsenal Football Club Ltd. v. Ende* [1979] A.C. 1.
[75] *Supra*, n. 58.
[76] See Lord Diplock at pp. 638–639; Lord Scarman at p. 649; Lord Roskill (with whom Lord Fraser expressly agreed) at pp. 657–658. See also Lord Wilberforce in the *Gouriet* case [1978] A.C. 435 at pp. 482–483.
[77] *Covent Garden Community Association Ltd. v. Greater London Council* [1981] J.P.L. 183 (certiorari refused on the merits); *R. v. Hammersmith and Fulham Borough Council, ex p. People Before Profit Ltd.* (1981) 80 L.G.R. 322 (*locus standi* for certiorari accepted, but leave refused in absence of a reasonable case to put forward); *R. v. Stroud District Council, ex p. Goodenough* (1982) 43 P. & C.R. 59 (mandamus).

challenge a decision by the Department of Health and Social Security on a matter concerning social security payments.[78]

Leave to apply for judicial review will be granted unless the applicant has no "reasonable" or "arguable" case to put forward.[79]

Once leave is granted, the application is made to a judge sitting in open court, unless the court directs that it should be made to a judge in chambers or to a Divisional Court of the Queen's Bench Division. In a criminal case, the application must be made to a Divisional Court.[80] The court may entertain interlocutory applications for orders such as those for discovery, interrogatories and cross-examination on affidavits.[81]

An application must be made promptly, and in any event within three months from the date when grounds for the application first arose, unless the Court considers there is good reason for extending the period.[82] In addition, section 31(6) of the Supreme Court Act 1981 provides that where the High Court considers that there has been undue delay in making an application for judicial review, the court may refuse to grant (a) leave for the making of the application; or (b) any relief sought on the application, if it considers that the granting of the relief sought would be likely to cause substantial hardship to, or substantially prejudice the rights of, any person or would be detrimental to good administration. This is stated to be without prejudice to any enactment or rule of court which has the effect of limiting the time within which an application or judicial review may be made.[83]

(a) *Mandamus*

12-37   The order of mandamus issues from the High Court to some person or body to compel the performance of a public duty imposed by law where no other effective means of redress is available. It may therefore be used to compel a local authority to carry out some duty cast upon it by statute or common law.[84] But there are several limitations on the power to issue an order. In the first place the duty must be an absolute one, and not one which may be exercised if the authority chooses. A council may not be compelled by this means to undertake some activity which is merely permissive (*e.g.* the making of by-laws), or which is discretionary. But

---

[78] *R. v. Secretary of State for Social Services, ex p. Greater London Council, The Times,* August 16, 1984: appeal by the G.L.C. dismissed on another ground: *The Times,* August 8, 1985.
[79] *R. v. Hammersmith and Fulham Borough Council, ex p. People Before Profit Ltd. supra; per* Lord Diplock in *Inland Revenue Commissioners* v. *National Federation of Self-Employed and Small Businesses Ltd.* [1982] A.C. 617 at p. 644.
[80] R.S.C. Ord. 53, r. 5(1), (2).
[81] *Ibid.* r. 8(1).
[82] *Ibid.* r. 4(1).
[83] Supreme Court Act 1981, s. 31(7). See *R. v. Stratford-on-Avon District Council, ex p. Jackson* [1985] 1 W.L.R. 1319.
[84] *e.g.* the duty to entertain an application for registration as the keeper of a common lodging-house: *R. v. Hounslow London Borough Council, ex p. Pizzey* [1977] 1 All E.R. 305.

mandamus lies to compel the exercise of a discretion in a way that extraneous considerations are excluded and that issues are dealt with on merit.[85] Secondly, the traditional principle is that the applicant for the order must show that he himself has a substantial, personal interest in the performance of the duty—it is not sufficient for him to show that a public duty has been neglected. How "substantial" that interest must be is not clear from the cases.[86] Thirdly, an order will not be made if there is some other remedy equally convenient, beneficial and effective. The following are examples of the use of mandamus:

R. v. Poplar Borough Council.[87] The borough council refused to pay sums under precepts issued by the London County Council and the Metropolitan District Asylums Board. *Held,* mandamus lay to compel the council to levy a rate to meet the precepts, for this was the only effective means of securing the performance of a public duty. The London Government Act 1899 (under which the London County precept was issued), did not provide a remedy for breach of duty: in the case of the precept of the Asylums Board, the remedy of distress (if in fact it were available) was wholly inadequate.

R. v. Braintree District Council, ex p. Willingham.[88] Section 71 of the Shops Act 1950 provides that it is the duty of every local authority to enforce the Act. The council decided not to prosecute the operators of a Sunday market for offences under the Act. The Divisional Court found that they had taken into account the expense of prosecuting and the fact that the market was popular in the locality. *Held,* these were irrelevant considerations, and mandamus should go, requiring the council to perform their duty under section 71. The council had no general discretion not to enforce the Act; the only scope for discretion was whether any particular proceedings were necessary to secure observance, and, as an aspect of that, the council could take account of the likelihood of failure.

The remedy is discretionary, and may be refused if, for example, the **12-38** applicant's motives are unacceptable,[89] or the authority's failure to meet a statutory obligation arises out of circumstances over which it has no control.[90] The order so far referred to is derived from the prerogative writ of mandamus which issued from the King's courts upon principles of law settled by decided cases. There are, however, several instances where mandamus is available by virtue of a specific statutory provision. The Secretary of State for Education and Science has, under section 99 of the Education Act 1944, a power to issue directions to a local education

---

[85] See *R. v. Flintshire County Council Licensing County (Stage Plays) Committee, ex p. Barrett* [1957] 1 Q.B. 350; *R. v. Stepney Corporation* [1902] 1 K.B. 317; *R. v. London County Council, ex p. Corrie* [1918] 1 K.B. 68; *Padfield* v. *Minister of Agriculture* [1968] A.C. 997.
[86] See *R. v. Paddington Valuation Officer, ex p. Peachey Property Corporation* (No. 2) [1966] 1 Q.B. 380; *R. v. Commissioner of Police of the Metropolis, ex p. Blackburn* [1968] 2 Q.B. 118; *R. v. Hereford Corporation, ex p. Harrower* [1970] 1 W.L.R. 1424, 1427.
[87] [1922] 1 K.B. 95.
[88] (1982) 81 L.G.R. 70.
[89] *e.g.* business rivalry: *R. v. Customs and Excise Commissioners, ex p. Cook* [1970] 1 W.L.R. 450.
[90] *Per* Scarman L.J. in *R. v. Bristol Corporation, ex p. Hendy* [1974] 1 W.L.R. 498 at p. 503.

authority, which, in his opinion, has failed to discharge its duties. These directions are enforceable, on the application of the Secretary of State, by mandamus. The court is bound to grant the application if the correct legal procedure is followed.

If a local authority disobeys an order of mandamus, whether derived from the prerogative writ or statute, the members of the authority responsible for the failure are liable to attachment, *i.e.* to arrest and to imprisonment until the order is obeyed.[91]

(b) *Prohibition and certiorari*

12-39   The orders of prohibition and certiorari issue from the High Court to prevent inferior courts from exceeding the limits of their legitimate powers or from otherwise acting unlawfully. Prohibition restrains an inferior court from acting unlawfully in the future or from completing an act already begun; certiorari enables a decision already made to be reviewed and if necessary quashed. These orders lie not only against inferior courts. It was held in *R. v. Electricity Commissioners*[92] that they extend to any body of persons who have a duty in law to act judicially, that they lie:

> "whenever any body of persons having legal authority to determine questions affecting the rights of subjects, and having the duty to act judicially, act in excess of their legal authority."

The House of Lords in *Ridge* v. *Baldwin*[93] discussed this statement at some length and expressed the view that there is in fact one ingredient only here, not two, and that where a tribunal is determining questions affecting the rights of subjects it has on that account a duty to act judicially.

The orders have relevance in local authority administration for there are many occasions when local authorities are called upon to "determine questions affecting the rights of subjects" and when accordingly they are acting in a judicial or quasi-judicial capacity.[94] Certiorari has been granted to quash a grant of planning permission to which *ultra vires* conditions had been attached.[95] An order of prohibition has been granted to restrain a local authority from increasing the number of taxicab licences in their area without hearing objections from existing cab owners.[96] Indeed, it has been stated that certiorari and prohibition are no

---

[91] *R.* v. *Worcester Corporation* (1905) 69 J.P. 296.
[92] [1924] 1 K.B. 171, *per* Atkin L.J. at p. 205.
[93] [1964] A.C. 40.
[94] See, *e.g. R.* v. *Hendon Rural District Council, ex p. Chorley* [1933] 2 K.B. 696; *R.* v. *Kent Police Authority, ex p. Godden* [1971] 2 Q.B. 662; *R.* v. *Barnsley Metropolitan Borough Council, ex p. Hook* [1976] 1 W.L.R. 1052.
[95] *R.* v. *Hillingdon London Borough Council, ex p. Royco Homes Ltd.* [1974] Q.B. 720.
[96] *R.* v. *Liverpool Corporation, ex p. Liverpool Taxi Fleet Operators' Association* [1972] 2 Q.B. 299.

longer limited to cases where there is a duty to act judicially.[97] The orders may lie if an authority acts or proposes to act without jurisdiction (*e.g.* in breach of natural justice). In addition, certiorari may be awarded where an error of law is apparent on the face of the record (see para. 12–32) or where an order is procured by fraud.[98] The courts traditionally have not applied a strict test for *locus standi.*[99] The remedies are discretionary, and may be refused, for example, where the plaintiff has delayed unreasonably,[1] or has been guilty of unreasonable conduct.[2] Moreover, they may be refused where another equally beneficial remedy is available,[3] where there would be no more than a theoretical prospect that the decision would be changed if the matter were remitted[4] or where the point of law is technical and without merit and the applicants have suffered no injustice.[5]

Declarations and injunctions

A declaratory judgment is, as the name implies, the finding of a court   **12–40** on a question of law or rights. An injunction is an order by which a party to the proceedings is required to do, or to refrain from doing, a particular thing.

Before the introduction of the application for judicial review, it had become increasingly common for persons wishing to challenge or test the legality of an act or decision of a public authority to proceed by commencing an action in the High Court for a declaration or injunction, in preference to seeking one of the prerogative orders. However, a litigant was faced with the difficulty that proceedings in respect of *public rights* were theoretically at the instigation of the Attorney-General, as the protector of public rights. It was necessary to ask the Attorney-General to consent to the institution of "relator proceedings."[6] Here, the proceedings were brought in the name of the Attorney-General "at the relation of" the

---

[97] See the *Royco Homes* case, *supra; O'Reilly* v. *Mackman* [1983] 2 A.C. 237, 239 (Lord Diplock); *cf. R.* v. *Barnet London Borough Council, ex p. Nilish Shah* [1983] 2 A.C. 309 (certiorari granted to quash a decision refusing a mandatory award to a student); *R.* v. *Manchester City Council, ex p. Fulford* (1982) 81 L.G.R. 292 (certiorari granted to quash a decision to abolish corporal punishment in schools: § 17–15).

[98] *R.* v. *Wolverhampton Crown Court, ex p. Croft* [1983] 1 W.L.R. 204.

[99] See Lord Denning M.R. in *R.* v. *Paddington Valuation Officer ex p. Peachey Property Ltd.* (No. 2) [1966] 1 Q.B. 380 at pp. 400–401, and *R.* v. *Liverpool Corporation, ex p. Liverpool Taxi Fleet Operators' Association* [1972] 2 Q.B. 299 at pp. 308–309.

[1] See *R.* v. *Stafford Justices* [1940] 2 K.B. 33; *R.* v. *Herrod, ex p. Leeds City Council* [1978] A.C. 403.

[2] *Ex p. Fry* [1954] 1 W.L.R. 730.

[3] *cf. R.* v. *Hillingdon London Borough Council, ex p. Royco Homes* [1974] Q.B. 720 (statutory right of appeal to the Secretary of State not as beneficial as certiorari where planning conditions are to be challenged on a point of law alone).

[4] *R.* v. *Secretary of State for the Environment, ex p. Stewart* (1979) 39 P. & C.R. 534; *cf. R.* v. *Greater Manchester Valuation Panel, ex p. Shell Chemicals U.K. Ltd.* [1982] Q.B. 255 at pp. 264–265.

[5] *R.* v. *Knightsbridge Crown Court, ex p. Marcrest Properties Ltd.* [1983] 1 W.L.R. 300.

[6] See *Ware* v. *Regent's Canal Co.* (1858) 3 De G. & J. 212 at p. 228, *per* Lord Chelmsford; *Att.-Gen., ex. rel. McWhirter* v. *Independent Broadcasting Authority* [1973] 1 Q.B. 629.

aggrieved party, but at the latter's expense. The Attorney-General had an absolute discretion as to whether he would lend his name.[7]

There were two exceptions to the rule that the Attorney-General was to be a party to proceedings in respect of public rights. A private party might sue in his own name (i) where the interference with the public right was such that some private right of his was at the same time interfered with, or (ii) where the plaintiff suffered special damage peculiar to himself from an interference with a public right.

> *Boyce* v. *Paddington Corporation.*[8] The plaintiff, shortly before the action, erected buildings on land abutting on an open space under the control of the borough council. The council resolved to erect a hoarding which would obstruct the access of light to the plaintiff's windows. The plaintiff brought an action to restrain the council from doing this. *Held*, that as the plaintiff was suing in respect of an alleged private right to the access of light, or in respect of an alleged interference with a public right from which he personally sustained special damage, he could sue without joining the Attorney-General as a plaintiff. The action failed on grounds unconnected with the right to sue.

There were a number of cases where a declaration or injunction was awarded to a person without these requirements being fulfilled, but where the point as to *locus standi* was not raised.[9] However, the House of Lords strongly reasserted the traditional position in *Gouriet* v. *Union of Post Office Workers.*[10]

As has been noted above,[11] a declaration or injunction may now be sought either on an application for judicial review under R.S.C. Ord. 53, or in ordinary proceedings in the High Court. However, under the principle of *O'Reilly* v. *Mackman,*[12] ordinary proceedings against a public authority will be struck out as an abuse of process, save in exceptional circumstances.

On an application for judicial review, the liberal "sufficient interest" test for *locus standi* is applicable.[13] Accordingly, a person may now seek a declaration or injunction in his own name under this procedure even though he has suffered no special damage or interference with his private rights in accordance with the tests applied in *Boyce* v. *Paddington Corporation.*[14] On the other hand, these tests remain applicable as the tests for *locus standi* where a declaration or injunction is sought in ordinary proceedings against a public authority.[15] Indeed these are among the few

---

[7] *Gouriet* v. *Union of Post Office Workers* [1978] A.C. 435.
[8] [1903] 1 Ch. 109.
[9] *e.g. Prescott* v. *Birmingham Corporation* [1955] 1 Ch. 210; *Lee* v. *Department of Education and Science* (1967) 66 L.G.R. 211.
[10] [1978] A.C. 435. See also *Gregory* v. *Camden London Borough Council* [1966] 1 W.L.R. 899.
[11] § 12–34.
[12] [1983] 2 A.C. 237: see § 12–34.
[13] *Inland Revenue Commissioners* v. *National Federation of Self-Employed and Small Businesses Ltd.* [1982] A.C. 617: see § 12–36.
[14] *Supra*, n. 8.
[15] *Barrs* v. *Bethell* [1982] Ch. 194. In this case, Warner J. disagreed with the view expressed by Webster J. in *Steeples* v. *Derbyshire County Council* [1985] 1 W.L.R. 256 that a person with "sufficient interest" under Order 53 would have *locus standi* in ordinary proceedings.

circumstances in which the courts will permit such proceedings to be brought.[16]

Statutory appeals

Many statutes give a right of appeal to a person aggrieved by a decision **12-41** of a local authority. A litigant relying on a statutory right must be able to bring his case within the statute—there is no discretionary power in any court to extend its jurisdiction beyond that specifically conferred. The following are examples of appeal provisions.

(a) *To a magistrates' court*

Private street works code.[17] A frontager may object to the proposals of a local authority on the ground, for example, that the works are insufficient or unreasonable, or that the street is not a private street. The authority must ask the court to determine the objection if it is not itself prepared to meet it. The court may quash the proposals in whole or in part or may amend them, or may adjourn the hearing or direct that further notices be given.

Building Act 1984, s. 79: A local authority may, in the interests of amenity, require the owner of a ruinous building to repair or to demolish it. An appeal against a requirement lies to the magistrates' court.

Statutes conferring jurisdiction on the justices usually provide a right of appeal on the part of a "person aggrieved" to the Crown Court. This is by the way of a rehearing of the case. Either party in a proceeding before the justices may require them to state a case to the High Court on a point of law or as to a want or excess of jurisdiction.[18]

(b) *To a county court*

Housing Act 1985, ss. 191, 269 and Sched. 10, para. 6: A person aggrieved by a notice requiring him to carry out works of repair, or by a demand for the recovery of expenses where the authority has acted in default, or by a demolition or closing order, may appeal to the county court. The court may quash or vary the notice, demand or order as it thinks fit.

(c) *To the Crown Court*

Highways Act 1980, s. 56: This section deals with the enforcement of a liability to maintain a highway and enables the complainant who claims that a highway maintainable at the public expense is out of repair first to require the authority to admit that the highway is in fact so maintainable. If this is disputed the complainant may ask the Crown Court for an order requiring the authority, if the court finds that the way is publicly maintainable and is out of repair, to put it in a state of proper repair.

---

[16] See § 12–34.
[17] Highways Act 1980, s. 209.
[18] See the Magistrates' Courts Act 1980, ss. 108, 111.

The Lotteries and Amusements Act 1976, Sched. 3: The grant of a permit for amusements with prizes is "at the discretion of the local authority." Paragraph 8 gives a right of appeal against refusal of a permit to the Crown Court.

(d) *To the High Court*

12-42   Acquisition of Land Act 1981, ss. 23, 24: An appeal lies to the High Court on the grounds that the purpose for which a compulsory purchase order is made is not one which is authorised by statute or that some statutory requirement has not been complied with to the substantial prejudice of the applicant.

There are a number of such appeal provisions on the statute book, mostly in the context of town and country planning and compulsory purchase. The grounds of challenge which may be raised under these procedures were stated as follows by Lord Denning M.R. in *Ashbridge Investments Ltd.* v. *Minister of Housing and Local Government,*[19] in relation to the Housing Act 1957, Sched. 4, para. 2 (now the Housing Act 1985, Sched. 22, para. 7):

> "The Court can only interfere on the ground that the Minister has gone outside the powers of the Act or that any requirement of the Act has not been complied with. Under this section it seems to me that the court can interfere with the Minister's decision if he has acted on no evidence; or if he has come to a conclusion to which on the evidence he could not reasonably come; or if he has given a wrong interpretation to the words of the statute; or if he has taken into consideration matters which he ought not to have taken into account, or vice versa; or has otherwise gone wrong in law. It is identical with the position when the court has power to interfere with the decision of a lower tribunal which has erred in point of law."

(e) *To a Minister*

12-43   Town and Country Planning Act 1971, s. 36: An applicant for planning permission may appeal to the Secretary of State for the Environment against a refusal or a conditional grant of planning permission by a local authority.

Town and Country Planning Act 1971, s. 88: A person on whom an enforcement notice is served or any other person having an interest in the land may appeal to the Secretary of State on any of eight specified grounds.

Locus standi and statutory appeals

12-44   Many appeals established by statute may only be brought by a "person aggrieved." This term has been considered by the courts on many occasions. The view most commonly relied on as to its meaning is that expressed by James L.J. in *ex p. Sidebotham*[20]:

---

[19] [1965] 1 W.L.R. 1320 at p. 1326.
[20] (1880) 14 Ch.D. 458 at p. 465. See also *Buxton* v. *Minister of Housing and Local Government* [1961] 1 Q.B. 278.

" . . . The words 'person aggrieved' do not really mean a man who is disappointed of a benefit which he might have received if some other order had been made. A 'person aggrieved' must be a man who has suffered a legal grievance, a man against whom a decision has been pronounced which has wrongfully deprived him of something, or wrongfully refused him something, or wrongfully affected his title to something."

The attitude of the court has, however, varied according to the context. In many areas of local government law, a local authority is empowered to serve a notice requiring a private person to have works done on his property, and a person aggrieved by the notice may appeal to a court. That private person is a "person aggrieved" by the notice, and by a decision of court upholding a notice. Is the local authority a "person aggrieved" by a decision of the justices against them? Apparently they are not, unless a legal burden has been placed upon them as a result of the decision. This is clearly so where the justices' decision throws a financial burden on the authority, as in *Phillips* v. *Berkshire County Council*,[21] where justices decided that a street was not a private street, and thus was maintainable at the public expense.

In recent cases concerning third parties affected by planning decisions, the courts have shown a less rigid attitude to the question of *locus standi*, while still emphasising that a person's interests must be prejudicially affected.[22]

Collateral challenges

An allegation that the act of a local authority is unlawful may be made **12-45** by way of defence to enforcement proceedings. For example, on a prosecution for breach of a by-law, it may be argued that the by-law is *ultra vires*, and on a prosecution for the offence of demolishing a building subject to a building preservation notice it may be argued that the notice was not validly served.[23] In *Allingham* v. *Minister of Agriculture*,[24] a notice requiring farmers to grow sugar beet on certain fields was held to be invalid because the task of specifying the fields had been delegated unlawfully by a county agricultural committee to an officer. A prosecution for non-compliance with the notice accordingly failed.[25]

G. EXCLUSION OF JUDICIAL REVIEW

Where Parliament wishes to reduce the scope for judicial intervention in **12-46** administrative decision-making, the technique most commonly adopted is to draft powers in a wide discretionary form. Alternatively, Parliament

---

[21] [1967] 2 Q.B. 991.
[22] See *Turner* v. *Secretary of State for the Environment* (1973) 72 L.G.R. 380.
[23] See *Maltglade* v. *St. Albans R.D.C.* [1972] 1 W.L.R. 1230.
[24] [1948] 1 All E.R. 780.
[25] See also *Stroud* v. *Bradbury* [1952] 2 All E.R. 76; *Canterbury City Council* v. *Bern* (1981) 44 P. & C.R. 178; *R.* v. *Jenner* [1983] 1 W.L.R. 873; *Wandsworth London Borough Council* v. *Winder* [1985] A.C. 461.

may seek expressly to exclude judicial review. By section 14(1) of the Tribunals and Inquiries Act 1971, any provision in an Act passed before August 1, 1958 that any order or determination shall not be called into question in any court, or any provision in such an Act which by similar words excludes any of the powers of the High Court, shall not have effect so as to restrict applications for certiorari or mandamus. Section 14(3), however, preserves exclusion clauses "where an Act makes special provision for application to the High Court . . . within a time limited by the Act." The special applications to quash orders discussed at para. 12-42 above must be brought within six weeks. No other administrative law remedies may be sought even within that period, and applications made after expiry of the six week period may not be entertained. Another "exclusion clause" expressly preserved by the forerunner of section 14(3)[26] was in issue in *Anisminic Ltd.* v. *Foreign Compensation Commission.*[27] Here, the House of Lords held that section 4(4) of the Foreign Compensation Act 1950, which provided that "the determination by the Commission of any application made to them under this Act shall not be called in question in any court of law," did not protect from judicial review a purported determination which was in truth a nullity as made in excess of jurisdiction. However, the House of Lords in *Smith* v. *East Elloe Rural District Council*[28] and the Court of Appeal in *R.* v. *Secretary of State for the Environment, ex p. Ostler*[29] have held that "time limit" clauses are effective to exclude judicial review on any ground. As a matter of strict logic, these two decisions are difficult to reconcile with *Anisminic*. It is significant that in *Anisminic* there was no provision for a statutory appeal even of a limited nature as in the other two cases.

2. *LEGAL PROCEEDINGS BY AND AGAINST LOCAL AUTHORITIES*

12-47   Section 222 of the Local Government Act 1972 provides that where a local authority consider it expedient for the promotion or protection of the interests of the inhabitants of their area they may:

(a) prosecute or defend or appear in any legal proceedings and, in the case of civil proceedings, may institute them in their own name; and

(b) in their own name, make representations in the interests of the inhabitants at any public inquiry.

These powers are available to local authorities including the Common Council of the City of London.[30]

---

[26] Tribunals and Inquiries Act 1958, s. 11(3).
[27] [1969] 2 A.C. 147. Applied in *Pearlman* v. *Keepers of Harrow School* [1979] Q.B. 56.
[28] [1956] A.C. 736.
[29] [1977] Q.B. 122.
[30] The power is not available to an urban development corporation: *London Docklands Development Corporation* v. *Rank Hovis McDougall Ltd., The Times*, July 25, 1985.

This section authorises the authority, for example, to commence or defend criminal prosecutions and proceedings in contract or tort.[31] A local authority may apply for judicial review of a decision of the Secretary of State or of another local authority.[32] Furthermore, the provision that civil proceedings may be instituted "in their own name" enables local authorities to seek an injunction or a declaration to protect the public without obtaining the consent of the Attorney-General. The authority must consider whether the institution of civil proceedings is in the interests of the inhabitants of their area, although there is a rebuttable presumption that this is so.[33] This last point has arisen in a number of cases where a local authority has sought an injunction to restrain a breach of the criminal law, such as contravention of a stop notice or enforcement notice[34] or infringement of the laws on Sunday trading.[35]

The special considerations that arise where it is sought to use the civil **12–48** law to restrain breaches of the criminal law were set out by Lord Templeman in *Stoke-on-Trent City Council* v. *B. & Q. (Retail) Ltd.*[36] (a Sunday trading case):

"The right to invoke the assistance of the civil court in aid of the criminal law is a comparatively modern development. Where Parliament imposes a penalty for an offence, Parliament must consider the penalty is adequate and Parliament can increase the penalty if it proves to be inadequate. It follows that a local authority should be reluctant to seek and the court should be reluctant to grant an injunction which if disobeyed may involve the infringer in sanctions far more onerous than the penalty imposed for the offence. In *Gouriet* v. *Union of Post Office Workers,*[37] Lord Wilberforce said[38] that the right to invoke the assistance of civil courts in aid of the criminal law is 'an exceptional power confined, in practice, to cases where an offence is frequently repeated in disregard of a, usually, inadequate penalty ... or to cases of emergency. ... '

It was said that the council should not have taken civil proceedings until criminal proceedings had failed to persuade the appellants to obey the law. As a general rule a local authority should try the effect of criminal proceedings before seeking the assistance of the civil courts. But the council were entitled to take the view that the appellants would not be deterred by a maximum fine which was substantially less than the profits which could be made from illegal Sunday trading. Delay while this was proved would have encouraged widespread breaches of the law by other traders, resentful of the continued activities of the appellants."

In this case, the company had traded in breach of the requirements of the Shops Act 1950 and an injunction was granted to restrain future breaches.

---

[31] See Chap. 10.
[32] As well as satisfying the requirements of s. 222, the authority must also have a sufficient interest under R.S.C. Ord. 53: see *R.* v. *Secretary of State for Social Services, ex p. Greater London Council* (1985) 129 S.J. 590: see § 12–36.
[33] *Stoke-on-Trent City Council* v. *B. & Q. (Retail) Ltd.* [1984] A.C. 754.
[34] See § 19–35.
[35] See t§ 22–29.
[36] [1984] A.C. 754 at p. 776.
[37] [1978] A.C. 435.
[38] At p. 481.

In *Runnymede Borough Council* v. *Ball*,[39] the Court of Appeal granted an interlocutory injunction to restrain the defendants from establishing a gipsy caravan site in contravention of enforcement and stop notices. No prosecutions had been brought. The penalties were not insubstantial, but the court accepted that prosecutions would have been too slow. The site would have been well established before the proceedings, including appeals, would be completed. The council were also justified in doubting the effectiveness of a financial penalty against gipsies. The control of the user of Green Belt land was a matter of public importance. The court's jurisdiction was not confined to cases where the defendant was "deliberately and flagrantly flouting the law." This expression appeared in Lord Fraser's speech in *Stoke-on-Trent City Council* v. *B. & Q. (Retail Ltd.)*[40] but did not form part of the *ratio* of Lord Templeman's leading opinion.

12-49   Local authorities may also take proceedings in their own name to protect the public where expressly permitted to do so by specific statutory provisions.[41]

12-50   Under section 223 of the Local Government Act 1972,[42] any member or officer[43] of a local authority[44] who is authorised by that authority to prosecute or defend on their behalf, or to appear on their behalf in proceedings before a magistrates' court, is entitled to do so, and, nothwithstanding anything in the Solicitors Act 1974, to conduct the proceedings although he is not a solicitor holding a current practising certificate.

The authorisation should be given by the authority before the commencement of court proceedings[45] and must be properly made.[46] If the authorisation is challenged, the proper method of proof is by production of the minute of proceedings that records the council's resolution authorising proceedings, or a certified copy thereof.[47]

---

[39] (1985) 135 New L.J. 889.
[40] [1984] A.C. 754 at p. 767, quoting Bridge L.J. in *Stafford Borough Council* v. *Elkenford Ltd.* [1977] 1 W.L.R. 324 at p. 330.
[41] See, *e.g.* the Public Health Act 1936, s. 100 (statutory nuisances; see § 16–32, *et seq.*); the Control of Pollution Act 1974, s. 58(8) (noise nuisances: see § 16–52).
[42] As amended by the Water Act 1973, Sched. 8, para. 98 and the Local Government Act 1985, Sched. 14, para. 21.
[43] Not a police officer: *Fisher* v. *Oldham Corporation* [1930] 2 K.B. 364.
[44] This power is also available to the Common Council, water authorities, joint authorities and the Inner London Education Authority, and, by virtue of the Local Government Act 1985, Sched. 13, para. 12(*f*) to residuary bodies.
[45] *Bowyer, Philpott and Payne Ltd.* v. *Mather* [1919] 1 K.B. 419. See § 4–57.
[46] *Bob Keats Ltd.* v. *Farrant* (1951) 49 L.G.R. 631.
[47] *Dee and Clwyd River Authority* v. *Parry* (1967) 65 L.G.R. 488. However, the court may not interfere if the magistrates' court expresses itself satisfied on less than strict proof that proceedings are authorised: *cf. R.* v. *Turner* [1910] 1 K.B. 346; *Westminster Coaching Services Ltd.* v. *Piddlesden* (1933) 31 L.G.R. 245.

CHAPTER 13

LOCAL ELECTIONS

THE following topics are considered in this Chapter: electoral areas; the **13-01**
franchise; the registration of electors; qualifications for candidature and
disqualifications; the conduct of elections; the questioning of elections;
election offences; and the filling of casual vacancies. The law relating to the
franchise, the registration of electors, the conduct of elections, the questioning of elections and election offences was consolidated in the Representation of the People Act 1983, and the regulations made thereunder.[1]
Certain changes were made by the Representation of the People Act 1985.
The law as to electoral areas, candidature and the filling of casual vacancies
is principally found in the Local Government Act 1972.

A. ELECTORAL AREAS[2]

The following table lists the various kinds of electoral units and the **13-02**
number of councillors elected for each:

Local government area	Electoral area	Representation
Counties	Electoral division	One councillor for each electoral division
Metropolitan districts	Ward	A number of councillors divisible by three
Non-metropolitan districts	Ward	Such number of councillors as may be provided by order
Parishes	The parish as a whole or wards of the parish	The number of councillors for each parish or ward of a parish is fixed by the district council
Communities	The community as a whole or wards of the community	The number of councillors as fixed under paragraph 4 of Schedule 5 to the Local Government Act 1972
London borough councils	Ward	Such number of councillors as is specified by order made under Part IV of the Local Government Act 1972[3]
Inner London Education Authority	Electoral division	Two councillors for each division for 1986; one councillor for each division thereafter[4]

[1] See the Representation of the People Regulations 1983 (S.I. 1983 No. 435).
[2] Local Government Act 1972, ss. 6, 16, 25 and 35 and Sched. 2, para. 7.
[3] Until an order is made the number is that specified in the borough's charter.
[4] Local Government Act 1985, s. 19 and Sched. 9.

Electoral areas in counties, districts and London boroughs may be, and usually are, further divided into polling districts.[5]

B. THE FRANCHISE[6]

13-03   A person is entitled to vote at a local government election who:

(i) at the qualifying date has a qualification based on residence or *alternatively* has a service qualification or a qualification as a merchant seaman or a qualification as a voluntary mental patient, and

(ii) on the qualifying date and the date of the poll is a Commonwealth citizen (or a citizen of the Republic of Ireland) and not suffering from a legal incapacity to vote, and

(iii) on the date of the poll is of voting age, *i.e.* is 18 years or over[7]

provided that he is registered as an elector. The qualifying date is defined as October 10 for elections falling within the period of 12 months beginning on February 16 in the following year.[8]

A person is qualified under (i) if on the qualifying date he is *resident* in the electoral area. The term "residence" was considered in *Fox* v. *Stirk*,[9] a case concerned with student residence. It was held that the word "residence" has no technical or special meaning but in the ordinary sense implies a degree of permanence. Lord Denning M.R. observed that the general principles in accordance with which the Representation of the People Act 1949 (now 1983) directs questions of residence as to the qualifying date are (1) that a person may have two residences, (2) that temporary presence at an address does not make a person resident there, and (3) that temporary absence does not deprive a person of his residence. A person may be resident in more than one place and where each such residence has the necessary degree of permanence he may be registered as an elector in more than one place.[10]

In *Hipperson* v. *Electoral Registration Officer for the District of Newbury*[11] it was held that a number of women who were living at the Greenham Common peace camp were "resident" there. The fact that camping on the land involved the commission of offences contrary to by-laws and the Highways Act 1980, s. 137 (obstruction of the highway) was

---

[5] Representation of the People Act 1983, s. 31.
[6] *Ibid.* ss. 2–7, 14–17.
[7] *Ibid.* ss. 2, 6, 14, 17.
[8] *Ibid.* s. 4.
[9] *Fox* v. *Stirk and Another; Ricketts* v. *Cambridge Electoral Registration Officer* [1970] 2 Q.B. 463.
[10] Though a person may have two residences it is an offence to vote in more than one electoral area in an ordinary election for councillors for a local government area which is not a single electoral area or to vote more than once in the same electoral area: Representation of the People Act 1983, s. 61.
[11] [1985] Q.B. 1060.

irrelevant: it was not necessary for the residence to be "lawful residence." Had any of the women been present on the land in breach of an injunction they could not have relied upon their residence there, but this was not the case on the facts.

The service qualification may be claimed by anyone who is a member of the forces or is employed in the service of the Crown or British Council in a post outside the United Kingdom or is the spouse of a person having a service qualification and (except in the case of spouses of members of the armed forces) who is resident outside the United Kingdom to be with his or her spouse.[12] A merchant seaman may be qualified as an elector in respect of an address at which he would be residing but for his occupation, or a hostel or club for merchant seamen where he normally stays in the course of his occupation.[13]

A mental patient, whether voluntary[14] or detained, who by the application of ordinary principles is regarded as resident at an address other than the mental hospital in which he is a patient or place where he is detained, is entitled to be registered at that other address. However, if by the application of those principles a voluntary mental patient would be regarded as resident only at the hospital, he may make a "patient's declaration" under section 7 of the Representation of the People Act 1983, provided that he is able to do so without assistance (other than assistance necessitated by blindness or other physical incapacity). The declaration must state, *inter alia*, the address where the declarant would be resident in the United Kingdom if he were not a voluntary mental patient or, if he cannot give any such address, an address (other than a mental hospital) at which he has resided in the United Kingdom. The declaration entitles the patient to be registered as an elector at that address. A detained mental patient may not be treated as resident at the place of detention.[15]

Legal incapacity is of two kinds, derived from common law and **13-04** defined in statute. At common law an idiot is debarred from voting[16] and also a person of unsound mind except during lucid periods.[17] The Forfeiture Act 1870[18] incapacitates a person convicted of treason who has been sentenced to death, preventive detention or corrective training or to a term of imprisonment exceeding 12 months, until he has suffered his punishment or been pardoned. A convicted person during the time that he is detained in a penal institution (prison, remand centre, detention centre or youth custody centre in the United Kingdom) in pursuance of

---

[12] Representation of the People Act 1983, s. 14.
[13] *Ibid.* s. 6.
[14] *i.e.* "a person who is a patient in a mental hospital but is not liable to be detained there by virtue of any enactment": Representation of the People Act 1983, s. 7(2).
[15] *Ibid.* s. 7(1).
[16] *Bedford (County) Case, Burgess' Case* (1785) 2 Lud.E.C. 381, 567.
[17] *Okehampton Case, Robin's Case* (1791) 1 Fras. 69, 162.
[18] s. 2, as amended.

his sentence is legally incapable of voting.[19] Persons guilty of corrupt practices and illegal practices are debarred from being registered as an elector or voting for five years—in the case of illegal practices the incapacity is effective only in the local government area in which the illegal practices took place.[20] Under the Public Bodies Corrupt Practices Act 1889[21] a person who is convicted for the second time of bribery or corruption of public officials is liable at the court's discretion to be disqualified for five years from being registered or from voting.

C. The Registration of Electors

13-05 A register of electors must be prepared each year. It is to be published not later than February 15 and is effective for elections occurring in the 12 months commencing February 16. Its preparation is dealt with in the Representation of the People Act 1983,[22] and the rules made thereunder.[23] The register serves both parliamentary and local government elections: the names of those who are entitled to vote only at local elections, *i.e.* peers of the realm, are appropriately marked. If a person reaches voting age during the currency of a register, the date of his eighteenth birthday is entered on the register, though he may not vote until an election which falls on or after that date.[24]

The compilation of the register falls to the registration officer, an officer appointed by each district and London borough council.[25] Where constituency boundaries and local government boundaries are not coterminous the appointment is dealt with by regulation.[26] The compilation of the register is based on a house-to-house or other sufficient inquiry and the registration officer has authority to require the giving of information. The lists on which the register is based are made available for public inspection on or before November 28 each year and persons aggrieved by an omission or entry in the lists may lodge a claim or objection in the prescribed form, and provision is made in the regulations for the claim or objection to be formally heard by the registration officer. An appeal lies to the county court against a decision of the registration officer in specific matters (generally speaking all matters connected with registration and non-registration) provided that the aggrieved person has first exercised his right to submit a claim or objection to the registration officer within the prescribed time.[27] There is a right of appeal from the county court to the Court of Appeal.

[19] Representation of the People Act 1983, s. 3.
[20] *Ibid.* s. 160.
[21] s. 2, as amended.
[22] ss. 9–13.
[23] Representation of the People Regulations 1983 (S.I. 1983 No. 435).
[24] Representation of the People Act 1983, s. 12(5).
[25] *Ibid.* s. 8.
[26] *Ibid.* Sched. 2, para. 1(1).
[27] *Ibid.* s. 56, as amended by the Representation of the People Act 1985, Sched. 2, para. 1 and Sched. 4, para. 16.

When the register as published "does not carry out the registration   **13-06** officer's intention" by omitting certain particulars from the register as published (*e.g.* because of printer's errors) the registration officer is authorised to make the necessary correction: any such correction is not effective at a particular election if it is made on or after the date of giving notice of election.[28]

The compilation of certain other lists falls to the registration officer—a list of persons who have been convicted or reported guilty of corrupt or illegal practices (this list is based on information supplied to the registration officer by the local authority), the absent voters list and proxy list.

D. Candidature[29]

A person is qualified to be elected to a local authority[30] if he is a British   **13-07** subject[31] or a citizen of the Republic of Ireland and on the "relevant day" he is 21 years of age and

(a) on that day he is and thereafter continues to be a local government elector for the area of the authority; or

(b) he has during the whole of the 12 months preceding that day occupied as owner or tenant any land or other premises in that area; or

(c) his principal or only place of work during that 12 months has been in that area; or

(d) he has during the whole of those 12 months resided in that area; or

(e) in the case of a member of a parish or community council he has during the whole of those 12 months resided either in the parish or community or within three miles of it.

The "relevant day" is the day of nomination and the day of the poll if there is one. Where an election is not preceded by nomination (where, for example, a parish councillor is co-opted) it is the day of election.

The foregoing are positive requirements; a person is disqualified if he: **13-08**

(i) holds any paid office or employment (other than the office of chairman, vice-chairman or deputy chairman) appointments to which are made or confirmed by the local authority or a committee or sub-committee of the authority, or by a joint board, joint authority or joint committee on which the authority is

[28] Representation of the People Act 1983, s. 11.
[29] Local Government Act 1972, ss. 79–81, as amended by the Local Government Act 1985, Sched. 14, paras. 2, 3 and Sched. 17.
[30] This term includes the Inner London Education Authority: s. 79(3), inserted by the Local Government Act 1985, Sched. 14, para. 2.
[31] *i.e.* now a Commonwealth citizen or British subject under the British Nationality Act 1981: see s. 5(1) and (3) of that Act.

represented, or by any person who is himself in the employment of the authority; or

(ii) is a person who has been adjudged bankrupt, or made a composition or arrangement with his creditors; or

(iii) has within five years before the election been surcharged by a district auditor to an amount exceeding £500 under Part X of the Local Government Act 1933[32]; or

(iv) has within five years before the day of election or since his election been convicted of any offence and has had passed on him a sentence of imprisonment (whether suspended or not) for a period of not less than three months without the option of a fine; or

(v) is disqualified from being elected or being a member of that authority under Part III of the Representation of the People Act 1983 (which relates to corrupt or illegal practices); or

(vi) is disqualified from membership for a specified period by order of the court because of his involvement in expenditure contrary to law[33]; or

(vii) is disqualified from membership for five years following an auditor's certificate that a loss or deficiency has been caused by his wilful misconduct while a member of a local authority.[34]

13-09 The disqualification attaching to a person by reason of his having been adjudged bankrupt ceases:

(i) on the date of annulment if the bankruptcy is annulled either on the ground that he ought not to have been adjudged bankrupt, or that his debts have been paid in full; or

(ii) if he is discharged with a certificate that the bankruptcy was caused by misfortune without any misconduct on his part, on the date of his discharge; or

(iii) in any other case on the expiration of five years from the date of his discharge.

The disqualification attaching to a person by reason of his having made a composition or arrangement with his creditors ceases:

(i) if he pays his debts in full, on the date on which payment is completed; or

(ii) in any other case, on the expiration of five years from the date on which the terms of the deed of composition or arrangement are fulfilled.

13-10 There are a number of particular rules on the matter of disqualification

---

[32] This provision was repealed by the Local Government Finance Act 1982, s. 38, but not so as to affect its application to accounts for any period beginning before the second appointed day (April 1, 1983) or any disqualification to which a person is subject immediately before the coming into force of the repeal.

[33] Local Government Finance Act 1982, s. 19: see § 7–20.

[34] *Ibid.* s. 20: see § 7–21.

and paid office.[35] A teacher or person otherwise employed in a school, college or other educational establishment maintained or assisted by a county council is not precluded from becoming a member of a district council on the grounds that the district council nominates members to the county education committee[36] and in any case may become a member of the education committee or a committee which discharges duties under the Public Libraries and Museums Act 1964.[37]

Employees of a passenger transport executive may not become members of the county council,[38] and an employee of a local authority who works under the direction of a committee of his employing authority on which there are representatives of other authorities is disqualified from membership of those other authorities. Similarly, employees who work under the direction of joint committees, joint authorities or joint boards may not serve on the constituent authorities.[39]

A teacher in a school maintained but not established by the authority (*i.e.* a voluntary school), is in the same position as a teacher employed directly by the authority—he is disqualified from membership.[40]

E. THE CONDUCT OF ELECTIONS

Election day and frequency of elections

Ordinary local government elections are held on the first Thursday in **13-11** May, unless the Secretary of State fixes another day by order made before February 1 in the previous year or, in the case of an order affecting more than one year, the first year.[41] Where the date of a general election is the same as the ordinary day for local government elections, any poll for the election of parish or community councillors is postponed for three weeks.[42]

County council elections take place every four years and all the councillors retire together. Those first elected in 1973 retired in 1977.[43] An election for metropolitan district councillors takes place in each year other than 1977 and every fourth year thereafter, and members retire by thirds.[44] Non-metropolitan district councils and district councils in Wales may, by the passing of a "requisite resolution" ask the Secretary of State

---

[35] As to disqualification for appointment to a joint authority, see the Local Government Act 1985, s. 35.
[36] Local Government Act 1972, s. 81(4), as amended by the Local Government Act 1985, Sched. 17. See hereon *Lamb* v. *Jeffries* [1956] 1 Q.B. 431 and *Boyd* v. *Easington Rural District Council* [1963] 1 W.L.R. 1281.
[37] Local Government Act 1972, s. 104(2).
[38] *Ibid.* s. 80(4). Repealed by the Transport Act 1985, Sched. 8, from a day to be appointed.
[39] *Ibid.* s. 80(2), as amended by the Local Government Act 1985, Sched. 14, para. 3.
[40] *Ibid.* s. 80(3).
[41] Representation of the People Act 1983, s. 37, as amended by the Representation of the People Act 1985, s. 18. In 1986, the date is May 8: *ibid.*
[42] Representation of the People Act 1985, s. 16.
[43] Local Government Act 1972, ss. 7 and 26.
[44] *Ibid.* s. 7(2), as amended by the Local Government Act 1985, Sched. 16, para. 3.

to make an order (a) providing for whole council elections, all the councillors retiring simultaneously, or (b) for a system of retirement by thirds.[45] Where the Secretary of State receives a request under (a), he may order simultaneous elections. Where he receives a request under (b) he may ask the Local Government Boundary Commission (for England or for Wales as the case may be) to make proposals as to the number, boundaries and names of wards into which the district is to be divided and the number of councillors to be elected for each ward. The "requisite resolution" is passed at a specially convened meeting of the council with notice of the object and a two-thirds majority is required. An option may not be exercised again for 10 years. Whole council elections took place in 1976 and 1979 and 1983, and will take place every four years thereafter in the year midway between county council elections. Elections which by order of the Secretary of State are to be by thirds are to take place in the year the order comes into force and in each year in which there is no county council election.

Parish councillors elected in 1973 held office for three years, retiring in 1976. Those elected in 1976 retired in 1979, and thereafter parish councillors have been elected for a four-year term.[46] Community councillors elected in 1974 served for five years, retiring in 1979. Thereafter, community councillors have also been elected for a four-year term.[47]

An election for London borough councillors took place in 1974 and 1978 and has taken place every fourth year thereafter.[48]

Procedure at elections

13-12   The principal steps to be taken in the conduct of an election are prescribed in detail in the Local Elections (Principal Areas) Rules 1973.[49] The latest time at which the various steps are taken is set out in the following table.

Proceeding	Latest time
Publication of notice of election	Twenty-fifth day before the day of election
Delivery of nomination papers	Noon on the nineteenth day before the day of election
Publication of statement as to persons nominated	Noon on the seventeenth day before the day of election

---

[45] Local Government Act 1972, ss. 7(4)–(7) and 26(2)–(5).
[46] Local Government Act 1972, s. 16.
[47] *Ibid.*s. 35.
[48] *Ibid.* Sched. 2, para. 6(3), as amended by the London Councillors Order 1976 (S.I. 1976 No. 213), altering previous arrangements.
[49] S.I. 1973 No. 79 as amended by S.I. 1976 No. 2065, S.I. 1983 No. 1154 and S.I. 1985 No. 1848. There are parallel provisions (with some differences) in the Local Elections (Parishes and Communities) Rules 1973 (S.I. 1973 No. 1910), as amended by S.I. 1974 No. 84, S.I. 1976 No. 2066 and S.I. 1983 No. 1153.

Proceeding	*Latest time*
Delivery of notices of withdrawals of candidature and appointment of election agents	Noon on the sixteenth day before the day of election
Applications and notices *re* postal and proxy voting	Eleventh day before the day of election[50]
Notice of poll	Sixth day before the day of election
Notice of appointment of polling or counting agents	Fifth day before the day of election
Polling	On the day of election

A Saturday, Sunday, day of the Christmas break,[51] of the Easter break or of a bank holiday or a day appointed for public thanksgiving or mourning are disregarded.

The conduct of elections is largely in the hands of the returning officer. **13-13** At district or county council elections, he is an officer appointed by the council. At parish or community elections he is an officer appointed by the district council in which the parish or community lies.[52] At elections for the London boroughs the returning officer is the proper officer of the borough.[53] A returning officer may appoint one or more persons to discharge all or any of his functions.

The first step in an election is the publication by the returning officer of the notice of election in the prescribed form.[54] It indicates, *inter alia*, where nominations are to be lodged, the latest time for lodging, and the latest date by which applications to be treated as absent voters, and other applications and notices about postal or proxy voting, must reach the registration officer.

A candidate is required to complete a nomination paper which follows **13-14** the prescribed form, signed by a proposer and seconder and by eight other electors of the electoral area as assenting to the nomination.[55] The signatures on the nomination form must be the usual signatures.[56]

Formerly, if the candidate's description were omitted the nomination was bad. It is now not essential to include any description at all. If a description is included (and it customarily is) it may contain a reference to a candidate's political activities or associations, but it may not in any event exceed six words in length. It is not the function of the returning officer to determine whether the description included is that which a candidate can properly claim to use.

It is the duty of the returning officer to decide, as soon as practicable after delivery, on the validity of the nomination paper.[57] A paper may be

---

[50] See the Representation of the People Regulations 1983 (S.I. 1983 No. 435), reg. 44.
[51] The term "break" is defined in r. 2.
[52] Representation of the People Act 1983, s. 35.
[53] *Ibid.*
[54] Local Elections (Principal Areas) Rules 1973 (S.I. 1973 No. 79), r. 4.
[55] r. 5. In the case of parish and community councils only a proposer and seconder are required: Local Elections (Parishes and Communities) Rules 1973 (S.I. 1973 No. 1910), r. 6.
[56] *Re Melton Mowbray (Egerton Ward) U.D.C. Election* [1969] 1 Q.B. 192.
[57] r. 8.

rejected as invalid on one or other of two grounds only, that the *particulars* of the candidate or person subscribing the paper are not as required by law or that the *paper* is not subscribed as required by law. The decision of the returning officer that a nomination paper is valid in form is final and may not be questioned in any proceeding whatsoever. The returning officer may not investigate the authenticity of particulars given which on their face are unobjectionable.[58] Objections on grounds other than form may be raised on an election petition.[59] If the returning officer decides the nomination paper to be bad his decision may also be reviewed by way of election petition. The formalities of nomination are complete when the candidate has submitted a consent to nomination in writing, attested by one witness, stating that he is qualified as required by law and giving particulars of his qualification.[60]

Under section 96 of the Representation of the People Act 1983[61], a candidate is entitled for the purpose of holding public meetings in furtherance of his candidature to the free use, at reasonable times between the notice of election and the day preceding the day of election, of any room which it is the practice to be let for public meetings and which is maintained wholly or mainly at public expense, and any suitable school room.

Election agent[62]

13-15 Except in the case of parish or community council elections the candidate is required to appoint an election agent; he may appoint himself and will be taken to have appointed himself if in fact he makes no appointment. The agent's office must be in the local government area, or in the constituency or one of the constituencies in which the area is comprised, or in a borough or district which adjoins it. The agent is to be generally concerned with the candidate's affairs, but certain specific duties are put on him by statute, particularly in the matter of expenses, the appointment of messengers, clerks and polling agents and the hiring of rooms. The following extract from the Final Report of the Committee on Electoral Reform on the requirement as to the appointment of election agents indicates an agent's functions[63]:

> "The object of the requirement is that there shall be an experienced person responsible to the candidate and to the public for the proper management of the candidature and in particular for the control of expenditure. The employment of an agent is of great benefit to the candidate, and a competent agent can do much to promote due observance of electoral law."

The responsibility of a candidate for the acts of his agent is considerably

---

[58] *Greenway-Stanley* v. *Paterson* [1977] 2 All E.R. 663.
[59] r. 8(7); *R.* v. *Election Court, ex p. Sheppard* [1975] 1 W.L.R. 1319 (address falsely given as a candidate's home address).
[60] r. 7.
[61] As substituted by the Representation of the People Act 1985, Sched. 4, para. 38.
[62] Representation of the People Act 1983, ss. 67, 69–71, as amended by the Representation of the People Act 1985, Sched. 4, paras. 20, 22, 23.
[63] Cmd. 7286 (1947–48).

greater than the responsibility normally flowing from the principal/agent relationship, where in general a principal is responsible only for the acts of his agent which come within the scope of the authority he has given. So far as responsibility is concerned, the relationship is more one of master and servant, the master being responsible for the acts of his servant within the course of his employment. Lush J. said in the *Harwich* case[64]:

> "The relation between a candidate and a person whom he constitutes his agent is much more intimate than that which subsists between an ordinary principal and an agent.... [T]he candidate is responsible for all the misdeeds of his agent committed within the scope of his authority, although they were done against his express directions, and even in wilful defiance of them. There is never any difficulty or doubt as regards this proposition."

Voting[65]

Electors record their votes in person at the polling stations to which **13-16** they are allotted by the returning officer, as published in the notice of poll. Exceptions are made in the case of persons falling within one of the following groups:

(1) An elector may vote by post if he is shown in the absent voters list as entitled to vote by post.

(2) An elector may vote by proxy if he is shown in the absent voters list as entitled to vote by proxy, unless, before a ballot paper has been issued for him so to vote, he applies at the polling station allotted to him for a ballot paper for the purpose of voting in person.

(3) An elector may vote in person at any polling station in the electoral area if
  (a) he is not entitled to an absent vote; and
  (b) he cannot reasonably be expected to go in person to the polling station allotted to him, by reason of the particular circumstances of his employment, either as a constable or by the returning officer, on the date of the poll, for a purpose connected with the election.

An elector may be entitled to an absent vote (1) for an indefinite period or (2) for a particular election. He will be eligible for an absent vote for an indefinite period:

(1) if he is or will be registered as a service voter; or

(2) if he cannot reasonably be expected to go in person to the polling station allotted or likely to be allotted to him, or to vote unaided there, by reason of blindness or other physical incapacity; or

---

[64] *Harwich* (1880) 3 O'M & H. 61 at p. 69.
[65] Representation of the People Act 1983, s. 46; Representation of the People Act 1985, ss. 5–9, Sched. 2.

(3) if he cannot reasonably be expected to go in person to that polling station by reason of the general nature of his occupation, service or employment or that of his spouse; or

(4) if he cannot go in person from his qualifying address to that polling station without making a journey by air or sea.

Applications must be made to the registration officer, and must meet the prescribed requirements. The officer must keep a record of successful applications.

An elector will be eligible for an absent vote at a particular election if his circumstances on the date of the poll will or are likely to be such that he cannot reasonably be expected to vote in person at the polling station allotted or likely to be allotted to him. Again, applications must be made to the registration officer and must meet the prescribed requirements. These provisions do not apply to a person eligible for an absent vote for an indefinite period, but such a person entitled to vote by post may apply, in respect of a particular election, to the registration officer (a) for his ballot paper to be sent to a different address in the United Kingdom, or (b) to vote by proxy. The officer must grant such an application if it meets the prescribed requirements.

The registration officer must, in respect of each election, keep an "absent voters list" of all persons entitled to vote by proxy or by post.

A person entitled to vote *as* proxy may do so in person at the polling station allotted to the elector unless he is included in the special list of such persons entitled to vote as proxy by post.

13-17   In a contested election the counting of votes is the responsibility of the returning officer.[66] This is done under conditions of secrecy in the presence of the candidates, their spouses, election agents and counting agents, and the official counting staff, and such other persons as may be approved by the returning officer after consultation with the agents. All such persons must make a formal declaration of secrecy. The decision of the returning officer on any question relating to the validity of a ballot paper or the voting or other mark thereon is final, but is subject to review on an election petition. If there is equality of votes he casts lots. When the result of the poll has been ascertained he must declare the result forthwith and as soon as possible publish it, with the number of votes given to each candidate, and the numbers of rejected ballot papers in the different categories. He then formally reports the result to the proper officer of the authority, to whom he hands over the election documents for custody. In an uncontested election, the returning officer is required to publish the result not later than 11 o'clock in the morning of the day of the election.

---

[66] Local Election (Principal Areas) Rules 1973 (S.I. 1973 No. 79), rr. 40 *et seq.*

Election expenses[67]

The total sum which a candidate may incur by way of election expenses **13-18**
is limited. Election expenses are expenses incurred before, during or after
an election on account of or in respect of the conduct or management of
the election. The maximum is £120 plus 2.4p for every entry in the
register. Where there are two joint candidates the maximum of each is
reduced by one-fourth; where there are more than two, by one-third.
Candidates are joint candidates for this purpose where they employ the
same election agent or employ the same clerks or messengers, or hire the
same committee rooms, or publish a joint election address.

A candidate or election agent who knowingly contravenes the rules is **13-19**
guilty of an illegal practice. All expenses (apart from the personal
expenses of the candidate and certain petty expenses) must be paid by or
through the election agent. No expenses may be incurred in holding
public meetings or organising public displays, or issuing advertisements,
circulars or publications, or otherwise presenting to the electors the
candidate or his views, or the extent or nature of his backing or
disparaging another candidate, with a view to promoting or procuring the
election of a candidate,[68] except by the candidate, his election agent and
persons authorised in writing by the election agent. A party political
broadcast is not an expense within the terms of section 63 of the
Representation of the People Act 1949 (now section 75 of the 1983 Act).[69]

All payments made by an election agent (except where they are less than
£20, or £10 in parish council elections) must be vouched for by a bill, stating
the particulars, and by a receipt, and all election expenses are to be paid
within 28 days of the declaration of the result of the election. Within 35 days
after the declaration of the election result, the election agent must deliver to
the returning officer a return as to election expenses, together with a
declaration as to the election expenses that to the best of his knowledge and
belief the return is true and correct. At the same time, or within seven days
afterwards, the candidate must deliver to the returning officer a declaration
in similar terms. If a candidate or agent makes a false declaration he is guilty
of a corrupt practice; a failure to send in the return or declaration within the
prescribed time is an illegal practice but relief against the consequences of
this failure may, in certain circumstances, be granted.

F. QUESTIONING AN ELECTION[70]

Election petition

An election may be challenged by means of an election petition **13-20**

---

[67] Representation of the People Act 1983, ss. 72–90, as amended by the Representation of the
People Act 1985, s. 14 and Sched. 4, paras. 24–33, 89. Section 76A, inserted by the 1985
Act, s. 14(4), empowers the Secretary of State to vary the specified maxima by statutory
instrument.

[68] It is sufficient to establish an intention to prevent the election of a candidate: *D.P.P.* v. *Luft*
[1977] A.C. 962 (literature advising the electorate not to vote for National Front candidates).

[69] *Grieve* v. *Douglas-Home* 1965 S.L.T. 186.

[70] Representation of the People Act 1983, ss. 127–157, as amended by the Representation of

presented in the prescribed form to the Queen's Bench Division of the High Court either by four or more persons who voted or were entitled to vote at the election, or by a candidate. A person whose election is questioned and a returning officer of whose conduct the petition complains may be made a respondent. The petition may be founded on one or more of the following grounds:

(i)   that the candidate was disqualified at the time of the election;
(ii) that the candidate was not duly elected;
(iii) that the election was avoided by corrupt or illegal practices;
(iv) that corrupt or illegal practices have so extensively prevailed that they may be reasonably supposed to have affected the result;
(v)   that the candidate or his election agent personally engaged as a canvasser or agent someone whom he knew or had reasonable grounds for supposing to be subject to incapacity by reason of his having been guilty of a corrupt or illegal practice or having been convicted more than once of bribery and corruption of members or officers of public bodies under the Public Bodies Corrupt Practices Act 1889.

13-21   A copy of the petition is forwarded by the court to the local authority for publication in the area.

It is for the court to decide on the evidence as a whole whether there has been a substantial compliance with the law as to elections or whether an act or omission affected the result.

Re Kensington North Parliamentary Election.[71] A parliamentary election petition was brought by Sir Oswald Mosley for a scrutiny of the votes recorded as having been cast in the election for the North Division of the Parliamentary Borough of Kensington, and for a determination that the Member in fact elected was not duly elected, and that his election and return were void on the ground that in the holding of the election divers illegal practices and breaches of the statutory rules governing the conduct of the election were committed by the returning officer and/or his servants or agents. *Held,* dismissing the petition, that, although certain breaches of the rules had been proved, there was no evidence that there had been a substantial breach, and that such breaches as there had been had not affected the result of the election. It was further held that the burden of proof in an election petition is not on the respondent to the petition; it is for the election court to decide on the evidence as a whole whether there has been a substantial compliance with the law as to elections or whether an act or omission affected the result.

No local government election is to be declared invalid by reason of any act or omission of the returning officer or any other person in breach of his official duty or otherwise of the local elections rules if it appears that

---

the People Act 1985, Sched. 4, paras. 48–51 and Sched. 5; Election Petition Rules 1960 (S.I. 1960 No. 543 as amended by S.I.s 1979 No. 543 and 1985 No. 1278). And see *Levers v. Morris* [1972] 1 Q.B. 221 for an example of this proceeding.
[71] [1960] 1 W.L.R. 762.

the election was so conducted as to be substantially in accordance with the law and that the act or omission did not affect its result.[72]

> *Gunn* v. *Sharpe*.[73] There was a failure to stamp ballot papers in a local election with the official mark. This disfranchised over half the voters at one polling station and resulted in two candidates being elected who otherwise would not have been. *Held*, the election was void as it had not been conducted substantially in accordance with the rules.
> *Morgan* v. *Simpson*.[74] Forty-four unstamped papers out of 24,000 resulted in a candidate having a majority of 11 votes, whereas had they been stamped and therefore counted, his opponent would have been elected with a majority of seven. *Held*, the election was void. Although it had been conducted substantially in accordance with the law, the result had in fact been affected by breaches of the rules.
> *Ruffle* v. *Rogers*.[75] The mere fact that a voter wrote the name of his chosen candidate on his ballot did not of itself invalidate the paper. The voter could not, on the facts, be clearly identified and he had made his intention clear. However, the failure to stamp four ballot papers had affected the result, as it would otherwise have been a tie: accordingly, the election was declared void.

Inspection of ballot papers can be obtained by order of a county court or an election court.[76]

Presentation of petition

13-22 A petition founded on a corrupt practice must be presented within 21 days from election day. This time is extended in certain circumstances. Where the petition alleges a corrupt practice relating to a payment or reward made or promised since the election, the time is 28 days after payment or promise. Where illegal practices are alleged, the latest time for presentation is 14 days after the receipt by the clerk of the return and declaration of election expenses; but where the illegal practice is the payment of money or other act done since the election, then the latest time for presentation is 28 days from the date of the payment or such act.

When the petition is presented, or within three days thereafter, the petitioner must give security for all costs which may become payable by him to any witness summoned on his behalf or to any respondent. The security is for an amount not exceeding £2,500 as the High Court directs, and must be by way of a surety[77] (or sureties) or deposit of money or a combination of both.

The election court

13-23 The election court consists of a commissioner sitting without jury. The commissioner is a barrister of at least 15 years' standing and is appointed

---

[72] Representation of the People Act 1983, s. 48.
[73] [1974] Q.B. 808.
[74] [1975] Q.B. 151; *cf. James* v. *Davies* (1977) 76 L.G.R. 189. (Election not void by reason of inconsistent election notices.)
[75] [1982] Q.B. 1220.
[76] Local Elections (Principal Areas) Rules 1973 (S.I. 1973 No. 79), r. 50.
[77] This must be a third party and not the petitioner himself: *Barrett* v. *Tuckman, The Times*, November 5, 1984.

by the judges on the rota for the trial of parliamentary election petitions. The trial normally takes place within the area of the authority for which the election was held. Provision is made for the stating of a special case for the determination of the High Court. At the conclusion of the trial the election court certifies to the High Court its decision as to whether the person whose election was complained of was duly elected or whether some other person was elected, or whether the election was void. This determination is final as to the matters at issue in the petition. Where an election has been declared void and no other person has been declared elected, a new election will be held in the same way as when a casual vacancy occurs. Where illegal or corrupt practices have been alleged a further report is required of the election court stating:

(i) whether any corrupt or illegal practice is proved to have been committed by or with the consent of the candidate and the nature of the corrupt or illegal practice;

(ii) whether any of the candidates has been guilty by his agents of any corrupt or illegal practice;

(iii) the names of all persons guilty of a corrupt or illegal practice; and

(iv) whether any corrupt practices have, or whether there is reason to believe that any corrupt practices have, extensively prevailed in the electoral area.

13-24   The election of a candidate is void if he is reported under (i) or (ii) or if it is shown that corrupt or illegal practices committed to procure his election have so extensively prevailed that they may be reasonably supposed to have affected the result. Other consequences may flow from this report. First, the report must be laid before the Director of Public Prosecutions (who is always to be present or represented at the trial of an election petition if the election court so requests, and who otherwise has a discretion to attend), and he may prosecute offenders before the election court, or some other competent court. Where information is given to the Director that a person has been guilty of an offence under the Representation of the People Act 1983, he must make such inquiries and institute such prosecutions as the circumstances of the case appear to him to require. Secondly, certain incapacities as to voting and holding office attach to persons who are reported guilty of corrupt or illegal practices. These matters are noted in earlier paragraphs.

All costs of and incidental to the presentation of an election petition and consequent proceedings are defrayed by the parties to the petition in the proportion which the election court or High Court determines.[78] The court may also direct that any costs incurred by vexatious conduct, unfounded allegations or unfounded objections shall be defrayed by the parties by whom they were caused, whether or not they were on the whole successful.

[78] See *R.* v. *Cripps, ex p. Muldoon* [1984] Q.B. 686.

G. Election Offences

It is customary to divide election offences into two groups, those **13–25** which stem from the common law and those from statute. The greater number of common law offences have now been defined in statute and for practical purposes it is the statutory offences which are important. Bribery at an election, for example, is an offence at common law; it is also an offence under the Representation of the People Act 1983, and whilst it is still open to proceed by way of the common law in the case of bribery at an election a prosecutor would normally choose the statutory procedure.

Statutory offences may be considered in three groups, corrupt practices, illegal practices, and other election offences. The distinction between a corrupt practice and an illegal practice lies more in the consequence which flows from the offence rather than in the offence itself. There is, however, this further point: speaking generally a corrupt practice involves a guilty intention; an illegal practice is something prohibited by the legislature whether it is done honestly or dishonestly. The statute law relating to corrupt and illegal practices is now contained in the Representation of the People Act 1983 and the following are corrupt practices: personation, incurring expense without authority of the candidate or agent; false declaration in relation to election expenses; bribery; treating; undue influence.[79]

Illegal practices and other election offences may be grouped under five **13–26** headings.[80] It will be noted that some offences are illegal practices only if committed by a candidate or agent.

(i) *Illegal payments:* Payments for the conveyance of electors to the poll, and to voters for exhibiting bills and notices, payments to induce withdrawal of a candidate, the provision of money for illegal payments; exceeding maximum expenses; failure to make a return and declaration as to expenses.

(ii) *Illegal hiring and employment:* The hiring of conveyances for voters, and certain premises for committee rooms (licensed premises); the employment of paid canvassers. These offences are illegal practices if committed by a candidate or agent.

(iii) *Restrictions on broadcasting during elections:* It is unlawful during the period commencing five weeks before polling day for an item about the electoral area to be broadcast or televised if any candidate who takes part does not consent; and, unless all candidates consent, any person taking part in the item broadcast for the purpose of promoting or procuring his election, is guilty of an illegal practice, unless the broadcast is without his consent. The

---

[79] Representation of the People Act 1983, ss. 60, 75, 82, 113, 114, 115.
[80] *Ibid.* ss. 61–66, 73, 75, 76, 78, 82–87, 92–94, 97, 99–102, 106–112, 168, 169, 175, 189, as amended by the Representation of the People Act 1985, Scheds. 3, 4, 5.

use of a wireless or television station abroad for election purposes is an illegal practice.

(iv) *Improper conduct of election campaign:* The publication of false statements of fact relating to the personal conduct or character of the candidate (unless the person concerned had reasonable grounds for supposing and did in fact believe that his statements were true); the publication of a false statement as to the withdrawal of a candidate; acting (or inciting others to act) in a disorderly manner at an election meeting for the purpose of preventing the transaction of business; inducing or procuring illegal practices. Under this heading may be included the failure to show the printer's name and address on election literature. This is an illegal practice if committed by a candidate or agent.

(v) *Voting offences:* It is an illegal practice to vote or to induce another to vote contrary to law.

13-27   A person guilty of a corrupt practice is liable to imprisonment or fine or both,[81] and other consequences and incapacities flow from a finding of guilt. He may be prosecuted before an election court which is hearing an election petition, or on indictment or summarily. A person guilty of an illegal practice, payment, employment or hiring is liable to a fine not exceeding level 5 on the standard scale.[82]

Provision is made in certain circumstances for the granting of relief from the consequences of wrongful acts. Where an illegal practice, payment, employment or hiring has been committed and the act or omission arises from inadvertence or accidental miscalculation or from some other reasonable cause of like nature, an application for relief may be made to the High Court or election court (or in certain cases to the county court).[83] The Director of Public Prosecutions or his assistant or representative may appear and make representations. An applicant must show that there has been no want of good faith, and notice of the application must be published locally. The effect of relief is to except the particular act or omission from being an illegal practice—the taint of illegality is removed so that no proceedings can be instituted in respect of that act or omission, either against the applicant or any other person.

13-28   Relief may also be granted by the High Court, an election court or a county court where a candidate or an agent fails to deliver the return and declaration as to election expenses, where the failure arises through the illness of the applicant or the absence, death, illness or misconduct of the election agent or by reason of inadvertence, provided that there is no want of good faith.[84] A candidate may also in certain circumstances avoid the consequences which would otherwise fall to him through the

---

[81] Representation of the People Act 1983, s. 168(1)–(4), as substituted by the Representation of the People Act 1985, Sched. 3, para. 8.
[82] *Ibid.* s. 169, 175.
[83] *Ibid.* s. 167. See *Re Berry* [1978] Crim. L.R. 357.
[84] *Ibid.* s. 86.

wrongful acts of his agent. Where such a candidate is reported by the election court to have been guilty *by his agents* of treating, undue influence or any illegal practice, and the election court further reports that the candidate has proved:

(i) that no corrupt or illegal practice was committed at the election by the candidate or his election agent and the offences mentioned in the report were committed contrary to the orders and without the sanction or connivance of the candidate or his election agent; and

(ii) that the candidate and his election agent took all reasonable means for preventing the commission of corrupt and illegal practices at the election; and

(iii) that the offences mentioned in the report were of a trivial, unimportant and limited character; and

(iv) that in all other respects the election was free from any corrupt or illegal practice on the part of the candidate and of his agents.

then the election is not avoided and the candidate suffers no incapacity.[85]

It was at one time suggested that an election address was the subject of **13-29** qualified privilege, being a communication from one elector to other electors on a matter of common interest which did not come within section 10 of the Defamation Act 1952: but this view has now been clarified and overruled. In ordinary circumstances, therefore, an election address is not privileged.[86]

A person who commits the offence of personation at an election is liable to imprisonment for a term not exceeding two years.[87]

H. Elections to Fill a Casual Vacancy[88]

The procedure for the filling of a casual vacancy is substantially the same **13-30** as that for an ordinary election. A casual vacancy may arise through the failure of an elected person to make a declaration of acceptance of office, or through the death or resignation of a member, or through the failure of a member to attend any meeting of the authority or of its committees or subcommittees for a period of six consecutive months (unless the failure was due to some reason approved by the authority), or because a member ceases to be qualified, or becomes disqualified. Where a casual vacancy arises because a member ceases to be qualified or becomes disqualified or because of his failure to attend meetings, the local authority is required forthwith to declare the office vacant, unless the High Court has already

---

[85] Representation of the People Act 1983, s. 158.
[86] *Plummer* v. *Charman* [1962] 1 W.L.R. 1469.
[87] Representation of the People Act 1983, s. 168(1), as substituted by the Representation of the People Act 1985, Sched. 3, para. 8.
[88] Local Government Act 1972, ss. 86, 87, 89, 90, 91, as amended by the Local Government Act 1985, Sched. 14, paras. 8–11. Sections 86–90 are applicable to the Inner London Education Authority.

made a declaration to this effect. In other cases, a vacancy may be declared by the local authority or the High Court or by notice in writing given to the proper officer by two local government electors for the area.[89] An election to fill a casual vacancy must be held within 42 days after the High Court or the council has declared the office to be vacant or within 42 days after written notice of the vacancy has been given to the authority by two electors for the area. Where a casual vacancy occurs within six months before the ordinary day of retirement from the office in which the vacancy arises, it is filled at the next ordinary election. If there is an election to fill several casual vacancies, the successful candidate with the fewer votes takes the shorter period; where the election is combined with an ordinary election of councillors and not contested, somewhat complex rules apply. A casual vacancy among parish councillors or community councillors is filled by election or by the parish or community council in accordance with the relevant election rules. Where there are so many vacancies among parish or community councillors that the council may be unable to act, the district council may by order make temporary appointments until other councillors are elected to take up office.[90]

[89] Local Government Act 1972, s. 89.
[90] *Ibid.* s. 91.

CHAPTER 14

HIGHWAYS

A HIGHWAY may be defined in simplest terms as a way over which all   **14-01**
members of the public have the right to pass and repass. Their use of the
way must be as of right, not on sufferance or by licence.
The law on this subject is considered under the following headings:
highway authorities; the creation of highways; the repair of highways and
bridges; private streets; rights related to highways; diversion and
extinguishment; nuisances and obstructions; lighting and cleansing;
transportation and traffic management; grants and reimbursements. The
principal Act is the Highways Act 1980.

A. HIGHWAY AUTHORITIES AND HIGHWAY CLASSIFICATION

The Secretary of State for Transport is the highway authority for trunk   **14-02**
roads.[1] These were described in the Trunk Roads Act 1936 as the
principal roads which constitute the national system of routes for through
traffic in Great Britain. A list of trunk roads appeared in Schedules to the
Trunk Roads Acts of 1936 and 1946; other existing roads can be
designated trunk roads and new trunk roads constructed under powers
conferred on the Secretary of State.[2] Although the Secretary of State is the
highway authority for these roads, much of the work is undertaken by
county councils and metropolitan district councils on an agency basis,
and county councils in turn may enter into arrangements with district
councils to undertake all or part of the work.[3]
Outside London, county councils and metropolitan district councils are   **14-03**
highway authorities for all roads except trunk roads, but much work in
non-metropolitan counties is undertaken by district councils on an
agency basis.[4] Some highway functions fall to district councils, parish
councils and community councils (they are noted in Appendices 1 and 2)
and district councils have certain rights in relation to highway maintenance—these are considered in paragraph 14-21.
In Greater London, London borough councils and the Common
Council are highway authorities for the roads in their areas other than for
roads for which the Secretary of State is responsible.[5]

[1] Highways Act 1980, s. 1; Local Government Act 1985, s. 8; Transfer of Functions
(Transport) Order 1981 (S.I. 1981 No. 238). The Minister in respect of Wales is the
Secretary of State for Wales; see Highways Act 1980, s. 329(1).
[2] Highways Act 1980, ss. 10, 24, Local Government Act 1985, Sched. 4, para. 53(2).
[3] Highways Act 1980, s. 6.
[4] This is done under s. 101 of the Local Government Act 1972.
[5] Local Government Act 1985, s. 8.

14-04   A highway authority of any category may be an authority for a special
road, namely, one reserved for particular classes of traffic (in the main
motorways). A scheme for the provision of a special road is made by a
highway authority and requires the confirmation of the Secretary of State
before it becomes effective, or is made by the Secretary of State himself.[6]

14-05   Two further road categories have relevance to highway administration,
namely, principal roads and classified roads. The Local Government Act
1966 introduced the first category, mainly for the purpose of the grant
system. A principal road was defined in Ministry of Transport Circular No.
Roads 9/66 as a road which is an essential route for traffic and which had a
sufficiently important place in the national highway system to justify
central government interest in its planning and Exchequer assistance
towards its improvement. Government assistance in respect of other roads
was provided, from April 1, 1967, by way of the rate support grant.

14-06   The second category, that of classified roads, is of less relevance, but
the term is constantly in use in connection with highway matters and is
therefore explained. Under the Local Government Act 1929, county
councils became the highway authority for all roads in rural districts and
for "classified roads" in non-county boroughs and urban districts. The
classification of roads stemmed from the Ministry of Transport Act 1919,
which empowered the Minister to classify roads for the purposes of grants
for construction, improvement and maintenance. All roads classified by
the Minister as coming within Class I and Class II (or declared not
inferior to these classes) became county roads in boroughs and urban
districts under the Act of 1929. In 1946 a further classification was added,
known as Class III, and all roads in this class became county roads.[7]
When the designation of principal roads was introduced by the Act of
1966 almost all the existing Class I classified roads became principal
roads.[8]

     The categories of principal road and classified road are retained in the
Highways Act 1980. The general provisions with regard to these roads
appear in section 12, and section 13 enables the Secretary of State for
Transport to change the designation of principal roads.

B. Creation of Highways

14-07 A highway may come into existence by dedication and acceptance under
the common law, or under statute.

Dedication and acceptance

     If an owner of land dedicates a right of passage across his land for use
by the public at large, and if the public accepts and uses the way as of

---

[6] Highways Act 1980, s. 16.
[7] Ministry of Transport Circular No. 595: see Ministry of Transport Circular No. 5/64.
[8] By s. 40 of the Local Government Act 1974 the classification of roads as principal roads
ceased to have relevance for grant purposes: see § 14–62 below.

right, then a public highway is created. Dedication may be express or implied—it is express, for example, where a formal deed is executed in favour of the highway authority, or where an owner constructs a road in developing an estate. It is implied where the owner is aware that the public is using a way across his land as of right, and acquiesces. Dedication, whether express or implied, contains several essential elements. There must be, in the first place, *animus dedicandi*—an intention to dedicate.[9] This intention is clearly expressed where dedication is embodied in a formal document; in other cases it may have to be inferred, but it can only be inferred where the acts of the owner conclusively point to an intention to dedicate.[10] The courts have sometimes drawn a distinction between *animus dedicandi* and tolerance. In *Steel* v. *Houghton*[11] Heath J. said:

> "It is the wise policy of the law, not to construe acts of charity, though continued and repeated for never so many years, in such a manner as to make them the foundation of legal obligation."

Secondly, the right of passage must be exercised by or granted to the public at large and not limited to particular groups or classes of people—a right of way restricted to residents of a given parish, for example, does not amount to a public highway.[12] Dedication may of course be subject to restrictions as to the mode of user—the way may be dedicated for use by pedestrians only, and it may be subject to physical restrictions and defects, to obstructions and nuisances, and the public in accepting the way will be taken to have accepted it as it is.[13] Finally, dedication will not be effective unless the grantor is capable of giving a right over his land for all time. A leaseholder, for example, would not be competent to do this, unless he obtained the consent of the reversioner (the person to whom the land reverts at the end of the lease). Generally speaking, only the owner of the fee simple (that is, the outright owner) can effectively dedicate. A public body can in general create a right of way for the public at large, provided that the use by the public would not be incompatible with the purpose of the public body.[14] **14-08**

Dedication itself is insufficient to create a public highway: there must be acceptance by user, and it must be acceptance as of right, not on sufferance or by licence. **14-09**

These two factors, dedication and acceptance by user are inter-related, for user may serve as *evidence* of dedication. If the public uses a way as of right and the owner knows of it and acquiesces, dedication may be inferred. Lord Blackburn said in *Mann* v. *Brodie*[15]: **14-10**

[9] *Simpson* v. *Att. Gen.* [1904] A.C. 476, *per* Lord Macnaghten at pp. 493, 494.
[10] *Ibid.*
[11] (1788) 1 H.Bl. 51 at p. 60.
[12] *Poole* v. *Huskinson* (1843) 11 M. & W. 827.
[13] *Fisher* v. *Prowse* (1862) 2 B. & S. 770.
[14] *British Transport Commission* v. *Westmorland County Council*; *Same* v. *Worcestershire County Council* [1958] A.C. 126.
[15] (1885) 10 App. Cas. 378 at p. 386.

"Where there has been evidence of a user by the public so long and in such a manner that the owner of the fee, whoever he was, must have been aware that the public were acting under the belief that the way had been dedicated, and has taken no steps to disabuse them of that belief, it is not conclusive evidence, but evidence on which those who have to find that fact may find that there was a dedication by the owner whoever he was."

The court will examine the circumstances as a whole, taking into account any evidence which negatives an *animus dedicandi*. Parke B. said in *Poole v. Huskinson*[16]:

"In order to constitute a valid dedication to the public of a highway by the owner of the soil, it is clearly settled that there must be an intention to dedicate—there must be an *animus dedicandi*, of which the user by the public is evidence, and no more; and a single act of interruption by the owner is of much more weight, upon a question of intention, than many acts of enjoyment."

The extent to which user can be relied on as *proof* of dedication was considered by the House of Lords in *Folkestone Corporation* v. *Brockman*[17] where Earl Loreburn said:

"Dedication may be and, indeed, ought to be presumed in the absence of anything to rebut the presumption from long-continued user of a way by the public. Two things have to be made good, that the user has been sufficient in its duration and character, and that the presumption then arising has not been rebutted."

14-11   The Rights of Way Act 1932 (as amended by the National Parks and Access to the Countryside Act 1949), simplified the common law rule under which dedication could be inferred from user by stating that certain assumptions should prevail unless the contrary was proved. These provisions are now contained in the Highways Act 1980.[18] Where a way has been actually enjoyed by the public as of right and without interruption for a full period of 20 years, the way is deemed to have been dedicated as a highway unless there is sufficient evidence to the contrary.[19] An owner may negative the inference of intention to dedicate by placing an appropriate notice on the way, and if it is torn down or defaced he may protect his rights by giving notice to the local authority (the council of a county, metropolitan district, London borough or the Common Council of the City of London[20]) that the way has not been dedicated. He may also submit to the authority maps of his land showing the ways which he admits to have been dedicated and may subsequently make declarations that no further ways have been dedicated, and in the

---

[16] (1843) 11 M. & W. 827 at p. 830.
[17] [1914] A.C. 338 at p. 378.
[18] Highways Act 1980, s. 31 (as amended by the Wildlife and Countryside Act 1981, s. 72(11)) and s. 32. These provisions were considered in *Gloucestershire County Council* v. *Farrow* [1985] 1 W.L.R. 741 where a market place constituted a highway.
[19] As to use as of right and without interruption, see *Lewis* v. *Thomas* [1950] 1 K.B. 438 and *Jones* v. *Bates* [1938] 2 All E.R. 237.
[20] Highways Act 1980, s. 31, as amended by the Local Government Act 1985, Sched. 4.

absence of proof to the contrary, these acts negative an intention to dedicate.

Whether or not a given way is a public highway is determined by **14-12** applying the principles described in the preceding paragraphs to the facts of a particular case. The issue will be settled on the basis of the evidence adduced, and as already noted the statutory provisions simplify the matter to some extent by stating that certain assumptions prevail unless the contrary is proved. In the case of public paths, however, there are further statutory provisions designed to resolve doubts as to status. The National Parks and Access to the Countryside Act 1949 required every county council, apart from the former London County Council, to undertake a survey of its area and to prepare and publish a definitive map and statement of public rights of way, that is footpaths, bridleways and roads used as public footpaths, within its area. That Act, as amended by the Countryside Act 1968, provided for the review at not less than five-yearly intervals of all the definitive maps and statements prepared by surveying authorities for their respective areas.

The Wildlife and Countryside Act 1981 introduced a new review procedure.[21] Definitive maps and statements are required to be kept under continuous review by surveying authorities,[22] and modified by way of orders as and when certain events occur, namely, when a way has been authorised to be stopped up, diverted, widened or extended, where a way of a particular description has ceased to be a way of that description, where a new right of way has been created, where new evidence affecting an entry is discovered, or where by the effluxion of time a presumption has arisen as to a public right of way. It is open to any person to apply to the surveying authority for an order to modify the definitive map and statement and in the event of a refusal there is a right of appeal to the Secretary of State.

A duty falls to surveying authorities to review particulars, in definitive **14-13** maps and statements, of roads used as public paths, and, if necessary, to modify those maps by order. Roads used as public paths must be specifically classified as (a) a by-way open to all traffic, (b) a bridleway, or (c) a footpath.

The marking of a definitive footpath is without prejudice to the existence of any greater rights over the same line.[23]

Creation of highways by or under Act of Parliament

Several statutes provide for the creation of highways and for the **14-14** construction of highways. The Highways Act 1980 is the most important.

---

[21] ss. 53 to 58.
[22] County councils, metropolitan district councils and London borough councils are surveying authorities for the purpose of these provisions: Wildlife and Countryside Act 1981, s. 66(1), as amended by the Local Government Act 1985, s. 6 and Sched. 3.
[23] This provision overruled the decision in *Suffolk County Council* v. *Mason* [1979] A.C. 705, H.L.

It enables the Secretary of State for Transport and local highway authorities to construct highways and to provide road ferries,[24] and empowers them to construct special roads, those reserved for particular classes of vehicles.[25] Provision is made for the creation of a particular species of highway, a walk-way—a way over, through or under buildings or structures. Such ways are created by dedication agreement (and in this respect take on certain characteristics of highways as commonly understood). But their use may be regulated by by-laws made by the local highway authority and by regulations made by the Secretary of State.[26]

Footpaths and bridleways may be created under the Highways Act 1980. The council of a county, district, London borough and a National Park joint planning board may enter into an agreement, called a public path agreement, for the dedication of a public path (*i.e.* a footpath or bridleway), and the agreement may provide for dedication subject to limitations and restrictions.[27] The authorities concerned may also exercise compulsory powers, subject to confirmation by the Secretary of State, creating a footpath or bridleway by means of a public path order.[28]

A highway for vehicles (other than a trunk road or principal road) may be converted into a public footpath or bridleway by an order made by the Secretary of State on the application of a local planning authority.[29]

14-15 The National Parks and Access to the Countryside Act 1949 has provisions as to long distance routes which enable the public to make extensive journeys on foot, horseback or bicycle over ways not principally used by vehicles.[30] Proposals for such routes are made to the Secretary of State for the Environment by the Countryside Commission, established under the Act, and are brought into effect by local authorities, with contributions from the Secretary of State. The Act facilitates public access to the countryside generally—it enables planning authorities to make access orders and access agreements and to acquire land for access purposes.[31] These powers are extended by the Countryside Act 1968: open country is made to include rivers, canals and waterways.[32]

The Cycle Tracks Act 1984 enables a highway authority by order to designate a footpath for which it is the highway authority as a cycle track. If the order is opposed it becomes effective only after confirmation by the Secretary of State for Transport.

---

[24] Highways Act 1980, s. 24. As to the acquisition of land for highway construction, see § 14–16, below.
[25] *Ibid.* s. 17 and Sched. 4.
[26] *Ibid.* s. 35.
[27] *Ibid.* s. 25, and the Wildlife and Countryside Act 1981, s. 64.
[28] *Ibid.* s. 26, and Local Government Act 1985, Sched. 5.
[29] Town and Country Planning Act 1971, s. 212.
[30] ss. 51–55; Countryside Act 1968, Sched. 3, para. 9(4).
[31] ss. 59 *et seq.*
[32] s. 16.

C. Repair and Improvement of Highways and Bridges

Highway authorities have wide powers of land acquisition.[33] They may   **14-16** purchase land, compulsorily or by agreement, for the construction and improvement of highways, and the land may lie outside the boundary of a highway or proposed highway.[34] They are empowered to acquire, compulsorily or by agreement, land needed to reduce the adverse effects of the existence or use of the highway on its surroundings; and they may acquire by agreement owner-occupied property which is severely affected by construction works or which is severely affected by the use of a new or improved road during the first 12 months.[35]

Highway authorities may carry out works to mitigate any adverse effect   **14-17** which the construction, improvement, existence or use of a highway has or will have on the surroundings of the highway.[36] This power includes the power to plant trees, shrubs or plants and to lay out any area as grass land. Where land is acquired for this purpose it may be developed or redeveloped for the purpose of improving the surroundings of the highway. Agreements may be entered into with frontagers to a highway as to the use of the land near to the highway and may contain appropriate financial provisions.[37] Authorities may acquire rights instead of titles.[38] They may be created over land for highway purposes by the use of compulsory powers. This provision may be of aid to highway authorities in the construction and maintenance of bridges over highways and tunnels under highways, the construction and maintenance of drains, the placing of apparatus in land and the construction of private accesses.

A highway may be repairable (i) by the local highway authority (the   **14-18** term "highways maintainable at the public expense" is used to describe these highways)[39]; (ii) by the Secretary of State for Transport; (iii) by private persons; or (iv) by no one, that is to say, there may be no one who has a duty in law to keep the way in repair. Public paths are dealt with somewhat differently and are considered at paragraph 14-27 below. The law as to the repair of bridges is broadly similar to that which applies to the repair of highways and is dealt with in paragraph 14-28. Paragraph 14-30 sets out the procedure available to enforce a duty of repair and the standard of repair which can be required where the duty to repair exists. This section ends with a note on the liability of highway authorities if they neglect to carry out their obligations to repair.

Highways maintainable at the public expense

At common law responsibility for the repair of all highways fell to the   **14-19**

---

[33] Highways Act 1980, Part XII.
[34] *Ibid.* ss. 238, 239, 249, 256 and Sched. 18.
[35] *Ibid.* s. 246.
[36] *Ibid.* s. 282.
[37] *Ibid.* s. 253.
[38] *Ibid.* s. 250.
[39] *Ibid.* s. 36.

inhabitants of the parish.[40] This rule was modified by the Highway Act 1835,[41] which provided that after the passing of the Act no new road should become publicly repairable unless the statutory formalities had been complied with. Broadly speaking, this rule still holds good. Highways are maintainable at public expense if they existed before 1836, or if since that time they have been adopted (a) under the procedure laid down in the 1835 Act or (b) under one of the subsequent statutes which provided for adoption.

The adoption procedure of the Highway Act 1835 was re-enacted in section 39 of the Act of 1959 but with a number of modifications to modernise procedure. It reproduced also section 49 of the National Parks and Access to the Countryside Act 1949, and therefore applied to public paths and other ways. Under this provision, which now appears in the Highways Act 1980,[42] a newly dedicated way may become maintainable at public expense if the highway authority certifies that the way has been dedicated and has been made up in a satisfactory manner. The procedure begins with a notice from the dedicator, and if the authority decides not to proceed the matter is settled by a magistrates' court.

14-20 The more important provisions under (b) were those relating to private street works, *i.e.* the Public Health Act 1875,[43] the Private Street Works Act 1892,[44] and the New Streets Act 1951.[45] These were reproduced in the Highways Act 1959 and the last two in the Highways Act 1980. An authority may adopt a private street after the execution of private street works[46] and may be required to make up and adopt a private street where payment has been made under the advance payments code.[47] In addition, a person liable to maintain a privately maintainable highway is enabled, on the payment of an appropriate sum, to have his liability taken over by the highway authority.[48] Where a privately maintainable highway is diverted by order of a magistrates' court, the substituted highway is maintainable at the public expense.[49]

14-21 A duty of maintenance lies upon the Secretary of State as respects trunk roads and on county councils and metropolitan district councils as respects all other publicly maintainable highways, and maintenance includes repair.[50] This duty may extend beyond keeping the surface of the highway in repair to include the removal of snow and ice or the taking of such protective measures as would render highways and paths safe for

[40] *Austin's Case* (1672) 1 Vent. 189.
[41] s. 23.
[42] s. 37.
[43] ss. 82 and 152. The Code of 1875 was repealed by the Local Government Act 1972, s. 188(5), Sched. 30.
[44] ss. 19 and 20.
[45] s. 6.
[46] Highways Act 1980, s. 228.
[47] *Ibid.* s. 229.
[48] *Ibid.* s. 53.
[49] *Ibid.* ss. 54 and 116.
[50] *Ibid.* ss. 41 and 329 and see below § 14–31.

vehicles and pedestrians in bad weather conditions.[51] In non-metropolitan counties, powers may be exercised by a district council.[52] In the case of footpaths, bridleways, and urban roads which are neither trunk roads nor classified roads but maintainable at public expense, the district council has powers of maintenance as of right. The district council will first inform the county council, in the manner laid down in the Act, of the highways or parts of the highways in respect of which it intends to exercise its powers. If the county council disagrees in any respect it may serve a counter-notice, and if agreement cannot be reached the Secretary of State for Transport himself decides. County councils are obliged to reimburse the expenses of district councils—only maintenance costs will be reimbursed. Anything above that is met by the district council. In exercising the powers of maintenance the district council stands in the shoes of the highway authority and is liable in tort for nonfeasance and misfeasance. In practice, a good deal of highway maintenance for which responsibility lies with county councils is exercised by district councils under agency agreements.

Authorities have a general power to improve highways for which they are responsible and to provide equipment for them,[53] and there are very many specific powers.[54]

There are several rules with respect to the precautions to be taken when   **14-22** works of repair and improvement are under way. The *statutory rules* are found in sections 174 and 175 of the Highways Act 1980. Section 174 prescribes the precautions to be taken in the carrying out of certain works in streets—they are additional to those contained in section 8 of the Public Utilities Street Works Act 1950. The section deals with the erection of barriers for preventing danger to traffic (a term which includes pedestrians and animals). It stipulates that works are to be properly guarded and lighted during the hours of darkness. Under section 175 a duty is placed on employees of local authorities to take all reasonable precautions where materials remain on the highway overnight. Section 175A, inserted by the Disabled Persons Act 1981, s. 1(1), obliges highway authorities, other authorities and other persons executing works in streets to have regard to the needs of disabled persons and blind persons.

The *common law rules* can be stated shortly. An authority when carrying out works of repair or improvement is under a duty to exercise care to prevent injury to the public. It must take reasonable care not to act

---

[51] *Haydon* v. *Kent County Council* [1978] Q.B. 343; *Bartlett* v. *Department of Transport* (1984) 83 L.G.R. 579. Failure to take measures to reduce the number of dogs straying on to the highway cannot be a failure of the duty to maintain: *Allison* v. *Corby District Council* [1980] R.T.R. 111.

[52] Highways Act 1980, s. 42 and Sched. 7.

[53] *Ibid.* s. 62.

[54] These appear in the Highways Act 1980, ss. 64–105 and ss. 115A, 115B, and 115C, inserted by the Local Government (Miscellaneous Provisions) Act 1982, Sched. 5, Part I. An authority may grant permission to a person to do those things which it is empowered itself to do under ss. 115B(1)–(3) and 115C.

in any way likely to endanger the lives and property of those who use the highway. In *Haley* v. *London Electricity Board*[55] the Board dug a trench under a power conferred by section 6 of the Public Utilities Street Works Act 1950, a provision which obliged them to fence and guard an excavation. They were therefore under a duty to take reasonable care. In order to meet this obligation they (through their workmen) put a punner hammer across the pavement to stop pedestrians walking into the trench. The handle rested on some railings two feet from the ground and the end rested on the pavement, about a foot from the outer edge. The plaintiff, a blind man, walking to work, missed the hammer with his stick and tripped over it, receiving injuries. The House of Lords held that the Board was liable at common law. Lord Reid said[56]:

> "It appears to me that the ordinary principles of the common law must apply in streets as well as elsewhere, and that fundamentally they depend on what a reasonable man, careful of his neighbour's safety, would do having the knowledge which a reasonable man in the position of the defendant must be deemed to have."

But there is no absolute duty to prevent accidents: the authority is never the insurer of highway users. It "does not have to cater for the man who walks with his head in the air and does not look where he is going."[57]

14-23   A distinction is to be drawn between liability to repair, discussed in the preceding paragraphs, and the liability of a highway authority for injury sustained by user of a highway through lack of repair or through negligent repair. These matters are examined below.[58]

Trunk roads

14-24   The second group consists of trunk roads, for which the Secretary of State for Transport is responsible, as highway authority. In practice, the work of maintenance, repair and improvement is generally carried out for him by local highway authorities, acting on an agency basis.

Highways privately repairable

14-25   In this group are those highways repairable other than by a highway authority. Liability may arise by prescription, *ratione tenurae or ratione clausurae*. The number of roads falling in these groups is small and the relevant law is therefore stated shortly. A prescriptive liability to repair might be imputed to persons or to an individual or a body which has as a matter of fact repaired the highway time out of mind. Liability to repair *ratione tenurae* (liability, that is, arising from tenure of particular lands) is an obligation which runs with the land, generally proved by evidence that

---

[55] [1965] A.C. 778.
[56] At p. 485.
[57] *Per* Lord Denning M.R. in the *Haley* case in the Court of Appeal [1964] 2 Q.B. 121 at p. 128.
[58] At § 14–31.

the occupier and his predecessors have for a lengthy period repaired the highway. It may arise, for example, where the Crown has granted a licence to the owner of certain lands to stop up a highway on condition that he made another, and that he and his heirs and assigns should keep the new road in repair.[59] Liability to repair *ratione clausurae* arises where the public have acquired a right to use open land adjoining a road to bypass the road when it becomes impassable or founderous, and where the owner encloses the open land, with the result that the public can no longer enjoy the right to deviate. The owner then becomes liable to keep the road in repair *ratione clausurae*.

Highways for the repair of which no one is responsible
This group consists mostly of roads which have come into existence **14–26** after 1835 and which have not been adopted by the highway authority as publicly repairable. In the case of these roads—known generally as private streets—there is no one on whom a duty to undertake *ordinary* repairs can be enforced. But the highway authority may require the owners of land fronting a private street to carry out urgent repairs, and the authority may execute the work in default, recovering the cost from the owners concerned.[60] The authority may itself execute works necessary to prevent or to remove the danger.[61] This power does not detract from the power of the authority to require the frontagers to execute repairs but it enables the authority to act in an emergency without prejudicing the question as to whether the road is publicly repairable or not. An authority may of course apply the private street works code to an unmade street.[62]

Footpaths and bridleways
Liability for repair of public paths was dealt with in section 47 of the **14–27** National Parks and Access to the Countryside Act 1949. Public paths in existence at the date of the commencement of that Act (December 16, 1949) were repairable by the inhabitants at large, and this was so even though other persons were liable for repair under statute, or by prescription, *ratione tenurae or ratione clausurae*. Such persons were not, however, relieved of their obligations, and could be required to meet the costs of repair incurred by the highway authority. Liability for paths coming into existence after December 16, 1949, fell to the highway authority only if dedicated to the public under a public path order or under a public path agreement; otherwise no one was under a duty to repair. Section 47 of the National Parks and Access to the Countryside Act 1949 was repealed by the Highways Act 1959, but the rules were continued by that Act and are now incorporated in the Highways Act 1980.[63]

---

[59] *Esher and Dittons Urban District Council* v. *Marks* (1902) 71 L.J.K.B. 309.
[60] Highways Act 1980, s. 230.
[61] *Ibid.* s. 230(7).
[62] See § 14–33, *et seq.*
[63] Highways Act 1980, ss. 36, 50 and 57.

A parish or community council has power to maintain bridleways and footpaths without detracting from the duty of the highway authority or any other person responsible for its maintenance.[64] An obligation is placed on highway authorities to signpost or mark footpaths and bridleways wherever they leave a metalled road.[65] A landowner is responsible for the repair of stiles but there is an obligation on the appropriate authority to contribute one quarter of the cost of expenses reasonably incurred in maintenance, and the authority may pay more if it wishes. If a landowner defaults in his duty the authority may, after notice, do the work itself, recovering the cost or part of the cost from the landowner.[66]

Bridges and level crossings

14-28   There has been much common law and statute law relating to bridges but it can be said in general that where a bridge across a river carries a road which is repairable at public expense, the responsibility for its repair rests with the authority which maintains the road. In non-metropolitan counties a bridge may be maintainable by a district council on an agency basis. Where a bridge crosses a highway authority boundary the two authorities may agree which one shall be the highway authority for the whole bridge, for the approaches and for the highway. In default of agreement, the Secretary of State for Transport may determine the issue. Where an approach to a bridge lies in a different highway authority area from the bridge, the highway authority for the approach is to be the same as the highway authority for the bridge.[67] The "approach" to a bridge is 100 yards from the end of the bridge.[68] Except in the case of trunk roads liability for repair may rest with persons other than the highway authority by prescription or *ratione tenurae*, and, as in the case of highways, there are bridges in respect of which no duty to repair exists.

The Level Crossings Act 1983 enables the Secretary of State for Transport to provide by order for the protection of persons using a level crossing.

Sections 93 and 94 of the Highways Act 1980 facilitate the reconstruction and improvement of privately maintainable bridges and make possible the transfer of such bridges to highway authorities. Wide powers are conferred on highway authorities to enter into agreements with owners of privately maintainable bridges with respect to their reconstruction, improvement and maintenance.

---

[64] Highways Act 1980, s. 43. See § 14–21 as to the powers of district councils.
[65] Countryside Act 1968, s. 27.
[66] Highways Act 1980, s. 146. The appropriate authority in the case of a footpath or bridleway maintained by a district council under s. 42 or s. 50 (see § 14–21), is the district council: in any other case it is the highway authority.
[67] *Ibid.* s. 3.
[68] *Ibid.* s. 3(4).

The responsibility of highway authorities and the Railways Board,   14-29
London Regional Transport and the Waterways Board with respect to
bridges carrying highways and with respect to such highways is set out in
sections 116 to 122 of the Transport Act 1968. Where a bridge belongs to
a board these provisions transfer from the board to the highway authority
responsibility for the maintenance of the highway running over it.
Responsibility for the bridge itself remains with the board. A duty is
placed on the particular board to ensure that any bridge has sufficient
load-bearing capacity to comply with any standards prescribed by the
Secretary of State, or where no standards have been prescribed, to bear
the weight of ordinary traffic using the bridge.

Standard of repair and enforcement procedure
Lindley J. said in *Burgess* v. *Northwich Local Board*[69]:   **14-30**

> "The duty of the highway surveyors is to repair and keep in repair; which
> means, I apprehend, to keep the road as dedicated to the public in such a state
> as to be safe and fit for ordinary traffic."

Lord Atkinson took the matter further in *Sharpness New Docks and
Gloucester and Birmingham Navigation Co.* v. *Att.-Gen.*[70] where he said:

> "It is the duty of road authorities to keep their public highways in a state fit to
> accommodate the ordinary traffic which passes or may be expected to pass
> along them. As the ordinary traffic expands or changes in character, so must the
> nature of the maintenance and repair of the highway alter to suit the change."

In the case of bridges the extent of the duty of repair will depend upon the
statutory provisions, if any, under which the bridge was built.[71] In any
case a duty of repair includes a duty to replace where the bridge is
destroyed or decayed.[72]

A person who alleges that a way or bridge is out of repair may serve a
notice on the highway authority or other person alleged to be liable for
maintenance requiring the way or bridge to be repaired.[73] If liability is in
issue (*i.e.* if the highway authority or other person alleged to be liable to
maintain the way disputes that liability or alternatively contends that the
way is not a highway) then the matter goes to the Crown Court. If liability
is admitted, the extent of repairs to be carried out may be settled, in case
of dispute, by the magistrates' court. Presumably an interested person can
still seek a declaration of the High Court as to the status of a highway or
as to liability to maintain it.

---

[69] (1880) 6 Q.B.D. 246 at p. 276.
[70] [1915] A.C. 654 at p. 665.
[71] *Ibid. British Oil and Coke Mills* v. *Company of Proprietors of Selby Bridge* [1976] J.P.L.
425.
[72] *R.* v. *Bucks (Inhabitants)* (1810) 12 East 192.
[73] Highways Act 1980, s. 56. A highway is "out of repair" when its surface is obstructed or
disturbed in some way: see *Hereford and Worcester County Council* v. *Newman* [1975] 1
W.L.R. 901.

A highway authority may repair a privately maintainable highway which is out of repair (if the way is a footpath or bridleway it may be *required* to undertake such repair) and in these circumstances the authority may recover the expense from the persons liable for maintenance.[74]

Failure to repair—civil liability

14-31 Until the coming into force of section 1 of the Highways (Miscellaneous Provisions) Act 1961 highway authorities were not, in general, liable to persons injured through a failure on their part to carry out the duty of repair and maintenance imposed upon them (this was called the doctrine of nonfeasance); though they were liable for the negligent or otherwise wrongful carrying out of their powers, that is to say, for misfeasance. The special defence of non-feasance was abrogated by section 1 of the Act of 1961 so that authorities became fully liable to those who suffer injury by failure to maintain and repair. Section 1 was replaced by section 58 of the Highways Act 1980. That section provides a defence to highway authorities: it is open to an authority to prove that it had taken such care as in all the circumstances was reasonably required to secure that the highway was not dangerous to traffic. For the purposes of this defence the court is required to have particular regard to a number of matters, including the character of the highway; the traffic which was reasonably expected to use it; the standard of maintenance appropriate for that highway; the state in which a reasonable person would have expected to find the highway; whether the authority knew, or could reasonably have been expected to know, that the condition of the highway was likely to cause danger to users; and, where the authority could not reasonably have been expected to carry out repairs before an accident occurred, whether warning notices had been displayed.

This provision, and the earlier common law standards, have been considered at length by the courts. In *Littler* v. *Liverpool Corporation*[75] Cumming-Bruce J. said:

"... what standard is a highway authority under a duty to maintain? ... where the cause of action of the plaintiff is that the plaintiff suffered personal injury by reason of the failure to maintain the highway, the plaintiff must make out a case that the highway was not reasonably safe, that is, was dangerous to the relevant traffic ... What, then, is the test of 'dangerous' in this context? ... The approach foreshadowed obiter in the speeches of the Court of Appeal in *Griffiths* v. *Liverpool Corporation*[76] has now become part of the law by the decision in *Meggs* v. *Liverpool Corporation*.[77] ... The test in relation to a length of pavement is reasonable foreseeability of danger. A length of pavement is only dangerous if, in the ordinary course of human affairs, danger may reasonably be anticipated from its continued use by the public who usually pass over it."

[74] Highways Act 1980, s. 57.
[75] [1968] 2 All E.R. 343 at p. 344.
[76] [1967] 1 Q.B. 374.
[77] [1968] 1 All E.R. 1137.

Repair and maintenance includes the provision of an adequate system of drainage,[78] but a transient danger due to the elements may not constitute a failure to maintain.[79] In *Rider* v. *Rider*[80] the Court of Appeal emphasised that whether a highway is a danger to traffic is a question of fact and degree, the type of user of that part of the highway being a relevant factor. Lawton J. said,

"In most cases proof that there were bumps or small holes in a road, or slight unevenness in flagstones on a pavement, will not amount to proof of a danger for traffic through failure to maintain. It does not follow, however, that such conditions can never be a danger for traffic. A stretch of uneven paving outside a factory probably would not be a danger for traffic but a similar stretch outside an old people's home, and much used by the inmates to the knowledge of the highway authority might be."

In *Griffiths* v. *Liverpool Corporation*[81] the Court of Appeal held that the duty of maintenance was strict, subject to the establishment by the authority of the statutory defences. In *Haydon* v. *Kent County Council*[82] the majority of the Court of Appeal[83] held that the onus was on the plaintiff to establish fault. The plaintiff had slipped on an icy path. Goff L.J. said[84]:

"In my judgment the plaintiff must prove either that the highway authority is at fault apart from merely failing to take steps to deal with the ice, or, which is the point in this case, that, having regard to the nature and importance of the way, sufficient time had elapsed to make it prima facie unreasonable for the authority to have failed to take remedial measures. Then the authority is liable unless it is able to make out the statutory defence."

The defence of contributory negligence continues to be available to highway authorities.

D. PRIVATE STREETS

A highway authority has statutory power to deal with the making up of **14-32** private streets under the private street works code[85] and the advance payments code.[86]

[78] *Burnside* v. *Emerson* [1968] 1 W.L.R. 1490.
[79] *Ibid. per* Lord Denning M.R. at p. 1494.
[80] [1973] Q.B. 505. See also *Burnside* v. *Emerson* [1968] 1 W.L.R. 1490; *Bird* v. *Pearce and Another, Somerset County Council* (1979) 77 L.G.R. 753; *Tarrant* v. *Rowlands* [1979] R.T.R. 144; *Bartlett* v. *Department of Transport* (1984) 83 L.G.R. 579.
[81] [1967] 1 Q.B. 374.
[82] [1978] Q.B. 343.
[83] Goff L.J. at p. 363 and Shaw L.J. at p. 365. Lord Denning M.R. agreed (at p. 357) with the view expressed in *Griffiths*. The statutory defences were not pleaded. In *Bartlett* v. *Department of Transport, supra,* Boreham J. expressed a preference for Lord Denning M.R.'s view, but held that he was bound by the view of the majority.
[84] At p. 363.
[85] Highways Act 1980, ss. 205 to 218. As to the meaning of the term "street" and "private street" see, *e.g. Jowett* v. *Idle Local Board* (1888) 36 W.R. 530; *Walthamstow Urban District Council* v. *Sandell* (1904) 68 J.P. 509; *Warwickshire County Council* v. *Adkins* (1967) 66 L.G.R. 486; *West End Lawn Tennis Club (Pinner)* v. *Harrow Corporation* (1965) 64 L.G.R. 35; *Att.-Gen. of Hong Kong* v. *Mightystream Ltd.* [1983] 1 W.L.R. 980.
[86] *Ibid.* ss. 219–225.

Private Street Works Code

14-33   An authority operating under this code may resolve to pave and sewer or light a private street, preparing plans and specifications of the works to be carried out, an estimate of the cost, and a provisional apportionment of these costs among the owners of the land fronting, adjoining and abutting on to the street. The resolution approving the plans, specifications and provisional apportionment must be published in a local newspaper in two successive weeks and posted in the street in each of three successive weeks, and a notice must be served on the owners within seven days of the first publication. In the month following first publication, the relevant documents are to be on deposit at the offices of the highway authority and, in the case of a street in a non-metropolitan district, at the offices of the district council.[87]

14-34   The authority may decide, in fixing the apportionment of expenses, to have regard to the greater or less degree of benefit which the premises derive from the works (charging some more and others less), but frontage must always be the overriding consideration.[88] The authority may have regard to the amount of any work already done in the street by owners or occupiers, and may bring into the apportionment premises which do not abut on to the street to be made up.[89] The authority is empowered to contribute the whole or part of the expenses of making up the private street.[90] An incumbent or minister or the trustees of a place of public religious worship (and burial ground if one adjoins) are freed from any payment—the amount involved is borne by the local authority.[91]

When the works have been completed the authority serves a notice of final apportionment of expenses on the owners affected.[92]

When the street has been made up as required, the authority may declare it to be maintainable at public expense, but if the majority of owners object the street must remain a private street unless the magistrates' court overrules the objection.[93]

Rights of appeal

14-35   An owner may object to a provisional apportionment and to a final apportionment on any of the grounds set out in the Act. He may object to a provisional apportionment for any of the following reasons but for no others[94]:

---

[87] Highways Act 1980, s. 205, as amended by the Local Government Act 1985, Sched. 4.
[88] *Parkstone Primrose Laundry Ltd.* v. *Poole Corporation* (1950) 48 L.G.R. 637, *per* Lord Goddard C.J. at p. 640.
[89] Highways Act 1980, s. 207.
[90] *Ibid.* s. 236.
[91] *Ibid.* s. 215.
[92] *Ibid.* s. 211.
[93] *Ibid.* s. 228.
[94] *Ibid.* s. 208: *Southampton Corporation* v. *Lord* (1903) 67 J.P. 189; *Brighton Borough Council* v. *Peachy Investments* [1957] J.P.L. 585.

(a) that the alleged street is not a street within the meaning of the Act;
(b) that there has been some material informality, defect, or error in respect of the resolution, notice, plans, sections or estimate[95];
(c) that the proposed works are insufficient or unreasonable;
(d) that the estimated expenses are excessive;
(e) that any premises ought to be excluded from or inserted in the provisional apportionment;
(f) that the provisional apportionment is incorrect in respect of some matter of fact, or in respect of the degree of benefit to be derived by any persons, or the amount or value of any work already done by the owner or occupier of any premises.

The meaning of the word "unreasonable" in the context of (c) was considered by the Court of Appeal in *Southgate Borough Council* v. *Park Estates (Southgate) Ltd.*[96] On the facts of this case it was held that the justices have power to determine that works, although reasonable in the future, are premature and therefore unreasonable if carried out at the time proposed. But the reasonableness must relate to the nature of the works and not to the burden placed on frontagers.[97] It would be appropriate under (f) to argue that land is *extra commercium* and not therefore chargeable.[98] An objection as to degree of benefit or as to the amount of work done can be raised only if the authority has taken these matters into account in fixing the apportionment.

An objection to a final apportionment may be made on one or more of **14-36** the following grounds[99]:

(a) that there has been an unreasonable departure from the specification, plans and sections;
(b) that the actual expenses have without sufficient reason exceeded the estimated expenses by more than 15 per cent.;
(c) that the final apportionment has not been made in accordance with the section.

The authority may apply to a court of summary jurisdiction to have objections against provisional or final apportionments heard and determined, and no objection which can be so raised in the magistrates' court may be raised elsewhere.[1]

An owner has a further right of appeal when he receives a demand for **14-37** payment. He may, within 21 days from the demand, lodge an appeal with the Secretary of State for the Environment and in this way he may raise objections which he could not have brought within the private street

---

[95] See hereon, *Ware Urban District Council* v. *Gaunt* [1960] 1 W.L.R. 1364.
[96] [1954] 1 Q.B. 359. See also *Bognor Regis Urban District Council* v. *Boldero* [1962] 2 Q.B. 448.
[97] *Allen* v. *Hornchurch Urban District Council* [1938] 2 K.B. 654, *per* Humphreys J. at p. 674.
[98] See *Herne Bay Urban District Council* v. *Payne and Wood* [1907] 2 K.B. 130.
[99] Highways Act 1980, s. 211.
[1] *Ibid.* ss. 209, 211 and 217.

works code—he may use this procedure, for example, where he claims that the authority should have invoked the "degree of benefit" provisions or should have made a contribution towards the cost of the works.[2] The Secretary of State for the Environment has the widest powers on appeal.

> *R.* v. *Minister of Housing and Local Government, ex p. Finchley Corporation.*[3] The council carried out private street works on a road adjoining vacant land belonging to the London Transport Executive. The Executive addressed a memorial to the Minister, who allowed the appeal. On a motion by the council for an order of certiorari to quash the decision it was held that the Minister on receiving the memorial had the widest powers and the largest discretion to decide what is equitable, and there is nothing to limit his powers. Devlin J. said[4]: "It may be an appealable decision because the local authority has acted outside its powers, or because it has not done something which it ought to have done under the Act, or because the decision is unfair or unjust. There is nothing, in my judgment, which limits the class of appealable decisions to one or the other or which excludes the Minister, once he has properly got seisin of the case, from reviewing any bad decision given in that case, no matter on what ground it was given."

Powers of recovery

14-38   If after demand, payment of private street works expenses is not made, an authority may proceed to recover the debt with interest in the magistrates' court (provided the action is begun within six months of the date of demand) or in the county court or the High Court.[5] If the sum involved exceeds £5,000 proceedings cannot be instituted in the county court.[6] Proceedings in the county court or High Court must be commenced within six years of the date of the first or any subsequent demand for payment, or within six years from the date of a part payment or acknowledgment of the debt by the debtor. The authority may declare the expenses to be payable by instalments.[7]

Private street works expenses become a charge on the premises. This means, generally speaking, that whoever is the owner of the premises is liable for whatever sums are outstanding.[8] The authority has the same powers as a mortgagee with a power of sale or lease under the Law of Property Act 1925, so that if the owner for the time being defaults in payment, the authority has a further remedy. It may sell or lease the land, taking from the proceeds what is due and paying the balance to the owner.

An owner cannot avoid liability by transferring land to a "man of straw." If an authority thinks that a transfer has been made for that

---

[2] Highways Act 1980, s. 233.
[3] [1955] 1 W.L.R. 29.
[4] At p. 35.
[5] Highways Act 1980, ss. 212 and 305.
[6] County Courts Act 1984, s. 16; County Courts Jurisdiction Order 1981 (S.I. 1981 No. 1123).
[7] Highways Act 1980, s. 212(4).
[8] *Ibid.* s. 212.

purpose it may in certain circumstances apply to the magistrates' court for an order requiring payment from the transferor.[9]

The advance payments code[10]

This code supplements the law as to the making up of private streets. **14-39** Two main principles are involved: before new buildings are erected in private streets a sum likely to be required to meet the cost of street works must be paid to the local authority, or security given for it; secondly, frontagers are able to call for street works to be carried out by the local authority and the street adopted when development has reached a certain stage. The authority is required to give notice of the amount due within six weeks after plans of the building have been passed under building regulations,[11] and interest is payable by the authority on sums deposited. An adjustment is made when the works are finished, the authority demanding more or making a refund as appropriate. If the street is made up by someone other than the local authority a refund is due to the person at whose expense the works were done, but the frontagers must be given an opportunity to make representations to the authority before the money is paid or the security released.

There are a number of exceptions to the general rule as to the need for deposit or security. The code does not apply, for example, where new buildings are erected within the curtilage of existing buildings, or where an owner has entered into an agreement under section 38 of the Highways Act 1980, under which new roads are constructed at his expense, or where the authority is satisfied that the development is isolated, or remote from made-up streets, or where development fills in gaps in a street already substantially built up, or where frontage property is substantially industrial.

If more than half of the total frontage of the street is built up and the provisions of the code have been applied to at least one building, the majority of the frontagers (either in number or in length of frontage) may call on the authority to exercise its powers to require the street to be made up, and in due course to adopt it.

The code applies in all outer London boroughs, in the areas of counties in which the code in the Highways Act 1959 was in force prior to 1 April 1974 and to any parish or community in which it is adopted by resolution of the county council.[12]

E. RIGHTS RELATED TO HIGHWAYS

This matter is considered in three parts: the rights of adjoining owners; **14-40** the rights of the public; the rights of highway authorities and statutory undertakers.

---

[9] Highways Act 1980, s. 235.
[10] *Ibid.* ss. 219–225.
[11] *Ibid.* s. 220. See § 16–23.
[12] *Ibid.* s. 204(2) and Sched. 15.

Rights of adjoining owners

When a highway is dedicated to the public the owners of the soil over which it passes do not divest themselves of ownership (subject, where the highway is maintainable at the public expense, to the rights of the highway authority in the "skin"),[13] and in the absence of evidence to the contrary it is to be assumed that the owners of the land on each side of the road own the soil to the middle of it.[14] It follows that an adjoining owner has a common law right to tunnel under the highway and to place beams over it. He has a right of access to it from any part of his premises, a right which he is required to exercise reasonably so as not to interfere with the reasonable exercise by the public of their rights of way.[15] But all these rights have been curtailed by statute. Under section 179 of the Highways Act 1980 an owner may not tunnel under a street except with the consent of the authority, and by section 178 the consent of the authority is required to place a beam, cable or other apparatus across a street. An owner's right of access is affected by the Town and Country Planning Act 1971—the formation and laying out of a means of access to a highway is development within the meaning of the Act—the consent of the planning authority is therefore needed before fresh access can be made.[16] An authority may ensure that, where an occupier of premises habitually crosses a footway with a vehicle, a carriage crossing is made at the occupier's expense.[17]

Rights of the public

14-41 These rights are limited to a liberty to pass and repass. A person using the highway for any other purpose may find that he has committed a trespass against the owner of the soil.

> *Harrison* v. *Duke of Rutland.*[18] The Duke owned certain moors intersected by highways. Harrison used the highway to frighten grouse so as to spoil the sport of the Duke's shooting party. He was asked to desist, refused to do so and was then held down on the ground by the Duke's keepers until the drive was over. He sued the Duke for assault. The Court of Appeal held that Harrison was a trespasser.

This rule must be construed reasonably. Lord Esher in the *Duke of Rutland* case said[19]:

> "I think it would be going too far to say that a person may pass along the highway, and that if he does anything more than so pass he is a trespasser. The public may pass and repass along highways, but certain things are done upon them which have come to be recognised as things done by the public in the

---

[13] See § 14–42, *infra.*
[14] *Beckett* v. *Leeds Corporation* (1872) 7 Ch. App. 421.
[15] Per Cozens-Hardy M.R. in *Tottenham Urban District Council* v. *Rowley* [1912] 2 Ch. 633 at p. 644.
[16] s. 22 and s. 290(1) in its definition of "engineering operations."
[17] Highways Act 1980, s. 184.
[18] [1893] 1 Q.B. 142; 62 L.J.Q.B. 117.
[19] 62 L.J.Q.B. at p. 120.

reasonable and usual mode of user of the highway, and if a person does no more than that, then he is not a trespasser."

The parking of a vehicle on the highway whilst a meal is taken is a reasonable user provided that no obstruction is caused.

Rodgers v. *Ministry of Transport.*[20] Lorry drivers made a practice of driving off the road on to the grass verge when calling at a restaurant for a meal. It was held (as part of a wider issue) that the verge was part of the highway and drivers were therefore entitled to leave their vehicles on it during a temporary stop for a legitimate purpose, *e.g.* for refreshment, provided that an obstruction was not caused.

Highway authorities have an obligation to "assert and protect the right of the public to the use and enjoyment of" highways.[21] Other councils have permissive powers in respect of all highways in their areas for which they are not the highway authority, and parish and community councils may make representations to the highway authority if the latter defaults.

Rights of highway authorities and statutory undertakers

In general, highways which are maintainable at public expense vest in the highway authority. The ownership of the authority is, however, limited to as much of the actual soil of the street as is necessary to preserve and maintain it to the top two spits, as Denning L.J. said in *Tithe Redemption Commission* v. *Runcorn Urban District Council.*[22] In *Tunbridge Wells Corporation* v. *Baird*, Lord Herschell said[23]: **14-42**

"It seems to me that the vesting of the street vests in the urban authority such property and such property only as is necessary for the control, protection and maintenance of the street as a highway for public use."

A local authority or a statutory undertaker has no inherent power to open a street for the laying of apparatus, and unless it can rely on a statutory authority it commits a nuisance. *Authority* for the breaking up of streets is generally found in the enactments which relate to the services provided—a power to break open streets, for example, is contained in the Third Schedule to the Water Act 1945. The *procedure* to be followed in all cases is that prescribed in the Public Utilities Street Works Act 1950. It applies wherever there is a statutory power to break open a street. There are two codes in the Act. The first is in Part I and is called the "street works code."[24] It prescribes a procedure to be followed when undertakers propose to lay down apparatus in a street or do any other works in **14-43**

---

[20] [1952] 1 All E.R. 634.
[21] Highways Act 1980, s. 130. See *R.* v. *Lancashire County Council, ex p. Guyer* (1977) 76 L.G.R. 290; [1980] 1 W.L.R. 1024, C.A.; *R.* v. *Surrey County Council, ex p. Send Parish Council* (1979) 40 P. & C.R. 390. As to common law powers and duties to prevent and remove obstructions, see *Bagshaw* v. *Buxton Local Board of Health* (1875) 1 Ch.D. 220 and *Reynolds* v. *Presteign Urban District Council* [1896] 1 Q.B. 604.
[22] [1954] Ch. 383 at p. 407.
[23] [1896] A.C. 434 at p. 442.
[24] ss. 1–20; Local Government Act 1972, Sched. 21, para. 98.

connection with the apparatus. The undertaker must give details of the proposed work to the highway authority or, if the street is not a publicly maintainable highway, to the street managers (the persons having the management or control of the street). If the authority or the managers reject the proposal or approve it with modification the undertaker may refer the matter to arbitration. Notice is not necessary in the case of emergency works. The code provides for the giving of notice when the works are to commence and for the supervision of reinstatement works by the authority or managers, and it enables the authority or street managers if they choose to do the works of reinstatement themselves.

14-44 The second code (in Part II of the Act[25]) is complementary to the street works code, and deals with the case where the highway authority proposes to carry out works which will disturb an undertaker's apparatus. The authority must give notice to the undertaker, and the undertaker may serve a counter-notice on the authority setting out the works which the undertaker must carry out to protect the services or supply. If a settlement cannot be reached by the parties the matter may be referred to arbitration. The cost of carrying out these protective works must be borne by the highway authority, except in two cases: first, where the works are undertaken to make good a subsidence for which no blame attaches to the authority; secondly, where the undertakers have placed or renewed apparatus in a road after they have had notice of the authority's works—this notice is effective if the works are commenced within two years after it is given. In two other circumstances a limitation is put to the costs which fall to the authority—where the undertakers use the opportunity to replace their apparatus by a better type or to renew apparatus placed in the road more than seven and a half years earlier.[26]

14-45 There is a relevant provision in the Highways Act 1980.[27] Subject to the exceptions mentioned below, statutory undertakers may not break up or open a carriageway during the 12 months following either (a) the end of any period during which a road has been closed to vehicular traffic, or the width reduced to less than two-thirds, for the carrying out of roadworks, or roadworks and other works, or (b) the completion of resurfacing extending to one-third or more of the width of the carriageway. This rule does not apply (a) where undertakers execute emergency works, or (b) where the highway authority consents. In cases where the undertakers consider that consent has been unreasonably withheld there is a procedure for the joint determination of any dispute by the Secretary of State for Transport and the minister in charge of the department concerned with the purposes for which the power to break open is conferred.

[25] ss. 21–25; Local Government Act 1972, Sched. 21, para. 98.
[26] s. 23.
[27] s. 156.

The powers contained in the Act of 1950 are exercisable not only in a highway proper but in what the Act calls "controlled land."[28] This is land which abuts on a maintainable highway or on a prospectively maintainable highway (one likely to become repairable at public expense), and which is destined for road purposes because the authority owns it or has authority to acquire it compulsorily or has reserved it by prescribing an improvement line under section 73 of the Highways Act 1980 (or under section 33 of the Public Health Act 1925, or section 72 of the Highways Act 1959, the antecedent provisions).

F. Diversion and Extinguishment

The Highways Act 1980[29] sets out a procedure to be followed for the **14-46** diversion or extinguishment of a highway. A magistrates' court may by order authorise a highway to be stopped up or diverted if it appears to the court that the highway is unnecessary or could be diverted to make it nearer or more commodious to the public. An application for an order may be made only by the highway authority. If the application concerns the stopping up or diversion of an unclassified road in a non-metropolitan county, the district council must be informed and its consent must be obtained. These rights apply equally to the councils of parishes and communities. A person may request the appropriate authority to initiate action and he may be required to meet the cost.

The rules with respect to the stopping up of footpaths and bridleways are somewhat different.[30] A highway authority, a district council, and a National Park joint planning board may make an order, called a public path extinguishment order, only if a path or way is not needed for public use. Such an order requires the confirmation of the Secretary of State for the Environment, who must satisfy himself that it is expedient to confirm the order having regard to the extent to which the path or way is used by the public and the effect of extinguishment on the lands served, and he must take into account the compensation provisions.

A highway authority, a district council and a joint planning board may **14-47** make a public path diversion order on the application of an owner, lessee or occupier of land, if satisfied that a diversion of a footpath or bridleway is in the interest of the owner or occupier or lessee of the land, or, alternatively, that the diversion is in the public interest.[31] An order is subject to the confirmation of the Secretary of State for the Environment

---

[28] Sched. 1.

[29] *Ibid.* ss. 116 and 117; Local Government Act 1985, Sched. 4.

[30] *Ibid.* s. 118; Public Paths Orders and Extinguishment of Public Right of Way Orders Regulations 1983 (S.I. 1983 No. 23)

[31] Highways Act 1980, ss. 118(7) and 119; Wildlife and Countryside Act 1981, s. 63 and Sched. 16; Public Path Orders and Extinguishment of Public Right of Way Orders Regulations 1983 (S.I. 1983 No. 23). Section 119 contemplates the diversion of a path to a *new* path, and not to an existing right of way—a road for example: *Lake District Special Planning Board, ex p. Bernstein, The Times* February 3, 1982.

and it creates a new way and extinguishes the old. Before deciding to make an order, the authority may require an applicant for an order to agree to defray or contribute towards any compensation payable, or to any expenses which the authority may incur in bringing the new path into a fit condition. Where an authority or board proposes to stop up or divert a footpath or bridleway there must be consultations with other authorities having like powers, or with the Countryside Commission in the case of a path or bridleway in a National Park.[32]

14-48 There are several other statutory provisions relating to closure and diversion of highways. A local authority may with the approval of the Secretary of State by order extinguish a public right of way over land purchased by the authority under Part IX of the Housing Act 1985 (which deals with clearance and development).[33] The Act provides that a public inquiry shall be held to deal with objections.

14-49 There is a generally expressed power in section 209 of the Town and Country Planning Act 1971 enabling the Secretary of State for the Environment by order to authorise the stopping up or diversion of any highway if he is satisfied that it is necessary to do so in order to enable development to be carried out in accordance with planning permission granted under Part III of that Act, or carried out by a government department. A similar power is conferred on planning authorities under section 210 in respect of the stopping up or diversion of footpaths or bridleways. Highways crossing or entering the route of a proposed new highway may be stopped up or diverted under section 211. Section 212 enables the Secretary of State for the Environment to make, on the application of a planning authority, an order extinguishing vehicular rights over a highway, thus converting a highway for vehicles into a public footpath or bridleway. The order may provide that vehicles of specified classes or in specified circumstances may nevertheless use it—this enables a highway to be converted into a pedestrian precinct, with provision for service vehicles at specified times. Local authorities generally may employ this section in respect of an area declared by them to be a general improvement area under housing legislation.[34] Section 214 provides for the extinguishment of public rights of way over land held for planning purposes.

The procedure to be followed where action is taken under sections 209, 211, 212 and 214 is set out in section 215 of the 1971 Act—publicity is given to the proposal and if objections are raised and not withdrawn a public inquiry is held.

Under section 32 of the Acquisition of Land Act 1981, footpath and bridleway rights may be extinguished by order made by an acquiring authority using, or which could use, compulsory powers. The authority

---

[32] Highways Act 1980, s. 120.
[33] Housing Act 1985, s. 294.
[34] See § 15–35.

must be satisfied that a suitable alternative right of way has been or will be provided, or that such provision is not required.

G. Nuisances and Obstructions

An interference with the highway, or the use of a highway, unless **14-50** authorised by law, may constitute (a) a criminal offence under a statutory provision (in the main the Highways Act 1980); (b) a criminal offence at common law, which can be dealt with by way of indictment; or (c) a common law nuisance, which may sustain a civil action for an injunction or damages or both.

Statutory offences

Many forms of interference and obstruction are made criminal offences under the Highways Act 1980—it is for example an offence under section 131 to cause damage to a highway or to plough up a footpath (section 134), or wilfully to obstruct the highway (section 137). *Mens rea* is not a necessary ingredient in the last-mentioned offence.

> *Arrowsmith* v. *Jenkins.*[35] A. held a public meeting on a highway, as a result of which those attending the meeting obstructed the highway. She was charged with wilful obstruction under section 121 of the Highways Act 1959. It was contended for the defendant, *inter alia*, that it was not sufficient to establish merely that the highway had been in part rendered less convenient or less commodious; it had to be shown that the obstruction was in fact intentional or the result of the defendant's conscious act. *Held*, that *mens rea* was not a constituent part of the offence, and that as A. had intentionally and by her free will done an act which caused an obstruction she was guilty of the offence charged.

The *de minimis* rule may apply in cases of this kind. Lord Parker of **14-51** Waddington C.J. said in *Seekings* v. *Clarke*[36]:

> "...Anything which substantially prevents the public from having free access over the whole of the highway which is not purely temporary in nature is an unlawful obstruction. There are, of course, exceptions to that. One possible exception would be on the principle of *de minimis*, which would no doubt cover the common case of the newsagent who hangs out a rack of newspapers, which though they project over the highway, project only fractionally."

User must be unreasonable for an offence to be committed.[37]

Criminal offence at common law

Procedure by way of indictment at common law is illustrated in the **14-52** case which follows.

---

[35] [1963] 2 Q.B. 561.
[36] (1961) 59 L.G.R. 268 at p. 269.
[37] *Nagy* v. *Weston* [1965] 1 W.L.R. 280; *Absalom* v. *Martin* [1974] R.T.R. 145; *Waltham Forest London Borough Council* v. *Mills* (1979) 78 L.G.R. 248. The *de minimis* principle was applied in *Putnam* v. *Colvin* [1984] R.T.R. 150, a case brought under s. 148(*c*) of the Highways Act 1980 which forbids the depositing of things on a highway.

R. v. *Clark* (*No.* 2).[38] The defendant was indicted on a charge that he had "unlawfully incited divers persons to commit a nuisance to the public by unlawfully obstructing the highway." It was held that, for the purposes of the offence of public nuisance by obstruction, the question is whether, in all the circumstances, there is or is not a reasonable user of the highway. The court applied *Lowdens* v. *Keaveney*[39] where it was held that there may be a considerable, even complete, obstruction (as in the case of a procession) and yet the use of the street might be quite reasonable.

It is seen that a different standard was applied in the *Clark* case from that in the *Arrowsmith* case.

Common law nuisance

14-53   An unlawful interference with the highway or with the use of a highway may give rise to a civil action for public nuisance. There are two forms of such actionable nuisance:

(i)   An obstruction of the highway, *i.e.* something which permanently or temporarily removes the whole or part of the highway from public use.[40]

(ii)   A danger to highway users, *i.e.* something which does not necessarily obstruct the highway physically but nonetheless renders the highway dangerous for public passage.[41]

A leading case is *Harper* v. *Haden & Sons Ltd.*[42] where the authorities were reviewed. The following propositions taken from that case appear to represent the law:

(a)   A permanent obstruction will necessarily be wrongful as it operates as a withdrawal of part of the highway from the public.

(b)   A temporary obstruction will not be actionable if it is reasonable in quantum and duration.

(c)   The fact that the highway authority has given its consent to such an obstruction affords no defence as such consent cannot legalise that which is otherwise illegal.

(d)   A private individual can only maintain an action in public nuisance if he can establish that he has suffered some particular, direct and substantial loss beyond that which is suffered by him in common with all other members of the public.[43]

Essentially, the law of nuisance depends upon the balancing of competing interests and an assessment as to whether one of those interests is unreasonably interfering with the other. In highway nuisance the issue is whether there is an unreasonable interference with the lawful rights of

---

[38] [1964] 2 Q.B. 315.
[39] [1903] 2 I.R. 82.
[40] See *Trevett* v. *Lee* [1955] 1 All E.R. 406.
[41] *Ibid.*
[42] [1933] 1 Ch. 298.
[43] For the position where an injunction is sought see below at § 14–54.

the public to pass and re-pass and to have access to the highway. Such interference may arise from the acts of adjoining landowners[44] or from other users of the highway.[45] It is a question of degree—whether the act or user complained of is unreasonable in its nature or by reason of its effects. The courts will have regard to the manner of creation of the interference, the status of its creator, the degree of fault, if any, attributable to its creation or continuance, and the physical or temporal extent of the interference.

The courts have had to consider whether it is necessary to prove fault or negligence on the part of the person causing the obstruction. The authorities are far from clear and it appears that the existence or absence of fault is just one of the factors to be assessed in determining whether the interference with the highway has been reasonable.[46]

To found an action for damages not only must there be loss suffered over and above that suffered by the public at large but the loss must be directly attributable to the nuisance itself.[47] In *Dymond* v. *Pearce*[48] a motor cyclist collided with a parked lorry at night. The lorry had been left for longer than was reasonable and without a justifiable reason and therefore constituted, prima facie, an obstruction. However, it was not proved that the nuisance was the cause of the accident: it was a result of the motor cyclist's own negligence.

In many cases an injunction may be a more appropriate remedy than **14-54** damages. An action for an injunction may be brought by the highway authority in its own name or by the Attorney-General on the relation of some other person. In these instances it is not necessary to prove special damage. In *Att.-Gen.* v. *Wilcox*,[49] the owner of land over which a towpath ran put up posts to prevent motor-cars, ice-cream barrows and the like from using it—their use had caused him annoyance and annoyance to pedestrians. A declaration was claimed by the Attorney-General in a relator action that the posts were an obstruction and a public nuisance, and an injunction was sought.

A complainant need not join with the Attorney-General if he suffers special injury, as compared with the public at large, or if a particular right of his has been infringed.[50]

Lyons, Son & Co. v. *Gulliver and Capital Syndicate Ltd.*[51] The access to the plaintiffs' premises was obstructed during important periods of the day because crowds assembled at the defendants' premises and there were queues at times

[44] See *Harper* v. *Haden & Sons (supra)*; *Hudson* v. *Bray* [1917] K.B. 520.
[45] *Dymond* v. *Pearce* [1972] 1 Q.B. 496. The Court of Appeal discussed the question of causation and the need for foreseeability in the different types of highway nuisance. See also *Wills* v. *T.F. Martin (Roof Contractors) Ltd.* [1972] R.T.R. 368.
[46] See *Hudson* v. *Bray (supra)*: *Maitland* v. *R.T. & J. Raisbeck & Hewitt Ltd.* [1944] K.B. 689: *Parish* v. *Judd* [1960] 3 All E.R. 33.
[47] *Wilkes* v. *Hungerford Market Co.* (1835) 2 Bing. (N.C.) 281.
[48] [1972] 1 Q.B. 496.
[49] [1938] Ch. 934 and see also *Att. Gen.* v. *Gastonia Coaches* [1977] R.T.R. 219.
[50] *Fineux* v. *Hovenden* (1599) Cro. Eliz. 664.
[51] [1914] 1 Ch. 631: and see also *Vanderpant* v. *Mayfair Hotel Company* [1930] 1 Ch. 138.

five deep. The plaintiffs complained that the collection of this crowd caused a
nuisance to them by the obstruction thereby occasioned to the free access to
and egress from their premises as a result of which they suffered damage by loss
of custom. It was held by the Court of Appeal (Cozens-Hardy M.R. and
Swinfen Eady L.J., Phillimore L.J. dissenting), that in the circumstances the
obstruction was an actionable nuisance and the defendants were liable to be
restrained by injunction, and that the failure of the police to prevent the
obstruction by regulating the crowd and keeping proper gaps for the passage of
the public through the queue did not afford a good defence. The Court
approved *Barber* v. *Penley*.[52] But Phillimore L.J. in his dissenting judgment
said[53]: "I believe that every trader has a right to make his shop window as
attractive as possible, and that he is not responsible for crowds assembling to
gaze at that shop window, and that it is for the police to regulate the traffic and
to make those persons, when they stand longer than they have any right to
stand on the highway, move on."

A highway authority has a common law right to remove an
obstruction,[54] and may obtain possession of the highway against
squatters.[55]

H. LIGHTING AND CLEANSING

14-55   The powers and duties in the matter of street lighting are statutory—the
common law imposes no duty. Highway authorities are empowered to
light the highways for which they are the highway authority.[56] But other
authorities, termed "lighting authorities"[57] have certain lighting powers.
They may maintain footway lighting (defined by reference to the height
and spacing of lamp standards), and may exercise other lighting powers
with the consent of the highway authority. A highway authority may
delegate its function of lighting to a lighting authority.[58]

14-56   A highway or street lighting authority acting under permissive powers
is not liable for accidents arising from a failure to light.

> *Sheppard* v. *Glossop Corporation*.[59] The council resolved that street lamps be
> extinguished at about 9 p.m. each night in the interests of economy. Because a
> lamp was unlit, the plaintiff strayed onto private land and then fell onto the
> highway from the private land over a retaining wall at a point where the level of
> the street was lower than the private land. The plaintiff sued the council for
> damages. *Held* that section 161 of the Public Health Act 1875 conferred on

---

[52] [1893] 2 Ch. 447.
[53] At p. 661.
[54] *Reynolds* v. *Urban District Council of Presteigne* [1896] 1 Q.B. 604.
[55] *Wiltshire County Council* v. *Frazer* (1984) 47 P. & C.R. 69. The procedure is by way of
Rules of the Supreme Court, Order 113.
[56] Highways Act 1980, s. 97.
[57] Lighting authorities are non-metropolitan district councils, parish councils, a parish
meeting where there is no parish council, and community councils: Public Health Act
1875, s. 161; Parish Councils Act 1957, s. 3 as amended by the Local Government Act
1972, Sched. 14, paras. 23 and 43; Highways Act 1980, s. 270. Their powers derive from
these provisions.
[58] Highways Act 1980, s. 98.
[59] [1921] 3 K.B. 132.

urban authorities a discretion, but imposed on them no obligation, to light the streets in their districts; consequently that the defendants, who had begun, were not bound to continue to light the street; and that having done nothing to make the street dangerous they were under no obligation, whether by lighting or otherwise, to give warning of danger. The defendants were not therefore liable.

If the authority places an obstruction in the highway, it is under an **14-57** obligation to give warning of it. There is no duty to provide lighting but to provide warning, whether by lighting or otherwise. Lord Greene M.R. said in *Fisher* v. *Ruislip-Northwood Urban District Council*[60]:

> "Lighting in such a case is no doubt the obvious and simplest measure of precaution during the hours of darkness. But the duty, if it exists, is, as I see it, not a duty to light (unless that be, in the circumstances, the only possible effective precaution) but a duty to take reasonable steps to prevent the obstruction becoming a danger to the public."

A highway authority is under a duty under section 22 of the Control of **14-58** Pollution Act 1974 to undertake the cleaning of highways for which it is the highway authority so far as the cleaning is necessary for the maintenance of the highways or the safety of traffic on them.

Litter authorities may provide bins for refuse in streets and public places, and may institute proceedings in a court of summary jurisdiction against persons who drop litter in any place in the open air to which the public are entitled or permitted to have access without payment.[61] A person guilty of an offence under this provision is liable to a fine not exceeding level 3 on the standard scale. The Refuse Disposal (Amenity) Act 1978[62] requires authorities to provide refuse dumps and empowers them to remove abandoned vehicles and other things.

I. TRANSPORTATION AND TRAFFIC MANAGEMENT

Municipal transport[62a]

Many authorities which operate transport systems do so under private **14-59** Acts. The general powers available to local authorities relate to light railways, tramways and omnibuses (there are no *general* powers to run trolley buses). An authority without powers and wanting now to create a transport undertaking would seek private Act powers.

An authority which operates a public service undertaking may grant travel concessions to qualified persons, a term which includes men over

---

[60] [1945] K.B. 584 at p. 593.
[61] Litter Act 1983, ss. 1 and 5. Litter authorities are the councils of counties, London boroughs, districts, parishes, communities, a National Park joint board and the Common Council of the City of London: *ibid.* s. 10.
[62] ss. 1, 3, 4 and 6.
[62a] The functions and powers of county and district councils in relation to passenger transport are to be substantially altered by ss. 63–71 of the Transport Act 1985 from a day to be appointed: *ibid.* s. 140(2).

65, women over 60, school children, the blind and disabled, and members of the authority travelling on "approved duties."[63]

(a) *Light railways*

The Secretary of State for the Environment may by order, on the application of a local authority, authorise the construction of a light railway, and where an order is made the authority may itself construct the railway or advance money to a light railway company.[64]

(b) *Tramways*

Local authorities may acquire a power to operate a tramway service (a) by means of an order of the Secretary of State made under section 3 of the Light Railways Act 1896, (b) by the promotion of a private Act which incorporates parts of the Tramways Act 1870, or (c) by way of provisional orders under the Tramways Act 1870.

(c) *Omnibuses*

An authority which operates a tramway, light railway, trolley vehicle or omnibus undertaking under any local Act or order is empowered, by the Road Traffic Act 1930,[65] to run public service vehicles, provided that consent is obtained from the Licensing Authority for Public Service Vehicles.

Passenger transport authorities and passenger transport co-ordination

14–60   The Transport Act 1968, in Part II,[66] enables the Secretary of State for the Environment to designate passenger transport areas to secure a properly integrated and efficient system of public transport, and to set up a passenger transport authority and passenger transport executive for each area. The former consists of members appointed by local authorities and members appointed by the Secretary of State for the Environment. The executive, the managing authority, is a body corporate with perpetual succession and a common seal. Its members are appointed by the passenger transport authority. Where an authority is in being in relation to an area, local authority passenger transport undertakings within the area are transferred to the executive and any deficiency in the running of the service is met from a precept made on authorities.

---

[63] Public Service Vehicles (Travel Concessions) Act 1955; Travel Concessions Act 1964; Transport Act 1968, s. 138; Local Government Act 1972, s. 186(5). These provisions are to be repealed from a date to be appointed by the Secretary of State, and replaced by ss. 93–105 of the Transport Act 1985; see *ibid.* ss. 139, 140(2); Sched. 6, para. 22, and Sched. 8.

[64] Light Railways Act 1896, s. 3.

[65] ss. 101–106, as amended by the Transport Act 1968, s. 31(1)(*b*).

[66] As modified by the Local Government Act 1972, s. 202, and Sched. 24, and the Transport Act 1983, ss. 1–10, and, from a date to be appointed by the Secretary of State, by the Transport Act 1985, Part IV, which makes substantial changes in the functions and duties of passenger transport authorities and executives and provides for the eventual transfer of bus undertakings of executives to companies owned by the authorities.

Under section 202 of the Local Government Act 1972, each metropoli-   **14-61**
tan county became a passenger transport area and the metropolitan
county council became the passenger transport authority. This came to an
end on March 31, 1986, as the Local Government Act 1985[67] created a
metropolitan county passenger transport authority in respect of each
metropolitan county. The authority is a body corporate and consists of
members of the constituent councils appointed by them to be members of
the authority.[68] The authority exercises the powers and duties of a
passenger transport authority under the Transport Act 1968 and
subsequent legislation.

London Regional Transport, a corporate body established by the
London Regional Transport Act 1984, is charged with the general duty,
in accordance with principles approved by the Secretary of State in
conjunction with the Railways Board, to provide or secure the provision
of public passenger transport services for Greater London.

Section 1 of the Transport Act 1978 imposes on the councils of non-   **14-62**
metropolitan counties the duty to promote the provision of a co-ordinated
and efficient system of passenger transport in their areas. District councils
with bus undertakings are required to operate them in accordance with
the policies developed by the county council, and if this involves them in
additional cost, there is provision for the county council to reimburse
them. All operators are required to co-operate with each other for the
purpose of co-ordinating the passenger transport services within the
county. County and district councils have a power to make grants
towards the cost incurred by any public transport operator. Section 2 of
the 1978 Act requires the council of each non-metropolitan county to
prepare a five-year county public transport plan in consultation with local
operators and district councils, and to revise it annually. County councils
may enter agreements with local operators.[69]

Traffic management

Principal responsibility for the discharge of traffic management   **14-63**
functions, including, for example, road safety and the making of traffic
regulation orders, falls to highway authorities.[70] There is a sharing of
functions with district and parish and community councils in the
provision, *inter alia,* of car parking.[71]

The Local Government Act 1985[72] has provisions intended to ensure a   **14-64**
properly co-ordinated system of traffic management in metropolitan
areas. The Secretary of State for the Environment, after consultation, is
empowered to designate roads in Greater London for the purpose of

[67] s. 28.
[68] *Ibid.* s. 29.
[69] s. 3.
[70] Local Government Act 1972, s. 186, and Sched. 19; Local Government Act 1985, s. 8.
[71] Road Traffic Regulation Act 1984, ss. 34 and 57.
[72] Sched. 5, para. 5.

facilitating the movement of traffic. The designated roads would form part of a strategic network of major roads for distributing traffic within London and for linking it with the national network of trunk roads and motorways. A London borough council may not exercise certain traffic functions in designated roads unless it has first given notice of its intention to the Secretary of State. The Secretary of State has powers to object or withhold consent.

London borough councils and metropolitan district councils are required to have regard to any guidance issued by the Secretary of State and to consult other local authorities whose areas would be directly affected by their traffic management proposals. The Secretary of State has reserve powers.[73]

J. GRANTS AND REIMBURSEMENTS

14-65   All expenditure on the maintenance of trunk roads is reimbursable (the Secretary of State for Transport being the highway authority) and grants are available towards the cost of the cleansing of trunk roads.

The Secretary of State is empowered, with the approval of the Treasury, to make advances to highway authorities for specified highway purposes, *inter alia*, for the construction of a highway which is to be a highway maintainable at the public expense, for the maintenance or improvement of a highway and for the acquisition of highway land.[74]

It is open to a non-metropolitan county council to contribute towards the expenses of the district council exercising the powers conferred on them by section 96 of the Highways Act 1980,[75] a provision under which, with the consent of the highway authority, a district council may plant trees and shrubs and lay out grass verges in highways maintainable at public expense. The Secretary of State for Transport may make grants to district councils for this purpose.[76]

A non-metropolitan district council may contribute towards any expenses incurred by a highway authority if, in the opinion of that council, the expenditure is, or will be, of benefit to the council's area.[77]

Section 7(1) of the Local Employment Act 1972 enables the Secretary of State to make grants towards the cost of improving roads in development and intermediate areas with a view to contributing to the development of industry in those areas.

Grants are payable to county councils and metropolitan district councils in respect of expenditure on transport purposes, defined as

---

[73] Local Government Act 1985, Sched. 5, para. 6.
[74] Highways Act 1980, s. 272. As to the limitation of this power, see *ibid.* subs. (4).
[75] *Ibid.* s. 273.
[76] *Ibid.* s. 272(5).
[77] *Ibid.* s. 274.

expenditure connected with public transport, highways, traffic regulation, and the provision of parking places. The aggregate amount of grant and the method by which it is apportioned is prescribed by regulation made by the Secretary of State for the Environment.[78]

[78] Local Government Act 1974, s. 6, as amended by the Local Government Act 1985, Sched. 17.

CHAPTER 15

HOUSING

15-01 Housing law is considered under the following headings: administering authorities; the provision and allocation of council housing; the council as landlord; assistance with house purchase; responsibilities concerning the private rented sector; responsibilities concerning housing associations; housing benefit; housing subsidy and accounting; general responsibilities concerning housing conditions.

A. ADMINISTERING AUTHORITIES

15-02 For the purposes of most of the discussion in this Chapter, the relevant housing authorities are the district councils, the Common Council of the City of London, and the London borough councils.[1] County councils have limited reserve powers relating to housing. A county council, acting either on its own initiative or following a request from one or more district councils, may, with ministerial consent, provide accommodation on behalf of a district council or councils.[2] Tenants of county councils are now generally "secure" (just like tenants of district or London borough councils), regardless of the powers under which the accommodation is provided, *i.e.* whether or not these "reserve" powers are operated.[3]

Social services authorities (*i.e.* non-metropolitan county councils, metropolitan district councils, London borough councils and the Common Council of the City of London[4]) have specific responsibilities to provide "residential accommodation for persons who by reason of age, infirmity or any other circumstance are in need of care and attention which is not otherwise available to them."[5]

The ministers most involved with the administration of housing legislation are the Secretary of State for the Environment and the Minister for Housing and Construction.

B. THE PROVISION AND ALLOCATION OF COUNCIL HOUSING

15-03 Housing authorities have a general duty to consider housing conditions and the need for the provision of further housing, including the special

[1] Housing Act 1985, ss. 1, 4.
[2] *Ibid.* s. 28; see also *ibid.* s. 29 (provision by county council of accommodation for its employees).
[3] *Ibid.* s. 80(1); "secure" tenancies are discussed below.
[4] Local Authority Social Services Act 1970, ss. 2(1), 3 and Sched. 1.
[5] National Assistance Act 1948, s. 21(1)(*a*); Local Government Act 1972, Sched. 23, paras. 2, 8; D.H.S.S. Circular 13/74, para. 4. See also § 18–10.

needs of the chronically sick and disabled.[6] They can provide accommodation by way of erection, conversion, acquisition, alteration, enlargement, repair, or improvement[7]; they also have ancillary powers concerning the provision (with ministerial consent) of shops, recreation grounds and other amenities, and the provision (without the need for ministerial consent) of furniture, board and laundry facilities.[8]

Allocation of accommodation

With regard to the allocation of their housing, authorities have a very broad discretion.[9] However, in selecting their tenants they must give a "reasonable preference" to persons who occupy insanitary or overcrowded houses, have large families or are living under unsatisfactory housing conditions[10]; and they must not discriminate, in operating their allocation policies, on grounds of race or sex.[11]

Every authority must publish a summary of its rules relating to allocations, transfers and exchanges, and must have a complete set of the rules readily available; a copy of the summary must be supplied on request free of charge, and a copy of each set of rules must be supplied on request upon payment of a reasonable sum.[12] In addition, an applicant for housing can require the authority to furnish him free of charge with details of the particulars which he has given to the authority and which it has recorded as relevant to his application.[13]

Rehousing

Specific rehousing duties are imposed on authorities with regard to persons displaced by various types of public action, where suitable alternative residential accommodation on reasonable terms is not otherwise available to them[14]; and authorities must use their best endeavours to provide suitable alternative accommodation for certain agricultural employees whose employers require their houses for other employees.[15]

---

[6] Housing Act 1985, ss. 8, 605; Chronically Sick and Disabled Persons Act 1970, s. 3(1); see also Housing Act 1985, ss. 289(4) (clearance areas), 334 (overcrowding).

[7] Housing Act 1985, ss. 9, 17.

[8] *Ibid.* ss. 10–12.

[9] *Ibid.* s. 21(1).

[10] *Ibid.* s. 22.

[11] Race Relations Act 1976, ss. 1, 3, 21(1), 71; Sex Discrimination Act 1975, ss. 1, 2, 30(1).

[12] Housing Act 1985, s. 106(1)–(2), (4).

[13] *Ibid.* s. 106(5).

[14] Land Compensation Act 1973, s. 39, discussed above at § 5–41; the public action covered includes acquisition by an authority possessing compulsory purchase powers, certain action under the unfitness provisions of the Housing Act 1985, and the service of an improvement notice under Pt. VII of the Housing Act 1985 (discussed below in relation to housing conditions).

[15] Rent (Agriculture) Act 1976, s. 28(7) (discussed below in relation to the authority's responsibilities concerning the private rented sector).

Homelessness

Authorities are subject to important rehousing duties under the Housing Act 1985 concerning certain homeless people. Where a duty to rehouse a homeless person is owed, then the authority's obligation is to secure that accommodation becomes available (for example in the private sector), and not necessarily to allocate a *council* house[16]; however, in the operation of its allocation scheme the authority must give a "reasonable preference" to all people who are homeless.[17] In applying the homelessness provisions, authorities must "have regard" to (but need not necessarily follow) ministerial guidance, currently in the form of a *Code of Guidance.*[18]

Issues involved concerning provision for the homeless

15-04   The key issues governing the extent of an authority's duties towards the homeless are those of "homelessness or threatened homelessness," "priority need," and "intentional homelessness."

Homelessness or threatened homelessness

If the authority has reason to believe that the applicant may be "homeless or threatened with homelessness," then it *must* make "appropriate inquiries" in order to satisfy itself on these key issues, and it *may* make inquiries regarding "local connections" with another authority's area.[19] In making these inquiries, the authority must act fairly, though the technical rules of evidence do not necessarily apply, and the courts do not demand "CID-type" investigations.[20] There is a preliminary duty to accommodate the applicant (and his family unit) pending further inquiries, where the authority has reason to believe that he may be "homeless" and in "priority need."[21] Criminal offences may be committed in connection with the application where the authority has been misled or relevant information has been withheld from it.[22]

"Homelessness" arises where there is no accommodation which the applicant (and his family unit) is entitled to occupy by virtue of an interest in it or of a court order, or which he has an express or implied licence to occupy, or which he is occupying under any enactment or rule of law giving him the right to remain in occupation or restricting the right

---

[16] Housing Act 1985, s. 69(1).

[17] *Ibid.* s. 22.

[18] *Ibid.* s. 71; *Housing (Homeless Persons) Act 1977 Code of Guidance (England and Wales)* DoE, 2nd ed., 1983; *De Falco* v. *Crawley Borough Council* [1980] Q.B. 460; *R.* v. *Police Complaints Board, ex p. Madden* [1983] 1 W.L.R. 447.

[19] *Ibid.* s. 62(1)–(2).

[20] See, *e.g. R.* v. *Wyre Borough Council, ex p. Joyce* (1983) 11 H.L.R. 73; *R.* v. *Southampton City Council, ex p. Ward* (1984) 14 H.L.R. 114; *Lally* v. *Kensington and Chelsea Borough Council, The Times*, March 27, 1980.

[21] Housing Act 1985, ss. 63, 75.

[22] *Ibid.* s. 74.

of any other person to recover possession.[23] Even if there is a legal right to occupy accommodation, it may be of such a temporary or "crisis" nature, or in such a poor or overcrowded state, that the applicant is "homeless" even while living in it.[24] Further, even if there is a legal right to occupy appropriate accommodation, the applicant may be *deemed* to be homeless if he cannot secure entry to it or occupation of it would probably lead to violence or threats of violence from some other person residing in it,[25] or if the relevant accommodation is outside Great Britain.[26] "Threatened homelessness" arises where it is "likely that [the applicant] will become homeless within 28 days"[27]; where a landlord is actively seeking possession from a tenant, the tenant is threatened with homelessness if it is clear that there is no defence to the landlord's claim, and the authority should not insist on a possession order.[28]

Priority need

"Priority need" arises[29] where there are dependent children who are residing with or might reasonably be expected to reside with the applicant, where there is an emergency such as flood, fire or any other disaster,[30] where there is vulnerability as a result of old age, mental illness or handicap or physical disability or other special reason,[31] or where there is pregnancy. The question of priority need is to be decided on the facts current when the council makes its decision.[32]

Intentional homelessness

"Intentional homelessness" arises where the applicant[33] "deliberately   **15-05** does or fails to do anything in consequence of which he ceases to occupy accommodation which is available for his occupation and which it would have been reasonable for him to continue to occupy" (and a similar definition applies in relation to intentionally *threatened* homelessness).[34] Each element of this definition must be satisfied if an intentionality

---

[23] *Ibid.* s. 58(2).
[24] See, *e.g. R.* v. *Ealing London Borough Council, ex p. Sidhu* (1982) 80 L.G.R. 534; but the standard is a low one: see *R.* v. *Hillingdon London Borough Council, ex p. Puhlhofer, The Times,* August 17, 1985.
[25] Housing Act 1985, s. 58(3).
[26] *Ibid.* s. 58(1).
[27] *Ibid.* s. 58(4).
[28] *Code of Guidance, op.cit.,* at § A 1.3; *Dyson* v. *Kerrier District Council* [1980] 1 W.L.R. 1205.
[29] Housing Act 1985, s. 59.
[30] A demolition order is not "disastrous" enough to come within the "emergency" head: *Noble* v. *South Herefordshire District Council* (1984) 17 H.L.R. 80.
[31] See, *e.g. R.* v. *Waveney District Council, ex p. Bowers* [1983] Q.B. 238; *R.* v. *Bath City Council, ex p. Sangermano* (1984) 17 H.L.R. 94.
[32] *R.* v. *Hillingdon Homeless Families Panel, ex p. Islam, The Times,* February 10, 1981.
[33] Not including a member of his family unit, unless there is reasonable evidence of acquiesence by the applicant in the member's acts or omissions: *R.* v. *Swansea City Council, ex p. Thomas, The Times,* April 14, 1983.
[34] Housing Act 1985, s. 60(1), (2).

finding is to be supported. For the act or omission to be "deliberate," it is not necessary for the applicant actually to have intended thereby to lose his accommodation, but there must have been an element of wilfulness[35]; and an act or omission "in good faith" on the part of an applicant who was unaware of any relevant fact is not to be treated as deliberate.[36] The words "in consequence" mean that although there must be a continuing causal connection between the relevant act or omission causing homelessness and the actual homelessness existing at the date of the inquiry, it is necessary to have primary regard to the position when the homelessness was caused rather than the position at the date of the inquiry[37]; however, an initially-forged "chain of intentionality" can be broken by subsequent events, such as the obtaining by the applicant of a settled residence.[38] The applicant must cease to occupy accommodation available for occupation by his family unit: thus the mere refusal of an authority's offer of accommodation cannot be a relevant "cessation" giving rise to intentionality,[39] nor can the leaving of accommodation in which it is not possible for the family unit satisfactorily to live together.[40] As regards the final limb of the definition of intentionality, in deciding whether it would have been reasonable for the applicant to have continued to occupy the vacated accommodation it would be relevant to consider (where appropriate) matters such as overcrowding, emotional stress, domestic violence, employment prospects, and whether there is a likely defence to a landlord's claim for possession[41]; in deciding this "reasonableness" issue the authority can have regard to the general housing circumstances of its area, although the courts have not welcomed arguments that poor housing conditions in an area should require applicants to remain in grossly overcrowded accommodation.[42] If an authority is in any doubt on the intentionality question, the applicant is entitled to the benefit of that doubt, and he should not be found intentionally homeless.[43]

---

[35] *R. v. Salford City Council, ex p. Devenport* (1983) 127 S.J. 306; *R. v. Wyre Borough Council, ex p. Joyce* (1983) 11 H.L.R. 73; *Code of Guidance, op.cit.*, at § 2.15.

[36] Housing Act 1985, s. 60(3); *R. v. Wandsworth London Borough Council, ex p. Rose* (1983) 11 H.L.R. 107.

[37] *Din v. Wandsworth London Borough Council* [1981] 1 A.C. 657; *R. v. Gloucester City Council, ex p. Miles* (1985) 17 H.L.R. 292.

[38] See, *e.g. Krishnan v. Hillingdon London Borough Council* [1981] L.A.G.Bul. 137; *R. v. Basingstoke and Deane District Council, ex p. Bassett* (1983) 10 H.L.R. 125.

[39] *R. v. Westminster City Council, ex p. Chambers* (1983) 81 L.G.R. 401.

[40] Housing Act 1985, s. 75; *Islam v. Hillingdon London Borough Council* [1981] 3 All E.R. 901; *R. v. Westminster City Council, ex p. Ali* (1983) 11 H.L.R. 83.

[41] *R. v. Eastleigh Borough Council, ex p. Beattie (No. 2)* (1984) 17 H.L.R. 168; *R. v. Wandsworth London Borough Council, ex p. Nimako-Boateng* (1983) 11 H.L.R. 95; *Charles v. Charles* [1984] Legal Action 81; *R. v. Hammersmith London Borough Council, ex p. Duro-Rama* (1983) 81 L.G.R. 702; *R. v. Surrey Heath Borough Council, ex p. Li* (1984) 16 H.L.R. 79; *Code of Guidance, op.cit.*, at §§ 2.16, A 1.3.

[42] Housing Act 1985, s. 60(4); *R. v. Westminster City Council, ex p. Ali, supra.*

[43] Housing Act 1985, ss. 65(2), (3), 66(2), (3); *R. v. Thurrock Borough Council, ex p. Williams* (1981) 1 H.L.R. 128; *R. v. West Dorset District Council, ex p. Phillips* (1984) 17 H.L.R. 336.

Duties of the council on completion of enquiries concerning homelessness

On completion of its inquiries, if the authority is satisfied that the   **15-06**
applicant is homeless or threatened with homelessness, it will be subject
to the following duties[44]:

(a) if it decides that the applicant does not have a priority need or has
become homeless or threatened with homelessness intentionally, it
must furnish advice and appropriate assistance;

(b) if it decides that the applicant is homeless, in priority need, but
intentionally homeless, it must (in addition to giving advice and
assistance) secure that accommodation becomes available for such
period as gives him a reasonable opportunity of himself securing
accommodation;

(c) if it decides that the applicant is threatened with homelessness, in
priority need, and not intentionally threatened with homelessness,
then it must take reasonable steps to secure that accommodation
does not cease to be available; and

(d) if it decides that he is homeless, in priority need, and not
intentionally homeless, then it must normally secure that accommodation becomes available on a permanent basis.

The decision must be notified to the applicant in writing, and contain
reasons if the authority considers that anything less than the permanent
accommodation duty is owed.[45]

As noted earlier, the accommodation offered does not necessarily have
to be council-owned[46]; but the accommodation must be available for the
relevant family unit,[47] of an adequate standard,[48] and situated in an
appropriate location.[49]

Transfer of duty towards the homeless

Exceptionally, where the full accommodation duty is owed (*i.e.* the   **15-07**
applicant is unintentionally homeless and in priority need), then
responsibility for rehousing may be transferred to another authority
under the "local connection" provisions, provided neither the applicant
nor any member of his family unit has a local connection with the area of
the authority to which he applied, either he or a member of his family
unit has a local connection with the area of another housing authority,
and there is no risk to him or his family unit of domestic violence in that
other authority's area.[50] While the transfer procedure is being carried out,

---

[44] Housing Act 1985, ss. 65–66.
[45] *Ibid.* s. 64.
[46] *Ibid.* s. 69(1).
[47] *Ibid.* s. 75.
[48] *R. v. Ryedale District Council, ex p. Smith* (1983) 16 H.L.R. 66; *R. v. Exeter City Council,
ex p. Gliddon* [1985] 1 All E.R. 493.
[49] *R. v. Wyre Borough Council, ex p. Parr* (1982) 2 H.L.R. 7.
[50] Housing Act 1985, ss. 61, 67–68.

the transferring authority remains under a duty to secure accommodation.[51] "Local connections" are based on residence, employment, family associations, or special circumstances.[52] The sparse statutory provisions on "local connection" transfers are filled out by a non-ministerial agreement entered into between the local authority associations in 1979.[53] If the authorities involved cannot agree on responsibility, then a referee will decide the local connection issue.[54]

Challenges to homelessness decisions

Challenges to an authority's decision on the key issues of homelessness, priority need and intentionality involve public law questions and must normally be heard by way of judicial review under Order 53 of the Rules of the Supreme Court, but "executive" issues like the location or quality of the accommodation offered involve private law questions and can proceed by way of ordinary action.[55]

C. THE COUNCIL AS LANDLORD

Rent-fixing

15-08   The "general management, regulation and control" of council housing is vested in each housing authority, which may, in particular, make such "reasonable charges" for its accommodation as it may determine.[56] There are very few legal restraints on council rent-fixing. Although there is a duty on the authority to review its rents "from time to time,"[57] council rents are outside the Rent Act 1977,[58] and are also outside the consultation and information duties concerning "secure" tenancies.[59] Moreover, the courts have proved most unwilling to interfere with an authority's discretion in this area.[60]

Secure tenancies

Outside the area of rent-fixing, the discretion of council landlords has been severely curtailed by the introduction in 1980 of statutory

---

[51] *Ibid.* s. 68(1).

[52] *Ibid.* s. 61.

[53] *Agreement on Procedures for Referrals of the Homeless—Revised,* June 6, 1979; *R.* v. *Eastleigh Borough Council, ex p. Betts* [1983] 2 A.C. 613; see also *Code of Guidance, op.cit.,* at §§ 2.20–2.22, 5.1–5.6.

[54] Housing Act 1985, s. 67(4)–(6); Housing (Homeless Persons) (Appropriate Arrangements) Order 1978 (S.I. 1978 No. 69); Housing (Homeless Persons) (Appropriate Arrangements) (No. 2) Order 1978 (S.I. 1978 No. 661).

[55] *Cocks* v. *Thanet District Council* [1983] A.C. 286; *Wandsworth London Borough Council* v. *Winder* [1985] A.C. 461.

[56] Housing Act 1985, ss. 21(1), 24(1).

[57] *Ibid.* s. 24(2).

[58] Rent Act 1977, ss. 14, 19(5)(a).

[59] Housing Act 1985, ss. 103(3), 105(2); see below, § 15–11.

[60] See, *e.g. Summerfield* v. *Hampstead Borough Council* [1957] 1 W.L.R. 167; *Evans* v. *Collins* [1965] 1 Q.B. 580; but *cf. Backhouse* v. *Lambeth Borough Council* (1972) 116 S.J. 802.

"charter rights" for "secure" tenants. A "secure" tenancy is one under which the property is let "as a separate dwelling,"[61] the landlord is a prescribed public landlord,[62] and the tenant is an individual who occupies the property as his "only or principal home."[63] Where there are joint tenants, in order for the tenancy to be secure each must be an individual and at least one must satisfy this occupation requirement.[64] Licences which are not granted temporarily to former trespassers can be treated as secure tenancies.[65] Even where these requirements are satisfied, the tenancy will not be "secure" if it falls within one of the exceptions listed in Schedule 1 to the 1985 Act: these include certain tenancies related to public employment,[66] tenancies of land acquired for development and used for temporary housing purposes,[67] and certain tenancies granted in pursuance of the temporary housing duties owed to homeless persons.[68]

Termination of secure tenancies

Where the tenancy is secure, it can nevertheless be terminated by the   **15-09** tenant by one of the traditional common law methods, such as surrender[69] or (where the tenancy is periodic) notice to quit.[70] However, the authority itself cannot end a periodic secure tenancy by serving notice to quit. Instead, it must serve the appropriate notice of intended proceedings[71] and then obtain a court order for possession on a prescribed ground,[72] whereupon the tenancy will only end on the date when the tenant is due to give up possession in pursuance of the order[73]; and if the tenancy is for a fixed term, the secure tenancy cannot be ended either by effluxion of time or forfeiture, but only by the court following the establishing by the

---

[61] Housing Act 1985, s. 79(1); thus the sharing of living accommodation (*e.g.* a kitchen or sitting-room) with people who are not members of the tenant's household will mean there is no secure tenancy, but the sharing of non-living accommodation (*e.g.* a bathroom or toilet) will not affect the existence of a secure tenancy.

[62] *Ibid.* s. 80 (the list includes district, county, and London borough councils).

[63] *Ibid.* s. 81; see *e.g. Peabody Donation Fund Governors* v. *Grant* (1982) 264 E.G. 925.

[64] *Ibid.* s. 81.

[65] *Ibid.* s. 79(3), (4); but *cf. Street* v. *Mountford* [1985] A.C. 809.

[66] *Ibid.* Sched. 1, para. 2.

[67] *Ibid.* Sched. 1, para. 3.

[68] *Ibid.* Sched. 1, para. 4; security will here normally attach after twelve months have run since the notification under s. 64 of the 1985 Act; see further *Family Housing Association* v. *Miah* [1982] L.A.G.Bul. 112; *Restormel Borough Council* v. *Buscombe* (1982) 14 H.L.R. 89; and *Eastleigh Borough Council* v. *Walsh* [1985] 1 W.L.R. 525.

[69] But *cf. Preston Borough Council* v. *Fairclough, The Times,* December 15, 1982; in the case of a joint tenancy, all the joint tenants must concur in the surrender: *Leek and Moorlands Building Society* v. *Clark* [1952] 2 Q.B. 788.

[70] One joint tenant can serve notice to quit on the authority and thereby terminate a periodic secure tenancy, even though the other joint tenants do not concur: *Greenwich London Borough Council* v. *McGrady* (1983) 46 P. & C.R. 223.

[71] Housing Act 1985, s. 83(1), (2); Secure Tenancies (Notices) Regulations 1980 (S.I. 1980 No. 1339); Secure Tenancies (Notices) (Amendment) Regulations 1984 (S.I. 1984 No. 1224).

[72] Housing Act 1985, ss. 82, 84 and Sched. 2, below.

[73] *Ibid.* s. 82(1), (2).

authority of a prescribed ground for possession.[74] The grounds for possession fall into three separate classes:

(i)   grounds on which the court can only make a possession order if it considers it reasonable to do so[75] (these grounds, most of which relate to the tenant's misconduct,[76] do not involve the need for the authority to establish the availability of suitable alternative accommodation, though it may be subject to its normal duties concerning the homeless[77]);

(ii)   grounds on which the court must make a possession order if it is satisfied as to "suitable accommodation"[78] ("suitable accommodation" is defined[79] by reference to accommodation which is itself subject to a secure tenancy, or a prescribed tenancy within the Rent Act 1977, and consideration has to be given to (*inter alia*) the relevant needs[80] and means of the tenant and his family); and

(iii) grounds on which the court can only make a possession order if it considers it reasonable to do so and it is satisfied as to suitable accommodation[81] (these grounds cover, in essence, accommodation currently occupied by persons who do not fall within the purpose for which it was originally provided).

Where possession is sought on a ground within categories (i) or (iii) above, the court has wide powers of adjournment, postponement and suspension[82]; but as regards the grounds in category (ii) above (*i.e.* the mandatory grounds), where the court makes the order it cannot postpone the giving up of possession for more than 14 days (or, in cases of exceptional hardship, six weeks).[83]

Disposals by secure tenant

15-10   Loss of a secure tenancy can also occur due to certain *inter vivos* disposals by the secure tenant. With regard to assignments, if the secure tenancy was for a fixed term and made before November 5, 1982, then the general rule is that following assignment the *secure* tenancy (and therefore the "package" of charter rights) will cease, although the *common law* tenancy will continue in the assignee on a purely contractual basis.[84] If the secure tenancy was periodic (whenever granted), or for a

---

[74] *Ibid.* ss. 82(1)–(3), 83 (2), (5), 86.

[75] *Ibid.* s. 84(2) and Sched. 2, Pt. I, gds. 1–8.

[76] As to whether it is "reasonable" to evict a tenant with rent arrears (within gd. 1), see *Woodspring District Council* v. *Taylor* (1982) 4 H.L.R. 95.

[77] Discussed above at § 15–06.

[78] Housing Act 1985, s. 84(2) and Sched. 2, Pt. II, gds. 9–11.

[79] *Ibid.* Sched. 2, Pt. IV.

[80] See *London Borough of Islington* v. *Metcalfe and Peacock* [1983] L.A.G.Bul. 105; *Enfield London Borough Council* v. *French* (1985) 49 P. & C.R. 223.

[81] Housing Act 1985, s. 84(2) and Sched. 2, Pt. III, gds. 12–16.

[82] *Ibid.* s. 85.

[83] Housing Act 1980, s. 89.

[84] Housing Act 1985, s. 91(1), (2).

fixed term and made on or after November 5, 1982, then the general rule is that the tenancy *cannot be assigned at all*, even as a common law contractual tenancy.[84a] However, whether the secure tenancy be fixed-term or periodic, and whenever it was granted, there are exceptional cases where the *secure tenancy itself* can be assigned[85]: basically these involve assignments to close family members, and "exchange" assignments (*i.e.* assignments, with the authority's consent, from one secure tenant to another secure tenant[86]); moreover, by an important "saving" provision, an assignment of a secure tenancy *prior to* August 26, 1984, to *anyone* is deemed retrospectively and effectively to have transferred the secure tenancy, although previous notices to quit and forfeiture proceedings are unaffected.[87] Subletting of the whole of the property by a secure tenant to anyone results in loss of the secure tenancy.[88] Subletting of part is permissible with the written consent of the council (which must not be unreasonably withheld[89]), but even if such consent is not obtained, the subletting of part will not cause the head tenancy to cease to be secure, but will merely give rise to a "reasonableness" ground for possession.[90] A secure tenant may take in lodgers without affecting his secure tenancy, and the authority's consent is not required.[91]

Death of secure tenant

Where the secure tenant dies, and he was not himself a "successor,"[92] then if the secure tenancy is periodic it can vest by virtue of the Housing Act 1985[93] (*i.e.* regardless of the terms of the tenant's will) in a prescribed member of his "family"[94] who satisfies stipulated residence requirements; there cannot be joint statutory succession: where there are competing claimants, the spouse has priority, and as between non-spouse claimants the authority must decide on the appropriate successor in cases of dispute.[95] Where a secure tenant dies holding a fixed-term tenancy, then in effect the tenancy will remain secure unless the relevant beneficiary under the dead tenant's will or intestacy is not a prescribed member of his "family."[96]

[84a] Housing Act 1985, s. 91(1), (2).
[85] *Ibid.* s. 91(3); in these exceptional cases, the secure tenancy will pass even if the assignment is absolutely prohibited by the individual tenancy agreement: *Governors of the Peabody Donation Fund* v. *Higgins* [1983] 1 W.L.R. 1091.
[86] Housing Act 1985, s. 92; consent to an "exchange" assignment can only be withheld on one or more of the prescribed grounds in Sched. 3.
[87] Housing (Consequential Provisions) Act 1985, Sched. 4, para. 8.
[88] Housing Act 1985, s. 93(2).
[89] *Ibid.* ss. 93(1)(*b*), 94.
[90] *Ibid.* Sched. 2, Pt. I, gd. 1.
[91] *Ibid.* s. 93(1)(*a*).
[92] *Ibid.* ss. 87–88.
[93] *Ibid.* s. 89.
[94] The prescribed members include heterosexual cohabitees (*ibid.* s. 113), but not homosexuals: *Harrogate Borough Council* v. *Simpson* (1984) 17 H.L.R. 205.
[95] Housing Act 1985, s. 89(2).
[96] *Ibid.* s. 90.

Information and consultation duties regarding secure tenancies

15-11   The 1985 Act imposes duties on the authority concerning the provision of information as regards secure tenancies: the authority must give each secure tenant a full written statement of all the actual terms of the tenancy other than those implied by law,[97] and must also give him up-to-date information explaining in simple terms the effect of the express terms of the tenancy, the "charter" rights in the 1985 Act, and certain of the landlord's implied repairing obligations under the Landlord and Tenant Act 1985.[98] The separate information duties concerning allocation, transfer and exchange schemes have already been discussed.[99]

The authority must, prior to October 3, 1981, have established (and thereafter have published) appropriate arrangements for consulting its secure tenants before it implements relevant changes in matters of "housing management" affecting the whole or a group of its secure tenants, although rents and other charges are excluded from these consultation duties.[1]

Variation of terms of secure tenancy

Where the authority wishes to vary the express terms of an individual secure tenancy, this can be achieved in one of three ways: by *ad hoc* agreement between the authority and the tenant; by unilateral action on the part of the authority or the tenant where this is permitted by the tenancy agreement and the change relates to the rent, rates or services; or by the authority alone, where the tenancy is periodic, pursuant to the prescribed notice of variation procedure (separate consultation duties are here imposed unless the change relates to rent, or payments in respect of rates, services or facilities).[2]

Other rights of secure tenants

15-12   Secure tenants have a right to carry out "improvements" (which are widely defined, and include external decoration) provided they obtain the written consent of the authority, which cannot be unreasonably withheld.[3] If the tenant carries out an improvement without the appropriate consent, the authority has a "reasonableness" ground for possession.[4] The authority cannot normally increase the rent of a secure tenancy on account of a tenant's improvements while the person who did them or a member of his "family" remains the secure tenant.[5] On the ending of a

---

[97] *Ibid.* s. 104(2)(*b*).
[98] *Ibid.* s. 104(1), (2)(*a*); the relevant repairing obligations are those in the Landlord and Tenant Act 1985, ss. 11–16, discussed below at § 15–12.
[99] Housing Act 1985, s. 106.
[1] *Ibid.* s. 105.
[2] *Ibid.* ss. 102, 103.
[3] *Ibid.* ss. 97–99.
[4] *Ibid.* Sched. 2, Pt. I, gd. 1.
[5] *Ibid.* s. 101.

secure tenancy, there is a power for the authority to reimburse the tenant or his personal representatives with a sum not exceeding the historic cost of an improvement lawfully carried out on or after October 3, 1980.[6] There is also a right for secure tenants to carry out certain "landlord's repairs" to the dwelling and then to recoup appropriate sums from the authority.[7] The Secretary of State has a power to implement arrangements in order to ensure that each secure tenant affected by an authority's district heating scheme does not bear an unreasonable proportion of the cost of running the scheme, and to enable secure tenants to receive information and inspect accounts relating to such schemes.[8]

Repairs and maintenance obligations of the council

Quite apart from its "charter" responsibilities in the 1985 Act concerning secure tenancies, an authority may be subject to wide-ranging repair and maintenance responsibilities towards its tenants (whether secure or non-secure), both at common law and by statute. Covenants to repair or maintain the dwelling can be implied, where appropriate, in the case of certain leases for less than seven years (including periodic tenancies),[9] certain leases at very low rents,[10] and furnished lettings.[11] Implied contractual obligations may also arise in respect of common parts (such as lifts and roofs in blocks of flats).[12] There may be separate liability in tort concerning the safety of the dwelling[13] and of the common parts.[14] Moreover, the occupier of a council property (be he a tenant, licensee or even perhaps a squatter) can, in an appropriate case, bring a private prosecution against the authority under the Public Health Act 1936 where the state of the property gives rise to a "statutory nuisance."[15]

D. ASSISTANCE WITH HOUSE PURCHASE

The following matters relating to house purchase will be discussed: (1)   **15-13**

---

[6] *Ibid.* s. 100.
[7] *Ibid.* s. 96; Secure Tenancies (Right to Repair Scheme) Regulations 1985 (S.I. 1985 No. 1493); but *cf.* the existing common law and equitable rights of tenants to set off repairing costs against the rent: see, *e.g. Lee-Parker* v. *Izzet* [1971] 1 W.L.R. 1688; *British Anzani (Felixstowe) Ltd.* v. *International Marine Management (U.K.) Ltd.* [1980] Q.B. 137.
[8] Housing Act 1985, s. 108.
[9] Landlord and Tenant Act 1985, ss. 11–16; see, *e.g. Brown* v. *Liverpool Corporation* [1969] 3 All E.R. 1345.
[10] Landlord and Tenant Act 1985, ss. 8, 10; see, *e.g. Summers* v. *Salford Corporation* [1943] A.C. 283.
[11] See, *e.g. Collins* v. *Hopkins* [1923] 2 K.B. 617.
[12] See, *e.g. Liverpool City Council* v. *Irwin* [1976] 2 W.L.R. 562.
[13] Defective Premises Act 1972, s. 4: see, *e.g. Smith* v. *Bradford Metropolitan Council* (1982) 80 L.G.R. 713; see also, as regards common law negligence, *Rimmer* v. *Liverpool City Council* [1985] Q.B. 1.
[14] Occupiers Liability Act 1957, ss. 1, 2; see also, as regards common law negligence, *Taylor* v. *Liverpool Corporation* [1939] 3 All E.R. 329.
[15] Public Health Act 1936, ss. 92(1)(*a*), 99; see, *e.g. Salford City Council* v. *McNally* [1976] A.C. 379. See further Chap. 16.

"right to buy" sales and mortgages; (2) sales and mortgages outside the "right to buy"; (3) assistance with obtaining mortgages from non-council lenders; (4) assistance with purchase and mortgage costs.

(1) "Right to buy" sales and mortgages
(a) *Sales*

15-14   A secure tenant who does not fall within specified excluded categories[16] can normally enjoy the right to buy and the right to a mortgage,[17] once he has been a "public sector tenant" for at least two years.[18] The right to buy is a right to acquire the freehold of the tenant's house, if the authority owns the freehold. If the authority does not own the freehold or the dwelling is a flat, then the right to buy is a right to be granted a long lease.[19] The price is generally the market value at the time when the tenant serves his initial claim notice, less the appropriate discount (which normally ranges on a sliding scale from 32 per cent. of the value in cases of less than three years' relevant occupation, to 60 per cent. after 30 years' relevant occupation).[20] The relevant occupation periods for the purpose of assessing the discount are generally the same as those used to assess basic right-to-buy eligibility.[21] Certain further disposals by the purchasing tenant or his successors in title within five years of acquisition under the right to buy will attract repayments of discount (or part thereof),[22] and this liability takes effect as a charge by legal mortgage (protected by notice or caution on the registered title) having priority immediately after any prescribed mortgage granted in connection with the right to buy.[23]

15-15   In outline, the right-to-buy procedure is as follows: the secure tenant serves on the authority a prescribed claim form (which must be provided to the tenant by the authority on request)[24]; after service of this form, the authority has (normally) four weeks to serve on the tenant a prescribed notice admitting or denying (with reasons) the right to buy.[25] Once the right has been established (following the authority's acceptance or a court decision), the authority must, within (normally) eight weeks thereafter, serve a second notice on the tenant stating the price,[26] the terms and other

---

[16] Housing Act 1985, ss. 120, 121 and Sched. 5.

[17] *Ibid.* ss. 118(1), 132(1).

[18] *Ibid.* s. 119 and Sched. 4.

[19] *Ibid.* s. 118(1).

[20] *Ibid.* ss. 126, 127, 129; however, the discount must not exceed £25,000: *ibid.* s. 131(2); Housing (Right to Buy) (Maximum Discount) Order 1980 (S.I. 1980 No. 1342); see also the "cost floor" provisions in *ibid.* s. 131(1).

[21] *Ibid.* s. 129(1) and Sched. 4.

[22] *Ibid.* s. 155.

[23] *Ibid.* s. 156; Housing (Right to Buy) (Priority of Charges) Order 1984 (S.I. 1984 No. 1554).

[24] *Ibid.* ss. 122, 176(1), (2); Housing (Right to Buy) (Prescribed Forms) Regulations 1984 (S.I. 1984 No. 1175).

[25] *Ibid.* s. 124(1), (2); Housing (Right to Buy) (Prescribed Forms) Regulations 1984 (S.I. 1984 No. 1175).

[26] Officials of the district valuer's office can be used to fix valuations on the authority's behalf, notwithstanding the district valuer's "appellate" role under *ibid.* s. 128, below; *R* v. *Secretary of State for the Environment, ex p. Norwich City Council* [1982] Q.B. 808.

prescribed particulars.[27] Within (normally) three months of service of this second notice, the tenant can choose to have the price reviewed by the district valuer.[28] If the title to the property is not already registered at the Land Registry, then there is a special conveyancing procedure leading to first registration even if the property is not in an area of compulsory registration.[29]

The authority's duty to complete the transaction, once all relevant matters have been decided, can be enforced by the tenant securing a county court injunction[30]; on execution of the deed of conveyance or the lease, the secure tenancy ends.[31] If the tenant fails to complete, the authority may (after the expiration of the relevant time limit) serve a notice requiring the tenant either to complete within not less than 56 days or to notify the authority of any outstanding matters within not less than 56 days[32]; failure to comply with this notice will entitle the authority to serve a second completion notice requiring completion within a further period of not less than 56 days, and if the tenant fails to comply with this second completion notice, then his right to buy notice is deemed to be withdrawn[33] (although he is under no liability to compensate the council for his failure to complete, and can immediately submit a new right-to-buy application).

Even where the transaction is completed, the secure tenant cannot be forced to pay the authority's costs in connection with the exercise of the right to buy and right to a mortgage, save for the costs of providing a mortgage, to a maximum of £50.[34]

The contents of the purchase deed or lease are governed by detailed **15-16** provisions in Schedule 6 to the 1985 Act; in particular, as regards the lease of a flat, the authority retains extensive liability for repairing the structure and exterior of the flat and the surrounding building, maintaining relevant services, and repairing relevant installations[35] (although a reasonable part of certain of these costs can be recovered from the tenant[36]). Where the property is situated in a National Park, an area designated as one of outstanding natural beauty, or a designated rural area, the conveyance or lease may contain a prescribed restrictive covenant or pre-emption clause whereby the authority can prevent "undesirable" dispositions by the purchasing tenant or his successors in title.[37]

---

[27] Housing Act 1985 s. 125.
[28] *Ibid.* s. 128.
[29] *Ibid.* s. 154.
[30] *Ibid.* ss. 138(1), (3), 181(1).
[31] *Ibid.* s. 139(2); see *Sutton London Borough Council* v. *Swann and others, The Times,* November 30, 1985.
[32] *Ibid.* s. 140.
[33] *Ibid.* s. 141.
[34] *Ibid.* s. 178; Housing (Right to Buy) (Mortgage Costs) Order 1980 (S.I. 1980 No. 1390).
[35] *Ibid.* Sched. 6, Pt. III, para. 14.
[36] *Ibid.* Sched. 6, Pt. III, para. 18.
[37] *Ibid.* s. 157.

(b) *Mortgages*

A secure tenant who exercises the right to buy also has the right to a mortgage from the authority,[38] the amount being the purchase price together with eligible mortgage costs and such of the tenant's own costs as the authority may agree to pay[39]; however, the tenant cannot in any event demand a mortgage which exceeds the prescribed multiple of his available annual income (aggregated with the incomes of other purchasers where there is a joint purchase).[40]

The mortgage is claimed by prescribed notice served on the authority not later than (normally) three months from the authority's own notice giving the terms of the purchase transaction.[41] "As soon as practicable" after the authority receives the mortgage application, it must send the tenant prescribed details of the mortgage.[42] If the tenant's mortgage entitlement is less than full (because of the income criteria), he may, within (normally) three months of service of the notice giving the mortgage details, serve a further notice on the authority claiming to defer completion and deposit the sum of £100.[43] The effect of this is threefold: the authority cannot serve an initial completion notice until (normally) two years have expired following service of the tenant's initial notice claiming the right to buy[44]; until a completion notice is served, the tenant may reapply for a mortgage[45]; and he may claim the right to be granted a shared ownership lease[46] so long as his initial right to buy notice remains in force.[47]

The mortgage term will normally be for 25 years.[48] Repayment must be by way of combined instalments of capital and interest, and the interest rate (which may be subsequently adjusted as appropriate[49]) must be (in effect) the higher of the cost of the council's own relevant borrowing plus $\frac{1}{4}$ per cent., or the rate currently recommended by the Building Societies Association.[50]

(c) *Shared ownership leases*

15-17   Where the secure tenant has established his right to buy, has claimed the right to a mortgage, and (due to a less than full entitlement) has

---

[38] Housing Act 1985, s. 132.

[39] *Ibid.* ss. 133, 178(2); Housing (Right to Buy) (Mortgage Costs) Order 1980 (S.I. 1980 No. 1390).

[40] *Ibid.* ss. 118(2), 123, 133(2)–(6); Housing (Right to Buy) (Mortgage Limit) Regulations 1980 (S.I. 1980 No. 1423).

[41] *Ibid.* s. 134(1)–(3); Housing (Right to Buy) (Prescribed Forms) (No. 2) Regulations 1980 (S.I. 1980 No. 1465).

[42] *Ibid.* s. 135(1)–(3).

[43] *Ibid.* s. 142(1)–(3).

[44] *Ibid.* s. 140(3)(c).

[45] *Ibid.* s. 142(4).

[46] Discussed below at § 15–17.

[47] *Ibid.* s. 143(1)(a).

[48] *Ibid.* Sched. 7.

[49] *Ibid.* Sched. 16, paras. 1(2), 3–6.

[50] *Ibid.* Sched. 16, paras. 1–4.

claimed to defer completion and deposited £100,[51] then (so long as his initial right-to-buy notice remains in force) he may serve notice on the authority claiming to exercise the right to be granted a "shared ownership lease"[52]; such a claim effectively blocks any completion notice from the authority under the normal right-to-buy provisions.[53] A shared ownership lease permits the buyer to reduce his mortgage commitments by paying a mixture of mortgage instalments and rent (in effect, he buys a lease for a premium representing a share of the market value of the property while paying rent on the remaining share, but he also has the right to buy up further shares at any time). The initial share must be not less than 50 per cent., and must be a multiple of $12\frac{1}{2}$ per cent.[54] The additional shares must each be $12\frac{1}{2}$ per cent. or some multiple thereof.[55] There are detailed provisions governing the quantification of the price for each share (taking account of discount entitlement[56]), the assessment of the rental element from time to time,[57] the repayment of discount and payment for any outstanding share on certain disposals,[58] the prohibition of certain disposals of part while any share is outstanding,[59] and the granting of further mortgage advances when the tenant wishes to acquire additional shares.[60] Further, many of the general right-to-buy provisions are incorporated into the shared ownership scheme (concerning, for example, the basic terms of the lease[61] and the Secretary of State's powers of intervention[62]). Once the right to a shared ownership lease has been claimed, a "mini-right to buy" purchase procedure is laid down, culminating in either completion by the authority, or the deemed withdrawal of the right to the shared ownership lease and the initial right-to-buy notice where the tenant fails to comply with a double dose of 56-day completion notices.[63]

(d) *Enforcement*

Where the authority fails properly to implement the right to buy, the right to a mortgage, or the right to a shared ownership lease, then the county court has general jurisdiction (including the power to issue injunctions and declarations).[64] The Secretary of State also has wide

[51] See above at § 15–16.
[52] *Ibid.* s. 143.
[53] *Ibid.* s. 144(3).
[54] *Ibid.* s. 145.
[55] *Ibid.* Sched. 8, para. 1(1).
[56] *Ibid.* s. 148 and Sched. 8, para. 3.
[57] *Ibid.* Sched. 8, para. 4; Housing (Right to a Shared Ownership Lease) (Repairs, Etc., Adjustment) Order 1984 (S.I. 1984 No. 1280).
[58] *Ibid.* s. 155(3) and Sched. 8, para. 6.
[59] *Ibid.* Sched. 8, para. 9.
[60] *Ibid.* Sched. 9.
[61] *Ibid.* s. 151(1)(*b*).
[62] *Ibid.* s. 164(1).
[63] *Ibid.* ss. 146–147, 150, 152–153.
[64] *Ibid.* ss. 138(3), 181(1)–(2).

powers to intervene on the tenant's behalf: he can (*inter alia*) provide assistance (including legal assistance) to the tenant, order the authority and its individual officers to co-operate, and even make a "vesting order" conveying the freehold or leasehold to the tenant (recovering the costs involved from the authority).[65]

(2) Sales and mortgages outside the "right to buy"

15-18 Ministerial consent is required for the disposal of council dwellings other than under the right to buy or by way of letting under a secure tenancy (or under what would be a secure tenancy if it did not fall within one of the prescribed statutory exemptions); general ministerial consents to disposals are given from time to time, and may provide for discounts (in which case provisions for repayment on premature disposal must be included in the purchase deed).[66] Even if a disposal is made without ministerial consent, the individual purchaser will normally be protected.[67] Separate provision has been made to encourage "build for sale" schemes, "improvement and sale" schemes, and voluntary "equity-sharing" schemes.[68]

Authorities have wide powers to grant mortgages for house purchase, whether or not the purchasers are acquiring council properties.[69] However, such mortgage advances are limited by central government's extensive controls on the ability of authorities to borrow money,[70] although certain "priority groups" of borrowers are approved from time to time.[71]

The rate of interest is generally calculated in accordance with the same formula as that already described in relation to "right-to-buy" mortgages.[72] However, there are special powers to grant "low-start" mortgages[73] (allowing for lower repayments in the early years of the mortgage), "maturity" loans[73a] (whereby "interest only" payments are made while the mortgage lasts and the capital is repaid as a lump sum on termination), and "homesteading" schemes[74] (under which authorities may, for a period of up to five years from the date of the mortgage, charge a lower rate of interest or waive interest payments entirely or dispense with repayments of capital, where the borrower undertakes specified repair or improvement work and the scheme has been approved by the Secretary of State). Authorities are recognised savings institutions for the

---

[65] *Ibid.* ss. 164–166, 169–170; see *R.* v. *Secretary of State for the Environment, ex p. Norwich City Council* [1982] Q.B. 808.
[66] *Ibid.* ss. 32–42; ministerial letters of June 2 and 4, 1981, as amended by DoE Circular 21/84, Annex C.
[67] *Ibid.* s. 44.
[68] *Ibid.* ss. 17(2), 32(4), 429; ministerial letter of June 2, 1981.
[69] *Ibid.* ss. 435, 437.
[70] See Chap. 7.
[71] See ministerial letter of August 10, 1979.
[72] Housing Act 1985, Sched. 16, discussed above at § 15–16.
[73] *Ibid.* s. 436(5)(*a*); ministerial consent is no longer necessary.   [73a] *Ibid.* s. 436(5)(*b*).
[74] *Ibid.* s. 441.

purpose of the scheme for assisting first-time buyers in sections 445–450 of the Housing Act 1985, whereby on complying with the necessary conditions, a first-time buyer of low-priced property can receive from central government funds, in addition to the normal mortgage advance, a tax-free bonus of up to £110 and an additional £600 loan which will be interest-free for five years.

(3) Assistance with obtaining mortgages from non-council lenders
Authorities which are short of mortgage funds may nominate **15-19** applicants (to whom they would normally lend) to a local building society under the non-statutory Building Societies' Support Lending Scheme established in 1976. Authorities also have the power, with ministerial consent, to enter into agreements guaranteeing the mortgagor's obligations under a mortgage made with a building society or other "recognised body" (and even to take over such mortgages if so provided for by agreement with the mortgagor and mortgagee)[75]; such guarantees can encourage mortgagees to advance loans on older properties and to low-income borrowers.

(4) Assistance with purchase and mortgage costs
Where a purchaser acquires a house from an authority, whether or not under the right to buy, and the authority advances the mortgage money, the purchaser's costs (including conveyancing costs) may be paid by the authority and added to the mortgage advance.[76] Further, authorities may contribute towards the costs (up to a maximum of £200) incurred by a purchaser in obtaining a mortgage advance from a prescribed lender (including a building society), provided the mortgage money is used *either* to finance the purchase of a dwelling sold by a specified public body (including a council), *or* to repay an advance obtained from a specified public body in connection with such a purchase.[77]

E. Responsibilities Concerning the Private Rented Sector

Quite apart from their responsibilities concerning the alleviation of poor **15-20** housing conditions,[78] authorities have several other disparate but important responsibilities concerning the private rented sector.
Authorities may prosecute for the offences of unlawful eviction and harassment of a "residential occupier" under the Protection from Eviction Act 1977.[79] A "residential occupier" is a person occupying

---

[75] *Ibid.* s. 442.
[76] *Ibid.* ss. 133(1), 437.
[77] *Ibid.* s. 443 (applying both to "right-to-buy" and "non-right-to-buy" purchases); Housing (Local Authority) (Contributions Towards Housing Costs) Order 1984 (S.I. 1984 No. 1174).
[78] Discussed below at § 15–25 *et seq.*
[79] Protection from Eviction Act 1977, s. 6; DoE Circular 15/73.

premises as a residence, whether under a contract or any enactment or rule of law giving him the right to remain or restricting the right of any other person to recover possession[80]; this definition covers current tenants and licensees, all former tenants who are holding over, and certain former licensees holding over by virtue of terminated "restricted contracts" within the Rent Act 1977.[81] Unlawful eviction involves depriving a "residential occupier" of his accommodation without a court order, even by peaceful means.[82] Harassment involves acts calculated to interfere with the peace or comfort of a residential occupier or members of his household, or the persistent withdrawal or withholding of services reasonably required for occupation of the premises as a residence, provided that (in either case) the defendant had the intent to cause the residential occupier to give up occupation or refrain from exercising any right or pursuing any remedy in respect of the premises.[83] In relation to *civil* proceedings which may arise in connection with unlawful eviction or harassment (for example, actions for breach of the implied covenant for quiet enjoyment or for trespass), the authority may exercise its general powers in the Local Government Act 1972 to underwrite the tenant's costs or undertake the action on his behalf.[84]

With regard to rent levels, where the occupier holds a "regulated tenancy" or a "restricted contract" under the Rent Act 1977, the authority may itself refer the rent to the rent officer or rent tribunal (as appropriate) for registration[85]; this power may prove particularly useful where the occupier is in receipt of housing benefit[86] or is wary of taking the initiative himself by applying for registration. There are also various offences created by the Rent Act 1977, for which the authority (and, sometimes, only the authority) may prosecute the landlord.[87]

15–21 Under the Rent (Agriculture) Act 1976, an authority is under a duty to use its best endeavours, in the interests of efficient agriculture, to provide suitable alternative accommodation for certain agricultural employees (who would otherwise have security of tenure), whose employers require their houses for other employees and cannot themselves provide the required alternative accommodation.[88] The employer's application to the authority may be referred to a local Agricultural Dwelling-House Advisory Committee: the Committee's decision must be taken into account by the authority, although the authority is not necessarily bound by it.[89]

---

[80] Protection from Eviction Act 1977, s. 1(1).
[81] *Ibid.* ss. 1–3, 8; Rent Act 1977, s. 19.
[82] Protection from Eviction Act 1977, s. 1(2); *R.* v. *Yuthiwattana* (1984) 128 S.J. 661.
[83] *Ibid.* s. 1(3); a single "act" will suffice (*R.* v. *Polycarpou* (1983) 9 H.L.R. 129), and need not amount to a breach of contract (*R.* v. *Yuthiwattana, supra*: refusal by landlord to replace tenant's lost key).
[84] Local Government Act 1972, ss. 111, 137, 222.
[85] Rent Act 1977, ss. 68, 77(1).
[86] Discussed below at § 15–23.
[87] See, *e.g.* Rent Act 1977, ss. 77(4), 81(5), 150.
[88] Rent (Agriculture) Act 1976, ss. 27–28.
[89] *Ibid.* ss. 28(3)–(5), 29.

Authorities may prosecute landlords and licensors who fail to provide rent books satisfying the requirements of the Landlord and Tenant Act 1985; proper rent books under this Act, containing prescribed information, must be supplied to tenants and licensees (whether or not covered by the Rent Act 1977) who pay their rent weekly (unless the rent includes payment for board the value of which forms a substantial part of the rent).[90]

Finally, authorities have the power[91] to publish information, for the assistance of landlords and tenants and others, as to their rights and duties under the Protection from Eviction Act 1977,[92] the Rent Act 1977, the private rented sector provisions of the Housing Act 1980, the Rent (Agriculture) Act 1976, and the provisions relating to rent books and service charges in the Landlord and Tenant Act 1985.

F. Responsibilities Concerning Housing Associations

Local authorities have various functions concerning housing associations.   **15-22**
They may finance the activities of an association by making grants or loans, or by subscribing for its shares or loan capital.[93] Where an association applies to an authority for a loan under these provisions, then if the association also wants to receive a housing association grant from the Secretary of State, it must first apply for this grant to the authority, whereupon the authority must forward the application to the Secretary of State together with its own comments.[94] Authorities frequently take an active part in promoting housing associations, and often acquire nomination rights to housing association dwellings, especially where they have helped to fund the relevant projects.

G. Housing Benefit

From April 1983, authorities have been obliged to operate a complicated   **15-23**
housing benefit scheme for certain low-income occupiers.[95] This comprises three separate benefits: rate rebates; rent rebates (for short-term tenants and licensees of housing authorities); and rent allowances (for short-term tenants and licensees whose landlords and licensors are not housing authorities).[96] A claimant who is not entitled to supplementary

---

[90] Landlord and Tenant Act 1985, ss. 4–7; Rent Book (Forms of Notice) Regulations 1982 (S.I. 1982 No. 1474). An authority in its capacity as landlord is bound to observe the requirements of the Act.
[91] Rent Act 1977, s. 149.
[92] Including the notice to quit provisions in s. 5 of the Protection from Eviction Act.
[93] Housing Associations Act 1985, s. 58.
[94] *Ibid.* s. 46.
[95] Social Security and Housing Benefits Act 1982; Housing Benefits Regulations 1985 (S.I. 1985 No. 677); Housing Benefits (Subsidy) Order 1985 (S.I. 1985 No. 440); Housing Benefits (Miscellaneous Amendments) Regulations 1985 (S.I. 1985 No. 1100).
[96] 1982 Act, s. 28(1); Housing Benefits Regs. 1985 (S.I. 1985 No. 677), reg. 2(4).

benefits from the D.H.S.S. can apply for housing benefit to the authority direct (the "standard" procedure); where the claimant is receiving supplementary benefits from the D.H.S.S., then the D.H.S.S. will issue a certificate to the authority confirming his entitlement to housing benefit (the "certificated" procedure).[97] Eligibility depends on the claimant being liable or treated as liable to pay rent or rates on a dwelling. In the case of rent rebates and rent allowances, the occupier need not necessarily be a tenant in the strict sense: certain licensees, and boarders who are not in receipt of supplementary benefits, are included.[98] Standard benefit is assessed by reference to the claimant's "needs allowance," "weekly income," "eligible rates" and/or "eligible rent."[99] There is generally no upper limit to benefit, save where the rent has been registered by the rent officer or rent tribunal under the Rent Act 1977,[1] or the authority considers the accommodation to be "unsuitable."[2]

With regard to the manner of payment, rent and rate rebates are normally given by simply waiving the requirement to pay the rent and rates for the relevant period,[3] while rent allowances are normally paid fortnightly or monthly.[4] In certain circumstances, payment of a rent allowance may be made by the authority direct to the occupier's landlord or licensor.[5]

Housing benefit is principally funded by subsidies from central government, supplemented by rate fund contributions.[6] Several changes to the housing benefit system have been proposed as part of the recent reviews of social security.[7]

H. HOUSING SUBSIDY AND ACCOUNTING

15–24 The current housing subsidy system[8] is based on "deficit financing," and is calculated by reference to three amounts: the "base amount" (being the amount of housing subsidy which the authority received in the previous year); the "housing costs differential" (representing increased costs, called "reckonable expenditure," as compared with the previous year, to the extent allowed by the Secretary of State); and the "local contribution differential" (this represents the amount by which the Secretary of State

---

[97] Housing Benefits Regs. 1985 (S.I. 1985 No. 677), reg. 9.
[98] 1982 Act, s. 28(1), (3); Housing Benefits Regs. 1985 (S.I. 1985 No. 677), regs. 5–7.
[99] Housing Benefits Regs. 1985 (S.I. 1985 No. 677), regs. 13–18; Housing Benefits (Increase of Needs Allowances) Regulations 1985 (S.I. 1985 No. 1244).
[1] Housing Benefits Regs. 1985 (S.I. 1985 No. 677), reg. 18(7); the authority may itself refer the rent for registration: Rent Act 1977, ss. 68, 77(1), discussed above.
[2] Housing Benefits Regs. 1985 (S.I. 1985 No. 677), reg. 19.
[3] *Ibid.* reg. 39.
[4] *Ibid.* reg. 42.
[5] *Ibid.* reg. 44.
[6] 1982 Act, ss. 32–34.
[7] *Reform of Social Security*, Cmnd. 9517 (1985); *Housing Benefit Review: Report of the Review Team*, Cmnd. 9520 (1985).
[8] Housing Act 1985, ss. 421–425.

expects rents and rates to have increased over the relevant period, rather than the income which the authority in fact receives). Before deciding on the local contribution differential, the Secretary of State has to consult the local authority associations. Housing subsidy is calculated by adding the housing costs differential to the base amount, and then subtracting from the resultant figure the local contribution differential. If the result of this process is a nil or negative figure, then no housing subsidy is payable for the year of account, though a nil or negative figure will be important in relation to a subsequent year's claim to subsidy, in providing a nil or negative base amount. If the local contribution differential is a nil or negative figure, then nothing may fall to be deducted on account of it, and indeed an amount may be added.

The Secretary of State may reclaim subsidy or part thereof, or withhold further subsidy, if it appears to him that the purpose for which it was paid has not been fulfilled, or has not been properly fulfilled, and the case falls within rules published by him.[9]

With regard to accounting, each authority must keep a housing revenue account of all housing income and expenditure. In this account the rents and other charges for services received by the authority in respect of its dwellings are credited, together with subsidies received, while loan charges attributable to housing provision are debited, together with the costs of repair, maintenance, supervision and management.[10] An authority may from time to time carry to the credit of its general rate fund the whole or part of any balance in its housing revenue account.[11] In addition, an authority may open a housing repairs account exclusively to deal with the repair or maintenance of its housing stock; this account must never be overdrawn, and any surplus may be credited, wholly or in part, to the housing revenue account.[12]

I. GENERAL RESPONSIBILITIES CONCERNING HOUSING CONDITIONS

The authority's responsibilities as landlord have already been discussed. **15-25** Authorities also have more general responsibilities concerning housing conditions, which can straddle the divisions of tenure. The following matters will be considered: (1) Fitness for habitation; (2) Compensation; (3) Improvements; (4) Overcrowding and multiple occupation.

(1) Fitness for habitation
(a) *The fitness standard*
The standard of "fitness for human habitation" (popularly called the **15-26** "nine-point standard") is defined by reference to the following nine

---

[9] Housing Act 1985, s. 427.
[10] *Ibid.* ss. 417–418 and Sched. 14.
[11] *Ibid.* Sched. 14, Pt. V, para. 1(1); the housing revenue account may show a profit which exceeds a mere working balance.
[12] *Ibid.* s. 419.

matters: repair; stability; freedom from damp; internal arrangement; natural lighting; ventilation; water supply; drainage and sanitary conveniences; and facilities for the preparation and cooking of food and for the disposal of waste water.[13] A house[14] is deemed unfit if and only if it is so far defective in respect of one or more of these matters that it is not reasonably suitable for occupation in that condition.[14a] There is no requirement that the specified matters must be dangerous to health,[15] and comparatively trivial matters have been held to give rise to unfitness.[16]

Once an authority is satisfied that there is unfitness, it is normally bound to take some action under the Housing Act 1985, and does not have the option of proceeding under the Public Health Act 1936 instead[17]; however, it cannot be required to operate the unfitness procedures in respect of its own properties.[18]

Unfit houses fall into two groups, those which can, and those which cannot, be made fit at reasonable expense. Those in the first group must be dealt with individually; those in the second group must either be dealt with individually or as part of a clearance area scheme.[19]

(b) *Unfit houses which are capable of repair at reasonable expense*

Where the authority is satisfied that a house is unfit but capable of repair at reasonable expense, it must serve a "repair notice" on the "person having control" (*i.e.* the person receiving the rack rent whether on his own account or as agent or trustee for any other person, or who would receive such rent if the house was let).[20] The notice requires the execution within a specified reasonable time of specified works to make the house fit.[21] Failure to comply is not an offence, but the authority may

---

[13] *Ibid.* s. 604; MHLG Circulars 55, 1954; 69, 1967; 68, 1969; see also *ibid.* s. 282 (underground rooms). A new fitness standard (including requirements for a fixed bath or shower and inside W.C.) was proposed in the Green Paper on *Home Improvement—A New Approach*, Cmnd. 9513 (1985), Annex II.

[14] This includes part of a house used or suitable for use as a dwelling: *ibid.* s. 205; a lodging-house, tenement block, or even a purpose-built block of flats, may qualify as a "house" for unfitness purposes: *Re Ross and Leicester Corporation* (1932) 30 L.G.R. 382; *Quiltotex Co.* v. *Minister of Housing and Local Government* [1966] 1 Q.B. 704; *Pollway Nominees Ltd.* v. *Croydon London Borough Council* [1985] 3 All E.R. 24.

[14a] *Supra*, n. 13.

[15] The separate provisions relating to poor housing in the Public Health Act 1936 are discussed below, Chap. 16.

[16] See, *e.g. Summers* v. *Salford Corporation* [1943] A.C. 283.

[17] *R.* v. *Kerrier District Council, ex p. Guppys (Bridport) Ltd.* (1976) 75 L.G.R. 129.

[18] *R.* v. *Cardiff City Council, ex p. Cross* (1982) 81 L.G.R. 105.

[19] Housing Act 1985, Pts. VI and IX; see also Land Compensation Act 1961, s. 10 and Sched. 2, paras. 1–2, which provide that where an authority purchases land otherwise than under the Housing Act 1985, it may seek an order from the Secretary of State that the houses are unfit for habitation.

[20] Housing Act 1985, ss. 189(1), 207; "rack-rent" means rent which is not less than two-thirds of the rateable value (*ibid.* s. 207); a freeholder who lets on long lease at a low ground rent cannot therefore be served with a repair notice: *Pollway Nominees Ltd.* v. *Croydon London Borough Council* [1985] 3 All E.R. 24. As to notices, see Housing (Prescribed Forms) Regulations 1972 (S.I. 1972 No. 228).

[21] *Ibid.* s. 189(2).

itself do the required work, recovering the cost by action or by instalments from the occupier; outstanding sums are a charge on the property.[22] Appeal lies to the county court. If the court finds expressly that the house cannot be made fit at reasonable expense, the authority can purchase the house by agreement or compulsorily, but it must then forthwith do all the work specified in the repair notice.[23] In deciding the issue of "reasonable expense,"[24] regard must be had to the estimated cost of the works necessary to make the house fit, and the estimated value of the house when the works are completed.[25] The open market value of the freehold must be taken into account.[26] Where the property is tenanted, the vacant possession value is not appropriate: the presence of the tenants must be recognised, having regard to such factors as their age and the extent of their protection under the Rent Act 1977.[27]

(c) *Unfit houses which are not capable of repair at reasonable expense*
Where the authority is satisfied that a house is unfit and incapable of **15-27** repair at reasonable expense, and the clearance area procedure[28] is not being operated, then it must serve a "time and place" notice on the person having control, the owner, and every mortgagee, giving the time and place of a meeting at which the condition of the house will be discussed.[29] If, following this meeting, the authority remains satisfied that the house is unfit and incapable of being made fit at reasonable expense, it must take one of four courses of action: acceptance of undertaking; demolition order; closing order; or purchase for temporary housing. The undertaking may be either to carry out work making the house fit, or not to use it for habitation until it has been made fit[30]; if either undertaking is broken, one of the three remaining courses of action must be taken.[31] A demolition order requires vacation of the house and its subsequent demolition within the time stated by the authority; failure to demolish the property is not an offence, but the authority must then enter and demolish it at the owner's expense.[32] A closing order prohibits the use of a house (or part thereof) for

---

[22] Housing Act 1985, ss. 193–194 and Sched. 10, para. 7; for charges, see § 24–02.
[23] *Ibid.* ss. 191–192.
[24] The Government has recently proposed the removal of the "reasonable expense" test, and its replacement with a requirement for the authority to consider the relative merits of available options, to be set out in a Departmental Code of Guidance: *Home Improvement—A New Approach, op.cit.,* at §§ 66–68.
[25] Housing Act 1985, s. 206; the authority need not consider detailed estimates, since s. 189(1) contains a presumption of reasonable expense: *Bacon* v. *Grimsby Corporation* [1950] 1 K.B. 272.
[26] *Inworth Property Co.* v. *Southwark London Borough Council* (1977) 76 L.G.R. 263.
[27] *F.F.F. Estates Ltd.* v. *Hackney London Borough Council* [1981] 1 Q.B. 503; *Phillips* v. *Newham London Borough Council* (1982) 43 P. & C.R. 54; *R.* v. *Ealing London Borough Council, ex p. Richardson* (1983) 265 E.G. 691.
[28] Discussed below.
[29] Housing Act 1985, s. 264(1).
[30] *Ibid.* s. 264(4).
[31] *Ibid.* s. 265.
[32] *Ibid.* ss. 267, 270–272; where a demolition order is made an authority may substitute a closing order for it, to enable the house to be used for a purpose other than housing: *ibid.* s. 275.

any purpose not approved by the authority, and must normally be made in two situations: where it is inexpedient to make a demolition order having regard to the effect on other property, and where any part of a dwelling is unfit and the authority would otherwise have made a demolition order or bought for temporary housing; failure to comply with the order is an offence.[33] If the authority considers an unfit house to be capable of providing adequate accommodation for the time being, despite its unfitness, then it may normally purchase the house (by agreement or compulsorily) instead of making a demolition or closing order[34]; the house need not be made fit by the authority,[35] but it must comply with basic public health standards[36]; further, the house can only be used for temporary accommodation pending its demolition: it cannot be treated as a permanent addition to the authority's stock.[37]

Appeal lies to the county court by a "person aggrieved" by a demolition or closing order or a purchase for temporary housing[38]; although short-term tenants cannot appeal to the county court, they can challenge the authority's decision by judicial review in the High Court.[39]

15-28   Where the owner gives an undertaking not to use the house for habitation, or the authority makes a demolition or closing order, then the occupiers will lose any Rent Act protection, even if the unfitness is due to the owner's breach of his repairing obligations,[40] but they may have rights to rehousing and financial benefits from the authority.[41] Where the authority purchases for temporary housing, the occupying tenants can become non-secure tenants of the authority.[42]

(d) *Clearance areas*

Where there are several unfit houses which cannot be made fit at reasonable expense, they may be dealt with by the authority as a group through the clearance area procedure, provided the authority is satisfied on all the following points:

(a) the houses are unfit, or are by reason of their bad arrangement, or the narrowness or bad arrangement of the streets, dangerous or injurious to health, and the other buildings (if any) in the area are similarly dangerous or injurious to health;

(b) the most satisfactory method of dealing with the conditions in the area is by demolition of all the buildings;

---

[33] Housing Act 1985, ss. 265(2), 266, 267(2), 277.
[34] *Ibid.* s. 300; MHLG Circular No. 55, 1954.
[35] *Ibid.* s. 302.
[36] *Salford City Council* v. *McNally* [1976] A.C. 379.
[37] *Victoria Square Property Co. Ltd.* v. *Southwark London Borough Council* [1978] 1 W.L.R. 463; see also *R.* v. *Birmingham City Corporation, ex p. Sale* (1983) 82 L.G.R. 69.
[38] *Ibid.* ss. 269, 300(2).
[39] *Ibid.* s. 269(2); *R.* v. *Ealing London Borough Council, ex p. Richardson* (1983) 265 E.G. 691.
[40] *Ibid.* ss. 264(5), 270(3), 276; *Buswell* v. *Goodwin* [1971] 1 W.L.R. 92.
[41] Under the Land Compensation Act 1973.
[42] Housing Act 1985, ss. 302(*a*), 583, and Sched. 1, para. 3.

(c) alternative accommodation can if necessary be made available for persons displaced;

(d) the authority has sufficient resources to carry out the procedure.[43]

A copy of the resolution declaring the clearance area must be sent to the Secretary of State.[44] The purpose of the procedure is to clear the property of its buildings; the authority must therefore proceed to purchase the land, compulsorily or by agreement, and then demolish the buildings.[45] The purchase may include land surrounded by the clearance area and land adjoining the clearance area if reasonably needed for satisfactory development.[46] Special compulsory purchase powers and procedures are prescribed.[47] Demolition of unfit houses within the clearance area can be postponed if the authority is satisfied that they are capable of providing adequate accommodation for the time being, provided retention is justified for some reason *other than* the mere need for housing accommodation[48]; but such houses must still comply with basic public health standards.[49] Occupiers displaced from clearance areas may be entitled to rehousing and financial benefits from the authority.[50]

(e) *Fit properties which are in disrepair*

Even if a house is not unfit, the authority may nevertheless serve a repair notice on the person having control if it is satisfied that the property is in such a state of disrepair that substantial repairs are needed to bring it up to a reasonable standard, having regard to its age, character and locality.[51] Further, even if a house is neither unfit nor in need of substantial repairs, the authority may at the request of the occupying tenant serve a repair notice on the person having control if it is satisfied that the property is in such a state of disrepair that its condition interferes materially with the tenant's personal comfort.[52] The general effects of these special repair notices, and the provisions for appeal, are the same as for repair notices served in respect of unfit houses.[53]

(2) Compensation

This topic is considered under the following headings: (a) compensa-   **15-29** tion where the property is not condemned as unfit (where, for example, it

[43] Housing Act 1985, s. 289.
[44] *Ibid.* s. 289(5).
[45] *Ibid.* s. 290(1).
[46] *Ibid.* s. 290(2).
[47] *Ibid.* Sched. 22.
[48] *Ibid.* s. 301; *R.* v. *Birmingham City Corporation, ex p. Sale* (1984) 82 L.G.R. 69.
[49] *Salford City Council* v. *McNally* [1976] A.C. 379.
[50] Under the Land Compensation Act 1973.
[51] Housing Act 1985, s. 190(1)(*a*); although there is no express "reasonable expense" qualification, this has been read in by the courts: *Hillbank Properties Ltd.* v. *Hackney London Borough Council* [1978] Q.B. 998. Yet policy considerations have on occasion outweighed the fact that the cost of repairs would exceed the increase in the property's value following completion of the work: *Kenny* v. *Kingston upon Thames London Borough Council* (1985) 274 E.G. 395.
[52] *Ibid.* s. 190(1)(*b*).
[53] *Ibid.* ss. 191, 193.

is included in a compulsory purchase order because the land on which it stands adjoins a clearance area and is needed for satisfactory redevelopment); (b) compensation where the property is condemned as unfit and is bought compulsorily by the authority; (c) compensation where the property is condemned as unfit but no compulsory purchase order is made; (d) relief in respect of mortgages.

(a) *Property other than condemned property*
Where property other than condemned property is purchased, the assessment of compensation follows the general principles discussed in Chapter 5, subject to certain special rules contained in the Housing Act 1985.[54]

(b) *Condemned property bought compulsorily*
15-30 Where an authority compulsorily acquires a house which is unfit (whether acquired as being individually unfit or as part of a clearance area), the amount of compensation to be paid to the owner is the value of the site cleared of buildings and available for development[55]; but this must not exceed the market value of the site with the property on it,[56] since a cleared site may be more valuable than a site with a house on it which in theory has no value. The cleared site basis of compensation is also used in several other situations where an authority compulsorily purchases houses and thereupon seeks an order from the Secretary of State that they are unfit.[57]

The cleared site basis of compensation is modified in certain circumstances. A "well-maintained payment" may be payable to the owner and/or occupier, depending, *inter alia*, on whether the interior or exterior or both has been well-maintained. The basic amount is the rateable value of the property multiplied by the appropriate factor (currently 14), but may not exceed the difference between the full compulsory purchase value and the site value; disputes are referable to the county court in the case of an individually acquired property, and to the Secretary of State in the case of property in a clearance area.[58] An "owner-occupier's supplement,"[59] representing the difference between site value and the full compulsory purchase value, is payable to an owner-occupier who has been in occupation as such for at least two years prior to the authority's action. The two years' qualification period may be satisfied through continuous occupation by successive owner-occupiers, and short breaks between the occupation of different owners will not

---

[54] Housing Act 1985, s. 578.
[55] *Ibid.* s. 585(1).
[56] *Ibid.* s. 589(1).
[57] Land Compensation Act 1961, Sched. 2, paras. 1–4.
[58] Housing Act 1985, s. 586 and Sched. 23; Housing (Payments for Well-Maintained Houses) Order 1982 (S.I. 1982 No. 1112).
[59] *Ibid.* s. 587 and Sched. 24, Pt. I.

affect the chain of continuity[60]; the two years' period is inapplicable where a purchaser bought the property after having made all reasonable inquiries and had no reason to believe that the unfitness action would be started within two years.[61] Further compensation may be payable where the house was occupied wholly or partly for business purposes.[62] If the overall compensation which an owner-occupier would receive comes to less than the gross value of the house, then the compensation is raised to that gross value.[63]

Quite separately, those displaced may be eligible for rehousing, home loss payments, disturbance payments, and certain other allowances in respect of disturbance and removal.[64]

(c) *Condemned property not compulsorily purchased*
Where the authority proceeds by way of a closing order or demolition order, there is no purchase for which the owner or occupier can be entitled to compensation; however, either the owner or occupier or both may be entitled (where appropriate) to a "well-maintained payment," an "owner-occupier's supplement," compensation for loss of business premises, rehousing, home loss payments, disturbance payments, and certain other allowances in respect of disturbance and removal.[65]

(d) *Relief in respect of mortgages*
The county court has jurisdiction to modify outstanding liabilities   **15-31**
under mortgages, charges or agreements to purchase by instalments, in respect of unfit houses which are condemned or compulsorily purchased.[66]

(3) Improvements
This topic is considered under the following sub-headings: (a) the   **15-32**
provision of standard amenities; (b) grants; (c) improvement areas.

(a) *The provision of standard amenities*
Even if a house is fit and in sound repair, it may lack one or more of the "standard amenities" (*i.e.* a fixed bath or shower with hot and cold water supply, a wash hand basin with hot and cold water supply, a sink with hot and cold water supply, and a W.C.—normally within the building[67]). In such a case, the authority may compel the person having control to

---

[60] *Laundon* v. *Hartlepool Borough Council* [1979] Q.B. 252; *Westerman* v. *St. Helens Metropolitan Borough Council* (1983) 46 P. & C.R. 236.
[61] Housing Act 1985, Sched. 24, Pt. I, para. 2(2).
[62] *Ibid.* s. 587 and Sched. 24, Pt. II.
[63] *Ibid.* s. 589(2).
[64] See Chap. 5.
[65] See above, and Chap. 5.
[66] *Ibid.* s. 591.
[67] *Ibid.* ss. 237, 508.

provide the missing standard amenities (and do other work necessary to improve the house to the required standard),[68] provided: (i) the dwelling is in a housing action area or general improvement area, or the occupying tenant requests the authority in writing to act; (ii) the dwelling is without the exclusive use of one or more of the standard amenities; (iii) the dwelling is capable at reasonable expense of improvement to a standard of reasonable repair, good insulation, fitness for habitation, possession of all the standard amenities for the exclusive use of the occupants, and probable future life of 15 years; and (iv) the dwelling was provided by erection or conversion before October 3, 1961.[69] The authority must be satisfied concerning the interim housing arrangements for the tenant while the work is being carried out.[70]

The procedure is by way of a system of provisional notices and improvement notices. Failure to comply with an improvement notice is not an offence, but the authority may carry out the work at the owner's expense.[71] Appeals against improvement notices lie to the county court.[72]

(b) *Grants*

15-33   There are four types of house renovation grants[73]: (i) intermediate grants: these are designed for the provision of missing "standard amenities,"[74] and are normally mandatory; (ii) repairs grants: these are designed to secure works of repair or replacement rather than improvement, and are discretionary, save that if the application satisfies the necessary conditions and relates to works required by an authority's "repair notice"[75] the authority must approve the grant; (iii) improvement grants: these are designed for general improvement (beyond mere repairs and the supply of standard amenities), or for the provision of a dwelling by conversion of a building, and are purely discretionary; (iv) special grants: these are designed for the improvement of a house in multiple occupation[76] by the provision of "standard amenities" and/or means of escape from fire, and are discretionary, save that if the application satisfies the necessary conditions and relates to works required by an authority's notice compelling the provision of standard amenities[76] or means of escape from fire,[76] the authority must approve the grant.

In May 1985 the government published a Green Paper[77] proposing wide-ranging reforms to house renovation grants: in particular, eligibility

---

[68] Housing Act 1985, Pt. VII.
[69] *Ibid.* ss. 209–210, 212, 215, 234, 236; as regards the "exclusive use" requirement, see *F.F.F. Estates Ltd.* v. *Hackney London Borough Council* [1981] Q.B. 503.
[70] *Ibid.* ss. 214(2)(*d*), 215(2)(*c*), 235.
[71] *Ibid.* s. 220 and Sched. 10.
[72] *Ibid.* s. 217.
[73] *Ibid.* Pt. XV.
[74] See above.
[75] *i.e.* under *ibid.* ss. 189–190 (discussed above).
[76] Discussed below.
[77] *Home Improvement—A New Approach*, Cmnd. 9513.

for grants would be means-tested; eligible applicants would then be entitled to mandatory grants for any improvement or repair work needed to bring the dwelling up to the new proposed fitness standard (which would include requirements for an inside W.C., a sink with hot and cold water supply, and a fixed bath or shower with hot and cold water supply); in the case of fit properties in need of improvement or repair, the authority would be able to offer a single type of discretionary financial assistance (again subject to means-testing), in the shape of an interest-free loan on an equity-sharing basis, covering any combination of repairs and improvements needed to put dwellings into reasonable repair and give them a 30-years life; transitional arrangements would be introduced to allow authorities to deal with applications made from April 1, 1984 under the existing system.

There is a separate system of grants administered by authorities which are designed to improve the thermal insulation of qualifying dwellings.[78]

There is another special system of grants and other financial relief **15–34** concerning defective dwellings acquired from the public sector.[79] These provisions allow certain purchasers of dwellings from authorities (whether or not under the right to buy) to claim assistance where the dwellings are of designated types[80] built with prefabricated reinforced concrete and have, subsequent to purchase, been found to be defective by reason of their construction or design. If the defective dwelling is a house (not a flat), and after reasonable expenditure on reinstatement would have a further life of 30 years and would be mortgageable with a private sector lending institution, then the owner is normally entitled to a "reinstatement grant" representing 90 per cent. of the reinstatement costs.[81] If any of these conditions is not met (i.e. in effect, the dwelling is a flat or the remedying of the defects is not economically viable), then the authority must offer to repurchase the dwelling at 95 per cent. of its defect-free value, must pay the owner's reasonable legal expenses, and must on being requested to do so grant him a secure tenancy of the house or flat in question or of other suitable accommodation.[82] Central government normally meets 90 per cent. of the repair costs paid by the authority under a reinstatement grant, or, in cases of repurchase, 75 per cent. of the difference between the price paid to the owner of the defective house and its defective value.[83]

---

[78] Housing Act 1985, ss. 521–522; see further: the Homes Insulation Scheme 1984, DoE Circular 13/84; Homes Insulation Grants Order 1984 (S.I. 1984 No. 838).
[79] Housing Act 1985, Pt. XVI.
[80] Designation can be by the Secretary of State (*ibid.* s. 528, DoE Circular No. 28/84, para. 3), or by an individual housing authority (*ibid.* s. 559). The designation must specify the "cut-off date" by which the existence of the defect became generally known; normally, the purchaser must have bought before the cut-off date, or within twelve months thereof and in ignorance of the defect: *ibid.* ss. 528(2)–(3), 531.
[81] *Ibid.* ss. 538, 541–545; there is a maximum level of eligible costs, currently £14,000: Housing Defects (Expenditure Limit) Order 1984 (S.I. 1984 No. 1705).
[82] *Ibid.* ss. 537, 547–558 and Sched. 20.
[83] *Ibid.* s. 569.

(c) *Improvement areas*

15-35   In recent years, authorities have tended to deal with groups of bad housing under improvement area schemes rather than by way of the declaration of clearance areas.[84] There are two classes of improvement area, the housing action area and the general improvement area.

A housing action area (which is not intended for alleviating the condition of the authority's own stock) may be declared by an authority in relation to an area consisting primarily of housing accommodation, following a report by a "qualified person" (which may be one of its own officers). The authority must be satisfied (having regard to the physical state of the housing and the social conditions) that the living conditions in the area are unsatisfactory, and can best be remedied within a period of five years by declaring the area to be a housing action area, in order to secure the improvement of the housing accommodation in the area, the well-being of the residents, and the proper and effective management and use of the accommodation.[85] The resolution must be registered as a local land charge, and a copy must be sent to the Secretary of State, who can veto the resolution.[86] The declaration of the housing action area normally lasts for five years, and there are the following consequences: the authority must provide information to owners and residents regarding its proposed action; the authority has special compulsory purchase powers, and special powers to carry out works in relation to property so acquired; the authority may spend money on environmental works (such as "enveloping"[87]) in the area, and recover a proportion of the expenditure from the Secretary of State; the authority can compel owners to provide standard amenities without the need for written requests from the tenants; and owners must notify the authority of certain disposals, of the service of notices to quit, and of the expiry of fixed-term tenancies.[88]

Declaration of a general improvement area is intended to encourage environmental development and improvement; the area must be predominantly residential, and the houses will generally be in better condition than those in housing action areas, with a greater proportion of owner-occupiers to tenants.[89] A general improvement area, like a housing action area, may be declared by an authority following a report from a "qualified person"; the authority must be satisfied that living conditions in the area can best be improved by the improvement of the amenities or the dwellings or both, and that such improvement ought to be effected or assisted by the authority.[90] Land in a clearance area or housing action

---

[84] See DoE Circular 13/75, para. 6.
[85] Housing Act 1985, s. 239.
[86] *Ibid.* ss. 239(5), 240(4), 241.
[87] *i.e.* a scheme whereby the authority improves the exteriors of houses in whole streets on a single contract and at no cost to the owners or tenants: DoE Circulars 29/82; 26/84.
[88] Housing Act 1985, ss. 210, 243–247.
[89] DoE Circular No. 13/75, para. 18.
[90] Housing Act 1985, s. 253(1).

area cannot be included.[91] Although a copy of the resolution must be sent to the Secretary of State, he has no power of veto.[92] A general improvement area has no maximum life span. The declaration has the following consequences: the authority must provide information to owners and residents; the authority may, for the purpose of furthering the objects of the general improvement area, carry out work on its own land or assist the carrying out of works on private land, acquire land by agreement or compulsorily, and recover a proportion of its relevant expenditure from the Secretary of State; and it can compel owners to provide standard amenities without the need for written requests from the tenants.[93]

The May 1985 Green Paper proposed a single type of improvement area, to be called a housing improvement area, designed for areas where "social and environmental problems exist side by side with poor housing"; declarations of the new areas would probably be subject to ministerial veto, and would be limited to periods of seven years.[94]

(4) Overcrowding and multiple occupation

There is a clear distinction in the legislation between the "overcrowd- **15-36** ing" provisions, which generally apply only to separate self-contained dwellings (which may themselves be part of a house), and the "multiple occupation" provisions, which apply to whole houses occupied by more than one household, whether or not the houses themselves are divided into separate dwellings; the same house may well be both overcrowded in its separate dwellings and in multiple occupation, but a house in multiple occupation will not necessarily be overcrowded in its separate dwellings (if any).

(a) *Overcrowding*

Authorities are under a duty, when occasion arises or the Secretary of State directs, to inspect their areas to discover overcrowding and to submit proposals to the Secretary of State for its abatement.[95] Only "dwellings," defined as premises used or suitable for use as a separate dwelling, can be overcrowded under these provisions[96]; in effect, for there to be a separate dwelling the occupiers must not share living accommodation with anyone else, but even a single room can satisfy this test. "Overcrowding" of such a "dwelling" arises if the statutory tests concerning either the sleeping arrangements or the "permitted numbers" of persons to rooms are infringed.[97] Both the owner and the occupier may commit an offence where they cause or permit overcrowding, and the

[91] Housing Act 1985, s. 253(2)–(3).
[92] *Ibid.* s. 254(4).
[93] *Ibid.* ss. 210, 254–257, 259.
[94] *Op.cit.*, at paras. 49–52.
[95] Housing Act 1985, s. 334.
[96] *Ibid.* ss. 324, 343.
[97] *Ibid.* ss. 324–326.

authority is under a duty to enforce these provisions.[98] However, the occupier may have a defence where (for example) the overcrowding arises through the "natural growth" of children and he applies to the authority for suitable alternative accommodation, or the authority gives a licence temporarily permitting the house to be overcrowded.[99] If the occupier is guilty of an overcrowding offence, he loses any Rent Act security,[1] and the authority itself can apply to the county court at the landlord's expense in order to obtain vacant possession for the landlord.[2] It is an offence for a landlord to omit prescribed information concerning overcrowding from a rent book.[3]

(b) *Multiple occupation*

15-37   Authorities must inspect their areas from time to time in order to determine what action to take relating to houses in multiple occupation.[4] A house in multiple occupation is one which is "occupied by persons who do not form a single household."[5] Thus even a single subletting can cause multiple occupation, though the mere taking of lodgers as "part of the family" would not normally do so; hostels will often constitute houses in multiple occupation, even if purpose-built.[6] In contrast to the overcrowding provisions, authorities normally have no duty to act in cases of multiple occupation; they do however have the following powers.

First, an authority may with the consent of the Secretary of State operate a registration scheme for houses in multiple occupation, and can attach "control provisions" preventing multiple occupation of an unregistered house or of a registered house where the number of households or occupiers exceeds the registered figure.[7] Under these "control provisions" the authority can refuse to register a house on stipulated grounds, or can require, as a condition of registration, that certain works are carried out. However, the "control provisions" cannot affect the continued occupation of a house by the number of households or persons occupying it when the provisions came into force, nor can they apply where there are only two households in the house, or no more than one household plus up to four individual persons.[8] Failure to comply with a registration scheme is an offence.[9]

---

[98] Housing Act 1985, ss. 327(1), 331(1), 339(1).
[99] *Ibid.* ss. 327–330.
[1] Rent Act 1977, s. 101; the position of the landlord here was discussed in *Zbytniewski* v. *Broughton* [1956] 2 Q.B. 673.
[2] Housing Act 1985, s. 338.
[3] *Ibid.* s. 332.
[4] *Ibid.* s. 605.
[5] *Ibid.* s. 345.
[6] *Simmons* v. *Pizzey* [1979] A.C. 37; *Silbers* v. *Southwark London Borough Council* (1977) 76 L.G.R. 421; *R.* v. *Camden London Borough Council, ex p. Rowton (Camden Town) Ltd.* (1983) 82 L.G.R. 614.
[7] Housing Act 1985, ss. 346–347(1).
[8] *Ibid.* ss. 347(3), 348(1).
[9] *Ibid.* ss. 346(6), 347(4).

Secondly, an authority may serve an "overcrowding notice" fixing the maximum number of persons who may occupy specified rooms in a house in multiple occupation (even though the house is not overcrowded in its separate dwelling units); contravention of the notice is an offence.[10] There is a separate power for the authority to make a direction fixing the maximum number of individuals or households who may occupy a house in multiple occupation which is defective in certain amenities and services having regard to the number of individuals or households living or likely to live there.[11] This direction does not affect the current occupiers, but merely prohibits any additional increase in numbers; again, contravention is an offence.

Thirdly, if an authority considers that a house in multiple occupation is in an unsatisfactory state because of failure to maintain proper management standards, it may make a "management order" directing the manager of the house to observe the prescribed "management code," which covers a wide range of requirements relating to the repair, maintenance and cleaning of common areas, responsibility for the installations for the supply of gas, electricity, lighting and heating for the common parts, means of escape from fire, etc; a management order is registrable as a local land charge; non-compliance is an offence, and the authority has powers to carry out works on the manager's default and at his expense.[12]

Fourthly, if an authority considers that a house in multiple occupation   **15-38** is defective with respect to certain amenities and services (such as lighting, ventilation, water supply, W.C.s and space heating) having regard to the number of individuals or households living there, then it may require the execution of works necessary to make the house suitable for such occupation.[13] Further, and quite separately, the authority may (and, as regards classes of houses in multiple occupation prescribed by the Secretary of State, *must*[14]) require the execution of any works to provide necessary means of escape from fire, and if there would be adequate means of escape if part of the house were not used for human habitation, the authority may secure that that part is not so used (by making a closing order or accepting the owner's undertaking as to non-user for habitation).[15] Again, non-compliance with any of these notices

[10] Housing Act 1985, ss. 358–364.
[11] *Ibid.* ss. 354–357.
[12] *Ibid.* ss. 369–373, 375–376; Housing (Management of Houses in Multiple Occupation) Regulations 1962 (S.I. 1962 No. 668).
[13] *Ibid.* s. 352.
[14] *Ibid.* ss. 365–368; the Secretary of State has made these provisions *mandatory* in the case of houses of at least three storeys (excluding basements) where the combined floor area (including staircases and basements) exceeds 500 square metres: Housing (Means of Escape from Fire in Houses in Multiple Occupation) Order 1981 (S.I. 1981 No. 1576). There is no "reasonable expense" qualification regarding the use by an authority of these fire escape provisions.
[15] *Ibid.*

requiring works is an offence, and the authority can carry out the work on the owner's default at his expense.[16]

Finally, where living conditions in a house in multiple occupation are so bad that immediate action is necessary to protect the safety, welfare or health of the residents, the authority may make a "control order" allowing it to act as manager of the house.[17] The order is registrable as a local land charge. Once the order is in force, the authority must take all steps immediately necessary to protect the occupants, including any action which would have been needed to obey any "management code" order, and may grant short leases or licences. Although the house is not regarded as part of the authority's own housing stock, new leases or licences created by the authority may well be "secure," and existing residents at the time when the order came into force will retain any security which they enjoyed under the Rent Act 1977.[18]

---

[16] Housing Act 1985, ss. 375–376.
[17] *Ibid.* ss. 379–394.
[18] *Ibid.*

CHAPTER 16

PUBLIC HEALTH

THE Public Health Acts of 1875 and onwards have dealt with a wide **16–01** variety of subjects not strictly related to public health, so that the term as used in local government law has acquired an extended meaning. In this chapter it is considered in the narrower sense of environmental hygiene and kindred matters. The law is found principally in the Public Health Act 1936. The Public Health Act 1961, the Clear Air Acts of 1956 and 1968 and the Control of Pollution Act 1974[1] conferred a number of additional public health powers on local authorities and strengthened or enlarged others. The Public Health (Control of Disease) Act 1984 consolidated enactments relating to the control of disease and the establishment and functions of port health authorities. The Building Act 1984 consolidated enactments relating to building control and building regulations, including Part II and most of Part III of the Housing and Building Control Act 1984, which had materially amended the previous law. The Water Act 1973 transferred to the newly constituted water authorities a number of functions exercised before April 1, 1974, by local authorities—these are noted in the appropriate places.

The subject is considered under the following headings: administering authorities; sanitation, buildings and sites; nuisances and offensive trades; air pollution; refuse collection; noise. A number of miscellaneous powers and duties are mentioned in the final paragraphs.

A. ADMINISTERING AUTHORITIES

Most public health functions fall to district councils, London borough **16–02** councils, the Common Council and the Under Treasurers of the Temples.[2] Certain functions (more particularly refuse disposal) are the responsibility of non-metropolitan county councils,[3] and a few may be discharged by parish and community councils—these are listed in Appendix II. Some functions traditionally regarded as public health functions are now undertaken by water authorities.

Public health functions may also be undertaken by joint boards and **16–03**

---

[1] This Act is being brought into force in stages. It is treated in the text as being in force, with footnotes to indicate where this is not the case at the time of going to press.
[2] Local Government Act 1972, s. 180 and Sched. 14; Building Act 1984, s. 126: definition of "local authority" substituted by the Local Government Act 1985, Sched. 8, para. 14(4)(*a*). These authorities are referred to as local authorities in this Chapter.
[3] *Ibid.* Sched. 14, para. 5, as amended by the Local Government Act 1985, Sched. 6, para. 2. See § 16–45.

port health authorities.[4] The Secretary of State for Social Services may by order constitute a union of districts to be administered for public health purposes by a joint board. The initiative must come from one or more authorities and unless all the authorities agree an order of the Secretary of State is subject to special parliamentary procedure. In general, whatever functions are conferred by the order on the joint board cease to be the responsibility of the constituent authorities.

16-04   The Secretary of State may by order constitute for the area of a customs port a port health authority. The order will constitute as this authority a local authority forming part of the port or adjoining it or a joint board consisting of representatives of more than one such authority.

Joint boards and port health authorities are bodies corporate with perpetual succession and a common seal, financed by way of precept issued on constituent authorities.

16-05   Exchequer grants are available towards the cost of schemes for the sewerage or the disposal of sewage in rural localities. These grants are payable under the Rural Water Supplies and Sewerage Acts 1944 to 1971.

16-06   A local authority cannot lawfully exercise its powers in relation to health and sanitation for purposes not connected with health and sanitation.

> *Pilling* v. *Abergele Urban District Council*.[5] The council refused to grant a licence under section 269 of the Public Health Act 1936 for the use of certain land as a site for movable dwellings on the ground that the use of the land in this way would be detrimental to the amenities of the neighbourhood. The justices confirmed this decision. *Held*, the council was wrong in taking town planning considerations into account in deciding whether or not to grant a licence. Where a provision relates to health and sanitation the council in exercising its discretion must have regard to these matters only.

16-07   If the appropriate Secretary of State is satisfied that any council, port health authority or joint board has failed to discharge its functions he may make an order declaring it to be in default and direct it to put matters right. He may enforce his order by mandamus or alternatively transfer the functions to himself, the defaulting authority bearing the cost of the work carried out on its behalf.[6]

---

[4] Public Health Act 1936, ss. 6, 7, 9, 10; Public Health (Control of Disease) Act 1984, ss. 2–8.
[5] [1950] 1 K.B. 636. See also *Chertsey Urban District Council* v. *Mixnam's Properties Ltd.* [1965] A.C. 735, § 16–61, *post.*
[6] Public Health Act 1936, s. 322 (as amended by the Local Government (Miscellaneous Provisions) Act 1976, Sched. 2) and ss. 324 and 325; Public Health (Control of Disease) Act 1984, s. 71.

B. Sanitation, Buildings and Sites[7]

(1) Sewers and drains and sewage disposal
Division of responsibility

In broad terms responsibility for the provision and maintenance of **16-08** public sewers and for sewage disposal falls to water authorities; the provision and maintenance of private sewers are matters of private concern and private persons have certain rights in relation to water authorities; local authorities are concerned, through the administration of the building regulations and in other ways, for the adequacy of drainage arrangements. These matters are considered in the following paragraphs, together with a note of the statutory requirements upon district councils to discharge certain functions of water authorities as their agents.

Sewers and drains

These terms are defined in the Public Health Act 1936[8]—"drain" means a drain used for the drainage of *one* building or of buildings or yards of buildings within the same curtilage; the term "sewer" does not include a drain as thus defined but otherwise includes "all sewers and drains used for the drainage of buildings and yards of buildings."[9] Drains are always a private responsibility; responsibility for sewers depends on whether they are public or private. Public sewers are defined in section 20 of the Public Health Act 1936 (as originally enacted) in somewhat complex terms by reference to the Public Health Act 1875 and other legislation, but broadly speaking sewers are public if constructed:

(i)   before October 1, 1937, except those constructed for profit (*i.e.* for some benefit apart from the taking away of sewage or other fluids) or as a land drain;

(ii) by the local authority (or acquired by them) and not draining only property belonging to the authority;

(iii) under a private street works procedure to the satisfaction of the authority; or

(iv) after October 1, 1937, and "adopted" under a declaration to that effect.

A new section 20 was substituted by the Water Act 1973.[10] By virtue of this new provision the following are public sewers

(i)   Sewers constructed by a water authority at its expense or vested in the authority in pursuance of arrangements under section 15 of the Water Act 1973 (see para. 16–14, *post*), or otherwise acquired by the authority;

---

[7] Public Health Act 1936, Part II; Public Health Act 1961, Part II; Water Act 1973, ss. 14–16; Control of Pollution Act 1974, Parts I and II; Building Act 1984. Provisions as to sewers and drains are still to be found in the 1936 and 1961 Acts, provisions as to building control in the 1984 Act.

[8] s. 343.

[9] See *Weaver* v. *Family Housing Association (York)* (1975) 74 L.G.R. 255, and *Cook* v. *Minion* (1979) 37 P. & C.R. 58.

[10] Sched. 8, para. 33.

(ii) Sewers constructed under Part XI of the Highway Act 1980, except sewers belonging to a road maintained by a highway authority;

(iii) Sewers and sewage draining works vested in the authority by a vesting declaration.

Sewers which are not public sewers falling within the categories above are private sewers.

Maintenance of sewers

16-09   The distinction between public and private sewers is of particular importance in the matter of maintenance. A duty is placed on all water authorities to maintain, cleanse and empty public sewers vested in them.[11] This duty relates to all public sewers, but in the following circumstances the cost of maintenance (defined for this purpose as repair, renewal and improvement) of a particular length of public sewer may be recovered from the owners of the lands through which that length of sewer passes[12]:

(1) where the sewer is one which prior to 1937 was repairable by persons other than the local authority under earlier legislation (particularly the Public Health Acts Amendment Act 1890, which enabled an authority to claim the cost of repairing what were called "single private drains," *i.e.* pipes laid in private land connecting two or more houses in separate ownership to a public sewer); or

(2) where the sewer lies in a garden, court or yard, or a private street used mainly as a means of access to the premises in it, and was not constructed by the authority.

Where several owners are involved the authority may apportion the costs, taking into account such matters as the benefit derived by the various owners and the responsibility for the act which made the work essential.

Provision of public sewers

16-10   A water authority is under a general duty to provide such public sewers as may be necessary for the effectual draining of its area.[13] In certain circumstances an authority may obtain from frontagers a contribution towards the cost of constructing a public sewer.[14] If an authority performs its duty negligently or improperly an action for damages may lie.[15]

16-11   Water authorities are under an obligation to discharge their functions under these provisions so as "not to create a nuisance."[16] These words were considered in the following case.

[11] Public Health Act 1936, s. 23; Water Act 1973, s. 14.
[12] Public Health Act 1936, s. 24, as amended by s. 15 of the Public Health Act 1961; Water Act 1973, s. 14.
[13] Water Act 1973, s. 14. This duty is qualified by s. 16(14) (*ibid.*).
[14] Public Health Act 1961, ss. 12–14; Water Act 1973, s. 14.
[15] *Fleming* v. *Manchester Corporation* (1881) 47 L.T. 517; *Dent* v. *Bournemouth Corporation* (1897) 66 L.J.Q.B. 395. For failure to perform statutory duty, see §§ 10–26 to 10–30.
[16] Public Health Act 1936, s. 31; Water Act 1973, s. 14.

Smeaton v. *Ilford Corporation.*[17] Because a sewer was overloaded sewage erupted from a manhole causing the plaintiff and his family grave inconvenience. There had been development in the area and owners of premises had exercised their right to connect with the sewerage system. The plaintiff brought an action founded on nuisance. *Held*, the defendants were not *"creating* a nuisance"; the section excluded liability for escapes in the absence of negligence.

The judgment in the *Ilford* case lays stress on the positive content of the words "creating a nuisance." The plaintiff might well have succeeded if the discharge of sewage onto his land was the result of active steps taken by the authority to deal with it.

A water authority is empowered to construct public sewers in streets, **16-12** after giving such notice as may be required under the Public Utilities Street Works Act 1950,[18] and through private land after giving reasonable notice to the owner and occupier.[19] Where a sewer is to run through private land compensation may be payable, assessed with reference to the Land Compensation Act 1961.[20] A water authority may also construct sewers outside its area.[21] If a private developer proposes to construct a drain or sewer he may be required by the authority to construct it so as to form part of a general system of drainage, any additional cost being met by the water authority.[22]

Rights of owners and occupiers

An owner or occupier is entitled to have his drains or sewers (except **16-13** where they contain trade effluent) drained into public sewers on giving notice to the water authority and he may be refused permission only if the mode of construction or the condition of the pipe would detrimentally affect the sewerage system. The owner himself may make the connection or the authority may elect to do it at his expense.[23]

Owners and occupiers may require the water authority to provide a public sewer for domestic purposes provided that certain conditions are satisfied. These conditions relate to the securing by the water authority that reasonable charges or any relevant deficit will be met by the persons requiring the sewer or sewer extension. If the water authority fails to provide a public sewer within six months (or a longer period which may be agreed) a penalty may be enforced against the authority unless it can show that the failure was due to unavoidable accident or other

---

[17] [1954] Ch. 450.
[18] See § 14–43.
[19] Public Health Act 1936, s. 15; Water Act 1973, s. 14. See hereon *Hutton* v. *Esher Urban District Council* [1974] Ch. 167.
[20] *Thurrock Grays and Tilbury Joint Sewerage Board* v. *Thames Land Co. Ltd.* (1925) 23 L.G.R. 648.
[21] Water Act 1973, s. 14.
[22] Public Health Act 1936, s. 19; Water Act 1973, s. 14.
[23] Public Health Act 1936, ss. 34 and 36; Water Act 1973, s. 14.

unavoidable cause.[24] Disputes as to the expense of providing a sewer, or as to the period within which it is to be laid, are determined by a referee.

Agency arrangements

16-14   It is the duty of every water authority and of every "relevant authority" whose area is wholly or partly in the area of the water authority to endeavour to make arrangements for the relevant authority to discharge in their area the water authority's sewerage functions, *i.e.* the authorities' functions under Part II of the Public Health Act 1936, other than those relating to sewage disposal.[25] The "relevant authority" means the council of a district or London borough or the Common Council of the City of London, or, in certain circumstances, a new town development corporation, the Development Board for Rural Wales or an urban development corporation. The arrangements must be made with a view to ensuring that the sewerage functions, taken as a whole, are carried out efficiently and must comply with any regulations made by the Secretary of State. The duty to make agency arrangements does not apply: (1) where the water authority and relevant authority concerned agree that it would be inexpedient: (2) where such arrangements have been ended within the past five years and either authority concerned regard it as inexpedient for them to be resumed; or (3) any relevant authority requesting the making of arrangments have had a similar request refused by the water authority within the previous five years, and the water authority regard such arrangements as inexpedient. Apart from these situations, a water authority may refuse a request by a relevant authority for such arrangements to be made where they are of the opinion that it would be inexpedient to do so, but the relevant authority may apply to the Secretary of State for the decision to be reviewed.

The regulations made by the Secretary of State[26] provide that where agency arrangements are made they must:

(1)   require the water authority to consult the relevant authority in formulating policies or proposals which significantly affect the latter's role and to have regard to any views expressed;

(2)   enable the water authority to set, and from time to time revise, limits to the costs and expenses to be incurred by the relevant authority, and require the relevant authority to ensure that such limits are not exceeded without the water authority's consent;

(3)   require the relevant authority to comply with all reasonable instructions or guidance given by the water authority;

---

[24] Water Act 1973, s. 16, as amended by the Local Government, Planning and Land Act 1980, ss. 105, 158. See *William Leech (Midlands) Limited* v. *Severn Trent Water Authority* (1981) 80 L.G.R. 102.

[25] *Ibid.* s. 15 and Sched. 4A, respectively as substituted and inserted by the Water Act 1983, s. 6 and Sched. 3.

[26] The Water (Sewerage Arrangements) Regulations 1984 (S.I. 1984 No. 1788).

(4) require that where the water authority have approved a capital works programme to be carried out by the relevant authority, that programme must be carried out within such time and in such manner as may be reasonably required by the water authority;

(5) require the relevant authority to comply with reasonable requests for a duly authorised officer of the water authority to be given information or access for inspection;

(6) require the water authority to reimburse the relevant authority in respect of costs and expenses reasonably incurred, other than those incurred in excess of any prescribed limit without consent;

(7) enable the water authority to refuse to reimburse the expenses incurred by the relevant authority in respect of the design and execution of capital works by persons regarded by the water authority as lacking the necessary skill, experience and resources.

The agency can be varied or ended at any time by agreement between the parties or in default of agreement on the application of either to the Secretary of State.

Independently of any agency agreement the water authority is obliged to consult the local authority before constructing, diverting or closing a public sewer and it is obliged in due course to inform the authority what has been done. This, amongst other things, enables the local authority to discharge its duty of keeping a map of public sewers.[27] Conversely, local authorities are required to notify the water authority of any proposal of which they themselves are notified for the erection or extension of a building over a public sewer.[28] The water authority may give directions to the local authority about the exercise of the latter's function with respect to consent to erection or extension of building over sewers.[29]

Sewage disposal

Every water authority is under an obligation to deal effectually with **16-15** the contents of its sewers by means of sewage disposal works or otherwise.[30] Broadly speaking, the rules as to the negligent or improper use of powers and the avoidance of nuisance apply to sewage disposal as to the construction and maintenance of sewers.

A local authority must not construct or use any sewer or drain for the purpose of conveying foul water into any natural or artificial stream, watercourse, canal, pond or lake until the water has been so treated as not to affect prejudicially the purity and quality of the water in that stream

---

[27] Public Health Act 1936, s. 32. In London, the duty under s. 32 falls on London borough councils and the Common Council: Water Act 1973, Sched 8, para. 36 (1) (2), as amended by the Building Act 1984, Sched. 7.

[28] Building Act 1984, s. 18(2). As to Inner London, see *ibid*, Sched 3.

[29] *Ibid.* s. 18(3). See n. 28.

[30] Water Act 1973, s. 14.

(etc).[31] This obligation may be enforced by an injunction.[32] There are also several criminal offences prohibiting, *inter alia*, the pollution of and discharge of sewage effluent into rivers and coastal waters.[33]

An authority which causes pollution may, of course, be liable in civil proceedings for damages at the instance of an injured party or it may be restrained at the instance of the Attorney-General or an injured party from committing or continuing to commit a wrongful act.[34]

Defective drainage

16–16   Where plans are submitted under building regulations the local authority must reject them unless adequate provision is made for drainage (or the authority is satisfied that the requirement can be dispensed with), but the authority cannot require that a drain be connected to a public sewer unless the sewer is within one hundred feet of the site of the building (unless it pays the extra cost) and the land between is land through which the developer is entitled to take a drain.[35]

If an existing building has no satisfactory drainage system, or if a drain or private sewer is insufficient or defective or prejudicial to health or a nuisance, the local authority may require the owner or occupier to carry out remedial works, but the authority cannot require a connection to a public sewer which is more than a hundred feet away unless it pays the extra cost involved.[36]

Section 17 of the Public Health Act 1961[37] provides a quick procedure to deal with stopped-up drains and the like. If it appears to a local authority that a drain, private sewer, water-closet, waste-pipe or soil pipe is not sufficiently maintained and kept in good repair, and can be sufficiently repaired at a cost not exceeding £250, they may, after giving not less than seven days' notice, cause it to be repaired, and recover the expenses from the persons concerned. If it appears that a drain, etc., is stopped-up they may by notice in writing require the owner or occupier of the premises to remedy the defect within 48 hours: if the notice is not complied with, the authority may carry out the necessary work and recover the expenses reasonably incurred from the person concerned. In either situation, where the expenses do not exceed £10, the local authority may remit the charge. In proceedings to recover expenses, the court may determine (1) whether the authority were justified in concluding that the drain was not sufficiently maintained and kept in good repair and whether any apportionment of expenses by the authority was fair and (2) whether any requirement contained in a notice in relation to stopped-up

---

[31] Public Health Act 1936, s. 30.
[32] See, *e.g. Att.-Gen.* v. *Ringwood Rural District Council* (1928) 92 J.P. 65.
[33] Control of Pollution Act 1974, ss. 31 and 32. See §§ 23–07—23–09.
[34] *Pride of Derby and Derbyshire Angling Association* v. *British Celanese Ltd.* [1953] Ch. 149.
[35] Building Act 1984, s.21. And see *Chesterton R.D.C.* v. *Thompson* [1947] K.B. 300.
[36] Building Act 1984, s. 59. See also ss. 59–63 for further provisions concerning drains.
[37] As substituted by the Local Government (Miscellaneous Provisions) Act 1982, s. 27.

drains, etc., was reasonable and whether the expenses ought to be borne wholly or in some part by some other person.

Section 17 of the 1961 Act is complemented by section 35 of the Local Government (Miscellaneous Provisions) Act 1976, under which a notice may be served on the owner or occupier of premises *served by* a sewer which is obstructed, requiring the obstruction to be removed within the period specified (not earlier than 48 hours after service of the notice). In default of compliance, the authority may remove the obstruction and recover reasonable expenses from the persons originally served in such proportions as the authority may determine having regard to the cause of the obstruction and any obligations arising from agreements between them.

A local authority may, on the application of the owner or occupier of any premises, undertake the cleansing or repair of any drains, water closets, sinks or gullies, and may make a reasonable charge for doing so.[38]

(2) Trade effluent

The Public Health (Drainage of Trade Premises) Act 1937, as amended **16–17** by the Public Health Act 1961,[39] and further modified by the Control of Pollution Act 1974,[40] contains special rules as to the discharge into public sewers of "trade effluent," which is defined as liquid, with or without particles of matter in suspension (excluding domestic sewage), produced in the course of any trade or industry or from farms, horticultural establishments and premises used for scientific research.[41] In certain circumstances trade effluent could formerly be discharged into the sewers as of right; in all others the authority's consent was required. Discharge was of right where an effluent of the same nature and composition was discharged immediately before the Act of 1937 came into force. But these privileged discharges were brought under control by the Public Health Act 1961,[42] and this control is extended by the Control of Pollution Act 1974. Discharges authorised by the first mentioned Acts now cease to be authorised and the consent of the water authority is required, except where deemed consent has been obtained. Deemed consent exists where an appropriate notice was served in accordance with section 43 of the Control of Pollution Act 1974. This deemed consent may be cancelled by notice and actual consent given, either unconditionally or subject to

---

[38] Public Health Act 1961, s. 22.

[39] ss. 55–70 and Water Act 1973, s. 14.

[40] ss. 43–45 and 52. ss. 45 and 52 were not in force at the time of going to press. See also the Control of Pollution (Discharges into Sewers) Regulations 1976 (S.I. 1976 No. 958).

[41] Public Health (Drainage of Trade Premises) Act 1937, s. 14, extended by the Public Health Act 1961, s. 63. See *Thames Water Authority* v. *Blue and White Launderettes Limited* [1980] 1 W.L.R. 700 (discharge from a launderette is a trade effluent). There is a power, not as yet exercised, for the 1937 Act to be applied to other liquid or matter discharged into public sewers: Public Health Act 1961, s. 64.

[42] ss. 55–57.

conditions which may be varied from time to time. These conditions may deal with terms of payment as well as technical matters.[43]

Where it is proposed to make a discharge, a notice called a trade effluent notice, stating the nature and composition of the effluent and the proposed rate of discharge, must be served on the authority. The authority may direct that no effluent shall be discharged until a specified date, and consent may be given unconditionally, or subject to conditions. These conditions may deal with terms of payment as well as technical matters.[44] They may be varied by the water authority by direction under section 60 of the Public Health Act 1961, although no such direction can be made within two years from the date of the consent or a previous direction, except where the owner of the trade premises agrees.[45] An earlier variation may, however, be made where the water authority considers it necessary to do so in order to provide proper protection for persons likely to be affected by discharges which would otherwise be lawful. Compensation is payable unless the direction is required in consequence of an unforeseeable change of circumstances.

16–18 There is a general right of appeal to the Secretary of State against an authority's decision, and it is open to him to state a case for the opinion of the High Court on any matter of law, and he may be required to do so by the court.[46]

(3) Sanitary accommodation

16–19 New buildings must be provided with sufficient sanitary conveniences.[47] Where existing buildings have insufficient or defective accommodation the authority may serve a notice on the owner requiring him to carry out remedial works.[48] Where a sufficient water supply and a sewer are available the authority may require the installation of water closets in place of other types of closets even though those closets are neither insufficient nor defective, but where this is done the cost involved is shared equally between the authority and the owner.[49] If a drain or other sanitary apparatus is believed by the authority to be defective, it may excavate for testing purposes, reinstating the land and making good any damage if the apparatus is in order.[50]

---

[43] Control of Pollution Act 1974, s. 44.
[44] Public Health (Drainage of Trade Premises) Act 1937, s. 2, as modified by the Public Health Act 1961, ss. 55–57, 59.
[45] Control of Pollution Act 1974, s. 45 (in force from a day to be appointed).
[46] Public Health (Drainage of Trade Premises) Act 1937, s. 3, as modified by the Public Health Act 1961, ss. 61 and 66.
[47] Building Regulations 1985 (S.I. 1985 No. 1065) Sched. 1, para. G4.
[48] Public Health Act 1936, s. 45; Building Act 1984, s. 64.
[49] Building Act 1984, s. 66.
[50] Public Health Act 1936, s 48, as amended by the Water Act 1973, Sched. 8.

(4) Buildings and sites
Building regulations
The Public Health Act 1936 (replacing a provision in the Public Health **16-20** Act 1875) enabled local authorities to make by-laws with respect to buildings (as to construction and materials, ventilation and the like). These by-laws were superseded by regulations made under the Public Health Act 1961 by the Secretary of State for the Environment, covering broadly the same field. The scope and coverage of building regulations was extended by the Health and Safety at Work, etc., Act 1974, Part III. The legislation on this topic has been consolidated in Part I of the Building Act 1984.[51] It is the duty of district and London borough councils, the Common Council of the City of London, the Sub-Treasurer of the Inner Temple and the Under Treasurer of the Middle Temple to carry the Act into execution, and, subject to Part II of the Act[52] it is the function of these authorities to enforce building regulations.[53]

Building regulations are made by the Secretary of State under section 1 of the Building Act 1984. The matters which they may cover are set out in Schedule 1 to the Act, and they may impose continuing requirements.[54] The regulations may exempt particular classes of buildings,[55] and State school-premises and buildings belonging to statutory undertakers are also generally exempt.[56] The regulations may exempt public bodies from procedural, but not substantive requirements.[57]

The Building Regulations 1985[58] differ from the 1976 Regulations by imposing less detailed control. Matters formerly covered in the regulations are now the subject of guidance contained in documents issued or approved by the Secretary of State or a body designated by him.[59] Failure to comply with an approved document does not of itself give rise to civil or criminal liability, but can be relied upon in evidence as tending to establish liability for a breach of a building regulation.[60]

The regulations apply to "building work"[61] and where there is a

---

[51] The whole of Part I came into force on December 1, 1984, apart from sections 12, 13, 38, 42(4) to (6) and 43(3) (except so far as they enable regulations to be made) and sections 20, 33, 42(1) to (3), 43(1) and (2), 44 and 45.

[52] Below, § 16-25.

[53] Building Act 1984, ss. 91 and 126 (definition of "local authority" substituted by the Local Government Act 1985, Sched. 7, para. 14(4)).

[54] *Ibid.* s. 2.

[55] *Ibid.* s. 3. See Sched. 3 to the Building Regulations 1985. The exempt buildings are those specified in n. 62 below, with the addition of certain kinds of small extension.

[56] *Ibid.* s. 4.

[57] *Ibid.* s. 5.

[58] S.I. 1985 No. 1065. These are operative from November 11, 1985. Provision is made for the charging of fees by local authorities: see the Building (Prescribed Fees, etc.) Regulations 1985 (S.I. 1985 No. 1576).

[59] Building Act 1984, s. 6.

[60] *Ibid.* s. 7. A set of approved documents was published by HMSO in August 1985.

[61] As defined by the Building Regulations 1985 (S.I. 1985 No. 1065), reg. 3. The definition includes the erection or extension of a building or the material alteration of a building such as by the insertion of cavity wall insulation or by underpinning.

"material change of use"[62] of a building. Building work must conform to any relevant requirements contained in Schedules 1 and 2 to the Regulations. Schedule 1 imposes requirements as to structure, fire precautions, site preparation and resistance to moisture, toxic substances, sound insulation, ventilation, hygiene, drainage and waste disposal, heat producing appliances, stairways, ramps and guards, and conservation of fuel and power. Schedule 2 imposes requirements as to facilities for disabled persons in offices and shops, and single storey buildings used as factories, schools and buildings to which the public are admitted. Where there is a material change of use, certain specified requirements of Schedule 1 apply.[63] Any building work must be carried out with proper materials and in a workmanlike manner.[64] No obligation arising under Schedule 1 (apart from those concerning conservation of fuel and power) and Regulation 7 shall require anything to be done beyond what is necessary to secure reasonable standards of health and safety.[65]

The Building Act 1984 enables a person who intends to carry out building work or make a material change of use (hereinafter referred to as a "builder") to elect whether the work is to be supervised (1) by the local authority or (2) by an "approved inspector" under Part II to the Act.

Supervision of work by the local authority

16-21 Where work is to be supervised by the local authority, the builder must either (1) give the authority a "building notice" or (2) deposit "full plans" with the authority.[66] The latter course must be adopted in certain cases where the building is to be put to a use designated under section 1 of the Fire Precautions Act 1971.[67]

A building notice must contain, *inter alia*, a description of the proposed work or change of use and particulars of the location of the relevant building and its use or intended use. In the case of the erection or extension of a building, the notice must be accompanied by a plan showing the size and position of the building and its relationship to adjoining boundaries, the boundaries of the curtilage, the position and use of any other building within the curtilage and the width and position of any streets on or within the boundaries of the curtilage, a statement of the number of storeys in the relevant building, and certain other particulars. There are also specific requirements where the work involves the insertion of insulating material into cavity walls or the provision of a

---

[62] As defined by the Building Regulations 1985, reg. 5. The definition includes change *to* use as a dwelling, hotel, institution or public building, the provision of a flat, and change *from* use as a building described in Sched. 3 to the Regulations (buildings controlled under other legislation, buildings not frequented by people, greenhouses and agricultural buildings, temporary buildings and mobile homes, ancillary buildings, small detached buildings).

[63] *Ibid.* reg. 6.

[64] *Ibid.* reg. 7.

[65] *Ibid.* reg. 8.

[66] *Ibid.* reg. 11(1). There is an exception for gas appliances installed by or under the supervision of the British Gas Corporation: reg. 11(3).

[67] *Ibid.* reg. 11(2) and see § 21–20.

hot water storage system. The local authority may require additional plans to be supplied. Neither a building notice nor accompanying plans are to be treated as having been deposited in accordance with building regulations.[68]

Full plans consist of all the information required in respect of a building notice and such other plans, if any, as are necessary to show that any work to be carried out complies with the building regulations, apart from those concerning heating systems.[69] As these plans are deposited in accordance with building regulations they are subject to passing or rejection by the local authority under section 16 of the Building Act 1984. Where they conform with the regulations and are not defective, the authority has no alternative but to approve them. If, however, the plans are defective or show that the proposed work would contravene any of the building regulations, the authority may either (1) reject the plans or (2) pass them subject to either or both of two conditions. The first condition is that such modifications as the local authority may specify shall be made in the deposited plans and the second is that such further plans as they may specify shall be deposited. Plans may, however, only be passed subject to conditions on the written request or with the written consent of the applicant. The authority may not reject plans for non-compliance with requirements as to structure or resistance to the passage of heat[70] if the deposited plans are accompanied by a certificate from an "approved person" that the proposed work will comply with those requirements, and a scheme of insurance approved by the Secretary of State applies to the certificate.[71]

There are, in addition, certain provisions specifically requiring the rejection of plans—they must be disapproved[72]:

(1) if it is proposed to erect a building over a sewer, unless the authority considers that consent can properly be given[73];

(2) unless satisfactory provision is made for drainage[74] and for a sufficient water supply[75];

(3) in the case of public buildings, where satisfactory means of ingress and egress are not available[76]; and

---

[68] Building Regulations 1985, reg. 12.
[69] *Ibid.* reg. 13.
[70] *Ibid.* Sched. 1, Part A and paras. L2 and L3.
[71] Building Act 1984, s. 16(9); the Building (Approved Inspectors etc.) Regulations 1985 (S.I. 1985 No. 1066), reg. 27. "Approved persons" are persons approved under *ibid.* regs. 3–7: see reg. 27(1).
[72] Provisions in the Building Act 1984 which specifically required or authorised the rejection of plans if there was inadequate provision of facilities for refuse (s. 23(1), (2)), closets (s. 26) bathrooms (s. 27) or food storage (s. 28) or where the site contained offensive materials (s. 29) were repealed by the Building Regulations 1985 (S.I. 1985 No. 1065) reg. 18. Requirements on these points (apart from the first and last) are now found in Sched. 1 to the Regulations, paras. G4, G2 and G1, respectively.
[73] Building Act 1984, s. 18.
[74] *Ibid.* s. 21.
[75] *Ibid.* s. 25.
[76] *Ibid.* s. 24.

(4) in the case of plans for buildings other than residences, shops and offices, unless the authority is satisfied that the height of the chimneys is adequate.[77]

16–22   An authority is empowered to declare the deposit of plans of no effect if the developer does not proceed within three years of deposit.[78]

If plans show that it is proposed to construct a building of materials which are short-lived it is open to the authority to fix a period at the end of which the building must be removed (unless an extension of time is given) and the authority may impose conditions which are relevant to the use of these materials (*e.g.* a condition to be imposed as to regular painting).[79] The materials to which this provision applies may be specified in the building regulations.

16–23   Notice of an authority's decision must be given within five weeks or such extended period (not exceeding two months) as may be agreed in writing.[80] If a question arises between a local authority and any person who proposes to carry out any work (1) whether plans of the proposed work are in conformity with building regulations or (2) whether the authority is prohibited from rejecting plans by virtue of a certificate of compliance under section 16(9) of the 1984 Act, that person may refer the question to the Secretary of State for his determination.[81] There is a right of appeal against the Secretary of State's decision to the High Court on a point of law and it is open to him in dealing with the issue to state a case for the opinion of the High Court on any question of law.[82]

16–24   Where work is to be supervised by the local authority, the builder must give the authority:

(1) not less than 48 hours notice before the commencement of operations;

(2) not less than 24 hours notice
    (a) before the covering up of any excavation for a foundation, any foundation, any damp-proof course or any concrete or other material laid over a site; and
    (b) before the haunching or covering up in any way of any drain or private sewer subject to the regulations;

(3) notice not more than seven days after such a drain or sewer has been laid;

(4) if a building or part of a building is occupied before completion, notice not less than seven days before occupation; and

(5) notice not more than seven days after completion of the work.

---

[77] s. 10 of the Clean Air Act 1956. See § 16–41, *post.*
[78] Building Act 1984, s. 32.
[79] *Ibid.* s. 20. This section is to come into force from a day to be appointed. Until such time reference should be made to *ibid.* s. 19.
[80] *Ibid.* s. 16(6), (12).
[81] *Ibid.* s. 16(10). A fee is payable: see the Building (Prescribed Fees, etc.) Regulations 1985 (S.I. 1985 No. 1576), reg. 18 and Sched. 4, paras. 1, 2.
[82] *Ibid.* s. 42.

Notice must be given in writing or in such other manner as is agreed between the builder and the authority. If the builder fails to give notice as required by (1)–(3), the local authority may by notice in writing require him within a reasonable time to cut into, lay open or pull down so much of the work as prevents the authority from ascertaining whether any of the regulations has been breached. If the authority give notice in writing specifying the manner in which any work contravenes the regulations, the builder must within a reasonable time of the completion of further work to secure compliance give notice in writing of its completion to the authority.[83]

The local authority may make such tests of any drain or private sewer and may take such samples of the material to be used in building work as may be necessary to establish whether they comply with the relevant requirements of the regulations.[84] In addition, there are general powers whereby the authority may require to be made or may carry out reasonable tests to ascertain whether work conforms or will conform to the regulations.[85] Where a person is required to carry out tests, that person must bear the expenses, unless the local authority agree to bear part or all of them. Disputes as to the reasonableness of a test or an authority's refusal to bear them are to be determined by a magistrates' court.[86]

Supervision of building work other than by local authorities
Under Part II of the Building Act 1984 an approved inspector may, at **16-25** the option of a person intending to carry out building work, supervise the work instead of the local authority. An "approved inspector" is a person approved under the building regulations by the Secretary of State or a body designated by him.[87] Approval may be limited to certain kinds of work. The approved inspector may act instead of the authority if "initial notice" is given to and accepted by the authority.[88] The notice must be given jointly by the developer and the approved inspector, and must be accompanied by such plans as are prescribed by building regulations[89] and a declaration signed by the insurer that an approved insurance scheme applies. The authority may not reject the notice except on prescribed grounds, but must do so if such grounds exist.[90] They may also impose requirements of a like kind to those which they may impose as a

[83] Building Regulations 1985 (S.I. 1985 No. 1065), reg. 14.
[84] *Ibid.* regs. 15, 16.
[85] Building Act 1984, s. 33. In force from a day to be appointed.
[86] *Ibid.*
[87] Building Act, 1984, s. 49. See the Building (Approved Inspectors) etc.) Regulations 1985 (S.I. 1985 No. 1066), regs. 3–7. References in the following footnotes are to this Act and these regulations, respectively, unless otherwise stated.
[88] s. 47.
[89] See reg. 8(1) and (2) and Sched. 2, forms 1 and 2.
[90] See reg. 8(3) and Sched. 3. The grounds include (1) deficiencies in the initial notice or the information supplied, (2) the lack of any necessary declaration or undertaking, and (3) deficiencies in the proposed work concerning drainage and building over sewers corresponding to the authority's power to reject plans under ss. 18 or 21(4) of the 1984 Act: see § 16–21 *ante*.

condition of passing plans. A notice not rejected within ten days is deemed to have been accepted.[91] So long as the notice is in force, the authority may not exercise their enforcement powers.[92]

The approved inspector must have no professional or financial interest in the work he supervises unless it is minor work.[93] He is required[94] to take such steps as are reasonable to enable him to be satisfied within the limits of professional skill and care that the work will comply with requirements of the Building Regulations,[95] that satisfactory provision is made for the conveyance of refuse water and rain water from roofs,[96] and that there is satisfactory provision for ingress and egress for any public building subject to section 24 of the Building Act 1984.[97] Where the Building Regulations impose requirements as to fire escapes,[98] and where the building is intended to be put to a use designated under section 1 of the Fire Precautions Act 1971, the approved inspector must consult the fire authority.[99] Where an approved inspector is satisfied that the plans are not defective and do not show that the proposed work would contravene the regulations he must at the request of the developer give a "plans certificate"[1] to that effect to the developer and the local authority. An initial notice may be combined with a plans certificate. The authority may not reject the certificate except on prescribed grounds, but must do so if the grounds exist. A certificate not rejected within ten days is deemed to have been accepted. The authority may rescind their acceptance if work is not commenced within three years.[2] If a question arises between the developer and the inspector it may be referred to the Secretary of State.[3]

On completion, the approved inspector must give a "final certificate" to the developer and the local authority, with respect to the completion of the work and the discharge of his functions. This is subject to acceptance by the authority on the same basis as a plans certificate. Upon acceptance, the initial notice ceases to apply, except that the authority's enforcement powers suspended on acceptance of the initial notice remain suspended.[4]

---

[91] s. 47(3), reg. 8(4).
[92] s. 48.
[93] reg. 9.
[94] By reg. 10.
[95] Building Regulations 1985 (S.I. 1985 No. 1065) regs. 4 and 6: see § 16–20 *ante.*
[96] *cf.* the authority's powers under s. 21(1) and (2) of the Building Act 1984. § 16–21 *ante.*
[97] See § 16–21 *ante.*
[98] Building Regulations 1985 (S.I. 1985 No. 1065), Sched. 1, para. B.1.
[99] S.I. 1985 No. 1066, reg. 11.
[1] See reg. 12 and Sched. 2, forms 2 and 3.
[2] s. 50; reg. 13 and Sched. 4. The grounds for rejection include deficiencies in form and information, absence of power to give certificate and lack of any necessary declaration.
[3] s. 50(2)(3): in force from November 11, 1985: S.I. 1985 No. 1602. An appeal lies on a point of law to the High Court and the Secretary of State has power to state a case on a point of law: *ibid.* s. 42.
[4] s. 51; reg. 15 and Sched. 5.

The initial notice otherwise continues in force until (1) it is cancelled[5] or (2) the occurrence or expiry of a prescribed period.[6] In either event, some or all of the authority's enforcement powers revive.[7] The approved inspector must give notice cancelling the initial notice (1) if he can no longer carry out his functions; or (2) if he considers that work is being carried out in a way which prevents him from carrying out his functions; or (3) if he considers that there is a contravention of the building regulations. The developer must cancel the initial notice if it appears that the inspector is no longer willing or able to carry out his functions. The authority may cancel the initial notice if the work has not been commenced within three years.[8]

Provision is made to enable public bodies to supervise their own work.[9]

A person aggrieved by an authority's rejection of an initial notice, plans certificate or final certificate (or the equivalents for public bodies) may appeal to a magistrates' court and then the Crown Court.[10] Local authorities must keep registers of notices and certificates available for public inspection.[11]

Contravention of regulations

Contravention of a building regulation is a summary offence, the **16-26** penalty being a fine not exceeding level 5 on the standard scale and £50 for each day on which the default continues after conviction.[12] The local authority may by notice under section 36 of the 1984 Act require an owner to pull down or remove, or, if he elects, alter work carried out in contravention of the regulations. If the notice is ignored the authority may pull down or remove or alter the work, charging their reasonable expenses to the owner. The notice must be served within twelve months of the completion of the works.[13] An appeal lies against a notice to a magistrates' court.[14] The Attorney-General or the authority or any other person may apply for an injunction for the removal or alteration of any work which contravenes a regulation or a requirement of the 1984 Act.

If work is executed in accordance with plans that have been passed or if notice of their rejection was not given within the prescribed time the authority may not serve a section 36 notice. This is without prejudice to

[5] s. 52; reg. 17.
[6] reg. 16.
[7] s. 53; reg. 18.
[8] s. 52.
[9] s. 54; regs. 19–26, Scheds. 6–8.
[10] s. 55.
[11] s. 56; reg. 28.
[12] s. 35. Proceedings may be taken before the completion of a building in respect of individual parts which contravene the regulations: *Sunley Homes Ltd.* v. *Borg* [1970] 1 Q.B. 115, *per* Lord Parker C.J. at p. 122. Contravention of the Building (Approved Inspectors, etc.) Regulations 1985 (S.I. 1985 No. 1066), other than reg. 18, is not an offence: *ibid.* reg. 29.
[13] s. 36(1)–(4).
[14] s. 40.

proceedings by an authority, the Attorney-General or any other person for an injunction, but if an injunction is granted, the court may order the authority to pay compensation to the owner.[15]

Relaxation of regulations

If in any particular case the Secretary of State considers that the operation of a regulation would be unreasonable, he can, after consulting with the local authority, give a direction dispensing with compliance. The exercise of this dispensing power has been delegated by the Secretary of State to local authorities.[16] The steps to be taken before a direction is made, including notifying affected persons and publicity, are prescribed by building regulations.[17] The Secretary of State may grant a relaxation of a requirement of building regulation in respect of a particular type of building matter, which may be of a general or class nature.[18] He may also by certificate approve any particular type of building matter as complying with particular parts of the regulations.[19] The power to approve may be delegated.[20] "Building matter" means any building or other matter to which building regulations are in any circumstances applicable.[21] If an application for relaxation is not dealt with by the authority, or the authority refuses to grant what the applicant seeks, an appeal will lie to the Secretary of State.[22] The Secretary of State may at his discretion afford the appellant and the local authority an opportunity of appearing before and being heard by a person appointed by him.[23]

Provision is made in the Second Schedule to the 1984 Act for relaxation to extend to certain cases of existing work, a concession, it would seem, to inadvertence. A developer cannot rely on this provision if, before an application is made, the authority had become entitled to pull down or alter the work under the enforcement rules of the Act.

Liability in tort

16-27 The negligence of a public authority in passing plans or of an inspector in supervising building work may give rise to civil liability.[24] However, the authority's power to ensure compliance with the plans was conferred to

---

[15] Building Act 1984, s. 36(5), (6).
[16] *Ibid.* s. 8, and the Building Regulations 1985 (S.I. 1985 No. 1065) reg. 10.
[17] *Ibid.* s. 10.
[18] *Ibid.* s. 11.
[19] *Ibid.* s. 12.
[20] *Ibid.* s. 13.
[21] *Ibid.* ss. 11(8), 12(12).
[22] *Ibid.* s. 39. The Secretary of State may state a case on a point of law to the High Court, and there is a right of appeal against his decision on a point of law to the High Court: *ibid.* s. 42.
[23] *Ibid.* s. 43: in force from a day to be appointed.
[24] In respect of the passing of plans, see *Dennis* v. *Charnwood Borough Council* [1983] Q.B. 409. In respect of the negligence of building inspectors, see *Dutton* v. *Bognor Regis Urban District Council* [1972] 1 Q.B. 373; *Anns* v. *Merton London Borough Council* [1978] A.C. 728 (see § 10–33); *Lyons* v. *Booth (F.W.) (Contractors) and Maidstone Borough Council* (1982) 262 E.G. 981; *Worlock* v. *S.A.W.S.* (1983) 265 E.G. 774.

safeguard the occupiers of houses built in their area and the members of the public generally against dangers to their health and safety: it was not conferred in order to safeguard building developers against economic losses. Accordingly, local authorities will not be liable where there is no danger or imminent danger to health and safety.[25] The cause of action accrues when physical damage occurs to the property,[26] not, as was at one time considered to be the case, when the damage could have been discovered with reasonable diligence.[27] An action will presumably lie against a private inspector.

There is, in addition, provision in the Building Act 1984[28] for a breach of the building regulations to be actionable so far as it causes damage, subject to any exemptions and any defences that may be prescribed, and without prejudice to any action at common law.

Provisions as to amenity and safety
The Building Act 1984 contains several provisions relating to the safety **16-28** and appearance of buildings and sites. If a structure is in a dangerous condition the authority may apply to a magistrates' court, and the court may order the owner to carry out remedial works or, if he so elects, to demolish the building and remove the rubbish. If the owner defaults, the authority may execute the order in the manner they think fit and recover their reasonable expenses from the owner. In addition the owner is liable to a penalty not exceeding level 1 on the standard scale.[28a]

If it appears to an authority that immediate action should be taken, the council may take such steps as may be necessary to remove the danger, recovering the cost from the owner through the magistrates' court.[29] But the council must first, if it is reasonably practicable, give notice to the owner and occupier. Where an authority uses this method the court may, in proceedings for the recovery of expenses, inquire as to whether the authority might reasonably have followed the procedure described in the preceding paragraph. The appropriate officer may take emergency measures without first being authorised so to do by the authority.

Local authorities may exercise a large measure of control over works of demolition.[30] With some minor exceptions, a person who intends to

---

[25] *Peabody Donation Fund (Governors of)* v. *Sir Lindsay Parkinson & Co. Ltd.* [1985] A.C. 210; *Bluett* v. *Woodspring District Council* (1982) 266 E.G. 220. The builder may be liable for such losses: see *Batty* v. *Metropolitan Property Realizations Ltd.* [1978] Q.B. 554; *Junior Books Ltd.* v. *Veitchi Co. Ltd.* [1983] 1 A.C. 520.
[26] In the case of an action against the local authority, the damage must be of such a nature as to pose an imminent danger to health and safety: see *Ketteman* v. *Hansel Properties Ltd.* [1984] 1 W.L.R. 1274.
[27] *Pirelli General Cable Works Ltd.* v. *Oscar Faber and Partners* [1983] 2 A.C. 1; *Ketteman* v. *Hansel Properties Ltd., supra.*
[28] s. 38: in force from a day to be appointed.
[28a] *Ibid.* s. 77.
[29] *Ibid.* s. 78.
[30] *Ibid.* ss. 80–83, 99, 102.

demolish a building must notify the authority, and the authority may require that action shall be taken on a number of points, such as the shoring up of adjacent buildings, weather-proofing of exposed surfaces, the removal of rubbish and the sealing or removal of drains and other pipes. An appeal lies to the magistrates' court against the terms of notice, and the authority may itself act if the recipient of the notice fails to do what is required of him and may, in addition or in the alternative, proceed for a fine.

16-29   Local authorities also have powers to deal with ruinous buildings[31] and vacant sites used as rubbish dumps.[32] If a building, because of its ruinous or dilapidated condition, is seriously detrimental to the amenities of the neighbourhood the authority may by notice require works of repair or restoration, or, if the owner chooses, its demolition. The authority may also require the site of the demolished building to be cleared up. In case of default the authority may itself do what is necessary and may seek a fine. An authority is also empowered to take such steps for the removal of rubbish from vacant sites as is considered necessary in the interests of amenity. Before taking action the authority must serve a notice on the owner or occupier stating what the authority proposes to do. The recipient may serve a counter-notice saying that he himself will take the necessary steps or he may appeal to the magistrates' court on the ground that the local authority's action is not justified. If a counter-notice is served, the authority must wait to see if steps are in fact taken within a reasonable time, or, if work is begun, if reasonable progress is made. Rubbish in this context does not include material accumulated in the course of any business or waste deposited in accordance with a disposal licence in force under Part I of the Control of Pollution Act 1974.

16-30   Further powers and duties with respect to rubbish are conferred on local authorities by the Refuse Disposal (Amenity) Act 1978. It is the duty of non-metropolitan county councils and metropolitan district councils in England and district councils in Wales to provide places where refuse (other than refuse from business activity) may be deposited, free by residents and, if the authority chooses, at a charge to others.[33] Powers are given to district councils to remove abandoned vehicles and to non-metropolitan county councils and metropolitan district councils in

---

[31] Building Act 1984, s. 79.
[32] Public Health Act 1961, s. 34, as amended by s. 26 of the Civic Amenities Act 1967. This power is also exercisable by county councils in England: see Local Government Act 1972, Sched. 14, para. 37.
[33] s. 1, as amended by the Local Government Act 1985, Sched. 6, para. 4(2). The power to charge is to be removed and a requirement to open sites at weekends imposed as from a date to be appointed: *ibid.* s. 1(8). Disposal functions under the Act in the areas of the London, Greater Manchester and Merseyside Waste Disposal Authorities are exercised by those authorities: 1978 Act, ss. 1, 3–5, as modified by the Waste Regulation and Disposal (Authorities) Order 1985 (S.I. 1985 No. 1884), Sched. 2, paras. 13–18. See further, §§ 16–46, 16–49.

England and district councils in Wales to deal with their disposal.[34] The Act imposes penalties for the unauthorised dumping of motor vehicles or anything else on a highway or elsewhere in the open.

The Control of Pollution Act 1974[35] makes it an offence to deposit controlled waste or cause or knowingly permit[36] controlled waste to be deposited on land unless the land is occupied by the holder of a disposal licence, authorising the deposit in question.[37] If the waste is poisonous, noxious or polluting and its presence is likely to cause an environmental hazard, such as danger to persons or animals, heavier penalties are applicable. Disposal licences are granted by disposal authorities[38] who must maintain a register of all licences containing particulars thereof. This procedure applies to all controlled waste not exempted by regulation.[39] Appeal to the Secretary of State lies in respect of an authority's decision regarding an application for a licence, or in respect of the revocation of a licence.[40]

Part II of the Mines and Quarries (Tips) Act 1969 confers certain powers on local authorities[41] so as to ensure that disused tips do not, by reasons of instability, constitute a danger to members of the public. They have a power to require the supply of information and have rights of entry to carry out exploratory tests.

If an authority, after consultation with the fire authority, is satisfied **16-31** that a theatre, hall or other building used as a place of public resort, or a restaurant, shop, store or warehouse to which members of the public are admitted and in which more than twenty persons are employed, is not provided with satisfactory means of ingress and egress, the authority may serve notice on the owner to take steps to rectify the matter, and if the

---

[34] ss. 3 and 4, as amended by the Local Government Act 1985, Sched. 6, para. 4.

[35] ss. 3 and 4.

[36] It is not necessary to prove that the defendant was knowingly acting in breach of licence conditions: *Ashcroft* v. *Cambro Waste Products Ltd.* [1981] 1 W.L.R. 1349.

[37] Provisions as to disposal licences are found in the 1974 Act, ss. 5–11, and the Control of Pollution (Licensing of Waste Disposal) Regulations 1976 (S.I. 1976 No. 732), as amended by the Control of Pollution (Licensing of Waste Disposal) (Amendment) Regulations 1977 (S.I. 1977 No. 1185).

[38] Non-metropolitan county councils, the Greater Manchester and Merseyside Waste Disposal Authorities, metropolitan district councils outside Greater Manchester and Merseyside and the London Waste Regulation Authority: s. 30 (1), as amended by, and s. 30(2A)–(2D), as inserted by, the Waste Regulation and Disposal (Authorities) Order 1985 (S.I. 1985 No. 1884), Sched. 2, para. 11. Sections 3 to 11 of the 1974 Act, concerning disposal licences, fall within the definition of "waste regulation provisions" inserted in s. 30(1) by *ibid.*

[39] s. 5, as amended by the Local Government, Planning and Land Act 1980, Scheds. 2 and 34 and the Local Government Act 1985, Sched. 6, para. 3(3), and see regulations noted *supra*, n. 37.

[40] s. 10, and see regulations noted n. 37, reg. 7.

[41] *i.e.* non-metropolitan county, metropolitan district and London borough councils, the Common Council and the Council of the Isles of Scilly: s. 11, as amended by the Local Government Act 1972, Sched. 30 and the Local Government Act 1985, Sched. 8, para. 27.

authority considers that immediate action should be taken it may apply to a magistrates' court for a temporary closing order.[42]

Authorities are under an obligation to require the provision of means of escape in case of fire in buildings of more than two storeys where an upper storey is more than 20 feet from the ground. This provision applies only to a building which:

(1) is let in flats, or tenements; or

(2) is used as an inn, hotel, boarding-house, nursing home, boarding school, children's home or other similar institution; or

(3) is used as a restaurant or shop, store or warehouse and has on any upper flore sleeping accommodation for persons employed on the premises,

unless a fire certificate under the Offices, Shops and Railway Premises Act 1963 or the Fire Precautions Act 1971 is currently in force. Where provision is inadequate the authority is required to serve notice on the owner specifying the steps to be taken by him. The authority is empowered to do the work in default and a penalty may be imposed by the court.[43]

An authority may require the provision of adequate means of escape in case of fire in houses in multiple occupation.[44] Where the house is of at least three storeys (excluding any storey lying wholly or mainly below the floor area of the principal entrance) and has a floor area of over 500 square metres, the exercise of this power is mandatory.[45]

C. NUISANCES AND OFFENSIVE TRADES[46]

(1) Statutory nuisances

16-32   A local authority is under an obligation to cause inspections to be made of its area to detect the existence of "statutory nuisances" and to take steps to see that they are abated. Section 92 of the Public Health Act 1936 lists the following as statutory nuisances:

(1) premises in such a state as to be prejudicial to health *or* a nuisance[47];

---

[42] Building Act 1984, s. 71. This control does not apply to premises for which a fire certificate is currently in force under the Offices, Shops and Railway Premises Act 1963 (see s. 76 of that Act) or under the Fire Precautions Act 1971 (see s. 30 of that Act). See also the transitional provisions contained in the Health and Safety at Work, etc., Act 1974, Sched. 8 (to come into force from a date to be appointed).

[43] Building Act 1984, s. 72.

[44] Housing Act 1985, s. 365.

[45] Housing (Means of Escape from Fire in Houses in Multiple Occupation) Order 1981 (S.I. 1981 No. 1576) made under Sched. 24, para. 1 to the Housing Act 1980 (now the Housing Act 1985, s. 365(2)).

[46] Public Health Act 1936, ss. 91–110; and the Public Health (Recurring Nuisances) Act 1969.

[47] It is not necessary to establish both conditions: *Betts* v. *Penge Urban District Council* [1942] 2 K.B. 154. The case appears to be good law on this point: *cf.* § 16–34.

(2) an animal kept in such a place or manner as to be prejudicial to health or a nuisance;

(3) an accumulation or deposit which is prejudicial to health or a nuisance;

(4) dust or effluvia[48] caused by any trade, business, manufacture or process and injurious, or likely to cause injury, to the public health or a nuisance[49];

(5) a workplace, which is not provided with sufficient means of ventilation, or in which sufficient ventilation is not maintained, or which is not kept clean or not kept free from noxious effluvia, or which is so overcrowded while work is carried on as to be prejudicial to the health of those employed therein.

Where proceedings are brought in respect of a statutory nuisance falling within the terms of (3) it is a defence to prove that the accumulation or deposit is necessary for the carrying on of a business and that all precautions have been taken. Where proceedings are brought in respect of a statutory nuisance under (4) it is a good defence to show that the best practicable preventive measures have been taken.[50]

Other nuisances are declared in other sections to be statutory **16-33** nuisances: a storage container for water used for domestic purposes so constructed or kept as to render the water liable to contamination and to be prejudicial to health[51]; a foul watercourse or a choked or silted watercourse which is prejudicial to health or a nuisance[52]; a tent, van, shed or similar structure used for habitation which is so overcrowded or is so deficient in sanitary accommodation as to be a nuisance or prejudicial to health.[53] Under section 16 of the Clean Air Act 1956 the emission of smoke in certain circumstances constitutes a statutory nuisance.[54]

The term "prejudicial to health or a nuisance" has been the subject of **16-34** much litigation. The words "prejudicial to health" are defined in the Act as injurious or likely to cause injury to health. The word "nuisance" was considered in *Betts* v. *Penge Urban District Council*[55] where it was held that if premises were in such a state as to interfere with the personal comfort of the occupiers a statutory nuisance existed. This can no longer be regarded as good law. It was disapproved of, *obiter*, by the House of Lords in *Salford City Council* v. *McNally*[56] and the view of the House of Lords was adopted in the following case:

---

[48] This term includes spent or ejected steam: Public Health Act 1961, s. 72.
[49] This head (s. 92(1)(*d*) of the 1936 Act) was amended by s. 26 of the Local Government (Miscellaneous Provisions) Act 1982.
[50] Public Health Act 1936, s. 94.
[51] *Ibid.* s. 141.
[52] *Ibid.* s. 259(1).
[53] *Ibid.* s. 268(2).
[54] See § 16–44.
[55] [1942] 2 K.B. 154.
[56] [1975] 1 W.L.R. 365.

National Coal Board v. *Thorne.*[57] Premises owned by the board were in a state of disrepair in that there were defective windows and gutters. The local authority considered that although the state of the premises was not such as to be prejudicial to health a statutory nuisance existed because the premises were in such a state as to interfere with the personal comfort of the occupier. This view was accepted in the court of summary jurisdiction. The Divisional Court (on a case stated) held that the magistrates were wrong. Watkins J. said[58]: "A nuisance cannot arise if what has taken place affects only the person or persons occupying the premises where the nuisance is said to have taken place. A nuisance coming within the meaning of the Public Health Act 1936 must be either a private or public nuisance as understood by common law."

Accordingly, for there to be a *statutory* nuisance there must either be a threat to health or a common law nuisance.

The words "prejudicial to health" were considered in *Coventry City Council* v. *Cartwright*[59] where it was held that an accumulation or deposit of matter was "prejudicial to health" as defined by section 343 of the Act if it was likely to cause a threat of disease or attract vermin but did not include inert matter, such as building waste or scrap iron, which could cause physical injury to people who walked on it. Nor could the visual impact of inert matter constitute a statutory nuisance within section 92(1)(c) of the Act—category (3) in paragraph 16–32 above.[60] Where a statutory nuisance exists by virtue of premises being in such a state as to be prejudicial to health or a nuisance under section 92(1)(a)—category (1) in paragraph 16–32 above, the fact that premises are empty is irrelevant, and the removal of the occupants will not constitute an abatement of the nuisance, unless perhaps the premises have been effectively rendered incapable of being occupied.[61]

16-35   If an authority is satisfied that a statutory nuisance exists, it may serve an abatement notice on the person by whose act, default or sufferance the nuisance arises or continues or, if the person cannot be found, on the owner or occupier of the premises on which the nuisance arises. The notice will require the nuisance to be abated and will state what works are necessary or what steps must be taken. Where a nuisance arises from a structural defect the notice must be served on the owner; and where the person responsible for the nuisance cannot be found and it is clear that the owner or occupier is not to blame, the authority may itself abate the nuisance.[62] Where a statutory nuisance has occurred and is likely to recur a prohibition notice may be served, and this may specify works necessary to prevent a recurrence. A prohibition notice may be served whether or not the nuisance is in existence at the time of service and whether or not an abatement notice has previously been served with respect to that

---

[57] [1976] 1 W.L.R. 543.
[58] *Ibid.* at p. 546.
[59] [1975] 1 W.L.R. 845.
[60] For a detailed discussion on this point, see *Encyclopedia of Environmental Health Law and Practice* (ed. Cross), pp. 1143 *et seq.*
[61] *Coventry City Council* v. *Doyle* [1981] 1 W.L.R. 1325.
[62] Public Health Act 1936, s. 93.

NUISANCES AND OFFENSIVE TRADES **16-36**

nuisance.[63] A prohibition notice and an abatement notice may be contained in the same document.

If an abatement notice or a prohibition notice is not complied with the **16-36** authority may apply under section 94 of the 1936 Act to a magistrates' court for a nuisance order, requiring the defendant to comply with the notice. The court may in addition impose a fine not exceeding level 4 on the standard scale, and is empowered to prohibit the use of a building as a dwelling-house where it is considered that the nuisance justifies this course.[64] If the justices are satisfied that a statutory nuisance exists, they are under a duty to make a nuisance order, but have a discretion as to its exact terms, for example as to the precise works to be done and the time within which they should be done.[65] Particular rules apply where the nuisance is alleged to come within the meaning of Part III of the Control of Pollution Act 1974, relating to noise (see *post*).

Any person aggrieved by an alleged statutory nuisance may complain under section 99 of the 1936 Act to a justice of the peace and the same procedures and penalties apply as in the case of complaint by the local authority.[66] In addition, the court may direct the authority to abate the nuisance. Proceedings under section 99 are regarded as criminal, not civil, and so should be commenced by way of information.[67] Whether there is a nuisance is to be judged in the light of the circumstances as at the date of the hearing before the magistrates, and not the date when the information was laid.[68] However, if a complainant under section 99 establishes that the nuisance existed at the time of the information he is entitled to payment of his reasonable expenses, even if the nuisance is abated by the time of the hearing.[69] Service of an abatement notice is not a necessary precondition to proceedings under section 99.[70] A person may institute proceedings under this section against a local authority if the authority has caused the nuisance.[71] It is no defence that the premises in question are within a clearance area in respect of which a deferment order under section 48(1) of the Housing Act 1957 (now section 301 of the Housing Act 1985) is operative, although that factor should be considered by the justices in exercising their discretion as to the terms of the nuisance order.[72]

---

[63] Public Health (Recurring Nuisances) Act 1969. See hereon *Peaty* v. *Field* [1971] 1 W.L.R. 387, where it was held that an authority does not have to wait until a recurrence of a nuisance takes place before authorising the issue of a complaint.

[64] Public Health Act 1936, s. 94; Criminal Justice Act 1982, ss. 38, 46. Proceedings under s. 94 are to be commenced by information: see the Magistrates' Courts Act 1980, s. 50.

[65] *Nottingham Corporation* v. *Newton* [1974] 1 W.L.R. 923.

[66] Under s. 94, *supra*.

[67] *R.* v. *Newham JJ., ex p. Hunt; R.* v. *Oxted JJ. ex p. Franklin* [1976] 1 W.L.R. 420.

[68] *Coventry City Council* v. *Doyle* [1981] 1 W.L.R. 1325, interpreting s. 94(2).

[69] *Ibid.*, by analogy with s. 94(3).

[70] *R.* v. *Newham JJ, ex p. Hunt, supra.*

[71] *R.* v. *Epping (Waltham Abbey) JJ, ex p. Burlinson* [1948] 1 K.B. 79; *cf. Salford City Council* v. *McNally* [1975] 1 W.L.R. 365; *Coventry City Council* v. *Doyle* [1981] 1 W.L.R. 1325.

[72] *Salford City Council* v. *McNally, supra; Nottingham Corporation* v. *Newton* [1974] 1 W.L.R. 923, *supra*, n. 65.

16-37   If a nuisance order is ignored the court may impose a fine not
exceeding level 5 on the standard scale and a further penalty not
exceeding £50 for each day on which the offence continues after
conviction.[73] Lack of finance cannot form any excuse for failure to
comply with a nuisance order.[74] The authority may itself do the work,
charging the expense to the person concerned, and it may do this whether
or not it has taken proceedings in a magistrates' court for failure to
comply with the nuisance order.

16-38   The Public Health Act 1961 introduced a speedier procedure for the
abatement of nuisances, now re-enacted in the Building Act 1984.[75] In
certain circumstances, if *premises* are considered to be prejudicial to
health or a nuisance and if it is considered that unreasonable delay in
remedying matters would be experienced if the 1936 Act procedure were
followed, then the authority may serve a notice, setting out the defects
and stating what it proposes to do. After nine days the authority may
undertake the work, recovering the cost. But the recipient of the notice
may serve a counter-notice within seven days, and if he does this the
authority may not proceed further unless the work is not begun within a
reasonable time or, if the work has been commenced, little progress has
been made. In proceedings to recover expenses the court has wide powers
of inquiry into the merits of the authority's action.

   If an authority considers that a prosecution in the magistrates' court is
an inadequate remedy it may take proceedings in the High Court for the
abatement or prohibition of the nuisance.[76]

(2) Offensive trades[77]

16-39   A person is liable to a fine not exceeding level 3 on the standard scale if
he establishes an offensive trade, as defined in the Public Health Act
1936, without the consent of the local authority. Consent must be given in
writing.[78] Section 107 lists what are offensive trades (*e.g.* blood-boiling,
fat-extracting, glue-making), and an authority may add to the list by
order confirmed by the Secretary of State. A person aggrieved by an
authority's refusal to give consent to the establishment of a trade, or by a
time limit attached to a consent, may appeal to a magistrates' court. An
authority may make by-laws with respect to the business of fish frying in
order to prevent any noxious or injurious effects of the trade, and may
make by-laws generally with respect to offensive trades.

---

[73] Public Health Act 1936, s. 95; Control of Pollution Act 1974, Sched. 2; Criminal Justice
Act 1982, ss. 37(2) and 46.
[74] *Saddleworth Urban District Council* v. *Aggregate and Sand* (1970) 69 L.G.R. 103.
[75] s. 76.
[76] Public Health Act 1936, s. 100. See, *e.g. Shoreham-by-Sea Urban District Council* v.
Dolphin Canadian Proteins Ltd. (1972) 71 L.G.R. 261.
[77] *Ibid.* ss. 107, 108; Local Government Act 1972, Sched. 14, paras. 11 and 12.
[78] Public Health Act 1936, s. 283(1); *Epping Forest District Council* v. *Essex Rendering* [1983]
1 W.L.R. 158.

D. AIR POLLUTION

The Clean Air Act 1956 repealed the provisions of the Public Health Act **16-40**
1936 which related to smoke nuisances and extended the control of local
authorities in this direction. The powers contained in the Act of 1956 were
further enlarged by the Clean Air Act 1968.

If dark smoke[79] is emitted from the chimney of any building the
occupier is guilty of an offence. Several defences are available to
him—that the contravention was solely due to the lighting up of
furnaces, and all practicable steps had been taken to prevent the
emission, or that the contravention was due to the failure of plant or to
the use of unsuitable fuel (no suitable fuel being obtainable).[80] The Act of
1968 extended this provision by making it an offence to emit dark
smoke from any industrial or trade premises *otherwise* than from a
chimney.[81]

A new industrial furnace must, so far as is practicable, be capable of **16-41**
operating without emitting smoke. Notice must be given to the local
authority of any proposals to instal a new furnace; there is no obligation
to submit plans and specifications to the authority, but if this is done and
the authority approves them, the plant is deemed to comply with this
provision.[82]

New furnaces must have plant to arrest grit and dust approved for this
purpose by the local authority. A person aggrieved by a decision of a local
authority may appeal to the Secretary of State.[83] The Secretary of State
may also prescribe limits on the quantities of grit and dust which may be
emitted from chimneys of premises, other than small domestic furnaces,
and where such limits are prescribed it is an offence to exceed the limit,
subject to the defence that the best practicable means have been used to
minimise the emission.[84]

The heights of chimneys are controlled. Chimneys serving processes
not involving the combustion of fuel are controlled by section 10 of the
Act of 1956. Where plans for the erection or extension of buildings (other
than residences, shops or offices) are submitted under the building
regulations the authority must reject the plans unless satisfied that the
height of the chimney will be sufficient to prevent, so far as practicable,
smoke, grit, dust or other gases from becoming prejudicial to health or a

---

[79] Dark smoke is defined in the Act by reference to a chart known as the Ringelmann
Chart.
[80] s. 1.
[81] Clean Air Act 1968, s. 1. This offence is applicable to the burning of debris by demolition
contractors: *Sheffield City Council* v. *A.D.H. Demolition* (1983) 82 L.G.R. 177.
[82] Clean Air Act 1956, s. 3.
[83] Clean Air Act 1956, s. 6, as amended by the Local Government Planning and Land Act
1980, Scheds. 2 and 34. Clean Air Act 1968, s. 2.
[84] Clean Air Act 1968, s. 2; the Clean Air (Emission of Grit and Dust from Furnaces)
Regulations 1971 (S.I. 1971 No. 162).

nuisance. There is a right of appeal to the Secretary of State against an authority's decision.[85]

16-42 The control of furnace chimneys is governed by section 6 of the Act of 1968. Where a new chimney is constructed or the capacity of a furnace served by an existing chimney is increased, it is an offence to use the chimney unless its height has been approved by the local authority. An approval may be subject to conditions and there is a right of appeal to the Secretary of State.

16-43 An authority may, by order, declare a part or the whole of its area a smoke control area, and where this is done it is an offence for smoke to be emitted from any building, and it is an offence to obtain solid smoke-producing fuel for use in a smoke control area, or to sell such fuel by retail for delivery to premises in such an area.[86] The order itself may limit the effect of this rule to specified classes of buildings and may exempt a particular building or classes of buildings or types of fireplace. The Secretary of State may also exempt any class of fireplace from the operation of the order, and may at any time relax the provisions of the order.[87]

16-44 If an owner or occupier is obliged to adapt a fireplace to avoid contravening a smoke control order the authority must repay him seven-tenths of the approved cost, and may pay him the whole or part of the remainder. Part of the local authority's expenditure is recoverable from the Exchequer.[88] A power is given to local authorities to make grants towards the cost of adapting fireplaces in churches, chapels and buildings used for charitable purposes.[89]

An authority may serve notice requiring the adaptation of fireplaces, doing the work in default and recovering not more than three-tenths of the cost.

The Secretary of State has power over defaulting authorities—he may require an authority to prepare for his approval a programme of smoke control, and when he approves it he may require the authority to carry it out.[90]

The Control of Pollution Act 1974 empowers the Secretary of State to make regulations imposing requirements as to the contents and composition of motor vehicle fuel and limiting the sulphur content of oil fuel used in furnaces or engines.[91] Regulations have been made limiting the

---

[85] This provision does not apply to an inner London borough: London Government Act 1963, Sched. 11, para. 31. The relevant powers are contained in the London Building (Amendment) Act 1935, s. 4(1).
[86] Clean Air Act 1956, s. 11 and Sched. 1, as amended by the Local Government Planning and Land Act 1980, Scheds. 2 and 34.
[87] Clean Air Act 1956, s. 11.
[88] Clean Air Act 1956, ss. 12–15, as amended by the Housing Act 1964, s. 95.
[89] Clean Air Act 1956, s. 15.
[90] Clean Air Act 1968, s. 8.
[91] ss. 75–77.

lead content of petrol[92] and the sulphur content of gas oil.[93] A duty to enforce these regulations is imposed on weights and measures authorities.[94] Regulations about the sulphur content of oil fuel[95] are enforceable by district and London borough councils.[96] Provision for the obtaining of information about atmospheric pollution is also made.[97]

Where the emission of smoke is a nuisance to the inhabitants of the neighbourhood it is a statutory nuisance, and the local authority may serve a notice under the Public Health Act 1936 requiring its abatement. There are two exceptions to this rule—the provision does not apply to smoke from private dwellings or to dark smoke (the emission of dark smoke, as noted earlier, is an offence without proof of nuisance). If it is thought that the nuisance is likely to recur an authority may apply to a magistrates' court for an order prohibiting the recurrence and requiring the execution of remedial works.[98]

E. REFUSE COLLECTION AND DISPOSAL

The collection and disposal of waste is still to a large extent governed by **16-45** sections 72–76 of the Public Health Act 1936. Provision has been made for the replacement of these sections by sections 12–14 of the Control of Pollution Act 1974, but this change has not been implemented. The two sets of provisions are considered in turn.

(i) *Public Health Act 1936, ss. 72–76*

The collection of refuse and waste is the function of district councils, London borough councils and the Common Council of the City of London, the Sub-Treasurer of Inner Temple and the Under Treasurer of Middle Temple. The disposal of refuse and waste is the function of non-metropolitan county councils, and metropolitan district councils in England, district councils in Wales, London borough councils, and the Common Council[99]

The Secretary of State has power in certain circumstances to establish a statutory authority in Greater London or any metropolitan county to discharge some or all of the refuse or waste disposal functions[1] otherwise exercisable by London borough councils or metropolitan district councils.

---

[92] Motor Fuel (Lead Content of Petrol) Regulations 1981 (S.I. 1981 No. 1523), as amended by S.I. 1985 No. 1728.

[93] Motor Fuel (Sulphur Content of Gas Oil) Regulations 1976 (S.I. 1976 No. 1989).

[94] Control of Pollution Act 1974, s. 75(5).

[95] Oil Fuel (Sulphur Content of Gas Oil) Regulations 1976 (S.I. 1976 No. 1988).

[96] Control of Pollution Act 1974, ss. 76(4) and 84. Enforcement in respect of furnaces subject to the Alkali, etc. Act 1906 is, however, the responsibility of the Alkali Inspectorate.

[97] ss. 79–83.

[98] Clean Air Act 1956, s. 16, as amended by Clean Air Act 1968, Sched. 1, para. 5.

[99] Public Health Act 1936, s. 1, as substituted by the Local Government Act 1972, Sched. 14, para. 1; 1972 Act, Sched. 14, paras. 5–7, as amended by the Local Government Act 1985, Sched. 6, para. 2.

[1] *i.e.* functions conferred by ss. 74 or 76 of the Public Health Act 1936, Part I of the Control of Pollution Act 1974, the Refuse Disposal (Amenity) Act 1978 or ss. 5 or 6 of the Litter Act 1983.

He may do this by order before April 1, 1986 if it appears to him that these councils could with advantage make joint arrangements for the discharge of these functions but have not made any or any satisfactory arrangements for that purpose before November 15, 1985. Otherwise, he may do this if it appears to him that satisfactory arrangements for that purpose have ceased or will cease to be in operation at any time after April 1, 1986. The Secretary of State has exercised this power to establish the London Waste Regulation Authority, to exercise waste regulation functions throughout Greater London, four authorities (the West London, North London, East London and Western Riverside Waste Authorities), to exercise waste disposal functions in the areas of 21 of the 33 London boroughs, and the Greater Manchester and Merseyside Waste Disposal Authorities exercising both regulation and disposal functions in their respective areas.[2]

16-46   A local authority may undertake the removal of house refuse from the whole or part of its area. If a council resolves to undertake this service any occupier may give notice to the council to carry out its duty and if without reasonable excuse it fails to do so within seven days the occupier may recover as a civil debt the sum of twenty-five pence for every day during which default continues.[3] The Secretary of State may require an authority to undertake the service and where this is done the authority may discontinue it only with his consent. An authority may make by-laws with respect to refuse removal.[4]

An authority may undertake the removal of trade refuse, making a reasonable charge for this service, and again an occupier may recover penalties in the case of continuing default. Any dispute as to what is trade refuse or as to reasonable charges may be determined by a magistrates' court.[5]

The distinction between house refuse and trade refuse cannot always readily be drawn.

> *Iron Trades Mutual Employers Insurance Association Ltd.* v. *Sheffield Corporation.*[6] The complainants used a converted dwelling house as an office. They contended that a large quantity of waste paper that had to be removed from the premises was "house refuse." The Divisional Court *held* that it was

---

[2] Local Government Act 1985, s. 10; Waste Regulation and Disposal (Authorities) Order 1985 (S.I. 1985 No. 1884). "Waste regulation" functions include those concerning hazardous waste and site licensing under the Control of Pollution Act 1974, ss. 3–11 (see § 16–30, n. 38). Disposal functions include those under ss. 74(2) and 76(1) of the Public Health Act 1936 and s. 2 of the 1974 Act (see § 16–48, nn. 14, 15, 20): S.I. 1985 No. 1884, Sched. 2, para. 3. Certain provisions of the Local Goverment Acts 1972 and 1985 are applied by the Order to these authorities. In Greater Manchester, disposal functions in Wigan are exercised by the district council rather than the waste disposal authority.
[3] The other possible remedy for breach of this duty is a complaint to the minister under the Public Health Act 1936, s. 322: the existence of these remedies has been held to exclude an application for mandamus: *R.* v. *Kensington and Chelsea (Royal) London Borough Council, ex p. Birdwood* (1976) 74 L.G.R. 424.
[4] Public Health Act 1936, s. 72, as amended by S.I. 1977 No. 336.
[5] *Ibid.* s. 73.
[6] [1974] 1 W.L.R. 107.

not. *Per* May J.[7]: "... house refuse ... is refuse produced by a house, and of the kind which one would ordinarily expect a house to produce occupied as a house." The court distinguished earlier cases[8] in which it was held that the distinguishing factor lay in the character of the refuse and not the character of the premises, on the ground that they were concerned with the interpretation of statutory definitions of "house refuse" and "trade refuse" which did not appear in the Public Health Act 1936.

This approach has been followed in subsequent cases in which it has been held that refuse emanating from a holiday site with chalets, caravans and pitches for touring caravans and tents,[9] and from a hostel,[10] was not house refuse.

A local authority may at the request of the owner or occupier of any **16–47** premises remove any refuse or clean any earth-closet, privy, ashpit or cesspool, which they are under no obligation to remove or cleanse, or may carry out such removal or cleansing more frequently than they are under any obligation to do. In either case, they may make such charge as they think fit. This power cannot, however, be relied upon as authorising the general collection of trade refuse.[11] It is used, for example, as authority for the collection of garden refuse.

Where an authority undertakes to remove house refuse it may require an owner or occupier to provide dustbins of the type approved by the authority. A person aggrieved by a requirement may appeal to a magistrates' court. If the owner appeals he may serve a copy of his notice of appeal on the occupier and the court may decide which of them should comply with the notice; similarly, if the occupier appeals he may send a copy of his notice of appeal to the owner and the court may similarly decide between them.[12]

If a notice is not complied with the authority may supply the bin and charge the cost to the person in default, and may in addition take proceedings against him in a magistrates' court, which has the power to impose a fine not exceeding level 1 on the standard scale. An authority may itself provide and maintain dustbins generally, making an annual charge, not exceeding £1[13] in respect of each bin provided, recovering this amount as part of the general rate.

---

[7] *Ibid.* p. 112.
[8] *Vestry of St. Martin's* v. *Gordon* [1891] 1 Q.B. 61; *Westminster Corporation* v. *Gordon Hotels Ltd.* [1906] 2 K.B. 39; *J. Lyons & Co. Ltd.* v. *London Corporation* [1909] 2 K.B. 588.
[9] *Pentewan Sands Ltd.* v. *Restormel Borough Council* (1980) 78 L.G.R. 642. *Cf. Rother District Council* v. *Coghurst Gardens Ltd.* (1980) 79 L.G.R. 476, where it was held that as the paramount occupancy of a caravan park was that of each individual pitch owner rather than the park owners, the refuse emanating from the caravans was house refuse; and *Craven District Council* v. *Brewer Properties Ltd., The Times*, May 7, 1985, where it was held that refuse from static caravans could be house refuse.
[10] *Exeter City Council* v. *Exeter Shilhay Community* (1981) 79 L.G.R. 605.
[11] Public Health Act 1936, s. 74(1).
[12] *Ibid.* s. 75, as amended by the Criminal Justice Act 1982, ss. 37, 46; Local Government (Miscellaneous Provisions) Act 1953, s. 8.
[13] *Ibid.*; Local Authorities (Charges for Dustbins) Order 1976 (S.I. 1976 No. 984).

16-48   Local authorities may at the request of the owner or occupier of any premises undertake to dispose of any refuse which he may deliver at a place appointed by them, and may make such charge, if any, for so doing as they think fit.[14] They may also provide places for the deposit of refuse and plant or apparatus for the treating or disposing of refuse.[15] In non-metropolitan counties in England, these powers are exerciseable by the county council.[16]

Local authorities may sell refuse received by them.[17] They have a duty to provide dumps for refuse, open to the public and free to their residents.[18]

Certain of the powers contained in the Control of Pollution Act 1974 have been brought into effect. If it appears to a collection authority that there is likely to be situated on any premises in its area commercial or industrial waste of a kind which is likely to cause a nuisance or to be detrimental to the amenities of the locality, they may serve a notice on the occupier requiring him to provide receptacles of a kind and number reasonably specified in the notice. Failure to comply with the requirements is a summary offence punishable by a fine not exceeding level 3 on the standard scale. The occupier may appeal against the notice to a magistrates' court.[19]

Finally, disposal authorities are under a duty to prepare and revise waste disposal plans dealing with specified matters after making appropriate consultations.[20]

(ii) *Control of Pollution Act 1974, ss. 12-14*

16-49   Part I of the Control of Pollution Act 1974 makes a similar division of responsibilities in respect of refuse and other waste on land between "collection authorities" and "disposal authorities". Collection authorities are the district and London borough councils, the Common Council of the City of London, the Sub-Treasurer of the Inner Temple and the Under Treasurer of the Middle Temple.[21] The disposal authorities are, generally speaking, the non-metropolitan county councils and metropolitan district councils in England, district councils in Wales, London borough councils and the Common Council. However, the London

---

[14] Public Health Act 1936, s. 74(2).
[15] *Ibid.* s. 76(1).
[16] Local Government Act 1972, Sched. 14, paras. 5–7, as amended by the Local Government Act 1985, Sched. 6, para. 2.
[17] Public Health Act 1936, s. 76(2); Local Government Act 1972, Sched. 14, para. 5(2)(*b*).
[18] See § 16–30, above.
[19] Control of Pollution Act 1974, s. 13(3) (5)–(8), as amended by the Local Government, Planning and Land Act 1980, Sched. 2 (which, *inter alia*, substituted new subsections (5), (5A), (7) and (7A)) and the Criminal Justice Act 1982, ss. 38 and 46.
[20] Control of Pollution Act 1974, s. 2, as amended by the Local Government Act 1985, Sched. 6, para. 2 and the Waste Regulation and Disposal (Authorities) Order 1985 (S.I. 1985 No. 1884), Sched. 2, para. 5.
[21] *Ibid.* s. 30(1).

Waste Regulation Authority, the four London Waste Authorities and the Greater Manchester and Merseyside Waste Disposal Authorities are disposal authorities for their areas.[22] When sections 12–14 of the 1974 Act are fully in force, collection authorities will be under a duty to arrange for the collection of household waste in their areas, and to collect commercial waste if so requested by the occupier of premises. Each English county disposal authority, the four London Waste Authorities and the Greater Manchester and Merseyside Waste Disposal Authorities and each collection authority will have power to arrange for the collection of industrial waste if so requested by the occupier of the relevant premises. Where the area of a collection authority in England is included in the area of a disposal authority, the collection authority may only exercise this power with the consent of the disposal authority. Where waste other than household waste is collected the person who makes the request is liable to pay a reasonable charge.[23] If an authority fails to perform any of its functions the Secretary of State can exercise his default powers to deal with the matter.[24]

The terms "household waste," "commercial waste" and "industrial waste" are defined by reference to the *source* of the waste.

An authority with a duty to collect household waste will have power by   **16–50** notice to require the occupier of premises to place the waste in receptacles of a kind and number reasonably specified in the notice. The recipient of the notice will have the right to appeal to a magistrates' court against the notice.

If a notice is not complied with, proceedings may be taken in a magistrates' court, which may impose a fine of up to level 3 on the standard scale. An authority may itself provide receptacles either free of charge or, with the agreement of the occupier, at his expense.

Receptacles may be provided by an English county disposal authority, the four London Waste Authorities, and the Greater Manchester and Merseyside Waste Disposal Authorities or any collection authority for commercial or industrial waste at the request of any person, and on payment of a reasonable charge, except that the authority may decide not to charge for a receptacle for commercial waste if that is considered appropriate.[25]

It will be the duty of each disposal authority to ensure that the arrangements made by the authority and other persons for the disposal of waste are adequate.[26]

Where a collection authority falls within the area of a disposal   **16–51**

---

[22] *Ibid.*, definition substituted S.I. 1985 No. 1884, Sched. 2, para. 11: *cf.* §16–45.
[23] Control of Pollution Act 1974, s. 12 (1)–(4), as amended by the Local Government Act 1985, Sched. 6, para. 3, and S.I. 1985 No. 1884, Sched. 2, para. 8.
[24] *Ibid.* s. 97.
[25] Control of Pollution Act 1974, s. 13(1)–(4), as amended by the Local Government, Planning and Land Act 1980, Sched. 2, the Criminal Justice Act 1982, ss. 38 and 46 and S.I. 1985 No. 1884, reg. 9.
[26] Control of Pollution Act 1974, s. 1.

authority, the collection authority will be required to deliver waste to such places as are directed by the relevant disposal authority. Agreements may be made between collection and disposal authorities for the dealing with waste by the collection authority subject to conditions as to payment or otherwise as specified in the agreement. A disposal authority will be entitled to recover from a collection authority the reasonable cost of disposing of commercial and industrial waste, and any dispute is to be settled by arbitration. If the place of delivery is unreasonably distant the disposal authority will be obliged to make a contribution to the collection authority's costs, and if there is a dispute the matter is settled by arbitration.[27]

Disposal authorities, and collection authorities which retain waste by agreement, are empowered to provide plant for treating and disposing of refuse and to sell refuse. Authorities may provide plant for dealing with waste paper collected separately from other refuse. They have a duty to provide dumps for refuse, open to the public and free to their residents.[28]

F. Noise

16-52 Part III of the Control of Pollution Act 1974[29] imposes duties on local authorities to deal with noise in their areas and confers extensive powers in this respect. Where a noise amounting to a nuisance exists an authority has a duty to serve a notice requiring its abatement and imposing other requirements where necessary. It is an offence not to comply with such a notice, punishable by a magistrates' court. Where this would afford an inadequate remedy proceedings may be taken in the High Court.[30] A person aggrieved by such a notice may appeal to a magistrates' court. A magistrates' court may also act on a complaint made by an occupier of premises that in his capacity as occupier of premises he is aggrieved by noise amounting to a nuisance. Special powers exist to control noise from construction sites, from loudspeakers in streets, and from plant and machinery. Areas may be designated as noise abatement zones in which noise from specified premises must be kept within permitted levels.[31] The maximum penalty for an offence against this Part of the Act is a fine not exceeding level 5 on the standard scale with a further fine not exceeding £50 per day where an offence continues after conviction.

---

[27] *Ibid.* s. 14 as amended by S.I. 1985 No. 1884, reg. 10.
[28] See § 16–30, above.
[29] ss. 57–74. The provisions as to penalties were amended by the Criminal Justice Act 1982, ss. 35, 38 and 46. See also Control of Noise (Appeals) Regulations 1975 (S.I. 1975 No. 2116); *Wycombe District Council* v. *Jeffways and Pilot Coaches (H.W.)* (1983) 81 L.G.R. 662; *Tower Hamlets London Borough Council* v. *Creitzman* (1984) 83 L.G.R. 72.
[30] See *Hammersmith L.B.C.* v. *Magnum Automated Forecourts* [1978] 1 W.L.R. 50.
[31] See *Morganite Special Carbons* v. *Secretary of State for the Environment* (1980) 256 E.G. 1105.

G. Miscellaneous Powers and Duties

There are several powers of a general nature which administering **16-53** authorities may exercise in carrying out their duties under the Public Health Acts. Where an authority requires an owner or occupier to undertake works the authority may by agreement itself execute them at the expense of the owner or occupier, and the authority may also undertake work in connection with drains on his behalf.[32] Authorised officers of a local authority have a right to enter premises at all reasonable hours on giving at least 24 hours' notice (this notice is not necessary in the case of a factory) and if refused may apply to a justice of the peace for a warrant.[33] This right of entry is not restricted to the premises on which the work is to be executed but includes the right to enter adjoining premises for the purposes of carrying out the work.[34]

If an authority incurs expenses on behalf of an owner the expense, and **16-54** any interest accruing, becomes a charge on the premises—this means that the authority has the powers of sale or lease of a mortgagee. It also has power to order the expenses and interest to be paid by instalments over a period not exceeding 30 years.[35] An authority may, apart from this provision, recover expenses as a simple contract debt (*i.e.* in the county court where the sum does not exceed £5,000 or in the High Court[36]). Generally speaking there is a right of appeal to the magistrates' court against any requirement of a local authority, and a further appeal from that court to the Crown Court.[37] These are general powers. Several specific powers and duties of a miscellaneous character are now given.

(1) Prevention of infectious disease and food poisoning[38]

Certain diseases are notifiable (they are listed in section 10 of the **16-55** Public Health (Control of Disease) Act 1984)[39] and where a person is suffering from one of these diseases or from food poisoning a duty is placed on the medical practitioner attending to inform the proper officer.

---

[32] Public Health Act 1936, s. 275.
[33] *Ibid.* s. 287.
[34] *Senior* v. *Twelves* (1958) 56 L.G.R. 239.
[35] Public Health Act 1936, s. 291. Establishment expenses may be included: Local Government Act 1974, s. 36.
[36] County Courts Act 1984, ss. 15, 145 and County Courts Jurisdiction Order 1981 (S.I. 1981 No. 1123); Public Health Act 1936, s. 293.
[37] Public Health Act 1936, s. 301; Courts Act 1971, Sched. 9.
[38] Public Health (Control of Disease) Act 1984 (a consolidation measure).
[39] Certain other diseases, *e.g.* tuberculosis, lassa fever, rabies and acquired immune deficiency syndrome (AIDS) have been made compulsorily notifiable by regulations made under the Public Health Act 1936, but these are not within the definition of "notifiable diseases" for the purposes of the 1984 Act: see the Public Health (Infectious Diseases) Regulations 1968 (S.I. 1968 No. 1366), as amended. Regulations are now made under s. 13 of the 1984 Act. They may apply any enactment relating to the notification of disease or to notifiable disease with or without modification. See, *e.g.* the Public Health (Infectious Diseases) Regulations 1985 (S.I. 1985 No. 434), applying certain provisions to AIDS.

An authority may extend the list of notifiable diseases by order approved by the Secretary of State for Social Services.[40] A penalty not exceeding level one on the standard scale may be imposed by a magistrates' court on anyone who exposes others to risk of infection by his conduct.[41] A justice of the peace may, on the application of an authority, order the removal to hospital of persons suffering from a notifiable disease where proper precautions to prevent the spread of infection cannot be taken and others are exposed to risk.[42] Similarly, a justice may order the detention in hospital of an infected person.[43]

A justice of the peace, on the certificate of a registered medical practitioner nominated by the local authority, may order a person, including a suspected carrier, to be medically examined,[44] and an authority may exclude children from places of public entertainment and assembly.[45] An authority may request a person to keep from work and a person who complies with this request can require the authority to compensate him.[46]

(2) Rag flock and other filling materials

16-56   The Rag Flock and Other Filling Materials Act 1951 is intended to secure the use of clean filling materials in upholstered articles and other articles which are stuffed or lined. Premises in which the filling materials are used are registrable with the local authority and an offence is committed if the business is carried on in unregistered premises or if unclean materials are used. Rag flock for filling purposes may be manufactured and kept only in premises licensed for the purpose by the local authority.

(3) Common lodging houses[47]

16-57   A person may not keep a common lodging house unless registered with the local authority and the authority may refuse registration if satisfied that the occupier is not a fit person, or that the premises are not suitable, or that the use of the premises in this way is likely to cause inconvenience or annoyance to neighbouring residents. An appeal against refusal lies to a magistrates' court.

(4) Rodent control

16-58   The Prevention of Damage by Pests Act 1949 imposes a duty on the local authority to take appropriate steps to secure as far as practicable

---

[40] Public Health (Control of Disease) Act 1984, s. 16.
[41] *Ibid.* s. 17.
[42] *Ibid.* s. 37.
[43] *Ibid.* s. 38.
[44] *Ibid.* ss. 35, 36.
[45] *Ibid.* s. 23.
[46] *Ibid.* s. 20.
[47] Public Health Act 1936, ss. 235–241, 246–248; Public Health (Control of Disease) Act 1984, ss. 39–42.

that its area is free from rats and mice. An obligation is placed on occupiers of land (other than agricultural land) to inform the local authority if the land is infested. Where an authority is satisfied that land (whether agricultural land or not) is infested a notice may be served on the owner or occupier requiring him to take appropriate steps, whether by undertaking repairs or by carrying out treatment. In case of default the authority may comply with the terms of the notice, charging the cost to the person at fault.

(5) Mortuaries[48]

A local authority (which in this case includes a parish council) may **16-59** provide mortuaries and post-mortem rooms and must do so if required by the Secretary of State for the Environment. The authority (which again includes a parish council) may provide for the interment of any body received in the mortuary. Under section 50 of the National Assistance Act 1948[49] it is the duty of district councils to bury or cremate the bodies of persons who have died or been found dead in their areas where it appears that no other suitable arrangements have been made.

(6) Movable dwellings, makeshift dwellings and caravan sites[50]

Local authorities have power to issue licences authorising the stationing **16-60** of movable dwellings and authorising the use of land as a site for movable dwellings. Conditions may attach to a licence, but they must have a bearing on public health.[51] It is an offence for a person to keep a movable dwelling on any site for more than 42 consecutive days or 60 days in any 12 consecutive months unless a licence is obtained from the local authority, but the Secretary of State for the Environment may grant general exemption from this provision to a recognised camping or other organisation.[52]

By-laws may be made with respect to tents, vans, sheds and similar structures used for human habitation; and where such structures are overcrowded or insufficiently provided with sanitary accommodation or for some other reason are prejudicial to health or a nuisance a "statutory nuisance" exists and may be dealt with as such.[53]

The Caravan Sites and Control of Development Act 1960 introduced, in Part I, a licensing system to regulate the establishment and operation of caravan sites, and it enables local authorities to provide and operate them if they choose.

An occupier of the land is guilty of an offence if he causes or permits

---

[48] Public Health Act 1936, s. 198.
[49] As amended by the Local Government Act 1972, Sched. 29, para. 44.
[50] Public Health Act 1936, ss. 268, 269; Caravan Sites and Control of Development Act 1960, Part I.
[51] See *Pilling* v. *Abergele Urban District Council* [1950] 1 K.B. 636, § 16–06, and *Mixnam's Properties Ltd.* v. *Chertsey Urban District Council* [1965] A.C. 735, § 16–61.
[52] Public Health Act 1936, s. 269. A caravan is excluded from this provision: Caravan Sites and Control of Development Act 1960, s. 30.
[53] Public Health Act 1936, s. 268.

any part of his land to be used as a caravan site unless he holds a site licence from the local authority. There are several exceptions to this broad rule and these are listed in Schedule 1. A licence is not needed, for example, where the use of a caravan site is incidental to the enjoyment as such of a dwelling-house within the curtilage of which the land is situated, or where the land is occupied by an organisation which holds a certificate of exemption from the Secretary of State for the Environment, or where the site is used by travelling showmen.[54]

The licensing authority is bound to issue a site licence if the use of land as a caravan site has planning permission and, indeed, may only issue a licence if the applicant has the benefit of a formal grant of planning permission other than by a development order. If the planning permission is a limited one in point of time, the authority is required to issue a licence if the consent has at least six months to run.

16-61　　The local authority may attach such conditions to the licence as it thinks necessary or desirable in the interests of the caravan dwellers, or other classes of persons, or the public at large. The power to impose conditions is in general terms, and, without prejudice to the generality of this power, the authority may regulate the number of caravans on any particular site and may impose conditions to secure that sites are properly equipped with sanitary and other facilities. Conditions cannot be imposed to control materials used in caravan construction. An appeal lies to the magistrates' court against conditions attached to a licence, but only on the ground that they are unduly burdensome.

> *Chertsey Urban District Council* v. *Mixnam's Properties Ltd.*[55] The council imposed conditions on a caravan site licence which sought to regulate not only the use of the site but the contractual relationship between the site occupier and the individual caravan dwellers. *Held*, by a majority of the House of Lords, despite the generality of the power to impose conditions, such conditions must be limited to the use of the site.

The local authority must consult the fire authority as to fire precautions appropriate to the land.[56] Model Standards have been issued by the Secretary of State.[57]

A site licence may not be limited in time unless planning permission is so restricted, but authorities may alter conditions imposed by them, on their own initiative (first giving the licensee a chance to make representations) or at the instance of the licensee, and a licensee may appeal to the magistrates' court against an altered condition or a refusal to make a variation.

---

[54] For this last exemption to apply, all the caravans on the site must be used by travelling showmen, not merely a predominant proportion: *Holmes* v. *Cooper* [1985] 1 W.L.R. 1060.
[55] [1965] A.C. 735.
[56] Caravan Sites and Control of Development Act 1960, s. 5(3A), (3B), (7), (8), inserted by the Local Government (Miscellaneous Provisions) Act 1982, s. 8.
[57] See DoE Circulars 119/77 (standards for static caravan sites) and 22/83 (standards for touring caravan sites).

Local authorities[58] may themselves provide caravan sites, and for this   **16-62**
purpose may acquire land compulsorily.[59] The fire authority must be
consulted. They may manage the sites or lease them to others and may
provide services and facilities for the health and convenience of
caravanners.

A duty is placed on county councils, metropolitan district councils and   **16-63**
London borough councils to provide adequate accommodation for
gipsies residing in or resorting to their areas. Outside London and the
metropolitan districts it is the duty of the district council to provide
services and facilities and to manage the sites made available by the
county council. The obligation upon metropolitan district councils and
London borough councils is to provide pitches for up to 15 caravans in
each metropolitan district or London borough.[60] The Secretary of State
may, if at any time it appears to him necessary to do so, give directions to
any authority in breach of its duty to provide sites. The existence of the
default power has been interpreted as excluding a private right of action
for breach of statutory duty[61] but not the right of a person with a sufficient
interest to apply for judicial review.[62] In *R. v. Secretary of State for the
Environment, ex p. Price,*[63] McCullough J. held that the duty to provide
sites was subject to an implied qualification that the authority is only
required to do that which is practicable, or reasonably practicable, or
reasonable, or that it must use its best endeavours. However, in *R. v.
Secretary of State for the Environment, ex p. Ward*[64] Woolf J. took a
different view[65]:

> "The duty is not, in my view, qualified precisely in this way. It is qualified by
> the fact that what is or is not adequate accommodation is a question in the first
> instance for the authority concerned, which has to make a value judgment,
> taking into account all the circumstances. It is also qualified by the fact that,
> except in exceptional circumstances, the court will not seek to enforce that duty,
> but leave the matter to the Secretary of State, who can be expected to only
> exercise his powers when it is appropriate to do so."

Gipsies are defined not by race but as persons of nomadic habit of life.[66]
There is a general power to provide working space for activities. In any
area where the Secretary of State considers either that adequate provision
has been made in the area for the accommodation of gipsies or that in all

---

[58] For this purpose the term includes county councils and joint planning boards: Caravan
Sites and Control of Development Act 1960, s. 24(8).

[59] *Ibid.*s. 24, as amended by the Local Government (Miscellaneous Provisions) Act 1982, s. 8.

[60] Caravan Sites Act 1968, ss. 6–9, as amended by Local Government, Planning and Land
Act 1980, s. 173, and Sched. 3, para. 13, and the Local Government Act 1985, Sched. 8,
para. 11. See also the 1980 Act, ss. 174–178; Local Government Act 1972, s. 190.

[61] *Kensington and Chelsea London Borough Council v. Wells* (1973) 72 L.G.R. 289.

[62] *R. v. Secretary of State for the Environment, ex p. Ward* [1984] 1 W.L.R. 834.

[63] [1984] J.P.L. 87.

[64] [1984] 1 W.L.R. 834.

[65] *Ibid.* pp. 849–850.Woolf J.'s view on this point was preferred by Mann J. in *R. v. Secretary
of State for the Environment, ex p. Lee* [1985] J.P.L. 724.

[66] Caravan Sites Act 1968, s. 16.

the circumstances it is not necessary or expedient to make any such provision he may "designate" that area. This enables the authority to obtain orders from the magistrates' court to remove unauthorised encampments and makes it an offence for a gipsy to station a caravan on the highway, on unoccupied land or on occupied land without the consent of the occupier.[67] Sites provided by local authorities for gipsies are excluded from the operation of the Mobile Homes Act 1983.[68]

(7) Canal boats[69]

16–64   It is an offence for a canal boat to be used as a dwelling unless it is registered, or for a boat to accommodate as a dwelling a greater number of persons, or a greater number of persons of either sex or any particular age, than is allowed in the certificate of registration. Local authorities and port health authorities whose districts include, or abut on, some part of a canal are responsible for registration and for enforcing the provisions of the 1984 Act as to canal boats.

(8) Public conveniences

16–65   Local authorities of all categories are empowered to provide conveniences in proper and convenient situations and have a measure of control over public conveniences in or accessible from streets—consent is needed from the highway authority for such provision.[70] Regard must be had to the needs of disabled persons.[71] A local authority (other than a county council) may require the owner or occupier of a "relevant place" to provide and maintain sanitary appliances. The term "relevant place" means (1) a place normally used as a place for public entertainment or for the sale of food or drink to members of the public; (2) a place used on some occasion or occasions for any such purpose; and (3) a betting office.[72] Provision must be made so far as practicable and reasonable for the needs of the disabled.[73]

---

[67] *Ibid.* ss. 10–12. ss. 11 and 12 were substituted by the Local Government, Planning and Land Act 1980, ss. 174 and 175, following the Cripps Report, *Accommodation for Gypsies* (H.M.S.O. 1976), and s. 12 was amended by the Local Government Act 1985, Sched. 8, para. 11.

[68] See s. 5(1): definition of "protected site."

[69] Public Health (Control of Disease) Act 1984, ss. 49–53; Canal Boats Regulations 1878–1931.

[70] Public Health Act 1936, s. 87, as amended by the Local Government Act 1985, Sched. 17; Local Government Act 1972, Sched. 14, paras. 9 and 10; Building Act 1984, s. 68.

[71] Chronically Sick and Disabled Persons Act 1970, s. 5.

[72] Local Government (Miscellaneous Provisions) Act 1976, s. 20.

[73] Chronically Sick and Disabled Persons Act 1970, s. 6.

CHAPTER 17

EDUCATION

Most of the law relating to education is found in the Education Acts 1944 **17-01**
to 1981. The Act of 1944 is the principal Act and unless a note to the
contrary appears the law stated here is from this source. The subject is
considered under the following headings: central administration; local
administration; the statutory system of education; ancillary powers and
duties; tortious liability.

A. Central Administration

Section 1 of the Act places a duty on the Secretary of State for Education **17-02**
and Science[1]:

> ... to promote the education of the people of England and Wales and the
> progressive development of institutions devoted to that purpose, and to secure
> the effective execution by local authorities, under his control and direction, of
> the national policy for providing a varied and comprehensive educational
> service in every area.

However, it has been stated that

> "the extent to which the Secretary of State is empowered to fetter a local
> authority's choice as to the method of implementing the national policy which
> it considers to be best suited to its own area is limited by the provisions of the
> Act."[2]

Two central advisory councils are established by section 4 of the Act, one
for England and the other for Wales, to advise the Secretary of State

> ... upon such matters connected with educational theory and practice as they
> think fit, annd upon any questions referred to them by him.

These councils have not, however, been reconstituted since their reports
in 1967. There have been a number of non-statutory standing advisory
bodies, including the Secondary Examinations Council, the School
Curriculum Development Committee and the Advisory Committee on
the Supply and Education of Teachers, and *ad hoc* bodies such as the
Taylor Committee on School Governors,[3] the Warnock Committee on
the Education of Handicapped Children and Young People[4] and the

---

[1] In Wales, the Secretary of State's functions are largely exercised by the Secretary of State
for Wales.
[2] *per* Lord Diplock in *Seccretary of State for Education and Science* v. *Metropolitan Borough
of Tameside* [1977] A.C. 1014 at p. 1063.
[3] *A New Partnership for Our Schools*, H.M.S.O. (1977).
[4] *Special Educational Needs*, Cmnd. 7212 (1978).

Swann Committee on the Education of Children from Ethnic Minority Groups.[5]

The powers of the Secretary of State to direct and control the work of local education authorities are significant, although some controls were removed by the Education Act 1980. In several cases his happroval is needed before an authority can give effect to its decisions,[6] and in others he may issue directions with which the authority must comply.

17-03   A general power is available to him under section 68. If he is satisfied that a local education authority, or the governors of any county or voluntary school, have acted or are proposing to act unreasonably in the exercise of any power or the performance of any duty, he may give such directions as to the exercise of the power or the performance of the duty as he considers expedient.

The extent of the Secretary of State's powers under section 68 was considered by the House of Lords in *Secretary of State for Education and Science* v. *Metropolitan Borough of Tameside.*[7] In this case the newly elected Council for the Metropolitan Borough of Tameside submitted to the Secretary of State in June 1976 their proposals for maintaining a form of pupil selection in secondary education. The Council's predecessors had already submitted and had approved a scheme of comprehensive education which was due to be implemented in September 1976. The Secretary of State indicated that he considered that a reversion to a principle of selection would at this late stage be harmful and that he considered the Council's proposed action to be unreasonable within the meaning of section 68. He issued a direction to the Council ordering it to implement the comprehensive scheme and subsequently he obtained an order of mandamus. The Court of Appeal allowed the Council's appeal and the House of Lords unanimously affirmed their decision. Lord Wilberforce recognised that the wording of section 68 was subjective and apparently made the Secretary of State the judge of unreasonableness. However, this did not mean that his decision was incapable of challenge in the courts:

> "If a judgment requires, before it can be made, the existence of some facts, then, although the evaluation of those facts is for the Secretary of State alone, the court must enquire whether those facts exist, and have been taken into account, whether the judgment has been made on a proper self direction as to those facts, whether the judgment has not been made on other facts which ought not to have been taken into account. If these requirements are not met, then the exercise of judgment, however *bona fide* it may be, becomes capable of challenge."[8]

Lord Diplock pointed out that in administrative law the word "unreason-

[5] *Education for All*, Cmnd. 9453 (1985).
[6] Examples may be found in the Education Act 1944, ss. 9(5), 15, 17, 42; Education Act 1946, s. 2; Education Act 1968, s. 3(4); Education (No. 2) Act 1968, s. 1; Education Act 1980, ss. 3, 12, 13, 14 and 27.
[7] [1977] A.C. 1014.
[8] At p. 1047.

able" when applied to the way in which a public authority has purported to exercise a discretion vested in it by statute had become a term of legal art:

> "To fall within this expression it must be conduct which no sensible authority acting with due appreciation of its responsibilities would have decided to adopt."[9]

Applying this test to the actions of the Tameside Metropolitan Borough Council there were no grounds on which the Secretary of State could conclude that the Council was acting unreasonably.

A somewhat similar power is given in section 99,[10] but in this case it is available only where the administering authority is in default. If the Secretary of State is satisfied:

> ... that any local education authority, or the ... governors of any county school or voluntary school, have failed to discharge any duty imposed upon them by or for the purposes of this Act, the Secretary of State may make an order declaring the authority, ... or governors, as the case may be, to be in default in respect of that duty, and giving such directions for the purpose of enforcing the execution thereof as appear to the Secretary of State to be expedient; and any such directions shall be enforceable on an application made on behalf of the Secretary of State by mandamus.

The Secretary of State has an appellate jurisdiction. Except where **17-04** special provision is made in the Act a dispute between the local education authority and the governors of a school may be referred to him for settlement, and he must determine disputes between local education authorities as to responsibility for the education of particular pupils or as to whether contributions in respect of particular pupils are payable.[11]

The Secretary of State has wide regulation-making powers. For example, the Education (School Premises) Regulations 1981 prescribe in some detail the standards to which premises are required to conform,[12] and the Education (Schools and Further Education) Regulations 1981,[13] require the use of certain radioactive substances and apparatus and the provision of new premises involving building work to be approved by the Secretary of State, and contain provisions as to the duration of the school year and day, leave of absence and the transfer of educational records.

The Secretary of State is under a duty to cause a periodic inspection to **17-05** be made of all educational establishments, and to arrange special inspections of particular establishments whenever he considers it desir-

---

[9] At p. 1064.
[10] For further examples of a power to give directions, see Education Act 1944, s. 62; Education Act 1946, s. 1.
[11] s. 67. For an example of appellate jurisdiction, see s. 37 in relation to school attendance orders.
[12] S.I. 1981 No. 909, made under s. 10. For other examples, see Education Act 1944, s. 80; Education Act 1962, ss. 1, 4 (as substituted by the Education Act 1980, Sched. 5); Remuneration of Teachers Act 1965; Education Act 1980, ss. 4, 12(1), 13(1), 15(3), 17(6), 18, 21, 27.
[13] S.I. 1981 No. 1086, as amended by S.I. 1983 No. 262.

able. Inspectors engaged on this work are appointed by the Crown on his recommendation,[14] and he is required to make an annual report to Parliament.[15] The reports of formal inspections are now published.[16]

B. LOCAL ADMINISTRATION

17–06 The form of local administration appears in section 192 of the Local Government Act 1972, and in section 6 and the First Schedule of the Act of 1944.[17] Councils of non-metropolitan counties and metropolitan districts are local education authorities, but the Secretary of State may by order create a joint education board for the area of two or more authorities if he considers this an advantage. A local public inquiry must first be held unless all the authorities concerned agree. A board so constituted becomes the local education authority; it consists of members appointed by the participating councils and is a corporate body with perpetual succession and a common seal, financed by precept issued on constituent authorities.

17–07 Every local education authority must appoint an education committee under an arrangement approved by the Secretary of State and must include on the committee persons with experience in education and persons acquainted with the educational conditions prevailing in the area for which the committee acts, but a majority must be council members. The committee may, subject to any restrictions imposed by the Secretary of State or the education authority, appoint such sub-committees constituted in such manner as the committee may determine, and may authorise them to exercise any of their functions. The authority may act only on a report of the education committee, except where the matter is urgent. If the authority acts without a valid report in a non-urgent case, its resolution will be *ultra vires*.[18] The authority may delegate functions to the education committee except the power to borrow money or levy a rate.[19] The general powers of a local authority and its committees to delegate[20] are excluded, except that the education *authority* may arrange for the discharge of education functions by an officer.[21] Accordingly, an education committee may not delegate functions to an officer,[22] and neither the authority nor an education committee may delegate to the

---

[14] s. 77.
[15] s. 5.
[16] D.E.S. Administrative Memorandum 2/83.
[17] As amended by the Local Government Act 1972, Sched. 30. As to education authorities in London, see Chap. 28.
[18] *R.* v. *Liverpool City Council, ex p. Professional Association of Teachers* (1984) 82 L.G.R. 648; *R.* v. *Brent London Borough Council, ex p. Gunning, The Times,* April 30, 1985.
[19] Sched. 1, Part II, as amended by the Local Government Act 1972, Sched. 30.
[20] Local Government Act 1972, ss. 101, 102: above §§ 4–04, 4–48—4–54.
[21] *Ibid.* s. 101(10).
[22] *R.* v. *Birmingham City Council, ex p. N.U.P.E., The Times,* April 24, 1984.

committee's chairman.[23] The authority must have a chief education officer.[24]

The Secretary of State may authorise local education authorities to **17-08** purchase compulsorily any land, within or without their areas, required for schools or colleges maintained or to be maintained by them or which they have power to assist, or for their other statutory functions. He must be satisfied, before authorising a purchase, that the authority will not ultimately bear expense which would have fallen to the governors of a voluntary school if the governors had purchased the land. Local education authorities are empowered to purchase by agreement land so required, provided again that an authority is not ultimately involved in expense which the governors of a voluntary school would have borne had they purchased the land.[25]

C. THE STATUTORY SYSTEM OF EDUCATION[26]

There are three progressive stages in the statutory system of public **17-09** education, known as primary education, secondary education and further education, and it is the duty of every local education authority:

... to contribute towards the spiritual, moral, mental, and physical development of the community by securing that efficient education throughout those stages shall be available to meet the needs of the population of their area.[27]

(1) Primary and secondary education[28]

Provision of schools

An obligation is placed on local education authorities to ensure that **17-10** there are sufficient schools in their areas for the provision of primary education (generally speaking for pupils under ten and a half years of age[29]) and secondary education (*i.e.* for senior pupils). By section 8(1) of the Act of 1944 the schools available for an area shall not be deemed to be sufficient unless they are sufficient in number, character and equipment to afford for all pupils opportunities for education offering such variety of instruction and training as may be desirable in view of their different ages, abilities and aptitudes.

In carrying out this duty regard must be had to the need for boarding

---

[23] *R.* v. *Liverpool City Council, ex p. Professional Association of Teachers, supra*; *R.* v. *Secretary of State for Education and Science, ex p. Birmingham City Council* (1984) 83 L.G.R. 79.

[24] s. 88, as amended by the Local Government Act 1972, Sched. 30.

[25] s. 90, as amended by the Acquisition of Land (Authorisation Procedure) Act 1946, ss. 6, 10, and Scheds. 4 and 6; the Education (Miscellaneous Provisions) Act 1948, s. 10(1); and the Education Act 1980, Sched. 1, para. 1, and Sched. 7.

[26] Part II of the Education Act 1944; Education (Miscellaneous Provisions) Act 1948; Education Acts 1964, 1980 and 1981.

[27] Education Act 1944, s. 7.

[28] *Ibid.* ss. 8–40.

[29] *Ibid.* s. 8, as amended by the Education (Miscellaneous Provisions) Act 1948, s. 3.

accommodation and for securing that special educational provision is made for pupils who have special educational needs.[30] The Education Act 1964 enables new county and voluntary schools[31] to be established in which the age of pupils will range from a point somewhere below ten and a half to a point somewhere above 12. Such schools are deemed to be either primary schools or secondary schools as the Secretary of State specifies: they are known as "middle schools."[32]

The Education Act 1976 required local education authorities to have regard to the "comprehensive principle" in carrying out their powers and duties.[33] These provisions were repealed by the Education Act 1979.[34]

The implementation of a system of comprehensive secondary education—as opposed to a system based on selection of pupils according to ability and aptitude—led to several attempts to challenge the policy of local education authorities in the courts.[35] In *Smith* v. *Inner London Education Authority*[36] a group of parents sought to challenge as *ultra vires* the proposals of the Inner London Education Authority to close St Marylebone's Grammar School as part of the authority's system of comprehensive education. It was argued that the wording of section 8(1) requiring local authorities to provide secondary schools sufficient "in . . . character" to give students education suited to their age, ability and aptitude imposed a duty on the Inner London Education Authority to ensure that in its area there were schools where pupils were *selected* according to ability and aptitude and schools which were smaller, as regards the number of pupils, than comprehensive schools. As the Act of 1944 laid down this general policy in section 8(1) the adoption of a comprehensive system was, it was argued, *ultra vires*. Although the parents obtained an interlocutory injunction at first instance, the Court of Appeal allowed the authority's appeal and discharged the injunction. The word "character" in section 8(1) did not refer to the method of selection for, or the size of, schools but rather what happened at, or the attributes of, schools: *e.g.* the type of pupil at them—girls, boys, or both sexes—

---

[30] *Ibid.* s. 8, as amended by the Education Act 1980, Sched. 7 and the Education Act 1981, s. 2(1). As to whether the duty imposed by s. 8 can be enforced in the courts (apart from invoking the Secretary of State's default powers under s. 99, *supra* § 17–03), see *Meade* v. *Haringey London Borough Council* [1979] 1 W.L.R. 637; *cf. R.* v. *Liverpool City Council ex p. Ferguson and others, The Times,* November 20, 1985 (decision to dismiss all Liverpool teachers *ultra vires* because it was the direct consequence of fixing an unlawful rate, was not taken for proper educational purposes and because its consequence would be a breach of the council's duty under s. 8).

[31] These terms are defined at § 17–13.

[32] See the Education (Middle Schools) Regulations 1980 (S.I. 1980 No. 918).

[33] Defined as the principle that secondary education is to be provided only in schools where the arrangements for the admission of pupils are not based (wholly or partly) on selection by reference to ability and aptitude: Education Act 1976, s. 1.

[34] s. 1.

[35] See *Bradbury* v. *Enfield London Borough Council* [1967] 1 W.L.R. 1311, *Wood* v. *Ealing London Borough Council* [1967] Ch. 364, *Legg* v. *Inner London Education Authority* [1972] 1 W.L.R. 1245, *Coney* v. *Choyce* [1975] 1 W.L.R. 422, and *Smith* v. *Inner London Education Authority* [1978] 1 All E.R. 411.

[36] *Supra.*

or the type of instruction available—academic, religious, or practical. The authority, therefore, was entitled under the Act of 1944 to have a policy of implementing the comprehensive system of education and to apply it to any individual school provided the proper procedure had been followed—which in this case it had. Nor could it be said that the authority was acting unreasonably.

The Education Act 1980[37] makes it clear that education authorities are empowered, but not obliged, to establish or assist nursery schools and day nurseries.

Where any provision for primary or secondary education is made by a local education authority for a pupil who belongs to the area of another education authority, the cost may be recouped.[38]

Section 12 of the Education Act 1980 lays down the procedure to be **17-11** followed where a local education authority intends:

(a) to establish a new county school;
(b) to commence maintaining a school as a county school;
(c) to cease to maintain any county school, or, except as provided by section 14 of the Education Act 1944, any voluntary school;
(d) to make any significant change in the character or enlargement of the premises of a county school; or
(e) to cease to maintain a nursery school established by it or a former authority.

The proposals have to be published[39] and submitted to the Secretary of State, whose approval is required if a voluntary school is involved, or he gives notice to that effect within two months of submission, or objections have been made and not withdrawn. Similar procedures are applied by sections 13 and 15 of the 1980 Act. Section 13 applies where it is proposed that a school should be maintained by the local education authority as a voluntary school, or the governors of a voluntary school intend to make a significant change in its character or enlargement of its premises. References in sections 12 to 14 to a change of character include changes resulting from education beginning or ceasing to be provided for pupils above or below a particular age, for boys as well as girls or for girls as well as boys, or from the making or alteration of arrangements for the admission of pupils by reference to ability or aptitude.[40] Section 15 of the 1980 Act applies where the number of first year places in a school is to be reduced (normally to four-fifths or less of the number in that age group in

---

[37] ss. 24 and 26.
[38] Education Act 1980, s. 31; the Education (Areas to Which Pupils Belong) Regulations 1980 (S.I. 1980 No. 917), as amended by S.I. 1980 No. 1862.
[39] In a local newspaper, and by being posted in at least one conspicuous place in the area and at or near the main entrance of any school to which the proposals relate: Education (Publication of School Proposals) (No. 2) Regulations 1980 (S.I. 1980 No. 658). See *Legg v. Inner London Education Authority* [1972] 1 W.L.R. 1245 and *Coney v. Choyce* [1975] 1 W.L.R. 422.
[40] Education Act 1980, s. 16(2).

the school year commencing in 1979). Where proposals are submitted under sections 12 or 13 for the establishment, maintenance, change of character or enlargement of a school, the premises require the approval of the Secretary of State.[41]

The discontinuance of a voluntary school is subject to the procedure set out in section 14 of the Education Act 1944 and requires not less than two years' notice.

17-12 In recent years, many schools have been closed or reorganised as a result of the reduction in the number of children of school age. D.E.S. Circular 5/77 requested local education authorities to assess future school population trends and to examine the educational opportunities provided in their schools, noted the educational disadvantages of maintaining schools with dwindling numbers and stated that the general policy of the Secretary of State was to approve proposals to cease to maintain under-used schools. Circular 2/81[42] stated that there was a need for faster progress and required authorities to inform the Department of Education and Science of their proposals to remove surplus places.[43] The Secretary of State has, however, indicated that he will not normally approve proposals which have as their consequence the closure of established school sixth forms which "have already proved their worth under existing arrangements."[44] Some proposals for the replacement of sixth forms in secondary schools by sixth form or tertiary colleges have accordingly been rejected.[45] Parents of school children whose schools are threatened with closure or amalgamation have a legitimate expectation and, accordingly, a right to be consulted by the local education authority before the decisions are taken.[46]

17-13 In order to fulfil its obligations an authority is empowered (a) to *establish and maintain* primary and secondary schools, (b) to *maintain* primary and secondary schools established by other bodies, and (c) under arrangements approved by the Secretary of State, to *assist* schools which the authority has not established and does not maintain, by making grants or by making payments for educational facilities which these schools provide. Schools which come under (a) are known as county schools. Those in (b) are known as voluntary schools and are of three kinds, controlled schools, aided schools and special agreement schools, differing one from the other mainly but not wholly in the degree to which the local education authority contributes to the cost of maintenance. Special agreement schools are those erected or extended under an

---

[41] Education Act 1980, s. 14.
[42] "Falling rolls and surplus places".
[43] See also D.E.S. Administrative Memorandum 4/84, "Proposals made under sections 12–16 of the Education Act 1980", which, *inter alia*, stresses the importance of local consultation.
[44] D.E.S. Circular 4/82, "Statutory proposals for secondary schools and falling rolls."
[45] See generally P. Meredith, "Falling Rolls and the Reorganisation of Schools" [1984] J.S.W.L. 208.
[46] *R.* v. *Brent London Borough Council, ex p. Gunning, The Times,* April 30, 1985.

agreement with the Secretary of State, which revives proposals made under the Education Act 1936 for the giving of assistance towards the cost of erection of what were then called non-provided schools.[47] In controlled schools (as, of course, in county schools) the local education authority is responsible for all expenditure; in aided schools internal repairs and repairs to playgrounds and playing fields are the responsibility of the local education authority, but the governors are responsible for other repairs and for any expense incurred in altering school buildings to make them conform to standards prescribed by regulation.[48] In special agreement schools rights and responsibilities in regard to repair and maintenance are similar to those which apply to aided schools.[49]

The Secretary of State is under a *duty* to pay to the governors of aided   **17-14** and special agreement schools maintenance contributions equal to 85 per cent. of the sums expended on such alterations and repairs that are the governors' responsibility under section 15(3) of the 1944 Act.[50]

In addition, the Secretary of State has *power* to pay to the governors of such schools a maintenance contribution or grant not exceeding 85 per cent. of capital expenditure incurred by them:

(1) in pursuance of proposals approved under section 13 of the Education Act 1980 for a significant enlargement of the school premises,[51] or for the establishment of a new school or the substitution of one or more existing ones[52]; or

(2) in pursuance of proposals approved under section 16 of the Education Act 1944 for the transfer of an existing school to a new site.[53]

In relation to proposals under section 13 of the 1980 Act, the governors are responsible for providing both the site and the school buildings; in relation to proposals under section 16 of the 1944 Act, the governors are only responsible for providing the buildings, the local education authority being responsible for providing the site.[54] No contribution or grant is, however, payable to the governors of a special agreement school in

---

[47] Education Act 1944, s. 15, and Sched. 3.
[48] These standards are given in the Education (School Premises) Regulations 1981 (S.I. 1981 No. 909).
[49] Education Act 1944, s. 15.
[50] Education Act 1944, s. 102, as amended by the Education Acts 1946, Sched. 2 and 1975, s. 3.
[51] Education Act 1944, s. 102, as amended by the Education Acts 1968, Sched. 1, 1975 s. 3, and 1980, Scheds. 1 and 3.
[52] Maintenance grant payable under the Education Act 1967, s. 1(2), as amended by the Education Acts 1968, Sched. 2, 1975, s. 3, and 1980, Scheds. 1 and 3.
[53] Maintenance grant payable under the Education Act 1944, s. 103, as amended by the Education (Miscellaneous Provisions) Act 1953, s. 8 and Sched. 2, and the Education Acts 1967, s. 1, 1975, s. 3 and 1980, Sched. 1.
[54] Education Act 1946, Sched. 1; Education Act 1980, s. 13(5). Where proposals are approved under s. 13 of the 1980 Act, it is the duty of the local education authority to implement so much of the proposals as relate to the provision of playing fields and buildings other than school buildings: s. 13(6).

respect of proposals to which the special agreement relates or the execution of repairs or alterations for which provision is made by the special agreement.[55] In the case of transfer under section 16 of the 1944 Act, sums accruing to the governors or trustees of the school in respect of disposal of the first site are to be taken into account by the Secretary of State in determining the amount of grant.[56]

Finally, the Secretary of State may make loans to the governors of aided or special agreement schools in respect of their share of the capital expenditure incurred for any of the above purposes or in pursuance of any special agreement.[57]

No fees may be charged in respect of admission to any school maintained by a local education authority or in respect of the education provided there.[58]

Administration[59]

17-15   The administration of primary and secondary schools is shared between the local education authority and a representative body appointed for each school (or group of schools), formerly called the managers in primary schools and governors in secondary schools, and, following the Education Act 1980, s. 1, called governors in both primary and secondary schools. The constitution of the representative body is contained in an instrument of government. It is made in the case of *county schools* by order of the local education authority, and in the case of *voluntary* schools by order of the Secretary of State for Education and Science.[60] As from September 1, 1985, instruments of government must contain provisions complying with the Education Act 1980, s. 2(2)–(8).[61] Accordingly, all school governing bodies must include governors appointed by the local education authority by whom the school is maintained. In the case of schools with less than three hundred registered pupils there must be at least one "teacher governor"; if there are three hundred or more pupils, there must be at least two. "Teacher governors" are persons who are elected by teachers at the school and who are themselves such teachers when elected. The head teacher is *ex officio* a

[55] Provisos to the Education Act 1944, ss. 102 and 103, as amended.
[56] Education Act 1944, s. 103(3). This also applies to grants payable under the Education Act 1967, s. 1(2): *ibid.* s. 1(3).
[57] Education Act 1944, s. 105, as amended by the Education Acts 1967, s. 1(5)(*a*), 1975, s. 3, and 1980, Sched. 1.
[58] Education Act 1944, s. 61(1). See *R.* v. *Hereford and Worcester Local Education Authority, ex p. Jones* [1981] 1 W.L.R. 768, where it was held that if tuition in playing musical instruments was offered as part of the school curriculum, this provision applied to prohibit the charging of fees.
[59] Education Act 1944, ss. 17–22, as amended; London Government Act 1963, s. 31(7); Education Act 1980, ss. 2–5.
[60] 1944 Act, s. 17(2).
[61] Superseding ss. 18 and 19 of the 1944 Act and part of s. 2(2) of the Education (No. 2) Act 1968. The Secretary of State has extended the requirements of s. 2 of the 1980 Act, in stages, to all maintained schools: see D.E.S. Circulars 4/81, 7/83 and 7/84.

member unless he or she chooses otherwise. In the case of aided or special agreement schools there must be at least one "parent governor"; in the case of county or controlled schools there must be at least two. "Parent governors" are persons who are elected by parents of registered pupils at the school and who are themselves such parents when elected. Elections of parents and teacher governors are arranged by the local education authority for county and controlled schools and by the governors for aided and special agreement schools. The governing body of a county or voluntary primary school serving an area in which there is a "minor authority" must include at least one governor appointed by that authority: this may be the community council, parish council or meeting or, otherwise, a non-metropolitan district council.[62] Finally, the governing body of a voluntary school must include "foundation governors." These are appointed other than by the local education authority or minor authority for the purpose of securing that the character of the school as a voluntary school is preserved and developed, and in particular that it is conducted in accordance with any trust deed relating to it.[63] They are commonly appointed by the church or denomination in which the school vests. In controlled schools, at least one-fifth of the governors must be foundation governors. In aided or special agreement schools, the foundation governors must outnumber the other members by two if the governing body has eighteen or fewer members and by three if it has more, and at least one of the foundation governors must be a parent of a registered pupil at the school at the time of appointment.

Schools may be grouped under a single governing body.[64] The Secretary of State may make regulations as to the proceedings and tenure of office of governors.[65]

The conduct of school affairs is governed by the articles of government. These indicate the respective functions of the local education authority, the governors, and the head teacher. They are made by the local education authority in the case of county primary, county secondary and voluntary primary schools (those relating to county secondary schools require the approval of the Secretary of State) and by the Secretary of State in voluntary secondary schools. The model Articles of Government issued by the Ministry of Education in 1945[66] provided that the local education authority "shall determine the general educational character of the school and its place in the local education system. Subject thereto the Governors shall have the general direction of the conduct and curriculum of the school." Subject to the Articles, the head teacher "shall control the

---

[62] Education Act 1944, s. 114(1): definition of "minor authority" substituted by the Local Government Act 1972, s. 192(4).
[63] Education Act 1944, s. 114(1), as amended by the 1980 Act, Sched. 1.
[64] Education Act 1944, s. 20; Education Act 1980, s. 3.
[65] Education Act 1980, s. 4; see D.E.S. Circular 4/81; Education (School Governing Bodies) Regulations 1981 (S.I. 1981 No. 809), as amended by S.I. 1981 No. 1180.
[66] Schedule to Administrative Memorandum No. 25, January 26, 1945.

internal organisation, management and discipline of the school. . . . ” Articles based on the model were considered in the following case:

> *R.* v. *Manchester City Council, ex p. Fulford.*[67] The schools sub-committee of the education committee resolved that corporal punishment should be abolished in all the city's schools. This resolution was confirmed by the education committee and the council. The Divisional Court *held* that the matter concerned the general direction of the conduct of the school rather than its general educational character and was thus for the school governors to determine and not the local education authority, in accordance with the Articles of Government for County Secondary schools. The governors had merely rubber-stamped the council's decision, and had not afforded head teachers the opportunity to make representations as required by the Articles of Government. The decisions of the council and the governors were quashed by certiorari.

Despite the issue of the model, present Articles have come to vary widely,[68] and the model has been withdrawn. The government intends to legislate to clarify and strengthen the functions of governing bodies.[69]

Syllabus[70]

17–16　Secular education is under the control of the local education authority except in aided secondary schools, where the governors exercise control. Religious instruction in *county* schools must conform to a syllabus agreed by a conference convened by the local education authority and consisting of representatives of the Church of England (except in areas in Wales), other religious denominations, teachers' associations and the authority itself.[71] If the conference unanimously recommends a syllabus, the authority may adopt it for use in the schools; if there is disagreement the Secretary of State may appoint a body to devise a syllabus. A parent may withdraw his child from religious instruction, and if he desires him to receive instruction of a kind not provided in the county school, the education authority may make arrangements for this to be done elsewhere, but the authority may not incur expenditure in so doing.

The agreed syllabus applies to *controlled schools*, except that parents may request that their children be given religious instruction in accordance with the trust deed of the school, or, where no deed exists, in accordance with the practice followed in the school before it became controlled, and where such requests are made the governors are required to make suitable arrangements where this is practicable. In *aided* and

---

[67] (1982) 81 L.G.R. 292.

[68] White Paper, *Better Schools*, Cmnd. 9469, (March 1985), para. 226.

[69] *Ibid.* Chap. 9. The White Paper also proposes further changes in the composition of governing bodies.

[70] See, generally: *The School Curriculum* (H.M.S.O. 1981), a paper issued by the D.E.S. and the Welsh Office offering guidance to local education authorities as to how the school curriculum could be further improved; D.E.S. Circular 6/81, which, *inter alia*, indicated that each authority should review its policy for the curriculum in the light of that paper; D.E.S. Circular 8/83, which asked for information on the steps undertaken in implementation of Circular 6/81; and Chapter 2 of the White Paper, *Better Schools, supra.*

[71] Education Act 1944, ss. 25–30 and Sched. 5; and London Government Act 1963, s. 31(7).

special agreement schools, religious instruction is under the control of the governors and must be given in accordance with the trust deed which relates to the school or with the practice formerly observed in the school if no trust deed exists. If a parent wishes his child to receive religious instruction on the basis of the agreed syllabus (*i.e.* the syllabus used in county schools) and this cannot conveniently be arranged elsewhere, then the instruction must be given in the school itself, through the governors if they are willing or by the local education authority. In all schools the day must begin with collective worship, but pupils may be excused attendance at the request of their parents.

Teachers[72]

The appointment of teachers in county schools, controlled schools and **17-17** special agreement schools is under the control of the local education authority unless other provision is made in the articles of government,[73] and a teacher may not be dismissed except by the authority. Accordingly, although the governors may properly conduct a hearing into complaints against a teacher and recommend his dismissal, the relevant education committee or sub-committee must rehear the matter and not merely consider whether the governors' recommendation can reasonably be supported.[74] In the case of controlled and special agreement schools, the authority must consult the governors as to the appointment of the head teacher and must satisfy the foundation governors as to the fitness and competence of persons whom it is proposed to appoint as reserved teachers (those who, in denominational schools, will give denominational religious instruction). In aided schools the governors appoint their own teachers but the number is determined by the local education authority. The authority may prohibit the dismissal of a teacher without its consent and may require the dismissal of any teachers. The case of *Hannam* v. *Bradford Corporation*[75] makes it clear that in an aided school there is no contract between the teacher and the local education authority. The employment and dismissal of teachers is now also governed by the concept of unfair dismissal. A detailed discussion of this area may be found in text books devoted to the law of employment.[76]

---

[72] Education Act 1944, s. 24.
[73] See *R.* v. *Powys County Council, ex p. Smith* (1982) 81 L.G.R. 342.
[74] See *R.* v. *Governors of Litherland High School, ex p. Corkish, The Times,* December 4, 1982. Conversely, the council may be entitled to dismiss a teacher, notwithstanding the governors' recommendation that he be reinstated: *Honeyford* v. *Bradford Metropolitan City Council, The Times,* November 14, 1985.
[75] [1970] 1 W.L.R. 937.
[76] See the Employment Protection (Consolidation) Act 1978; the Sex Discrimination Act 1975; the Race Relations Act 1976; *Ahmad* v. *Inner London Education Authority* [1978] Q.B. 36; *Beard* v. *St. Joseph's School* (1978) 77 L.G.R. 278, E.A.T.; *Lake* v. *Essex County Council* (1979) 77 L.G.R. 708, C.A.; *Birmingham City Council* v. *Elson* (1979) 77 L.G.R. 743, E.A.T.; *Nothman* v. *Barnet London Borough Council* (1978) 77 L.G.R. 89; *Pearson* v. *Kent County Council* (1979) 77 L.G.R. 604; *Ford* v. *Warwickshire County Council* [1983] 2 A.C. 71. See also *R.* v. *Liverpool City Council, ex p. Ferguson and others, The Times,* November 20, 1985, n. 30, *supra.*

The Secretary of State may by regulations under section 27 of the Education Act 1980 make provision:

(1) for requiring teachers at schools to possess such qualifications as may be determined by or under the regulations, and for requiring such teachers to serve probationary periods;

(2) with respect to the teaching staff to be provided in schools;

(3) for imposing requirements as to the health and physical capacity of teachers; and

(4) for prohibiting or restricting the employment or further employment of persons as teachers on medical grounds, in cases of misconduct, and on educational grounds.

Such regulations apply in respect of any school maintained by a local education authority and any special school whether or not so maintained, and, in addition, they apply as regards (3) and (4) to any other teachers employed by local education authorities. The relevant regulations,[77] *inter alia*, enable the Secretary of State to bar the employment of a particular person as a teacher or direct a dismissal or suspension, after consultation with the local education authority and after affording the person concerned an opportunity to make representations.[78] Employment as a teacher is normally restricted to qualified persons.

The remuneration of teachers is fixed by order of the Secretary of State and in making orders he is advised by committees approved by him and appointed by bodies representative of local education authorities and teachers respectively.[79]

Children with special educational needs

17-18   The Education Act 1981 makes provision for children with "special educational needs."[80] A child has such needs if he has a "learning difficulty" which calls for "special educational provision" to be made for him.

There is a "learning difficulty" if a child:

(1) has a significantly greater difficulty in learning than the majority of children of his age; or

(2) has a disability which prevents or hinders him from using educational facilities generally provided in local schools for children of his age; or

[77] The Education (Teachers) Regulations 1982 (S.I. 1982 No. 106).
[78] See D.E.S. Administrative Memorandum 3/82.
[79] Remuneration of Teachers Act 1965, and the numerous orders made thereunder. And see *Lewis* v. *Dyfed County Council* (1978) 77 L.G.R. 339; *R.* v. *Central Arbitration Committee, ex p. Gloucestershire County Council* (1980) 79 L.G.R. 412.
[80] This Act was passed following the Report of the Warnock Committee of Enquiry into the Education of Handicapped Children and Young People entitled *Special Educational Needs*, Cmnd. 7212 (1978). See D.E.S. Circular 8/81, "Education Act 1981"; D.E.S. Circular 1/83, "Assessments and statements of special educational need"; Education (Special Educational Needs) Regulations 1983 (S.I. 1983 No. 29).

(3) is under five, and is, or would be if special educational provision were not made for him, likely to fall within (1) or (2) when over five.

Difficulty arising solely because he is or will be taught in a language different from that spoken at home is specifically excluded.

"Special educational provision" is defined in the case of a child of two or over as educational provision that is additional to or different from that made generally for children of his age in local maintained schools.[81]

In certain circumstances, local education authorities are under a duty to identify children with special educational needs. This duty applies to:

(1) children registered as pupils in schools maintained by them or in pursuance of arrangements made under section 6 of the Education (Miscellaneous Provisions) Act 1953; and

(2) children who are brought to their attention as having, or as probably having, special educational needs and who are either (a) registered as a pupil at a school other than under (1), or (b) are not registered as a pupil at a school and are aged between two and sixteen.

If the authority are of opinion that such a child has or probably has special educational needs, they must make an *assessment* of his needs under section 5.[82] The authority must serve notice on the child's parent[82a] of the proposal to make an assessment and the parent has the right to make representations.

Where an assessment has been made, the authority must decide whether they are required to determine the special educational provision that should be made for the child. If they decide that they are not so required, the parent may appeal to the Secretary of State and the Secretary of State may direct the authority to reconsider.[83] If they decide that they are so required, they must make a *statement of his special educational needs* under section 7.[84] Before making the statement, the authority must serve a copy of the proposed statement on the parent. If the parent disagrees with any part of it, he has the right to make representations. If a statement is made, it is the authority's duty to arrange that the special educational provision specified in the statement is made for the child, unless the parent has made suitable arrangements. Under section 8, the parent may appeal against a statement to an appeal committee constituted under Schedule 2 to the Education Act 1980,[85] and there is a further right of appeal to the Secretary of State.

---

[81] 1981 Act, s. 1.
[82] See also Sched. 1, Part I.
[82a] The term "parent" includes a guardian and every person who has the actual custody of the child: Education Act 1944, s. 114, applied by the 1981 Act, s. 21(2).
[83] 1981 Act, s. 5(6)–(8).
[84] See also Sched. 1, Part II.
[85] See below, § 17–19 and *R.* v. *Surrey County Council Education Committee, ex p. H* (1984) 83 L.G.R. 219.

Under section 6, if a local education authority are of the opinion that a child under two has special educational needs they may make an assessment if the parent consents, and must do so if the parent so requests. The formal procedures under section 5 are not necessary as no assessment can be made without parental consent. A section 6 assessment must be made in such a manner as the authority consider appropriate. After such an assessment is made, they may make a statement of the child's special educational needs, and maintain it, again in such manner as they consider appropriate.

Where special education provision must be arranged, the authority must secure that the child is educated in an ordinary school, provided that this is compatible with the provision of efficient education for the other children and the efficient use of resources. The school governors must use their best endeavours to ensure that the special provision is made and that the teachers are aware of the relevant educational needs. If reasonably practicable, the child should engage in school activities together with children who do not have special educational needs.[86] If education in an ordinary school is inappropriate, the child may be educated at a "special school" approved by the Secretary of State under section 12, or an independent school approved by the Secretary of State under section 13.[87]

The 1981 Act also makes special provision for the discontinuance of maintained special schools[88] and school attendance orders made in respect of children in respect of whom the authority maintain a statement under section 7.[89]

Special schools maintained by a local education authority are governed by governors constituted by an instrument of government and in accordance with articles of government, both made by order of the local education authority.[90]

Wishes of parents

17-19   A local education authority is under an obligation in carrying out its power and duties to:

> have regard to the general principle that, so far as is compatible with the provision of efficient instruction and training and the avoidance of unreasonable public expenditure, pupils are to be educated in accordance with the wishes of their parents.[91]

This provision does not create an absolute obligation to educate pupils in accordance with a parent's wishes, nor is an authority bound to have regard exclusively to those wishes.

---

[86] 1981 Act, s. 2.
[87] See the Education (Approval of Special Schools) Regulations 1983 (S.I. 1983 No. 1499) and D.E.S. Circular 6/83, "The approval of special schools."
[88] 1981 Act, s. 14; D.E.S. Circular 3/82.
[89] 1981 Act, ss. 15, 16.
[90] Education (No. 2) Act 1968.
[91] Education Act 1944, s. 76.

Watt v. *Kesteven County Council.*[92] The plaintiff wished to have his sons educated, at the full cost of the local education authority, at a Roman Catholic boarding school. The council did not provide a secondary grammar school in the plaintiff's area, but education was made available at an independent school and the local education authority paid the fees of boys qualified to attend. *Held*, the council had discharged its duty. Denning L.J. said[93]: "section 76 . . . lays down a general principle to which the county council must have regard. This leaves it open to the county council to have regard to other things as well, and also to make exceptions to the general principle if it thinks fit to do so. It cannot therefore be said that a county council is at fault simply because it does not see fit to comply with the parent's wishes. And that is all that the father's complaint comes to in this case."

In *Wood* v. *Ealing London Borough Council*[94] Goff J. held that section 76 merely qualified the powers and duties of local education authorities and of the Minister under the Act as a whole and that breach of it could not of itself give rise to a right of action. In section 76 "education" must refer to the curriculum and "whether it includes any, and if so what, religious instruction and whether co-educational or single sex and matters of that sort and not to the size of the school or the conditions of entry."[95]

Section 6 of the Education Act 1980 (which applied from autumn 1982) provides that it is the duty of the education authority and the governors of a county or voluntary school to comply with parental wishes as to the school at which his or her child is to be educated. This does not apply if compliance (a) would prejudice the provision of efficient education or the efficient use of resources, or (b) would be incompatible with admission arrangements between the governors of an aided or special agreement school and the authority, or (c) would be incompatible with arrangements for selection by reference to ability or aptitude. The parents may appeal against an allocation decision to an appeal committee.[96] The committee consists of three, five or seven members nominated by the local authority from among those persons appointed by the authority to a panel. The panel comprises (a) members of the authority or of any of its education committees and (b) other persons who have experience in education, are acquainted with the educational conditions in the area or are parents of registered pupils at a school. It must not include any person employed by the authority other than as a teacher. In the case of aided or special agreement schools, the arrangements are made by the governors. The committee's decision is binding on the authority or governors as the case may be.[97] Information as to schools and admission arrangements must be

[92] [1955] 1 Q.B. 408. Followed in *Cumings* v. *Birkenhead Corporation* [1972] Ch. 12.
[93] At p. 424.
[94] [1967] Ch. 364.
[95] At p. 384. See further *Winward* v. *Cheshire County Council* (1978) 77 L.G.R. 172.
[96] 1980 Act, s. 7 and Sched. 2.
[97] The committees are subject to the jurisdiction of the Council on Tribunals and the Local Commissioners: 1980 Act, s. 7(6),(7). For comment by the latter on complaints against committees, see Report of the Commission for Local Administration in England (1983–84) pp. 30–32; D. Bull, [1985] J.S.W.L. 189. A Code of Practice was issued in August 1981 after consultation between the Council and local authority associations and other organisations concerned. A number of unreported cases concerning committees are considered in T. Buck, "School Admission Appeals" [1985] J.S.W.L. 227.

published annually.[98] These provisions do not apply to nursery or special schools, or children under five at the time of their proposed admission.[99]

School attendance

17-20   Parents and guardians of children of compulsory school age (*i.e.* between five and sixteen years)[1] are under a duty to cause them to receive efficient full-time education suitable to their age, ability and aptitude and any special educational needs they may have, either by attendance at school or otherwise, and to see that they attend school regularly.[2] Where it appears that a parent or guardian has failed in the first of these duties the authority may make a school attendance order requiring the registration of the child as a pupil at a school named in the order. The local education authority must serve written notice of their intention to serve an order. The notice must specify the school they intend to name in the order and, if they think fit, one or more other schools which they regard as suitable alternatives. Aided or special agreement schools cannot be named without the consent of the governors. If the parent selects one of the named schools within 14 days, that school will be specified in the order. The parent may make an alternative proposal. If it amounts to an application for the child to attend at a different maintained school, the procedure under sections 6 and 7 of the Education Act 1980[3] will apply. If an alternative proposal either is not made or is not successful, the authority will name the school originally specified in the attendance order. Section 11 of the Education Act 1980 makes parallel provision for the amendment of existing school attendance orders where the parent subsequently applies for a place at a different school. Failure to observe the provisions of an order is an offence unless it is shown that the child is receiving efficient full-time education otherwise than at school suitable to his age, ability and aptitude and any special educational needs. The 1944 Act does not give an express power for inspection in the home to ensure that education there is sufficient. It has been held, however, that while it would be wrong for an education authority to say that, as a matter of policy, they will only be satisfied by such an inspection, there can be cases

---

[98] 1980 Act, s. 8; Education (School Information) Regulations 1981 (S.I. 1981 No. 630), as amended by S.I. 1983 No. 41.

[99] 1980 Act, s. 9. ss. 6–9 were brought into force from October 1, 1980; ss. 6–8 applied to admissions from the autumn school term 1982: see S.I. 1980 No. 959.

[1] Raising of School Leaving Age Order 1972 (S.I. 1972 No. 444); see also Education Act 1962, s. 9, as amended by the Education (School Leaving Dates) Act 1976, s. 1.

[2] Education Act 1944, ss. 35–37, 39–40, as amended by the Education (Miscellaneous Provisions) Act 1953, s. 10, the Children and Young Persons Act 1969, s. 72, Scheds. 5 and 6, the Education Act 1980, Sched. 3 para. 2 and the Education Act 1981, Sched. 4; Education Act 1980, ss. 10, 11. It was held in *Hinchley* v. *Ranking* [1961] 1 W.L.R. 421 that a child does not "attend regularly" if he is not regularly present for the periods laid down for attendance at the school in question. Truancy of which the parent is unaware is no defence although it may be accepted as mitigation: *Crump* v. *Gilmore* (1969) 68 L.G.R. 56. A child is not absent from school "with leave" if he is suspended because of his parents' refusal to return him to school: *Happe* v. *Lay* (1977) 76 L.G.R. 313.

[3] See § 17–19, above.

where the other methods invoked are so unsatisfactory that the authority is entitled to indicate that they will only be satisfied if they are permitted to inspect in the home.[4]

A parent or guardian who neglects the second of these duties (to ensure **17-21** regularity of attendance) is guilty of an offence unless the absence is due to sickness or other unavoidable cause, or to the fact that the day in question was set apart for religious observance by the religious body to which the parent belongs, or that the school at which the child is registered is not within walking distance[5] from his home and that no suitable arrangements have been made by the local education authority for transport or for boarding accommodation. "Sickness" in this context refers to the sickness of the child and "unavoidable cause" means a cause affecting the child, and imports an element of emergency.

> *Jenkins* v. *Howells.*[6] A child failed to attend school regularly in order to give domestic help to her widowed mother unable on health grounds to do any work. *Held*, these facts did not constitute unavoidable cause within the meaning of the section; the mother was therefore guilty of an offence in not causing the child to be sent to school.

It is not a question as to whether a cause of absence is reasonable but whether the cause comes within the section.

> *Spiers* v. *Warrington Corporation.*[7] A headmistress refused to admit a girl wearing slacks unless a medical note was produced to the effect that this kind of clothing was necessary in the interests of the child's health. *Held*, the list of excuses in section 39(2) of the Actt of 1944 is exhaustive. In acting as she did the headmistress was only acting in a matter of discipline which must be within the competence of a headmistress and accordingly in persistently sending his daughter to school in slacks the father was not causing her to attend school regularly and was guilty of an offence.

Failure to comply with a school attendance order or to secure the **17-22** regular attendance of a child at school is an offence punishable on summary conviction with a fine not exceeding level 3 on the standard scale or imprisonment for a term not exceeding one month.[8] Proceedings may be brought only by the local education authority. The authority must first consider whether it would be appropriate, instead of or as well as instituting proceedings, to bring the child before a juvenile court as in need of care or control under section 1 of the Children and Young Persons Act 1969. Where proceedings are taken, the court, if it convicts for a breach of a school attendance order, or if it deals with a charge of failure to secure regular attendance, may direct the authority to bring the child before a juvenile court as in need of care or control.[9]

---

[4] *R.* v. *Surrey Quarter Sessions Appeal Committee, ex p. Tweedie* (1963) 61 L.G.R. 464.
[5] See § 17–31.
[6] [1949] 2 K.B. 218.
[7] [1954] 1 Q.B. 61. See also *Jarman* v. *Mid-Glamorgan Education Authority* (1985) 82 L.S. Gaz. 1249, D.C.
[8] s. 40(1), as modified by the Criminal Justice Act 1982, ss. 35, 46.
[9] s. 40(2)–(4), as substituted by the Children and Young Persons Act 1969, Sched. 5. See also the Child Care Act 1980.

In *Re S. (A Minor)*[10] the Court of Appeal considered the principles which should apply to the making of a care order in these circumstances. In this case parents who were opposed to the system of comprehensive education refused to send their son to the local education authority's schools which had adopted the comprehensive system. The authority obtained a care order in respect of the child. On appeal to the Court of Appeal the order was confirmed. Lord Denning M.R. considered whether a care order could be appropriate where a child had a perfectly good home. Care proceedings went beyond the consideration of physical and moral well-being. The child's welfare was the paramount consideration and this involved him receiving a proper education. If he was not receiving suitable full-time education he was in need of "care and control" within the meaning of section 1(2) of the Children and Young Persons Act 1969.

The Court of Appeal in the following case considered the jurisdiction of the Chancery Division of the High Court as to wardship in relation to children whose education is the responsibility of the local education authority. The case dealt specifically with school attendance, but the principles discussed in it are of wider interest.

17-23   *Re Baker (Infants).*[11] A mother refused to send her children to school despite repeated prosecutions and school attendance orders. The authority applied for an order that the infants be made wards of court and that directions be given as to their education. *Held*, although the court had jurisdiction to continue the wardship of the children, the court would not do so in the present case for the following reasons—

  (i) (*per* Ormerod L.J., Pearson L.J. concurring) the prerogative of the Crown in relation to infants had been restricted in that it might no longer be exercised in relation to the particular matters placed by the Education Act 1944 within the ambit of the local education authority's discretion and powers.

  (ii) (*per* Upjohn and Pearson L.JJ.) the Education Act 1944 had established a comprehensive code which it was the duty of local education authorities to carry out and it would not be proper for the court to exercise wardship jurisdiction solely to assist a local education authority in the enforcement of their statutory functions or, in the absence of special circumstances, to exercise the court's discretionary control over a ward in a sphere of activity which had been entrusted by statute to a local education authority.

  (iii) (*per* Ormerod and Pearson L.JJ.) moreover the remedy provided by the statute had not been fully used.

(2) Further education[12]

17-24   Every local education authority is under a duty to secure the provision of adequate facilities for further education—full-time and part-time

---

[10] [1978] Q.B. 120.
[11] [1962] Ch. 201.
[12] Part II of the Act, ss. 41–42, and London Government Act 1963, s. 31(1)(*c*), (4). See also the Education No. 2 Act 1968, as to government of institutions providing full-time further education and the Further Education Act 1985. Sections 43–46 of the 1944 Act concern county colleges, but it is now extremely unlikely that such colleges will be established.

education for persons over compulsory school age, and leisure-time occupation, in organised cultural training and recreative activities, for persons over compulsory school age who are able and willing to profit by the facilities. Each authority is required by the Act to prepare a scheme for further education, taking into account existing facilities offered by universities and other bodies, and the scheme as approved by the Secretary of State becomes the working plan to which the authority must conform.[13]

Arrangements vary from one area to another but normally include colleges of further education offering vocational courses for young people between the ages of 16 and 19. Provision may also be made for area colleges providing facilities for technical and specialist education at or near degree level for full-time and part-time students. Thirty colleges or groups of colleges have been designated by the Secretary of State as polytechnics and provide a wide range of full-time and part-time courses for degrees approved by the Council for National Academic Awards and for professional qualifications of a similar standard.[14] The governing body of a college or polytechnic generally comprises representatives from the maintaining local education authority and other local education authorities in the area with representatives from industry, commerce, the professions, trade unions, academic staff and students, and each institution is required to have its own instrument of government.[15]

The Secretary of State has similar powers to make regulations in **17-25** relation to further education establishments and their staff, as he does in relation to schools.[16] In addition, he may make regulations concerning the provision of, and the fees to be charged for, courses of further education, including requirements for his approval of the provision of courses of "advanced further education" as designated under the regulations. Accordingly, his approval is necessary for the provision of courses for the further training of teachers, postgraduate or first degree courses, courses for the Diploma of Higher Education and various other courses of a standard above that of O.N.C or G.C.E. "A" level, and he may direct that such courses cease to be provided. Furthermore, he may give directions as to the numbers and categories of students to be admitted to teacher training courses.[17]

A local authority may supply goods or services through further education establishments and may make loans for such purposes to a company in which they have at least a 20 per cent. holding, to other

---

[13] According to P. Liell and J.B. Saunders, *The Law of Education* (9th ed, 1984), § B40, no schemes of further education exist in Wales and most such schemes in England are out of date.

[14] See White Paper, *A Plan for Polytechnics*, Cmnd. 3006 (1966).

[15] See the Education (No. 2) Act 1968, s. 1, D.E.S. Circular 7/70, and *Winder* v. *Cambridgeshire County Council* (1978) 76 L.G.R. 176.

[16] See Education Act 1980, s. 27; Education (Schools and Further Education) Regulations 1981 (S.I. 1981 No. 1086) as amended by S.I. 1983 No. 262; Education (Teachers) Regulations 1982 (S.I. 1982 No. 106).

[17] S.I. 1981 No. 1086, regs. 14–17, Scheds. 2, 3 (3 as substituted by S.I. 1983 No. 262).

persons or bodies who provide further education establishments, or to companies in which such persons or bodies have at least a 20 per cent. holding.[18]

Since 1958, expenditure on advanced further education has been funded by a pooling arrangement. All local education authorities contribute to a fund according to a formula, and the fund is used to reimburse authorities which have incurred expenditure. This arrangement is effected by adjustments to the block grant. In *R.* v. *Secretary of State for Education and Science, ex p. Inner London Education Authority*[19] it was held that the formula used was unlawful to the extent that it took relative ratable resources into account. Each authority's contribution should relate to demand for advanced further education in its area.

Local education authorities have a duty under section 1 of the Education Act 1962,[20] to make awards in accordance with regulations made by the Secretary of State to persons ordinarily resident in their area who attend designated courses at a university, college or other institution in the United Kingdom, and a power under section 2 to make awards to persons over compulsory school age attending other courses. Relying on the advice of the Department of Education and Science,[21] many local authorities decided that students from overseas who had been given leave by the immigration authorities to enter the country for the purpose (for example) of receiving secondary education, were not ordinarily resident in the United Kingdom for the prescribed three year period before entering higher education. A "real home" test was applied. However, in *R.* v. *Barnet London Borough Council, ex p. Nilish Shah*[22] the House of Lords held that the term "ordinary residence" was to be given its natural and ordinary meaning and that the question was whether the applicant had habitually and normally resided in the United Kingdom from choice and for a settled purpose throughout the prescribed period, apart from temporary and occasional absences. Accordingly, such students as those mentioned above could be regarded as ordinarily resident. In response to this decision, the Secretary of State (1) advised local education authorities to be prepared to reconsider cases where an award had been refused for a course beginning in 1979/80 or later, but not any case earlier save in exceptional circumstances[23]; and (2) amended the relevant regulations, removing the duty to make an award, in respect of courses beginning in 1982/83 and 1983/84 (which education authorities had not yet decided),

---

[18] Further Education Act 1985, ss. 1, 2.
[19] *The Times*, June 20, 1985.
[20] As substituted by the Education Act 1980, s. 19, Sched. 5 and amended by the Education (Grants and Awards) Act 1984.
[21] D.E.S. Awards Circular Letter 1/78.
[22] [1983] 2 A.C. 309.
[23] D.E.S. Awards Circular Letter 2/83, March 30, 1983. See *R.* v. *Hertfordshire County Council, ex p. Cheung*; *R.* v. *Sefton Metropolitan Borough Council, ex p. Pau, The Times,* July 15, 1985, where McNeill J. held that the authorities' refusal to reconsider decisions to refuse awards for the years before 1979–80 was *ultra vires*.

where residence in the United Kingdom had been wholly or mainly for the purposes of receiving full time education.[24]

Under the Education (Fees and Awards) Act 1983, the Secretary of State may make regulations (1) requiring or authorising the charging of higher fees to overseas students by universities and maintained further education establishments; and (2) excluding such students from eligibility for certain discretionary awards.[25]

Awards for postgraduate students are made directly by the Secretary of State.[26]

D. ANCILLARY POWERS AND DUTIES

(1) Medical inspection and treatment[27]

It is the duty of the Secretary of State (in practice, the Secretary of State **17-26** for Social Services) to provide for the medical and dental inspection, at appropriate intervals, of pupils attending schools maintained by local education authorities and for their treatment. The Secretary of State also has a power, but not a duty, to make similar arrangements for the medical and dental inspection and treatment of senior pupils at educational establishments other than schools maintained by local education authorities and at which full-time further education is provided. Provision may also be made for the inspection and treatment of children and young persons receiving education otherwise than at school. The Secretary of State undertakes his duties through district health authorities—these are described in paragraph 18–05. Parents of pupils are under a duty to submit their children for inspection and they commit an offence if they fail to do this without reasonable excuse, for which the penalty is a fine not exceeding level 1 on the standard scale. An authority is empowered to ensure the cleanliness of pupils in schools maintained by them.[28]

(2) Clothing, milk and meals

Section 5 of the Education (Miscellaneous Provisions) Act 1948[29] **17-27** enables a local education authority to provide clothing for any pupil

---

[24] S.I. 1983 No. 477, amending the Education (Mandatory Awards) Regulations 1982 (S.I. 1982 No. 954). See now the Education (Mandatory Awards) Regulations 1985 (S.I. 1985 No. 1126) reg. 13(1)(a),(b). See *R.* v. *Hereford and Worcester County Council, ex p. Wimbourne* (1983) 82 L.G.R. 251 (revised regulations held applicable to a British citizen); *MacMahon* v. *Department of Education and Science* [1983] Ch. 227 (three year residence requirement cannot lawfully be applied to E.E.C. national); *cf. R.* v. *Inner London Education Authority ex p. Hinde* (1984) 83 L.G.R. 695.

[25] See the Education (Fees and Awards) Regulations 1983 (S.I. 1983 No. 973) as amended by S.I. 1984 No. 1201.

[26] See the State Awards Regulations 1978 (S.I. 1978 No. 1096) as amended by S.I.s 1979 No. 333 and 1983 Nos. 188, 920.

[27] National Health Service Act 1977, s. 5(1) and Sched. 1; Education Act 1944, ss. 48(4), as amended and 69(2) as amended by the Criminal Justice Act 1982, ss. 38 and 46.

[28] s. 54, and London Government Act 1963, s. 32(7).

[29] As amended by the Education (Miscellaneous Provisions) Act 1953, Sched. 1, the Education Act 1980, s. 29 and the Education Act 1981, Sched. 3 para. 7. See the Education (Provision of Clothing) Regulations 1980 (S.I. 1980 No. 545.)

boarding at an educational institution maintained by the authority or attending nursery schools or nursery classes maintained by the authority. Clothing may also be supplied to a pupil attending any other school maintained by the authority or attending a special school whether maintained by the authority or not if the pupil is unable by reason of the inadequacy or unsuitability of his clothing to take full advantage of the education provided. The authority is expected to recover contributions from the parents to cover the cost or part of the cost of the clothing supplied if they are able to pay without financial hardship.

A local education authority has power under section 22 of the Education Act 1980 to provide pupils at schools maintained by it with milk, meals or other refreshment. This power must be exercised in relation to pupils whose parents receive supplementary benefit or family income supplement, and these pupils may not be charged. Charges may otherwise be made. The authority may remit the whole or part of any charge that would otherwise be made if, having regard to the particular circumstances of any pupil or class of pupils, it considers it appropriate to do so.[30]

(3) Facilities for recreation and social and physical training[31]

17-28   Every local education authority must see that facilities for primary, secondary and further education include adequate provision for recreational and social and physical training, and is empowered to provide camps, holiday classes, playing fields, play centres, and other places (including playgrounds, gymnasiums and swimming baths not appropriated to any school or college). The authority may itself provide these facilities or help others to do so. This power, in conjunction with section 41,[32] is relied upon as authority for Youth Service provision by local authorities.[33]

(4) Careers services[34]

17-29   Local education authorities have a duty to make arrangements for providing certain careers services. These comprise a vocational guidance service for persons attending, either full-time or part-time, educational institutions other than universities, and an employment service for persons leaving such institutions or universities. The duty does not apply to part-time evening students. Authorities are required to consult and co-operate with each other and may operate a joint service. Records must be

---

[30] See the Seventh Report from the Education, Science and Arts Committee for 1981–82, *School Meals* (1981–82 H.C. 505), and the Government Response, Cmnd. 8740.

[31] s. 53, as amended by the Education (Miscellaneous Provisions) Act 1948, s. 11, and Part I of Sched. 1 and the Education Act 1980, Sched. 7. See also § 20–20 as to provision of these facilities.

[32] § 17–24, above.

[33] See *Experience and Participation: Report of the Review Group on the Youth Service in England,* Cmnd. 8686 (1982); Government Response: D.E.S. Circular 1/85.

[34] Employment and Training Act 1973, ss. 8–10, as amended by S.I. 1981 No. 494.

kept of vocational advice given and be transferred when a person moves into the area of another authority. Local education authorities are required to perform their functions in accordance with such advice of a general character as the Secretary of State may give and to provide him with such information as he may request.

It is unlawful for a local education authority to do any act in the performance of its functions under section 8 of the Employment and Training Act 1973 which constitutes unlawful discrimination under the Sex Discrimination Act 1975 or the Race Relations Act 1976. This does not apply if the discrimination only concerns employment which the employer could lawfully refuse to offer the person in question, and the authority is not liable if it reasonably relies on a statement made to it by an employer that the employment is of this nature.[35]

The Youth Training Scheme is managed by the Manpower Services Commission, which was established by the Employment and Training Act 1973[36] and is under the supervision of the Secretary of State for Employment.[37] The Scheme came into operation in 1983, replacing the Youth Opportunities Programme. The aim is to provide a year's programme of planned work experience integrated with work-related training or further education for 16-year old school leavers, 17-year old school leavers who remain or become unemployed and some 18-year olds. There are two methods of arranging training. Under Mode A, young people are placed with public and private sector employers, including local authorities. Alternatively, the training is organised by the Commission, some programmes being run through community projects, training workshops or Information Technology Centres (Mode B1) and others through colleges, training associations and similar organisations (Mode B2).

A local authority may enter into arrangements with the Manpower Services Commission or the Secretary of State under any provision of the Employment and Training Act 1973.[38]

(5) Employment of children and young persons
The Children and Young Persons Act 1933 empowers a local authority **17-30** to make by-laws with respect to the employment of children, and, subject to those by-laws, no child under the age of 13 may be employed in any way.[39] There are restrictions on employment in street trading (in general

---

[35] Sex Discrimination Act 1975, s. 15; Race Relations Act 1976, s. 14.
[36] ss. 1, 2.
[37] s. 3. See generally M. Freedland, (1983) 12 I.L.J. 220.
[38] Local Government (Miscellaneous Provisions) Act 1982, s. 45.
[39] Children and Young Persons Act 1933, s. 18, as amended by the Children and Young Persons Act 1963, s. 34, Sched. 3, para. 4, and the Children Act 1972, s. 1. The Employment of Children Act 1973 transfers to the Secretary of State, on a day to be appointed, the powers of local authorities to make by-laws with respect to the employment of children. Regulations made by him will take their place.

no one under 17 years of age may be engaged on this work)[40] and the use of children in entertainments for which a charge is made to the audience.[41] The local authority for the purpose of these provisions is the local education authority, except in the case of the City of London where (other than in respect of licences for entertainment) the Common Council is the authority.[42]

Under section 59 of the Education Act 1944[43] a local education authority may, by notice served on an employer, prohibit or restrict employment of any child if the authority considers the employment to be prejudicial to his health or education. The Young Persons (Employment) Acts 1938 and 1964 regulate the employment of persons under the age of eighteen and impose on local authorities the duty of enforcement.

(6) Transport facilities

17-31 A local education authority must make such arrangements as it thinks necessary or as the Secretary of State directs to provide free transport to facilitate the attendance of pupils at schools or at courses provided under a scheme for further education.[44] It is a valid excuse for failure to attend school to show that the pupil's home is not within walking distance from his school and that no suitable arrangements have been made for his transport by the authority. "Walking distance" is two miles in the case of children under eight years and three miles in other cases.[45] In *Surrey County Council* v. *Ministry of Education*[46] it was held that the council had not discharged its duty by providing that no child should have to travel a longer distance than three miles unaided; it was not sufficient merely to pay for the transport of the child to within the three-mile limit. A route which is unsafe to the extent that a responsible parent would not permit his or her child to use it is not an "available route" for these purposes.[47]

Apart from the *duty* to make arrangements already mentioned, there is a *power* to pay the whole or any part of the reasonable travelling expenses of any pupil in attendance at any such school or course for whose transport no arrangements are made.

(7) Training of teachers

17-32 It is the duty of the Secretary of State to make arrangements for

[40] Children and Young Persons Act 1933, s. 20, as amended by the Children and Young Persons Act 1963, s. 35.
[41] Children and Young Persons Act 1963, s. 37, as amended by the Licensing Act 1964, Sched. 14, para. 1 and the Cable and Broadcasting Act 1984, Sched. 5, para 12.
[42] Children and Young Persons Act 1933, ss. 96 and 97; Local Authority Social Services Act 1970, Sched. 2, para. 1.
[43] Repealed by the Employment of Children Act 1973 from a day to be appointed.
[44] Education Act 1944, s. 55, as amended by the Education (Miscellaneous Provisions) Act 1948, s. 11, and Sched. 1, Part 1.
[45] *Ibid.* s. 39.
[46] [1953] 1 All E.R. 705.
[47] *Rogers* v. *Essex County Council* [1985] 1 W.L.R. 700.

securing sufficient facilities for the training of teachers, and for this purpose he may direct a local education authority to establish, maintain or assist any college of further education or other institution or to provide or assist in the provision of other facilities. Where a direction is given to one authority the Secretary of State may require other authorities to contribute towards the expenses incurred.[48] Local education authorities are also required to make awards and grants to students accepted for courses for the initial training of teachers, and the Secretary of State may make grants to education authorities in respect of school teachers undergoing further training as such and further education teachers undergoing training as such, whose remuneration is paid by them.[49]

Colleges for teacher-training (known as colleges of education) are managed by governors established under an instrument of government and in accordance with articles of government made by the local education authority with the approval of the Secretary of State.[50]

(8) Nuisance and disturbance on educational premises

Any person who, without lawful authority, is present on the premises of **17-33** a school maintained or further education establishment provided by a local education authority and causes or permits nuisance or disturbance to the annoyance of persons who lawfully use those premises, commits a summary offence, punishable by a fine not exceeding level 2 on the standard scale. The term "premises" includes playgrounds, playing fields and other premises for outdoor recreation. A police constable or a person authorised by the education authority (or, in the case of an aided or special agreement school, by the governors), may remove any person reasonably suspected to be committing or to have committed an offence.[51]

(9) Unlawful discrimination

It is unlawful for a local education authority or governors, in relation to **17-34** an educational establishment maintained by the authority, to discriminate against a person on the ground of her sex:

(a) in the terms on which they offer to admit her as a pupil;

(b) by refusing or deliberately omitting to accept an application for her admission as a pupil; or

(c) where she is a pupil, in the way in which they afford her access to any benefits, facilities or services, or by refusing or deliberately

---

[48] Education Act 1944, s. 62; Local Government Act 1974, s. 2, Sched. 2.
[49] Education Act 1962, as substituted by the Education Act 1980, s. 19 and Sched. 5; Education (Teacher Training Awards) Regulations 1983 (S.I. 1983 No. 481), as amended by S.I.s 1984 No. 893 and 1985 No. 1220; Education (Grants for Teacher Training) (No. 2) Regulations 1985 (S.I. 1985 No. 1883).
[50] Education (No. 2) Act 1968, s. 1.
[51] Local Government (Miscellaneous Provisions) Act 1982, s. 40, as amended by the Criminal Justice Act 1982, s. 46.

omitting to afford her access to them or by excluding her from the establishment or subjecting her to any other detriment.[52]

Furthermore, it is unlawful for a local education authority in carrying out its other functions to do any act which constitutes sex discrimination,[53] and such authorities are under a general duty to secure that facilities for education provided by it, and any ancillary benefits or services, are provided without sex discrimination.[54] There are exceptions in respect of single-sex establishments and further education courses in physical training.[55]

Similarly worded provisions, without the exceptions, apply to prohibit racial discrimination.[56] Proceedings were taken under the Race Relations Act 1968[57] against the London Borough of Ealing to prevent the "bussing" of Asian children from Southall to "white" schools elsewhere in the borough other than on educational grounds.[58] An out of court settlement was reached and the policy was phased out.[59] In a Formal Investigation Report on Secondary School Allocations in Reading in February 1983, the Commission for Racial Equality found that while the arrangements were not discriminatory, the authority had taken insufficient account of their duties under sections 19 and 71 of the Race Relations Act 1976.

E. Tortious Liability

17-35 Pupils of a school come within the category known in the common law of tort as invitees: the duty which the occupier of school premises has towards pupils attending the school is therefore the "common duty of care" owed to "lawful visitors" as defined in section 2 of the Occupiers' Liability Act 1957. This section is printed in full at paragraph 10–37. Put briefly, it is a duty to take such care as in all the circumstances of the case is reasonable to see that the visitor will be reasonably safe in using the premises and to be prepared for children to be less careful than adults. The common law duty of an occupier to invitees is somewhat similar to that now imposed by statute—cases decided on common law principles

---

[52] Sex Discrimination Act 1975, s. 22. For what constitutes discrimination see ss. 1, 2 and 4; for enforcement provisions see Part VII of the Act. The provisions apply equally to discrimination against males: s.2. These requirements apply also to establishments designated by the Secretary of State, which include assisted schools, polytechnics and colleges of education: Sex Discrimination (Designated Education Establishments) Order 1975 (S.I. 1975 No. 1902), as amended by S.I. 1980 No. 1860.

[53] Sex Discrimination Act 1975, s. 23. See *R.* v. *Secretary of State for Education and Science, ex p. Keating, The Times,* December 3, 1985.

[54] *Ibid.* s. 25.

[55] *Ibid.* ss. 26–28, s. 28 as amended by the Further Education Act 1985, s. 4.

[56] Race Relations Act 1976, ss. 17–19.

[57] s. 2 (discrimination in the provision of goods, facilities or services). There was no equivalent in the 1968 Act to ss. 17–19 of the 1976 Act.

[58] See *Commission for Racial Equality* v. *London Borough of Ealing* [1978] 1 W.L.R. 112.

[59] Report of the Commission for Racial Equality for 1978, at p. 101.

may therefore be relevant in the interpretation of the statutory duty, and one of these cases is cited.

Fryer v. *Salford Corporation*.[60] The plaintiff, a pupil aged 11 years attending a cookery class, sustained injury by fire when approaching a gas stove. A guard had not been provided for the stove. *Held*, the corporation was liable in damages, for the danger was one which might reasonably have been anticipated and could have been guarded against.

Parents who visit a school in connection with the work of the school or in the interests of their children as pupils may also be classed as invitees,[61] and therefore "lawful visitors," and the "common duty of care" imposed by section 2 of the Act of 1957 would apply. The duty of care lies primarily on the occupier of the premises—in a voluntary school it would therefore fall on the governors.

Teachers owe a duty of care to the pupils under their charge of a **17-36** standard equal to the care which parents might be expected to show their children.[62]

Lord Esher M.R. said in *Williams* v. *Eady*[63]:

" . . . as to the law on the subject there could be no doubt; and it was correctly laid down by the learned judge, that the schoolmaster was bound to take such care of his boys as a careful father would take of his boys, and there could not be a better definition of the duty of a schoolmaster."

This dictum was quoted with approval in *Rich* v. *London County* **17-37** *Council*,[64] a decision of the Court of Appeal. There have, however, been several judgments of the Queen's Bench Division which suggest a somewhat different standard. In *Lyes* v. *Middlesex County Council*[65] it was held that the common law duty of the schoolmaster to his pupil is that of a prudent parent not in the context of the home but in the circumstances of school life. And in *Beaumont* v. *Surrey County Council*[66] Geoffrey Lane J. said[67]:

"The duty of a headmaster towards his pupils is said to be to take such care of them as a reasonably careful and prudent father would take of his own children. The standard is a helpful one when considering, for example, individual instructions to individual children in a school . . . but that standard when applied to an incident of horseplay in a school of 900 pupils is somewhat unrealistic if not unhelpful. . . . In the context of the present action it appears to me to be easier and preferable to use the ordinary language of the law of negligence, that is, it is a headmaster's duty, bearing in mind the known propensities of boys . . . to take all reasonable and proper steps to prevent any of the pupils under his care from suffering injury from inanimate objects, from the

---

[60] [1937] 1 All E.R. 617.
[61] *Griffiths* v. *Smith* [1941] A.C. 170.
[62] See *Clerk and Lindsell on Torts*, 15th ed., § 10–64; and see *ibid.* § 10–65 as to the duty in *negligence* of those in charge of a school.
[63] (1893) 10 T.L.R. 41 at p. 42.
[64] [1953] 1 W.L.R. 895 at p. 900.
[65] (1962) 61 L.G.R. 443.
[66] (1968) 66 L.G.R. 580.
[67] At p. 585.

actions of their fellow pupils, or from a combination of two. That is a high standard.[68]

17-38 The "ordinary language of the law of negligence" was applied in the case which follows:

> *Barnes* v. *Hampshire County Council.*[69] An infant school operated a system whereby children were handed over to their parents at 3.30 p.m. The plaintiff (five years old) was released from the school early and before her mother reached the gate. She set out alone and was injured on the main road nearby at 3.29 p.m. *Held*, it was the duty of the school authorities not to release the children before the official closing time, since although a premature release would very seldom cause an accident, it foreseeably could, and in the present case it did cause an accident. The five minute period did not come within the *de minimis* rule and the defendants were liable in negligence.

17-39 Liability for an absence of care in the matter of supervision may extend beyond a pupil to third parties.

> *Carmarthenshire County Council* v. *Lewis.*[70] A child of four years attending a nursery school strayed from the school to the highway and the respondent's husband who was driving a lorry struck a telegraph post in an attempt to avoid the child, and he was killed. The respondent sued the council for damages, claiming that the death was due to the authority's negligence or that of the teacher who had left the child unattended for a short while. *Held*, the duty of the teacher was the same as that of a careful parent and she acted as she might have been expected to act (her absence was due to a call to treat another child) and she could not therefore be held liable. But that did not conclude the matter so far as the county council was concerned, for the fact that the child could reach the street indicated some lack of care or of precautions which might reasonably be required.

If an absence of care is due to the fault of the school authority (as in the *Carmarthenshire* case), then only the authority can be sued for damages in case of injury; if the teacher is at fault, then an action may lie against the authority as well as against the teacher, for a master is responsible for the tortious acts of his servants.[71] In *Smith* v. *Martin and Hull Corporation*[72] the corporation was held liable for the negligence of a teacher who directed a child to attend to a fire in the teachers' common room, notwithstanding the fact that only the teacher was at fault.

17-40 Regulations have been made under section 10 of the Act of 1944 prescribing standards to which school premises must conform[73] and a duty is imposed on local education authorities to secure that schools

---

[68] But *cf. Crouch* v. *Essex County Council* (1966) 64 L.G.R. 240.
[69] [1969] 1 W.L.R. 1563. The duty of supervision may not extend to play before school; *Ward* v. *Hertfordshire County Council* [1970] 1 W.L.R. 356. For other cases involving supervision, see *Butt* v. *Cambridgeshire County Council* (1969) 68 L.G.R. 81; *Jacques* v. *Oxfordshire County Council* (1967) 66 L.G.R. 440; *Butt* v. *Inner London Education Authority* (1968) 66 L.G.R. 379; *Mays* v. *Essex County Council* (1975) 125 New L.J. 1065 and *Moore* v. *Hampshire County Council* (1981) 80 L.G.R. 481.
[70] [1955] A.C. 549.
[71] See Chap. 10 as to vicarious liability.
[72] [1911] 2 K.B. 775.
[73] Education (School Premises) Regulations 1981 (S.I. 1981 No. 909). reg. 24.

maintained by them comply with these requirements. The regulations require that premises shall be of such design and construction that the health and safety of the occupants "are reasonably assured." A cause of action will lie for a breach of this duty, and the same facts may sustain an action founded on negligence and breach of common duty of care imposed by the Occupiers' Liability Act 1957 (referred to above).

> *Reffell* v. *Surrey County Council.*[74] A girl hurrying along a corridor in a controlled school put out her hand to stop a swing door that was swinging towards her, and she was injured. The plaintiff succeeded in a claim for damages for breach of statutory duty under section 10 of the Education Act 1944, and regulation 51 of the Standards for School Premises Regulations 1959.[75] Veale J. held that these provisions imposed an absolute duty of which the test of breach was an objective test, *viz.* that there would be a breach of duty if safety were not reasonably assured, and, on the facts, safety had not been reasonably assured. The local education authority was also liable in negligence and for a breach of its common duty of care under the Occupiers' Liability Act 1957. What the pupil had been doing was perfectly natural. There had been similar accidents in the authority's schools and the risk was one that could reasonably have been foreseen.

In spite of the view of Veale J. in *Reffell's* case it is doubtful whether the duty under the Education Act and the regulations is any more strict than at common law. In *Ward* v. *Hertfordshire County Council,*[76] where a boy aged eight was injured when he stumbled and hit his head against a jagged part of a brick and flint wall, Salmon L.J. said[77]:

> "No question really arises under the Standards for School Premises Regulations 1959. Under these regulations it would be necessary for the plaintiff to show that the wall was not reasonably safe. If it were not, there would be no necessity in the circumstances of this case to rely on the regulations because the plaintiff would have his remedy at common law."

Tortious liability can also arise in the field of nuisance. In *Dunton* v. *Dover District Council*[78] it was held that the noise from a children's playground constituted a nuisance when it was used from dawn to dusk by children of all ages. The owner of a hotel adjoining a housing estate including a playground adjacent to the hotel garden was awarded damages and was granted an injunction against the Council stipulating that the playground should be open only between 10 a.m. and 6.30 p.m. to children under the age of 12.

---

[74] [1964] 1 W.L.R. 358.
[75] Reg. 51 was expressed in similar terms to S.I. 1981 No. 909, reg. 24, *supra.*
[76] [1970] 1 W.L.R. 356.
[77] At p. 361.
[78] (1977) 76 L.G.R. 87.

CHAPTER 18

THE HEALTH AND SOCIAL SERVICES

18-01   THE following topics are considered in this Chapter—the health services provided under the National Health Service Act 1977; social and other services provided by local authorities including the care of children; mental health.

A. THE HEALTH SERVICES

18-02   The National Health Service Reorganisation Act 1973[1] gave effect to the proposals contained in the White Papers *National Health Service Reorganisation: England,* Cmnd. 5055, and *National Health Service Reorganisation: Wales,* Cmnd. 5057, published in 1972. It brought together under one unified administration (a) the hospital and specialist services formerly administered by the Regional Hospital Boards, Hospital Management Committees and Boards of Governors; (b) the family practitioner services formerly administered by Executive Councils; (c) the personal health services formerly administered by local authorities; and (d) the school health service formerly administered by local education authorities.

18-03   A duty falls to the Secretary of State for Social Services to provide throughout England and Wales, to such extent as he considers necessary to meet all reasonable requirements, hospital and other related accommodation, medical, dental, nursing and ambulance services, facilities for care of expectant and nursing mothers and young children, and facilities for the prevention of illness and for care and after-care. He is required to make provision for the medical and dental inspection and treatment of school children, and to provide a family planning service.[2]

18-04   England is divided, for the purposes of the Act, into 14 regions and the regions into districts.[3] Regional health authorities administer the first and district health authorities the second. In Wales the district health authorities are in direct relationship with the Welsh Office.

General medical and dental practitioners, ophthalmic medical practitioners, opticians and pharmacists are independent contractors. The Secretary of State is required to set up a family practitioner committee to administer these contracts.[4]

---

[1] Now see the consolidating National Health Service Act 1977.
[2] National Health Service Act 1977, ss. 3 and 5.
[3] *Ibid.* s. 8, as amended by the Health Services Act 1980, s. 1.
[4] *Ibid.* ss. 10 and 15, as amended by s. 5 of the Health and Social Security Act 1984.

Under these general arrangements, the Department of Health and Social Security undertakes central strategic planning and monitoring and it settles national health policies, objectives and priorities. Each regional health authority has a regional planning responsibility and settles priorities where there are competing claims between districts. The basic unit of planning and operational control is the district authority. At each level—national, regional and district—there is a unified administration covering the whole span of the national health service.

Two further bodies, local advisory committees[5] and community health councils, were established by the 1977 Act.[6] The former provide professional advice to health authorities. The latter represent the interests in the health service of the public in the districtts to which they are related.

Each regional authority consists of a chairman appointed by the **18–05** Secretary of State and of such number of other members appointed by him as he thinks fit after consultation with various bodies. District health authorities consist of a chairman appointed by the regional authority after consultation, and a specified number (not less than four) of members appointed by the corresponding local authorities. Family practitioner committees consist of people appointed by the Secretary of State. They are accountable to the Secretary of State for the services they provide, but rely on district health authorities for their staffing and accommodation.[7] At least half the members of a community health council are appointed by the local authorities concerned, and at least one comes from each authority. Not less than a third of the membership is appointed by voluntary bodies. Members of a health authority cannot be members of a community health council.

A duty is placed on health authorities and local authorities to co- **18–06** operate with one another in order to secure and advance the health and welfare of the people of England and Wales.[8] To facilitate this, the Act requires the appointment of joint consultative committees to advise district health authorities and related local authorities on the perform-ance of their duties and on the planning and operation of services of common concern.

There are many points at which services are inter-related. Child guidance, for example, involves child psychiatry, available within the hospital services, social work provided by the local authority social service department, and educational psychology, which falls to local education authorities. District health authorities have comprehensive health education powers and there are complementary powers available to local authorities in the provision of environmental health services and

---

[5] National Health Service Act 1977, s. 19.
[6] *Ibid.* s. 20.
[7] *Ibid.* s. 10 and Sched. 5, Part II, as amended by the Health and Social Security Act 1984, s. 5, Sched. 3.
[8] *Ibid.* s. 22, as amended by the Health and Social Services and Social Security Adjudications Act 1983, s. 12 and Sched. 5.

to local education authorities for health education within schools. Environmental health functions (described in Chapter 16) include measures for the prevention of the spread of communicable diseases; local authorities have powers relating to food safety and hygiene (see Chapter 22) and they have responsibility for the enforcement of certain requirements concerning health and safety at work (see Chapter 27) and the employment of children and young persons (see para. 17-30).

18-07   Health Service Commissioners for England and Wales have been appointed under Part V of the Act. They have the same kind of responsibilities as the Local Government Commissioners for England and Wales, referred to at paragraph 4-64.

B. THE SOCIAL SERVICES

18-08   Local authority social services are those listed in Schedule 1 to the Local Authority Social Services Act 1970, and include the welfare services and child care. The responsible authorities are the councils of non-metropolitan counties, metropolitan districts, London boroughs and the Common Council of the City of London.[9] Authorities are required to appoint a social services committee and to refer to that committee the functions listed in Schedule 1.[10] They may, however, refer matters concerned with social services functions to other committees on the ground that the service relates to a general service of the authority, but the authority must first consider a report of the social services committee with respect to the subject matter of the proposed reference. Additionally, matters other than those concerned with the social services may be referred to or delegated to the social service committee.[11] A social services committee may, subject to the approval of the authority, establish sub-committees and may delegate to them any of the functions of the committee.[12] An authority is required to appoint a director of social services.[13]

18-09   Under legislation in force prior to April 1, 1974, authorities discharged their health and welfare functions in accordance with proposals and schemes made by them and approved by the Secretary of State. The Local Government Act 1972[14] simplified the situation. The requirement to submit proposals and schemes was removed. Instead, local authorities may, with the approval of the Secretary of State, and to such extent as he may direct, make arrangements for carrying out the functions to which those proposals and schemes related, except in so far as from April 1,

---

[9] Local Authority Social Services Act 1970, s. 1; Local Government Act 1972, s. 195.
[10] Local Authority Social Services Act 1970, s. 2; Local Government Act 1972, s. 101(8).
[11] Local Authority Social Services Act 1970, ss. 2, 3 and 3A; Local Government, Planning and Land Act 1980, s. 183.
[12] *Ibid.* ss. 2–5; Local Government Act 1972, s. 101(9)(*f*).
[13] Local Authority Social Services Act 1970, s. 6; Local Government Act 1972, s. 112(4).
[14] Local Government Act 1972, s. 195(3).

1974, they became the responsibility of the national health service. Additionally, local authorities are required, in the exercise of their social services functions, including the exercise of any discretion conferred on them, to act under the general guidance of the Secretary of State.[15]

Welfare services

(a) *The provision of accommodation*[16]

Social services authorities have a power (and, if directed by the **18-10** Secretary of State, a duty) to provide residential accommodation for those who because of age, infirmity, mental disorder[17], or other circumstances are in need of care and attention not otherwise available to them. The authority may itself provide accommodation or may make arrangements with another authority or voluntary organisation. A standard charge for the use of the accommodation must be fixed, but in particular cases a lower rate may be charged, not less than the minimum which the Secretary of State prescribes.[18] In assessing ability to pay, only the resources listed in Part III of Schedule 1 to the Supplementary Benefits Act 1976 must be disregarded.

The authority liable to provide residential accommodation is the authority of the area where the person is ordinarily resident, but if he has no settled place of residence or if the need is urgent, the authority in whose area the needy person happens to be is responsible for providing accommodation. The authority which provides the service may, however, recover the costs involved from the authority of the area where the person is ordinarily resident, and any dispute as to where a person is ordinarily resident is settled by the Secretary of State.

(b) *The provision of welfare services*[19]

An authority may make arrangements for promoting the welfare of **18-11** persons who are blind, deaf or dumb, and other persons who are substantially and permanently handicapped by illness, injury, or congenital deformity, and this power may be exercised for the benefit of mentally disordered persons of any description.[20] The Secretary of State may direct

---

[15] Local Authority Social Services Act 1970, s. 7(1).
[16] National Assistance Act 1948, ss. 21–27; London Government Act 1963, s. 46; Local Government Act 1972, Sched. 23, paras. 2 and 8; National Health Service Act 1977, s. 21, Sched. 8. As to provision of accommodation for homeless persons, see §§ 15–03, *et seq.*
[17] The provisions of s. 21 of the National Assistance Act 1948 are extended by s. 8 of the Mental Health Act 1959 to include persons suffering from mental disorder. And see National Health Service Act 1977, s. 21 and Sched. 8.
[18] National Assistance (Charges for Accommodation) Regulations 1985 (S.I. 1985 No. 1317).
[19] National Assistance Act 1948, ss. 29–32; National Assistance (Amendment) Act 1959, s. 1; Local Government Act 1972, Sched. 23, para. 2; National Health Service Act 1977, s. 21 and Sched. 8.
[20] s. 29 of the National Assistance Act 1948 is extended by s. 8 of the Mental Health Act 1959 to include persons suffering from mental disorder. It does not authorise the provision of residential accommodation: *Vandyk* v. *Oliver* [1976] A.C. 659.

an authority to make arrangements for persons ordinarily resident in the authority's area. Arrangements may include the provision of recreational facilities and home instruction, and facilities for earning a living (at home or in workshops) and for selling the products, and hostels may be provided to accommodate those engaged in the workshops. Authorities may with the approval of the Secretary of State, and to such extent as he may direct, make arrangements for promoting the welfare of old people, and charges may be made.[21] They may employ registered voluntary organisations[22] as their agents and may also contribute to the funds of such organisations. Authorities have a duty to provide a home help service.[23]

18–12   The Chronically Sick and Disabled Persons Act 1970 greatly extended the duties of welfare authorities.[24] They must make particular arrangements for persons in the disabled categories to meet their particular needs, giving practical assistance in their homes, making provision for wireless, television or other recreational facilities inside and outside their homes, providing travelling facilities to enable them to take advantage of welfare and other services available to them, giving assistance in works of adaptation to give their homes greater safety, comfort and convenience, helping with meals and holidays, and the provision of telephone facilities. Authorities are under a duty to discover how many disabled persons are in their areas and to ensure that these persons know what services are available to them.[25]

In *Wyatt* v. *Hillingdon London Borough Council*[26] the Court of Appeal dismissed the appeal of a registered disabled person who claimed damages for negligence and breach of statutory duty under section 2 of the Act of 1970 for failure to provide her with an adequate home help service. The remedy in such cases lies in the default powers of the Secretary of State under section 36 of the National Assistance Act 1948.

18–13   Contributions may be made to voluntary organisations which provide recreation or meals for old people and authorities may themselves provide these services.[27]

(c) *Registration and other functions*

18–14   Homes for disabled persons and aged persons must be registered as "residential care homes" with local authorities, and wide powers are given to inspect and control homes and to refuse or to cancel registration if the personnel of the homes or the conduct of affairs or the state of the

---

[21] Health Services and Public Health Act 1968, s. 45; Health and Social Services and Social Security Adjudications Act 1983, s. 17.
[22] See below as to registration.
[23] National Health Service Act 1977, Sched. 8 para. 3.
[24] ss. 1 and 2.
[25] s. 1.
[26] (1978) 76 L.G.R. 727.
[27] Health and Social Services and Social Security Adjudications Act 1983, s. 29, Sched. 9, Pt. II. This power is available to district councils.

premises are in the council's view unsatisfactory.[28] A decision to refuse or to cancel registration is subject to appeal to a Registered Homes Tribunal. It is possible for an establishment to be registered both as a residential care home and as a nursing home or mental nursing home.

Authorities are under a duty to safeguard the moveable property of **18-15** persons admitted to hospitals or to accommodation provided under the National Assistance Act 1948 where the property is in danger of loss or damage and no other suitable arrangements are made.[29]

Where a person is suffering from chronic disease, or, being old or incapacitated, is living in insanitary conditions and is not receiving adequate care and attention, the local authority (in this case the council of a London borough or district or the Common Council of the City of London) may apply to a magistrates' court for an order requiring the patient's removal to hospital or other place.[30]

A duty falls to authorities to bury or cremate those who die in their areas where no other suitable arrangements are made; the authorities here are the councils of districts and London boroughs and the Common Council of the City of London.[31]

The care of children

Local authorities have a number of statutory powers and duties with **18-16** respect to the care of children: under the Child Care Act 1980[32] for the care and welfare of orphans, deserted children and other children deprived, temporarily or permanently, of a normal life with their parents; under the Foster Children Act 1980[33] with respect to private foster children; under the Adoption Acts 1958 to 1976 and the Children Acts 1958 to 1975 with respect to adoption; under the Children and Young Persons Act 1933 to 1969[34] in respect of juvenile offenders and children and young persons in need of care or control and in respect of the provision of community homes; under the Mental Health Acts 1959 and 1983 in respect of mentally disordered children. They also have responsibilities towards children under care or supervision orders made under the Matrimonial Causes Act 1973, the Domestic Proceedings and Magistrates' Courts Act 1978, the Family Law Reform Act 1969 and the Guardianship Act 1973. They, with the Department of Health and Social Security, may engage in or assist research.[35]

Authorities are under a general duty to make available such advice, **18-17**

---

[28] Registered Homes Act 1984, s. 1; Residential Care Homes Regulations 1984 (S.I. 1984 No. 1345).
[29] s. 48, as amended by the Local Government Act 1972, Sched. 23, para. 2.
[30] National Assistance Act 1948, s. 47; London Government Act 1963, s. 46; National Assistance (Amendment) Act 1951, s. 1; Local Government Act 1972, Sched. 23, para. 47.
[31] Public Health (Control of Disease) Act 1984, s. 46.
[32] By virtue of S.I. 1980 No. 1935 this Act came into force on April 1, 1981.
[33] A consolidating measure which came into force on April 1, 1981.
[34] And see the Child Care Act 1980.
[35] Child Care Act 1980, s. 77.

guidance and assistance as may promote the welfare of children by diminishing the need to receive or keep them in care or to rely on other proceedings[36]: in discharging this obligation authorities prevent or forestall family breakdown and other situations which give rise to use of other statutory powers.

(a) Care of deprived children

18-18   Section 2 of the Child Care Act 1980 imposes a duty on local authorities to receive into their care children in their areas under the age of 17 and who are without parents or guardians, or who have been abandoned or lost, or whose parents or guardians are unfit or unable to look after them, provided that the intervention of the authority is necessary in the interests of the child's welfare. Those received into care may remain the responsibility of the authority until they reach the age of 18, which can be extended under certain circumstances, but wherever it is consistent with the welfare of a child an effort must be made to have the care entrusted to a parent, guardian, relative or friend, and if a parent asks for the child, the authority must usually return him.[37]

A parent or guardian may not take away a child who has been in care of the local authority throughout the preceding six months unless the authority consents or the parent or guardian has given the authority not less than 28 days notice of his intention to take the child.[38] Restrictions are also placed on the removal of a child from the care of a voluntary organisation, whether resident in a voluntary home or boarded out with foster parents.

An authority which has received a child into its care under section 2 of the 1980 Act may pass a resolution under section 3 of that Act vesting in itself parental rights and duties with respect to that child. The grounds for passing a resolution under section 3 are:

    (a)   that his parents are dead and he has no guardian or custodian; or

    (b)   that a parent of his—

        (i)   has abandoned him, or

        (ii)   suffers from some permanent disability rendering him incapable of caring for the child, or

        (iii) while not falling within sub-paragraph (ii) of this paragraph, suffers from a mental disorder (within the meaning of the Mental Health Act 1983), which renders him unfit to have the care of the child, or

---

[36] Child Care Act 1980, s. 1. "Assistance" includes the provision of temporary accommodation: see *Att.-Gen. (ex rel. Tilley)* v. *Wandsworth L.B.C.* [1981] 1 W.L.R. 854.

[37] In *Lewisham Borough Council* v. *Lewisham Juvenile Court Justices* [1980] A.C. 273, the House of Lords held that the power of a local authority to keep a child in their care under s. 2 was not automatically terminated when a parent notified the authority of his or her desire to take over the care of the child. See further below.

[38] Child Care Act 1980, s. 13(2). See *Wheatley* v. *Waltham Forest L.B.C.* (Note) [1980] A.C. 311.

(iv) is of such habits or mode of life as to be unfit to have the care of the child, or

(v) has so consistently failed without reasonable cause to discharge the obligations of a parent as to be unfit to have the care of the child; or

(c) that a resolution under paragraph (b) above is in force in relation to one parent of the child who is, or is likely to become, a member of the household comprising the child and his other parent; or

(d) that throughout the three years preceding the passing of the resolution, the child has been in the care of a local authority under section 2, or partly in the care of a local authority and partly in the care of a voluntary organisation.

Notice of the resolution must be served on the parent or guardian, and they may object by counter-notice served on the local authority within one month. If objection is raised, the resolution ceases to have effect, but the authority may complain to the juvenile court, and the court may order that the resolution shall remain in operation. A resolution assuming parental rights continues in force until the child becomes 18, but it may at any time be rescinded by the authority if it appears to be for the benefit of the child, or by the juvenile court on the initiative of a parent or guardian, or if the child is adopted.

An appeal lies to the High Court from the making by a juvenile court of an order confirming or terminating a resolution or from refusal to make such an order.[39]

The House of Lords reviewed the cases on the assumption of parental rights by a local authority and the jurisdiction of the juvenile court in the following case:

Lewisham London Borough Council v. *Lewisham Juvenile Court Justices*.[40] M. was born into a one-parent family in January 1976 and 18 months later was received into care at his mother's request. The mother left the child in care until April 1978 when she gave the local authority four weeks notice that she would be taking him home the following month. Seven days after receipt of the letter the authority resolved that parental rights and duties of the mother be vested in the council under section 2 of the Children Act 1948 (section 3 of the 1980 Act) on the grounds that the mother had so consistently failed without reasonable cause to discharge the obligations of a parent as to be unfit to have the care of her child. Two weeks later the mother served a counter-notice on the local authority which made a complaint to the juvenile court. The juvenile court refused to hear the complaint, holding that it had no jurisdiction in view of the Court of Appeal decision in *Johns* v. *Jones*.[41] On the same day as their complaint was made to the juvenile court, the local authority took out a wardship summons in the Family Division of the High Court. A wardship order was made and the child became a ward of court. In proceedings for judicial review of the justices' decision declining jurisdiction the House of

[39] Child Care Act 1980, s. 6.
[40] [1980] A.C. 273.
[41] [1979] Q.B. 411. In this case it was held that the communication of a parent's desire to take over the care of her child terminated local authority care.

Lords, overruling *Johns* v. *Jones,* unanimously allowed the appeal of the local authority and remitted the question of whether or not the local authority's resolution of assumption of parental rights should stand. Lord Scarman said[42]:
"The encouragement and support of family life are basic. The local authority is given duties and powers primarily to help, not to supplant, parents. A child is not to be removed from his home or family against the will of his parents save by the order of a court, where the parent will have the opportunity to be heard before the order is made. Respect for parental rights and duties is, however, balanced against the need to protect children from neglect, ill treatment, abandonment and danger; for the welfare of the child is paramount. Even in the system of 'voluntary' care under the Act of 1948 [now the Act of 1980], the local authority has the power in circumstances of danger to the child's welfare to pass a resolution vesting in itself the parental rights and duties in respect of the child. If the parent does not object or has disappeared, there will be no need to go to court. If the parent objects and serves his counter-notice, the juvenile court will decide whether the resolution is to lapse, in which event the parent's rights and duties over-ride those of the local authority, or is not to lapse in which event the parent must, so long as the resolution is in force, yield to the local authority. The parent is, however, never totally excluded. He or she can always come back. The local authority may, while the resolution continues, entrust the child to the parent . . . and the resolution may at any time be rescinded."

18-19   The relationship between the parental rights assumed by a local authority and the ancient prerogative of the Crown as *parens patriae* as regards minors (now exercised by way of ward of court procedure in the Family Division of the High Court) was considered in the following case:

Re M. (An Infant).[43] The local authority requested the return of a child boarded out with a foster mother. The foster mother refused and the authority issued a summons for an order of habeas corpus. The foster mother thereupon made application that the child become a ward of court. The authority applied for an order that the child should cease to be a ward of court. The local authority succeeded. It was held that the decision as to the best interests of the child lay in the exclusive jurisdiction of the local authority, not the court. Lord Evershed M.R. said[44]: "The prerogative right of the Queen as *parens patriae* in relation to infants within the realm is not for all purposes ousted or abrogated as the result of the exercise of the duties and powers by local authorities under the Children Act 1948: in particular the power to make an infant a ward of court . . . is unaffected. But even where a child is made a ward of court . . . the judge in whom the prerogative power is vested will, acting on familiar principles, not exercise control in relation to duties or discretions clearly vested by statute in the local authority, and may, therefore, and in a case such as the present normally will, order that the child cease to be a ward of court. . . . There remains the right (and duty) of the judge in whom the prerogative power is vested, to control the activities of a local authority in cases where the local authority is shown to be acting in some way in breach or in disregard of its statutory duties."

18-20   The High Court will not normally review the merits of the authority's

---

[42] At p. 539.
[43] [1961] Ch. 328, approved by the House of Lords in *A.* v. *Liverpool City Council* [1982] A.C. 363 and *Re W. (A Minor) (Wardship Jurisdiction)* [1985] A.C. 791.
[44] At p. 345.

decisions affecting the child by virtue of its wardship jurisdiction, but the Court will exercise a supervisory role in respect of any abuse of discretion.[45] These principles are applicable where there is a section 3 resolution or where the child has been committed to the care of the local authority by a juvenile court (see paras. 18-34, *et seq.*).[46] Where a child has been received into care under section 2 of the 1980 Act the Court is more likely to exercise its wardship jurisdiction.

> *Re S (An Infant).*[47] A boy in the care of a local authority was entrusted by the authority to foster parents, who agreed that the boy could be removed from them when required. The foster parents heard that the boy's mother had made a request to the local authority to take the boy back and they applied by originating summons to make him a ward of court, and the boy became a ward of court. The authority claimed that the court had no jurisdiction to review such decision as it might make. *Held,* the jurisdiction of the court over the boy as a ward of court was not ousted by the fact that the authority had received him into care under section 1 of the Children Act 1948 (section 2 of the Child Care Act 1980), and the judge should have considered the evidence so as to ascertain the facts and to determine whether the case was one in which the wardship should be continued. Here, the authority had, in the words of Lord Denning, M.R., a "transient care."[48]

The wardship jurisdiction of the High Court may be invoked *by* the **18-21** local authority.[49] In *Re. B. (a Minor),*[50] Lane J. said that local authorities "are sometimes faced with difficult and onerous decisions concerning children in their charge; responsible officers of their welfare departments may be subject to various pressures from within or from outside the authority itself. I consider that there would be no abandonment of, or derogation from, their statutory powers and duties were they to seek the guidance and assistance of the High Court in matters of difficulty, as distinct from the day to day arrangements with which, as the authorities show, the court will not interfere."

If a child ordinarily resident in one area is received into care by an **18-22** authority elsewhere, a transfer may be made with an appropriate financial adjustment, the Secretary of State deciding any dispute as to the place of ordinary residence.

Under section 43 of the Matrimonial Causes Act 1973, section 4 of the **18-23** Guardianship Act 1973, section 10 of the Domestic Proceedings and Magistrates' Courts Act 1978, and section 7 of the Family Law Reform Act 1969, the court may commit a child under 17 to the care of a local authority where it appears that there are exceptional circumstances making it impracticable or undesirable for the child to be entrusted to

---

[45] *Re W. (minors) (Wardship: jurisdiction)* [1980] Fam. 60.
[46] *Re M. (An Infant)* [1961] Ch. 328, and the cases cited in n. 43, *supra.*
[47] [1965] 1 All E.R. 865.
[48] *Ibid.* at p. 867.
[49] *Re Baker (Infants)* [1962] Ch. 201; *Re B. (A Minor) (Wardship: Child in Care)* [1975] Fam. 36, 43; *Re D. (A Minor) (Justices' Decision) (Review)* [1977] Fam. 158.
[50] [1975] Fam. 36.

either of the parties to the marriage or to any other individual. Such an order ceases to have effect when the child reaches the age of 18.

18-24 Under sections 33–46 of the Children Act 1975[51] a custodianship order may be made by the court awarding the legal custody of a child to a person, other than a natural parent, with whom the child has had his home for the preceding three months and for a minimum period of three years (one year where the applicant has the consent of a person entitled to legal custody), or to a relative or step-parent with whom the child has had his home for the preceding three months and who has the consent of a person entitled to legal custody. Notice of a custodianship application must be given to the local authority for the area where the child is living within seven days of the issue of proceedings and the local authority is required to inquire into and report on the case. On revocation of a custodianship order, the court may order that a child be committed to the care of a specified local authority or that the child shall be under its supervision.

18-25 Authorities may become responsible for the care of children in another way. Under Part I of the Children and Young Persons Act 1969 (referred to in greater detail under (d) below), a juvenile court has power to commit a child or young person to the care of the local authority. A child so committed is dealt with as a deprived child although he may have appeared before a court as an offender or in need of care or control.

In reaching any decision relating to a child in their care, a local authority shall give first consideration to the need to safeguard and promote the welfare of the child throughout his childhood, and shall, so far as practicable, ascertain the wishes and feelings of the child regarding the decision and give due consideration to them having regard to his age and understanding. The local authority may act in a manner inconsistent with this duty if this appears necessary to protect members of the public.[52]

Children in care may be boarded out, or may be sent home or they may be placed in homes maintained by the authority, *i.e.* community homes, or by voluntary organisations, or the authority may make some other appropriate arrangement.[53] The Secretary of State has made regulations as to the welfare of children who are boarded out[54] and as to the supervision and administration of homes.[55]

18-26 Under provisions of the Child Care Act 1980, a local authority may pass a parental rights resolution in respect of a child who is in the care of a voluntary organisation. The parental rights and duties which vest in the

---

[51] Which came into force on December 1, 1985 (S.I. 1985 No. 779).
[52] Child Care Act 1980, s. 18; see *R.* v. *Solihull M.B.C., ex p. C. and others* [1984] F.L.R. 363.
[53] Child Care Act 1980, s. 21. See § 18–39 as to community homes. A child in care may not be placed in secure accommodation (see § 18–41) unless certain conditions are fulfilled, and may not be so kept for longer than 72 hours without the order of a juvenile court: see Child Care Act 1980, s. 21A; Secure Accommodation (No. 2) Regulations 1983 (S.I. 1983 No. 1808).
[54] Boarding-out of Children Regulations (S.I. 1955 No. 1377), as amended by S.I. 1965 No. 654.
[55] Community Homes Regulations 1972 (S.I. 1972 No. 319).

voluntary organisation may be transferred to the local authority if it considers that the organisation is no longer able to provide the care the child needs.[56]

An authority may provide accommodation in a community home for persons over compulsory school age and under 21 whether or not they are or have been in the authority's care: this is primarily to enable them to live near their work or place of education or training.[57] Financial assistance may be given to young people of certain categories towards expenses of maintenance, education or training.[58]

The parents of a child or young person committed to the care or **18-27** received into the care of a local authority are liable to contribute towards his maintenance until he reaches 16—the young person himself becomes liable at that age. When a court makes an order committing a child or young person to the care of a local authority, it may then make a contribution order. At any time thereafter, the magistrates' court for the place where the person liable is residing may make such an order, and may deal with any complaint as to non-compliance by the contributee.[59]

A local authority cannot be required by magistrates to pay a fine imposed on a child for offences committed while in care and resident in one of its homes,[60] or while allowed home on trial.[61]

(b) *Child protection and child-minders*

Children who are cared for by people other than their parents or **18-28** relatives are protected by several statutory codes. Local authorities are required by the Nurseries and Child-Minders Regulation Act 1948[62] to keep a register of nurseries where children are taken for the day or for part of a day exceeding two hours or for longer periods not exceeding six days and of persons who for reward receive for similar periods a child under the age of five of whom they are not the relatives. The authority may impose conditions as to registration and may cancel registration.

The second statutory code relates to foster children and is contained in **18-29** the Children and Young Persons Act 1969, the Children Act 1975 and the Foster Children Act 1980. A duty is placed on authorities to satisfy themselves as to the well-being of foster children in their areas, ensuring that whenever there is a need the children are visited, and that advice is available.[63] A foster child is one below the upper limit of compulsory school age whose care and maintenance is undertaken by someone other

[56] Child Care Act 1980, ss. 64, 65. Appeals lie to the juvenile court and thence to the High Court: s. 67.
[57] Child Care Act 1980, s. 72.
[58] Child Care Act 1980, s. 27.
[59] Child Care Act 1980, ss. 45–49.
[60] For liability in tort for damage caused by a child in care, see *Vicar of Writtle* v. *Essex County Council* (1979) 77 L.G.R. 656.
[61] *Leeds City Council* v. *West Yorkshire Metropolitan Police* [1983] 1 A.C. 29.
[62] s. 1, as amended by s. 60 of the Health Services and Public Health Act 1968; Local Government Act 1972, Sched. 23, para. 4.
[63] Foster Children Act 1980, s. 3.

than his parent or relative, whether or not payment is made.[64] There are a number of exceptions to this broad rule: they take account, amongst other things, of those who look after children occasionally, on holidays and in emergencies for example, and exempt from the rules children in homes, residential schools where they receive full-time education, and in hospitals and nursing homes. The general effect of the rules and the exceptions to the rules is broadly this. If a person is a "regular" foster parent, then if he takes a child for six days or more he must act in accordance with the statutory code. If he is not a "regular" foster parent, then if he takes a child for less than 27 days he is exempt from the requirements of the code. The principal duty under the code is the giving of notice to the authority whenever a person becomes or ceases to be a foster parent.[65]

18-30   The foster parent is required to keep the authority informed of any change in his permanent address and to notify the authority if the child dies or if, in certain circumstances, he is removed from the foster parent's care.[66] The officers of the authority who are authorised to visit foster children may inspect the premises where they live, and where premises are used wholly or partly for the keeping of foster children the authority may impose requirements as to the following: the number of children who may be kept; the accommodation and equipment to be provided; the medical arrangements to be made for protecting the health of the children; the giving of particulars of the person in charge of the children; the number, qualifications or experience of those employed to look after them; the fire precautions to be taken; the keeping of records and the giving of information of any foster child received or any change in the number or identity of the children kept in the premises. An authority may prohibit the taking of a child if it is of the opinion that the person or premises are unsuitable or that the arrangement would be detrimental to the child.[67] A person aggrieved by a prohibition or requirement may appeal to the juvenile court, and where the court allows the appeal it may vary the requirement or may substitute a requirement for a prohibition.[68]

18-31   A local authority may make complaint to a juvenile court where it considers that a foster child is kept in unsuitable surroundings, and if the court is satisfied that the person in charge of the child is unfit to have his care, or that a requirement imposed by the authority is not being observed, or that the environment of the child is detrimental to him, the court may make an order for his removal to a place of safety until he can be restored to a parent, relative or guardian, or until other arrangements are made for him. In case of imminent danger an order may be made by a

[64] Foster Children Act 1980, s. 1.
[65] *Ibid.* s. 5.
[66] *Ibid.* ss. 5, 6.
[67] *Ibid.* ss. 8–10.
[68] *Ibid.* s. 11.

justice sitting singly. A child removed in these circumstances may be received into the care of the local authority.[69]

These provisions apply where children in independent boarding schools stay at school during the holidays. The person in charge must notify the authority of the fact, giving an estimate of the number of children who will stay at school, but the authority may grant exemptions from the requirement as to the giving of notice.[70]

Local authorities have a duty to secure the well-being of "protected **18-32** children." Protected children fall into two classes—those who are awaiting adoption (the responsibility of an authority towards these children is considered later) and those who are placed with strangers. A child comes within the second group where arrangements are made for him to be placed in the care of one who is not a parent, guardian or relative of his, and another person, not being a parent or guardian, takes part in the arrangements. The authority has a similar responsibility towards him, and has similar powers to protect him, as it has in connection with foster children.[71]

(c) *Adoption of children*

Local authorities have responsibilities in regard to the adoption of **18-33** children.[72] First, they may themselves arrange adoptions, acting through the committee discharging its functions under the Local Authority Social Services Act 1970.[73] Secondly, they have a duty to register adoption societies, and may refuse to register or may cancel registration on any of the grounds set out in the Act.[74] Thirdly, an adoption order cannot be made in respect of a child who was not placed for adoption by an adoption agency unless the applicant has given at least three months notice to the local authority within whose area he has his home that he intends to apply for the order.[75] On giving of the notice the child becomes a "protected child" and the authority must then investigate and submit a report to the adoption court.[76] Whilst the child is a "protected child" the authority has the appropriate powers and responsibilities in relation to him.[77] Fourthly, an authority may be called upon to act in adoption proceedings. Adoption is effected by order of a court (the Family Division of the High Court, a county court or a domestic court), and

---

[69] Foster Children Act 1980, s. 12.

[70] *Ibid.* s. 17.

[71] Adoption Act 1958, ss. 37 (as amended by s. 52 of the Children and Young Persons Act 1969), 38, 41, 43. The law relating to the adoption of children has been consolidated in the Adoption Act 1976, which has not yet been brought into force.

[72] Adoption Act 1958, s. 28; London Government Act 1963, s. 47(1); Local Government Act 1972, Sched. 23, para. 8.

[73] Adoption Act 1958, s. 28; Local Government Act 1972, Sched. 23, para. 8.

[74] Children Act 1975, ss. 4–6.

[75] *Ibid.* s. 18(1).

[76] *Ibid.* s. 18(2).

[77] Children Act 1958, ss. 38–45.

when an application is before the court it may appoint a guardian *ad litem* to safeguard the interests of the child.

(d) *Care of children and young persons through court proceedings*

18-34   Part I of the Children and Young Persons Act 1969[78] confers powers and duties on local authorities in relation to children and young persons in need of care or control. A person will come within this category if he is neglected, or is living in a home where some other child has been dealt with under these provisions or where a person convicted of an offence against a child is living and where it is likely that he too will suffer unless something is done,[79] or if he is being exposed to moral danger, or if he is beyond control or is not attending school,[80] or if he has committed an offence other than homicide, and also that he is in need of care or control which he is unlikely to receive unless the court makes an order in respect of him.

18-35   Proceedings in the juvenile court may be commenced only by the police or local authority or the National Society for the Prevention of Cruelty to Children, but the Society may not initiate proceedings where the child has committed an offence. An authority about to take proceedings must first initiate an inquiry unless satisfied that this is not needed, and if the National Society or police begin proceedings they must notify the local authority.

The court may do one of a number of things. It may deliver the child to the parents, requiring from them a recognisance to take proper care of him and to exercise proper control over him: the parents are "bound over" as it were. It may make a supervision order—this requires the local authority or a probation officer to advise, assist and befriend the supervised person.[81] The order may stipulate a number of requirements, as to the person with whom the supervised person should live, or as to activities in which he must join. The court may instead make a care order, committing the child to the authority until he is 18 or, if the order was made when he had attained the age of 16, until he is 19, or it may make a hospital or guardianship order under the Mental Health Act 1983, to which reference is made later.

18-36   Another course is open to the court—it may make an interim order if it is not sure what to do. The order will commit the person to the care of the local authority temporarily and may require the child to be brought back to court on a given date: if the child is an unruly boy of 15 or more, the committal may in certain circumstances be to a remand centre.

18-37   A juvenile remanded in custody may be put in the care of the local authority.[82] A child of 10 or over[83] may be prosecuted for a criminal

---

[78] ss. 1–24; Criminal Justice Act 1972, Sched. 5.

[79] See hereon *R. v. Birmingham Juvenile Court, ex p. S. (an infant)* [1984] Fam. 93.

[80] See *Re S. (A Minor) (Care Order: Education)* [1978] Q.B. 120, above, § 17–22.

[81] The existence of a supervision order will not prevent the High Court from exercising its wardship jurisdiction on the application of the local authority. In *Re D. (A Minor) (Justices' Decision) (Review)* [1977] Fam. 158.

[82] Children and Young Persons Act 1969, s. 23.

[83] There is a conclusive presumption that no child under 10 can be guilty of an offence: Children and Young Persons Act 1933, s. 50.

offence. Care proceedings are rarely used where an offence has been committed.[84]

(e) Mentally disordered children

The Mental Health Acts of 1959 and 1983 enable authorities to deal **18-38** with children and young persons suffering from mental disorder. Such a child may be received into a community home although he is not in the care of the local authority under Part III of the Children Act 1980.[85] This provision enables a child suffering from mental disorder to be dealt with in the child care services if he can suitably mix with other children.

A duty is placed on the authority to arrange for the visiting of certain mentally disordered persons who are in hospital, namely, children and young persons in respect of whom parental rights and powers vest in the authority.[86] These powers so vest where (a) the child has been committed to its care under the Children and Young Persons Act 1969[87]; (b) the authority has assumed parental rights under section 3 of the Child Care Act 1980; (c) a person is subject to the guardianship of the authority under Part II of the Mental Health Act 1983; or (d) the functions of the nearest relative under the Act of 1983 are transferred to the authority under section 29 of that Act. The authority must not only arrange for the child or young person to be visited—it must take such other steps as may be expected of parents.

(f) Accommodation for children in care

The Children and Young Persons Act 1969 gives local authorities a **18-39** discretion to make whatever arrangements they consider appropriate for securing that community homes are available to accommodate children in their care and for purposes connected with the welfare of children, whether in their care or not.[88] The statutory duty imposed on local authorities to establish regional planning committees for the purpose of planning for the provision and maintenance of community homes is abolished, although these committees could continue to operate if all of the constituent local authorities agreed that this would be the means by which they would fulfill their obligations to provide community homes. Community homes may be provided by voluntary organisations. They are of two kinds, controlled homes and assisted homes, differing in the extent to which the local authority shares in the management.[89] In

---

[84] s. 4 of the Children and Young Persons Act 1969, which prohibits criminal proceedings for offences by children, has not been brought into effect.

[85] Mental Health Act 1959, s. 9 as amended by the Children and Young Persons Act 1969, Sched. 5, para. 37, the Child Care Act 1980, Sched. 5, para. 12 and Local Government Act 1972, Sched.3, para. 9.

[86] Mental Health Act 1983, s. 116.

[87] Child Care Act 1980, ss. 10 and 11.

[88] Child Care Act 1980, s. 31, as substituted by the Health and Social Services and Social Security Adjudications Act 1983, s. 4(1).

[89] Child Care Act 1980, ss. 35, 37, 38.

controlled homes responsibility for management, equipment and maintenance falls to the local authority, and two-thirds of the membership of the management committee are appointed by the authority. In assisted homes responsibility falls to the voluntary organisation, and one-third of the managers are appointed by the authority. Staffing in a controlled home is principally a matter for the authority, and in assisted homes for the voluntary organisation.

18-40   The Secretary of State is empowered to make regulations with respect to the conduct of community homes and for securing the welfare of children in their care[90] His powers are widely drawn—those particularly stated include requirements as to accommodation, equipment, medical services, religious instruction—and he has power to direct that particular premises shall cease to be used as a community home.

18-41   Provision is made in section 81 of the Child Care Act 1980 for the Secretary of State to pay grants to local authorities in respect of expenditure incurred in providing secure accommodation in community homes. "Secure accommodation" means accommodation provided for the purposes of restricting the liberty of children in a community home.

(g) *Inquiries*

18-42   Section 76 of the Child Care Act 1980 empowers the Secretary of State to cause an inquiry to be held into any matter relating to:

(a) the functions of the social services committee of a local authority, in so far as those functions relate to children;

(b) the functions of an adoption agency;

(c) the functions of a voluntary organisation in relation to voluntary homes;

(d) a home maintained by the Secretary of State for the accommodation of children who are in the care of local authorities;

(e) the detention of a child under section 53 of the Children and Young Persons Act 1933.

Such inquiries will normally be held in private at the discretion of the Secretary of State or the person holding the inquiry.

C. MENTAL HEALTH

18-43   It will have been observed from earlier paragraphs that provision is made in section 9 of the Mental Health Act 1959 for extending the welfare and child care services to include services more particularly for those who suffer from mental disorder. The Mental Health Act 1983 provides for the treatment and care of mentally disordered persons, a term used to describe persons suffering from mental illness, arrested or incomplete

---

[90] Child Care Act 1980, s. 39; Community Homes Regulations 1972 (S.I. 1972 No. 319).

development of mind, psychopathic disorder, or any other disorder or disability of mind.

Under Part II of the 1983 Act compulsory admission to hospital, whether for assessment or treatment, is founded on the written recommendation of two medical practitioners, but admission informally and without powers of detention is possible and is the method used in the majority of cases. A person may be received into guardianship, under a procedure similar to that applying to compulsory admission to hospital, where this is necessary in his interests or for the protection of other persons.[91] The person named as guardian in the application may be either a local authority or any other person (including the applicant himself), but an application in which a person other than a local authority is named as guardian has no effect unless it is accepted on behalf of that person by the authority. Where guardianship is accepted by an authority it has certain specific powers which are limited to restricting the liberty of the person under guardianship only to the extent necessary to ensure that various forms of treatment, social support, training, education or occupation are undertaken.

It is the duty of an approved social worker appointed by the local **18-44** authority to make an application for admission to hospital or an application for guardianship in respect of a patient where he is satisfied that it ought to be made and is of opinion, having regard to any wishes expressed by relatives of the patient or any other relevant circumstances, that it is necessary or proper for the application to be made by him. An application for admission to hospital can only be made if the approved social worker is satisfied that detention in a hospital is the most appropriate way of providing for the patient's needs.[92]

A county court may designate an authority the "nearest relative" of a patient,[93] and when this is done the authority has responsibilities, among others, with regard to the making of an application for admission or an application for guardianship, or for an order for the discharge of the patient from detention or guardianship.

Nursing homes and mental nursing homes are to be registered and **18-45** inspected by district health authorities under the Registered Homes Act 1984.[94]

A Mental Health Review Tribunal is appointed for the area of each **18-46** regional health authority[95] The Tribunals are appointed by the Lord Chancellor and must include legal and medical members. A person admitted or detained in hospital otherwise than voluntarily, or who has been placed under guardianship, has the right to ask the Tribunal to review his case. Mental Health Review Tribunals are within the

---

[91] Mental Health Act 1983, s. 7.
[92] *Ibid.* s. 13.
[93] *Ibid.* s. 29.
[94] Registered Homes Act 1984, s. 23; Nursing Homes and Mental Nursing Homes Regulations 1984 (S.I. 1984 No. 1578).
[95] Mental Health Act 1983, s. 65.

supervision of the Council of Tribunals established under the Tribunals and Inquiries Act 1971.[96]

A special health authority, the Mental Health Act Commission, has been established to keep the Mental Health Act 1983 under review and to visit patients and investigate complaints.[97]

[96] Mental Health Act 1983, Sched. 1.
[97] *Ibid.* s. 121.

CHAPTER 19

PLANNING, NEW TOWNS AND TOWN DEVELOPMENT

1. *PLANNING*

The law on this topic is considered under the following headings: the **19-01**
Minister; planning authorities; development plans; control of development; control of advertisements; financial background to planning;
powers in relation to trees and waste land; buildings of special
architectural or historic interest; conservation areas; the powers of the
High Court to review certain orders and decisions; government grants.

A. THE MINISTER

The Minister primarily concerned with town and country planning in **19-02**
England is the Secretary of State for the Environment. He has many
specific powers under the Town and Country Planning legislation
including a number of default powers. He may, to take one example,
prepare or alter a structure or local plan or a unitary plan if a local
planning authority fails to submit such a plan after a specified period.[1] In
Wales, the Minister primarily concerned is the Secretary of State for
Wales.

B. PLANNING AUTHORITIES

(1) Non-metropolitan counties
In non-metropolitan counties, both county councils and district **19-03**
councils are local planning authorities.[2] The broad division of function
between them is stated shortly in this paragraph, though the terms may
not be understood until all the Chapter has been read. County planning
authorities, in consultation with district planning authorities, are responsible for the preparation of structure plans and for development plan
schemes, which allocate responsibility for making local plans. District
planning authorities, subject to any contrary provision in the structure
plan or development plan scheme, are responsible for the preparation of
local plans, and they deal directly with most matters of planning control

---

[1] Town and Country Planning Act 1971, s. 17; Local Government Act 1972, Sched. 16,
para. 4; Local Government Act 1985, Sched. 1, para. 13.
[2] Town and Country Planning Act 1971, s. 1, as amended by the Local Goverment Act 1972,
s. 182 and the Local Government Act 1985, s. 3. And see App. 1.

except in national parks. This means that the county planning authorities are concerned with general strategic policies, and district councils with the character of development within their own areas.

The Secretary of State may by order establish a joint board as the planning authority for the area of two or more counties or parts of counties and he may establish a joint board as the district planning authority for the area of two or more districts, or parts of districts.[3] The Secretary of State must hold a local inquiry before he makes an order unless all the councils concerned have agreed to it. In national parks all planning functions are exercisable by the county planning authority or joint board as the case may be, subject to a few exceptions.

(2) Metropolitan counties

19-04   In metropolitan counties the council of each metropolitan district is the planning authority for the district for all purposes. Thus it is responsible for preparing a unitary development plan, which takes the place of structure and local plans, and for planning control.[4]

(3) Greater London

19-05   In Greater London, each London borough council is the local planning authority for the borough for all purposes, as is the Common Council of the City of London for the City. It is responsible for the preparation of a unitary development plan for the borough, or for the City, and for planning control.[5] But co-ordination of planning policy for a metropolitan region such as Greater London is very desirable. Accordingly, the London borough councils and the Common Council of the City are required to establish a joint committee (a) to advise them on matters of common interest relating to the development and planning of Greater London, (b) to inform the Secretary of State of the views of these authorities concerning such matters, and (c) to inform local planning authorities for other areas in the vicinity of Greater London, or any body on which those authorities and the Greater London authorities are represented (in this context the South East Regional Planning Conference) of the views of the Greater London authorities on matters of common interest in planning and development.[6]

The Historic Buildings and Monuments Commission for England is also given certain functions relating to the preservation of buildings of special architectural or historic interest.[7]

---

[3] Town and Country Planning Act 1971, s. 1, as amended, and Sched. 1. See also Local Government Act 1972, Sched. 17.
[4] Local Government Act 1985, s. 3.
[5] *Ibid.*
[6] *Ibid.* s. 5.
[7] *Ibid.* s. 6.

C. Development Plans

The basis of planning control in any area is the development plan. The **19-06**
operative development plan for any area consists of a number of maps,
diagrams and documents, which may be amended or replaced from time
to time.[8]

(1) Old system development plans
   The concept of the development plan was introduced by the Town and **19-07**
Country Planning Act 1947. The relevant provisions of this Act were re-
enacted in the Town and Country Planning Act 1962[9] and now appear in
Schedule 5 to the 1971 Act. They provided for a development plan to
indicate how it was proposed that land in the area should be used and the
stages by which development should be carried out. By regulations[10]
made under these earlier provisions the development plan was to consist
of (1) a county map, town maps, comprehensive development area maps,
and various other maps, defining the sites of proposed roads, parks,
public and other buildings and works, and allocating areas for residential,
industrial, commercial and other uses, and (2) a written statement
concerning the proposals embodied in the maps. All these maps were of a
precise nature which tended to attract numerous objections, and every
map and written statement had to be approved by the Secretary of State
after consideration of, and the holding of an inquiry or hearing into, any
objections, before becoming operative. This produced great delay, and
the Town and Country Planning Act 1968, the relevant provisions of
which are now contained in Part II of the 1971 Act, provided for a new
system.

(2) New system development plans
   Under the new system, development plans consist of a structure plan **19-08**
and local plans. The structure plan consists of a written statement only of
general policies diagrammatically illustrated, and which, while still
requiring the approval of the Secretary of State, is less likely to attract
detailed objections. A local plan provides for the detailed application of
the structure plan general policies and for other detailed matters but,
generally, does not require the approval of the Secretary of State. Thus it
was hoped to speed up the planning process. For a transitional period a
development plan will contain some plans and statements under the 1962
Act system and some under the new system, but the former will gradually
be phased out.
   The new system has applied to all counties, non-metropolitan and
metropolitan, and has also applied, with modifications, to the Greater

---

[8] Town and Country Planning Act 1971, ss. 20 and 21 and Sched. 7, and Local Government
   Act 1985, Sched. 1, para. 15 and Part II.
[9] ss. 4–11.
[10] Town and Country Planning (Development Plans) Regulations 1965 (S.I. 1965 No. 1453).

London area. However, the Local Government Act 1985, which abolished the Greater London Council and the metropolitan county councils, has introduced yet a further new system for use in Greater London and the metropolitan counties in the form of the "unitary development plan." So, for the future, plan preparation for non-metropolitan counties must be considered separately from that for the Greater London area and the metropolitan counties.

(3) The non-metropolitan counties

19-09   Under the system, first introduced by the Act of 1968, each county planning authority must prepare a structure plan, and this must be accompanied by an explanatory memorandum summarising the reasons for every policy and general proposal in it and explaining the relationship of these to expected development in neighbouring areas.[11]

In fact, structure plans are now in force over much the greater part of England and Wales, so that the procedure described below has for the most part already been carried out. But the county planning authority must keep matters expected to affect the development of their area under review and may (if required by the Secretary of State, must) submit to the Secretary of State proposals for the alteration, or repeal *and* replacement, of the structure plan.[12] The procedure in relation to such proposals is, for the most part, similar to that described below for the original structure plan, and, in particular, proposals must be accompanied by a similar explanatory memorandum. Thus a structure plan may be kept up to date.

The structure plan procedure starts with the authority's instituting a survey of its area, examining matters expected to affect the development of the area, and (as mentioned above) it must keep these matters under review. Adequate publicity must be given to the matters to be included in the structure plan and to the proposed content of the explanatory memorandum so that representations can be made to the authority with respect to these matters *before* the content of the structure plan is finally determined for submission to the Secretary of State.

In the light of the results of the survey, any representations made, the planning policies of the region and the resources available, the county planning authority finally prepares the structure plan. The plan is not strictly a plan but a written statement supplemented by diagrams and illustrations which formulates the authority's policy and general proposals for development in its area, including measures for the improvement of the physical environment and the management of traffic, and it must contain such other matters as the Secretary of State may prescribe or

---

[11] Town and Country Planning Act 1971, ss. 6–10, as amended by Local Government, Planning and Land Act 1980, Sched. 14.
[12] Town and Country Planning Act 1971, s. 10 as substituted by the Local Government, Planning and Land Act 1980, Sched. 14.

direct. The Secretary of State may prescribe by regulations the form and content of structure and local plans.[13]

19-10 The structure plan must be submitted to the Secretary of State for approval and copies of it and of the explanatory memorandum are made available for public inspection. Before the Secretary of State proceeds to consider the plan he must satisfy himself that adequate steps have been taken to publicise the plan proposals and the proposed content of the explanatory memorandum and he must take into account the representations submitted to the authority thereon. If not so satisfied he must return the plan to the authority with a direction as to the further action it must take. These provisions enable the Secretary of State to ensure that there has been an adequate measure of public participation in the preparation of structure plans.

The Secretary of State must consider any objections to the plan and was formerly required to hold a local inquiry or hearing into objections. The latter requirement has now been replaced under section 3 of the Town and Country Planning (Amendment) Act 1972 by a public examination into such matters as he considers ought to be considered. In the case of proposals for alteration he need not hold an examination in public if it appears to him that there are no matters in the proposals which require it. After the examination, at which persons or bodies may only take part if invited to do so, the Secretary of State may approve the plan in whole or in part and with or without modifications or reservations, or he may reject it. The explanatory memorandum is not part of the plan and does not have to be approved by the Secretary of State.

19-11 The appropriate planning authority (see para. 19-03) may at any time after the preparation of a structure plan has begun prepare a local plan for any part of the area.[14] Once a structure plan has been approved, the appropriate planning authority must consider whether it is desirable to make a local plan for any part of its area and must make a local plan in any case where the Secretary of State so directs. A local plan may deal with planning matters generally in the area it covers or be an action area plan, being a plan for an area selected by the authority for comprehensive development, redevelopment or improvement, or a subject plan dealing with particular developments or uses of land.[15] It comprises a map called "the proposals map," with any appropriate inset maps to a larger scale, and a written statement, which must contain a written justification for the proposals. Proposals contained in the local plan are to conform generally with the structure plan, and it may not be adopted until after the structure

---

[13] Town and Country Planning (Structure and Local Plans) Regulations 1982 (S.I. 1982 No. 555) For the procedure generally see DoE Circular No. 22/84.

[14] Town and Country Planning Act 1971, ss. 11–15 as amended by the Local Government, Planning and Land Act 1980, Sched. 14; Local Government Act 1972, Sched. 16.

[15] Town and Country Planning (Local and Structure Plans) Regulations 1982 (S.I. 1982 No. 555) regs. 10–13. Prior to the Local Government, Planning and Land Act 1980 an action area had to be indicated as such on the structure plan before a local plan for it could be prepared.

plan has been approved except where the Secretary of State so directs.[16]

The authority when preparing a local plan must take similar action as in the case of the structure plan to satisfy the Secretary of State that adequate steps have been taken as to publicity and that there has been opportunity for representations to be made during its preparation. An opportunity must be given for the making of objections: they are submitted to the planning authority and it is the duty of the authority to consider these objections. A local inquiry or other hearing must be held into objections duly made unless the objectors do not desire one. The authority must send a copy of the local plan to the Secretary of State and he may give a direction that the plan should be submitted to him for approval. Unless this happens the planning authority may by resolution adopt the plan, with or without modification, or may reject it.

Local plans may be altered, repealed or replaced by following a similar procedure, but if the plan has been approved by the Secretary of State, the proposal to amend it requires his consent.[17]

Where any authority fails to carry out a survey or prepare or submit any structure or local plan, or proposals for alteration of any such plan, which it is required to do, the Secretary of State may, after holding a local inquiry, undertake such work in default or, alternatively, authorise another local planning authority which appears to have an interest in the proper planning of the area to do this.[18]

19-12   A person who is aggrieved by a structure or local plan as approved or adopted may question its validity in the High Court as described in paragraph 19–60.

(4) Greater London and the metropolitan counties

19-13   Until April 1, 1986, the new (1968) planning system described above also applied in the Greater London area, though under separate provisions in the 1971 Act and with modifications.[19] Thus the Greater London Development Plan is the structure plan for Greater London,[20] and the London borough councils and the Common Council of the City were empowered to prepare local plans. In the metropolitan counties the new (1968) system worked as for the non-metropolitan counties (structure plans are in force in all the metropolitan counties).

However, section 4 and Part I of Schedule 1 to the Local Government Act 1985 substitute for the 1968 system plans and machinery (as they now

---

[16] Town and Country Planning Act 1971, s. 14 and ss. 15A and 15B added by the Local Government, Planning and Land Act 1980, s. 88.

[17] *Ibid.* s. 15.

[18] Town and Country Planning Act 1971, s. 17.

[19] *Ibid.* s. 19 and Sched. 4, as substituted by the Town and Country Planning (Amendment) Act 1972 and amended by the Local Government, Planning and Land Act 1980. See also the Town and Country Planning (Local Plans for Greater London) Regulations 1983 (S.I. 1983 No. 1190) and the Town and Country Planning (Structure and Local Plans) (Amendment) Regulations 1984 (S.I. 1984 No. 6).

[20] 1971 Act, Sched. 4, para. 5.

appear in the Town and Country Planning Act 1971) a new form of development plan and new machinery for its preparation for each London borough and the City and for each metropolitan district in a metropolitan county. The new plan, which the council of each borough, the City or district is to prepare, is the "unitary development plan." Part I of this is to consist of a written statement formulating the authority's general policies and Part II is to consist of a written statement formulating detailed proposals for development, a geographical map showing these proposals, and a reasoned justification of the general policies in Part I and the proposals in Part II. In short, Part I is rather like a structure plan and Part II rather like a local plan. The procedure is set out in Part I of Schedule 1 to the 1985 Act and provides opportunity for objections and their hearing, but neither part of the plan will require the approval of the Secretary of State unless he calls it in for approval. There is a similar limited right to apply to the High Court as for the 1968 system plans.

Part II of Schedule 1 to the 1985 Act continues in force the Greater London Development Plan and any existing structure and local plans until the new unitary plan for the area concerned becomes operative.

(5) Planning blight

In certain circumstances public authorities are obliged to purchase **19-14** interests affected by proposals appearing in the structure or any local plan or a unitary development plan. An owner-occupier who tries to sell his property and cannot do so except at a much deflated price because the plan indicates that it is likely to be purchased compulsorily by a public authority may require the authority to buy the property forthwith. Certain conditions must be fulfilled before this provision can be invoked.[21] These provisions apply also to cases where the blight arises otherwise than from the development plan, the most common case being where it arises from certain proposals of a highway authority for road construction.

First, the claimant must fall within one of the following classes: a *resident* owner-occupier of the property affected, or an owner-occupier of an agricultural unit, or an owner-occupier of a hereditament whose annual value does not exceed a limit prescribed by regulation (the upper limit has been fixed at £2,250 by the Town and Country Planning (Limit of Annual Value) Order 1973).[22] A mortgagee with an exercisable power of sale may stand in the shoes of a qualified owner-occupier[23] as may a personal representative of a deceased owner-occupier.[24]

---

[21] Town and Country Planning Act 1971, ss. 192–207; Local Government Act 1972, Sched. 16, para. 45; Land Compensation Act 1973, Part V; Local Government, Planning and Land Act 1980, Sched. 15 and s. 147; Local Government Act 1985, Sched. 1, Part I.
[22] S.I. 1973 No. 425.
[23] Town and Country Planning Act 1971, s. 201.
[24] *Ibid.* s. 200 and the Land Compensation Act 1973, s. 78.

Secondly, the land must be under a "blight": in broad terms, it must appear in the development plan as required for the purposes of a public body, or, apart from any plan, be subject to a compulsory purchase order where notice to treat has not been served or be shown in proposals of the appropriate highway authority as required for highway purposes.[25]

Thirdly, the owner-occupier must have made reasonable efforts to sell and been unable to sell except at a price much deflated by the blight. If these conditions are satisfied the owner-occupier may serve a "blight" notice on the authority responsible for the blighting proposal, requiring the purchase of the land to be carried through.

The authority may, within two months serve a counter-notice objecting on certain specified grounds.[26] The authority may, for example, say that it does not propose to acquire the property or any part of it. It is then open to the owner-occupier to require that the objection be sent to the Lands Tribunal to be determined. Where the objection is to the effect that the authority does not intend compulsorily to acquire the land in question, or to acquire compulsorily any part of it within the next 15 years, the Tribunal will uphold the objection only if it is shown to be well founded.

The forms of notice and counter-notice are prescribed in the Town and Country Planning General Regulations 1976.[27]

In calculating compensation for property acquired under these provisions no regard will be had to the "blight."[28]

D. Control of Development

19-15 Part III of the Act of 1971 and the regulations made under it provide for the control of development through local planning authorities, and confer a number of powers on the Secretary of State, including an appellate jurisdiction.

(1) The meaning of development

The term "development" is defined as "the carrying out of building, engineering, mining or other operations in, on, over or under land, or the making of any material change in the use of any buildings or other land...."[29] Certain operations and uses are declared *not* to be development for the purposes of the Act, and these are:

(1) works of maintenance, improvement or other alteration which affect only the interior of a building or do not materially affect the

---

[25] Cases of blight are listed in the 1971 Act, s. 192, as supplemented by ss. 68 to 76 of the Land Compensation Act 1973. And see the Local Government Act 1985, Sched. 1, Part I.

[26] Town and Country Planning Act 1971, s. 194; Land Compensation Act 1973, ss. 75, 86, Sched. 3; Local Government, Planning and Land Act 1980, Sched. 15.

[27] S.I. 1976 No. 1419.

[28] Land Compensation Act 1961, s. 9.

[29] Town and Country Planning Act 1971, s. 22(1).

external appearance, unless the alteration provides additional space below ground[30];

(2) road repairs and improvements by a highway authority within the boundaries of a road;

(3) repairs to public services (*e.g.* the renewing of sewers and water mains);

(4) the use of buildings or other land within the curtilage of a dwelling-house for a purpose incidental to the enjoyment of the house;

(5) the use of land for agriculture or forestry;

(6) a change of use within a specified "use class."[31]

The "use classes" referred to in (6) are contained in the Town and Country   **19-16** Planning (Use Classes) Order 1972.[32] The Order lists a number of classes, and a change from one use to another if within one of the classes is deemed not to be development. For example, one of the classes is "use as a light industrial building for any purpose." This means that a building which is used for light industry of one kind can be used for light industry of another kind without there being any development as defined in the Act.

For the avoidance of doubt it is stated that the use as more than one separate dwelling of any building previously used as a single dwelling involves a material change of use, and tipping on what is already a tip is development if the height is raised or the area extended.[33]

The definition of development in section 22(1) of the 1971 Act comprises two kinds covering, respectively, "operations" and "material changes in use." A number of terms in the definition are themselves the subject of further definition in section 290(1). The term "building" includes any structure or erection, and any part of a building as so defined, but does not include plant or machinery. The term "building operations" includes rebuilding operations, structural alterations of or additions to buildings and other operations normally undertaken by a person carrying on business as a builder.[34] The term "engineering

---

[30] See *Kensington and Chelsea Royal London Borough Council* v. *C.G. Hotels* (1980) 41 P. & C.R. 40 (fixing of floodlights and an electric cable held not to affect the external appearance of a hotel).

[31] Town and Country Planning Act 1971, s. 22(2).

[32] S.I. 1972 No. 1385, as amended in relation to hazardous substances by the Town and Country Planning (Use Classes) (Amendment) Order 1983 (S.I. 1983 No. 1614). See *Brooks and Burton Ltd.* v. *Secretary of State for the Environment* [1977] 1 W.L.R. 1294 (intensification of a use within a use class held not to constitute development); *Forkhurst* v. *Secretary of State for the Environment* (1982) 46 P. & C.R. 89 (use classes not to be interpreted restrictively): *cf. Tessier* v. *Secretary of State for the Environment* (1975) 31 P. & C.R. 161.

[33] Town and Country Planning Act 1971, s. 22(3).

[34] The term "building operations" connotes an alteration of the physical character of the land (*Cheshire County Council* v. *Woodward* [1962] 2 Q.B. 126 : installation of a large mobile hopper and conveyer held not to constitute a building operation), although this test should not be applied so as to exclude a proper consideration of the definitions contained in s. 290(1) (*Barvis Ltd.* v. *Secretary of State for the Environment* (1971) 22 P. & C.R. 710). See also *James* v. *Brecon County Council* (1963) 15 P. & C.R. 20.

operations" includes the formation or laying out of means of access to highways. The term "mining operations" is not defined in the 1971 Act, although "minerals" are defined in section 290(1) as including all minerals and substances in or under land of a kind ordinarily worked for removal by underground or surface working, but with the exception of peat cut for purposes other than sale.[35] Mining operations are regarded as continuous, the extraction of each shovelful constituting a separate mining operation.[36]

The demolition by itself of a building is generally not considered to be development but partial demolition may be regarded as a building operation materially affecting the external appearance.[37]

Whether there is a material change of use is not always easy to decide. The matter is principally one of fact and degree for the Secretary of State to determine.[38] The test has relation to the character of the use and not the particular purpose of the particular occupier,[39] and an increase in intensification of use may well amount to a material change of use if it changes the character of the use.[40] It is also related to the planning unit, which is *prima facie* the unit of occupation, *e.g.* if the use of a building on a farm is changed, whether the change is material must be decided by reference to the whole of the farm occupied by the farmer and not just by reference to the building itself.[41] Where a site has a "primary" use and a number of "ancillary" or "incidental" uses, there will normally only be a material change in use if the primary use is changed.[42] However, this does not apply if the link between the ancillary and primary uses is broken, for

---

[35] The scope of "mining operations" is extended to include the removal of minerals from certain deposits by s. 22(3A) of the 1971 Act, inserted by the Town and Country Planning (Minerals) Act 1981 (in force from a day to be appointed).

[36] *Thomas David (Porthcawl) Ltd.* v. *Penybont Rural District Council* [1972] 1 W.L.R. 1526.

[37] See *Coleshill and District Investment Co. Ltd.* v. *Minister of Housing and Local Government* [1969] 1 W.L.R. 746 (removal of embankment and blast walls around ammunition depot held to constitute engineering and building operations); *cf. Iddenden* v. *Secretary of State for the Environment* [1972] 1 W.L.R. 1433 (demolition of nissen huts held not to constitute development).

[38] See, *e.g. Bendles Motors Ltd.* v. *Bristol Corporation* [1963] 1 W.L.R. 247.

[39] *Marshall* v. *Nottingham Corporation* [1960] 1 W.L.R. 707; *East Barnet Urban District Council* v. *British Transport Commission* [1962] 2 Q.B. 484, per Lord Parker C.J. at p. 491, approved by the House of Lords in *Westminster City Council* v. *Great Portland Estates plc.* [1985] 1 A.C. 661.

[40] *Birmingham Corporation* v. *Minister of Housing and Local Government and Habib Ullah* [1964] 1 Q.B. 178; *Peake* v. *Secretary of State for Wales* (1971) 22 P. & C.R. 889; *Brooks and Burton* v. *Secretary of State for the Environment* [1977] 1 W.L.R. 1294; *Royal Borough of Kensington and Chelsea* v. *Secretary of State for the Environment and Mia Carla Ltd.* [1981] J.P.L. 50.

[41] *Burdle* v. *Secretary of State for the Environment* [1972] 1 W.L.R. 1207; *Hilliard* v. *Secretary of State for the Environment* [1978] J.P.L. 41; *Winton* v. *Secretary of State for the Environment* (1982) 46 P. & C.R. 205; *cf. Wakelin* v. *Secretary of State for the Environment* [1978] J.P.L. 768.

[42] *Emma Hotels Ltd.* v. *Secretary of State for the Environment* (1979) 250 E.G. 157; (1980) 41 P. & C.R. 255 (non-residents' bar held to be incidental to hotel use); *cf. Lydcare Ltd.* v. *Secretary of State for the Environment* (1984) 49 P. & C.R. 186 (provision of film viewing facilities not incidental to shop use).

example where the primary use ceases,[43] or where the ancillary use grows so that it becomes a separate use in its own right.[44]

If a person is not sure whether a proposal constitutes development he may ask the local planning authority to determine the question, and if he is aggrieved by the authority's decision he may appeal to the Secretary of State. In dealing with an application of this kind account must be taken of the facts of the case in relation to the definition of development—no consideration is given to the merits of the proposal.[45] A further appeal on a point of law lies from the Secretary of State's decision to the High Court,[46] but generally the question of whether there has been a material change of use is a question of fact and degree and not of law.

(2) Permission for development

No development may lawfully take place unless permission is first **19-17** obtained,[47] and this may be given in one of two ways.

First, the Secretary of State is empowered to make development orders which have the effect themselves of granting permission for development.[48] The order may apply in general to England and Wales or be limited to a special area or areas. An example of the former is the Town and Country Planning General Development Order 1977,[49] and of the latter the Town and Country Planning (New Towns) Special Development Order 1977.[50]

The General Development Order specifies classes of development which are permitted by the order itself and which may be carried out by a developer without obtaining permission from the local planning authority or from the Secretary of State, though he may need consent under some other statutory provision. Some examples of permitted development under the order are the enlargement of a dwelling-house so long as the original cubic content is not exceeded by more than 70 cubic metres or 15 per cent., whichever is the greater (50 cubic metres or one-tenth in the case of terrace houses), subject to a maximum of 115 cubic metres; the erection of gates and fences not exceeding one metre in height where they abut on a highway used for vehicular traffic, or two metres in any other case; the use of land for any purpose, except as a caravan site, on not more than 28 days (no more than 14 days of which may be for motorcar or motorcycle racing or markets) in total in any calendar year. The

---

[43] *Barling (David W.) Ltd.* v. *Secretary of State for the Environment* [1980] J.P.L. 594.
[44] *Peake* v. *Secretary of State for Wales* (1971) 70 L.G.R. 98 (repairing vehicles is incidental to use of a private garage, but change from part-time to full-time vehicle repairing held to constitute an intensification in use amounting to a material change); *cf. Trio Thames Ltd.* v. *Secretary of State for the Environment* [1984] J.P.L. 183.
[45] Town and Country Planning Act 1971, s. 53.
[46] *Ibid.* s. 247.
[47] *Ibid.* s. 23.
[48] *Ibid.* s. 24. For permission on Crown land, see the Town and Country Planning Act 1984.
[49] S.I. 1977 No. 289, as amended by orders of 1981 (S.I. 1981 No. 245), 1983 (S.I. 1983 No. 1615), 1985 (S.I. 1985 Nos. 1011 and 1981).
[50] S.I. 1977 No. 665.

permissions granted by the order are subject to certain conditions and limitations set out in the order. Furthermore, some of the permissions are modified in their application to certain landscape areas by the Town and Country Planning (Landscape Areas Special Development) Order 1950[51] and in relation to other special areas by the Town and Country Planning (National Parks, Areas of Outstanding Natural Beauty and Conservation Areas) Special Development Order 1981[52] and another such Order of 1985.[53] If either the Secretary of State or the local planning authority is satisfied that development in any of the classes specified in the order should not be carried out in any particular area unless permission is specifically granted, either may direct that permission granted by the order shall not apply, but the Secretary of State's consent is needed, with certain exceptions, if the direction is made by a local authority. The direction may relate (1) to all or any development in all or any of the classes in a particular area, or (2) to a particular development falling within any of the classes.[54] Permission may not be withdrawn by a direction after it has been implemented.[55]

19-18   Secondly, permission may be obtained from the local planning authority.[56] If development is not permitted by the General Development Order, then the developer must submit an application for planning permission to the district planning authority.

19-19   Most decisions relating to planning control outside national parks are given by district planning authorities. They deal with (a) applications for planning permission, (b) applications for a determination as to whether an application for permission is required (see para. 19–16) and (c) applications for a certificate of established use (see para. 19–36). In general terms, the district planning authority deals with all cases which do not relate to land in national parks *or*, in non-metropolitan counties, to "county matters." "County matters"[57] include mineral working, prospecting and disposal, and certain related activities, the development of land partly in and partly outside a national park, and, finally, development which has been prescribed, or is within a class which has been prescribed, by the Secretary of State by order. Such orders may be made generally or in relation to a particular area. The use of land in England for the disposal of waste has been so prescribed.[58]

---

[51] S.I. 1950 No. 729.
[52] S.I. 1981 No. 246.
[53] S.I. 1985 No. 1012, as amended by S.I. 1985 No. 1982.
[54] Town and Country Planning General Development Order 1977 (S.I. 1977 No. 289), art. 4; *Spedeworth Ltd.* v. *Secretary of State for the Environment* (1972) 71 L.G.R. 123; *Thanet District Council* v. *Ninedrive Ltd.* [1978] 1 All E.R. 703.
[55] *Cole* v. *Somerset County Council* [1957] 1 Q.B. 23.
[56] Town and Country Planning Act 1971, ss. 29 and 30.
[57] Local Government Act 1972, Sched. 16, para. 32, as amended by the Local Government, Planning and Land Act 1980, s. 86. Appendix 1 sets out broadly the division of functions between county councils and district councils in non-metropolitan areas.
[58] The Town and Country Planning (Prescription of County Matters) Regulations 1980 (S.I. 1980 No. 2010).

Applications and decisions must be registered in a register open for public inspection free of charge.[59]

The General Development Order describes in detail how applications **19-20** should be made. They are to be sent to the district council. By section 87 of the Local Government, Planning and Land Act 1980, the Secretary of State may prescribe a fee to be paid to the council.[60] A decision must be reached within eight weeks, and if no decision is made within that period or within an agreed extended period, the applicant may lodge an appeal with the Secretary of State.

The applicant must give the local planning authority a certificate in one of four alternative forms:

(a) that he was the sole owner of the land 21 days before the date of application;

(b) that notice has been given to all persons owning any of the land 21 days before the date of application;

(c) that he has notified all the known owners of any of the land, has taken reasonable steps to identify the others and has published notice of the application in a local newspaper; or

(d) where none of the owners are known, that he has taken reasonable steps to identify them and has published notice of the application in a local newspaper.

In the case of agricultural land, both the owner and the tenant must be informed.[61] A grant of planning permission may be quashed if the certificate is defective.[62]

An applicant may apply for outline planning permission for the erection of a building and the planning authority may, if it wishes, grant the application subject to the reservation for subsequent approval by the authority of matters not particularised in the application.[63] Applications for approval of these reserved matters must be made within three years, or such other time as the authority may specify, of the grant of outline permission.[64] More than one application may be made in respect of different reserved matters or as alternatives of the same reserved matter, or in respect of different parts of the site.[65] Whether an application is for

---

[59] Town and Country Planning Act 1971, s. 34; Town and Country Planning General Development Order 1977 (S.I. 1977 No. 289), art. 21. See *Steeples* v. *Derbyshire County Council* [1985] 1 W.L.R. 256, 278–281.

[60] For current fees see the Town and Country Planning (Fees for Applications and Deemed Applications) Regulations 1983 (S.I. 1983 No. 1674) as amended by Regulations of 1985 (S.I. 1985 No. 1182).

[61] Town and Country Planning Act 1971, s. 27, as amended by the Local Government, Planning and Land Act 1980, s. 90, Sched. 15.

[62] *Main* v. *Swansea City Council* (1984) 49 P. & C.R. 26.

[63] Town and Country Planning General Development Order 1977 (S.I. 1977 No. 289), art. 5. "Reserved matters" may relate to siting, design, external appearance, means of access or the landscaping of the site: see the definition in art. 2(1) of the General Development Order.

[64] Town and Country Planning Act 1971, s. 42(2)(*a*), (4) and (5).

[65] *Heron Corporation Ltd.* v. *Manchester City Council* [1978] 1 W.L.R. 937.

outline or full permission, the planning authority may reserve these or other matters for their subsequent approval by attaching an appropriate condition.[66]

19-21　　A person who applies for permission to carry out any development which falls within certain specified classes must give notice of his application in a newspaper and on the site.[67] The classes are specified in the General Development Order[68] and include the construction of public conveniences, the construction of buildings or use of land for the disposal of refuse or as a scrap yard or coal yard or for winning minerals or for the purpose of sewage disposal, the construction of buildings higher than 20 metres, the construction of buildings or use of land as a slaughterhouse or for plucking poultry, and the construction and use of buildings as a funfair, bingo hall, theatre, cinema, music hall, dance hall, skating rink, swimming bath, gymnasium or turkish bath.

Publicity in the local press and on the site must also be given by the authority for development affecting a conservation area or the setting of a listed building[69] (see paras. 19–57 and 19–59). Publicity must be given to development departing from the development plan (see para. 19–23).

19-22　　By section 67 of the 1971 Act[70] an application for planning permission for the construction of a building of any prescribed class, or the change of use of existing premises to use as such a building, is to be of no effect without an industrial development certificate from the Secretary of State (in this case the Secretary of State for Industry). The object of this provision was to enable central government to regulate the distribution of industry in England and Wales. Prior to January 9, 1982, regulations prescribed all classes of industrial buildings, with certain exemptions, but as from that date the then current regulations were revoked,[71] and IDC control has ceased to have effect, though it could be re-introduced by new regulations.

A similar control, by means of office development permits, applied to office development in certain areas, but this control ceased to have effect on August 6, 1979.[72]

19-23　　Assuming that the application is in order, the planning authority must determine it, but the Secretary of State may direct that an application be referred to him for decision.[73] Here it is important to bear in mind the link

---

[66] See, *e.g. Sutton London Borough Council* v. *Secretary of State for the Environment* (1975) 29 P. & C.R. 350.

[67] Town and Country Planning Act 1971, s. 26. See *Wilson* v. *Secretary of State for the Environment* [1973] 1 W.L.R. 1083; *McMeechan* v. *Secretary of State for the Environment* (1974) 232 E.G. 201.

[68] S.I. 1977 No. 289, art. 8.

[69] Town and Country Planning Act 1971, s. 28, as amended.

[70] Further provisions as to this control are contained in ss. 68–72 of the Act.

[71] By the Town and Country Planning (Industrial Development Certificates) (Prescribed Classes of Building) Regulations 1981 (S.I. 1981 No. 1826).

[72] Town and Country Planning Act 1971, ss. 73–85; Control of Office Development (Cessation) Order 1979 (S.I. 1979 No. 908).

[73] Town and Country Planning Act 1971, s. 35.

between the development plan and development control. The plan by itself neither permits nor prohibits anything. But in determining an application the authority must "have regard to the development plan, so far as material to the application, and to any other material considerations." "To have regard to" does not mean "slavishly adhere to," and in any case the authority must have regard to other material considerations as well.[74] Such an other consideration must be a planning consideration and one material to the application. For example, material considerations may include the protection of existing uses, (but not simply the protection of the occupation of a particular occupier[75]), or of neighbours,[76] financial considerations, such as the planning consequences of granting permission for a development that is not financially viable,[77] the planning history of the site,[78] and, in exceptional circumstances, personal hardship.[79] Central government policy may also be a material consideration.[80] In addition, however, to the duty to have regard to the plan the Local Government, Planning and Land Act 1980, section 86(3), has imposed a duty on the authority, in determining the application, "to seek the achievement of the general objectives of the structure plan for the time being in force for their area." Nevertheless, on the whole, the plan is only a guide which, subject to observance of the section 86(3) duty, need not be followed. But if the plan is to be departed from a special procedure has to be followed as laid down in the Town and Country Planning (Development Plans) (England) Direction 1981, contained in Department of the Environment Circular 2/1981 providing, *inter alia*, for the giving of

---

[74] s. 29; *Enfield London Borough Council* v. *Secretary of State for the Environment* (1975) 233 E.G. 53; *Niarchos (London) Ltd.* v. *Secretary of State for the Environment* (1977) 35 P. & C.R. 259.

[75] See, *e.g. Clyde & Co.* v. *Secretary of State for the Environment* [1977] 1 W.L.R. 926 (permission validly refused for a change from residential use to office use); *cf. Westminster City Council* v. *British Waterways Board* [1985] 1 A.C. 676, *per* Lord Bridge at p. 682–683: to justify refusal of permission for use B on the sole ground that use A ought to be preserved there must be at least a balance of probability that if permission is refused for use B, the land will be effectively put to use A; *Westminster City Council* v. *Great Portland Estates plc* [1985] 1 A.C. 661.

[76] *Stringer* v. *Minister of Housing and Local Government* [1970] 1 W.L.R. 1281.

[77] See *J. Murphy & Sons Ltd.* v. *Secretary of State for the Environment* [1973] 1 W.L.R. 560, but *cf. Hambledon and Chiddingfold Parish Councils* v. *Secretary of State for the Environment* [1976] J.P.L. 502; *Sovmots Investments Ltd.* v. *Secretary of State for the Environment* [1977] 1 Q.B. 411; *Tonbridge and Malling District Council* v. *Secretary of State for the Environment* [1981] J.P.L. 757; *Sosmo Trust Ltd.* v. *Secretary of State for the Environment* [1983] J.P.L. 806.

[78] *Spackman* v. *Secretary of State for the Environment* [1977] 1 All E.R. 257 (existing planning permission); *South Oxfordshire District Council* v. *Secretary of State for the Environment* [1981] 1 W.L.R. 1092 (expired planning permission); *Tower Hamlets Borough Council* v. *Secretary of State for the Environment* [1983] J.P.L. 315.

[79] *Great Portland Estates plc* v. *Westminster City Council* [1985] 1 A.C. 661; *per* Lord Scarman at p. 670.

[80] *e.g. Kent County Council* v. *Secretary of State for the Environment* (1976) 33 P. & C.R. 70. See also the cases on validity of conditions in §§ 19-24, 19-25, and, generally, for a full analysis, *Encyclopedia of Planning Law and Practice*, §§ 2-875-2-877.

publicity to the application.[80a] Section 86(2) of the 1980 Act contains provisions requiring a district council to consult the county council before determining an application for development which may affect the structure plan, and in certain other cases.

Having considered the application the authority may grant it unconditionally (subject to what is said in the next paragraph) or subject to conditions or may refuse it.[81] They must give reasons for any conditions imposed or for a refusal.[82]

Every planning permission, with a few exceptions, is granted, or deemed to have been granted, subject to the condition that the development authorised must be begun within five years or such other period as the planning authority may direct.[83]

19-24   In the cases which follow the courts have considered the legitimate scope of conditions attaching to planning permissions.

> In *Pyx Granite Co. Ltd.* v. *Ministry of Housing and Local Government*[84] Lord Denning said[85]: "Although the planning authorities are given very wide powers to impose 'such conditions as they think fit,' nevertheless the law says that those conditions, to be valid, must fairly and reasonably relate to the permitted development. The planning authority are not at liberty to use their powers for an ulterior object, however desirable that object may seem to them to be in the public interest."

19-25   The Court of Appeal's decision in this case was reversed by the House of Lords, but these words of Lord Denning have been approved by the House on several occasions since, including the following two cases:

> *Fawcett Properties* v. *Buckingham County Council.*[86] A company challenged the validity of a condition attached to a consent given by the county council for the erection of a pair of farm workers' cottages, limiting occupation to persons employed in agriculture, or in forestry, or in an industry mainly dependent upon agriculture, and including also their dependants. *Held*, the condition was valid, for it was not unrelated to or inconsistent with the policy underlying the planning proposals; nor was it shown that the council had taken account of matters which were irrelevant or had disregarded the relevant considerations.
>
> *Newbury District Council* v. *Secretary of State for the Environment.*[87] The District Council had imposed a condition on a planning permission for the use of certain war-time aircraft hangars as warehouses requiring that the hangars be removed at the end of a limited period specified in the permission. The House of Lords held that for certain reasons the permission was not required, but they also expressed opinions on the validity of planning conditions. For

---

[80a] See *R.* v. *St. Edmundsbury Borough Council, ex p. Investors in Industry Commercial Properties Ltd.* [1985] 1 W.L.R. 1168.

[81] Town and Country Planning Act 1971, ss. 29 and 30. And see DoE Circular No. 1/85 on the use of conditions in planning permissions.

[82] Town and Country Planning General Development Order 1977 (S.I. 1977 No. 289), art. 7(7).

[83] Town and Country Planning Act 1971, s. 41. For outline permissions, see s. 42.

[84] [1958] 1 Q.B. 554.

[85] At p. 572.

[86] [1961] A.C. 636, at pp. 674 and 685; see also *Chertsey U.D.C.* v. *Mixnam's Properties Ltd.* [1965] A.C. 751. *per* Lord Reid at p. 761.

[87] [1981] A.C. 578 at pp. 607 and 619. And see § 19–60 n. 67 for the Court of Appeal's later emphasis on the strictness of the *Wednesbury* test.

example, Lord Fraser of Tullybelton said: "In order to be valid, a condition must satisfy three tests. First it must have a planning purpose. It may have other purposes as well as its planning purpose. But if it is imposed solely for some other purpose or purposes, such as furtherance of the housing policy of the local authority, it will not be valid as a planning condition: see *R.* v. *Hillingdon London Borough Council, ex p. Royco Homes Ltd.*[88] Second, it must relate to the permitted development to which it is annexed. The best known statement of these two tests is that by Lord Denning in *Pyx Granite Co Ltd.* v. *Ministry of Housing and Local Government*[89] which has been followed and applied in many later cases.... Thirdly, the condition must be 'reasonable' in the rather special sense of *Associated Provincial Picture Houses Ltd.* v. *Wednesbury Corporation.*[90] Thus it will be invalid if it is 'so clearly unreasonable that no reasonable planning authority could have imposed it' as Lord Widgery said in *Kingston-upon-Thames Royal London Borough Council* v. *Secretary of State for the Environment.*[91]"

In the *Royco Homes*[92] case, the condition which was held void required houses built under the permission to be occupied by persons on the council's waiting list and that such occupants should have security of tenure for 12 years. If the void condition is fundamental to the permission the whole **19-26** permission will fall with it; if not fundamental it may be severed from the permission and the permission will stand without it. It is not easy in any particular case to say whether a condition is fundamental or not.[93]

It is sometimes possible for an owner applying for planning permission **19-27** to overcome possible reasons for the authority to object to granting permission, or to give a planning benefit compensating for a planning disadvantage resulting from the proposed development, by entering into an agreement with the authority restricting the use of his land or undertaking to carry out certain works. Section 52 of the 1971 Act in the case of restrictive agreements and section 33 of the Local Government (Miscellaneous Provisions) Act 1982 in the case of positive agreements enable agreements to be made which are binding on successors in title. Such agreements are often given in exchange for planning permission.[94]

Development by local authorities and statutory undertakers

The general rules as to planning permissions are somewhat different **19-28** where the developer is a local authority or a statutory undertaker.[95] In

---

[88] [1974] Q.B. 720.
[89] [1958] 1 Q.B. 554 at p. 572. And see § 19–24.
[90] [1948] 1 K.B. 223, 229.
[91] [1973] 1 W.L.R. 1549, 1553.
[92] See n. 88.
[93] See *Hall & Co.* v. *Shoreham-by-Sea Urban District Council* [1964] 1 W.L.R. 240; *Allnatt London Properties Ltd.* v. *Middlesex County Council* (1964) 62 L.G.R. 304 and the opinions of the House of Lords in *Kent County Council* v. *Kingsway Investments (Kent) Ltd.* [1971] A.C. 72, where the Law Lords were divided 3 to 2.
[94] See *e.g. Tarmac Properties Ltd* v. *Secretary of State for Wales* (1977) 241 E.G. 765. And see *Royal Borough of Windsor and Maidenhead* v. *Brandrose Investments Ltd.* [1981] 1 W.L.R. 1083.
[95] Town and Country Planning Act 1971, ss. 40 and 270 and Sched. 21; Town and Country Planning General Regulations 1976 (S.I. 1976 No. 1419), Parts I and II; Town and Country Planning General Development Order 1977 (S.I. 1977 No. 289). See *Steeples* v. *Derbyshire County Council* [1985] 1 W.L.R. 256, at pp. 272–275.

broad terms, if the proposed development requires the authorisation of a government department, then the department may give planning consent along with the authorisation. A principal council may also, except in certain cases, give itself deemed planning permission by resolving to carry out the proposed development, publicising it, and then, after considering any objections received, resolving to carry out the development. In other cases, *e.g.* where the development affects a building listed as of architectural or historic importance, the council must apply to the Secretary of State for permission.

Much of the ordinary development carried out by local authorities and statutory undertakers is permitted development.

(3) Rights of aggrieved persons

19-29   An applicant who is aggrieved by a decision of a local planning authority to refuse permission, or approval of details, or to impose conditions, or who has not received a decision within the prescribed period or agreed extended period, may appeal to the Secretary of State.[96] An appeal must be lodged within six months of the notice of decision or of the expiry of the appropriate period if no decision has been made, or within such longer period as the Secretary of State allows. The Secretary of State may allow or dismiss the appeal or may reverse or vary any part of the decision, dealing with the case as though it were an application before him in the first instance. He must afford the authority and the applicant an opportunity of being heard if either party so desires, but a very large proportion of appeals is now decided, by agreement of the parties, by written representations. Where a hearing is held, it usually takes the form of a public local inquiry.[97] Appeals, except certain appeals by statutory undertakings, are in fact now determined by an inspector or other person appointed by the Secretary of State unless the Secretary of State otherwise directs.[98]

A decision of the Secretary of State on appeal may in certain circumstances be challenged in the High Court.[99]

19-30   An aggrieved person has another remedy. Where permission has been refused or granted subject to conditions and the owner is able to claim that the land has become incapable of reasonably beneficial use in its existing state he may serve a "purchase notice" on the district council, requiring the authority to purchase his interest in the land.[1] In *R. v. Minister of Housing and Local Government, ex p. Chichester Rural District*

---

[96] Town and Country Planning Act 1971, ss. 36, 37.
[97] And see the Planning Inquiries (Attendance of Public) Act 1982.
[98] Town and Country Planning Act 1971, s. 36(8) and Sched. 9; Town and Country Planning (Determination of Appeals by Appointed Persons) (Prescribed Classes) Regulations 1981 (S.I. 1981 No. 804).
[99] Town and Country Planning Act 1971, ss. 242, 245. See further § 19-61.
[1] *Ibid.* ss. 180-187; Local Government Act 1972, Sched. 16, paras. 37, 38. And see DoE Circular No. 13/83.

Council,[2] it was held that in considering whether a purchase notice should be confirmed, the test was whether the land in its existing state had become incapable of reasonably beneficial use, and the fact that the land was less useful in its present state than if developed was not the correct test. Furthermore, the Secretary of State is not concerned with what has brought about the existing state of the land, except that the provisions do not apply where the land has become incapable of reasonably beneficial use by reason of unlawful activities on the part of the owner.[3] If part only of a piece of land is incapable of reasonably beneficial use, the owner cannot require the local authority to purchase the whole.[4]

If the authority (or some other authority or statutory undertaker) is willing to accept the notice, the authority or undertaker, as the case may be, is deemed to be authorised to acquire the interest compulsorily. If this is not the case a copy of the notice is sent by the authority to the Secretary of State, who may confirm it or confirm it with a direction that some other authority shall be required to buy the land. He may, for example, name the local education authority as the purchasing authority where refusal is based on the needs of the education service. Alternatively, he may grant the permission which the local planning authority refused or may vary the conditions or grant permission for other development which would render the land capable of reasonably beneficial use. The Secretary of State must give notice to the parties concerned of what he proposes to do (including, if it be the case, that he proposes not to confirm the order) and if objections are raised he must provide an opportunity for the views of the parties to be heard. When this has been done he may come to a conclusion different from the one he had proposed.

(4) Revocation of permission and powers in relation to authorised uses

Unless the contrary is stated, a planning permission enures for the   **19-31** benefit of the land and of all persons for the time being interested in it.[5] This means that if a permission is given for development and the land is sold, the purchaser may take advantage of the permission already given. A local planning authority may, however, by order revoke or modify a permission it has given[6] where the works to which it relates are not completed or a change of use has not been effected. An opposed order is

---

[2] [1960] 1 W.L.R. 587.
[3] *Purbeck District Council* v. *Secretary of State for the Environment* (1982) 46 P. & C.R. 1. However, this principle does not apply if enforcement proceedings can no longer be brought in respect of those activities: *Balco Transport Services* v. *Secretary of State for the Environment* [1985] 3 All E.R. 689.
[4] *Wain* v. *Secretary of State for the Environment* (1981) 44 P. & C.R. 289.
[5] Town and Country Planning Act 1971, s. 33(1). Accordingly, a valid permission capable of implementation cannot be abandoned by the conduct of an owner or occupier of the land: *Pioneer Aggregates (U.K.) Ltd.* v. *Secretary of State for the Environment* [1985] 1 A.C. 132.
[6] Town and Country Planning Act 1971, ss. 45, 46; Local Government 1972, Sched. 16, para. 24; Local Government Act 1974, Scheds. 6 and 7. And see the Town and Country Planning (Minerals) Act 1981.

not effective until confirmed by the Secretary of State. An unopposed order may, after advertisement, become operative without confirmation by the Secretary of State. Compensation may be payable (see para. 19–53).

A local authority may by order require the alteration or removal of buildings or works or the discontinuance of a use, or it may make the use the subject of fresh conditions.[7] Such an order is not effective until confirmed by the Secretary of State, and if there are objectors to it he must give them an opportunity of being heard. Compensation will be payable (see para. 19–54).

In certain circumstances a purchase notice may be served where an authority takes action under these provisions.[8]

(5) Enforcement provisions[9]

19-32   If development takes place without permission or if conditions attaching to a permission are not complied with, the local planning authority may issue an enforcement notice and serve copies on the owner and occupier of the land in question and on any other person having an interest in the land which is materially affected, specifying the breach of planning control, and the steps required to remedy the breach or alleviate any injury to amenity. An enforcement notice alleging development which involves building, engineering, mining or other operations, or failure to comply with any condition involving such operations, must be served within four years from the time of such development or the breach of condition as the case may be. In the case of unauthorised change of use or any other development in breach of planning control there is no time limit—the only limitation is that the breach must have commenced after 1963. But there is one case of change of use to which the four-year rule applies, namely, a change of use of any building to use as a single dwelling-house; and the rule also applies to any breach of a condition which would prevent such a change.

19-33   The enforcement notice must also specify (a) the date on which it is to take effect and (b) the period or periods within which the steps specified in it must be taken (different periods may be specified for different steps). The copy notices must be served not later than 28 days after the date of issue of the notice and not later than 28 days before the date at (a). At any time before the date at (a) the owner, the occupier, or other person having

---

[7] Town and Country Planning Act 1971, s. 51. And see the 1981 Act.
[8] Town and Country Planning Act 1971, ss. 188 and 189.
[9] *Ibid.* ss. 87–88B (as substituted or inserted by the Local Government and Planning (Amendment) Act 1981), s. 89 (as amended by the 1981 Act), s. 90 (as substituted by the Town and Country Planning (Amendment) Act 1977), ss. 91, 92 and 92A (inserted by the 1981 Act), and ss. 93–95, 243. For special enforcement notices on Crown land, see the Town and Country Planning Act 1984.

an interest in the land[10] may appeal to the Secretary of State. In general the burden of proof in enforcement appeals lies on the appellant.[11]

Eight grounds of appeal are listed in the Act[12]: (*a*) that permission should be granted for the development to which the notice relates or the infringed condition discharged; (*b*) that the matters alleged in the notice do not constitute a breach of planning control; (*c*) that the breach of planning control has not taken place; (*d*) that in the cases to which the four year rule applies, (see para. 19-32), the four year period has expired, (*e*) that in any other case the breach of control was out of time because it began before 1964, (*f*) that any copy of the notice was not properly served; (*g*) that the requirements of the notice are excessive; and (*h*) that the period allowed for compliance is too short.

Whether or not ground (*a*) is pleaded, the appellant is deemed to have made an application for planning permission (and consequently a fee is payable on the appeal, see para. 19-20) so that the Secretary of State is enabled to judge on the merit of the development to which the notice relates and to grant permission for it if he chooses.

The validity of a notice cannot be challenged, except on appeal to the Secretary of State, on any of the grounds (b) to (h). An appeal lies from the Secretary of State to the High Court on matters of law.

If an enforcement notice (other than one requiring the discontinuance of **19-34** a use) is not complied with, the authority may enter the land, remedy the breach as required by the notice and charge the costs to the owner.[13] Alternatively, or in addition, the authority may take proceedings in the magistrates' court against the person who owned the land when the copy notice was served on him. The court may impose a fine not exceeding £2,000 on summary conviction with a further daily fine not exceeding £100 if the contravention still persists; if conviction is on indictment, the fines are unlimited. If the contravention relates to a use or a breach of condition, the only remedy is to take proceedings in the magistrates' court for similar penalties. In these two cases proceedings lie against any person who uses or permits the land to be used in a way which contravenes the notice.[14]

As noted in an earlier paragraph the validity of an enforcement notice **19-35** cannot be challenged on certain grounds other than by way of an appeal to the Secretary of State, and so the recipient of a copy of a notice cannot on these grounds in the magistrates' court raise any substantial defence. But there is no doubt that if an enforcement notice is bad on the face of it and therefore a nullity (if it is materially defective in form, for example),

---

[10] This includes a person occupying with a written licence: Town and Country Planning Act 1984, s. 4.
[11] *Nelsovil Ltd.* v. *Minister of Housing and Local Government* [1962] 1 W.L.R. 404 and *Thrassyvoulou* v. *Secretary of State for the Environment* [1984] J.P.L. 732.
[12] s. 88(2).
[13] Town and Country Planning Act 1971, s. 91. An authority may take *some only* of the necessary steps: *Arcam Demolition and Construction Co.* v. *Worcestershire County Council* [1964] 1 W.L.R. 661.
[14] Town and Country Planning Act 1971, s. 89.

the person on whom the notice is served can ignore it annd may challenge its validity if prosecuted.[15]

The High Court has jurisdiction to grant an injunction when there is a persistent breach of an enforcement notice.

> *Att.-Gen.* v. *Bastow.*[16] Bastow was fined for contravening an enforcement notice. On the third occasion he failed to pay and was imprisoned. The Attorney-General brought an action at the relation of the council. While the action was pending he was fined a fourth time and sentenced to three months imprisonment for non-payment. *Held,* the court had jurisdiction to grant an injunction where, as in this case, the Attorney-General was suing for the purpose of enforcing a public right, although this right was conferred by a statute that prescribed remedies for its infringement.

An injunction may be sought to restrain a flagrant and deliberate breach without necessarily exhausting the specific remedies under the 1971 Act.[17]

Under section 222 of the Local Government Act 1972 an authority may now obtain an injunction in its own name.[18]

Where an enforcement notice has been issued, planning permission is not required for the use of that land for the purpose for which it could lawfully have been used if that development had not been carried out.[19] This provision only applies in respect of the immediately preceding use, and provided that it was lawful.[20] The mere fact that a use was immune from enforcement proceedings does not render it "lawful" for these purposes.[21]

19-36   As noted in paragraph 19–32, the four-year limitation period for enforcement notices does not apply, with one exception, to a change of use. But a person having an interest in land may apply to the planning authority for an "established use certificate" certifying that a particular use claimed has become established.[22] A use of land is to be regarded as established if:

(a) it was begun before the beginning of 1964 without planning permission in that behalf and has continued since the end of 1963; or

---

[15] *Mead* v. *Chelmsford R.D.C.* [1953] 1 Q.B. 32 and *Miller-Mead* v. *Minister of Housing and Local Government* [1963] 2 Q.B. 196, *per* Upjohn L.J. at pp. 226–227, 232–233, and Diplock L.J. at pp. 234–235. The Secretary of State has power under s. 88A of the Town and Country Planning Act 1971, as inserted by the Local Government and Planning (Amendment) Act 1981, to correct on appeal any informality, defect or error if satisfied that it can be done without injustice.

[16] [1957] 1 Q.B. 514.

[17] *Westminster City Council* v. *Jones* (1981) 80 L.G.R. 241 and *Stoke-on-Trent City Council* v. *B and Q (Retail) Ltd.* [1984] A.C. 754.

[18] *Stoke-on-Trent City Council* v. *B and Q (Retail) Ltd.* [1984] A.C. 754.

[19] Town and Country Planning Act 1971, s. 23(9).

[20] *Young* v. *Secretary of State for the Environment* [1983] 2 A.C. 662.

[21] *L.T.S.S. Print and Supply Services Ltd.* v. *Hackney London Borough Council* [1976] Q.B. 663.

[22] Town and Country Planning Act 1971, ss. 94 and 95 and Sched. 14.

(b) it was begun before the beginning of 1964 under a planning permission in that behalf granted subject to conditions or limitations, which either have never been complied with or have not been complied with since the end of 1963; or

(c) it was begun after the end of 1963 as the result of a change of use not requiring planning permission and there has been, since the end of 1963, no change of use requiring planning permission.

The granting of such a certificate means that the use thereby certified as established is not open to challenge by enforcement procedure. An appeal against refusal of a certificate lies to the Secretary of State and he must, if either the applicant or the planning authority so desire, afford each of them an opportunity of being heard.

Where a planning authority has served a copy of an enforcement notice **19-37** the authority may at any time before the notice takes effect serve a stop notice prohibiting the carrying out or continuing of any specified operations, or, with certain exceptions, any activity which was begun not more than 12 months earlier, which are alleged to be in breach of planning control.[23] A breach of a stop notice renders the person concerned liable on summary conviction to a fine not exceeding £2,000, and, if continued, to a daily fine of up to £100; on conviction on indictment the fines are unlimited. The stop notice ceases to have effect when the period for compliance with the enforcement notice expires or the enforcement notice is withdrawn by the authority or quashed. There is provision for compensation for loss resulting from the stop notice if the enforcement notice is quashed on grounds, other than the grant of planning permission, indicating that its service was unjustified, or if the stop notice is withdrawn.[24]

The district planning authority is required to keep a public register of **19-38** enforcement and stop notices.[25]

E. Control of Advertisements

The rules which apply to advertisement control and the procedure to be **19-39** followed in applying them are set out in detail in the Town and Country Planning (Control of Advertisements) Regulations 1984,[26] operative under section y63 of the Town and Country Planning Act 1971. The word "advertisement" as defined in the regulations has a wider meaning than is ordinarily given to it—the definition would include, for example, a doctor's name-plate. It also includes hoardings and lettered balloons used for the display of advertisements.

[23] *Ibid.* s. 90, as substituted by the Town and Country Planning (Amendment) Act 1977, as amended by the Criminal Law Act 1977, s. 28(2) and the Local Government and Planning (Amendment) Act 1981, s. 1 and Sched. 3, para. 3.

[24] Town and Country Planning Act 1971, s. 177, as amended by the Town and Country Planning (Amendment) Act 1977.

[25] Town and Country Planning Act 1971, s. 92A, as inserted by the Local Government and Planning (Amendment) Act 1981.

[26] S.I. 1984 No. 421. Special regulations may be made for conservation areas (see § 19-59).

Generally speaking, an advertisment may not be displayed unless consent is given by the regulations themselves or expressly given by the local planning authority or the Secretary of State. Special rules apply to certain areas, called "areas of special control," and these are referred to later. Somewhat different rules, not here discussed, apply to advertisements of local planning authorities, travelling circuses and fairs, and to advertisements displayed within buildings and visible from without. The local planning authority for all purposes, except in national parks, is the district council.[27]

(1) Advertisements permitted by the regulations

19–40   There are several classes which come within this title. First, advertisements which were displayed on August 1, 1948; secondly, advertisements which continue to be displayed after express consents have expired, provided in any particular case that the consent itself did not impose a condition to the contrary, and renewal has not been refused; thirdly, election notices, statutory advertisements and traffic signs; and, fourthly, advertisements which fall within the following classes specified by the regulations.

Class I: Advertisements of local authorities, statutory undertakers and public transport undertakers required for the proper performance of their functions.

Class II: Certain advertisements relating to the premises on which they are displayed—advertisements which identify or warn, or relate to a profession, business or trade or to churches, recreational institutions, hotels and the like.

Class III: Certain advertisements of a temporary character, *e.g.* relating to the sale of property.

Class IV: Advertisements on business premises relating to the business carried on or goods sold on or from the premises.

Class V: Advertisements on the forecourts of business premises.

Class VI: Flag advertisements.

Class VII: Advertisements displayed on hoardings enclosing certain building sites.

The regulations prescribe (except in the case of Class I) maximum sizes for advertisements, and if a particular advertisement exceeds the prescribed size, express consent must be obtained from the local planning authority. The Secretary of State may, subject to consideration of objections, on his own initiative or at the request of the local planning authority direct that advertisements in any of these classes (or in any particular case) shall not be displayed in any area except with consent expressly given.

19–41   Where consent is given by the regulations, the local planning authority may, if it considers it expedient in the interests of amenity or public

---

[27] Local Government Act 1972, Sched. 16, para. 25, as amended by the Local Government, Planning and Land Act 1980, Sched. 15.

safety, serve a notice requiring the discontinuance of the display of the advertisement in question within a specified period and giving the authority's reasons. There is a right of appeal to the Secretary of State under regulation 22 as if the person served with the notice had applied for consent and had been refused for the reasons stated in the notice. Where this procedure is successfully invoked in relation to an advertisement displayed or an advertisement site used on August 1, 1948, a claim for compensation may be made on the local planning authority for the amount of expenditure incurred in carrying out the requirements of the authority. There are three exceptions to the discontinuance notice procedure—election notices, statutory advertisements and traffic signs may not be dealt with in this way.

(2) Advertisements requiring express consent

If it is proposed to display an advertisement which is not permitted by **19-42** the regulations, an application for consent must be made to the local planning authority in the way prescribed by the regulations, and the authority in reaching a decision must have regard to, and only to, the interests of amenity (taking into account the general characteristics of the locality, including the presence of historical and architectural features) and public safety. The authority may refuse the application or grant it subject to conditions.

Certain conditions attach to any consent—these are termed the standard conditions and relate to tidiness and safety and are prescribed in the regulations. Other conditions may be imposed by the local planning authority. A consent runs for five years unless the local planning authority specify a shorter or longer period in the consent. Any limit of time is deemed to be a condition attaching to the consent.

If the local planning authority fails to give a decision within two months, or if an applicant is aggrieved by the authority's decision, an appeal may be lodged with the Secretary of State, and he may deal with the case as though it were before him in the first instance. He must give the parties concerned an opportunity of being heard unless he considers himself sufficiently informed.

(3) Revocation

The local planning authority may by order revoke or modify an express **19-43** consent at any time before the display is begun. The order is not effective until it has been confirmed by the Secretary of State and the parties involved must have had an opportunity to put their views to a person appointed by the Secretary of State for that purpose. Compensation may be payable for any loss directly attributable to the revocation or modification other than any depreciation in the value of any interest in the land.

(4) Enforcement provisions[28]

19-44   The provisions of the regulations are enforced by prosecution in a court of summary jurisdiction. A person who contravenes the regulations is liable on summary conviction to a fine not exceeding £200, and if the offence continues the court may impose an additional daily penalty of £20. The Act itself provides that persons whose goods are advertised and the occupier and owner of land on which the advertisement appears are liable equally with the person directly responsible for the display, but it is a good defence to anyone other than those directly responsible to show that what was done was done without his knowledge and consent.

(5) Areas of special control[29]

19-45   The local planning authority must from time to time consider whether any part of its area should be defined as an area of special control, and if as a result an order is made defining such an area, the display of advertisements is governed by special rules. An order defining the area is not effective unless confirmed by the Secretary of State, and the regulations provide for the giving of public notice and for a hearing by a person appointed by the Secretary of State if an objection is lodged. An order may only be made in the interests of amenity having regard to the general characteristics of the area, including features of historic, architectural or cultural interest. Where an area has been defined, the broad rule is that no advertisements may be displayed. There are several exceptions: those advertisements which fall into specified classes referred to above (but with added restrictions as to height and size of lettering), election notices, statutory advertisements, traffic signs, advertisements inside buildings and visible from without, and advertisements relating to travelling circuses and fairs—consent for these is given by the regulations. The local planning authority may expressly approve advertisements relating to local activities, for announcement or direction in relation to buildings or land in the locality, and advertisements required for public safety.

F. FINANCIAL BACKGROUND TO PLANNING

(1) Development value

19-46   Development value is the value which land may have for development or redevelopment over and above its value for its current use, the two together making up its value in the market. For example, if land is worth £3,000 a hectare if it could be used for agriculture only but £30,000 if it

---

[28] Town and Country Planning Act 1971, s. 109, as amended by the Local Government and Planning (Amendment) Act 1981, Sched., para. 16, s. 109A (control of fly-posting) as inserted by the Local Government (Miscellaneous Provisions Act) 1982, s. 36, and the Town and Country Planning (Control of Advertisements) Regulations 1984 (S.I. 1984 No. 421), reg. 8.

[29] Town and Country Planning Act 1971, s. 63.

could be developed by building houses, its development value would be £27,000 a hectare. There is a financial problem inherent in a planning system—the compensation and betterment problem. A grant of planning permission is the key to the realisation by an owner of the development value in his land, and the question is this—is an owner who is refused planning permission to develop his land to be compensated for the loss of his development value, and is an owner who receives permission to pay something for the benefit of being able to realise this? Without some overall solution the compensation would greatly exceed the betterment because development value is a floating value and, say, three owners might be refused permission and need to be compensated before the development concerned was finally permitted on the land of a fourth.

The Town and Country Planning Act 1947 attempted to solve the problem by transferring to the State all development value in land in Great Britain. This it did by prohibiting the carrying out of development under a planning permission unless a development charge, fixed by order under the Act at 100 per cent. of the development value, was paid to the Central Land Board set up by the Act. Correspondingly, where planning permission was refused no compensation was payable. Accordingly no owner, whether granted permission or refused it, in theory, received any development value. The Act did, however, provide for a few kinds of development listed in Schedule 3 to the Act, now represented by Schedule 8 to the 1971 Act, to be included in the current use value of land, so that owners retained the development value of this development and compensation might be, and still may be, payable if permission for it was refused. The Act set up a £300M fund out of which payments were to be made to owners whose development value was thus transferred to the State; an owner had to make a claim under Part VI of the Act for such loss. **19-47**

The Town and Country Planning Act 1953, however, abolished development charge and suspended the making of any payments out of the £300M fund. Then the Town and Country Planning Act 1954 translated these payments into "unexpended balances of established development value" attached to the land to which the corresponding Part VI claims related and provided that these unexpended balances should be used for compensating owners who were refused planning permission for the development of their land. These provisions have been retained in subsequent legislation and now appear in the 1971 Act. The loss the subject of a Part VI claim was, however, calculated on 1947 values and the balances only represent 1947 values, plus one-seventh. This, coupled with the fact that most land does not have a balance attached to it anyway, makes these provisions of little practical importance. **19-48**

The abolished development charge was replaced in 1967[30] by a betterment levy, and this in turn was abolished in 1971.[31] Then at the end of 1973 development value realised by an owner was taxed as part of the

[30] Land Commission Act 1967.
[31] Land Commission (Dissolution) Act 1971.

owner's income by "development gains tax" provisions.[32] These have been superseded in turn by taxing realised development value by a new tax—the development land tax.[33] This was chargeable whenever the owner realised development value, other than for Schedule 8 and certain other development, by disposing of his interest, and, apart from an actual disposal, he was deemed to dispose of his interest if he started to carry out material development, which involved most kinds of development other than Schedule 8 development. But this tax has now also been abolished as regards any disposal, including a deemed disposal, taking place on or after March 19, 1985.[34]

19-49   The current financial background to planning at the present day is, therefore—(1) if an owner is prevented from realising his development value by being refused planning permission, then (a) if the development is included in the current use value of land, *i.e.* Schedule 8 development, he may in one way or another recover full compensation, or (b) if it is not, but is for other development, which in the Act is called "new development," he is entitled to compensation only if there is an unexpended balance of established development value attached to the land and only up to the amount of that balance; and (2) increases in land value and development gains are left to be taxed by the ordinary income, capital gains and corporation taxes.

(2) Compensation for planning refusals or restrictions—new development[35]

19-50   If planning permission is refused for, or restrictive conditions are imposed on, development other than Schedule 8, Part I and Part II development, *i.e.* new development as mentioned in paragraph 19–49, a claim may be made under Part VII of the 1971 Act if the land has an unexpended balance of established development value. There are, however, a number of exceptions to this broad rule, *e.g.* no claim may be made for a refusal of planning permission to change the use of land.[36]

19-51   Claims for compensation in the prescribed form[37] are to be submitted to the local planning authority for sending to the Secretary of State, by whom the compensation is payable for the amount of the depreciation up to the amount of the balance.

The Secretary of State is empowered to review the planning authority's decision and give permission for other development. In this way he may avoid the payment of compensation. A claimant who disputes the findings of the Secretary of State on compensation may require the matter

---

[32] Finance Act 1974.
[33] Development Land Tax Act 1976.
[34] Finance Act 1985.
[35] Town and Country Planning Act 1971, ss. 146–163.
[36] *Ibid.* ss. 147–149.
[37] *Ibid.* s. 154, and Town and Country Planning (Compensation and Certificates) Regulations 1974 (S.I. 1974 No. 1242).

to be referred to the Lands Tribunal for determination. If the amount exceeds £20 a notice to that effect is given to the local authority and becomes registrable in the local land charges register,[38] and if the land is subsequently developed, the Secretary of State may require the compensation to be repaid to him, in whole or in part.[39]

(3) Compensation for planning refusals or restrictions—development within "current use"

If planning permission is refused for, or restrictive conditions are   **19-52**
imposed on, development which falls within the scope of "current use," then a claim may be made under section 169 of the Act of 1971. As mentioned in paragraph 19–47 there are certain kinds of development which are included in the "current use" of land—*e.g.* the enlargement and improvement of buildings so long as the cubic content or gross floor space is not increased by more than one-tenth (or in the case of a dwelling by that amount or, 1,750 cubic feet, whichever is the greater)—the full list appears in Part II of Schedule 8 to the Act of 1971.[40] Application for compensation must be made to the local planning authority. The application for permission must have been dealt with by the Secretary of State, by reference to him or on appeal. Compensation will be payable by the local planning authority for any depreciation in the value of the land resulting from the refusal or restrictive conditions.

Part I of Schedule 8 contains other development which falls within the current use, *e.g.* the rebuilding of a building; compensation cannot be claimed under section 169 for the refusal of Part I development, but the development value for Part I development may be recovered in the purchase price if a successful purchase notice (see para. 19–30) is served.[41]

(4) Compensation for modification and revocation of planning permission[42]

In this case a claim may be made in respect of abortive expenditure and   **19-53**
loss or damage arising out of the revocation or modification. In addition a claim may be made for loss of development value but in this case it is not necessary to show that an unexpended balance of established development value attaches to the land. A claim may be made by "a person interested in the land." This is not confined to persons with a legal or equitable interest but includes a person with a contractual right who suffers loss.[43] The compensation is payable by the local planning authority, but, if the land has an unexpended balance, the Secretary of

[38] Town and Country Planning Act 1971, s. 158.
[39] *Ibid.* ss. 159 and 160.
[40] As modified by s. 278 of that Act and by the Town and Country Planning (Compensation) Act 1985.
[41] Town and Country Planning Act 1971, s. 180.
[42] *Ibid.* ss. 45, 46, 164, and 165 as amended by the Local Government Act 1974, Scheds. 6 and 7 and the Town and Country Planning (Compensation) Act 1985.
[43] *Pennine Raceway Ltd.* v. *Kirklees Metropolitan Borough Council* [1983] Q.B. 382.

State may make a contribution up to the amount of the balance towards the loss of development value.[44] Alternatively a purchase notice may be served if the land has become incapable of reasonably beneficial use in its existing state.[45]

(5) Compensation for alteration or removal of authorised buildings or extinguishment of authorised uses[46]

19-54   Where an order is made which requires the alteration or removal of an authorised building or which extinguishes, or places conditions on, an authorised use an owner may claim compensation from the local planning authority for depreciation of the value of his interest in the land, calculated in accordance with the provisions of section 5 of the Land Compensation Act 1961, and for disturbance in the enjoyment of his land. He may, as an alternative, serve a purchase notice on the local authority under section 189 of the Act of 1971, if the land has become incapable of reasonably beneficial use in its existing state.

G. Powers in Relation to Trees and Waste Land

(1) Preservation of trees[47]

19-55   A local planning authority is empowered in the interests of amenity to make tree preservation orders controlling the felling, lopping, uprooting, or wilful destruction or damaging of individual trees, groups of trees or woodlands. An order may itself provide for the replanting of any woodland after forestry operations, or the planning authority may impose a condition requiring replanting on any consent to fell given in pursuance of an order. There is a general requirement to replace any tree protected by an order which is uprooted or felled otherwise than with express consent, and this is enforceable by notice served on the owner of the land by the planning authority within four years of the failure to replant.[48] Where an application for consent to fell or lop a protected tree is refused by the planning authority, an appeal lies to the Secretary of State as in the case of refusal of planning permission, and compensation may be payable.

Regulations prescribe the procedure to be followed in the making of an order.[49] By virtue of the Local Government, Planning and Land Act 1980,

---

[44] Town and Country Planning Act 1971, s. 167.

[45] *Ibid.* s. 188. See also § 19–30.

[46] Town and Country Planning Act 1971, s. 170.

[47] *Ibid.* s. 59 and s. 60, as amended by the Town and Country Amenities Act 1974, s. 61 as amended by the Local Government, Planning and Land Act 1980, s. 61A as inserted by the 1974 Act, and s. 62 as amended by the 1974 Act and the Town and Country Planning (Amendment) Act 1985. For co-ordination of this control with the felling licensing powers of the Forestry Commission, see the Forestry Commission Act 1967, s. 9, as amended.

[48] Town and Country Planning Act 1971, s. 62 as amended by the Town and Country Planning (Amendment) Act 1985, and s. 103 as amended by the Local Government and Planning (Amendment) Act 1981.

[49] The Town and Country Planning (Tree Preservation Order) Regulations 1969 (S.I. 1969

such an order does not require confirmation by the Secretary of State, whether opposed or not. The order must be confirmed by the authority, but not, in the case of an opposed order, until after the authority has considered any objections. An authority may make an order immediately operative pending confirmation by special direction included in the order.[50] A person who contravenes an order by cutting down a tree or damaging it in a manner likely to destroy it, is liable on summary conviction to a fine not exceeding £2,000 or twice the value of the tree, whichever is the greater, or on conviction on indictment to an unlimited fine; in the case of any other contravention the penalty is £500. Where the offence continues the offender is liable to an additional daily penalty not exceeding £5.[51] A tree which is not protected by order but which is in a conservation area (see para. 19-59) may not be felled or lopped without six weeks prior notice to the district or London borough council.[52]

(2) Waste land

Where the amenity of an area is seriously injured by the condition of **19-56** any open land the local planning authority may by notice require the owner and occupier to abate the injury.[53] This is so even where the condition complained of is brought about by an existing use of the land.[54] An appeal against a notice lies to the magistrates' court. The powers of enforcement are generally similar to those available to an authority following the service of an enforcement notice.

H. BUILDINGS OF SPECIAL ARCHITECTURAL OR HISTORIC INTEREST[55]

The Secretary of State is empowered by section 54 of the Town and **19-57** Country Planning Act 1971 to compile lists of buildings of special architectural or historic interest or may approve such lists compiled by

---

No. 17) as amended by the Town and Country Planning (Tree Preservation Order) (Amendment) and (Trees in Conservation Areas) (Exempted Cases) Regulations 1975 (S.I. 1975 No. 148) and the Town and Country Planning (Tree Preservation Order) (Amendment) Regulations (S.I. 1981 No. 14).

[50] Town and Country Planning Act 1971, s. 61, as amended by the Local Government, Planning and Land Act 1980, Sched. 15.

[51] Town and Country Planning Act 1971, s. 102, as amended by the Criminal Law Act 1977 and the Criminal Justice Act 1982.

[52] Town and Country Planning Act 1971, s. 61A, inserted by the Town and Country Amenities Act 1974, s. 8.

[53] Town and Country Planning Act 1971, ss. 65 (as amended by the Local Government Act 1974, Sched. 6 and the Local Government, Planning and Land Act 1980, Sched. 15), 104–107, in the case of s. 104 as substituted by the Local Government and Planning (Amendment) Act 1981 and amended by the Criminal Justice Act 1982, s. 38, and in the case of ss. 106 and 107 as amended by the 1981 Act. See also Public Health Act powers relating to vacant sites, considered at § 16–29, and *Stephens* v. *Cuckfield Rural District Council* [1960] 2 Q.B. 373, as to the meaning of open land.

[54] *Britt* v. *Buckinghamshire County Council* [1964] 1 Q.B. 77.

[55] ss. 54–58 of the Town and Country Planning Act 1971; Local Government Act 1972,

others. By section 54A, added by Schedule 15 to the Local Government Planning and Land Act 1980, a person may in certain circumstances obtain from the Secretary of State a certificate of intention not to list a building. The certificate will give five years' protection against listing, and against service of a building preservation notice (see below) but not against conservation area restrictions (see para. 19–59).

It is an offence to demolish a listed building or to alter or extend a listed building in a way which would affect its character as a building of special architectural or historic interest unless the work has been authorised by a "listed building consent" issued by the local planning authority or the Secretary of State and, in the case of demolition, notice has been given to the Royal Commission on Historic Monuments in England or the Royal Commission on Ancient Monuments in Wales.

19-58   The procedure for applying for listed building consent is similar to that for a normal planning permission but the local planning authority must give local publicity to applications; in England it must notify the Historic Buildings and Monuments Commission for England as required by the Secretary of State,[56] and carry out consultations as directed by him.[57] The Secretary of State must be notified of an application to demolish, or in certain cases to carry out alterations, which the authority proposes to grant, so that he may decide whether or not to call in the application for determination. If an application is refused or a consent is granted subject to conditions there is a right of appeal to the Secretary of State. Furthermore, if an owner claims that the refusal or conditions imposed have rendered the land incapable of reasonably beneficial use he may serve a purchase notice on the appropriate local authority. Compensation may alternatively be claimed in certain limited circumstances.

Where unauthorised works of demolition or alteration have been carried out to a listed building, the planning authority may require works of restoration by serving an enforcement notice.[58] There is a right of appeal to the Secretary of State.

If a non-listed building is regarded as of special architectural or historic interest and is in danger of demolition or alteration affecting its special character, the planning authority may serve a "building preservation notice" on the owner and occupier which will have the effect of imposing immediate control, but limited to six months to enable the Secretary of

Sched. 16, paras. 25 and 26, and Sched. 30; Town and Country Planning (Amendment) Act 1972, ss. 7(1); s. 277A of the 1971 Act, inserted by the Town and Country Amenities Act 1974 brings the demolition of unlisted buildings in conservation areas under control. See the Local Government Act 1985, s. 6, as to Greater London.
[56] Town and Country Planning Act 1971, s. 28, as amended by the National Heritage Act 1983; and see DoE Circular 23/84.
[57] Town and Country Planning (Listed Buildings and Buildings in Conservation Areas) Regulations 1977 (S.I. 1977 No. 228) and DoE Circular 23/77.
[58] Town and Country Planning Act 1971, ss. 96–100.

State to decide whether or not to list the building.[59] If he decides not to list it compensation for loss or damage resulting from the notice may be payable by the authority.[60]

If a principal council considers a listed building is not being properly preserved, it may serve upon the owner a repairs notice specifying the works considered necessary for the preservation of the building, and in default of compliance, the Secretary of State may authorise the council to acquire the building compulsorily. Compensation for such acquisition may be reduced to "minimum compensation" if it can be shown that the building has been deliberately neglected with a view to demolition and redevelopment.[61]

I. CONSERVATION AREAS

Where there are areas of special architectural or historic interest, the **19-59** character or appearance of which should be preserved or enhanced, the local planning authority may designate such areas as conservation areas and special attention must then be paid to these areas when exercising planning control functions—applications for planning permission have to be publicised, unlisted buildings may not be demolished without consent, trees not protected by tree preservation orders may not be felled or lopped without six weeks' prior notice to the district council and special advertisement regulations may be made.[62] Exchequer grants or loans may be available for expenditure making a significant contribution towards the preservation of a conservation area.[63]

J. POWERS OF THE HIGH COURT

An *application* may be made to the High Court to question the validity of **19-60** (a) a structure, local or unitary development plan,[64] and (b) certain specified orders, decisions or directions made by local planning authorities or the Secretary of State.[65] The following are examples: an order revoking or modifying a planning permission, a tree preservation order, a planning decision given by the Secretary of State under section 35 where he has directed the application to be referred to him, a decision of the

---

[59] Town and Country Planning Act 1971, s. 58, as amended by the Local Government, Planning and Land Act 1980, Sched. 15, and other Acts.

[60] Town and Country Planning Act 1971, s. 173.

[61] *Ibid.* ss. 115–117 and Town and Country Amenities Act 1974, s. 6.

[62] Town and Country Planning Act 1971, ss. 28, 277, 277A, 277B (as amended by the Local Government, Planning and Land Act 1980, Sched. 15), 61A and 63 (as amended by the Town and Country Amenities Act 1974).

[63] Town and Country Planning (Amendment) Act 1972, s. 10 as amended by the Local Government, Planning and Land Act 1980, Sched. 15; DoE Circular 12/81, paras. 31–39 and DoE Circular 23/77, para. 121 as amended by Circular 12/81.

[64] Town and Country Planning Act 1971, ss. 242 and 244 as amended by the Local Government Act 1985, Sched. 1, para. 16.

[65] Town and Country Planning Act 1971, ss. 242, 244 and 245.

Secretary of State in an appeal against a planning decision. The right of challenge subsists for six weeks[66] and is available only if it is alleged (a) that the plan or order or decision is *ultra vires*[67] or (b) that the interests of the applicant have been substantially prejudiced by a failure to comply with the requirements of the Act.

19-61   An *appeal* lies to the High Court (a) from a decision of the Secretary of State on an appeal against an enforcement notice or a listed building enforcement notice,[68] and (b) against a determination of the Secretary of State under section 53 of the Act of 1971 as to whether a given set of facts constitutes development.[69] An appeal is available under (b) where the Secretary of State has dealt with the matter by way of appeal from a decision of the local planning authority under section 36, or where the matter comes to him in the first instance under section 35. An appeal under (a) or (b) lies only on a point of law.

19-62   Where one of the statutory remedies is not applicable, the courts have in the past controlled the action, or inaction, of ministers and local authorities by orders of certiorari, prohibition and mandamus, or the grant of declarations or injunctions, and Order 53 of the Rules of the Supreme Court now provides the means of securing such remedies by application for judicial review.[70] (See paras. 12–34 *et seq.*)

19-63   An action for damages for negligence will not lie against a local planning authority in relation to the decision making process,[71] but the existence of a statutory remedy or the application for judicial review will not bar a common law action for negligence against an authority if such an action will otherwise lie.[72]

19-64   However, injustice suffered as a result of maladministration in planning matters may be complained of to the local government ombudsman (paras. 4–64 *et seq.*); indeed a large proportion of such complaints have related to planning matters.

---

[66] See *Griffiths* v. *Secretary of State for the Environment* [1983] 2 A.C. 51.

[67] This would include the plans being so unreasonable that *no* reasonable planning authority *could* have adopted them within the principles of the *Wednesbury* case (§§ 12–20 and 19–25): *Sand and Gravel Association* v. *Buckinghamshire County Council* [1985] J.P.L. 634, where the Court of Appeal specifically emphasised that the *Wednesbury* test of "reasonableness" should not be relaxed in its strictness so as to permit of a plan's being quashed for some lesser degree of unreasonableness.

[68] Town and Country Planning Act 1971, s. 246, as amended by the Local Government and Planning (Amendment) Act 1981.

[69] Town and Country Planning Act 1971, s. 247.

[70] See, *e.g. R.* v. *Hillingdon London Borough Council, ex p. Royco Homes Ltd.* [1974] Q.B. 740 (appeal to the Secretary of State against a condition held not to be as beneficial as an application to the High Court for certiorari for the condition to be quashed, where only a point of law is involved); *R.* v. *Hendon Rural District Council, ex p. Chorley* [1933] 2 K.B. 696, *Steeples* v. *Derbyshire County Council* [1985] 1 W.L.R. 256, *R.* v. *Amber Valley District Council, ex p. Jackson* [1985] 1 W.L.R. 298, and *R.* v. *Sevenoaks District Council, ex p. Terry* [1985] 3 All E.R. 226 and *R* v. *St. Edmundsbury Borough Council, ex p. Investors in Industry Commercial Properties Ltd* [1985] 1 W.L.R. 1168 (questions of bias).

[71] *Strable* v. *Borough Council of Dartford* [1984] J.P.L. 329.

[72] *Davy* v. *Spelthorne Borough Council* [1984] A.C. 262 (allegation that alleged negligence by the council lost appellant his right of appeal against an enforcement notice).

K. GOVERNMENT GRANTS

Certain grants are available from central sources. Under section 250 of **19-65** the Town and Country Planning Act 1971, grants may be made for comprehensive development or redevelopment and under section 253 for research and education in planning and design; contributions may be made under section 254 towards compensation on decisions taken by local planning authorities in the interests of Government departments. In England, the Historic Buildings and Monuments Commission for England, and elsewhere the Secretary of State, may make grants for the repair of buildings of outstanding architectural or historic interest, or the acquisition of such buildings in need of repair, and to make grants or loans for the preservation or enhancement of the character or appearance of conservation areas.[73] Special financial assistance for certain inner urban areas is available under the Local Government Grants (Social Need) Act 1969 (para. 19-70). Grants for the improvement of derelict, neglected or unsightly land in certain areas may be made by the Secretary of State in England under the Derelict Land Act 1982 and in Wales under section 16 of the Welsh Development Agency Act 1975, as substituted by section 2 of the 1982 Act, by the Agency.

2. NEW TOWNS AND TOWN DEVELOPMENT

The New Towns Act 1981 consolidated earlier legislation, providing **19-66** for the creation of new towns by means of development corporations. The area of a new town is designated in an order made by the Secretary of State—it may include the area of an existing town or other centre of population and in no way alters local government areas or boundaries.

If after hearing any objections to a draft of the order (which has to be **19-67** published) the Secretary of State makes the order he will then establish a development corporation consisting of a chairman, deputy chairman and other members not exceeding 11. It is the duty of the development corporation to secure the layout and development of the new town, and for this purpose it is empowered to acquire land and other property, compulsorily and by agreement, to carry out building operations, to provide public services, and to carry on any business or undertaking for the purposes of the town.

At the present time there is no proposal for the creation of any further new town though some existing new towns have still to be completed (see para. 19-70).

---

[73] Historic Buildings and Ancient Monuments Act 1953; Town and Country Planning (Amendment) Act 1972, s. 10, as amended by the Local Government, Planning and Land Act 1980, Sched. 15 and the National Heritage Act 1983. See DoE Circular 23/77, Part V as amended in Circular 12/81.

19-68   When the purposes of the corporation are achieved, the corporation may be dissolved by order of the Secretary of State and on dissolution the assets and undertakings of the corporation vest in a commission, called the Commission for the New Towns. Special provision is made for the transfer of sewerage and sewage disposal undertakings to the water authority, and a local authority may, at the request of the Commission, do work on its behalf in respect of its functions, and may lend its officers or servants to the Commission.

The Commission is subject to the directions of the Secretary of State. The general duty of the Commission is to maintain and enhance the value of the land transferred to it, and it must have regard to the purpose for which the new town was developed and to the convenience and welfare of persons residing, working or carrying on business there.[74]

Schemes may be made for the transfer to the appropriate district councils of the ownership of dwellings and associated assets held by new town corporations and the Commission, the district councils to be responsible for servicing the relevant debt but receiving subsidies on the dwellings transferred.

19-69   The purpose of the Town Development Act 1952[75] was to encourage town development in districts to relieve congestion and over–population outside the county comprising the district or districts in which the development is carried out. The Act formed the basis for more than 60 schemes to alleviate over-population and congestion in London and other major urban areas.

19-70   In 1976, however, the Government's attention began to turn towards the problems of declining population and employment in the inner urban areas of major towns, with the result that in 1977 the Secretary of State announced a curtailment of the new towns programme, and in 1978 he initiated proposals for winding up outstanding schemes under the Town Development Act 1952. Government efforts were directed more towards revitalising such inner urban areas, and, to assist this, the Inner Urban Areas Act 1978 was passed. Under this Act, if the Secretary of State is satisfied that special social need exists in an inner urban area, he may designate the district for the purposes of the Act, and this gives a designated district authority various powers to make loans for the acquisition of land and the carrying out of works which would benefit the district and also to declare industrial or commercial areas within the district as improvement areas. The Act gives additional powers for the authority to make loans, and also to make grants, for various works in such improvement areas. The Act also contains provisions for partnership arrangements between Ministers and authorities with areas of special social need to determine the action to be taken to relieve the conditions giving rise to the need. If an area is both a partnership area and a designated district the Secretary of State may designate it a special area,

---

[74] New Towns Act 1981, ss. 35–41.
[75] *Ibid.* ss. 42–57.

and yet further powers to make loans and grants then arise. Local authority expenditure under the Act may be grant–aided from the urban programme under the Local Government Grants (Social Need) Act 1969. This transfer of emphasis from the new towns to the inner urban areas **19-71** is emphasised further by the Local Government, Planning and Land Act 1980. On the one hand, sections 126 and 127 (now repealed and replaced by the New Towns Act 1981, sections 63 and 64) in Part XV of the Act enabled the Secretary of State to direct a development corporation or the Commission to pay specified sums to him and empowered the corporation or Commission, for the purpose of complying with such a direction, to dispose of land. The Government's intention appeared to be to encourage the sale of new town assets on the market and sections 128–130 (now repealed and replaced by the New Towns Act 1981, s. 2 and Sched. 2), also in Part XV of the 1980 Act, gave the Secretary of State power to make orders reducing the designated areas of new towns.

On the other hand, Part XVI of the Act enables the Secretary of State by order to be approved by both Houses of Parliament to designate an area as an urban development area if he considers it in the national interest to do so, and by another order to appoint an urban development corporation for the area for the purpose of regenerating it. The powers of urban development corporations are modelled for the most part on those of new town development corporations. In England an area to be designated must be in a metropolitan district or in an inner London borough or partly in such a borough and partly in an adjoining outer London borough. The Merseyside Development Corporation and the London Docklands Development Corporation are the only corporations so far established under these powers.

Part XVIII of the 1980 Act provides for the establishment of enterprise zones, where simplified planning procedures will operate and certain financial advantages, such as freedom from rates for most non-domestic hereditaments will be available, to encourage industry and other activity in run-down areas. An enterprise zone results from an invitation from the Secretary of State to a local authority or development corporation to prepare a draft scheme, which is advertised and, after consideration of any representations received, may be adopted and sent to the Secretary of State. A scheme may be the subject of an application within six weeks of adoption to the High Court to quash it on grounds of *ultra vires* or prejudicial non-compliance with procedure. After a scheme has been adopted the Secretary of State may, if he thinks fit, by order designate the area in the scheme as an enterprise zone. The effect of the order, among other things, is to grant planning permission for development specified in the scheme, or for any class of development so specified, subject to any directions, conditions or limitations specified in the scheme, and any structure or local plan has to be reviewed in the light of the scheme. A considerable number of enterprise zones have been established under these provisions.

CHAPTER 20

THE RECREATIONAL SERVICES

20-01 THE law relating to the following services is considered in this Chapter: libraries and museums; parks, recreation grounds and open spaces; allotments; other recreational facilities.

A. LIBRARIES AND MUSEUMS

The law on this topic is contained in the Public Libraries and Museums Act 1964, as amended by the Local Government Act 1972.[1] The councils of non-metropolitan counties, metropolitan districts, London boroughs and the Common Council of the City of London are library authorities in England: in Wales the library authorities are the councils of counties and such districts as may be constituted library authorities by order of the Secretary of State for Wales.[2]

20-02 Library authorities are under a duty to provide a comprehensive and efficient service[3] and may include pictures, records and films in the facilities they offer. They have an obligation to lend their books to those who live or work within their areas or who study full-time there.[4] Charges may be made for the loan of gramophone records and the like, but not for books borrowed by those who reside, work, or study full-time in the area of the library authority. There is statutory authority to levy a "fine"[5] and there is direct authority (if it were needed) to use library premises for meetings and exhibitions, concerts, and other events of an educational or cultural character, and charges for admission may be made.[6]

20-03 The 1964 Act introduced a measure of central control over the library service. It became the duty of the Secretary of State "to superintend, and promote the improvement of, the public library service . . . , and to secure the proper discharge by local authorities of the functions in relation to libraries conferred on them. . . . " A duty is placed on library authorities to furnish such information, and provide such facilities for the inspection of library premises, stocks and records, as the Secretary of State may

---

[1] s. 208.
[2] ss. 206, 207.
[3] See *Standards of Public Library Service*, (HMSO 1962); *Public Library Service Points*, (HMSO 1973); *The Staffing of Public Libraries*, Library Information Series No. 7 (HMSO 1976).
[4] Public Libraries and Museums Act 1964, s. 7.
[5] *Ibid.* s. 8.
[6] *Ibid.* s. 20.

require for carrying out his duty.[7] The Act provides for the setting up of two National Advisory Councils, one for England and one for Wales, to advise the appropriate Minister on library questions, and for the constitution of regional councils for inter-library co-operation.[8] The appropriate Minister is given default powers.[9]

The Public Lending Right Act 1979 gives a right to authors to payments in respect of loans of their books from public libraries. A scheme has been prepared[10] based on the number of occasions on which books are lent from particular libraries. The scheme is administered by a Registrar of Public Lending Right appointed by the Chancellor of the Duchy of Lancaster. Payments due to authors and administration expenses of the scheme are met from a central fund provided by Parliament and controlled by the Registrar. A register is kept by the Registrar of books and authors in respect of which the public lending right exists.

The councils of counties, districts, London boroughs and the Common **20-04** Council of the City of London are empowered to provide museums and art galleries, and these authorities, whether providing a service or not, may contribute to the expenses of some other authority.[11] Parishes and communities may provide this service.

By-laws regulating the use of facilities provided under the Act of 1964 are subject to the confirmation of the appropriate Minister.[12]

Under Part V of the Local Government Act 1985, the control and funding of the Museum of London[13] is shared between the Corporation of the City of London and the Government,[14] the three London Historic House Museums (Kenwood House, Marble Hill House and Ranger's House) were transferred from the Greater London Council to the Historic Buildings and Monuments Commission for England[15] and the Horniman and Geffrye museums were transferred from the Greater London Council to the Inner London Education Authority.[16] There was power for the establishment of a body of trustees to own and administer any

---

[7] Public Libraries and Museums Act 1964, s. 1. The powers of the Secretary of State under the Act in relation to England were transferred to the Chancellor of the Duchy of Lancaster by the Transfer of Functions (Arts, Libraries and National Heritage) Order 1984 (S.I. 1984 No. 1814).

[8] 1964 Act, ss. 2 and 3. In 1981, the Library Advisory Council (England) was enlarged and strengthened, given wider terms of reference, and renamed the Library and Information Services Council.

[9] *Ibid.* s. 10.

[10] Public Lending Right Scheme 1982 (Commencement) Order 1982 (S.I. 1982 No. 719), Appendix, as amended by S.I. 1983 No. 1688, S.I. 1984 No. 1847 and S.I. 1985 No. 1581.

[11] Public Libraries and Museums Act 1964, ss. 12, 25; Local Government Act 1972, s. 206, as amended by the Local Government Act 1985, Sched. 17.

[12] Public Libraries and Museums Act 1964, s. 19.

[13] See the Museum of London Act 1965, as amended by the Local Government Act 1985, s. 43(3)–(6) and Sched. 17.

[14] Local Government Act 1985, s. 43(1),(2). These functions were formerly shared with the Greater London Council.

[15] *Ibid.* s. 44. The Commission was established under the National Heritage Act 1983.

[16] Local Government Act 1985, s. 45.

collection of works of art, or objects of historical or scientific interest, which belonged to a metropolitan county council and which, in the opinion of the Chancellor of the Duchy of Lancaster, was of national importance.[17]

B. Parks, Recreation Grounds and Open Spaces

20-05 The law on this subject is contained in a number of statutory provisions, extending over many years and beginning with the Public Health Act 1875. Under these various provisions local authorities (now the councils of counties, districts, London boroughs, parishes and communities) may lease or purchase land for use as public walks and pleasure grounds and may support or contribute to the support of public walks and pleasure grounds provided by other bodies, even though the land is not within the boundaries of the contributing authority. Powers of compulsory purchase may be used except by parish and community councils.[18] Open spaces held on trust and disused burial grounds may in certain circumstances be transferred to local authorities and managed by them as open spaces.[19]

20-06 Authorities may set aside parts of public parks for ice skating, and for cricket, football and other games, allowing exclusive use to particular clubs. They may provide apparatus for games and recreation, making a charge if thought fit, and may equip and maintain reading rooms, pavilions and other buildings.[20]

Authorities may provide boating lakes in parks and pleasure grounds, including ancillary buildings and equipment, operating these facilities or letting out the right to others.[21] Caravan sites may be provided by local authorities.[22]

20-07 These provisions have been applied to Greater London by section 58 of the London Government Act 1963.[23] In general, the primary authorities for parks and open spaces are the councils of London boroughs and the Common Council of the City of London.

---

[17] Local Government 1985, s. 46.

[18] Public Health Act 1875, s. 164; Public Health Acts Amendment Act 1890, s. 45; London Government Act 1963, s. 58; Local Government Act 1972, s. 121, Sched. 14, paras. 18 and 27; Local Government (Miscellaneous Provisions) Act 1976, s. 19. A district council may purchase land compulsorily on behalf of a parish or community council: see § 5–02.

[19] Open Spaces Act 1906, ss. 2–8.

[20] Public Health Acts Amendment Act 1907, s. 76, as amended by the Public Health Act 1961, s. 52, and the Local Government Act 1972, Sched. 14, para. 32.

[21] Public Health Acts Amendment Act 1890, s. 44; Public Health Act 1961, s. 54; Local Government Act 1972, Sched. 14, para. 27.

[22] Caravan Sites and Control of Development Act 1960, s. 24, as amended by s. 93(1) of the London Government Act 1963, and Sched. 18, Pt. II and the Local Government (Miscellaneous Provisions) Act 1982, s. 8(2). A grant may be made by the Secretary of State: Local Government, Planning and Land Act 1980, s. 70.

[23] As amended by the Local Government Act 1972, Sched. 30, and the Local Government Act 1985, Sched. 17.

National parks, country parks and commons

A non-metropolitan county council or metropolitan district council, **20-08** whose area consists of or includes the whole of a national park, has a duty to establish a National Park committee. Where a national park is comprised in the areas of two or more such councils, then either one council must appoint the committee, by agreement with the others, or a committee must be jointly appointed. These obligations do not apply if there is a joint planning board or special planning board.[24] A board or committee must appoint a National Park Officer and was required to produce a National Park Plan formulating their policy for the management of the park and the exercise of their functions in respect of it, within three years of April 1, 1974, or the date of establishment. The plan must be reviewed at least every five years.[25] The committee or board may make arrangements for securing the provision of accommodation, meals and refreshments (where existing facilities are inadequate), camping sites and parking places, and they may improve waterways in the park to facilitate their use by the public for sailing, boating, bathing, fishing or other forms of recreation.[26]

Powers are available to principal councils to provide, or to join in providing, country parks, and a wide range of facilities in them, including specifically camping sites and picnic sites and facilities for sailing, bathing and fishing.[27] They are empowered to provide facilities in connection with common lands, and to acquire compulsorily adjacent land needed to carry out their functions.

The Commons Registration Act 1965 provides for the registration of common land and town and village greens, for the disposal of disputed claims and for the vesting of unclaimed land in local authorities.

Management

The management of parks and recreation grounds rests with the local **20-09** authority and by-laws relating to their use may be made.[28] An authority may enclose or set apart a part of a park or pleasure ground for the provision of entertainment.[29]

---

[24] The only such authorities are the Peak Park Joint Planning Board and the Lake District Special Planning Board, constituted, respectively, under the Town and Country Planning Act 1971, s. 1, and the 1972 Act, Sched. 17, para. 3. On the composition of a committee or board, see the 1972 Act, Sched. 17, paras. 8–14, as amended by the Wildlife and Countryside Act 1981, s. 46 and the Local Government Act 1985, Sched. 3.

[25] 1972 Act, Sched. 17, paras. 15–21, as amended by the 1985 Act, Sched. 3, para. 5.

[26] National Parks and Access to the Countryside Act 1949, ss. 12 and 13; Local Government Act 1972, Sched. 17, paras. 5, 8, as amended by the Local Government Act 1985, Sched. 3, para. 5. As to grants available, see Local Government Act 1974, s. 7, as amended by the 1985 Act, Sched. 5, para. 6.

[27] Countryside Act 1968, ss. 6–10.

[28] See, *e.g.* the Public Health Act 1875, s. 164 (public walks or pleasure grounds). For other relevant by-law making powers, see Appendix 5 under the heading "Parks, Recreational Facilities and Open Spaces."

[29] Public Health Acts Amendment Act 1890, s. 44, as amended by the Public Health Act 1961, s. 53, and the Local Government Act 1972, s. 145, and Sched. 14, para. 27.

20-10   There are two legal issues which sometimes confront administering authorities: the extent of their liability to users of a park for injury suffered in it, and the extent of their liability for acts of nuisance committed by members of the public. Both these issues belong to the law of tort. The duty of a person to another who comes on his premises with his permission or at his invitation is laid down in the Occupiers' Liability Act 1957. Section 2 (1) reads:

> "An occupier of premises owes the same duty, the "common duty of care," to all his visitors, except in so far as he is free to and does extend, restrict, modify or exclude his duty to any visitor or visitors by agreement or otherwise."

The full text of section 2 appears at paragraph 10–37 and should be read in the light of the following comments. The "common duty of care" referred to involves reasonable foresight and prudence, and what is reasonable must depend on particular circumstances, and especially, in the case of parks and recreation grounds, on the age of the visitor. In applying the test of reasonableness the courts may well look to the body of case law out of which have grown those rules of common law which this statute has replaced. Several cases decided on the common law rules are given.

20-11   *Ellis* v. *Fulham Corporation.*[30] The corporation had given instructions that a children's paddling pool should be raked daily so that dangerous objects might be detected and removed. A child aged nine years cut his foot on a piece of glass whilst paddling in the pool. It was proved that the pool had been raked on the day in question, but ineffectively. The corporation was held liable in damages. Slesser L.J.[31] said: "I think it is clear that the injury . . . was due to a danger which was obvious to the corporation. They had . . . put up a notice for the very purpose of preventing this kind of danger arising; and, moreover, there is specific evidence that one of their agents, a park-keeper, had been informed not more than ten days or a fortnight before the infant plaintiff was injured that another child had suffered a cut while paddling in this very pond. Therefore there is clear evidence to my mind that this corporation knew and anticipated this danger of glass, and indeed, as my Lord has pointed out, sought to guard against it. Now, the method by which they sought to guard against it was to employ a rake adapted for what they conceived to be the purpose they had in view. On that, the evidence is uncontradicted, and indeed it is the evidence of their own witness responsible primarily for the cleansing of this pond, . . . that whenever the sand is heavy the rake would be quite useless."

Sutton v. *Bootle Corporation.*[32] A child caught her finger in the mechanism of a swing in the council's recreation ground. The accident was of so unlikely a nature that its occurrence could not reasonably have been foreseen or guarded against. *Held*, the council was not liable in damages.

An authority has a particular responsibility in regard to "allurements"—there may well be liability unless there is adequate warning and

---

[30] [1938] 1 K.B. 212. And see also *Parks* v. *Walthamstow Borough Council* (1934) 151 L.T. 30.
[31] At p. 231.
[32] [1947] K.B. 359, applied in *Dyer* v. *Ilfracombe Urban District Council* [1956] 1 W.L.R. 218. And see also *Pearson* v. *Lambeth Borough Council* [1950] 2 K.B. 353.

protection.[33] On this point Asquith L.J. said in the *Bootle* case[34]:

"I must briefly deal with the issue raised by the word 'allurement.' ... The presence of this element, which is of course only relevant when the entrant on the defendant's premises is a child, would seem, where it exists, to affect the occupier's duty to this extent, that a danger which is patent to an adult may not be apparent to a child; to a child it may be a concealed trap; accordingly that a warning or other preventive measure may be called for in the case of a child, when it would not be called for in the case of an adult, or a warning of a more emphatic or coercive character than would suffice in the case of an adult."

The following is the leading case on the matter of responsibility for   **20-12** "allurements."

Glasgow Corporation v. *Taylor*.[35] A boy died from eating berries of a poisonous shrub growing in public gardens in Glasgow. The corporation knew that the berries were deadly poison but, it was alleged, took no steps to warn the children of the danger of picking the berries or to prevent them from doing so. *Held*, these facts if true disclosed a good cause of action against the corporation. Lord Atkinson said[36]: "The liability of defendants in cases of this kind rests, I think, in the last resort upon their knowledge that by their action they may bring children of tender years, unable to take care of themselves, yet inquisitive and easily tempted, into contact, in a place in which they, the children, have a right to be, with things alluring or tempting to them, and possibly in appearance harmless, but which, unknown to them and well known to the defendants, are hurtful or dangerous if meddled with. I am quite unable to see any difference in principle between placing amongst children a dangerous but tempting machine,[37] of whose parts and action they are ignorant, and growing in the vicinity of their playground a shrub whose fruit is harmless in appearance and alluring, but, in fact, most poisonous. I think, in the latter case, as in the former, the defendant would be bound, by notice or warning or some other adequate means, to protect the children from injury." Lord Shaw of Dunfermline said[38]: "When the danger is familiar and obvious, no special responsibility attaches to the municipality or owner in respect of an accident having occurred to children of tender years. The reason for that appears to me to be this, that the municipality or owner is entitled to take into account that reasonable parents will not permit their children to be sent into the midst of familiar and obvious dangers except under protection or guardianship. The parent or guardian of the child must act reasonably; the municipality or guardian of the park must act reasonably. This duty rests upon both and each; but each is entitled to assume it of the other."

It would appear from *Bates* v. *Stone Parish Council*[39] that if an   **20-13** authority excludes young children from a part of a park where there are things dangerous to young children (such as play equipment), or alternatively makes it a condition (either express or implied) that young children must be accompanied by a competent adult when using that part

---

[33] See Occupiers' Liability Act 1957, s. 2(4)(*a*), as to warning against danger: § 10–37.
[34] At p. 368.
[35] [1922] 1 A.C. 44, applied in *Phipps* v. *Rochester Corporation* [1955] 1 Q.B. 450.
[36] At p. 58.
[37] His Lordship was referring to *Cooke* v. *Midland Great Western Ry. Co. of Ireland* [1909] A.C. 229.
[38] At p. 61.
[39] [1954] 1 W.L.R. 1249.

of the park, then liability can be avoided. If a young child enters that part of the park he becomes a trespasser.[40]

Liability may also be contested where the danger is manifest, on the principle of *volenti non fit injuria*.[41]

Liability for nuisance caused by visitors to a park is linked with the question of occupation, and on this issue it has been held that local authorities are not *occupiers* of parks and recreation grounds dedicated to the use of the public, but rather trustees. They cannot therefore be liable for a nuisance caused by members of the public to adjoining landowners.

> *Hall v. Beckenham Corporation*.[42] People were in the habit of flying power-driven model aircraft in the council's recreation ground. The plaintiff, who lived nearby, brought an action against the council alleging nuisance and claiming damages and an injunction. *Held*, the council was not in occupation of the recreation ground, but merely its custodian, and an action would not accordingly lie against the corporation. Finnemore J. said[43]: "I think that the corporation are the trustees and guardians of the park, and that they are bound to admit to it any citizen who wishes to enter it within the times when it is open. I do not think they can interfere with any person in the park unless he breaks the general law or one of their by-laws. . . . Their proper attitude to such a complaint is to say that the complainer must take action against the person who is said to be committing the nuisance."

20-14   It might well have been different if the council could have prevented the nuisance but did not, or actively caused a nuisance. In the *Beckenham* case Finnemore J. said[44]:

> "Whether a person occupies land in the strict sense, or has the management and control of it, he must occupy or manage and control it so that it is not a nuisance. In some circumstances a statute may authorise a nuisance, but the fact that something is done by statutory authority does not entitle the person doing it to disregard others' rights, or to create a nuisance to others, unless the Act itself authorises things to be done which cannot be done otherwise than by creating a nuisance. . . . So long, however, as there is a way of carrying out a statutory obligation, or, particularly, a statutory permission without affecting other people's rights, that way must be adopted."
>
> *Kinney v. Hove Corporation*.[45] The plaintiffs complained that the corporation proposed to allow a circus and menagerie to be held in a public park for ten days. The plaintiffs failed in the *quia timet*[46] action—the court was not satisfied, having in mind the restrictions to be imposed, that the circus would substantially interfere with the comfort and convenience of the average person living in the neighbourhood.

---

[40] See § 10–39 as to liability of occupiers to trespassers.

[41] *Giles* v. *London County Council* (1903) 68 J.P. 10, in which a cricketer ran into an iron indicator which identified the pitches.

[42] [1949] 1 K.B. 716.

[43] At p. 728.

[44] At p. 727.

[45] (1950) 49 L.G.R. 696.

[46] A *quia timet* action is a proceeding by which a person may obtain an injunction to prevent or restrain some threatened act being done which, if done, would cause him substantial damage, for which money would be no adequate or sufficient remedy.

C. ALLOTMENTS

The law as to allotments is contained in a number of statutes known **20-15** collectively as the Allotments Acts 1908 to 1950. Allotment authorities are the councils of London boroughs, districts, parishes and communities.[47] A district council is precluded from providing allotments in a parish. Default powers are conferred on the Secretary of State.[48]

There is a distinction between an allotment and an allotment garden: **20-16** the former is a parcel of land not more than five acres in extent, cultivated as a garden or farm,[49] the latter is a parcel of land not exceeding 40 poles, cultivated by the occupier for the provision of vegetables and fruit crops for himself and his family.[50] Most "allotments"—certainly in urban areas—are therefore allotment gardens. Whilst an authority *may* provide allotments and allotment gardens there is a statutory obligation except in the case of inner London boroughs to provide allotment gardens sufficient to meet the demand.[51]

The administration of allotments largely rests with the administering **20-17** authorities and there are few statutory provisions to be observed.[52] There are no special rules as to the determination of the tenancy of an *allotment*[53]—the matter will usually be dealt with in an agreement between the council and the tenant; in the case of *allotment gardens* there are special rules. Under section 1 of the Allotments Act 1922 a tenancy of an allotment garden may not be determined, notwithstanding an agreement to the contrary, except:

(1) by a 12 months'[54] or longer notice to quit expiring on or before April 6 or on or after September 29 in any year; or
(2) after three months' notice, under a power of re-entry in the contract of tenancy, on account of the land being required for building, mining or industrial use or for roads and sewers necessary in connection with such development;
(3) where land is required by a public undertaking, provided there is a term to this effect in the contract, after three months' notice has been given (except in case of emergency);
(4) where the land is required by the local authority for statutory purposes, after three months' notice has been given;
(5) in case of non-payment of rent or breach of condition.

---

[47] London Government Act 1963, ss. 1(6) and 55(4); Small Holdings and Allotments Act 1908, ss. 23 and 61(4); Local Government Act 1972, Sched. 29, paras. 9–11.
[48] Allotments Act 1922, s. 20; London Government Act 1963, s. 55(4); Local Government Act 1972, Sched. 30; Secretary of State for the Environment Order 1970 (S.I. 1970 No. 1681).
[49] Allotments Act 1925, s. 1.
[50] Allotments Act 1922, s. 22.
[51] s. 23 of Small Holdings and Allotments Act 1908 and s. 9 of Allotments Act 1950.
[52] See *Harwood* v. *Borough of Reigate and Banstead* (1982) 43 P. & C.R. 336, where a steep increase in rent was held to be unreasonable and unjustifiable on the ground that it was out of line with the general rise in charges for other recreational activities.
[53] Unless an allotment is also a "holding" to which the Agricultural Holdings Act 1948 applies.
[54] 12 months was substituted for 6 months by s. 1 of the Allotments Act 1950.

20–18   Section 30 of the Small Holdings and Allotments Act 1908 provides for the recovery of possession of allotments (including allotment gardens) on one month's notice if the rent is in arrear, or if a tenant fails to observe any of the rules made by the authority, or if a tenant is residing more than a mile from the authority's area.

20–19   There are several provisions relating to compensation on the determination of a tenancy. Under section 47 of the Small Holdings and Allotments Act 1908 the tenant of an allotment (but not an allotment garden)[55] may claim against the authority for any improvement referred to in Part I of the Second Schedule to that Act—the list includes the planting of fruit trees and the erection of buildings. The measure of compensation is the value of the improvements to an incoming tenant.[56] The tenant of an allotment garden has, under section 2 of the Allotments Act 1922, a right to compensation if notice to quit is given between April 6 and September 29 or if the landlord re-enters in the circumstances mentioned in (2), (3) or (4) above. The measure of compensation is related to the crops growing on the land and to manure applied to it. Compensation for disturbance may also be claimed under section 3 of the Allotments Act 1950 where the landlord re-enters under (2),(3) or (4) above. Compensation under this head will equal one year's rent, and the tenant has in addition certain rights as to the removal of crops and fruit trees. Under section 4 of the Allotments Act 1950 compensation may be payable by a quitting tenant to the local authority—the authority may claim for deterioration of the land due to bad cultivation equal to the cost of making the land good.

D. Other Recreational Services

20–20   Section 19 of the Local Government (Miscellaneous Provisions) Act 1976 empowers local authorities to provide such recreational facilities as they think fit both within and outside their areas. Apart from this wide general power, local authorities are given particular powers in the section to provide:

(a)   indoor facilities consisting of sports centres, swimming pools, skating rinks, tennis, squash and badminton courts, bowling centres, dance studios and riding schools;

(b)   outdoor facilities consisting of pitches for team games, athletic grounds, swimming pools, tennis courts, cycle tracks, golf courses, bowling greens, riding schools, camp sites and facilities for gliding;

(c)   facilities for boating and water ski-ing on inland and coastal waters and for fishing in such waters;

(d)   premises for the use of clubs or societies having athletic, social or recreational objects;

(e)   staff, including instructors;

---

[55] This is the effect of s. 2(8) of the Allotments Act 1922.
[56] Agricultural Holdings Act 1948, s. 51.

(*f*) such facilities in connection with any other recreational facilities as the authority considers it appropriate to provide including facilities by way of parking spaces and places at which food, drink and tobacco may be bought from the authority or another person.

The powers conferred include powers to provide buildings, equipment, **20-21** supplies and assistance of any kind. Local authorities may make the facilities available for use by such persons as they think fit, either free or on payment of a charge, and may make grants and loans to voluntary organisations providing similar facilities.

Local authorities are empowered by section 145 of the Local **20-22** Government Act 1972[57] to provide entertainment of any nature and facilities for dancing, to establish theatres, concert halls, dance halls and other premises for the holding of entertainments, to maintain a band or orchestra and to foster the arts and crafts. It is permissible to enclose or set apart an area within a park for these purposes and to hire out premises provided under the section, giving the hirers a right to charge for admission. Section 144 of the Local Government Act 1972[58] gives wide powers to authorities to attract visitors and to provide facilities for conferences, fairs and the like. The powers conferred by these provisions may be exercised by an authority outside its area.

The Education Act 1944 imposes a duty on local education authorities **20-23** to provide facilities for recreation and physical training and enables those authorities to provide swimming baths or to co-operate with others in this matter.[59]

Authorities (other than parish or community councils) may acquire land by agreement or compulsorily when providing recreational facilities.[60]

---

[57] See also s. 57 of the London Government Act 1963. This power may be exercised by the Inner London Education Authority so far as it considers it expedient to do so for the benefit of persons under the age of 26: Local Government Act 1972, s. 146A(2), inserted by the Local Government Act 1985, Sched. 14, para. 16.
[58] As amended by the Local Government (Miscellaneous Provisions) Act 1976, Sched. 2, the Local Government, Planning and Land Act 1980, s. 190 and the Local Government Act 1985, Sched. 17.
[59] s. 53, as amended by the Local Government, Planning and Land Act 1980, Sched. 7.
[60] Local Government Act 1972, ss. 120 and 121.

CHAPTER 21

POLICE, FIRE AND CIVIL DEFENCE SERVICES

A. POLICE

21-01 THE law on this topic is considered under the following headings: police authorities; police administration; complaints and discipline; the status and powers of constables; the tortious liability of constables; the liability of police authorities in case of civil disturbance; central control and grants-in-aid. Much of the law is contained in the Police Act 1964, which introduced radical changes in police administration and gave effect to many of the recommendations of the Royal Commission on the Police.[1] The law relating to police powers has been reformed by the Police and Criminal Evidence Act 1984.

(1) Police authorities

21-02 The police area is the county or a combined area constituted by an amalgamation scheme or the Northumbria police area, and the appropriate authority is the police committee of the county council (in the case of a non-metropolitan county), the metropolitan county police authority constituted under Part IV of the Local Government Act 1985 (in the case of the metropolitan counties other than Tyne and Wear), the combined police authority constituted in accordance with the amalgamation scheme, or the Northumbria Police Authority constituted under Part IV of the 1985 Act (for Tyne and Wear and Northumberland).[2]

The police committee of a non-metropolitan county council consists of members of the county council appointed by that body, and of magistrates appointed by the magistrates' courts committee. Two-thirds of the membership comes from the former group, one-third from the latter. It will be observed that the *committee* is the police authority in a non-metropolitan county. Statutory duties imposed on the police authority are imposed directly on the committee and the committee is not accountable in any way to the council. What control there is is by way of finance and questions on police administration, referred to later.

The police authorities constituted under Part IV of the Local Government Act 1985 are composed, as to two-thirds, of members of the constituent metropolitan district councils appointed by those bodies and,

---

[1] Cmnd. 1728.
[2] Police Act 1964, ss. 1, 2, 3, as amended by the Local Government Act 1972, s. 196(2) and Sched. 30, and the Local Government Act 1985, Sched. 11, para. 1; Local Government Act 1972, ss. 101; Courts Act 1971, s. 53(5); Police Authorities (Appointment of Magistrates) Rules 1973 (S.I. 1973 No. 733).

as to one-third, of magistrates appointed by joint magistrates' courts committees.[3]

A combined police authority is composed, as to two-thirds, from **21-03** members of the constituent councils, and, as to one-third, of magistrates in the constituent areas. If all the constituent authorities prefer it, the combined police authority may be a committee of one of the constituent councils. The Secretary of State for the Home Department has power to make an amalgamation scheme, effected by statutory instrument, on the representation of the police authorities concerned or on his own initiative.[4] A scheme may be amended or revoked by a subsequent scheme approved or made by the Secretary of State.[5] A combined police authority is a corporate body: it precepts upon constituent councils.

The metropolitan police district is defined in section 76 of the London Government Act 1963[6] and in this area the Secretary of State is the police authority.[7] He is answerable to Parliament for the administration of the metropolitan force, and can be questioned in the House. The executive authority under the Secretary of State is the Commissioner of Police of the Metropolis, appointed by the Crown under section 1 of the Metropolitan Police Act 1829.[8] Assistant Commissioners of Police are appointed by the Crown under the Metropolitan Police Act 1856. Under the Police Act 1964,[9] the police authority within the City is the Common Council.

(2) Police administration

The detailed management of a force is to a very large extent controlled **21-04** by regulations made by the Secretary of State.[10] They deal with "government, administration and conditions of service of police forces" and cover fully and minutely almost every aspect of police administration, providing a comprehensive code of practice. This rule-making power is in the widest terms, but there are in addition specific matters upon which regulations may be made, e.g. ranks, qualifications, promotion,[11] retirement, discipline,[12] records, duties, pay and allowances.

The Act of 1964 lays down the spheres of responsibility of the police authority and the chief constable.[13] The authority is charged with the duty of maintaining an adequate and efficient police force for the area and

---

[3] See further the Local Government Act 1985, ss. 23–25 and 29–37; see also § 4–03.
[4] Police Act 1964, s. 21; Local Government Act 1972, s. 196 and Sched. 30. A large number of such schemes have been made.
[5] Police Act 1964, s. 22.
[6] As amended by the Local Authorities, etc. (Miscellaneous Provision) Order 1974 (S.I. 1974 No. 482).
[7] Metropolitan Police Acts 1829–1963.
[8] As amended by the Administration of Justice Act 1973, ss. 1(9), 5, and Sched. 1, para. 10.
[9] s. 62(b), Sched. 8.
[10] Police Act 1964, ss. 33–36. Police Regulations 1979 (S.I. 1979 No. 1470), as amended.
[11] Police (Promotion) Regulations 1979 (S.I. 1979 No. 991), as amended.
[12] Police (Discipline) Regulations 1985 (S.I. 1985 No. 518), Police (Discipline) (Senior Officers) Regulations 1985 (S.I. 1985 No. 519).
[13] Police Act 1964, ss. 4, 5, 6.

may provide and maintain such buildings, vehicles and equipment as may be required for police purposes. The authority must appoint a chief constable, a deputy chief constable[14] and, if it so chooses, assistant chief constables. These appointments are all subject to the approval of the Secretary of State, and those of deputy and assistant are made after consultation with the chief constable. The chief constable is responsible for the direction and control of the force, and he makes all appointments in ranks below that of assistant chief constable, and all appointments of special constables.[15] Traffic wardens, appointed under the Road Traffic Regulation Act 1984[16] to undertake specified duties in connection with road traffic and vehicles, are under the direction of the chief constable but are deemed to be employed by the police authority.

21-05   Each authority must establish a separate fund, called a police fund, out of which all expenditure is met,[17] and, in the case of a county council, all payments out of this fund require the approval of the council. This is the instrument of control in the hands of the council itself and will customarily be exercised in the budgeting process. There are several exceptions to the general rule. Approval is not required (a) in respect of pay and allowances, (b) in respect of sums required to satisfy a judgment or order of a court, and (c) sums directed to be paid by statute. Under (c) would come part or all of the costs of disciplinary appeal if so ordered by the Secretary of State. The general administrative provisions applicable to local authorities are applied, with modifications, to police authorities.[18]

21-06   Questions on police administration may be asked in the meetings of councils of counties, and constituent councils in the case of a combined police authority or a joint authority.[19] They may deal with matters concerning the discharge of the police authority's functions, but not matters which come within the province of the chief constable. The spokesman for the police authority is a member of the council appointed for that purpose by the police authority.

A chief constable is under a duty to submit an annual report to the police authority on the policing of the area, and he must submit reports

[14] Section 6 of the 1964 Act was amended by the Police and Criminal Evidence Act 1984, s. 108, to provide for a *rank* of deputy chief constable rather than an office. Section 6A, inserted by s. 109 of the 1984 Act, sets out the circumstances in which a force may have more than one person of that rank, but provides that one of them must be designated as having power to act as chief constable under s. 6(1) in the latter's absence, incapacity, etc.

[15] Police Act 1964, ss. 7 and 16. Constables giving assistance to the Royal Ulster Constabulary under the Police Act 1969 are under the control and direction of that force: see s. 1.

[16] ss. 95–97, and the Functions of Traffic Wardens Order 1970 (S.I. 1970 No. 1958).

[17] Police Act 1964, s. 8, as amended by the Local Government Act 1972, s. 196(3) and Sched. 30, and the Local Government Act 1985, Sched. 11, para. 1(5); Local Government Act 1972, s. 107.

[18] Local Government Act 1972, ss. 107 and 196; Local Government 1985, s. 84 and Sched. 14.

[19] Police Act 1964, s. 11, as amended by the Local Government Act 1972, Sched. 30, and the Local Government Act 1985, Sched. 11, para. 1(6); Local Government Act 1985, s. 41.

from time to time on specific matters if the authority so requests.[20] If the chief constable considers that the information called for ought not, in the public interest, to be disclosed, or is not needed for the discharge of the functions of the police authority, he may ask the authority to refer the matter to the Secretary of State, and if this is done the requirement has no effect until the Secretary of State has given his confirmation.

Arrangements must be made in each police area for obtaining the **21-07** views of the people in their area about matters concerning the policing of the area and for obtaining their co-operation with the police in preventing crime. The arrangements are to be made by the police authority after consulting the chief constable, and must be reviewed from time to time. If it appears to the Secretary of State that they are not adequate, he may require the authority to submit a report to him, and after consideration of the report he may require the authority to review the arrangements and submit a further report. In London, the arrangements are to be made by the Metropolitan Police Commissioner, in the light of guidance from the Secretary of State and after consultation with London borough councils and the councils of districts within the Metropolitan Police District. In the City, the Commissioner of Police for the City of London is to make arrangements in the light of guidance from the Common Council.[21]

Collaboration agreements may be entered into between the chief **21-08** constables of various forces on matters within their jurisdiction, and between police authorities on matters concerning them.[22] The Secretary of State may himself direct that such agreements be made if he thinks this right after considering representations made to him by those concerned. *Ad hoc* aid may be given by one force to another, and again the Secretary of State may order this. Special police services may be given to any premises or in any locality on payment.[23]

On occasion, "mutual aid" arrangements have been co-ordinated by a National Reporting Centre, located at New Scotland Yard and operated by a team under the direction of the President of the Association of Chief Police Officers, a senior Home Office official and a representative of H.M. Chief Inspector of Constabulary. The Centre was used during the urban riots of 1981 and the miners' strike of 1984–5.[24] It has no specific statutory status.

(3) Complaints and discipline

The arrangements for the handling of complaints against police officers **21-09** and the conduct of disciplinary proceedings have been remodelled by Part IX of the Police and Criminal Evidence Act 1984.[25] Where a

---

[20] Police Act 1964, s. 12.
[21] Police and Criminal Evidence Act 1984, s. 106.
[22] Police Act 1964, s. 13.
[23] *Ibid.* s. 14.
[24] Report of H.M. Chief Inspector of Constabulary for 1981, 1981–82 H.C. 463, at p. 4.
[25] See V. Bevan and K. Lidstone, *A Guide to the Police and Criminal Evidence Act 1984*, Chap. 9; the Police (Complaints) (General) Regulations 1985 (S.I. 1985 No. 520) and the Police (Anonymous, Repetitious, Etc. Complaints) Regulations 1985 (S.I. 1985 No. 672).

complaint is made by or on behalf of a member of the public, it must be recorded by the "appropriate authority." This means (1) in relation to a complaint concerning an officer of the metropolitan police, the Metropolitan Police Commissioner; (2) in relation to a chief constable or deputy or assistant chief constable, the police authority; and (3) in relation to another officer, the chief constable.[26] Where the complaint does not concern a senior officer, it may be subject to "informal resolution"[27] if the member of the public concerned consents and the chief officer is satisfied that the conduct complained of, even if proved, would not justify a criminal or disciplinary charge. Otherwise, it must be investigated formally.[28] A complaint against a senior officer may be dealt with according to the appropriate authority's discretion, if the authority is satisfied that the conduct complained of, even if proved, would not justify a criminal or disciplinary charge. Otherwise it must be investigated.[29]

Investigations must be conducted by an officer of the same or another force of at least (1) the rank of chief inspector and (2) the rank of the officer against whom the complaint is made. The appropriate authority:

(1) *must* refer to the Police Complaints Authority[30] any complaint alleging that the conduct complained of resulted in death or serious injury or alleging assault occasioning actual bodily harm, an offence under section 1 of the Prevention of Corruption Act 1906 or a serious arrestable offence[31];

(2) *must* refer any complaint required to be submitted by the Police Complaints Authority[32];

(3) *may* refer any other complaint[33]; and

(4) *may* refer any matter which appears to indicate that an officer may have committed a criminal or disciplinary offence, and is not the subject of a complaint, if it appears that it ought to be referred by reason of its gravity or of exceptional circumstances.[34]

The Police Complaints Authority must supervise the investigation of complaints in category (1) above, and, if they consider it desirable in the public interest, any other complaint or any matter referred to them under

---

[26] Police and Criminal Evidence Act 1984, s. 84. These are also the discipliinary authorities for the respective ranks. A chief constable may delegate most of his functions under this part of the Act to a deputy or assistant chief constable and similar arrangements may be made in London: S.I. 1985 No. 520, reg. 13; 1984 Act s. 101(5), (9).

[27] See the Police (Complaints) (Informal Resolution) Regulations 1985 (S.I. 1985 No. 671).

[28] 1984 Act, s. 85.

[29] *Ibid.* s. 86.

[30] An independent statutory body established by s. 83 of and Schedule 4 to the 1984 Act.

[31] *Ibid.* s. 87(1)(*a*); the last three were specified by the Police (Complaints) (Mandatory Referrals, Etc.) Regulations 1985 (S.I. 1985 No. 673).

[32] *Ibid.* s. 87(2).

[33] *Ibid.* s. 87(1)(*b*).

[34] *Ibid.* s. 88.

section 88.[35] The Authority must also be informed of the result of investigations not supervised by them.[36]

An investigation may lead to (1) the institution of a criminal prosecution by the Director of Public Prosecutions; (2) the institution of disciplinary proceedings by the chief officer; or (3) no action. The Police Complaints Authority may require a report to be sent to the Director of Public Prosecutions or direct the institution of disciplinary proceedings.[37]

Regulations made under section 33 of the Police Act 1964[38] establish a **21-10** code of discipline with seventeen disciplinary offences, including discreditable conduct, disobedience to orders, neglect of duty and racially discriminatory behaviour, and prescribe the procedure for the investigation of alleged offences and the conduct of disciplinary hearings.[39] Disciplinary charges against lower ranks are normally heard by the chief officer,[40] but in some cases they are heard by a tribunal comprising the chief officer and two members of the Police Complaints Authority.[41] Cases must be remitted to another chief officer if the chief officer concerned is interested in the case otherwise than in his official capacity, or is a material witness, and may be so remitted if it is otherwise considered appropriate.[42] A punishment of dismissal, requirement to resign or reduction in rank may not be awarded unless the officer concerned has been given the opportunity to be legally represented.[43] Contested charges against senior officers are heard by a tribunal consisting of a single person appointed by the police authority from a list nominated by the Lord Chancellor, sitting with one or more assessors.[44] The officer may be legally represented.

An appeal lies from a decision of a deputy chief constable to the chief constable, and from the chief constable or a tribunal to the Secretary of State.[45]

Every police authority in carrying out its duty with respect to the maintenance of an adequate and efficient police force must keep itself

---

[35] Police and Criminal Evidence Act 1984, s. 89.
[36] *Ibid.* s. 90(9).
[37] *Ibid.* ss. 91, 93.
[38] See also the Police and Criminal Evidence Act 1984, ss. 101, 102.
[39] The Police (Discipline) Regulations 1985 (S.I. 1985 No. 518) enact the discipline code applicable to all police officers, and the disciplinary procedures for non-senior officers; the Police (Discipline) (Senior Officers) Regulations 1985 (S.I. 1985 No. 519) prescribe the disciplinary procedures for officers above the rank of superintendent.
[40] Or, in minor cases, the deputy chief constable.
[41] Police and Criminal Evidence Act 1984, s. 94.
[42] *Ibid.* s. 101(3), (4); S.I. 1985 No. 518, reg. 14.
[43] *Ibid.* s. 102.
[44] S.I. 1985 No. 519, reg. 12.
[45] Police Act 1964, s. 37 and Sched. 5, as substituted by s. 103 of the Police and Criminal Evidence Act 1984; Police (Appeals) Rules 1985 (S.I. 1985 No. 576). Exceptionally, the decision of a disciplinary tribunal may be challenged on an application for judicial review notwithstanding that rights of appeal have not been exhausted: *R.* v. *Chief Constable of Merseyside Police, ex p. Calveley, The Times,* November 28, 1985.

informed as to the working of the provisions of the 1984 Act as to the handling of complaints in relation to the force.[46]

Natural justice, or the duty to act fairly, must be observed where a police officer is dismissed or compulsorily retired.[47]

(4) The status and powers of constables

21-11 Every constable is required to make a declaration that he will well and truly serve the Sovereign and will cause the peace to be kept and preserved.[48] A constable has a common law duty to preserve the Queen's peace and if he has reason to suppose that the peace will be broken he may arrest the person causing or provoking the breach.[49]

He has a wide variety of specific powers, some conditional on the grant of a warrant, to enter premises, to search for and seize property, and to arrest persons.[50] For example, a constable has wider powers than a member of the public to arrest without warrant persons guilty, or reasonably suspected of being guilty, of an "arrestable offence," *i.e.* one for which the sentence is fixed by law or for which a person may be sentenced to imprisonment for a term of five years.[51] A member of the public may only arrest in relation to past "arrestable offences" where an offence has actually been committed by someone—a constable need only reasonably suspect that the offence has been committed. A constable, unlike a member of the public, may arrest a person who is, or whom he, with reasonable cause, suspects to be, about to commit an arrestable offence. Whilst a constable, whether acting under statute or common law, is not required to have a prima facie case for conviction before arrest without a warrant, he has a duty, before making an arrest, to make such inquiries as in the circumstances of the case are reasonable. In *Dumbell* v. *Roberts*[52] damages were awarded for false imprisonment against two constables who failed to observe this principle. Where a constable acts under a justice's warrant in circumstances in which the grant of the warrant was beyond the justice's jurisdiction, the constable is nevertheless protected.[53]

21-12 In carrying out their duty to enforce the law the police have a discretion with which the courts will not ordinarily interfere. Two cases illustrate the principles involved.

---

[46] 1984 Act, s. 95.
[47] *Cooper* v. *Wilson* [1937] 2 K.B. 309; *Ridge* v. *Baldwin* [1964] A.C. 40; *R.* v. *Kent Police Authority, ex p. Godden* [1971] 2 Q.B. 662; *Chief Constable of the North Wales Police* v. *Evans* [1982] 1 W.L.R. 1153.
[48] Police Act 1964, s. 18 and Sched. 11.
[49] *Timothy* v. *Simpson* (1835) 1 Cr.M. & R. 757; *R.* v. *Howell* [1982] Q.B. 416.
[50] See generally L. H. Leigh, *Police Powers* (2nd ed, 1985); V. Bevan and K. Lidstone, *A Guide to the Police and Criminal Evidence Act 1984* (1984)
[51] Police and Criminal Evidence Act 1984, s. 24.
[52] [1944] 1 All E.R. 326.
[53] Constables' Protection Act 1750.

R. v. Commissioner of Police of the Metropolis, ex p. Blackburn.[54] In consequence of a policy decision made by the Commissioner of Police of the Metropolis, the police did not attempt to enforce section 31(1)(*a*) of the Betting, Gaming and Lotteries Act 1963 in gaming clubs in London. The applicant applied for an order of mandamus directing the Commissioner to reverse his policy decision. It was argued on behalf of the Commissioner that he owed no duty to the public to enforce the law and had an absolute discretion not to prosecute. *Held*, that the respondent did owe a duty to the public to enforce the law which he could be compelled to perform, and (*per* Lord Denning M.R. and Salmon L.J.) while he had a discretion not to prosecute, his discretion to make policy decisions was not absolute. Lord Denning M.R. said[55]:

"Although the chief officers of police are answerable to the law, there are many fields in which they have a discretion with which the law will not interfere. For instance, it is for the Commissioner of Police of the Metropolis, or the chief constable, as the case may be, to decide in any particular case whether inquiries should be pursued, or whether an arrest should be made, or a prosecution brought. It must be for him to decide on the disposition of his force and the concentration of his resources on any particular crime or area. No court can or should give him direction on such a matter. He can also make policy decisions and give effect to them, as, for instance, was often done when prosecutions were not brought for attempted suicide. But there are some policy decisions with which, I think, the courts in a case can, if necessary, interfere. Suppose a chief constable were to issue a directive to his men that no person should be prosecuted for stealing any goods less than £100 in value. I should have thought that the court could countermand it. He would be failing in his duty to enforce the law."

As the policy decision was withdrawn, an order of mandamus was not in fact made.

R. v. Commissioner of Police of the Metropolis, ex p. Blackburn (No. 3).[56] Mr. Blackburn sought an order of mandamus to be directed to the Commissioner of Police of the Metropolis requiring him to secure the enforcement of law against illegal publishing and selling of pornographic material both by the seizure of the material and by prosecuting the publishers and sellers. Counsel for the Commissioner and for the Attorney-General conceded that the action taken against shopkeepers in Soho had been relatively ineffective. *Held*, that although the evidence disclosed that obscene material was widely available for sale in shops the applicant had not established that it was a case for the court to interfere with the discretion of the police in carrying out their duties. Lord Denning M.R. said[57]:

"In *R. v. Commissioner of Police of the Metropolis, ex p. Blackburn* we made it clear that, in the carrying out of their duty of enforcing the law, the police have a discretion with which the courts will not interfere. There might, however, be extreme cases in which he was not carrying out his duty. And then we would. I do not think this is a case for our interference. In the past the Commissioner has done what he could under the existing system and with the available manpower. The new Commissioner is doing more. He is increasing the number of the Obscene Publications Squad to eighteen and he is reforming it and its administration. No more can reasonably be expected."

[54] [1968] 2 Q.B. 118.
[55] At p. 136.
[56] [1973] Q.B. 241. See also *R. v. Chief Constable of Devon and Cornwall, ex p. Central Electricity Generating Board* [1982] Q.B. 458.
[57] At p. 254.

21–13   The legal relationship which exists between a constable and the police authority cannot be stated shortly, for the ordinary rules of master and servant relationships do not apply.[58] In one respect a constable enjoys an independent status: in other respects he is a wage-earner subject to a highly developed code of discipline. These two aspects of a constable's status are not easily reconcilable, not the least because of dicta appearing in several leading cases.

The fundamental nature of a constable's status was dealt with in *Fisher* v. *Oldham Corporation*,[59] where McCardie J. said[60] (after reviewing the common law status of police officers):

> "Prima facie, therefore, a police constable is not the servant of the borough. He is a servant of the state, a ministerial officer of the central power, though subject, in some respects, to local supervision and local regulation."

The idea of a constable as being a "servant of the state" appeared in the Australian case, *Enever* v. *The King* (a case based on English decisions), in which Griffith C.J. said[61]:

> "At common law the office of constable or peace officer was regarded as a public office, and the holder of it as being, in some sense, a servant of the Crown. . . . A constable, therefore, when acting as a peace officer, is not exercising a delegated authority, but an original authority, and the general law of agency has no application."

It is submitted that the terms "servant of the state" and "servant of the Crown" in these cases mean no more than this, that the constable has sworn allegiance to the Crown. This was the meaning given it by the House of Lords in *Att.-Gen. for New South Wales* v. *Perpetual Trustee Co.*[62] Moreover, it is clear that a constable is not an officer, agent or servant of the Crown as understood by section 2(6) of the Crown Proceedings Act 1947, for a constable is not appointed directly or indirectly by the Crown or paid wholly out of the Consolidated Fund or from money voted by Parliament: the Crown could not therefore be liable for his tortious acts.

A constable has all the powers and privileges of constable throughout England and Wales, a special constable in his own and contiguous police areas.[63]

(5) The tortious liability of constables

21–14   Under the Police Act 1964 a chief constable is liable for torts committed by constables under his direction and control and in the performance or purported performance of their functions in the same

---

[58] See G. Marshall, *Police and Government* (1965), Chap. 3 and G. Marshall, *Constitutional Conventions* (1984), Chap. VIII.
[59] [1930] 2 K.B. 364.
[60] At p. 371.
[61] (1906) 3 C.L.R. 969 at pp. 975, 977.
[62] [1955] A.C. 457, *per* Viscount Simonds at p. 489.
[63] Police Act 1964, s. 19; Local Government Act 1972, s. 196(5).

way as a master is liable for the torts committed by his servants in the course of their employment.[64] The chief constable is therefore to be treated as a joint tortfeasor. The Act provides that there shall be paid out of the police fund any damages or costs awarded against the chief constable in any proceedings brought against him under this provision, and any sum required in connection with the settlement of a claim against the chief constable under this provision if the settlement is approved by the police authority. The authority has a discretion to order payment out of the police fund of damages or costs awarded against a member of the force or any special constable in proceedings for a tort committed by him, and to pay out any sum in settlement. This would apply where an action was brought directly against a constable in respect of a tort committed by him. The police authority's discretion to order payments out of the police fund applies even though the tort was not committed in the performance or purported performance of the constable's duties. If it were found that the matter complained of had not arisen in the course of duty or in the intended execution of duty, the action could succeed only against the constable.

(6) Liability of police authorities in civil disturbance

21-15
There is a liability to pay compensation where damage or loss is sustained in civil commotion. Section 2(1) of the Riot (Damages) Act 1886,[65] reads:

> Where a house, shop, or building in any police district has been injured or destroyed, or the property therein has been injured, stolen, or destroyed, by any person riotously and tumultuously[66] assembled together, . . . compensation . . . shall be paid out of the police fund of such district to any person who has sustained loss by such injury, stealing, or destruction; but in fixing the amount of such compensation regard shall be had to the conduct of the said person, whether as respects the precautions taken by him or as respects his being a party or accessory to such riotous or tumultuous assembly, or as regards any provocation offered to the persons assembled or otherwise.

(7) Central control and grants in aid

21-16
Section 28 of the Police Act 1964 defines the "general duty" of the Secretary of State—he is required to exercise his powers under the Act in such manner and to such extent as appears to him to be best calculated to promote the efficiency of the police. This means that questions may be raised in Parliament on certain matters of police administration which formerly were excluded. He is given a number of specific powers of supervision and control and as noted earlier he has wide regulation-making powers. He has a direct relationship with the police authority and

---

[64] s. 48. See, *e.g. Rigby* v. *Chief Constable of Northamptonshire* [1985] 1 W.L.R. 1242.
[65] As amended by the Police Act 1964, Sched. 9; and see S.R. & O. 1921 No. 1536.
[66] The assembly must be riotous *and* tumultuous. The words are cumulative: see *Dwyer (J. W.)* v. *Metropolitan Police District Receiver* [1967] 2 Q.B. 970.

with the chief constable. He may require a police authority to call for the retirement of the chief constable in the interests of efficiency.[67] Where this is done, the officer must be given an opportunity to make representations to the Secretary of State and an inquiry must be held to consider representations and to report to the Secretary of State. There must be one independent member of the board of inquiry. The Secretary of State may call for reports from a chief constable on any matter connected with the policing of his area and the chief constable must submit an annual report to him. Since the reports concern matters not within the jurisdiction of the police authority, they will cover a wider field than those for which the police authority can call.[68]

21–17 The Secretary of State may order a local inquiry into any matter connected with the police, and he decides whether or not the inquiry shall be held in public.[69] The report of the findings need not be published, but if they are not published a summary of them must be "made known" by the Secretary of State. The appropriate provisions of the Local Government Act 1972 are incorporated here, so that witnesses may be subpoenaed.

Her Majesty may appoint such number of inspectors (known as "Her Majesty's Inspectors of Constabulary") as the Secretary of State may, with the consent of the Treasury, determine, and one of them may be appointed Chief Inspector.[70] They are under a duty to inspect all forces, including that of the City of London, and to report to the Secretary of State.

Section 31 of the Police Act 1964 authorises the payment of grants to police authorities subject to such conditions as the Secretary of State may with approval of the Treasury by order determine. The Police (Grant) Order 1966[71] provides for a grant of 50 per cent. of approved expenditure "conditional upon the Secretary of State being satisfied that the police area in question is efficiently policed, that adequate co-operation is afforded by the police to other police forces, that the police service is efficiently and properly maintained, equipped and administered, and that the rates of pay and allowances of the force are as prescribed or approved by him." The same formula is used in connection with the grant to the metropolitan police force, except that an additional sum is paid each year in respect of the special services which the force renders to the state, such as the provision of personal protection to the Royal Family, certain Ministers of the Crown and distinguished visitors. A grant of one-third of net expenditure is paid in respect of the City of London police.

The Home Office provides several common police services—the police college, district police training centres, the Home Office forensic science

---

[67] Police Act 1964, s. 29.
[68] *Ibid.* s. 30.
[69] Police Act 1964, s. 32. Inquiries under this provision are subject to the Tribunals and Inquiries Act 1971, ss. 1 and 11; see S.I. 1975 No. 1879, art. 3 and Schedule.
[70] Police Act 1964, s. 38.
[71] S.I. 1966 No. 223, as amended.

laboratories and the Home Office wireless depots. The cost of these services is shared between the Home Office and the police authorities.

B. THE FIRE SERVICE

(1) Fire authorities and their statutory obligations
The law relating to the fire service is contained in the Fire Services Acts **21-18** 1947 to 1959 and in regulations made by the Secretary of State. The fire authority in each non-metropolitan county is the county council.[72] The fire authority in each metropolitan county is the metropolitan fire and civil defence authority, and in Greater London, the London Fire and Civil Defence Authority, these being joint authorities established under Part IV of the Local Government Act 1985.[73] Provision is also made for the combination of fire areas.[74] Where two or more fire authorities wish to combine for fire fighting purposes they may submit a combination scheme to the Secretary of State for his approval, and he himself may make a scheme if he considers one is necessary in the interest of efficiency and the authorities themselves have not taken the initiative. A combined authority is a body corporate consisting of representatives of each of the constituent areas as prescribed in the scheme, and it exercises all the powers of a fire authority. Following reorganisation, all existing combination schemes came to an end on April 1, 1974.[75]

The Act of 1947 imposes specific duties on fire authorities and combined fire authorities. Each authority is required to make provision for fire fighting purposes and particularly to secure that the service adequately meets all normal requirements and can be summoned efficiently, that personnel are properly trained, that advice as to fire prevention is available, that the brigade is familiar with the area and with the availability of water supplies, and with the steps they should take to mitigate damage to property when tackling fire.[76] An authority is also under a duty, so far as is practicable, to join in the making of reinforcement schemes to render mutual aid. Where an authority cannot obtain the agreement of another authority as to a reinforcement scheme the Secretary of State may, at its request, intervene.[77]

An authority may discharge its functions through other authorities or **21-19** persons, and where agreement cannot be reached the Secretary of State may be asked to determine what arrangements should be entered into,

---

[72] Fire Services Act 1947, s. 4, as amended by the Local Government Act 1972, Sched. 30 and the Local Government Act 1985, Sched. 11, para. 2(3).
[73] Local Government Act 1985, Sched. 11, para. 2(1),(2). See also *ibid.* ss. 23, 26, 27, 29–37, 41, 42 and § 4–03 and 28–07.
[74] Fire Services Act 1947, ss. 5 to 10; London Government Act 1963, s. 48(1); Local Government Act 1972, ss. 179 and 197.
[75] Fire Services (Revocation of Combination Schemes) Order 1974 (S.I. 1974 No. 389).
[76] Fire Services Act 1947, s. 1.
[77] *Ibid.* s. 2, as amended by the Fire Services Act 1959, s. 2.

and he may himself take the initiative if he thinks this necessary in the interests of efficiency.[78]

The rules as to the liability of local authorities for failure to carry out statutory duties, where failure results in loss or injury, are discussed in Chapter 10. In general, a right of action for damages will not lie at the suit of a private person if a duty is owed to the public at large, as is the case in duties imposed by statute on fire authorities. If, however, an authority carries out its duties negligently (if there is a misfeasance as distinct from nonfeasance) an action might well lie.[79]

> *Dawson* v. *Bingley Urban District Council.*[80] The Public Health Act 1875 placed a duty on urban authorities to provide and maintain fire plugs and to mark the situation of them. The Bingley Council put up an indication plate in a wrong place and when a fire broke out on the plaintiff's property his loss was greater because the fire brigade lost time in finding the fire plug. *Held*, in putting up a misleading indication plate the council was guilty of an act of misfeasance and it was therefore liable for the extra loss caused as a result of the breach of statutory duty. Vaughan Williams L.J. said[81]: "... although well-established authorities make it clear that public bodies representing the public are not liable to be sued by an individual member of the public who has sustained injury in consequence of the omission of such a body to perform a statutory duty created for the benefit of a class of which such person is one, yet the public body will be liable if by its acts it alters the normal condition of something which it has a statutory duty to provide or maintain and in consequence some person of a class for whose benefit the statutory duty is imposed is injured."

21–20   Fire authorities have a number of specifically expressed duties in regard to fire prevention. The Fire Precautions Act 1971 greatly extended the scope of statutory fire precautions. It is necessary for premises which are put to certain uses to have a fire certificate from the fire authority.[82] A fire certificate may impose requirements as to means of escape, means for fighting fire, warnings in case of fire, instruction of employees, the number of persons who may be in the premises at any one time, and other fire precautions.[83] The classes of use within this rule are those designated by the Secretary of State from the following classes of uses: use for any purpose involving sleeping accommodation; use for entertainment, recreation or instruction, or for the purposes of any club or society; use for purposes of teaching, training or research; use for any purpose involving access to the premises by the public and use as a place of work.[84] The Fire Precautions (Hotels and Boarding Houses) Order 1972 brought

---

[78] Fire Services Act 1947, s. 12, as amended by the Fire Services Act 1959, s. 4.
[79] As to the liability of fire authorities for the negligence of firemen, see *Ward* v. *London County Council* [1938] 2 All E.R. 341.
[80] [1911] 2 K.B. 149.
[81] At p. 154.
[82] See the Fire Precautions (Application for Certificate) Regulations 1976 (S.I. 1976 No. 2008). See also *Hallett* v. *Nicholson* 1979 S.C.1 on the liability of fire authorities in tort in respect of the exercise of their functions under the 1971 Act.
[83] Fire Precautions Act 1971, s. 6.
[84] *Ibid.* s. 1(2) as amended by the Health and Safety at Work, etc., Act 1974, s. 78(2).

the first group of uses within the requirements of the Act.[85] Factories, offices, shops and railway premises were brought within the Act by the Fire Precautions (Factories, Offices, Shops and Railway Premises) Order 1976.[86] In the case of factories, offices, shops and railway premises within a specified list of special hazards, enforcement and certificating functions are exercised by the Health and Safety Executive rather than fire authorities.[87]

Local authorities have a discretionary power to advance loans to those incurring expenditure as a result of the Act of 1971.[88]

(2) The administration of the Fire Service

The management of the service by a fire authority is subject to certain **21-21** controls which the Act confers on the Secretary of State. In the first place fire brigade establishment schemes are to be notified annually to the Secretary of State (an establishment scheme gives details of fire stations, equipment and the number and ranks of firemen). No variation in an establishment involving the closing of a fire station or the reduction of personnel and appliances kept ready to attend fires can be made except with the consent of the Secretary of State.[89] If the Secretary of State considers a scheme unsatisfactory, or if none is submitted, he may himself make a scheme.

Secondly, the Acts confer on the Secretary of State regulation-making **21-22** powers, more particularly in regard to personnel matters. The Fire Service (Appointments and Promotion) Regulations[90] govern the method of appointment of chief officers of fire brigades and the qualifications for appointment and promotion generally. The Fire Service (Discipline) Regulations[91] prescribe a procedure to be followed in cases of breach of discipline, the punishments which may be imposed, and the rights of appeal available. Alleged breaches of discipline must be referred to an investigating officer nominated by the chief officer, except that in the case of the ranks of assistant chief officer or above, the matter must be referred to the fire authority. There is provision for preliminary investigation and, in cases of gross misconduct, for summary dismissal, including in both cases a right to a hearing. The investigating officer or fire authority, as the case may be, must decide whether the officer should be charged with an offence. Depending on the circumstances, cases may be heard by the fire authority's disciplinary tribunal (a committee or sub-committee of the

---

[85] S.I. 1972 No. 238.
[86] S.I. 1976 No. 2009.
[87] Fire Certificates (Special Premises) Regulations 1976 (S.I. 1976 No. 2003).
[88] Fire Precautions Act 1971, s. 31, Fire Precautions (Loans) Act 1973, and the Fire Precautions (Loans) Regulations 1973 (S.I. 1973 No. 1271).
[89] Fire Services Act 1947, s. 19, as amended by the Fire Services Act 1959, s. 7; Local Government Act 1972, s. 197.
[90] S.I. 1978 No. 436, as amended by S.I. 1981 No. 787 and S.I. 1985 No. 1176.
[91] S.I. 1985 No. 930.

authority, the chief officer, or, in minor cases, another nominated officer). There is a right of appeal against all awards other than a reprimand or caution. Appeals lie from the tribunal to an appeal committee of the fire authority, and from the chief officer to the tribunal. A further appeal lies to the Secretary of State against any dismissal, requirement to resign or reduction in rank.

The courts are less reluctant than formerly to review decisions taken in the exercise of disciplinary functions.

> *Ex p. Fry*.[92] A fireman refused to obey an order to clean an officer's uniform and was punished by caution. The fireman contended that the order was not a lawful one and that he had been denied a fair trial. The Divisional Court *held* that the chief officer of a fire brigade exercising disciplinary authority was not acting judicially or quasi-judicially.[93] The Court of Appeal dismissed F.'s appeal, but on the different ground that certiorari should not be granted in the exercise of the court's discretion. *Per* Singleton, L.J.[94]:
> "The applicant disobeyed that order. He might have dealt with it otherwise; he might have obeyed the order and then have put forward to the fire authority, or, if necessary, to the Secretary of State, the question whether, in view of the instruction which had been issued, this order was lawful and one with which a fireman was bound to comply. He did not do that; he disobeyed the order, and so the case was made the subject-matter of a charge. I cannot help feeling that it was extraordinarily foolish conduct. In these days it behoves everyone to act reasonably. If every fireman or every policeman is to take it upon himself to disobey an order of this kind and to say: 'I do not think it is lawful,' it will become almost impossible to carry on any public service."
> *Buckoke and Others* v. *Greater London Council*.[95] The plaintiffs, 20 members of the fire brigade, disobeyed orders to man vehicles, on the ground that Order 144/8 of the London brigade was unlawful. The Order accepted that drivers might in an emergency ignore traffic lights at red, stated that it was essentially the driver's decision, and instructed the use of extreme caution in such circumstances.
> Disciplinary proceedings were instituted against the firemen, who sought interim injunctions to restrain implementation of Order 144/8 or of the disciplinary proceedings. Plowman J. held that the order was lawful, and (applying *Ex p. Fry*[96]) that the court would not exercise its discretion to grant an injunction interfering with the exercise of a disciplinary power. The Court of Appeal agreed that the Order was lawful. On the other point, Lord Denning M.R. stated[97]:
> "The judge devoted a considerable part of his judgment to *Ex parte Fry*, but that case was not canvassed before us. It does not warrant the proposition that the rules of natural justice do not apply to disciplinary bodies. They must act fairly just the same as anyone else: and are just as subject to control by the courts. If the firemen's disciplinary tribunal were to hold an order to be a lawful order, when it was not, I am sure that the courts could interfere: or, if it proceeded contrary to the rules of natural justice in a matter of serious import,

---

[92] [1954] 1 W.L.R. 730.
[93] This view was expressly disapproved by the Court of Appeal in *R.* v. *Board of Visitors of Hull Prison, ex p. St. Germain* [1979] Q.B. 425 at pp. 446–447, 455–456, 461–462.
[94] At p. 735.
[95] [1971] 1 Ch. 655.
[96] [1954] 1 W.L.R. 730.
[97] At p. 669.

so also the courts could interfere.[98] But in this case the order was lawful and the tribunal will, I have no doubt, do what is just. So there is no ground whatever for interfering."

In disciplinary proceedings the correct standard of proof is the civil **21-23** standard.

> *R. v. Hampshire County Council, ex p. Ellerton.*[99] The fire authority's appeal tribunal held that disciplinary proceedings against a fire officer for corrupt practice should be decided on the civil standard of proof. The officer sought certiorari, arguing that the criminal standard of proof beyond reasonable doubt should have been applied. The Court of Appeal *held* that the civil standard of proof on the balance of probabilities was the correct standard, although it was to be applied flexibly: "the degree of probability required to tip the balance will vary according to the nature and gravity of the issue."[1] This last point was explained as follows by Slade L.J.[2]: "My understanding of the concept of the flexible standard of proof . . . is *not* that it involves proof on, say, a 51:49 balance of probabilities in some cases and, say, a 75:25 probabilities in others; any sliding scale of this nature will lead to intolerable uncertainty in application. My understanding . . . is simply that the relative seriousness of the allegation is a relevant factor, on occasions a highly relevant factor, in considering whether or not the civil burden of proof on the balance of probabilities has been discharged in any given case."

Inspectors of Fire Brigades are appointed by the Crown to enable the **21-24** Secretary of State to obtain information as to the way in which fire authorities are carrying out their functions, and as to technical matters relating to those functions.[3]

C. CIVIL DEFENCE

Civil defence functions are conferred by the Civil Defence Act 1948 on **21-25** Ministers of the Crown,[4] local authorities and police authorities.[5] The statute refers throughout to the "designated Minister" as the responsible Minister. This expression means such Minister as may be designated by Order in Council, and different Ministers may be designated for different purposes or different provisions of the Act. If and in so far as provision is not so made, the expression means the Secretary of State for the Home Department.[6] It is the duty of the designated Minister to take such steps as appear to him to be necessary or expedient for civil defence purposes, including the organisation of civil defence forces and services.

---

[98] The decision of a sub-committee of the fire authority in disciplinary proceedings was quashed for breach of natural justice in *R. v. Leicestershire Fire Authority, ex p. Thompson* (1978) 77 L.G.R. 373.

[99] [1985] 2 All E.R. 599.

[1] *Per* Lord Scarman in *R. v. Secretary of State for the Home Department, ex p. Khawaja* [1984] A.C. 74 at pp. 113–114, cited by May L.J. at p. 606.

[2] At p. 608.

[3] Fire Services Act 1947, s. 24.

[4] s. 1.

[5] s. 2.

[6] s. 9(2). See S.I. 1950 No. 1650.

The precise functions of local authorities and police authorities are not specified in the Act—they are such as the designated Minister may prescribe by regulation, and if an authority fails or refuses properly to comply with the regulations, the designated Minister may by virtue of regulations himself discharge the functions or transfer them to another authority, in either case at the expense of the defaulting authority.[7] All regulations under the Act are made by statutory instrument requiring an affirmative resolution of both Houses of Parliament.[8]

21-26 In 1968, the Government decided that civil defence should be placed on a care and maintenance basis, authorities being restricted to a planning function. Regulations were made to provide for the compensation of persons who suffered loss of employment, or diminution of emoluments as a result of this decision.[9]

The Civil Defence (Planning) Regulations 1974[10] imposed certain planning functions on county councils and the Greater London Council. However, in 1982 a large number of county councils refused to co-operate in a major civil defence exercise, Operation "Hard Rock," which the government was accordingly forced to cancel. In response, new regulations were introduced designed to extend and make more explicit the obligations of local councils. The Civil Defence (General Local Authority Functions) Regulations 1983[11] provide that it is the function of every non-metropolitan county council, metropolitan county fire and civil defence authority and the London Fire and Civil Defence Authority:

(a) to make, keep under review and revise plans for matters specified in Schedule 2 to the Regulations;

(b) to establish, equip and maintain emergency centres[12] in which to control and co-ordinate action to be taken by them in the event of hostile attack or a threat of hostile attack;

(c) to arrange for the training of an appropriate number of suitable members of staff[13] to carry out civil defence functions;

(d) to arrange for the attendance of staff at training courses provided by the designated minister;

(e) to take part in any training exercise in civil defence organised by or on behalf of the designated Minister which provides for their participation;

---

[7] s. 2.
[8] s. 8.
[9] Civil Defence (Compensation) (General) Regulations 1968 (S.I. 1968 No. 1344). The Civil Defence Corps was disbanded: Civil Defence Corps (Revocation) Warrant 1968.
[10] S.I. 1974 No. 70.
[11] S.I. 1983 No. 1634, modified by the Local Government Act 1985, s. 38(1)–(3).
[12] At two places in non-metropolitan counties (in different districts); at one place in a metropolitan district; at five places in Greater London (not more than one in any one London borough or the City of London).
[13] Including in the case of non-metropolitan counties staff from each district council and in the case of the London Fire and Civil Defence Authority staff from each London borough and the City of London.

(f) to make arrangements for enabling persons to serve as volunteer assistants in the performance of civil defence functions and training such persons;

(g) at the request of the designated Minister, (i) to take such preparatory steps as may be necessary to ensure that plans made under (a) can be carried out; and (ii) to carry out any of these plans.[14]

The matters specified in Schedule 2 are:

(a) collecting information on the results of hostile attack and distributing such information; (b) controlling and co-ordinating action necessary as a result of hostile attack; (c) instructing and advising the public on the effects of hostile attack and on protective measures to be taken; (d) utilising such buildings, structures, excavations and other features of land in their area as are suitable for use as public civil defence shelters; providing and maintaining services in their area for use in the event of hostile attack for: (e) the rescue of persons from damaged buildings and debris; (f) the temporary accommodation and maintenance of persons made homeless; (g) the prevention of disease or the spread of disease, including the provision of facilities for emergency sanitation and the disposal of refuse; (h) the distribution, conservation and control of food; and (i) the urgent repair, replacement or demolition and clearance of property on streets; (j) providing facilities for the disposal of human remains; (k) providing and maintaining any other services essential to the life of the community; and (l) securing the assistance of voluntary organisations and other persons volunteering their services.

When making or revising plans, a non-metropolitan county council or metropolitan fire and civil defence authority and the London Fire and Civil Defence Authority must consult any county, district or London borough council, or the Common Council of the City of London, whose area may be affected by such plans.[15]

It is the function of every district and London borough council and the **21-27** Common Council (a) to supply information at the request of the relevant county council, fire and civil defence authority or the London Fire and Civil Defence Authority; (b) to assist those authorities in making, revising and implementing plans and in accepting and training volunteers; (c) to establish, equip and maintain an emergency centre in their area; (d) to arrange for the training of an appropriate number of suitable staff for these purposes; (e) to make available the staff for whom training is arranged by the relevant county, the London Fire and Civil Defence Authority or the designated minister; and (f) to take part in any training exercise in civil defence organised by or on behalf of the designated minister which provides for their participation.[16]

---

[14] reg. 4(1),(3).
[15] reg. 4(2).
[16] reg. 5.

As respects the exercise of any functions conferred on a local authority, the authority shall comply with any directions given by the designated minister.[17]

The Civil Defence (Grants) Regulations[18] provide for the reimbursement to police authorities and local authorities of all expenditure incurred for purposes specified in a schedule to the regulations (for example, the provision of communications equipment, training, attendance at training courses provided by or on behalf of the designated minister and the reimbursement of expenses incurred by volunteers in taking part in training) and of 75 per cent. of approved expenditure in all other cases.

[17] reg. 6.
[18] S.I. 1953 No. 1777, as amended by S.I. 1974 No. 69 and S.I. 1983 No. 1633.

CHAPTER 22

FOOD, DRUGS AND POISONS, SHOPS, CONSUMER PROTECTION

A. Food

THE law on this subject is for the most part found in the Food Act 1984, **22-01** which consolidated earlier legislation concerning food. It is considered under the following headings: administering authorities; general provisions as to food; milk and dairies; enforcement; slaughterhouses.

(1) Administration

The councils of non-metropolitan counties, metropolitan districts, **22-02** London boroughs and the Common Council of the City of London are "food and drugs authorities" for the purposes of the Act of 1984.[1] District councils, London borough councils and the Common Council of the City of London are "local authorities" for the purposes of the Act.[2] In non-metropolitan areas, the district council's functions are mainly concerned with food hygiene and food safety. The county council functions are those which are more akin to consumer protection. In metropolitan counties, the district councils were required to establish, by September 1, 1985, a joint committee to co-ordinate the exercise by these councils of their enforcement functions as food and drugs authorities and weights and measures authorities, with a view to securing uniformity throughout the county, and to co-ordinate the employment, provision or use of staff, property and facilities. If after April 1, 1986, it appears to the Secretary of State to be necessary or expedient to do so, he may by order establish in a metropolitan county a single authority for the discharge of these functions. The metropolitan district councils must be consulted.[3]

Several Ministers have administrative responsibility in relation to the **22-03** provisions of this Act. The Minister of Agriculture, Fisheries and Food and the Secretary of State for Social Services acting jointly are concerned, for example, with matters relating to the composition, labelling, marking and advertising of food, the Minister of Agriculture, Fisheries and Food with slaughterhouses and meat inspection, the Secretary of State for the Environment with the provision and regulation of markets, and the Secretary of State for Trade with regulations as to labelling and marking

---

[1] Food Act 1984, s. 71, as amended by the Local Government Act 1985, Sched. 8, para. 15(2).
[2] *Ibid.* s. 72. On the division of responsibilities see the 1984 Act, s. 74 and Sched. 6.
[3] Local Government Act 1985, Sched. 8, para. 15(6)(7), as amended by the Weights and Measures Act 1985, Sched. 12, para. 11. This provision also applies to enforcement of the provisions of the Agriculture Act 1970, relating to fertilisers and feeding stuffs.

of food as respects weight, measure and number. The Ministers are advised by the Food Advisory Committee on matters relating to the composition, labelling and advertising of food, and additives, contaminants and other substances which are or may be present in food or used in its preparation.

22-04   Every food and drugs authority must appoint a public analyst having the qualifications prescribed by the Ministers.[4]

If the Minister of Agriculture, Fisheries and Food considers that a food and drugs authority has failed to carry out its duties he may by order authorise an officer of his department to see to the execution and enforcement of the provisions in question, the authority bearing the cost involved.[5] A separate default power is available in respect of other local authorities with duties under the Act.[6]

(2) General provisions as to food

Offences related to injurious foods.

22-05   The general provisions are contained in Part I of the 1984 Act. It is an offence:

(i) to add to, or abstract constituents from, or treat food intended for sale for human consumption if it is thereby rendered injurious to health; or

(ii) to sell for human consumption, or to offer, expose, advertise or possess for sale any such injurious food.

In determining whether an article of food is injurious to health, regard shall be had not only to the probable effect of that article on the health of the person consuming it, but also the probable cumulative effect of articles of substantially the same composition on the health of a person consuming such articles in ordinary quantities.[7]

Other offences

22-06   An offence is also committed in the following circumstances:

(i) Where a person sells any food[8] which is not of the nature, substance, or quality demanded,[9] if the purchaser is prejudiced by the sale.[10] Where a

---

[4] Food Act 1984, s. 76; Public Analysts Regulations 1957 (S.I. 1957 No. 273).
[5] *Ibid.* ss. 114, 115.
[6] *Ibid* ss. 113, 115.
[7] *Ibid.* s. 1.
[8] This includes drink, and also the supply of something in the erroneous belief that it is an item of food or drink: *Meah* v. *Roberts* [1977] 1 W.L.R. 1187 (caustic soda supplied instead of lemonade).
[9] See *Goldup* v. *John Manson Ltd.* [1982] Q.B. 161 (the opinion of an expert witness cannot be evidence of the quality demanded by a purchaser); *cf. T. W. Lawrence & Sons Ltd.* v. *Burleigh* (1981) 80 L.G.R. 631.
[10] Food Act 1984, s. 2. There are three distinct offences here: see *Bastin* v. *Davies* [1950] 2 K.B. 579; *Moore* v. *Ray* [1951] 1 K.B. 98; *cf. Preston* v. *Greenclose Ltd.* (1975) 139 J.P. 245.

food is not of the quality demanded because of the presence of extraneous matter, it is not necessary to show that the matter is deleterious.[11] A sale is to the prejudice of a customer if he "gets an article inferior to that which he demands and pays for"[12]; it is otherwise if notice is given to the purchaser before the sale of the true nature of the commodity offered him.[13] A sale may be to the prejudice of the purchaser although the purchaser has special knowledge, not derived from information given by the seller, that the article sold is not of the nature, substance or quality demanded. The test is whether a sale would have been to the prejudice of the purchaser who had not that special knowledge.[14] It is a defence to prove that the operation in question was not carried out fraudulently and that the article was sold with a label or in a wrapper stating explicitly the nature of the operation, but this defence is not available if the food has been rendered injurious to health.[15] If proceedings are taken on the ground that a food contains extraneous matter it is a good defence to show that the presence of the matter was an unavoidable consequence of the process of collection or preparation[16] although it is not sufficient to show that all reasonable precautions have been taken.[17]

(ii) Where a food is sold or exposed for sale with a label or in a **22-07** container which falsely describes the article or is calculated to mislead. There is no offence if the seller can show that he did not know, and could not with reasonable diligence have known, of the deception.[18]

(iii) Where a false or misleading advertisement relating to a food is published. It may be raised as a defence that the advertiser did not know of, and could not with reasonable diligence have ascertained, the deception, or that he received the advertisement in the ordinary course of his business.[19]

(iv) Where food unfit for human consumption is sold or offered for sale or is consigned for sale by another. A consignor may plead as a defence that he gave notice to the consignee that the food was unfit, or alternatively that when he consigned the food he did not know and could not with reasonable diligence have known of its condition.[20]

The term "unfit for human consumption" was considered in *Miller* v. *Battersea Borough Council*[21] and *Chibnall's Bakeries* v. *E. J. Cope*

---

[11] *Barber* v. *Co-operative Wholesale Society Ltd.* (1983) 81 L.G.R. 762.
[12] *Hoyle* v. *Hitchman* (1879) 4 Q.B.D. 233, *per* Mellor J. at p. 237.
[13] *Sandys* v. *Small* (1878) 3 Q.B.D. 449.
[14] *Pearks, Gunston & Tee Ltd.* v. *Ward* [1902] 2 K.B. 1.
[15] Food Act 1984, s. 3(1).
[16] *Ibid.* s. 3(2).
[17] *Smedley's Ltd.* v. *Breed* [1974] A.C. 839 (caterpillar in a tin of peas); *Greater Manchester Council* v. *Lockwood Foods Ltd.* [1979] Crim. L.R. 593 (beetle in a tin of strawberries: defence rejected, but defendants given an absolute discharge).
[18] Food Act 1984, s. 6(1); Food Labelling Regulations 1984 (S.I. 1984 No. 1305).
[19] Food Act 1984, s. 6(2).
[20] *Ibid.* s. 8.
[21] [1956] 1 Q.B. 43.

Brown.[22] In the first case it was held that the presence of a piece of metal in a chocolate bun did not make the bun "unfit for human consumption"; this term applied to putrid or unwholesome food. The facts may, however, have sustained a charge under a provision relating to the sale of food not of the nature or substance or quality demanded, to the prejudice of a purchaser. The appellants in the second case, a firm of bakers, sought to rely on this decision when charged with selling a loaf unfit for human consumption in that it contained a used and dirty bandage, but failed and were convicted.

Regulations

22-08   Wide powers are conferred on the Minister of Agriculture, Fisheries and Food and the Secretary of State for Social Services acting jointly to make regulations for securing the observance of sanitary and cleanly conditions and practices in connection with—

(1) the sale of food for human consumption, and
(2) the importation, preparation, transport, storage, packaging, wrapping, exposure for sale, service or delivery of food intended for sale or sold for human consumption,

or otherwise for the protection of the public health in connection with these matters.[23] The Food Hygiene (General) Regulations 1970[24] made under this section contain detailed rules in relation to premises where a food business is carried on, to persons engaged in the handling of food, to stores from which foods are sold, and to the transport of food. From the wording of the statute it is clear that the regulations are made for the purpose of protecting public health and they must be construed accordingly. This proposition emerges from *MacFisheries Ltd.* v. *Coventry Corporation*[25] where the effect of what is now regulation 9 of the Food Hygiene (General) Regulations was under review. The regulation is in the following terms:

> "A person who engages in the handling of food shall while so engaged take all such steps as may be reasonably necessary to protect the food from risk of contamination, and in particular (without prejudice to the generality of the foregoing)—(*a*) shall not so place the food as to involve any risk of contamination;..."

> *MacFisheries (Wholesale and Retail) Ltd.* v. *Coventry Corporation.*[26] The company constructed a new shop and permitted fish to be exposed for sale in this shop. There was a risk of contamination to the food, *e.g.* from customers in the shop, but the risk was only of contamination which was not of such nature as to be injurious to health. The corporation contended that the prosecution had to prove no more than risk of contamination, but did not have to prove

---

[22] [1956] Crim. L.R. 263.
[23] Food Act 1984, s. 13.
[24] S.I. 1970 No. 1172.
[25] [1957] 3 All E.R. 299.
[26] *Ibid.*

actual contamination or that such contamination if it did occur would be injurious to health. *Held,* no offence had been committed, for the words "risk of contamination" in the regulation must be construed as risk of such contamination as might be injurious to public health.

The regulations are administered by "local authorities" as defined in paragraph 22-02[27] and these authorities may make by-laws as to the handling and sale of food.[28] The Ministers are also empowered to make regulations as to the composition of food[29] and as to the labelling and description of food.[30]

Closure orders

Where a person is convicted of an offence under regulations made **22-09** under section 13 in respect of premises or a stall which are insanitary, or where food is exposed to the risk of contamination, the local authority may apply to the court for a closure order.[31] The court may grant the order if satisfied that food is likely to continue to be dealt with at the premises or stall, and that the carrying on of a food business there would be dangerous to health. The order prohibits the handling of food until the local authority certifies that such specified measures as the court considers necessary to remove the dangers have been carried out. An emergency order may be made prior to conviction if there is an imminent risk of danger to health.[32] Compensation is payable by the local authority where the court determines that at the date of the emergency order there was no such imminent risk, and is satisfied that loss has been caused by the order.[33] Appeal lies to the Crown Court.[34]

Food unfit for human consumption

An authorised officer of a council is empowered to examine and seize **22-10** any food suspected of being unfit for human consumption, whether in transit or otherwise. The officer must bring the food to a justice of the peace, and if the justice considers it unfit he must order its destruction, but if he refuses to condemn the food the council must compensate the owner.[35]

Registration of premises

Premises used for the manufacture, storage or sale of ice cream and for **22-11**

---

[27] Food Act 1984, s. 72, 74(2), and Sched. 6.
[28] *Ibid.* s. 15.
[29] *Ibid.* s. 4.
[30] *Ibid.* s. 7.
[31] *Ibid.* s. 21. This supplements the power of a court to disqualify a caterer from using premises as catering premises, under s. 14 of the 1984 Act.
[32] *Ibid.* s. 22.
[33] *Ibid.* s. 23.
[34] *Ibid.* s. 24.
[35] *Ibid.* s. 9. A justice acting under this section must act fairly: *R.* v. *Birmingham City Justice, ex p. Chris Foreign Foods (Wholesalers) Ltd.* [1970] 1 W.L.R. 1428.

the preparation or manufacture of sausages and preserved foods are required to be registered by the local authority. If the authority proposes to refuse or to cancel registration the applicant must be informed of this and given an opportunity to appear before the authority. If he is aggrieved by the decision ultimately reached he may appeal to a magistrates' court.[36]

Food poisoning

22-12   Cases of food poisoning must be notified to the local authority by medical practitioners, and if it is suspected that certain food is likely to cause poisoning its sale may be forbidden until investigations are complete. If the notice is withdrawn, the owner must be compensated: if, on the other hand, suspicions are confirmed, the food may be dealt with as unfit for human consumption.[37]

(3) Milk and dairies[38]

22-13   The Milk and Dairies (General) Regulations[39] provide for the registration of dairy farms and dairy farmers by the Minister of Agriculture, Fisheries and Food, and for the registration by district councils of distributors and dairies other than dairy farms. Detailed rules relate to buildings and water supplies and to the conditions under which milk may be produced, treated and distributed. It is an offence under the Food Act 1984 to sell milk from diseased cows or to adulterate milk or to sell adulterated milk.[40] The Milk (Special Designation) Regulations[41] prescribe special designations of milk and make provision for the granting of licences to producers and consumers. Council Regulation 1411/71/E.E.C. and the Drinking Milk Regulations 1976[42] restrict the delivery of milk for sale for human consumption to specified categories, and prohibit alteration in the composition of drinking milk.

(4) Enforcement

22-14   As noted in earlier paragraphs the administration of the Food Act 1984 is shared between food and drugs authorities and "local authorities": in general the enforcement of any particular provisions falls to the authority responsible for its administration.[43] A private person may, however,

---

[36] Food Act 1984, ss. 16–20.
[37] *Ibid.* s. 31; Public Health (Control of Disease) Act 1984, s. 11. See also s. 18 of the Public Health (Control of Disease) Act 1984 as to the giving of information in food poisoning cases.
[38] Food Act 1984, ss. 32–49.
[39] S.I. 1959 No. 277; S.I. 1962 No. 1288; S.I. 1973 No. 1064; S.I. 1977 No. 171; S.I. 1979 No. 156; S.I. 1982 No. 1703.
[40] ss. 35, 36.
[41] S.I. 1977 No. 1033, as amended by S.I. 1980 No. 1863, S.I. 1982 No. 1359, S.I. 1982 No. 1702, S.I. 1983 No. 1510, S.I. 1985 No. 530.
[42] S.I. 1976 No. 1886, as amended by S.I. 1982 No. 1703.
[43] See § 22–02.

institute proceedings for a contravention of the Act.[44] The initial work of enforcement will fall to "authorised officers"—officers authorised in writing by the council to do this work. No officer may be authorised to act in relation to the examination and seizure of meat unless he has a prescribed qualification.[45]

Authorised officers may procure samples, by taking or purchase, for bacteriological or other examination,[46] and any person who purchases an article of food may submit a sample of it to the food and drugs authority for analysis.[47]

Authorised officers have power to enter premises used as a private dwelling-house, on giving notice, and other premises at all reasonable times, and if admission is refused a justice of the peace may issue a warrant authorising the officer to enter, by force if necessary.[48]

Where a person is charged with an offence under the Act or under a **22-15** regulation and he alleges that the contravention was due to the default of another, he may require that other person to be brought before the court. If the original defendant can prove that the other was in fact responsible and that he himself used all diligence to observe the law, then he may be acquitted and the other convicted. Alternatively, the authority may proceed against the person actually responsible.[49]

There may be a succession of moves back to the party originally at fault.

British Fermentation Products Ltd. v. *British Italian Trading Co. Ltd.*[50] An information was laid against a grocer for selling an article with a label containing a false description. The grocer laid an information so as to bring the middleman to court, and the middleman similarly brought in the original supplier. *Held*, this reaching back was within the Act. Lord Caldecote C.J. said[51]: "There is no reason why Parliament should not have intended to allow this procedure to be followed down a chain of persons."

In certain circumstances a defendant may plead warranty.[52] If he **22-16** himself purchased the article under the name or description under which he sold it and if he had from the vendor a written warranty to that effect, then provided he had no reason to believe that the warranty was false, and provided that the article was in the same state when he sold it as when he bought it, this defence may be pleaded. The person by whom the warranty is alleged to have been given is entitled to appear in court and give evidence.

[44] *Snodgrass* v. *Topping* (1952) 116 J.P. 312.
[45] Food Act 1984, s. 73.
[46] *Ibid.* s. 78.
[47] *Ibid.* s. 79.
[48] *Ibid.* s. 87.
[49] *Ibid.* s. 100.
[50] [1942] 2 K.B. 145.
[51] At p. 148.
[52] Food Act 1984, s. 102. A brand name in an invoice may amount to a written warranty: *Rochdale Metropolitan Borough Council* v. *F.M.C. (Meat) Ltd.* [1980] 1 W.L.R. 461. See also *Laidlaw* v. *Wilson* [1984] 1 Q.B. 74.

22-17   As a general rule a master is not liable for an offence committed by his servant without his knowledge or authority; the servant alone can be prosecuted. Offences under the Food Act constitute an exception to this rule. An employer can be charged although the wrongful act was committed by his servant, and this is so even if he had no knowledge of the servant's wrongdoing[53] and even though he may have taken steps to prevent a breach of the law.[54] In *Parker* v. *Alder*[55] this principle was taken further and a milk dealer was convicted of selling adulterated milk although he had delivered the milk in a pure condition to the servants of the railway company and the milk was watered down in transit. In *Quality Dairies (York) Ltd.* v. *Pedley*[56] a milk distributor was held liable for an offence against regulation 26 of the Milk and Dairies Regulations 1949 (which provided for the cleanliness of vessels), notwithstanding the fact that the milk was handled at all stages by a sub-contractor.[57] A servant or sub-contractor can, of course, be prosecuted as the actual wrongdoer, and where an employer or principal is charged he may invoke the procedure available under section 100 referred to earlier for offences under the Act.[58]

(5) Markets

22-18   Part III of the Food Act 1984[59] relates to markets: this subject is dealt with in Chapter 27.

(6) Slaughterhouses, knackers' yards and the slaughter of animals

22-19   The local authorities which administer the law relating to these matters are district councils, London borough councils and the Common Council of the City of London.[60] Premises may not be used as a slaughterhouse or a knackers' yard unless they are licensed by the authority.[61]

An application for a slaughterhouse licence must be granted if the authority is satisfied that the requirements of relevant regulations and by-laws[62] are, or within reasonable time will be, complied with.[63] An application for the grant or renewal of a licence must be refused if it is

---

[53] *Pearks, Gunston & Tee Ltd.* v. *Ward* [1902] 2 K.B. 1.
[54] *Brown* v. *Foot* (1892) 66 L.T. (N.S.) 649.
[55] [1899] 1 Q.B. 20.
[56] [1952] 1 K.B. 275.
[57] See, however, *United Dairies (London) Ltd.* v. *E. Fisher & Sons Ltd.* [1961] 1 All E.R. 579, where a milk dealer was exonerated from liability for ash in a bottle of milk filled by a farm producer because under the appropriate regulations the producer was made directly responsible for the filling and sealing of the bottles and the dealer was directly responsible for selling the milk with the seals unbroken.
[58] See *United Dairies (London) Ltd.* v. *E. Fisher & Sons Ltd.*, *supra*, as to the distinction between offences under the Act and offences under regulations.
[59] Food Act 1984, ss. 50–61.
[60] Slaughterhouses Act 1974, ss. 41, 45.
[61] *Ibid.* s. 1.
[62] Made under *ibid.* s. 12.
[63] *Ibid.* s. 2(1).

made in respect of a building part of which is or is proposed to be used or adapted for use as a dwelling, unless the authority is satisfied that it will not in fact be so used while the licence is in force.[64] This provision does not apply where a licence was first granted before August 1, 1958, unless the holder had been convicted of an offence of permitting a part of a building which contains a slaughterhall to be used as a dwelling.[65]

The authority has a discretion whether to grant an application for a knackers' yard licence. It may refuse a licence if it is not satisfied that the requirements of by-laws, or of regulations made under section 13 of the Food Act 1984, are or will be complied with, and must refuse an application unless satisfied that construction regulations made under section 38 of the Slaughterhouses Act 1974 are or will be complied with.[66]

Reasons for refusal of a licence must be given in the case of an application for a slaughterhouse licence, and in other cases reasons must be given if so required by the applicant within 14 days.[67] A person aggrieved by a refusal may appeal to a magistrates' court. The court may declare a refusal of a slaughterhouse licence to be of no effect if satisfied that the authority acted unreasonably, and in any other case may vary or reverse the authority's decision. A further appeal lies to the Crown Court.[68]

Local authorities have power to provide slaughterhouses either by acquiring existing facilities and making them public or by making direct provision themselves.[69] They may make by-laws in regard to the management of public slaughterhouses[70] and as to private slaughterhouses and knackers' yards.[71] Authorities are empowered to provide cold stores and refrigerators in connection with any public slaughterhouse.[72]

Part II of the Slaughterhouses Act 1974 makes provision, *inter alia*, for **22-20** the humane and scientific slaughter of animals. Local authorities are responsible for the enforcement of these provisions[73] and for the granting of licences to slaughtermen,[74] and authorised officers have a right to enter slaughterhouses and knackers' yards.[75]

B. Drugs and Poisons

Prior to the coming into force of the Medicines Act 1968, certain of the **22-21** offences relating to the preparation and sale and false labelling and

---

[64] Slaughterhouses Act 1974, s. 3.
[65] Contrary to s. 11(1) of the 1974 Act.
[66] Slaughterhouses Act 1974, s. 4.
[67] *Ibid.* s. 5.
[68] *Ibid.* s. 6.
[69] *Ibid.* s. 14.
[70] *Ibid.* s. 16.
[71] *Ibid.* s. 12.
[72] *Ibid.* s. 18.
[73] *Ibid.* s. 41.
[74] *Ibid.* ss. 39, 40.
[75] *Ibid.* s. 42.

advertising of food applied also to drugs.[76] However, the 1968 Act repealed all references to drugs in the Food and Drugs Act 1955,[77] and the régime for the control of medicines and drugs is now distinct from that of food.

The Medicines Act 1968 regulates the manufacture, distribution and importation of (1) medicines for human use; (2) medicines for administration to animals; and (3) medicated animal feeding stuffs. The responsible minister is the Secretary of State for Social Services in respect of (1), and the Minister of Agriculture, Fisheries and Food in respect of (2) and (3). They are advised by the Medicines Commission. The Act is for the most part enforced by Inspectors of the Medicines Division of the Department of Health and Social Security, the Investigation Branch of the Ministry of Agriculture, Fisheries and Food and the Pharmaceutical Society.[78] Food and drugs authorities have power, concurrently with the appropriate minister, to enforce sections 53 (sale or supply of medicinal products on general sale list) and 54 (sale of medicinal products from automatic machines) of the 1968 Act, and the Medicines (Sale or Supply) (Miscellaneous Provisions) Regulations 1980[79] in their application to most premises other than registered pharmacies.[80] In addition they have a duty[81] to enforce provisions relating to the proper labelling or description of medicated feeding stuffs[82] and orders made prohibiting the sale, supply or importation of specified animal feeding stuffs.[83] There is a general power, not as yet exercised, for the appropriate minister to delegate concurrent enforcement powers in relation to other provisions of the 1968 Act to food and drugs authorities.[84] However, *ad hoc* arrangements have been made for a food and drugs authority to investigate and prosecute alleged breaches of provisions relating to the sale or supply of medicinal products by persons other than registered pharmacies.[85]

22-22   The Poisons Act 1972 provides for a "Poisons List" of non-medicinal poisons to be maintained. Substances may be added to or removed from the list by the Secretary of State, acting on the advice of the Poisons Board. Poisons on Part I of the list may only be sold by persons lawfully conducting a retail pharmacy business; poisons on Part II may be sold by such persons or by a person whose name is entered in a list kept by the local authority, (*i.e.* the council of a non-metropolitan county, metropolitan district or London borough or the Common Council of the City of

---

[76] Food and Drugs Act 1955, ss. 1, 2, 6.
[77] Hence the title "Food Act" for the 1984 consolidation, above.
[78] Medicines Act 1968, s. 108.
[79] S.I. 1980 No. 1923.
[80] Medicines Act 1968, s. 108(4)(7); S.I. 1980 No. 1923, reg. 2(1).
[81] Medicines Act 1968, s. 108(8).
[82] *Ibid.* s. 90.
[83] *Ibid.* s. 62(1).
[84] *Ibid.* s. 108(2).
[85] *Butterworths' Law of Food & Drugs* (1985), para. S(592). Pharmacists are subject to the supervision of the Pharmaceutical Society.

London[86]) under section 5 of the Act. It is also the duty of such an authority to secure compliance with the Poisons Act 1972 and the Poisons Rules 1982,[87] in respect of the sale of Part II poisons by persons other than pharmacists.[88]

C. SHOPS

Most of the law as to closing hours and conditions of employment is   **22-23** found in the Shops Acts 1950 to 1965. The councils of districts and London boroughs, and the Common Council of the City of London are under a duty to enforce the provisions of these Acts.[89] This duty is enforceable by mandamus.[90] Each local authority must appoint inspectors for this purpose and may authorise such inspectors to carry on any proceedings under the Acts on their behalf.[91] This does not, however, prevent the authority from authorising another person, such as their solicitor, to institute proceedings.[92] The responsible Minister is the Secretary of State for the Home Department.

(1) Hours of closing

(a) *Early closing days*[93]
   As a general rule every shop must close for the serving of customers not   **22-24** later than one o'clock on one day each week. The First Schedule lists a number of businesses exempt from this requirement (the list includes the sale of refreshments, newspapers, confectionery, tobacco and smokers' requisites and articles of a perishable nature[94]). Every shopkeeper affected by the rules as to early closing days must choose a day on which to close not later than one o'clock, and he must display a notice specifying the chosen day. He may vary the selected day, but not more frequently than once in three months. An authority may exempt any particular class of shop in any area from the requirement as to half-day closing if satisfied that a majority of shopkeepers within the class desire it.

(b) *General closing hours*[95]
   The Act specifies general closing hours for shops, but enables an   **22-25**

---

[86] Poisons Act 1972, s. 11(2), definition of "local authority" for the purposes of the Act, as amended by the Local Government Act 1985, Sched. 8, para. 16.
[87] S.I. 1982 No. 218, as amended by S.I. 1985 No. 1077.
[88] Poisons Act 1972, s. 9.
[89] Shops Act 1950, ss. 71 and 73, the latter as substituted by the Local Government Act 1972, Sched. 29, para. 43.
[90] *R.* v. *Braintree District Council, ex p. Willingham* (1982) 81 L.G.R. 70.
[91] Shops Act 1950, s. 71(2).
[92] *Kirklees Metropolitan Borough Council* v. *Wickes Building Supplies Ltd.* (1983) 82 L.G.R. 467.
[93] Shops Act 1950, s. 1 and Sched. 1, the Shops (Early Closing Days) Act 1965, and S.R. & O. 1912, No. 316.
[94] The meanings of the terms "confectionery" and "perishable nature" were considered in *London County Council* v. *Welford's Surrey Dairies Co. Ltd.* [1913] 2 K.B. 529. Butter was held in this case to be an article of a perishable nature.
[95] Shops Act 1950, ss. 2–11 and Sched. 2, and S.R. & O. 1912, No. 316.

authority by order, called a closing order, to substitute earlier hours either generally or in relation to shops of a particular class or in a particular area. The time fixed may not be earlier than 7 p.m. and the order cannot be made to apply to any transaction listed in the Second Schedule (the lists includes the sale of meals, tobacco, newspapers and newly cooked provisions). Public notice must be given of an intention to make an order and the authority must consider objections which may be raised and must be satisfied that at least two-thirds of the shopkeepers approve of it. A closing order may be revoked by the local authority either absolutely, or, if a majority of any class of shop to which the order applies are opposed to it, so far as it affects that class.[96] A later closing hour may be fixed for tobacco shops if at least two-thirds of the traders concerned desire this, and special provisions apply to sweet shops. General closing hours and closing orders may be altered on special occasions (at Christmas, for example) and during exhibitions.[97]

In a holiday resort the local authority may suspend the weekly half-day closing rule and in addition may order later closing hours than those prescribed in the Act if satisfied that a majority of shopkeepers want it. These modifications may not operate for more than four months in any year.[98]

The weekly half-day closing provision and the general closing hours do not apply to shops at certain airports designated by the Secretary of State for Transport.[99]

(c) *Application of rules as to closing*

22-26   The rules as to closing apply to a "shop," which is defined as including "any premises where any retail trade or business is carried on."[1] "Retail trade or business" is defined as including the business of a barber or hairdresser, the sale of refreshments or intoxicating liquor, the business of lending books or periodicals when carried on for purposes of gain, and retail sales by auction, but not the sale of programmes or catalogues or similar sales at theatres and places of amusement.[2] In addition, it is unlawful to carry on a retail trade or business in a "place" not being a shop at a time when it would be unlawful to keep a shop open for that trade or business.[3] But in *Kahn* v. *Newberry*[4] it was held that a

---

[96] Shops Act 1950, s. 11, substituted by the Local Government, Planning and Land Act 1980, Sched. 4, para. 1(4).
[97] *Ibid.* ss. 42, 43.
[98] *Ibid.* ss. 40, 41.
[99] Shops (Airports) Act 1962, s. 1; Airport Shops Order 1977 (S.I. 1977 No. 1397); East Midlands Airport Shops Order 1977 (S.I. 1977 No. 1919); Airport Shops Order 1985 (S.I. 1985 No. 654); Airport Shops (No. 2) Order 1985 (S.I. 1985 No. 1739).
[1] Shops Act 1950, s. 74. This includes a video-hire shop: *Lewis* v. *Rogers; Gardner* v. *Duffell* (1984) 82 L.G.R. 670; *cf. M. & F. Frawley Ltd.* v. *The Veribest Co. Ltd.* [1953] 1 Q.B. 318.
[2] Shops Act 1950, s. 74.
[3] Shops Act 1950, s. 12. Most of the provisions of the Act relating to Sunday trading extend to any place where any retail trade or business is carried on as if that place were a shop: *ibid.* s. 58.
[4] [1959] 2 Q.B. 1.

costermonger selling apples from a barrow (moved on whenever a policeman came in sight) had not committed an offence under the Shops Act 1950, for neither the barrow, nor the ground on which it stood, was a "place"; it required more than a casual sale to constitute a piece of ground a "place." Donovan J. concluded his judgment with these observations[5]:

> "Two things, perhaps, might finally be said. First, the present case is not one where a stall is regularly erected on the same piece of land so that an aspect of some permanency is given to the site as one where goods are regularly sold by retail. It may be that such a place would be within the language of section 12 and section 58 of the Shops Act 1950. That case can be left to be decided if and when it arises. Secondly, the case of the itinerant hawker is not, in my view, the case which Parliament had in mind in passing the various Shops Acts. I say that because of the language of those Acts, which, as has been pointed out before in this court, seems to contemplate shops in the ordinary sense of the word, and other places not being shops but with sufficient aspect of permanence about them to warrant them being treated as shops, and also because, although this court held over twenty years ago that a mobile selling vehicle was not within the Shops Act, Parliament has taken no steps to bring such a contrivance within this legislation."

It was held in *Stone* v. *Boreham*[6] that a mobile van is not a *shop* and the **22-27** place at which it stops is not a *place* where retail trade is carried on, and in *Greenwood* v. *Whelan*[7] it was held that a market stall, even if almost permanently stationed in one place, is not a *shop*. In *Maby* v. *Warwick Corporation*[8] it was held that a stall erected and on which business was done on a single day each week had a sufficient degree of permanence to be a place where retail trade or business is carried on.

In *Jarmain* v. *Wetherell*[9] a stall at a coin and stamp fair which was set up on one Sunday morning and taken down the same evening did not have a sufficient degree of permanence to be a "place" within section 58. However, in *Newark District Council* v. *E. & A. Market Promotions Ltd.*[10] the Court of Appeal held that the Act did apply to traders at Sunday markets organised by the first defendant on three separate sites on a farm owned by the second defendant. The intention was to use different sites on successive Sundays so that no one site would be used more than once a month. The court held that any trader who regularly or frequently rented a stall each Sunday at the market, on whichever site, showed a sufficient continuity of the trade or business for the stall to be a "place" within section 58. Each stall counts as a separate "place"; the market as a whole does not.[11]

---

[5] At pp. 12, 13.
[6] [1959] 1 Q.B. 1.
[7] [1967] 1 Q.B. 396. This case was concerned with s. 12 of the Pharmacy and Medicines Act 1941. The point at issue was whether it was a shop. No question arose as to whether it could be regarded as a place.
[8] [1972] 2 Q.B. 242.
[9] (1977) 75 L.G.R. 537.
[10] (1978) 77 L.G.R. 6.
[11] *Chichester District Council* v. *Flockglen* (1977) 122 S.J. 61; *Thanet District Council* v. *Ninedrive Ltd.* [1978] 1 All E.R. 703, 710; *cf.* Lord Denning M.R. in *Stafford Borough Council* v. *Elkenford* [1977] 1 W.L.R. 324, 328 and the *Newark* case, *supra*, at pp. 12, 13.

A fully automatic launderette is not within the rules as to closing, for though it is a shop it is not, when open, "open for the serving of customers," for "serving" means "personal serving."[12] Moreover, a showroom may lawfully be open for the purposes of silent inspection and viewing only. Where a showroom for purpose-built kitchen furniture was open, but the only element of trading would be the taking of potential customers' names and addresses, no transaction taking place without a home visit, the showroom was held not to be open for the serving of customers.[13] Where a shop is permitted to be open for limited purposes, an isolated act of serving for the purpose of a prohibited transaction does not necessarily mean that the shop is open for the prohibited purpose: for the latter there has to be a degree of repetition from which it can be said that the shop was open as a matter of business or practice for that purpose.[14]

(2) Sunday trading[15]

22-28   There are a number of exemptions to the general rule that shops must close on Sundays. The Fifth Schedule contains a list of transactions for the purpose of which a shop may be kept open—the list includes the sale of fruit and vegetables (unless bottled or tinned),[16] the sale of intoxicating liquors and the sale of meals and refreshments[17] whether or not for consumption on the premises. The Sixth Schedule contains a list of transactions which may be permitted on Sundays up to 10 a.m. provided the authority has made a partial exemption order. The sale of bread, confectionery, fish and groceries are among the transactions which may be included in this order. In holiday resorts the authority may permit Sunday trading of the kind listed in the Seventh Schedule for not more than eighteen Sundays in any one year. This list includes the sale of toys, souvenirs and fancy goods, books, stationery and photographic supplies, and any article of food.

22-29   Where a shopkeeper is a person of the Jewish faith he may apply for the registration of his shop by the local authority as a Jewish trader's

---

[12] *Ilford Corporation v. Betterclean (Seven Kings) Ltd.* [1965] 2 Q.B. 222.

[13] *Bury Metropolitan Borough Council v. Law; Same v. Cowburn* (1983) 82 L.G.R. 170. See also *Betta Cars Ltd. v. Ilford Corpn.* (1959) 124 J.P. 19.

[14] *Waterman v. Wallasey Corporation; Hesketh v. Same* [1954] 1 W.L.R. 771; *Monaco Garage Ltd. v. Watford Borough Council* [1967] 1 W.L.R. 1069.

[15] Shops Act 1950, Part IV, ss. 47–66, and Scheds. 5, 6 and 7. And see the *Ilford, Jarmain* and *Newark* cases, *supra*, and the cases cited in the previous two footnotes, which related to Sunday trading.

[16] The sale of a carrot at a price reflecting the selling price of items of furniture selected by a customer, with the furniture being handed over as a "free gift," has been held to be in reality a sale of furniture and accordingly not within Sched. 5: *Waller v. Hardy* (1972) 70 L.G.R. 331.

[17] In *Binns v. Wardale* [1946] K.B. 451, a loaf of bread sold from a "general" shop was held to be a "refreshment" or a "meal." In *Newberry v. Cohen's (Smoked Salmon) Ltd.* (1956) 54 L.G.R. 343, a raw kipper was held to be a "meal" or "refreshment" while a packet of tea or flour was not.

shop, and where this is done the shop may be open for business until 2 p.m. on Sundays, but it must be closed on Saturdays. The applicant is required to make a statutory declaration to the effect that he conscientiously objects on religious grounds to carrying on trade or business on the Jewish Sabbath.[18]

Contravention of the Sunday trading laws is an offence.[19] In addition to prosecutions for offences, a local authority may sue in the High Court in its own name to obtain an injunction to restrain continuing breach of law.[20]

(3) Conditions of employment[21]

The Act requires that a half holiday each week shall be given to shop **22-30** assistants and that meal intervals shall be arranged in accordance with the provisions of the Third Schedule. Where there is Sunday employment some additional or compensatory holiday must be given, and the total hours which persons under eighteen years of age may work in any week are restricted.[22]

D. Consumer Protection

Former weights and measures or public control departments of local **22-31** authorities are now commonly described as trading standards or consumer protection departments, and their officers may carry similar titles. This reflects the widening of the enforcement responsibilities of local authorities under modern consumer legislation. Weights and measures authorities, as defined by section 69 of the Weights and Measures Act 1985, have been given the duty of enforcing the provisions of a series of statutes passed to protect the interests of the consumer. In various contexts they work closely with the Director General of Fair Trading and his Office, established under the Fair Trading Act 1973. Much information is supplied to the Director on a voluntary basis. For example, the results of criminal prosecutions are notified to the Director, although the statutory obligations as to notification apply only to proposed proceedings.[23]

A local weights and measures authority has express power to make or **22-32** assist in the making of arrangements to provide advice to consumers of

---

[18] Shops Act 1950, s. 53.
[19] *Ibid.* s. 59.
[20] *Stafford Borough Council* v. *Elkenford* [1977] 1 W.L.R. 324; *Solihull Metropolitan Council* v. *Maxfern* [1977] 1 W.L.R. 127; *Ibid.* (*No. 2*) (1976) 75 L.G.R. 392; *Thanet District Council* v. *Ninedrive Ltd.* [1978] 1 All E.R. 703; *Stoke-on-Trent City Council* v. *B. & Q. (Retail) Ltd.* [1984] A.C. 754 (see §§ 12–47, 12–48). Enforcement powers under the Town and Country Planning Acts may also be used in respect of Sunday markets: *Tidswell* v. *Secretary of State for the Environment* (1976) 34 P. & C.R. 152; the *Thanet* case, *supra.*
[21] Shops Act 1950, ss. 17–36.
[22] Young Persons (Employment) Act 1938; s. 1; Young Persons (Employment) Act 1964.
[23] Annual Report of the Director General of Fair Trading for 1977, pp. 16–18 (1977–78 H.C. 228); § 22–50, *infra.*

goods and services in their area.[24] A number of local authorities have
established consumer advice centres which offer advice about consumer
goods, provide information about consumer affairs generally, and give
assistance in relation to complaints about faulty goods. Most are linked to
local authority consumer protection departments.[25] Central Government
grants for such centres were, however, withdrawn in 1980.

In 1976, a co-ordinating body, the Local Authorities Co-ordinating
Body on Trading Standards (LACOTS) was established by agreement
between the Association of County Councils and the Association of
Metropolitan Authorities.[26]

Legislation enforceable by weights and measures authorities is
considered under the following headings: weights and measures; trade
descriptions; consumer credit; other statutes. This section concludes with
a note on the relevance of the unfair trading provisions to the consumer
protection work of local authorities.

(1) Weights and measures

22-33   The law as to weights and measures is for the most part found in the
Weights and Measures Act 1985, a consolidation measure. Local
authorities for the purpose of the statute are the councils of non-
metropolitan counties, metropolitan districts and London boroughs, the
Common Council of the City of London, the Temples and the Council of
the Isles of Scilly.[27]

22-34   A duty is placed on local authorities to appoint a chief inspector of
weights and measures and a sufficient number of other inspectors holding
Department of Trade certificates of qualification,[28] and to provide
standards of measure and weight so that weights and measures in
use in the area may be verified.[29] The responsibility for verification
and stamping falls directly on the inspectors (not the employing
authorities)[30] and inspectors have power to enter premises for the purpose
of testing, provided they have the written authority of a justice of the
peace.[31]

22-35   A number of offences in relation to weighing and measuring for trade
are created by Part II of the Weights and Measures Act 1985. It is, *inter
alia*, an offence:

---

[24] Weights and Measures Act 1985, s. 69(5). See also Local Government Act 1972, s. 137
(expenditure for purposes not otherwise authorised) and s. 142 (provision of information
about local services), which powers are available to all local authorities. s. 32 of the
Greater London Council (General Powers) Act 1973 empowers a London borough
council to establish a consumer advisory and protection service.
[25] See B. W. Harvey, *The Law of Consumer Protection and Fair Trading* (2nd ed, 1982),
pp. 45–46.
[26] *Ibid.* p. 45.
[27] Weights and Measures Act 1985, s. 69. See also § 22–02.
[28] Weights and Measures Act 1985, ss. 72, 73.
[29] *Ibid.* ss. 4, 5.
[30] *Ibid.* s. 11.
[31] *Ibid.* s. 79.

(1) for any person to use for trade[32] any unit of measurement not included in Parts I to V of Schedule 1 to the Act[33];

(2) for any person to use for trade, or have in his possession for trade, any measure or weight not included in Schedule 3 to the Act[34]; or any weighing or measuring equipment not verified and stamped by an inspector[35];

(3) for any person to forge, counterfeit, alter or remove any stamp, or make any alteration in equipment after it has been stamped such as to make it false or unjust, or to use equipment knowing of any such circumstances[36];

(4) for any person to use for trade or have in his possession[37] for trade any weighing or measuring equipment which is false or unjust[38];

(5) for any person to commit fraud in the use of any weighing or measuring equipment for trade.[39]

It is a defence to a prosecution under section 17(1) for the person to show that he used the equipment only in the course of his employment by some other person and that he neither knew, nor might reasonably have been expected to know, nor had any reason to suspect, the equipment to be false or unjust.[40] Equipment used in the commission of an offence[41] is liable to be forfeited.[42]

Further offences are created by Part IV of the 1985 Act in respect of certain transactions in goods. Schedules 4 to 7 apply special requirements to transactions in particular kinds of goods (respectively, sand and ballast, solid fuel, miscellaneous goods and composite goods and collections of articles). Furthermore, the Secretary of State may make regulations in relation to transactions in specified goods requiring, for example, that they be sold only in certain quantities, or only if pre-packaged in a container of a certain size, or in a container marked with certain specified information.[43] Failure to comply with these requirements

[32] The term "use for trade" is defined in s. 7 as essentially the transferring of money or money's worth in consideration for money or money's worth, provided the transaction is by reference to quantity and the use is for the purpose of the determination or statement of that quantity. The term "use" carries a wider meaning than in road traffic legislation: accordingly, it includes the use of a vehicle operated by an independent contractor: *F. Charman Ltd.* v. *Clow* [1974] 1 W.L.R. 1384.

[33] Weights and Measures Act 1985, s. 8(1)(*a*).

[34] *Ibid.* s. 8(1)(*b*).

[35] *Ibid.* s. 11.

[36] *Ibid.* s. 16.

[37] See *Bellerby* v. *Carle* [1983] 2 A.C. 101, where licensees were held not to be in possession of equipment owned and maintained by a brewery company and provided under a contract between that company and the licensees' employers.

[38] Weights and Measures Act 1985, s. 17(1). Acquiescence by the purchaser is no defence: *London County Council* v. *Payne & Co.* [1904] 1 K.B. 194.

[39] *Ibid.* s. 17(3).

[40] *Ibid.* s. 17(2).

[41] Or in circumstances where a defence is available under *ibid.* s. 17(2).

[42] *Ibid.* ss. 8(4), 11(3), (14),13, 16(4), 17(1),(3).

[43] *Ibid.* s. 22.

is an offence.[44] Furthermore, there are a number of "short weight" offences. It is, *inter alia,* an offence:

(1) for any person, in selling or purporting to sell any goods by weight or other measurement or by number, to deliver or cause to deliver to the buyer a lesser quantity than that purported to be sold or than corresponds with the price charged[45];

(2) for any person to make any misrepresentation as to quantity or to do any other act calculated to mislead as to quantity[46];

(3) for any person to be in possession for sale or to be the seller of goods of a quantity less than that marked on their container.[47]

In any proceedings for an offence under Part IV, warranty may be pleaded as a defence.[48] It is also a defence for the person charged to prove that he took all reasonable precautions and exercised all due diligence to avoid commission of the offence,[49] and there are a number of further specific defences.[50] It is, however, no defence that the purchaser was not deceived.[51]

22-36   An offence is committed by a person whose goods are exposed for sale short weight even though he does not know about the deficiencies of weight. In *Winter* v. *Hinckley and District Industrial Co-operative Society Ltd.*[52] a servant had stolen coal from sacks exposed for sale. It was held that the society had committed an offence, although they knew nothing about the matter (the employee having stolen from the bags after they had left the society's premises). It was held that *mens rea* (*i.e.* an evil intention, or a knowledge of the wrongfulness of the act) was not necessary to constitute the offence.

A defence under the original version of section 34 was successfully maintained in *Bibby-Cheshire* v. *Golden Wonder.*[53] A bagging machine produced six underweight packets in 10,000. The manufacturers had exercised all due diligence. The machines, normally accurate and reliable, had, for no anticipated reason, proved inaccurate.

22-37   It is the duty of a local weights and measures authority to enforce the obligations imposed on packers and importers by Part V of the Weights

---

[44] Weights and Measures Act 1985, s. 25.

[45] *Ibid.* s. 28. See, *e.g. Bennett* v. *Markham* (1982) 81 L.G.R. 60 (prosecution for selling a short measure pint of beer failed as the head of froth was held to be part of what was purported to be sold as the pint). When in force, s. 43 of the 1985 Act will provide that the head will be disregarded when ascertaining the quantity of beer or cider.

[46] *Ibid.* s. 29. The representation need not be made by a party to the contract of sale: *Collett* v. *Co-operative Wholesale Society Ltd.* [1970] 1 W.L.R. 250.

[47] *Ibid.* s. 30.

[48] *Ibid.* s. 33; *cf.* § 22–16.

[49] *Ibid.* s. 34. This formula is less onerous than the original version of the defence.

[50] *Ibid.* ss. 35, 36.

[51] *Sopp* v. *Co-operative Retail Services Ltd.* (1969) 68 L.G.R. 106.

[52] [1959] 1 W.L.R. 182.

[53] [1972] 1 W.L.R. 1487. See also *Kinchin* v. *Haines* [1979] Crim. L.R. 329. *Smedleys Ltd.* v. *Breed* [1974] A.C. 839, § 22–06, under the differently worded provisions of the Food and Drugs Act 1955 (now the Food Act 1984).

and Measures Act 1985 (formerly the Weights and Measures Act 1979) in relation to the control of quantities in packaged goods.[54]

The 1979 Act was passed in order to implement E.E.C. Directives.[55] It **22-38** enables a packer or importer of manufactured pre-packaged goods to comply with the law if the goods conform *on average* to a stated weight. A batch of pre-packaged goods is acceptable if (1) the actual contents of a sample are not less on average than the stated or "nominal" quantity, and (2) the number of non-standard packages in the sample is not greater than the number prescribed as acceptable. The Act imposes a series of duties on packers and importers,[56] non-performance of which is an offence.[57] Moreover, it is an offence for a person to have in his possession for sale, to agree to sell or to sell a package which is "inadequate"[58] if either (1) he is the packer or importer, or (2) he knows that the package is inadequate. The offences applicable to packers and importers are strict, subject to certain defences, including one that the defendant took all reasonable precautions and exercised all due diligence to avoid the commission of the offence in question.[59] The Weights and Measures (Packaged Goods) Regulations 1979[60] provide that the "average weight" regime must be adopted in respect of certain kinds of goods (Class A) and can be adopted in respect of others (Class B).

Local authorities may be supplied with information and advice by, and may be required to supply information to, the National Metrological Co-ordinating Unit.[61] The Unit may require an authority to arrange for the performance by an inspector of certain specified functions.[62] The powers of inspectors and weights and measures authorities under Part V of the Act are set out in Schedule 8.

Proceedings for offences under the Weights and Measures Act 1985 may be instituted only by a weights and measures authority or a chief of police.[63]

(2) Trade descriptions

Local weights and measures authorities have enforcement duties under the Trade Descriptions Act 1968 and 1972.

---

[54] Weights and Measures Act 1985, s. 52.
[55] Council Directives 75/106/E.E.C. and 76/211/E.E.C. See also the Weights and Measures (Packaged Goods) Regulations 1979 (S.I. 1979 No. 1613) as amended.
[56] Weights and Measures Act 1985, ss. 47–49.
[57] *Ibid.* s. 50.
[58] *i.e.* if the quantity of goods it contains is less than the nominal quantity by more than twice the permitted margin for error: *ibid.* s. 68(2).
[59] *Ibid.* s. 51.
[60] S.I. 1979 No. 1613, as amended.
[61] Established by s. 55 and Sched. 9. All the members of the Unit must be members of a local authority.
[62] *Ibid.* s. 59(1)(*b*).
[63] *Ibid.* s. 83.

(a) *False trade descriptions*

22-39   Section 1 of the Trade Descriptions Act 1968 renders it illegal for any person, in the course of a trade or business,[64] to apply a false trade description to any goods, or to supply or offer to supply any goods to which a false trade description is applied. Several of these expressions are amplified in the subsequent sections: "trade description"[65]; "false trade description"[66]; "applying a trade description to goods"[67]; and "offer to supply."[68] A false trade description is one which is false "to a material degree."[69] "Misleading" descriptions are deemed to be false.[70] An oral statement may amount to the use of a trade description.[71] A person exposing or possessing goods for supply is deemed to offer to supply them.[72] The hiring of goods amounts to the "supply" of them.[73] Section 1 imposes strict liability, subject to the defences mentioned in paragraph 22–43.[74] The section applies to buyers as well as sellers.[75]

22-40   Examples of false trade descriptions include incorrect car mileometer readings[76] (unless there is an effective disclaimer, which has to be as bold, precise and compelling as the trade description itself[77]); the description of an unsafe car with seventeen substantial defects as in "excellent condition throughout"[78]; the description of shoes as all leather where they were not, notwithstanding that the word "all" was crossed out at the cash desk[79]; and the description of a car as having had "one owner" where it had been owned by a leasing company and leased in turn to five hirers.[80] Repairs which have the effect of concealing a significant defect without removing

---

[64] See *Blakemore* v. *Bellamy* [1983] R.T.R. 303; *Davies* v. *Sumner* [1984] 1 W.L.R. 1301 and *Corfield* v. *Sevenways Garage Ltd.* [1985] R.T.R. 109.

[65] Trade Descriptions Act 1968, s. 2.

[66] *Ibid.* s. 3.

[67] *Ibid.* s. 4.

[68] *Ibid.* s. 6.

[69] *Ibid.* s. 3(1).

[70] *Ibid.* s. 3(2).

[71] *Ibid.* s. 4(2).

[72] *Ibid.* s. 6.

[73] *Cahalne* v. *Croydon London Borough Council* (1985) 149 J.P. 561.

[74] *Macnab* v. *Alexanders of Greenock* 1971 S.L.T. 121; *Alec Norman Garages Ltd.* v. *Phillips* [1985] R.T.R. 164.

[75] *Fletcher* v. *Budgen* [1974] 1 W.L.R. 1056 (false statement by car dealer to a private customer that his car was fit only for scrap).

[76] The *Macnab* case, *supra; Tarleton Engineering Co. Ltd.* v. *Nattrass* [1973] 1 W.L.R. 1261; *R.* v. *Hammerstons Cars Ltd.* [1976] 1 W.L.R. 1243; *Holloway* v. *Cross* [1981] 1 All E.R. 1012.

[77] *Norman* v. *Bennett* [1974] 1 W.L.R. 1229; *Zawadaski* v. *Sleigh* [1975] R.T.R. 113; *Waltham Forest London Borough Council* v. *T. G. Wheatley (Central Garage) Ltd.* [1978] R.T.R. 157, 333; *Corfield* v. *Starr* [1981] R.T.R. 380. The defence of a disclaimer is not available in respect of offences under s. 1(1)(*a*) (applying a false trade description), but only s. 1(1)(*b*) (the supply, or offer to supply, of goods to which a false trade description is applied): *Newman* v. *Hackney London Borough Council* (1981) 80 L.G.R. 611.

[78] *Chidwick* v. *Beer* (1974) 138 J.P. 210.

[79] *Haringey London Borough Council* v. *Piro* [1976] Crim. L.R. 462.

[80] *R.* v. *Inner London JJ. ex p. Wandsworth London Borough Council* [1983] R.T.R. 425.

it may amount to the application of a false trade description.[81] The words "extra value" on the wrappers of chocolate bars have been held not to constitute a "trade description" as the matters specified in section 2, the indicating of which amounts to a trade description, concern only the physical characteristics and history of goods.[82]

The Act covers only false trade descriptions in relation to the sale or supply of goods, and not descriptions given incidentally in providing the service of advising in regard to some matter affecting those goods.[83] A statement made after the actual sale is concluded may not be the basis of a prosecution.[84] It is not, however, necessary that the statement be made by a party to the contract of sale or supply.[85]

(b) *False indications as to price*

It is an offence under the Trade Descriptions Act 1968 for a person **22–41** offering to supply goods to give (i) any false indication that the price at which the goods are offered is equal to or less than a recommended price or the price at which the goods or goods of the same description were previously offered by him.[86] or (ii) any indication likely to be taken as an indication that the goods are being offered at a price less than that at which they are in fact being offered.[87] This section applies only to transactions of a commercial nature notwithstanding that the words "in the course of a trade or business" do not appear expressly.[88] The advertisement of a price for a mini bus without an indication that value added tax was extra was held to be an offence under section 11(2) in *Richards* v. *Westminster Motors Ltd.*,[89] the test being the effect on the mind of the person to whom the vehicle was being offered.[90] An indication by a person that goods were previously offered at a higher price or at a particular price is to be treated as indicating, unless the contrary is expressed, (i) that they were so offered by that person and (ii)

---

[81] *R.* v. *Ford Motor Co. Ltd.* [1974] 1 W.L.R. 1220; *cf. Cottee* v. *Douglas Seaton (Used Cars) Ltd.* [1972] 1 W.L.R. 1408; § 22–44.
[82] *Cadbury Ltd.* v. *Halliday* [1975] 1 W.L.R. 649.
[83] *Wycombe Marsh Garages Ltd.* v. *Fowler* [1972] 1 W.L.R. 1156 (false statement in a M.o.T. car test certificate).
[84] *Hall* v. *Wickens Motors (Gloucester) Ltd.* [1972] 1 W.L.R. 1418.
[85] *Fletcher* v. *Sledmore* [1973] Crim. L.R. 195 (statement by car owner to prospective purchaser introduced by car dealer through whom the car would be sold).
[86] Trade Descriptions Act 1968, s. 11(1). Note also the restrictions contained in the Price Marking (Bargain Offers) Order 1979 (S.I. 1979 No. 364), considered in *Comet Radiovision Services Ltd.* v. *Williamson* [1983] 1 W.L.R. 766 and *West Yorkshire Metropolitan County Council* v. *M.F.I. Furniture Centre Ltd.* [1983] 1 W.L.R. 1175.
[87] *Ibid.* s. 11(2).
[88] *John* v. *Matthews* [1970] 2 Q.B. 443 (sale of cigarettes in a working men's club).
[89] [1976] R.T.R. 88.
[90] See also *Doble* v. *David Greig Ltd.* [1972] 1 W.L.R. 703; *Read Bros. Cycles (Leyton) Ltd.* v. *Waltham Forest London Borough Council* [1978] R.T.R. 397; *Barnes* v. *Watts Tyre and Rubber Co. Ltd. (Note)* [1978] R.T.R. 405.

that they were so offered within the preceding six months for a continuous period of not less than 28 days.[91]

(c) *Other offences*

22-42   There are also offences in relation to false representations as to royal approval or award,[92] false representations that any goods or services supplied are of a kind supplied to any person,[93] and the making knowingly or recklessly[94] of a false statement as to services,[95] accommodation[96] or facilities[97] provided in the course of any trade or business.[98] The last provision does not apply to promises as to the future as distinct from representations as to existing fact, although the latter may include a representation as to the present intention of the person making it.[99] Save in exceptional cases, the supply of goods does not fall within the words "services" or "facilities."[1] Moreover, a false statement "as to" services etc. provided does not cover a false statement as to the terms (*e.g.* price) on which such services etc. are provided.[2]

(d) *Defences*

22-43   It is a defence in relation to any prosecution under the Act for the person charged to prove (a) that the commission of the offence was due to a mistake or to reliance on information supplied to him or to the act or default of another person,[3] an accident or some other cause beyond his control, and (b) that he took all reasonable precautions and exercised all due diligence to avoid the commission of such an offence by himself or any person under his control.[4] In relation to false trade descriptions, it is a defence for the person charged to prove that he did not know, and could not with reasonable diligence have ascertained, that the goods did not

---

[91] Trade Descriptions Act 1968, s. 11(3). Under (ii), the onus lies on the prosecution to show that during the six month period there was no offer at a higher price for a period of 28 days: *House of Holland* v. *Brent London Borough Council* [1971] 2 Q.B. 304. Moreover, it is not necessary for the goods to have been so offered at the same premises; it is sufficient that they have been so offered at other premises owned by the relevant person: *Westminster City Council* v. *Ray Alan (Manshops) Ltd.* [1982] 1 W.L.R. 383.

[92] Trade Descriptions Act 1968, s. 12.

[93] *Ibid.* s. 13.

[94] A dishonest intention is not necessary: *M.F.I. Warehouses Ltd.* v. *Nattrass* [1973] 1 W.L.R. 307. See also *Dixons Ltd.* v. *Roberts* (1984) 82 L.G.R. 689.

[95] *e.g.* a statement that reservation of an airline seat was certain where there was a policy of overbooking: *British Airways Board* v. *Taylor* [1976] 1 W.L.R. 13.

[96] *e.g.* a statement that a hotel was air-conditioned: *Wings Ltd.* v. *Ellis* [1985] A.C. 272.

[97] *e.g.* a guarantee to effect repairs in a car: *Bambury* v. *Hounslow London Borough Council* [1971] R.T.R. 1.

[98] Trade Descriptions Act 1968, s. 14. The offences under s. 14 are absolute as regards the actual making of the statement: *Wings Ltd.* v. *Ellis* [1985] A.C. 272.

[99] *Beckett* v. *Cohen* [1972] 1 W.L.R. 1593; *R.* v. *Sunair Holidays Ltd.* [1973] 1 W.L.R. 1105.

[1] *Newell* v. *Hicks* [1984] R.T.R. 135; *Dixons Ltd.* v. *Roberts* (1984) 82 L.G.R. 689.

[2] *Ibid.* A prosecution might be brought under s. 11(2): *Newell* v. *Hicks, supra,* at p. 150.

[3] Who may be an employee, see *Beckett* v. *Kingston Brothers (Butchers) Ltd.* [1970] 1 Q.B. 606; *Tesco Supermarkets Ltd.* v. *Nattrass* [1972] A.C. 153.

[4] Trade Descriptions Act 1968, s. 24(1): *Naish* v. *Gore* [1971] 3 All E.R. 737; *Simmons* v. *Potter* [1975] R.T.R. 367; *Nattrass* v. *Timpsons Shops Ltd.* [1973] Crim. L.R. 197.

conform to the description or that the description had been applied to the goods.[5] As regards proceedings in respect of the publication of an advertisement, it is a defence for a person charged to prove that he is a person whose business it is to publish or arrange for the publication of advertisements, and that he received the advertisement for publication in the ordinary course of business and did not know and had no reason to suspect that its publication would constitute an offence.[6]

Where the commission by any person of an offence under the Act is **22-44** due to the act or default of some other person, that other person is guilty of the offence, and may be convicted whether or not proceedings are taken against the first-mentioned person.[7] The first-mentioned person must have committed an offence for this provision to operate. In *Cottee v. Douglas Seaton (Used Cars) Ltd.*[8] the owner of a car treated it for rust with plastic filler and sold the car to the defendants, who smoothed down the filler and repainted the interior body work to match the original colours. The defendants sold the car to a dealer, W., who in turn sold the car to S. The defendants were charged in respect of the sale by W. to S. The court held that W. had not committed an offence as he neither covered up the existence of the car's defective condition nor knew of that condition, and accordingly had not applied a false trade description. The defendants might have been convicted on a charge relating to the sale by themselves to W. Lord Widgery C.J. stated[9] that "an alteration of goods which causes them to tell a lie about themselves may be a false trade description. . . . "

(3) Consumer credit

Local weights and measures authorities are enforcement authorities **22-45** (together with the Director General of Fair Trading) under the Consumer Credit Act 1974.[10] They are under a duty to enforce the provisions of the Act and regulations made under it. The Act regulates many aspects of the provision of credit and the supply of goods on hire or hire-purchase.

(a) *Licensing*

Part III of the Act provides for the licensing of credit and hire **22-46** businesses. Local authorities are exempt from this control.[11] Most of these provisions apply similarly to ancillary credit businesses,[12] which are defined in Part X to include credit brokerage, debt-adjusting, debt-

---

[5] Trade Descriptions Act 1968, s. 24(3). See, *e.g. Simmons* v. *Ravenhill* [1984] R.T.R. 412 (D. should have been put on inquiry by low odometer reading: defence rejected).
[6] *Ibid.* s. 25.
[7] *Ibid.* s. 23.
[8] [1972] 1 W.L.R. 1408.
[9] At p. 1416.
[10] Consumer Credit Act 1974, s. 161, as amended by the Local Government, Planning and Land Act 1980, s. 1 and Sched. 4.
[11] *Ibid.* s. 21(2).
[12] *Ibid.* s. 147.

counselling, debt-collecting and the operation of a credit reference agency.[13] The licensing authority is the Director General of Fair Trading, who must grant a licence if satisfied by the applicant that he is a fit person to engage in the activities covered by the licence, and that the name or names under which he applies to be licensed are not misleading or otherwise undesirable.[14] Licence application forms are obtainable from trading standards officers. A requirement that applicants send notice of their applications to trading standards officers in the areas where they intended to operate was abandoned in November 1976 as an economy measure.[15] Nevertheless, the Director takes account of the information concerning consumer complaints, local practice and prosecutions which is regularly supplied to the Office of Fair Trading by trading standards officers. It is an offence for a person to operate without a licence in circumstances where a licence is required.[16]

(b) *General controls over business methods*

22-47   Part IV imposes various controls as to methods of seeking business. For example, it is an offence to canvass debtor-creditor agreements away from trade premises[17] except in response to a request made on a previous occasion.[18] It is also an offence to send to a minor, with a view to financial gain, any document inviting him to borrow money or obtain credit, or to seek information on such matters.[19]

(c) *Controls in relation to specific agreements*

22-48   Parts V to VII contain provisions as to entry into credit or hire agreements, matters arising during their currency, and default and termination. Part VIII concerns securities, and Part IX judicial control of agreements which are, for example, extortionate.[20] Sections 157 to 160 impose various obligations as to the collection and keeping of information by credit reference agencies.[21] A debtor or hirer may require a creditor, owner or negotiator to disclose the name and address of any credit reference agency from which the latter has sought information about the former's financial standing during antecedent negotiations. A credit reference agency must disclose on request information on its files concerning a consumer. There is a procedure whereby wrong information can be corrected. Failure to comply with obligations imposed by these sections is an offence.

---

[13] Consumer Credit Act 1974, s. 145(1).
[14] *Ibid.* s., 25(1).
[15] Annual Report of the Director General of Fair Trading for 1976, pp. 23–24 (1976–77 H.C. 195).
[16] Consumer Credit Act 1974, s. 39(1).
[17] *Ibid.* s. 49.
[18] *Ibid.* ss. 48(1)(*b*), 49(2).
[19] *Ibid.* s. 50.
[20] *Ibid.* ss. 137–140: in force from May 16, 1977.
[21] In force from May 16, 1977. See also S.I. 1977 Nos. 329 and 330.

(d) *Offences*

The Act creates 35 new offences.[22] The intention is that local **22-49** enforcement authorities will prosecute in respect of offences of a local character, and the Director General of Fair Trading will prosecute in cases which raise important questions of general policy, or which raise issues of a national character (*e.g.* advertisements in national newspapers).[23] Part XI contains the usual provisions as to entry and inspection, test purchases, and obstruction of authorised officers. It is a defence for a person to prove that his act or omission was due to a mistake or to reliance on information supplied to him, or to an act or omission by another person, or to an accident or some other cause beyond his control, and that he took all reasonable precautions and exercised due diligence to avoid such an act or omission by himself or any person under his control.[24]

A local weights and measure authority must notify the Director **22-50** General of Fair Trading of intended proceedings in respect of most offences under the Act. It must give a summary of the facts on which the charges are to be founded, and postpone institution of the proceedings until either 28 days have expired since notice was given, or the Director notifies the authority of receipt of the notice and summary. Failure to comply with these obligations does not, however, invalidate a prosecution.[25] The Director may require a local weights and measures authority to report to him in such form and with such particulars as he specifies on the exercise of its functions under the Act.[26]

(4) Other statutes

Weights and measures authorities are under a duty (*inter alia*) to **22-51** enforce the following provisions: (i) orders made by the Secretary of State under section 22 of the Fair Trading Act 1973 concerning a trade practice which the Consumer Protection Advisory Committee has found adversely to affect the economic interests of consumers in the United Kingdom[27]; (ii) the Hallmarking Act 1973, which regulates the composition, assaying, marking and description of articles of or containing precious metal, and which also may be enforced by the British Hallmarking Council and assay offices[28]; (iii) safety regulations for goods made by the Secretary of State under the Consumer Safety Act 1978.

---

[22] They are listed in Sched. 1.

[23] Annual Report of the Director General of Fair Trading for 1975, p. 39 (1975–76 H.C. 288).

[24] Consumer Credit Act 1974, s. 168(1).

[25] *Ibid.* s. 161(2). There are similar requirements in respect of offences under the Fair Trading Act 1973, s. 23, and most offences under the Trade Descriptions Act 1968: Fair Trading Act 1973, s. 130.

[26] Consumer Credit Act 1974, s. 161(3).

[27] Fair Trading Act 1973, s. 27.

[28] Hallmarking Act 1973, s. 9.

(5) Unfair trading

22-52   Under Part III of the Fair Trading Act 1973, where it appears to the Director General of Fair Trading that a person in the course of his business has persisted in an unfair course of conduct detrimental to the interests of consumers, he may seek a written assurance from that person that he will refrain from continuing that course of conduct and from carrying on any similar course of conduct in the course of that business.[29] Conduct is regarded as unfair if it consists of contraventions of the civil or criminal law.[30] If the Director is unable to obtain such an assurance or if an assurance is not observed, the Director may bring proceedings in the Restrictive Practices Court[31] or a county court,[32] and the court may accept an assurance, or make an order in similar terms.[33] Breach of an order or an undertaking given to the courts constitutes contempt of court. Assurances and orders are publicised in the Annual Report of the Director. In this Report for 1977 the Director stated[34] that there were encouraging indications that increasing numbers of trading standards officers and environmental health officers were beginning to look upon his power to seek assurances as a valuable supplement to their own work, especially where persistent complaints could not adequately be dealt with by prosecution under the Trade Descriptions Act or the Food and Drugs Act (now the Food Act 1984).

---

[29] Fair Trading Act 1973, s. 34(1).
[30] *Ibid.* s. 34(2).
[31] *Ibid.* s. 35.
[32] *Ibid.* s. 41.
[33] *e.g. Director General of Fair Trading* v. *Smith's Bakeries (Westfield) Ltd., The Times,* May 12, 1978.
[34] At p. 14.

CHAPTER 23

WATER RESOURCES, POLLUTION OF WATERS, LAND DRAINAGE, COAST PROTECTION

A. Water Resources

THE Water Resources Act 1963 introduced a comprehensive system of **23-01** management of the water resources of England and Wales and made provision for the appointment of river authorities to undertake responsibilities in relation to water resources and to discharge the land drainage, fisheries and prevention of river pollution functions formerly exercised by river boards established under the River Boards Act 1948.[1] Twenty-seven river authorities were established by orders made by the Minister of Housing and Local Government and the Minister of Agriculture, Fisheries and Food, acting jointly, and these authorities, with the Thames Conservancy and the Lee Conservancy Catchment Board, covered the whole of England and Wales. River authorities were composed principally of persons appointed by the councils of counties and county boroughs and by the two ministers.[2]

This system was wholly changed by the Water Act 1973. Its main **23-02** purpose was to provide for the establishment of new authorities to carry out all functions relating to water, namely: water conservation; water supply; sewerage and sewage disposal; prevention of river pollution; fisheries; land drainage and water recreation.

An overall responsibility for a national policy for water falls to the Secretary of State and the Minister of Agriculture, Fisheries and Food.[3] It is the duty of the first to secure the effective execution of the national policy so far as it relates to the following:

(a) the conservation, augmentation, distribution and proper use of water resources, and the provision of water supplies;

(b) sewerage and the treatment and disposal of sewage and other effluents;

(c) the restoration and maintenance of the wholesomeness of rivers and other inland water;

(d) the use of inland water for recreation;

(e) the enhancement and preservation of amenity in connection with inland water; and

---

[1] Water Resources Act 1963, ss. 5 and 99.
[2] Water Resources Act 1963, s. 6.
[3] Water Act 1973, s. 1. The functions of the Secretary of State are discharged by the Secretary of State for the Environment in relation to English water authority areas, and the Secretary of State for Wales in relation to the area of the Welsh authority.

(f) the use of inland water for navigation.

It is the duty of the second-named minister to secure the effective execution of the national policy so far as it relates to land drainage and to fisheries in inland and coastal waters.

23-03   Nine regional water authorities were established under the Act—they came into being by orders of the Secretary of State—and, for Wales, there is the Welsh National Water Development Authority.[4] Each regional water authority consists of a chairman appointed by the Secretary of State, two members appointed by the Minister of Agriculture, Fisheries and Food and not less than six nor more than twelve other members appointed by the Secretary of State. The Welsh authority consists of a chairman and not less than eight nor more than fourteen other members appointed by the Secretary of State. Members appointed by the Minister must be persons who appear to him to have had experience of, and shown capacity in, agriculture, land drainage or fisheries. Members appointed to regional water authorities by the Secretary of State must be persons who appear to him to have had experience of, and shown capacity in, some matter relevant to the functions of water authorities. Similar requirements apply to appointments to the Welsh authority. In making appointments regard must be had to the desirability of members being familiar with the requirements and circumstances of the authority's area.[5] There is no longer any provision for the appointment of members by local authorities, but the government is committed to the appointment of between two and four members with local government experience, and has undertaken that county and district councils should have the opportunity to make nominations for these places.[6] Members, whether full-time or part-time, are paid salaries.

23-04   A further body was established under the 1973 Act—the National Water Council, consisting of a chairman appointed by the Secretary of State, the chairmen of the water authorities, and other members (not more than 10) appointed by the Ministers. It was the duty of the Council to advise any minister and water authorities on matters relating to water, to promote the efficient performance by water authorities of their functions (in particular those relating to research and the preparation of plans), to consult the bodies concerned with a view to the establishment of a scheme for the testing and approval of water fittings, and to prepare a scheme for training and education. The Council was dissolved by an Order under the Water Act 1983.[7] Its functions were transferred to the following non-statutory bodies,[8] incorporated under the Companies Acts:

---

[4] Water Act 1973, s. 2.
[5] *Ibid.* s. 3, substituted by the Water Act 1983, s. 1. Further administrative and financial provisions are contained in Schedule 3, Parts I and II to the 1973 Act (Part I as substituted by the Water Act 1983, s. 1(3) and Sched. 1).
[6] DoE Circular 16/83, paras. 6,7.
[7] S.I. 1983 No. 1927.
[8] National Water Council (Transfer of Property, etc.) Order 1983 (S.I. 1983 No. 1320); DoE Circular 16/83.

(1) The Water Authorities Association, in which all the water authorities are equal shareholders, and which provides a forum for discussion between the authorities and other organisations including the government, and also provides certain common services. It inherited all the property, rights and liabilities of the Council, except in relation to the following.

(2) The Water Industry Training Association, which has central training responsibilities for the water industry.

(3) The Water Research Centre, which is responsible for the scheme for the testing and approval of water fittings.

(4) British Water International Ltd., which has taken over the responsibilities of the Council's International Advisory Services.

The Ministers may give directions of a general nature to water authorities—a direction may relate to one authority in particular or to water authorities generally.[9] All these matters are contained in Part I of the 1973 Act.

Part II deals with the functions of water authorities, and they are **23-05** summarised here. First, the water authorities took over the functions of river authorities.[10] Secondly, they have duties with respect to water conservation, sewers and sewerage.[11] Thirdly, it is the duty of the water authority to supply or secure the supply of water in its area.[12] This matter is considered in Chapter 25. Fourthly, they have responsibilities in regard to river pollution, fisheries and land drainage.[13] Finally, in discharging their obligations they are to take all reasonable practical steps to put their rights to the use of water to the best use for recreational purposes.[14] Authorities and ministers are to have regard to the desirability of preserving natural beauty and conserving the countryside and buildings of architectural, archeological and historic interest and to consider the effect which proposals would have on the beauty or amenity of any area, whether rural or urban.[15]

Each water authority must (1) conduct a survey of the water in the **23-06** authority's area, its management, the purposes for which it is being used and its quality in relation to its existing and likely future uses, and prepare a report setting out the results; (2) prepare an estimate of future demand; and (3) prepare a plan of action for securing more efficient management of the water in its area. These matters must be kept under review, and the report, estimate and plan revised at least every seven years. Each authority must also prepare one or more programmes of a

[9] Water Act 1973, s. 5.
[10] s. 9.
[11] ss. 10, 14.
[12] s. 11.
[13] Control of Pollution Act 1974, Pt. II; Salmon and Freshwater Fisheries Act 1975, s. 28; Land Drainage Act 1976.
[14] Water Act 1973, ss. 20, 21.
[15] s. 22.

general nature for the discharge of its functions, and submit them for the approval of the appropriate minister or ministers. The authority must consult every local authority in its area and have regard to any structure, local or development plan made under the Town and Country Planning Act 1971. Copies of any report prepared in consequence of a survey must be sent to the appropriate minister or ministers and each local authority in the area, and be available for inspection by or sale to the public.[16] Arrangements must be made for the representation of the interests of consumers in its area, and these are subject to the approval of the Secretary of State.[17] Each water authority must make such provision for advancing the skill of its employees as it considers to be appropriate.[18]

Part III of the Act deals with the financing of water services. In general terms they are to be financially self-supporting. It is the duty of each authority so to discharge its functions as to secure that, taking one year with another, its revenue is not less than sufficient to meet its total outgoings properly chargeable to the revenue account. Revenue is raised by charges for all services, rights and facilities except those relating to land drainage.[19] Revenue for land drainage is raised by precept and drainage charges, as under earlier law, except that since March 31, 1978, a water authority may apply for an order under which it will use a system of charges as for its other functions.[20]

B. POLLUTION OF WATERS

Statutory provisions

General powers to prevent pollution

23-07   The Control of Pollution Act 1974, Part II, repeals and replaces most of the provisions of the Rivers (Prevention of Pollution) Acts 1951 to 1961.[21] The Act applies to:

(a) "controlled waters,"[22] which means the sea within three nautical

---

[16] s. 24, as amended by the Control of Pollution Act 1974, Sched. 8, and the Water Act 1983, Sched. 5.

[17] s. 24A, inserted by the Water Act 1983, s. 7; in force from a day to be appointed.

[18] s. 26, as amended by the Water Act 1983, Sched. 4.

[19] s. 30, as amended by the Water Charges Act 1976, s. 2.

[20] Land Drainage Act 1976, Pt. IV.

[21] It is intended that the phased programme or implementation of Part II will be substantially complete by 1986: DoE Circular 17/84. See, *inter alia*, the Control of Pollution Act 1974 (Commencement No. 17) Order 1984 (S.I. 1984 No. 853) and (Commencement No. 18) Order 1985 (S.I. 1985 No. 70). For transitional arrangements see the 1974 Act, s. 40, the Control of Pollution (Exemption of Certain Discharges from Control) Order 1983 (S.I. 1983 No. 1182) and the Control of Pollution (Consents: Transitional Provisions) Regulations 1985 (S.I. 1985 No. 5). Certain provisions of Part II apply to the non-radioactive elements of radioactive waste: Control of Pollution (Radioactive Waste) Regulations 1984 (S.I. 1984 No. 863).

[22] s. 56.

miles of the coast, such other parts of the territorial sea adjacent to Great Britain as are prescribed, and any other tidal waters; and

(b) "specified underground water,"[23] which means water specified by a water authority; and

(c) "streams," which term includes any river, water-course or inland water, except lakes or ponds which do not discharge into a stream.

The collective term for these waters is "relevant waters."[24]

A person commits an offence under section 31 of the Act if he causes or knowingly permits[25]:

(a) any poisonous, noxious or polluting matter to enter any relevant waters; or

(b) any matter to enter a stream so as to tend either directly or in combination with similar acts (whether his own or another's) to impede the proper flow of the water of the stream in a manner leading or likely to lead to a substantial aggravation of pollution due to other causes or of the consequences of such pollution; or

(c) any solid waste matter to enter a stream or restricted water.[26]

A person guilty of an offence under (a) or (b) is liable on conviction on **23-08** indictment to imprisonment for a term not exceeding two years or a fine or both, or on summary conviction to imprisonment for a term not exceeding three months or a fine not exceeding the prescribed sum[27] or both. For an offence under (c) a magistrates' court may impose a fine not exceeding level 4 on the standard scale. The Act specifies the circumstances when such actions shall not amount to an offence, for example, when the entry is authorised by a disposal licence or consent given by the Secretary of State or a water authority, or the entry is caused by an emergency in order to avoid danger to the public.

A person commits an offence under section 32 of the Act if he causes or knowingly permits:

(a) trade effluent or sewage to be discharged into relevant waters or through a pipe to the sea outside controlled waters or into any land, lake or pond not discharging into a stream; or

(b) any other matter to be discharged from a sewer into relevant waters; or

---

[23] *Ibid.* Control of Pollution (Underground Water) (Specification) Regulations 1984 (S.I. 1984 No. 582).

[24] *Ibid.*

[25] The phrase "causes or knowingly permits" is considered in *Alphacell Ltd.* v. *Woodward* [1972] A.C. 824. See also *Moses* v. *Midland Railway* (1915) 84 L.J.K.B. 2181, *Impress (Worcester)* v. *Rees* [1971] 2 All E.R. 357 and *F. J. H. Wrothwell* v. *Yorkshire Water Authority* [1984] Crim. L.R. 43.

[26] "Restricted waters" are controlled waters in certain tidal rivers and moorings designated in regulations: s. 56. The law relating to the acceptance of trade effluent is considered in Chap. 16.

[27] See the Magistrates' Courts Act 1980, s. 32(2) and the Criminal Penalties, etc. (Increase) Order 1984 (S.I. 1984 No. 447), art. 2(1), Sched. 1), under which the sum is £2,000.

 (c) any other matter to be discharged into relevant waters from a drain kept open under section 100 of the Highways Act 1980, where the water authority has given notice that these provisions apply to it,

unless the discharge is made with the consent of the water authority.

23–09 A water authority is deemed to have caused the discharge of sewage under (a) where it was bound to receive it into works or a sewer either unconditionally or subject to conditions which were observed. The penalty for an offence under this section is the same as that mentioned for an offence under section 31((a) and (b) above).

The Secretary of State may make regulations as to precautions to be taken by persons having control of poisonous, noxious or polluting matter,[28] and where he considers it appropriate may make regulations prohibiting or restricting activities in a particular area so as to avoid such matter entering relevant waters.[29] Water authorities have wide powers to forestall or remedy the pollution of water.[30]

23–10 A person commits an offence under section 49 of the Act, and is liable on summary conviction to a fine not exceeding level 4 on the standard scale, if:

 (a) without the consent of the water authority (which may not be unreasonably withheld), he cleanses any part of the channel or bed of a stream from a deposit accumulated by reason of any dam, weir, or sluice holding back the water of the stream, and does so by causing the deposit to be carried away in suspension in the water of the stream; or

 (b) by his wilful default, and without the consent of the water authority (which may not be unreasonably withheld), any substantial amount of vegetation cut or uprooted in the stream, or so near to the stream that it falls in, is allowed to remain in the stream.

Regulations may be made applying this provision to any controlled waters. Any question as to whether consent is unreasonably withheld is to be determined by the Secretary of State.

By-laws

23–11 A water authority is empowered by sections 31 and 33 of the Act to make by-laws[31]:

 (a) for prohibiting or regulating the washing or cleaning in any stream or controlled waters of things of a kind specified in the by-laws;

---

[28] Control of Pollution Act 1974, s. 31(4).
[29] *Ibid.* s. 31(5).
[30] *Ibid.* s. 46: subss. (1)–(3), (8) in force from a day to be appointed.
[31] As to procedure see Water Act 1973, Sched. 7.

(b) for prohibiting or regulating the keeping or use on a stream or restricted waters of vessels of a specified kind provided with sanitary appliances.

Before making by-laws the water authority must have regard to certain specified matters (*e.g.* the character, flow and use of the stream), and is required to give reasonable notice to bodies representative of affected interests and designated as such by the minister. A person who contravenes a by-law made under paragraph (a) or (b) is liable on summary conviction to a fine not exceeding level 4 on the standard scale.

Discharge consents

It is unlawful to discharge trade or sewage effluent into relevant waters **23-12** without the consent of the water authority. Public notice must be given of applications for consent.[32] Conditions may be imposed, *inter alia*, as to the point of discharge, composition, temperature, volume and rate of discharge, the provision of facilities for sampling and inspection, the keeping of records and the making of returns to the authority. Consent may not be unreasonably withheld or unreasonable conditions imposed, and there is an appeal to the Secretary of State. If consent is neither given nor refused within three months (or such longer time as is agreed between applicant and authority) the application is deemed to be refused.[33] The Secretary of State has power to call in an application for his determination and a hearing or local inquiry may be held.[34] His determination is final.[35] Consents must be reviewed from time to time by the water authority, and the authority has power to revoke or modify them.[36] However, the authority must specify a reasonable period of not less than two years within which there may normally be no revocation or modification.[37] Revocation or modification within that period is permissible in exceptional circumstances to protect third parties, but requires either (1) the agreement of the person making the discharge in pursuance of the consent or (2) (unless there has been an unforeseen change of circumstances) the payment of compensation.[38]

Water authorities must maintain registers, *inter alia*, of applications for consent, consents and information derived from samples. These must be

[32] Control of Pollution Act 1974, s. 36; Control of Pollution (Consents for Discharges) (Notices) Regulations 1984 (S.I. 1984 No. 864).
[33] Control of Pollution Act 1974, ss. 34, 39; the Control of Pollution (Consents for Discharges) (Secretary of State Functions) Regulations 1984 (S.I. 1984 No. 865). On an appeal, the Secretary of State may hold a hearing or local inquiry and may state a case for the opinion of the High Court on a point of law: S.I. 1984 No. 865, reg. 10 and 1974 Act, s. 39(8).
[34] *Ibid.* s. 35.
[35] *Ibid.* s. 39(1).
[36] *Ibid.* s. 37.
[37] *Ibid.* s. 38(1), (2).
[38] *Ibid.* s. 38(3)–(5): in force from a day to be appointed.

open to public inspection.[39] The Secretary of State may grant exemption from publicity if that would prejudice to an unreasonable degree some private interest by disclosing information about a trade secret, or would be contrary to the public interest.[40]

Discharges by water authorities require the consent of the Secretary of State.[41]

If action is taken without the authority's consent the authority may impose such conditions as might have been imposed if an application had been made.[42] Proceedings may be taken where a discharge is made without consent or where conditions are not observed.

Other statutory provisions

23-13   There are several other statutory provisions relating to the purity of rivers. It is an offence:

(i)   to discharge oil into waters (including inland waters) which are navigable by sea-going ships,[43] or

(ii) to throw into a river or stream the carcass of an animal which has died of disease or has been slaughtered as diseased or suspected,[44] or

(iii) to put any liquid or solid matter into any water containing fish to such an extent as to cause the water to be poisonous or injurious to fish.[45]

23-14   A statutory nuisance exists under the Public Health Act 1936[46] where a pond or watercourse is so foul or is in such a state as to be prejudicial to health or a nuisance or where any part of a water-course is so choked or silted as to obstruct or impede its proper flow, thereby causing a nuisance or giving rise to conditions prejudicial to health.[47] Effluent from alkali works is subject to particular legislation.[48]

At common law

23-15   The rights of riparian owners at common law are stated by Lord Macnaghten in *John Young & Co.* v. *Bankier Distillery C.*[49] He said:

---

[39] Control of Pollution Act 1974, s. 41; Control of Pollution (Registers) Regulations 1985 (S.I. 1985 No. 813). Registers must be open to inspection after July 31, 1985.

[40] *Ibid.* s. 42.

[41] *Ibid.* s. 55; Control of Pollution (Discharges by Authorities) Regulations 1984 (S.I. 1984 No. 1200).

[42] *Ibid.* s. 34(3): in force from a day to be appointed.

[43] Prevention of Oil Pollution Act 1971, s. 2.

[44] Animal Health Act 1981, s. 35(4).

[45] Salmon and Freshwater Fisheries Act 1975, s. 4.

[46] See Chap. 16 as to statutory nuisances.

[47] Public Health Act 1936, s. 259(1).

[48] Alkali, etc., Works Regulation Act 1906.

[49] [1893] A.C. 691 at p. 698. This is now subject to rights of abstraction under the Water Resources Act 1963, ss. 23–25, as amended by the Water Act 1973, but is not affected by any consent given under the Control of Pollution Act 1974.

"The law relating to the rights of riparian proprietors is well settled. A riparian proprietor is entitled to have the water of the stream, on the banks of which his property lies, flow down as it has been accustomed to flow down to his property, subject to the ordinary use of the flowing water by upper proprietors, and to such further use, if any, on their part in connection with their property as may be reasonable under the circumstances. Every riparian proprietor is thus entitled to the water of his stream, in its natural flow, without sensible diminution or increase and without sensible alteration in its character or quality. Any invasion of this right causing actual damage or calculated to found a claim which may ripen into an adverse right entitles the party injured to the intervention of the court."

23-16 A riparian owner whose rights have been infringed can bring an action for an injunction and damages, and he may do this without proof of actual damage. The pollution of the river may sustain an action in nuisance; the deposit of faecal matter, whether carried by current or wind, may sustain an action in trespass.

> *Jones* v. *Llanrwst Urban District Council.*[50] Sewage was taken in a crude state without any treatment into the River Conway opposite to the plaintiff's premises. The plaintiff alleged first that this sewage seriously polluted the water of the river opposite his property, infringing his rights as a riparian owner, and secondly that faecal matter from the sewer outfalls was deposited along his banks in such quantities as to occasion a serious nuisance, and that such deposit was a trespass on his land. *Held*, as to the first complaint, that a riparian owner is entitled to the flow of the stream past his land in a natural state of purity, undeteriorated by noxious matter discharged into it by others. The plaintiff could therefore maintain an action without proving that he had actually been damaged. As to the second complaint it was held that anyone who turns faecal matter or allows faecal matter collected by him or under his control to escape in a river in such manner or under such conditions that it is carried, whether by the current or the wind, on to his neighbour's land, is guilty of trespass.

If the action lies in nuisance a prescriptive right acquired for 20 years' usage provides a defence, but not if the discharge is illegal by reason of any of the pollution prevention statutes.[51]

23-17 Any authority is responsible at common law in the same way as any private person for the escape of its sewage to the injury of others, whether the injury consists of fouling the water of a river in the infringement of the rights of riparian owners, or of in the deposit of offensive matter on their land.[52] In earlier cases a distinction has been drawn between the non-feasance and the misfeasance of authorities where the authority has inherited drains constructed by a predecessor,[53] but in the light of *Pride of Derby and Derbyshire Angling Association Ltd. and Another* v. *Derby Celanese Ltd. and Others*[54] it is doubtful whether this distinction now has

[50] [1911] 1 Ch. 393.
[51] *Hulley* v. *Silver Springs Bleaching and Dyeing Co. Ltd.* [1922] 2 Ch. 268.
[52] *Supra.* n. 50.
[53] *Glossop* v. *Heston and Isleworth Local Board* (1879) 12 Ch.D. 102; *Att.-Gen.* v. *Dorking Guardians* (1882) 20 Ch. D. 595; *Robinson* v. *Workington Corporation* [1897] 1 Q.B. 619; *Hesketh* v. *Birmingham Corporation* [1924] 1 K.B. 260.
[54] [1953] Ch. 149.

relevance in an action founded on nuisance. This case, and the principles of non-feasance and misfeasance, are considered in Chapter 10.

Authorities (including water authorities) cannot plead as a defence that they are performing duties imposed upon them under Part II of the Public Health Act 1936 (which, *inter alia*, deals with the powers and duties of authorities in relation to sewers and sewage disposal). Section 30 of that Act reads:

> Nothing in this Part of this Act shall authorise a local authority to construct or use any public or other sewer, or any drain or outfall, for the purpose of conveying foul water into any natural or artificial stream, watercourse, canal, pond or lake, until the water has been so treated as not to affect prejudicially the purity and quality of the water in the stream, watercourse, canal, pond or lake.

Neither is it a defence for any discharger to prove that consent to the polluting discharge has been granted under the Control of Pollution Act 1974. The consents absolve him merely from criminal liability. A riparian owner and anyone claiming under him can still sue for damages and for an injunction.

C. LAND DRAINAGE[55]

Authorities

23-18   A duty falls to the water authority to exercise a general supervision over all matters of land drainage in its area.[56] Each water authority is required to establish a regional land drainage committee, consisting of a chairman and a number of other members appointed by the Minister, two members appointed by the water authority and a number of members appointed by or on behalf of constituent councils.[57] It falls to the regional land drainage committee to submit to the water authority a local land drainage scheme for the creation of local land drainage districts and for the constitution of local land drainage committees.[58]

The functions of the water authority in regard to land drainage are exercised by regional land drainage committees, except the making of drainage charges, the levying of precepts[59], the borrowing of money and the making of an application for a water charges option order. The water authority may give directions to the regional land drainage committee on matters affecting materially the water authority's overall water policy— but directions may not be given in relation to internal drainage functions.[60]

---

[55] Most of the law on this subject has been consolidated in the Land Drainage Act 1976, as amended by the Local Government Act 1985, Scheds. 7 and 17.
[56] Land Drainage Act 1976, s. 1: and see § 23–29, below.
[57] *Ibid.* s. 2; Sched. 1.
[58] *Ibid.* ss. 4 and 5; Sched. 1.
[59] *Ibid.* s. 1.
[60] *Ibid.*

Within water authority areas are internal drainage districts, each with an internal drainage board. The board exercises general supervision over all matters relating to the drainage of land within its district, and has the powers and duties conferred on it by the Land Drainage Act, 1976.[61]

The Thames River (Prevention of Floods) Acts 1879–1962, the Thames **23-19** Barrier and Flood Protection Act 1972, and the Land Drainage Act 1976 confer powers and impose duties on the councils of London boroughs in relation to flood works, flood protection and land drainage.[62] The functions of the Greater London Council as the principal land drainage and flood prevention authority in the London Excluded Area, and in relation to the Thames Barrier, were transferred to the Thames Water Authority by order under the Local Government Act 1985.[63]

Functions

Water authorities and those authorities operating under their overall **23-20** supervision have the following general responsibilities:[64]

(a) to maintain existing works, that is to say, to cleanse, repair or otherwise maintain in a due state of efficiency any existing watercourse or drainage work;

(b) to improve any existing works, that is to say, to deepen, widen, straighten or otherwise improve any existing watercourse, or remove or alter mill dams, weirs or other obstructions to watercourses, or raise, widen or otherwise improve any existing drainage work;

(c) to construct new works, that is to say, to make any new watercourses or drainage work or erect any machinery or do any other act not already referred to, required for the drainage of the area comprised within their district.

These authorities have powers to secure the proper flow of water- **23-21** courses,[65] they may enforce obligations arising from tenure, custom, prescription or otherwise to repair watercourses, bridges and drainage works,[66] and they have power with the consent of the Minister of Agriculture, Fisheries and Food to commute such obligations,[67] and, in relation to a main river, there is a duty to commute.[68]

A water authority has power to maintain, improve or construct **23-22** drainage works for the purpose of defence against sea water or tidal

---

[61] Land Drainage Act 1976, ss. 6 and 7; Sched. 2.
[62] See Land Drainage Act 1976, Sched. 5, and London Government Act 1963, s. 62(2), Sched. 14, paras. 7, 15(1).
[63] ss. 11(2), 103.
[64] Land Drainage Act 1976, s. 17. As to powers of entry, see *Pattinson* v. *Finningley Internal Drainage Board* [1970] 2 Q.B. 33.
[65] *Ibid.* s. 18.
[66] *Ibid.* s. 24.
[67] *Ibid.* s. 26.
[68] *Ibid.* A "main river map" or maps are kept by water authorities under the Water Act 1973, Sched. 2, Part II.

water, and this power is exercisable anywhere in the water authority's area, whether or not the works are in connection with a main river.[69]

Compensation and tortious liability

23-23   If injury is caused through the use of the general powers conferred by section 17 of the Act of 1976 the authority or board is liable to make compensation. This is the only remedy available to a person who suffers injury (this term includes injury and damage to land) unless he can prove negligence in the *manner of carrying out the work*: he may then have an action in tort.

> *Marriage* v. *East Norfolk Rivers Catchment Board*.[70] The Board had dredged the River Waveney in the exercise of a statutory power and had deposited the spoil on the south bank, raising the level of the bank. This prevented the water at a time of flood from escaping over the south bank as had happened before, and as a consequence a by-pass channel on the north side received an abnormal spate, which swept away the plaintiff's bridge. The plaintiff claimed damages for nuisance, alternatively for negligence. *Held*, the injury was of the kind contemplated in the Act, and the plaintiff's sole remedy was therefore a claim for compensation. On the question of negligence, Singleton L.J. said[71]: "It seems to me that in order to establish a right of action against the catchment board the plaintiff must prove affirmatively that there was negligence in the manner of carrying out the work which had been undertaken.... In such circumstances, the damage would be shown to arise from the negligence of those carrying out the work rather than from the operations authorised by the section." His Lordship then added this comment: "It may be questionable how far it is worth while going into such matter in any particular case if the person who has sustained damage can recover full compensation under section 34(3)."

23-24   The functions referred to are permissive functions, and in *East Suffolk Catchment Board* v. *Kent and Another*[72] it was held that since the Board operated under a permissive power and not under an imperative duty it could not be made liable for damages sustained through a failure to exercise that power. The authority of this case must now be in some doubt since *Anns* v. *Merton London Borough Council*[73] where it was held that despite the fact that there was a statutory power rather than a duty it did not follow that failure to act could not constitute a breach of duty of care and that it was irrelevant to the existence of the duty of care whether what was created was a duty or a power. The *East Suffolk* case may have been correctly decided on its own particular facts but the propositions of law made therein must now be suspect.

Drainage rates

23-25   The expenses of an internal drainage board, in so far as they are not met by contributions from a water authority, are raised by means of

---

[69] Land Drainage Act 1976, s. 17.
[70] [1950] 1 K.B. 284.
[71] At p. 299.
[72] [1941] A.C. 74.
[73] See further §§ 10–31 to 10–35.

drainage rates. These are of two kinds: (a) an owner's drainage rate, which is raised for the purpose of defraying expenses incurred in connection with new works or the improvement of existing works and any contributions to be made by the drainage board to the water authority; and (b) an occupier's drainage rate, a rate raised for the purpose of defraying any other expenses or charges. The whole rate is levied in the first instance on the occupier, and he in turn is entitled to recover from the owner the amount of the owner's drainage rate.[74] In certain circumstances the rate may be levied on the owner instead of the occupier.[75] In an urban area the rating authority may pay to the board the sum that would otherwise have been levied on occupiers in the urban area.[76] In certain circumstances a water authority may contribute to the expenses of an internal drainage board,[77] and a local authority may contribute to the expenses of a drainage authority in carrying out drainage works, to an extent thought proper having regard to the public benefit to be derived from them.[78] Grants may be paid by the Minister of Agriculture, Fisheries and Food towards the cost of drainage schemes.[79]

Drainage charges

The Land Drainage Act 1976[80] enables water authorities to levy a **23-26** drainage charge on agricultural land and agricultural buildings within that part of their areas which does not fall within an internal drainage district. Provision is also made for the making of a special drainage charge in respect of particular works carried out to watercourses in accordance with a scheme prepared by the authority and approved by the Minister. A scheme must be one which the authority considers necessary in the interests of agriculture.

Precepts

A water authority's main income for drainage purposes is derived from **23-27** precepts on the councils of non-metropolitan counties, metropolitan districts and London boroughs, the amount being calculated by reference to the penny rate product of so much of their areas as lies within the authority's area.[81] Internal drainage boards are required to make such contributions towards the expenses of the water authority as the water authority considers fair,[82] and grants may be paid by the Minister of

[74] Land Drainage Act 1976, ss. 63 and 72.
[75] *Ibid.* s. 73.
[76] *Ibid.* s. 81.
[77] *Ibid.* s. 84.
[78] *Ibid.* s. 102.
[79] *Ibid.* s. 91.
[80] ss. 48–61.
[81] *Ibid.* s. 45, as amended by the local Government Act 1985, Sched 7, para. 5; s. 46, as amended by the Local Government, Planning and Land Act 1980, s. 181.
[82] *Ibid.* s. 84.

Agriculture, Fisheries and Food towards expenses incurred in the improvement of existing works or the construction of new works.[83]

A water authority may also issue precepts on internal drainage boards.[84]

Charges option orders

23–28   A water authority may apply to the Minister of Agriculture, Fisheries and Food for a "water charges option order" to be made. Once such an order is made, the water authority will no longer issue precepts or impose general drainage charges, but will raise revenue by charging for services performed, facilities provided or rights made available.[85]

Powers of local authorities

23–29   The councils of counties and London boroughs and the Common Council have certain powers in relation to land drainage. They may undertake schemes for the drainage of small areas where they consider that the land is capable of improvement by drainage works and where the constitution for that purpose of an internal drainage district would not be practicable. Before works are undertaken the council must prepare a scheme setting out, *inter alia*, the estimated cost of the works, the maximum amount recoverable by the authority in respect of those expenses, and the manner in which it is proposed to apportion the expenses. The relevant water authority must be consulted. If there are objections the confirmation of the Secretary of State is required, and he may cause a public inquiry to be held into the objections or give objectors an opportunity of being heard.[86] The power to make schemes under this provision is exercisable by water authorities as well as by local authorities.[87]

The councils of the above-mentioned local authorities and district councils have the powers of drainage boards in relation to the maintenance of watercourses under section 18 of the Land Drainage Act 1976, subject to prior notice of the exercise of any such power being given to the appropriate internal drainage board or water authority.[88] The councils of districts and London boroughs have the powers of drainage boards to undertake drainage works against flooding.[89] The consent of the water authority is required for drainage works affecting a watercourse.

---

[83] Land Drainage Act 1976, s. 90.
[84] *Ibid.* s. 85.
[85] *Ibid.* s. 62. And see Water Act 1973, ss. 29–32.
[86] *Ibid.* s. 100.
[87] *Ibid.* ss. 30, 31.
[88] *Ibid.* s. 97.
[89] *Ibid.* s. 98, as amended by the Local Government Act 1985, Sched. 7, para. 6. Certain powers are also available to non-metropolitan county councils.

D. COAST PROTECTION

Coast protection authorities under the Coast Protection Act 1949 are **23-30** the councils of maritime districts.[90] Coast protection authorities are given a general power to carry out such protective works as they consider necessary or expedient and to acquire land, by agreement or compulsorily.[91] This general power merely confers a *capacity* to do what would otherwise be beyond the powers of the authority. A council cannot, in exercising these general powers, do something which apart from these powers would be actionable.

Public notice must be given by an authority proposing to undertake **23-31** coast protection works, other than works of repair and maintenance or urgently needed works, and provision is made for the holding of public inquiries by the Minister[92] where objections are lodged and not withdrawn.[93]

Where in the opinion of an authority works of repair or maintenance are necessary the authority may serve notice on the owner and occupier specifying the works to be done: if they default, or if the works become urgently necessary, the authority may take the necessary steps and may recover the cost from the owner or occupier. There is a right of appeal to a magistrates' court against the requirements of a notice served under this provision.[94]

The consent of the coast protection authority is required to carry out any coast protection work and an authority has power to cause the removal or alteration of works which are undertaken without consent.[95]

For the safety of navigation the consent of the Department of Trade may be required for coast protection works to be carried out below high-water-mark of ordinary spring tides.[96]

The Minister has power to make grants towards the cost of coast protection works,[97] and may exercise default powers where a coast protection authority has failed to take sufficient protective measures.[98]

---

[90] Coast Protection Act 1949, s. 1; Local Government Act 1972, Sched. 29, para. 17.

[91] Coast Protection Act, ss. 4, 5, 14. See *Webb* v. *Minister of Housing and Local Government* [1965] 1 W.L.R. 755, where a compulsory purchase order was held to be invalid, in that it was proposed to acquire a strip of land not entirely for coast protection but for the inclusion of a promenade.

[92] By the Transfer of Functions (Secretary of State and Minister of Agriculture, Fisheries and Food) Order 1985 (S.I. 1985 No. 442), the functions of the Secretary of State under the 1949 Act were transferred to the Minister.

[93] The procedure to be followed is prescribed in the Coast Protection (Notices) Regulations 1950 (S.I. 1950 No. 124).

[94] Coast Protection Act 1949, ss. 12 and 13.

[95] *Ibid.* s. 16.

[96] *Ibid.* ss. 34 and 35, and the Transfer of Functions (Shipping and Construction of Ships) Order 1965 (S.I. 1965 No. 145).

[97] Coast Protection Act 1949, ss. 20 and 21; Local Government Act 1972, Sched. 29, para. 17.

[98] Coast Protection Act, s. 29; Local Government Act 1972, Sched. 30.

Chapter 24

LOCAL LAND CHARGES

24-01   Local authorities in a variety of ways acquire charges against privately owned land which cast a responsibility on the owners for the payment of certain expenses or oblige them to observe conditions or restrictions in the use of the land. Under the system of local land charges many of these incumbrances are registrable, and where they are registrable they are binding upon those who subsequently acquire the land whether or not they actually search in the register and whether or not the charge has actually been registered. Under this system prospective purchasers are enabled, by means of a search of the register, to find out whether certain burdens attach to the land they propose to buy. It may be noted in passing that the registration of local land charges forms part of a wider system. There are other charges and incumbrances which run with the land and which are registrable at H.M. Land Registry by the Chief Land Registrar. The charges registered there are broadly those which run with the land but which may not be revealed when title is being investigated. Local land charges are not registrable in the Land Charges Register.[1]

The law relating to this subject is contained in the Local Land Charges Act 1975[2] and the rules made thereunder.[3] It is the duty of each registering authority (district councils, London borough councils, and the Common Council of the City of London) to keep the local land charges register and an index whereby all registered entries can readily be traced.[4] Neither the register nor the index need be kept in documentary form.[5]

Registrable charges

24-02   A charge is a local land charge if it falls within any of the categories set out in section 1 of the 1975 Act provided it does not fall within any of the exclusionary categories set out in section 2. These charges may be summarised as follows:

(i)   Any charge acquired before or after August 1, 1977, by a local

---

[1] Land Charges Act 1925, s. 2(4), (5), as amended by the Local Land Charges Act 1975, s. 17.
[2] The system of local land charges was altered considerably in consequence of the Law Commission's Report on Local Land Charges (Law. Com. No. 62, 1974) which led to the introduction of the Local Land Charges Act 1975. The Act came into force on August 1, 1977 (S.I. 1977 No. 984). For a detailed and practical exposition of the system, see J. F. Garner, *Local Land Charges* (9th ed.) and see [1976] 40 Conv. 106.
[3] Local Land Charges Rules 1977 (S.I. 1977 No. 985), as amended by S.I. 1978 No. 1638 and S.I. 1985 No. 221.
[4] Local Land Charges Act 1975, ss. 3 and 16(1).
[5] *Ibid.* s. 3(3), as substituted by the Local Government (Miscellaneous Provisions) Act 1982, s. 34.

authority, water authority or new town development corporation under the Public Health Acts, the Highways Act 1980, or the Building Act 1984, or a similar charge under any other Act being a charge which is binding on successive owners of the land affected by the charge.

(ii) Prohibitions and restrictions on the use of land which are binding on successive owners and are imposed or enforceable by a local authority or government department.

(iii) Positive obligations affecting land that are enforceable by a Minister of the Crown, government department or local authority under agreements and covenants made after August 1, 1977, and which are binding on successive owners.

(iv) Any other charges expressly made local land charges under any other statutory provision.

A sum recoverable from successive owners or occupiers under (i) above is to be treated as a charge whether the sum is expressed to be a charge on the land or not.[6] This provision avoids a difficulty experienced under earlier law—now all registrable interests are local land charges and there is no registrable interests which are by statute "deemed" to be so. A charge registered under (i) above takes effect as if it had been created by a deed of charge by way of legal mortgage within the meaning of the Law of Property Act 1925, but without prejudice to its priority.[7] This appears to have the effect of tpreserving the view that such a charge is a charge on the property and not on the interests therein and accordingly such a charge can take priority over earlier incumbrances and interests.[8]

Exclusions
There are eight matters stated in the Act not to be local land charges[9]:   **24-03**

(a) a prohibition or restriction enforceable under a covenant or agreement made between a lessor and a lessee;

(b) a positive obligation enforceable under a covenant or agreement made between a lessor and a lessee;

(c) a prohibition or restriction enforceable by a Minister of the Crown, government department or local authority under any covenant or agreement, being a prohibition or restriction binding on successive owners of the land affected by reason of the fact that the covenant or agreement is made for the benefit of land of the Minister, government department or local authority;

---

[6] Local Land Charges Act 1975, s. 1(2).
[7] s. 7; Law of Property Act 1925, s. 101.
[8] *Paddington Borough Council* v. *Finucane* [1928] Ch. 567; *Westminster City Council* v. *Haymarket Publishing Ltd.* [1981] 1 W.L.R. 677 (rating surcharge held to take priority over mortgage). This does not affect building society mortgages, however, which cannot be given on security of land subject to a prior charge. It is statutorily provided that a prior charge, in favour of a local authority under an Act of Parliament or an instrument made under an Act does not prevent a building society loan: Building Societies Act 1962, s. 32 and Sched. 5.
[9] s. 2.

(d)   a prohibition or restriction embodied by any by-laws;

(e)   a condition or limitation subject to which planning permission was granted at any time before August 1, 1977 or was or is (at any time) deemed to be granted under any statutory provision relating to town and country planning, whether by a Minister of the Crown, government department or local authority;

(f)   a prohibition or restriction embodied in a scheme under the Town and Country Planning Act 1932 or any enactment repealed by that Act;

(g)   a prohibition or restriction enforceable under a forestry dedication covenant entered into pursuant to section 5 of the Forestry Act 1967;

(h)   a prohibition or restriction affecting the whole of any of the following areas:

     (i)   England, Wales or England and Wales;

     (ii)   England, or England and Wales, with the exception of, or of any part of, Greater London;

     (iii)   Greater London.

Local land charges register

24-04   There are 12 parts to the register: they are listed in the Local Land Charges Rules made by the Lord Chancellor.[10] These rules deal with the form and contents of the register, scales of fees and other administrative arrangements. In addition to placing the duty to keep the register on the registering authority the Act makes it the duty of any body or person (called the "originating authority") entitled to the benefit of a charge to apply to have the charge registered.[11] The originating authority is defined as "the Minister of the Crown, government department, local authority or other person by whom the charge is brought into existence or by whom, on its coming into existence, the charge is enforceable."[12] As will be noted in the paragraph which follows, several statutory bodies have registrable rights, as do individuals.[13]

Contents of the register[14]

24-05   *Part 1.* General charges falling within section 6(2) of the 1975 Act and any scheme registrable by virtue of the Coast Protection Act 1949 which does not specify the person by whom the coast protection charges are to be paid. Under section 6(2) at any time before a specific charge comes into existence a general charge may be made against the land. A provisional apportionment under the private street works code is an example of a general charge.[15]

Part 2. Specific financial charges falling within (i) in the list of registrable charges set out in paragraph 24–02 above, or a scheme falling within section 8(8) or 13(6) of the Coast Protection Act 1949 which specifies the persons by whom the coast protection charges are to be paid.

---

[10] S.I. 1977 No. 985, *supra.*

[11] s. 5(1), (2).

[12] s. 5(4).

[13] In particular see Parts 8, 9 and 11 of the register.

[14] S.I. 1977 No. 985, *supra*, r. 3, and see the definition in r. 2.

[15] See § 14–33.

A final apportionment under the private street works code[16] and rating surcharges[17] are examples of charges registrable under this Part.

Part 3. Planning charges which are charges (not falling within section 54(6) of the Town and Country Planning Act 1971 relating to lists of buildings of special architectural or historical interest) which are

(a) prohibitions, restrictions or conditions on the use of land by virtue of any provisions of the Act of 1971 imposed *after* August 1, 1977, the Community Land Act 1975 or any other statutory provision relating to town and country planning;

(b) notices deposited under section 158 of the Act of 1971 (registration of compensation);

(c) resolutions passed under section 23(2) of the Act of 1975 (disposal notification areas); or

(d) notices of intention to acquire land under paragraph 4 or 5 of Schedule 7 to the Act of 1975.

Part 4. Miscellaneous charges being those not made registrable in any other part of the register.

Part 5. Charges falling within section 8(4) of the Agriculture (Miscellaneous Provisions) Act 1941 ("fenland ways maintenance charges").

Part 6. Charges falling within section 8(4) and section 52(8) of the Land Compensation Act 1973 ("land compensation charges").

Part 7. Charges falling within section 1(4) or 9 of the New Towns Act 1965[18] ("new towns charges").

Part 8. Charges falling within section 33 of the Civil Aviation Act 1949, section 21 of the Civil Aviation Act 1968 and section 16(2) of the Civil Aviation Act 1971 ("civil aviation charges").[19]

Part 9. Charges falling within section 11(1) or 16(6) of the Opencast Coal Act 1958 ("opencast coal charges").

Part 10. Charges falling within section 54(6) of the Town and Country Planning Act 1971 ("listed building charges").

Part 11. Charges falling within section 2(4) of the Rights of Light Act 1959 ("light obstruction notices").

Part 12. Charges falling within section 31(4) of the Land Drainage Act 1976 ("drainage scheme charges").

Effect of non-registration

The Local Land Charges Act 1975 altered the law in regard to the **24–06** effect of non-registration, about which there had formerly been some doubt.[20] Some charges were enforceable notwithstanding non-registration and non-financial charges could be reimposed. The effect of non-

---

[16] See § 14–33.
[17] See § 8–33.
[18] See now the New Towns Act 1981, ss. 1(5) and 12.
[19] See now the Civil Aviation Act 1982, s. 55(1).
[20] See Law Commission's Report, above, at § 24–01.

registration of a financial charge was to avoid the charge but to leave the debt still recoverable. It is now provided in the Act[21] that failure to register a local land charge or failure to disclose a charge on an official certificate of the result of search shall not affect its enforceability. This system is then complemented by a system of compensation payable in certain situations.

Compensation

24–07   Compensation is available to a purchaser[22] for any loss he suffers in consequence of the charge not being registered in the appropriate register or not being disclosed by an official search certificate as registered in that register. It is provided that either a material personal search[23] or material official search[24] must be made before the relevant time and that in the case of the former search the charge was in existence but not registered, and in the case of the latter search the charge was in existence but (whether registered or not) was not shown on the official certificate of search.[25] Thus more protection is afforded if an official certificate of search is requisitioned. Generally speaking the relevant time is the time when a contract is made which preceded the acquisition of the interest in the land.[26] It follows therefore that compensation is available generally only to a purchaser who effects a search before making the contract and that search fails to disclose a charge which was in existence at the time of the search. The linking of the relevant time to the contract rather than the acquisition of the interest is more satisfactory since it accords with the conveyancing practice of making the contract subject to local land charge entries.[27]

The compensation is paid by the registering authority who will then have a right of recourse against an originating authority in certain

---

[21] s. 10(1).

[22] For the purposes of section 10 a person purchases land where, for valuable consideration, he acquires any interest in land or the proceeds of sale of land, and this includes cases where he acquires as lessee or mortgagee and cases where an interest is conveyed or assigned at his direction to another person (s. 10(3)(*a*)). See *Peffer* v. *Rigg* [1977] 1 W.L.R. 285, concerning a purchaser for valuable consideration within s. 3(xxi) of the Land Registration Act 1925.

[23] A personal search is material if it is made by or on behalf of the purchaser or, before the relevant time, the purchaser or his agent has knowledge of the result of it (s. 10(3)(*c*)).

[24] An official search is material if it is requisitioned by or on behalf of the purchaser or before the relevant time the purchaser or his agent has knowledge of the contents of the official search certificate (s. 10(3)(*d*)).

[25] s. 10(1)(*a*), (*b*). Under s. 10(1)(*aa*), as inserted by the Local Government (Miscellaneous Provisions) Act 1982, s. 34, where the register is kept otherwise than in documentary form (*i.e.* on a computer), and a material personal search is made before the relevant time, a right to compensation arises if the registering authority fails to make the portion of the register which the person wishes to examine available to inspection in visible and legible form (see s. 8(1A)).

[26] s. 10(3)(*b*).

[27] For difficulties in respect of local land charges entries see *Aquis Estates* v. *Minton* [1975] 1 W.L.R. 1452.

circumstances.[28] A county court has jurisdiction if the amount claimed is within its jurisdictional limits. If a claim is dismissed a claimant is not to be ordered to pay the authority's costs unless the action was unreasonable.[29] There are particular provisions where the claim relates to land subject to a mortgage or is held on trust for sale or is settled land.[30]

The amount of compensation which may be claimed is the amount of **24-08** loss suffered by reason of non-registration or non-disclosure. Probably all the common law rules of causation and mitigation will apply. If a purchaser discovers elsewhere the possibility of a charge and does not resolve an inconsistency with a search he has made, his compensation may be affected. This may, however, be a difficult view to uphold on a proper meaning of mitigation as opposed to causation.[31] A problem may occur in the measure of compensation in the case of non-financial charges.

An authority making payments cannot recover them from a third party unless under insurance or on the grounds of fraud.[32]

Discovering local land charges

A crucial matter is the time that a local land charge comes into **24-09** existence.[33] If the charge was not in existence at the time of the search, but comes into existence subsequent to the search but before the contract, no compensation is payable. It is clear from the Act that a charge can come into existence before registration[34] and it is likely that a charge will come into existence by virtue of a resolution of the council or its creation by agreement. Some charges (*e.g.* town planning enforcement notices) will not come into force for a considerable time after the local authority's resolution. A purchaser's certificate of search therefore is only good on the day that the search is made. There is now no priority period in respect of the search, and the certificate of search reveals entries up to and including the day of the certificate,[35] but advance warning may be obtained through the supplementary enquiries customarily made by an intending purchaser, referred to below.

---

[28] s. 10(4) and (5). By s. 10(5) the registering authority can recover from the originating authority if an application is not made in time for it to be practicable for the registering authority to avoid incurring liability for compensation. By r. 5 it is regarded as practicable for a registering authority to register a charge on the day on which the application is delivered or deemed to be delivered. If delivered between the time when an office closes and it next re-opens, the application is deemed to be delivered immediately after the time when the office is closed.

[29] s. 10(8) and (9).

[30] s. 11.

[31] See J. E. Adams, [1976] 40 Conv. 119.

[32] s. 10(6).

[33] See J. E. Adams, [1976] 40 Conv. 118.

[34] See s. 10(1)(*a*) and (*b*).

[35] See Form C in the rules.

Searches

24-10   A search may be made in person.[36] It is more common, however, to make an official search, a requisition for which is made in writing on the form prescribed by the rules.[37] No other form may be used.[38] Office copies of the entries are available,[39] and such office copies are admissible evidence to the same extent that the original would be.[40] A solicitor or trustee, personal representative, agent or other person in a fiduciary position is not answerable for any loss occasioned by reliance on an erroneous official search certificate or erroneous office copy entry.[41]

Registered land

24-11   Local land charges are overriding interests until protected on the register of the title in question.[42] Local land charges are not generally entered on the register and accordingly a search is required in the local land charges register just as if the title were unregistered.[43]

Supplementary enquiries

24-12   It is common practice for intending purchasers to make a number of supplementary enquiries of the registering authority. This is done on a form agreed between the Law Society and the local authority associations, and an agreed fee is charged. As the transaction is based on a contract (in contrast with searches in the local land charges register, which depend on statute) the local authority is able to include in the form a disclaimer of legal liability. It is stated that the information given in the replies is on the distinct understanding that neither the district council nor the county council nor any officer of either council, is legally responsible for it except for negligence.[44]

---

[36] s. 8.
[37] s. 9 and r. 11.
[38] r. 13.
[39] r. 12.
[40] s. 12. Any reference in the Act to an office copy of an entry includes a reference to the reproduction of an entry in a register kept on a computer: see s. 16(1A), inserted by the Local Government (Miscellaneous Provisions) Act 1982, s. 34.
[41] s. 13.
[42] s. 70(1)(*i*), Land Registration Act 1925.
[43] See also s. 10(3)(*b*).
[44] See hereon § 10–42 and J. F. Garner, *Local Land Charges* (9th ed. 1982), at p. 94.

CHAPTER 25

WATER SUPPLY

IN considering the law with respect to water supply it is necessary to have regard to the law which applied before April 1, 1974. Until that date responsibility fell to statutory water undertakers—these included water companies, local authorities and joint water boards.[1]

A. THE SYSTEM PRIOR TO APRIL 1, 1974

Water companies

Many of the older water companies were incorporated by private Acts **25-02** of Parliament. It was the normal practice for these Acts to adopt the provisions of the Waterworks Clauses Acts 1847 and 1863 relating to the supply of water, provisions of the Companies Clauses Acts 1845–89 governing the conduct of companies' affairs, and provisions of the Lands Clauses Act 1845–83 containing powers to acquire land.

A simpler method of establishing water companies was later provided by the Gas and Water Facilities Acts 1870–73. This was by a provisional order confirmed by Parliament, followed by incorporation under the current Companies Act. The provisional order would normally adopt provisions of the Clauses Acts.

The adoption of sections of the Clauses Acts, and the use of similar provisions in private Acts, resulted in a fairly uniform code. Moreover, the Secretary of State was empowered to repeal or amend provisions of local enactments relating to the supply of water,[2] a process by which further uniformity could be achieved. Finally, some of the provisions of the Water Acts 1945–58 applied to the companies.

Local authorities and joint water boards

Many local authorities were also statutory water undertakers. Some **25-03** derived powers from private Acts of Parliament, usually adopting provisions of the Waterworks Clauses Acts. The Public Heath Act 1936 and the Water Acts 1945–58 gave powers to all local authorities who were statutory water undertakers and to joint water boards, and imposed duties on local authorities to ensure adequate supplies and empowered them to supply water. Incorporated in the power to supply were parts of the code contained in the Waterworks Clauses Acts. The powers and duties of these public authorities were governed principally by the Water Act 1945,

---

[1] See the definition given in the Water Act 1948, s. 1.
[2] Water Act 1945, s. 33, and Water Act 1973, Sched. 6, para. 15.

Sched. 3, but many still retained powers granted by local Acts of Parliament, and some gained further powers by more recent local Acts.

B. The System after April 1, 1974

25-04 The new system of water management introduced by the Water Act 1973 has already been considered.[3] So far as water supply is concerned, the Secretary of State for the Environment[4] exercises powers of general supervision, and the regional water authorities[5] are the principal executive bodies. Local authorities lost their powers to supply water, but the water companies and joint authorities remained in existence to supply water on behalf of the water authorities.

25-05 Under the Act, the Secretary of State for the Environment and the Minister of Agriculture, Fisheries and Food have a duty to promote jointly a national policy for water, and the Secretary of State is to secure the execution of that policy so far as it relates to "the conservation, augmentation, distribution and proper use of water resources, and the provision of water supplies."[6] To enable him to secure the effective execution of this part of the national policy he is empowered to give directions of a general character to water authorities.[7]

Water authorities

25-06 Water authorities must take such steps as they consider necessary or expedient, or as directed under the Water Resources Act 1963[8] or Water Act 1973,[9] to conserve, redistribute or augment water resources in their areas, to secure the proper use of those resources or to transfer them to the areas of other water authorities.[10] For this purpose they have the power to license abstractions of water within their areas,[11] to receive water in bulk from other persons within their areas, and to transfer water in bulk to or from other statutory water undertakers.[12] If it appears to the Secretary of State that it is expedient that one water authority should give to another a supply of water in bulk, and the transfer cannot be secured by agreement, he may require that the arrangement be made, and on a complaint made to him he may exercise certain default powers.

---

[3] See § 23–02 above.

[4] The Secretary of State for Wales for the area of the Welsh National Water Development Authority.

[5] The Welsh National Water Development Authority for Wales.

[6] Water Act 1973, s. 1.

[7] *Ibid.* s. 5.

[8] ss. 105, 107 and Water Act 1973, s. 9(*a*).

[9] ss. 5(2) and (3), 11(5), 24(11).

[10] Water Act 1973, s. 10.

[11] Water Resources Act 1963, ss. 23–25. There are certain exceptions and persons entitled to licences as of right.

[12] Water Act 1945, ss. 12, 13 and 13A, as substituted by the Water Act 1973, Sched. 4, para. 12.

It is the duty of every water authority itself to supply water in its area,[13] except that where any part of its area is within the limits of supply of a statutory water company the authority must supply water through that company.[14] In the latter case the authority must take all reasonable steps to make available to the company sufficient water to enable it to meet foreseeable demands of consumers within its area of supply.[15]

Statutory water companies

Each water authority is required to enter into an arrangement with   **25-07** every statutory water company whose limits of supply fall wholly or partly within the authority's area.[16] Under the arrangement the company is to undertake to supply water within the limits of its supply on behalf of the authority. The arrangement is to provide for such incidental, supplementary and consequential matters as the authority thinks desirable and may include provision (a) for the management or operation of sources of supply, (b) for the supply of water in bulk by or to the company, and (c) for the company's charges for the supply of water.[17]

In default of agreement between the parties, the Secretary of State is empowered to settle the arrangement, but is required to fix the company's charges so that it can make a reasonable return on paid-up capital.[18]

The duties of the water company under the arrangement may be enforced by default powers exercised by the water authority. On a complaint being made to the authority, or where it considers that an investigation is necessary, it may cause a local inquiry to be held. The authority may thereafter declare the company to be in default, direct them to remedy the default, and on a failure to do so transfer to itself such functions of the company as it thinks fit.[19]

The acquisition of further powers[20]

The Secretary of State may by order confer additional powers on   **25-08** statutory water undertakers, including water authorities, authorising the carrying out of works of construction or alteration, the raising of capital and the borrowing of money, and land may be acquired by agreement with his approval, or compulsorily by means of a compulsory purchase order. A licence from the water authority is required by undertakers to abstract water from any source of supply or to commence works for the impounding of water.[21]

---

[13] Water Act 1973, s. 11(1).
[14] *Ibid.* s. 12(1).
[15] *Ibid.* s. 12(7).
[16] *Ibid.* s. 12(2).
[17] *Ibid.* s. 12(3).
[18] *Ibid.* s. 12(4) and (6).
[19] *Ibid.* Sched. 4, para. 13(2) (4) and (6).
[20] Water Act 1945, ss. 23–25, as amended by the Water Act 1948 and the Water Act 1973, s. 11(6).
[21] Water Resources Act 1963, Pt. IV; Water Act 1973, s. 9.

The Drought Act 1976, ss. 1 and 2, enables the Secretary of State to give temporary powers to meet supply deficiencies in time of drought. An order under section 1 may authorise, *inter alia*, the taking of water from a specified source for a period not exceeding six months, or may suspend for a similar period any restriction or obligation to which an undertaker is subject as to the taking of water from any source, the discharge of compensation water,[22] or filtration or other treatment. An order conferring additional powers may be made where the deficiency threatens to impair the economic or social well-being of persons in an area. Such an order remains in force for no longer than three months but orders under both sections 1 and 2 can be extended. Water taken or impounded by virtue of such an order is treated as if authorised by a licence granted by the water authority.[23] The Secretary of State may by order enable an undertaker for a period not exceeding six months to supply water by means of stand-pipes or water tanks and to erect this equipment in any street. The procedure to be followed in the making of orders is given in the First Schedule to the Act.[24]

25-09   By-laws may be made for preventing waste, undue consumption, misuse and contamination and pollution of water.[25] A model code is issued by the Secretary of State and generally speaking he will confirm only those by-laws which conform to this code.

The obligation to supply

25-10   Water companies are not under statutory obligation to supply water, except by means of hydrants for extinguishing fires, for cleansing sewers and for certain other public purposes.[26] Their duties to supply water are those set out in the arrangements with the water authorities.

Water authorities are under a duty to supply water for domestic purposes to premises within their areas, and in this they are governed by the Water Act 1945, Sched. 3, Parts VII and IX.[27] They must lay mains for that purpose if owners or occupiers of premises require it and agree to take a supply of water for at least three years, provided the aggregate annual water rates payable in respect of those premises are not less than one-eighth of the cost of laying the mains.[28] Under section 37(1) of the Water Act 1945, as amended by section 46 of the Housing Act 1949, an owner of land on which he proposes to erect buildings may require the water authority to lay necessary mains[29] for a supply of water needed for

---

[22] "Compensation water" is the term used to describe the regular flow of water which undertakers must ensure is sent down a river or stream from which they have abstracted water.
[23] Water Resources Act 1963, s. 128.
[24] See also the Drought Orders (Inquiry Procedure) Rules 1984 (S.I. 1984 No. 999).
[25] Water Act 1945, ss. 17–20; Water Act 1973, s. 36 and Sched. 7, Pt. II.
[26] Water Act 1973, s. 12(8); Water Act 1945, Sched. 3, Pt. VIII.
[27] Applied by the Water Act 1973, s. 11(7)(*b*).
[28] Water Act 1945, Sched. 3, Pt. VII, para. 29.
[29] See *Royco Homes Ltd.* v. *Southern Water Authority* [1979] 1 W.L.R. 1366.

domestic purposes to such point as will enable the buildings to be connected at a reasonable cost. The authority may require the owner to undertake to pay an annual contribution towards the cost of providing and laying the necessary mains and to make an initial deposit in respect of the cost. An owner or occupier may undertake to lay a supply pipe at his own expense.[30] If it is not practicable to supply water in pipes, but it is practicable at a reasonable cost to supply it otherwise, the water authority is under a duty to do so, bringing it within a reasonable distance of the premises concerned.[31]

The authorities must cause water in all pipes giving supplies for domestic purposes, or on which hydrants are fixed, to be laid on constantly and at such pressure as will cause the water to reach the top of the top-most storey of every building in its area. But this is subject to the proviso that they are not required to deliver water at a height greater than that to which it will flow by gravitation through the mains from a service reservoir or tank, and the authority may determine from which reservoir or tank the supply shall be taken.[32] Where the authority is required to supply water in pipes for domestic purposes, it must be sufficient for those purposes.[33]

All water supplied for domestic purposes must be wholesome.[34] An **25-11** authority which supplies unwholesome water may be liable in damages to persons who suffer injury. The principles involved are considered at length in *Read and Another* v. *Croydon Corporation*,[35] a summary of which appears at paragraph 25–12. Liability may be founded in the first place on the failure of the undertaking to discharge its statutory obligation, notwithstanding the fact that penalties are prescribed in the statute for such a failure. As will have been noted in Chapter 10 under the heading "Failure to perform statutory duties," it is a fairly general rule that if a statute prescribes a remedy it is to be the only remedy available, but that each statute must be examined as a whole. The *Croydon* case has decided this issue in relation to an undertaker's duty in regard to the supply of wholesome water—an action for damages will lie based on the failure of an undertaking to discharge this obligation.

In the second place, an action may lie at common law founded on the **25-12** failure of the undertaking to discharge its common law duty to exercise care to prevent an injury to consumers from a cause known to the undertaking or which ought to have been known to the undertaking. This

---

[30] Water Act 1945, Sched. 3, Pt. X. [31] Water Act 1973, s. 11(3).
[32] Water Act 1945, Sched. 3, Pt. IX, para. 39. [33] *Ibid.* Sched. 3, Pt. VII, para. 31.
[34] *Ibid.* as applied by the Water Act 1973, s. 11(7)(*b*). The words "pure" and "wholesome" were considered in *Att.-Gen of New Zealand* v. *Lower Hutt Corporation* [1964] A.C. 1469, a Privy Council case. It was held that the addition of fluoride added no impurity to already pure water. *Cf. McColl* v. *Strathclyde Regional Council* [1984] J.P.L. 351, where the Court of Session held that fluoridation was *ultra vires* as it did not facilitate the supply of wholesome water. Express power to add fluoride to water supplies was conferred by the Water (Fluoridation) Act 1985.
[35] [1938] 4 All E.R. 631.

again was decided in the *Croydon* case, and it was held that an action in common law is not excluded merely because a statutory duty is identical with, or wider than, the common law duty.

> *Read and Another* v. *Croydon Corporation*.[36] The corporation supplied water under a private Act which incorporated provisions for the Waterworks Clauses Act 1847. Due to the negligence of the undertaking the water supply became contaminated with typhoid bacilli, and an epidemic broke out. The daughter of Mr. Read, the person who paid the water rate, contracted typhoid fever. The daughter claimed damages for the pain and suffering she had undergone and Mr. Read claimed damages for the expense to which he had been put. The plaintiffs alleged breach of contract, breach of statutory duty, and breach of common law duty. As to the first allegation it was held that the water was supplied under a statutory obligation and not under contract. There could be no claim therefore for breach of warranty, express or implied, that the water supplied should be pure. On the second allegation, the court considered (a) the class of persons to whom the duty is owed and (b) the nature of the duty. As to (a) it was held that the duty lay to the "persons entitled to demand and receive a sufficient supply of water for domestic purposes, having paid or tendered the water rate."[37] Mr. Read fell in this class and could succeed in this claim based on the failure to discharge a statutory duty. But the daughter was outside this class and her claim in this part was ill-founded. As to (b), the nature of the duty, the court held it not to be an absolute one. Stable J. said[38]: "I hold that the obligation on the corporation is not an absolute obligation, but is limited to the exercise of all reasonable care and skill to ensure that the water provided accords with the provisions of the Act. I have no doubt that the standard of care and skill required of an authority engaged on a matter so vital to public health is a high one, but, if that standard is maintained, I do not think that, on the true construction of the Act, the corporation can be held to be liable for the consequences of the presence in the water supplied by it at the point where it reaches the consumer of some impurity which no care or skill could have prevented."

25-13　　　　On the third allegation, it was held that an action could lie at common law and that Miss Read's claim under this head was well founded. The court rejected the contention of the corporation that the statutory remedy must be exclusive of any other remedy. Stable J. said[39]: "The scope of the two duties may have been identical, or the scope of the statutory duty may have been wider than that of the common law duty, but the class of persons to whom they were respectively owed was different, and their origin was different. The fact that a statute imposes a duty does not absolve the person on whom the duty is cast from his obligation in the performance of the duty to observe the common law rights of third persons, unless the statute expressly so provides. . . . Wholly apart from the statute, and irrespective of whether or not it imposed any duties, or of the scope of the duties, or of the class of persons to whom the duties were owed, if the corporation supplied water for drinking purposes to Mr. Read's house which they knew would be consumed by him and the members of his household and failed to exercise the requisite degree of care or skill in the course of that operation, with the result that what they supplied was not drinking water but poison, the person injured would, in my judgment, have a complete cause of action at common law for the damage sustained as a result of that negligence."

[36] [1938] 4 All E.R. 631.
[37] Waterworks Clauses Act 1847, s. 53.
[38] At p. 651.
[39] At p. 654.

The obligations of undertakers to consumers at common law were   **25-14**
considered further in the case which follows.

> *Barnes* v. *Irwell Valley Water Board*.[40] The Board supplied water to the
> plaintiffs: it was pure and wholesome in the Board's mains, but on its way from
> the mains to the plaintiff's premises it absorbed lead and became contaminated.
> *Held*, although the Board had fulfilled its statutory duty in that pure and
> wholesome water had been supplied in the mains it had failed in its common
> law duty to warn the plaintiffs of the danger arising from the fact that the water
> leaving the Board's mains passed through old leaden pipes which could render
> the water injurious to health. Greer L.J. said[41]: "They (the Board) were content
> with saying: 'When the water gets to the position where the tenant may insert
> his pipe and take it into his premises for consumption by means of a lead pipe,
> it exhausts all our responsibility in the matter. We are not responsible for
> anything that happens after that.' I think it would be lamentable if the law
> were such as to disable users of water for domestic purposes from saying that, if
> reasonable precautions had been taken, then the damage which occurred to the
> tenant and to his wife, who are the plaintiffs in this action, would never have
> happened. I think there is an obligation upon them that reasonable precautions
> should be taken." Slesser L.J. said[42]: "I think that they owed a duty to those
> persons who were closely and directly affected by their acts, to quote the
> language of Lord Atkin in *M'Allister* (or *Donoghue*) v. *Stevenson*[43] to take
> reasonable care to supply them with water which was proper in quality, or at
> least to warn them that it was not, and that it needed purification." The
> omission to warn constituted negligence, and the board was liable in damages.

A local authority may agree with a water authority to make periodic or   **25-15**
other payment, or to guarantee payment, on condition that the authority
provides a supply of water to a part of the authority's area and executes
any works that may be necessary.[44] Where payment of this kind is made
by a "receiving district" under the Town Development Act 1952 the
Secretary of State may make a grant to the authority.[45]

Water authorities have a duty to give a supply of water for non-   **25-16**
domestic purposes on reasonable terms and conditions, but are relieved of
this duty where they cannot meet their existing obligations to supply
water for *any purposes*, or probable future requirements to supply water
for *domestic purposes*, without incurring unreasonable expenditure on the
construction of new waterworks.[46]

Supplies of water for public purposes

Part VIII of the Third Schedule to the Water Act 1945 prescribes the   **25-17**
duty of water authorities in regard to the services to be given to fire
authorities—there is an obligation to fix and maintain fire hydrants to the
water mains at points convenient for fire fighting. The cost falls to the fire

---

[40] [1938] 2 All E.R. 650.
[41] At p. 656.
[42] At p. 660.
[43] [1932] A.C. 562 at p. 580.
[44] Public Health Act 1936, s. 123.
[45] Town Development Act 1952, s. 2(2).
[46] Water Act 1945, s. 27.

authority, but no charge may be made for the supply of water to extinguish fires.[47] In every pipe on which a hydrant is fixed the undertakers must provide a supply of water at an agreed rate and upon agreed terms and conditions for the cleansing of sewers and drains, for cleansing and watering highways and for supplying public pumps, baths and washhouses.[48] An authority which fails to comply with these requirements (unless prevented by an unavoidable cause) is liable to a fine not exceeding level 3 on the standard scale and to additional penalties for continuing default.[49]

25-18   If a person is aggrieved by the failure of an undertaking to discharge its duty *under these provisions* his only remedy is to proceed for the fine or penalty: he cannot bring an action for damages.

> *Atkinson* v. *Newcastle and Gateshead Waterworks Co.*[50] A brought an action against the Water Company for not keeping supply pipes charged as required by section 42 of the Waterworks Clauses Act 1847. Because of the lack of pressure A's premises had been destroyed by fire. *Held*, the Act gave no right of action to the plaintiff: he had no remedy other than that prescribed in the statute. Lord Cairns L.C. said[51]: "Apart, then, from authority, I should say, without hesitation, that it was no part of the scheme of this Act to create any duty which has to become the subject of an action at the suit of individuals to create any right in individuals with a power of enforcing that right of action; but that its scheme was, having laid down certain duties, to provide guarantees for the due fulfilment of them, and where convenient to give the penalties or some of them, to the persons injured, but, where not convenient so to do, there simply to impose public penalties, not by way of compensation, but as a security to the public for the due performance of the duty."

Local enactments

25-19   Although the Water Act 1945, Schedule 3, Parts VII and IX, now provides a code governing the supply of water throughout water authority areas, many local enactments remain in force. The Water Act 1973[52] provides that, notwithstanding the transfer of functions and abolition of bodies it effects, any local statutory provisions in force on April 1, 1974, continue to apply. They will apply to the same areas as before, but because of the transfer of functions they may thereafter apply to the water authority. They will have effect subject to any provision to the contrary made by or under the 1973 Act, and may be repealed, revoked or amended by the Secretary of State, or extended so as to apply to any part or all of the water authority area. In this way he may remove obsolete or unnecessary provisions and make others operate harmoniously within the area of application.

---

[47] Water Act 1945, Sched. 3, Part VIII, para. 36; Fire Services Act 1947, ss. 13 and 14.
[48] Water Act 1945, Sched. 3, Part VIII, para. 37; Waterworks Clauses Act 1847, s. 37.
[49] Water Act 1945, Sched. 3, Part VIII, para. 38; Waterworks Clauses Act 1847, s. 43.
[50] (1877) 2 Ex.D. 441.
[51] At p. 446.
[52] Sched. 6, para. 11.

A study of the provisions governing the supply of water in any particular water authority area therefore necessarily involves a study not only of the Water Acts, but of local enactments and of any subsequent Ministerial Orders which may affect them.

Water charges

A water authority is empowered to fix such charges for services **25–20** performed, facilities provided or rights made available by them as it thinks fit, although it is to have regard to the cost involved.[53] This includes a power to make charges for water supplied. The charges may be fixed either by agreement or according to a "charges scheme," which must show the principles on which charges are made and be given adequate publicity. The authority may make different charges for the same services, but the charges must not show undue preference to or discrimination against any class of persons. The Secretary of State may give directions to an authority as to the services for which charges may be made, and the criteria by reference to which the charges are to be fixed. In *Daymond* v. *South West Water Authority*,[54] the House of Lords held that section 30 of the Water Act 1973 (as originally enacted), which omitted to specify the persons from whom charges could be recovered, was subject to the implied limitation that charges could only lawfully be recovered from those who availed themselves of the authority's services. The Water Charges Act 1976 accordingly (1) provided for the refund of charges for sewerage and sewage disposal levied in 1974–75 and 1975–76 on properties not connected to public sewers; and (2) substituted new subsections (1), (1A) and (1B) in section 30 of the 1973 Act. These subsections provide that charges may be recovered by water authorities:

(a) for services performed, facilities provided or rights made available in the exercise of any of their functions from persons for whom they perform the services; and

(b) for services performed, etc., in the exercise of sewerage and sewage disposal functions, from persons liable to be rated in respect of hereditaments, provided that

(i) the hereditament is drained by a sewer or drain connecting, either directly or through an intermediate sewer or drain, with a public sewer provided for foul or surface water or both; or

(ii) the person has the use, for the benefit of the hereditament, of facilities which drain to a sewer or drain so connecting; or

(iii) the hereditament is subject to special rating; and

---

[53] Water Act 1973, ss. 30 (as amended by the Water Charges Act 1976) and 31. A local authority which agrees to collect water charges may collect them with the general rate: *ibid.* s. 32A, added by the Local Government Act 1974, s. 38.

[54] [1976] A.C. 609.

(c) for services performed, etc., in the exercise of specified functions (including recreation, conservation and amenity functions under the Water Act 1973 and functions under the Control of Pollution Act 1974) from all persons liable to be rated in respect of hereditaments in their area, or particular classes of such persons.

In *South West Water Authority* v. *Rumble's*[55] the House of Lords held that the rateable occupiers of a ground floor shop which had no separate water supply, appliances or facilities, were nevertheless liable to pay charges under (b)(ii) as the shop had the benefit of drainage into a public sewer of water falling on the roof of the premises above the shop.

Water authorities are also empowered to instal in any premises meters to measure the volume of water supplied so that they may charge accordingly.[56] They may make agreements as to charges for the supply of water for non-domestic purposes and special charges for spray irrigation.[57]

Grants

25-21 The Rural Water Supplies and Sewerage Acts 1944–1971 enable the Secretary of State to contribute towards expenses of water authorities in providing a supply of water, or improving an existing supply in a rural locality.

Safety of reservoirs

25-22 Where the Waterworks Clauses Act 1863[58] is incorporated in a water undertaking's local Acts, an interested person may complain to two justices that a reservoir is in a dangerous state. The justices are then required to make inquiry into the truth of the complaint, and if it is well founded they may take steps provided in the Act to secure the repair. Two justices may make inquiry on their own initiative, without complaint by any person.

The Reservoirs Act 1975[59] provides that no large raised reservoir[60] shall be constructed or altered so as to increase its capacity, unless a qualified civil engineer who is included in the appropriate panel of engineers established under the Act[61] is employed to design and supervise its construction or alteration.

---

[55] [1985] A.C. 609.
[56] Water Act 1973, s. 32.
[57] *Ibid.* s. 31(6); Water Act 1945, s. 27; Water Resources Act 1963, s. 63.
[58] ss. 3–10.
[59] This Act repeals and replaces the Reservoirs (Safety Provisions) Act 1930 as from a day to be appointed. Until such day reference must still be made to the 1930 Act. The 1975 Act is being implemented in stages. See S.I. 1983 No. 1666 and S.I. 1985 No. 176. See also DoE Circular 5/85, where it is stated that it is intended to implement the entire Act by April 1, 1986, in non-metropolitan areas and by April 1, 1987, in Greater London and in metropolitan areas.
[60] As defined in s. 1.
[61] Four panels have been established: see S.I. 1984 No. 1874, S.I. 1985 No. 175 and S.I. 1985 No. 1086.

A duty is laid on undertakers to arrange for the periodical inspection of **25-23** all large raised reservoirs by independent qualified civil engineers on the panel of engineers, and to give effect to any recommendations made. If undertakers are aggrieved by recommendations contained in a report, they may refer their complaint to an independent qualified civil engineer appointed by agreement between them and the engineer who made the report, or in default of agreement to such person as the appropriate ministers may appoint. Undertakers are required as soon as practicable to give effect to the recommendations as finally settled. In addition the undertakers are required to keep a record of such matters as water levels, depth of water, leakages and repairs. A qualified civil engineer must also be employed to supervise the reservoir and to keep the undertakers advised as to its safety.

Local authorities in whose area reservoirs lie are the bodies responsible for enforcing the Act, the relevant councils being the councils of counties, metropolitan districts and London boroughs.[62] They must maintain a register of large raised reservoirs in their area, and must report to the Secretary of State every two years on the enforcement of the Act.[63] Provision is made for the supplying of them with engineers' reports and other relevant documents. Local authorities have reserve powers to act themselves if undertakers fail to comply with enforcement notices or to deal with emergencies or dangerous situations.

Failure to comply with the provisions of the Act is an offence rendering the undertakers liable on conviction on indictment to a fine, or in the case of summary conviction to a maximum fine not exceeding the prescribed sum, or level 4 or 5 on the standard scale, depending upon the provision broken.[64]

Where damage or injury is caused by the escape of water from a reservoir constructed after the year 1930 under statutory powers granted after July 1930, the fact that the reservoir was so constructed shall not exonerate the persons for the time being having the management and control of the reservoir from any indictment, action or other proceedings to which they would otherwise have been liable.[65] The effect of this section, where it applies, is to make an undertaker liable for an escape of water *without proof of negligence.* Apart from the section it might have been set up as a defence that the works were authorised by statute and that liability could arise only in case of negligence. The section restores the common law rule as to absolute liability to be found in *Rylands* v. *Fletcher.*[66]

---

[62] Reservoirs Act 1975, s. 2(1), as amended by the Local Government Act 1985, s. 11(3).
[63] *Ibid.* ss. 3, 4; Reservoirs Act 1975 (Registers, Reports and Records) Regulations 1985 (S.I. 1985 No. 177) (applicable to non-metropolitan counties).
[64] *Ibid.* s. 22, as amended by the Magistrates' Courts Act 1980, s. 32(2) and the Criminal Justice Act 1982, ss. 38, 46.
[65] *Ibid.* s. 28, Sched. 2.
[66] (1868) L.R. 3 H.L. 330.

Functions of local authorities

25-24   Although local authorities no longer supply water, every district and London borough council and the Common Council of the City of London has a duty to take such steps as from time to time may be necessary for ascertaining the sufficiency and wholesomeness of water supplies within its area, and to notify the water authority of any insufficiency or unwholesomeness.[67]

25-25   A local authority must reject under the building regulations plans for new houses unless satisfactory provision is made for a supply of wholesome water for domestic purposes, and if a house is built without any adequate supply the authority may by notice forbid its use for human occupation.[68] The powers of local authorities extend to houses already occupied—if an authority is satisfied that a house is inadequately supplied a notice may be served on the owner requiring him to take appropriate action provided the authority is satisfied that this can reasonably be done.[69]

Where in the opinion of a local authority water for use for domestic purposes is polluted, an application may be made to a court of summary jurisdiction for an order forbidding this use or restricting it.[70]

Public wells and pumps used for providing a gratuitous supply of water vest in the local authority,[71] and parish and community councils are empowered to utilise wells, springs or streams for obtaining water, and to execute works, including works of repair and improvement, incidental to this use.[72]

---

[67] Water Act 1973, s. 11(2), (10), as amended by the Local Government Act 1985, Sched. 17. See also Water Act 1945, s. 29 and Sched. 3 and Public Health Act 1936, s. 123.
[68] Building Act 1984, s. 25.
[69] *Ibid.* s. 69.
[70] Public Health Act 1936, s. 140.
[71] *Ibid.* s. 124.
[72] *Ibid.*

CHAPTER 26

BURIALS AND CREMATION

A. BURIAL AUTHORITIES

THE law with respect to burials and cremation was greatly simplified by **26-01** the Local Government Act 1972.[1] Under earlier legislation, authorities outside of London provided burial grounds under the Burial Acts 1852–1906—there were 16 of them and they were adoptive—or under the Public Health (Interments) Act 1879, and some authorities made provision under both of these codes. The Act of 1972 established one code in place of the two. The earlier Acts were largely repealed[2] and replaced.[3] Additionally, the Secretary of State was given power by order to make provision with respect to the management, regulation and control of cemeteries. An order under this provision may amend or repeal other enactments or any instrument made under an enactment and may impose fines for contravention of the order. Before making an order, the Secretary of State is required to consult local authority associations and other interested bodies, and an order so made requires an affirmative resolution of each House of Parliament.

The following authorities are burial authorities: district councils, **26-02** London borough councils, the Common Council of the City of London, parish and community councils, and, in England, the parish meetings of parishes having no parish council, whether separate or common. District councils and, where they exist, parish and community councils and parish meetings have concurrent powers. The Act abolished a large number of ad hoc burial authorities—burial boards, joint burial boards, joint committees established under section 53 of the Local Government Act 1894, or subsequent legislation, and burial boards constituted under local Acts. The successor authorities are defined in Schedule 26 to the Act of 1972.[4]

The power under section 6 of the Public Health Act 1936 to establish joint boards for the carrying out of public health functions is extended so as to include burial authorities and burial functions.[5] This provision makes it possible for parish and community councils and, in England, parish meetings, to participate in a joint board providing a cemetery or crematorium.

Where a parish or community council or parish meeting operates as a

[1] Local Government Act 1972, s. 214.
[2] *Ibid.* Sched. 30.
[3] *Ibid.* s. 214 and Sched. 26.
[4] Para. 1.
[5] Sched. 26, para. 3.

burial authority it may charge its expenses as burial authority on a part of its area.[6]

26–03   Burial authorities may provide and maintain cemeteries outside their areas, but in the case of a district council, a London borough council and the Common Council of the City of London before constructing a cemetery or crematorium beyond its boundaries it must give notice to the local authority of the district in which the cemetery or crematorium will be.[7] Where there are objections the matter is settled by the Secretary of State after a public local inquiry.

By-laws with respect to the management of cemeteries may be made by the council of a district or London borough or the Common Council of the City of London, and a parish or community council or meeting may adopt these by-laws for any cemetery provided by them.[8] The Secretary of State is the confirming authority.

A code of management for cemeteries dealing with such matters as the distance of a cemetery from dwelling-houses, approach roads, chapels, consecration of land, burial rights and rights to erect memorials and fees is contained in an order made by the Secretary of State under section 214 of the Local Government Act 1972.[9]

26–04   A burial authority may charge such fees as it thinks proper, and in fixing fees may take account of the fact, if it be the case, that burial expenses have been declared to be special expenses.[10]

All burials in cemeteries provided and maintained by a burial authority under section 214 of the 1972 Act must be recorded in a register maintained by the authority.[11] All burials according to the rites of the Church of England other than in such a cemetery[12] must be registered under the Parochial Registers and Records Measure 1978.[13]

B. The Care and Use of Disused Burial Grounds

An Order in Council, made under section 1 of the Burial Act 1853,[14] may provide for the discontinuance of burials in any burial ground or churchyard.

26–05   A local authority may, under sections 9 to 11 of the Open Spaces Act 1906, acquire a freehold, leasehold or other interest in a burial ground, and may control and manage it, holding it in trust for the public as open space. If the ground is consecrated, the powers of management may not be exercised until the bishop's faculty or licence is obtained. If it is

---

[6] Local Government Act 1972, Sched. 26, para. 6.
[7] *Ibid.* para. 10 and s. 15 of the Public Health Act 1936.
[8] *Ibid.* para. 11.
[9] Local Authorities Cemeteries Order 1977 (S.I. 1977 No. 204).
[10] Sched. 6, para. 15(1); and see § 7–02 as to special expenses.
[11] Registration of Burials Act 1864, s. 1; Local Authorities' Cemeteries Order 1977, art. 11.
[12] Or in a cemetery to which an Act incorporating the Cemeteries Clauses Act 1847 applies.
[13] 1978 No. 2, s. 3; 1864 Act, s. 1.
[14] As amended by the Local Government Act 1972, Sched. 30.

intended to use consecrated ground for games and sports, a further faculty or licence of the bishop is required; where unconsecrated ground is to be used in this way the authority must first secure the sanction of the persons from whom the land or interest in the land was acquired, and those persons may specify conditions.

The Disused Burial Grounds Act 1884 imposed a general prohibition   **26–06** on the erection of secular buildings on disused burial grounds except for the enlargement of places of public worship. This general restriction has been considerably modified by town and country planning legislation. Broadly speaking a burial ground which has been acquired by a local authority or a statutory undertaker under Part VI of the Town and Country Planning Act 1971, or has been appropriated by a local authority under section 122 of the Town and Country Planning Act 1971, may be used in any way which conforms with planning control; if land is acquired by a minister under these provisions he may use it for any purpose for which it was acquired. The use of burial grounds in this way is subject to conditions imposed by regulations[15] having effect under section 128 of the Town and Country Planning Act 1971, which include a requirement as to the removal and re-interment of human remains.

An order for the discontinuance of burials provided in or for any part of Greater London may be made under the Burial Act 1853,[16] and London borough councils are able to utilise disused burial grounds for public recreation.[17]

A parochial church council which is liable to maintain a closed churchyard may serve a written request on the parish or community council for the area to take over the maintenance of the churchyard. Three months after the service of the request the maintenance of the closed churchyard must be taken over by the authority upon whom the request was served. Responsibility may, however, be transferred to the district council by the parish or community council. Somewhat different rules apply where there is no parish or community council.[18]

C. CREMATION

The Cremation Acts 1902 and 1952 enable burial authorities except   **26–07** parish meetings to provide and maintain crematoria.

[15] Town and Country Planning (Churches, Places of Religious Worship and Burial Grounds) Regulations 1950 (S.I. 1950 No. 792). The 1884 Act is also relaxed in respect of unconsecrated disused burial grounds belonging to a church or other religious body by the Disused Burial Grounds (Amendment) Act 1981.

[16] s. 1: applied by the Local Government Act 1972, Sched. 26, para. 15.

[17] Ministry of Housing and Local Government Provisional Order Confirmation (Greater London Parks and Open Spaces) Act 1967. Additional powers are available to London borough councils under the London County Council (General Powers) Act 1951, s. 33, and to the Common Council under the City of London (Various Powers) Act 1952, ss. 4 and 5.

[18] Local Government Act 1972, s. 215.

A crematorium may not be constructed nearer to a dwelling-house than 200 yards except with the consent in writing of the owner, lessee and occupier, nor within 50 yards of a public highway, nor in the consecrated part of the burial ground of any burial authority.[19] The Secretary of State has made regulations under section 7 of the Cremation Act 1902[20] as to the maintenance and inspection of crematoria, the conditions under which cremations may take place (including the notices and certificates to be given and the appointment by the Secretary of State on the nomination of the cremation authority of a medical referee and a deputy medical referee), and as to registration of cremations.[21] Fees and charges are fixed by the authority.[22]

[19] Cremation Act 1902, s. 5, as modified for Greater London by the London County Council (General Powers) Act 1935, s. 64 and S.I. 1965 No. 540, art. 4, and Greater London Council (General Powers) Act 1971, s. 7.
[20] As amended by the Cremation Act 1952, s. 2.
[21] Cremation Regulations 1930 (S.R. & O. 1930 No. 1016), as amended by the Cremation Regulations 1952 (S.I. 1952 No. 1568), 1965 (S.I. 1965 No. 1146), 1979 (S.I. 1979 No. 1138) and 1985 (S.I. 1985 No. 153).
[22] Cremation Act 1902, s. 9, as amended by the Local Government Act 1972, Sched. 30.

Chapter 27

MISCELLANEOUS POWERS, DUTIES AND SERVICES

A. Administration of Justice

THE areas of counties are units for certain judicial purposes[1]—the historic **27–01** connection between counties and the administration of justice at the level of assize and quarter sessions was brought to an end by the Courts Act 1971.

Each county has a Lord Lieutenant, a sheriff and a coroner. The **27–02** Crown must appoint a Lord Lieutenant for each county[2] and for Greater London. The Lord Lieutenant is appointed by commission and usually holds in addition the office of *custos rotulorum* (the keeper of the records). He is the Queen's personal representative in the county.[3] The Lord Lieutenant appoints such persons as he thinks fit to be deputy lieutenants (provided the Queen does not disapprove) and with her consent he may appoint one of the deputy lieutenants to be vice-lieutenant and to act in his place. The Queen may appoint other lieutenants within any county or Greater London.[4]

The sheriff is appointed by the Crown.[5] His functions include the executing of judgments within the county, and he acts as returning officer in Parliamentary elections in county constituencies.[6] He is required to appoint an under-sheriff to act as his deputy for all purposes except his functions as returning officer at Parliamentary elections.[7] The Local Government Act 1972, designated the sheriff as "high sheriff."[8]

Coroners must be appointed for each non-metropolitan county by the **27–03** county council and for the City (including the Temples) by the Common Council.[9]

---

[1] Local Government Act 1972, s. 216.
[2] "County" here means any metropolitan or non-metropolitan county: Local Government Act 1972, s. 270(1), and remains so notwithstanding the abolition of councils for the metropolitan counties: see the Local Government Act 1985, Sched. 16, para. 8.
[3] Reserve Forces Act 1980, s. 130.
[4] *Ibid.* ss. 130, 133, 135.
[5] Sheriffs Act 1887, s. 6; Local Government Act 1972, s. 219.
[6] Representation of the People Act 1983, s. 24.
[7] Sheriffs Act 1887, s. 23; Representation of the People Act 1983, s. 28(6).
[8] Local Government Act 1972, s. 219. There are special provisions with respect to the counties of Greater Manchester, Merseyside and Lancashire. The sheriff of Lancashire is appointed by the Queen in right of the Duchy of Lancaster. The sheriff of Cornwall is appointed by the Prince of Wales as Duke of Cornwall.
[9] Local Government Act 1972, s. 220(1), as amended by the Local Government Act 1985, s. 13(1). On qualifications for appointment see the Coroners (Amendment) Act 1926, s. 1.

Where a coroner's district consists of or is included in a metropolitan district or London borough, the appointment is made by the council of that district or borough. If a coroner's district consists of two or more metropolitan districts or London boroughs, the appointment is made by one of the relevant councils designated by the Secretary of State after consultation with the others. In either case, the appointment must be approved by the Secretary of State.[10] The Lord Chief Justice and the judges of the High Court are coroners *ex officio*.[11] The duty of the coroner is to hold inquiries into sudden deaths and treasure trove.

27-04　　There is a separate commission of the peace for each county, both metropolitan and non-metropolitan, for the City of London and for each of the five commission areas of Greater London.[12] Justices are appointed by the Crown either on the recommendation of the Lord Chancellor or, in the county of Lancaster, on the advice of the Chancellor of the Duchy of Lancaster. It is common practice for local advisory committees, appointed by the Lord Chancellor, to advise him on the filling of appointments.

27-05　　Magistrates' courts committees are established in each non-metropolitan county, metropolitan district, outer London borough and the City of London.[13] These committees are responsible for the general administration of the courts within their areas, for appointment of clerks to the justices (the approval of the Secretary of State for the Home Department is required for appointment and dismissal), for the provision of courses of instruction for magistrates and for the submission to the Secretary of State of schemes for the division of the area into petty sessional divisions.[14] The Secretary of State for the Home Department may make general regulations about the constitution, procedure and quorum of magistrates' courts committees. In Inner London, similar functions are performed by a "committee of magistrates."

27-06　　Stipendiary magistrates may be appointed by the Crown, on the advice of the Lord Chancellor, holding office during Her Majesty's pleasure.[15] They must be barristers or solicitors of not less than seven years' standing.

A stipendiary magistrate when sitting alone has the powers of a justice of the peace sitting in petty sessions; when sitting with other justices he has no special powers. He may not sit in the Crown Court.[16]

27-07　　Costs incurred in the provision and maintenance of magistrates' courts, including salaries of justices' clerks and their staffs and expenses of

---

[10] Local Government Act 1985, s. 13(2)–(4), and see the Coroners' Districts (Designation of Relevant Councils) Order 1985 (S.I. 1985 No. 1933).

[11] Coroners Act 1887, s. 34; and see the Supreme Court Act 1981, s. 44.

[12] Justices of the Peace Act 1979, ss. 1, 2(1). The Justices of the Peace Act 1979 was a consolidating measure and relates to justices of the peace, justices' clerks and the administrative and financial arrangements for magistrates' courts, and connected matters.

[13] Justices of the Peace Act 1979, ss. 19–24, as amended by the Local Government Act 1985, s. 12(4)–(8).

[14] Justices of the Peace Act 1979, ss. 35–38.

[15] Justices of the Peace Act 1979, ss. 13–16. As to the Inner London Area, see *ibid.* ss. 31–34.

[16] Justices of the Peace Act 1979, s. 16.

magistrates' courts committees, are paid by the councils of each non-metropolitan county, metropolitan district and outer London borough. The amounts of such costs are determined by the magistrates' courts committee after consultation with the relevant council or councils. A council dissatisfied with the determination of a committee may appeal to the Secretary of State.[17] Fines are payable to the Secretary of State for the Home Department and grants are made by him to the councils concerned of an amount not exceeding 80 per cent. of the authority's expenditure.[18]

B. DISEASES OF ANIMALS

Most of the law relating to this matter is contained in the Animal Health **27-08** Act 1981,[19] and the orders made thereunder. Local authorities for the purposes of the Act are non-metropolitan county councils and metropolitan district councils. In London the Common Council of the City of London is the authority for the City of London and for the whole of Greater London in regard to the provisions relating to imported animals; in relation to other provisions the London borough councils are responsible.[20] Where the area of an authority includes part of a port or aerodrome, the Minister may by order make another body responsible for imported animals.

In broad terms, the Act imposes on the Minister of Agriculture, Fisheries and Food the duty of devising and putting into operation measures for the control and eradication of contagious disease in animals and the Minister has wide powers to make regulations to effect these purposes. The enforcement of the Act falls broadly on local authorities and the police.

Local authorities are under a duty to appoint inspectors and other officers as the authority thinks necessary for the execution and enforcement of the Act, and the Minister has default powers.[21]

An authority may provide wharves, sheds and other places for the landing, reception, sale, slaughter or disposal of imported or other animals, carcasses and other things,[22] and may purchase land compulsorily or by agreement for wharves or for use for the burial of carcasses.[23]

C. HEALTH AND SAFETY AT WORK

The law on this subject is now largely contained in the Health and Safety **27-09** at Work, etc., Act 1974 which followed the Report of the Robens

[17] Justices of the Peace Act 1979, ss. 55–58, as amended by the Local Government Act 1985, s. 12(9) and Sched. 17.
[18] *Ibid.* ss. 59, as amended by the Local Government Act 1985, s. 12(10), and 61.
[19] As amended by the Animal Health and Welfare Act 1984, and the Local Government Act 1985, Sched. 8, para. 18.
[20] *Ibid.* s. 50.
[21] *Ibid.* ss. 52, 59.
[22] *Ibid.* s. 54.
[23] *Ibid.* s. 55.

Committee on Safety and Health at Work 1972.[24] It is intended that the Act will eventually replace the old law contained in the Factories Act 1961, the Offices, Shops and Railway Premises Act 1963 and other enactments, referred to in the 1974 Act as "the existing statutory provisions,"[25] which the committee regarded as unsatisfactory.

The new system is to be based on regulations and Codes of Practice supplementing the provisions of the 1974 Act under which new responsibilities are imposed not only on employers and managers, but also on employees themselves and the self employed, aimed at maintaining and improving standards of health, safety and welfare of people at work and others affected by the activities of people at work. The 1974 Act is much wider in scope than the earlier legislation. It applies to people rather than to premises and covers all employed persons, apart from domestic workers in private employment, thus bringing in many persons who were outside the scope of the former statutory protection.

27–10   One of the main criticisms of the earlier legislation was the large number of different authorities administering different aspects of the health, safety and welfare of people at work and the Robens Committee recommended that, if possible, all the administration of this body of law should be undertaken by a single organisation. The recommendation was dealt with in the 1974 Act by the establishment of a new hierarchy under the overall control of the Secretary of State for Employment.

27–11   The Act provides for the establishment of a Health and Safety Commission which is a corporate body consisting of a chairman and between six and nine other members appointed by the Secretary of State.[26] The Commission has the general duty of making arrangements for operating the Act, including assisting and encouraging persons concerned with the general administration of the Act, the conduct of research and the provision of information and advice.[27] The Secretary of State may issue directions to the Commission with respect to its functions and the Commission is required to give effect to any such directions.[28] With the consent of the Secretary of State, the Commission may approve and issue Codes of Practice.

The Act also establishes a Health and Safety Executive consisting of a Director, appointed by the Commission with the approval of the minister, and two other persons appointed by the Commission with the approval of the Director. The Executive has the duty of implementing the advisory functions of the Commission and of enforcing the relevant statutory provisions by means of inspectors which the Executive may appoint.[29]

---

[24] Cmnd. 5034.
[25] s. 53, Sched. 1. The Schedule lists some 30 enactments.
[26] s. 10.
[27] s. 11.
[28] s. 12.
[29] s. 10 and s. 18.

The Secretary of State has power by regulation to make local **27-12** authorities responsible for the enforcement of "relevant statutory provisions"[30] to such extent as may be prescribed. The Health and Safety (Enforcing Authority) Regulations 1977[31] provide for district councils, London borough councils and the Common Council of the City of London to be the enforcing authorities where the main activities in any premises are the sale or storage of goods for retail or wholesale distribution (with certain exceptions), office activities, catering services, the provision of residential accommodation, consumer services provided in shop premises (except dry cleaning, radio or television repairs or the maintenance or repair of motor vehicles), dry cleaning in coin–operated units in launderettes and similar premises and the keeping of wild animals for exhibition to the public (other than for the purposes of a circus).

Responsibility for enforcement may be transferred by agreement from the Executive to the local authority or vice versa. To remove uncertainty as to the respective responsibility of the Executive or a local authority in any particular case, either body may apply to the Health and Safety Commission which may assign the responsibility to whichever authority it considers appropriate. Liaison at the national level is provided by the Health and Safety Executive and Local Authority Enforcement Liaison Committee, comprising senior staff of the Executive and representatives of local authority associations. At the local level, a principal inspector of factories advises local authorities on enforcement matters.[32]

Every enforcing authority may appoint as inspectors, under whatever **27-13** title it may determine, such persons having suitable qualifications as it thinks necessary for carrying into effect the "relevant statutory provisions" within its field of responsibility.[33] The powers of inspectors are widely defined in sections 20–26 of the Act and include the issue of improvement and prohibition notices for remedying contraventions of the statutory provisions, directing the cessation of activities involving risk of serious injury and dealing with the cause of imminent danger, as well as the general duties imposed by Part I of the 1974 Act and the provisions of health and safety regulations made under Section 15 of that Act.

The provisions of the Factories Act 1961, the Offices, Shops and Railway Premises Act 1963 and other "existing statutory provisions" remain in force for the time being subject to the new enforcement machinery of the 1974 Act.

---

[30] s. 53 and Sched. 1; these include the Factories Act 1961, the Offices, Shops and Railway Premises Act 1963 and 28 other enactments relating to health and safety in various industries and employments, as well as the general duties imposed by Part I of the 1974 Act and the provisions of health and safety regulations made under s. 15 of that Act (1983).

[31] S.I. 1977 No. 746, as amended by S.I. 1980 No. 1744 and S.I. 1985 No. 1107.

[32] See C. D. Drake and F. B. Wright, *Law of Health and Safety at Work: The New Approach* (1983), p. 59.

[33] s. 19.

27-14   Local fire authorities also have responsibility for fire precautions at places of employment under the Fire Precautions Act 1971. Factories, offices, shops and railway premises have been designated under section 1 of the 1971 Act as requiring a fire certificate from the fire authority.[34] The requirement does not apply to premises where not more than 20 persons are employed to work at any one time or not more than 10 persons are so employed elsewhere than on the ground floor but in these premises certain provisions as to fire precautions are laid down in regulations.[35]

D. SAFETY OF SPORTS GROUNDS

27-15   Under the Safety of Sports Grounds Act 1975, the Secretary of State may, by order, designate as a stadium requiring a safety certificate under the Act any stadium which in his opinion has accommodation for more than 10,000 spectators.[36] Applications for a safety certificate must be directed to the local authority for the area in which the stadium is situated, and in this context "local authority" means London borough council, the Common Council of the City of London, metropolitan district council or non-metropolitan county council.[37] A certificate may be either a "general safety certificate," covering specified activities for an indefinite period, or a "special safety certificate" covering specified activities on an occasion or series of occasions. It must contain such terms and conditions as the local authority consider necessary or expedient to secure reasonable safety, and, without prejudice to this, must specify the maximum number of spectators to be admitted to the stadium, may specify the maximum number to be admitted to different parts, and must include terms and conditions as to entrances and exits and crush barriers.[38] If the applicant is "a person likely to be in a position to prevent contravention of the terms and conditions of a certificate," the local authority *must* issue a general safety certificate to him if no such certificate is already in operation, and, where a general safety certificate is in operation, they *may* issue a special safety certificate to him.[39] The authority must consult the local chief officer of police and in the case of non-metropolitan counties, the district council, and in the case of Greater London or a metropolitan county, the fire authority.[40] The local authority may, in any case where it appears

---

[34] Fire Precautions (Factories, Offices, Shops and Railway Premises) Order 1976 (S.I. 1976 No. 2009). See also § 21–20, above.

[35] Fire Precautions (Non-Certificated Factory, Office, Shop and Railway Premises) Regulations 1976 (S.I. 1976 No. 2010).

[36] s. 1.

[37] s. 17(1), definition of "local authority" substituted by the Local Government Act 1985, Sched. 8, para. 7(3).

[38] s. 2.

[39] s. 3(1), (2).

[40] s. 3(3), as amended by the Local Government Act 1985, Sched. 8, para. 7(1), and s. 17(1) (definition of "building authority" substituted by the Local Government Act 1985, Sched. 8, para. 7(2)).

appropriate to them do so, amend a certificate by notice in writing to the holder, or replace a certificate.[41] Appeal against refusal of a certificate lies to the Secretary of State, and a hearing or inquiry may be held.[42] While a general safety certificate is in force, safety provisions in certain other Acts covering the same matters do not apply.[43]

If a magistrates' court is satisfied, on the application of the local authority, that the risk to spectators at a sports ground is so great that their admission ought to be prohibited or restricted until steps have been taken to reduce it to a reasonable level, the court may order accordingly. An appeal lies to the Crown Court.[44]

The Act creates a series of criminal offences in respect of non-compliance with its requirements or with the provisions of a certificate.[45]

The Secretary of State has power to extend provisions of the Act to sports grounds other than sports stadia.[46]

The Secretary of State has progressively increased the list of stadia designated under the Act, so that it now extends to all Football League grounds,[47] Wembley Stadium, Twickenham Rugby Union Ground and Cardiff Arms Park, and certain Rugby League Grounds.[48]

E. LICENSING AND REGISTRATION

Local authorities have a number of functions in relation to licensing and registration: some of the more important are noted here and a list of licensing functions appears in Appendix 4.   **27-16**

The substantive law on each of these functions is to be found in the parent statute but, subject to the procedures therein laid down, a number of general principles have emerged from the case law on the subject.

The judicial nature of many licensing functions requires that authorities in exercising them must have regard to the principles of natural justice.[49] Where an authority lays down a policy to govern the way in which applications will be dealt with, that policy must not be applied so rigidly as to amount to a refusal to consider an individual case on its merits. A licensing authority must not take irrelevant considerations into account in dealing with applications.[50] Where power is given to impose

---

[41] s. 4.
[42] ss. 5, 7.
[43] s. 9.
[44] s. 10.
[45] s. 12.
[46] No such order has been made at the time of writing.
[47] Third and Fourth Division clubs not previously designated were included by the Safety of Sports Grounds (Association Football Grounds) (Designation) Order 1985 (S.I. 1985 No. 1063), following the fire at the Valley Parade Ground, Bradford, in that year.
[48] Safety of Sports Grounds (Rugby Football Grounds) (Designation) Order 1985 (S.I. 1985 No. 1064).
[49] See further Chap. 12.
[50] *Pilling* v. *Abergele U.D.C.* [1950] 1 K.B. 636 and *Chertsey U.D.C.* v. *Mixnam's Properties Ltd.* [1965] A.C. 735; see also §§ 16–06 and 16–61.

"such conditions as the authority thinks fit," the conditions must be fairly within the powers of the statute and must not be so unreasonable that no reasonable authority could have imposed them.[51]

There may possibly be circumstances in which an applicant for a statutory licence has a right to damages if his application is refused on malicious grounds, or if in some other way there has been a malicious misuse of statutory power.[52]

Theatres and public entertainments

27-17   Premises in which stage plays are performed are required to be licensed under the provisions of the Theatres Act 1968, unless the Crown has given authority by letters patent.[53] District and London borough councils and the Common Council of the City of London are the licensing authorities.[54]

In granting, renewing or transferring a licence, the authority may not impose any term, condition or restriction as to the nature of the plays which may be performed under the licence or as to the manner of performing the plays.[55]

An appeal against an authority's decision lies to the magistrates' court.[56]

The licensing of public entertainments in Greater London—music, dancing, boxing and wrestling—is governed by Schedule 12 to the London Government Act 1963.[57]

27-18   The licensing of public entertainments outside Greater London is governed by Part I of and Schedule 1 to the Local Government (Miscellaneous Provisions) Act 1982. Public dancing or music or any other public entertainment of a like kind must not be provided, except under and in accordance with the terms of a licence granted by the district council or the Council of the Isles of Scilly. There are exemptions from this requirement for music in a place of public religious worship or performed as an incident of a religious meeting or service, entertainments held in a pleasure fair and entertainments which take place wholly or mainly in the open air. There are similar licensing requirements for any entertainment which consists of or includes any public display of boxing, wrestling, judo, karate or similar sports. The council may resolve to apply licensing requirements to public musical entertainments held wholly or mainly in the open air and on private land. In deciding whether to grant a licence, the council must have regard to any observations submitted by

---

[51] *Associated Provincial Picture Houses* v. *Wednesbury Corporation* [1948] 1 K.B. 223; see also § 12–20, *ante*.
[52] See § 10–43.
[53] ss. 12, 17.
[54] s. 18, as amended by the Local Government Act 1972, s. 204(6), and the Local Government Act 1985, Sched. 8, para. 3.
[55] s. 1.
[56] s. 14.
[57] As amended by the Local Government Act 1985, Sched. 8, para. 1.

the chief officer of police or the fire authority. In most cases, the applicant must pay a reasonable fee as determined by the council, although no fee is payable if the application relates to a church or village hall or similar building, and the fee may be remitted where, in the opinion of the council, the entertainment is of an educational or like character or is given for a charitable or other like purpose. The council may attach conditions to a licence, and has power to prescribe standard conditions. When dealing with an application for a licence, the council must inform the applicant of the substance of any objection and give him the opportunity to make representations in reply.[58] An appeal lies against refusal to the magistrates' court.

Cinemas

The Cinemas Act 1985 provides that a film exhibition may not be given **27-19** unless the regulations made by the Secretary of State for the Home Department[59] as to safety and the health and welfare of children attending are complied with, and unless the premises in which the exhibition is given are licensed for the purpose.[60] District councils, London borough councils and the Common Council are licensing authorities[61] and they may grant licences to such persons as they think fit, and on such terms and conditions as they determine, subject to the regulations made by the Secretary of State.[62] Certain exhibitions are exempted from these requirements: (1) those given in a private dwelling house to which the public is not admitted and which either are not promoted for private gain or are held to demonstrate any product, advertise any goods or services or to provide information, education or instruction[63]; and (2) certain other non-commercial exhibitions.[64] In considering applications for a licence, the licensing authority are to have regard to any observations submitted to them by the fire authority or by the chief officer of police.[65] Authorities are under a duty when granting a licence to impose conditions prohibiting or restricting children from the showing of unsuitable films[66] and are empowered to control the use of premises for film exhibitions organised wholly or mainly for children.[67] A licensing authority may attach conditions requiring admission to a film to

---

[58] *R.* v. *Huntington District Council, ex p. Cowan* [1984] 1 W.L.R. 501.

[59] s. 4, and the Cinematograph (Safety) Regulations 1955 (S.I. 1955 No. 1129) as amended by S.I. 1958 No. 1530, S.I. 1965 No. 282 and S.I. 1976 No. 1315.

[60] s. 1. The operation of a video amusement game constitutes an exhibition of moving pictures for these purposes and the premises must therefore be licensed: *British Amusement Catering Trades Association* v. *Greater London Council* [1985] 1 W.L.R. 840.

[61] Cinemas Act 1985, ss. 3(10) and 21, as amended by the Local Government Act 1985, Sched. 8, para. 4.

[62] Cinematograph (Children) (No. 2) Regulations 1955 (S.I. 1955 No. 1909).

[63] Cinemas Act 1985, s. 5.

[64] *Ibid.* s. 6.

[65] *Ibid.* s. 3(3).

[66] *Ibid.* s. 1(3).

[67] *Ibid.* s. 2.

be in accordance with the film's classification[68] by the British Board of Film Censors, a non-statutory body established by the manufacturers of films: however, the authority must reserve the right to review the Board's classification.[69]

A licensing authority may allow cinema shows to be given on Sundays, subject to such conditions as the authority thinks fit and to a compulsory condition that an employee may not work on Sunday if he has worked on each of the six preceding days in the cinema.[69a]

Premises may not be used for the storing of raw celluloid or cinematograph film unless the occupier has given to the local authority in writing a statement of his name, the address of the premises and the nature of the business carried on there.[70] The occupier is required to observe the provisions appearing in Schedule 1 and in regulations made by the Secretary of State for the Home Department and the duty to see that these provisions are carried out falls to local authorities,[71] *i.e.* the councils of non-metropolitan counties, London boroughs and the Common Council of the City of London, and in metropolitan counties, the fire and civil defence authority. The Health and Safety Executive may grant exemption from any requirement of the Act or regulations.[72]

Charities

27-20   The Charities Act 1960 confers three powers on local authorities under the heading "Provisions for inquiring into, making known and co-ordinating charitable activities."[73] First, there is a provision enabling local authorities to keep indexes of local charities. The information upon which the index is based comes from the Charity Commissioners, who under section 4 of the Act are required to compile a central register of all charities other than those specifically excluded in the Act or by regulation: among those excluded by the Act are charities having neither a permanent endowment nor an income from property amounting to more than £15 a year, nor the use and occupation of any land.

Secondly, authorities are enabled to review the working of local charities, in co-operation with the trustees concerned, reporting to the

---

[68] Currently: U—Universal: suitable for all; PG—Parental Guidance: some scenes unsuitable for young children; 15: passed only for persons of 15 years and over; 18: passed only for persons of 18 and over; R18: passed only for restricted distribution through segregated premises to which no-one under 18 is admitted. The R18 category is for films certified for showing at private clubs and licensed sex cinemas.
[69] *Mills* v. *London County Council* [1925] 1 K.B. 213; *R.* v. *Greater London Council, ex p. Blackburn* [1976] 1 W.L.R. 550.
[69a] Cinemas Act 1985, s. 9.
[70] Celluloid and Cinematograph Film Act 1922, s. 1, as amended by S.I. 1974 No. 1841; London Government Act 1963, s. 62(1)(*b*).
[71] *Ibid.* ss. 4, 9, as amended by the Local Government Act 1985, Sched. 11, para. 6.
[72] Celluloid and Cinematograph Film Act 1922 (Exemptions) Regulations 1980 (S.I. 1980 No. 1314).
[73] ss. 10–12. As to the application of the Act to Greater London, see London Government Act 1963, s. 81(8).

Commissioners as the council and trustees think fit. This provision enables authorities to encourage and permit the co-operation of statutory and voluntary services by bringing the various agencies together.

Thirdly, provision is made for the co-ordination, in the interests of the beneficiaries, of the welfare services provided by charities and local authorities, and for the exchange of information.

The powers with respect to registration and review are available to the councils of districts, London boroughs and the Common Council of the City of London. The powers with respect to co-ordination may be exercised by any authority providing services similar to those given by local charities.[74]

The Charities Act 1985 requires charities for the relief of poverty to send copies of statements of account to any local authority for an area which is for the area of benefit or within which the whole or any part of the area of benefit falls. "Local authority" for these purposes means non-metropolitan county, metropolitan district and London borough councils, and the Common Council of the City of London. The authority must keep the statement for at least two years, and during that time open to public inspection. The local authority must also be notified of resolutions of charity trustees for such charities to alter the objects of the charity or to transfer all the property to another charity.

Charity property may be held by a local authority as trustee and expenditure may be incurred by a local authority in making contributions to the funds of a charity in furtherance of its work in the United Kingdom.[75]

Hackney carriages and private hire vehicles[75a]

The licensing of hackney carriages and their drivers outside the **27-21** Metropolitan Police District and the City of London is governed by sections 37–68 of the Town Police Clauses Act 1847, section 76 of the Public Health Act 1925 and Part II of the Local Government (Miscellaneous Provisions) Act 1976. District councils which have resolved to apply the provisions of the 1847 Act have power to licence within their area such number of hackney carriages as they think fit.[76] Where a district council has, additionally, resolved to apply the provisions of Part II of the Local Government (Miscellaneous Provisions) Act 1976 the authority may attach such conditions as it thinks fit, including one requiring the vehicle to be of such design and appearance and bear such distinguishing marks as shall clearly identify it as a

---

[74] Local Government Act 1972, s. 210.
[75] *Ibid.* s. 210 and s. 137(3)(*a*); and see *Manchester City Council* v. *Greater Manchester Council* (1980) 78 L.G.R. 560.
[75a] As from a day to be appointed, the relevant statutory provisions are modified by ss. 10–13 of the Transport Act 1985: *ibid.* s. 140.
[76] *Ibid.* ss. 60–62.

hackney carriage.[77] Charges may be made for the licensing of cabs and cab drivers.[78]

In the Metropolitan Police District and the City of London the power to license hackney carriages and their drivers is vested in the Secretary of State for the Home Department and is exercised by an Assistant Commissioner of Police.[79]

In districts where the Town Police Clauses Act 1847 is in force and where the district council has, in addition, applied the provisions of Part II of the Local Government (Miscellaneous Provisions) Act 1976 to its area, private hire vehicles, drivers of private hire vehicles, and operators of private hire vehicles require to be licensed by the district council. In the case of any licence, whether for vehicle, driver or operator, the council may impose such conditions as it thinks reasonably necessary.

A person aggrieved by a refusal of a licence or by any condition attached to a licence may appeal to the magistrates' court.

In deciding whether or not to grant a licence the council must act fairly and be ready to hear persons or bodies whose interests are affected.[80]

Sex establishments

27-22   A local authority (for these purposes, district and London borough councils and the Common Council of the City of London) may resolve to apply licensing requirements to sex cinemas and sex shops under Schedule 3 to the Local Government (Miscellaneous Provisions) Act 1982. The Schedule comes into force on the day specified in the resolution, which must not be before the expiration of one month from the day on which the resolution was passed. The council must publish notice that a resolution has been passed on two consecutive weeks in a local newspaper circulating in their area, and the first publication must not be later than 28 days before the Schedule is to come into force in the area.[81] The council must give to an applicant an opportunity of being heard by a committee or sub-committee,[82] and has a discretion to afford such an opportunity to objectors.[83] Intelligible reasons must be given for

---

[77] Local Government (Miscellaneous Provisions) Act 1976, s. 47.

[78] If Part II of the 1976 Act has been adopted this may be done by virtue of s. 70 of that Act; if it has not, this may be done by virtue of s. 35 of the Transport Act 1981.

[79] Metropolitan Police Carriage Act 1869, s. 9, the London Cab Order 1934 (S.R. & O. 1934 No. 1346), as amended by S.I. 1977 No. 2030.

[80] *R.* v. *Liverpool Corporation, ex p. Liverpool Taxi Fleet Operators' Association* [1972] 2 Q.B. 299; *cf. R.* v. *Metropolitan Police Commissioner, ex p. Parker* [1953] 1 W.L.R. 1150; see also § 12–29, above.

[81] s. 2. These requirements are mandatory: *R.* v. *Swansea City Council, ex p. Quietlynn Ltd., The Times,* October 19, 1983; *R.* v. *Birmingham City Council, ex p. Quietlynn Ltd.* (1985) 83 L.G.R. 461.

[82] 1982 Act, Sched. 3, para. 19.

[83] *R.* v. *Chester City Council, ex p. Quietlynn Ltd.* (1984) 83 L.G.R. 308; *R.* v. *Birmingham City Council, ex p. Quietlynn Ltd., supra.*

refusal of a licence.[84] The applicant must pay a reasonable fee as determined by the council. Conditions may be attached to a licence and there is power to prescribe standard conditions. An appeal against refusal lies to a magistrates' court.

F. Markets

27-23

The council of a district or London borough may establish a market within its district or may acquire an existing market by lease or purchase, providing, in either event, a market place and other buildings.[85] A market authority may make such charges in respect of the market and the weighing and measuring of articles and vehicles as they may from time to time determine.[86] If they are not paid the authority may distrain on animals or other articles or may recover the sum due as a civil debt in the magistrates' court, or in the county court as a simple contract debt. The authority may restrict street sales within the market area and may make by-laws as to the use of its markets.

Many authorities own and administer markets under a franchise acquired by Grant or Charter and many have private Acts incorporating the Markets and Fairs Clauses Act 1847.

At common law a franchise market is entitled to be protected from disturbance by a rival market held within $6\frac{2}{3}$ miles. Local authority markets established under statute are entitled to the same protection,[87] whether the rival market is held inside or outside the authority's district.[88] The establishment of a rival market on the same day within the limit is actionable without proof of damage[89]: if it is established on another day, actual or apprehended damage must be proved.[90] Whether the rival concern is a "market," the essential feature of which is the provision of facilities for a concourse of buyers and sellers, is a question of fact.[91] It is a good defence that the rival market is held by statute or with the consent of the owner of the older franchise.[92]

---

[84] 1982 Act, Sched. 3, para. 20. *R.* v. *Birmingham City Council, ex p. Quietlynn Ltd., supra.* This decision deals with a number of other points arising under Schedule 3. See also *Westminster City Council* v. *Croyalgrange Ltd.* [1985] 1 All E.R. 740 in respect of offences under the Schedule and *Lambeth London Borough Council* v. *Grewal, The Times,* November 26, 1985, on the definition of "sex shop."

[85] Food Act 1984, ss. 50–61.

[86] The council is entitled to fix the charges so as to make a profit for the benefit of the general rate fund: *Ricketts* v. *Havering London Borough Council* (1980) 79 L.G.R. 146.

[87] *Wakefield City Council* v. *Box* [1982] 3 All E.R. 506 (interlocutory injunction granted).

[88] *Halton Borough Council* v. *Cawley* [1985] 1 W.L.R. 15.

[89] *Tamworth Borough Council* v. *Fazeley Town Council* (1978) 77 L.G.R. 699; *Sevenoaks District Council* v. *Pattullo & Vinson Ltd.* [1984] Ch.211.

[90] *Leicester Corporation* v. *Maby* (1971) 70 L.G.R. 209.

[91] *Scottish Co-operative Wholesale Society Ltd.* v. *Ulster Farmers' Marts Co. Ltd.* [1960] A.C. 63; *Northampton Borough Council* v. *Midland Development Group of Companies Ltd.* (1978) 76 L.G.R. 750 (interlocutory injunction granted); *Kingston upon Hull City Council* v. *Greenwood* (1984) 82 L.G.R. 586; *Manchester City Council* v. *Walsh* (1985) 82 L.S. Gaz.1716.

[92] *Tamworth Borough Council* v. *Fazeley Town Council, supra.*

Where the council of a district or London borough resolve that the requirement shall apply in their area, a person intending to hold a temporary market and the occupier of land who intends to permit the land to be used for this purpose must give at least one month's notice to the council. No notice is required if the proceeds are to be applied for charitable, social, sporting or political purposes.[93]

G. REGISTRATION OF BIRTHS, DEATHS AND MARRIAGES

27-24 The law as to the administration of this service is contained in the Registration Service Act 1953.

The unit of administration is the registration district in the charge of a superintendent registrar of births, deaths and marriages. There is one or more such district in every non-metropolitan county and metropolitan district,[94] and each district has one or more sub-districts in the charge of a registrar of births and deaths—this officer may also be a registrar of marriages if the appropriate powers are conferred on him by the local scheme.

A general responsibility for the registration service falls on the Registrar-General, an officer appointed by the Crown and holding office at the pleasure of the Crown.[95] He is empowered to make regulations prescribing, inter alia, the duties of superintendent registrars, registrars of births and deaths and registrars of marriages, and the duties under the Registration Acts of officers appointed under local schemes.[96]

Superintendent registrars and registrars are appointed by the local authority and hold office at the pleasure of the Registrar-General.[97] Superintendant registrars are not employed by the local authority. If a superintendant registrar is in breach of any of his statutory duties the authority is not entitled to withhold part of his salary; the only remedy lies in the Registrar-General's power of dismissal.[98] It is the responsibility of the local authority to provide and maintain register offices.[99]

The law as to registration of births and deaths is to be found in the Births and Deaths Registration Act 1953, and as to marriages in Part IV of the Marriage Act 1949, as amended by the Marriage Act 1983.

Provision for a reorganisation of local registration services in and around Greater London was made by the London Authorities (Registration Service) Order 1964.[1]

---

[93] Local Government (Miscellaneous Provisions) Act 1982, s. 37.
[94] Local Government Act 1972, Sched. 29, para. 41; Local Government (Registration Service) Order 1973 (S.I. 1973 No. 1654).
[95] Registration Service Act 1953, s. 1.
[96] Registration of Births, Deaths and Marriages Regulations 1968 (S.I. 1968 No. 2049) as amended by S.I. 1971 No. 1218, S.I. 1974 No. 571, S.I. 1976 No. 2081, S.I. 1977 No. 1912, S.I. 1982 Nos. 265, 955, S.I. 1983 No. 460 and S.I. 1985 Nos. 568 and 1133.
[97] Registration Service Act 1953, s. 6.
[98] Miles v. Wakefield District Council [1985] 1 W.L.R. 822.
[99] Ibid. s. 10.
[1] S.I. 1964 No. 2066.

H. SMALLHOLDINGS

Under Part III of the Agriculture Act 1970, a duty is placed on county **27-25**
councils[2] to provide smallholdings to enable persons to become farmers
on their own account. Wide powers are given to trade in machinery,
stock, seeds and other requisites for the benefit of smallholding occupiers,
but an authority may not proceed with the creation and equipment of
smallholdings except in accordance with a scheme approved by the
Minister of Agriculture, Fisheries and Food, and holdings must be let at a
full fair rent. If it appears to the Minister that an authority has not
exercised its functions in accordance with the rules of good estate
management he may issue directions to the authority, and if they are
disregarded the Minister may arrange for the carrying out of work at the
cost of the authority. The Minister is also empowered to transfer to
himself the functions of a defaulting authority.

The Minister is empowered to make contributions partly to offset losses
incurred by smallholdings authorities in carrying out their schemes.[3]

I. OFFICES OF HONOUR[4]

A principal council may, by a resolution passed by not less than two- **27-26**
thirds of the members voting thereon at a meeting of the council specially
convened for the purpose, confer the title of honorary aldermen on
persons who have, in the opinion of the council, rendered eminent
services to the council as past members.

The council of a London borough or a district having the status of city,
borough or royal borough, and any parish or community which by grant
under the Royal Prerogative has the status of city or the style of royal
town may similarly admit to be honorary freemen persons of distinction
and persons who have, in the council's opinion, rendered eminent services
to the area.

J. WAR MEMORIALS

A local authority has no power to provide or erect a war memorial, but **27-27**
may incur reasonable expenditure in the maintenance, repair and
protection of a memorial, whether or not it has vested in the

---

[2] Greater London Council and metropolitan county council smallholdings were transferred
to adjacent non-metropolitan counties by an order under s. 100 of the Local Government
Act 1985.

[3] Forms and procedure are given in the Small Holdings (Contributions Towards Losses)
Regulations 1949 (S.I. 1949 No. 1815), as amended.

[4] Local Government Act 1972, s. 249, as amended by the Local Government, Planning and
Land Act 1980, s. 180.

authority[5]—ownership may be acquired by acceptance as a gift under the Local Government Act 1972.[6]

K. LOCAL LOTTERIES

27–28   Local authorities have power under the Lotteries and Amusements Act 1976 to promote local lotteries in accordance with a scheme approved by the local authority itself (not by a committee, sub-committee or officer under delegated powers) and registered with the Gaming Board.[7] The lottery may be promoted for any purposes for which the local authority has power to incur expenditure under any enactment, including section 137 of the Local Government Act 1972. Publicity must be given to bring the object of the lottery to the attention of persons purchasing tickets.[8] All receipts, after deduction of the expenses of promotion and sums required for prizes, must be paid into a separate lottery fund for each lottery.[9] Not more than 52 lotteries may be held in any period of 12 months and at least seven days must elapse between the promotion of each lottery.[10] Restrictions are placed on the maximum price of tickets sold and on the proportion of proceeds allocated to prizes and to promotion expenses.[11]

L. DIRECT LABOUR SERVICES

27–29   Local authorities commonly operate direct labour departments to carry out works of maintenance and construction for their own functions under powers contained in section 111 of the Local Government Act 1972 to which reference is made in paragraph 1–10. Such direct labour organisations, as they are called, may also carry out work for other authorities and bodies in accordance with agency arrangements under section 101 of the Local Government Act 1972, sections 5 and 18 of the London Government Act 1963, or under local legislation. Works of maintenance, but not construction, may also be carried out for other authorities under the Local Authorities (Goods and Services) Act 1970 dealt with in paragraph 10–02.

Part III of the Local Government, Planning and Land Act 1980[12] introduced a system of control by the Secretary of State over the power of local authorities to enter into agreements to carry out construction and

---

[5] War Memorials (Local Authorities' Powers) Act 1923, s. 1.
[6] Local Government Act 1972, s. 139.
[7] s. 6; see also the Lotteries Regulations 1977 (S.I. 1977 No. 256) as amended by S.I. 1981 No. 109.
[8] s. 7.
[9] s. 8.
[10] s. 10.
[11] s. 11.
[12] As amended by the Local Government Act 1985, Sched. 17. See also the Local Government (Direct Labour Organisations) (Competition) Regulations 1983 (S.I. 1983 No. 685) and DoE Circulars 10/81, 6/82 and 19/83.

maintenance work for other bodies, referred to in the Act as "works contracts," and over functional work carried out by direct labour organisations for their parent authorities.

Works contracts

A works contract comprises: **27-30**

- (a) an agreement under
    - (i)   section 5(3)(c) of the London Government Act 1963[13] (agreements between London authorities for the carrying out of works of maintenance by one party in connection with land or buildings for the maintenance of which another party is responsible), or
    - (ii)   section 1 of the Local Authorities (Goods and Services) Act 1970 which provides for the carrying out by a local authority of certain works of maintenance; or
- (b) an agreement made by virtue of any other enactment (including a provision of a local Act) which provides for the carrying out by a local authority of any construction or maintenance work.[14]

A local authority may not enter into a works contract whose value exceeds an amount prescribed by the Secretary of State except as a result of acceptance of a tender where the invitation to tender was extended to at least three other persons. In the case of contracts at or below the prescribed amount, conditions prescribed in regulations made by the Secretary of State must be complied with. Such regulations may prescribe the manner in which the value of a contract is to be determined, exclude certain descriptions of contract and vary the number of persons tendering.

Functional work

Functional work means construction or maintenance work undertaken   **27-31** by a local authority otherwise than under a works contract for the performance of, or in connection with:

- (a) their functions; or
- (b) their obligations under any arrangements, agreement or require- ment made under any enactment and providing for the discharge by them of any functions of:
    - (i)   a Minister of the Crown; or
    - (ii)   a water authority; or
    - (iii) a local authority under Part VI of the Local Government Act 1972 (discharge of functions, *e.g.* by delegation under section 101).

---

[13] As amended by the Local Government Act 1985, Sched. 17.
[14] This term is defined in s. 20. It includes painting: *Wilkinson* v. *Doncaster Metropolitan Borough Council, The Times,* July 23, 1985.

It does not include work done by placing a contract with another person, either directly or through a sub-contractor, unless the work done under such a contract is dependent upon, or incidental or preparatory to, other work undertaken or to be undertaken by persons in the employment of the local authority.

When a local authority is about to undertake functional work it must first prepare a written statement of the amount which will be credited to the direct labour organisation revenue account (to which reference is made below) or of a method by which it intends that the amount to be so credited shall be calculated. In the case of functional work of the type prescribed by the Secretary of State the authority may not proceed to undertake the work until it has invited at least three other persons to tender for it.

If an authority is asked by any person to furnish him with a written statement showing the tender figures and who is to undertake the work and its estimated cost, the authority must comply with the request.

Accounting and financial provisions

27–32 There are rules laid down as to accounting practice. Each authority undertaking construction or maintenance work under works contracts or by way of functional work must keep a revenue account and such other accounts as the Secretary of State may direct in respect of the following descriptions of work:

(a) general highway works and works in connection with the construction or maintenance of a sewer;

(b) works of new construction, other than general highway works or works in connection with the construction of a sewer, the cost of which in the estimation of the authority or development body will exceed £50,000;

(c) works as in (b), the cost of which in the estimation of the authority or development body will not exceed £50,000; and

(d) works of maintenance within the meaning of the Act of 1970, other than such works of maintenance in connection with highways or sewers.[15]

An authority may not credit any revenue account in respect of the cost of carrying out functional works with a sum in excess of the appropriate amount, that is to say, the amount appearing in the written statement referred to above or calculated in accordance with the method in that statement.

Authorities are required to secure such positive rate of return on capital as the Secretary of State may direct and he may deprive authorities of the power to maintain direct labour organisations where the prescribed rate

---

[15] 1980 Act, s. 10(2), as substituted by the Local Government (Direct Labour Organisations) (Accounts) Regulations 1981 (S.I. 1981 No. 339).

of return has not been achieved. A deficit in a revenue account is charged, in the first instance, against any direct labour organisation reserve fund established by the authority: otherwise the deficit falls to be met by the general rate fund.

Authorities are under a duty to prepare, not later than September 30 in respect of the preceding financial year, a balance sheet, a revenue account, and a statement of rate of return. In addition, each authority which has undertaken construction or maintenance work under works contracts or by way of functional work or both is obliged to prepare an annual report not later than September 30 in the financial year following that to which it relates.

CHAPTER 28

LOCAL GOVERNMENT IN GREATER LONDON

28-01   The administrative area of Greater London is comprised of the area
of 32 London boroughs, the City of London and the Temples, and is
administered by (a) the London borough councils, (b) the Corporation of
the City of London, (c) the Inner and Middle Temples, and (d) a number
of ad hoc authorities. The 12 London boroughs whose areas, together
with the City of London, formed the administrative county of London are
known as "inner London boroughs"; the remaining area of Greater
London is made up of the "outer London boroughs."

The law relating to administration in Greater London is found in the
London Government Act 1963, as amended, in statutory provisions which
that Act applies and in the Local Government Acts of 1972 and 1985.

The Act of 1963 abolished the London County Council, the Middlesex
County Council, 28 metropolitan borough councils, and all other local
authorities (except the Corporation of the City of London and the
Temples) within the area of Greater London. It established the Greater
London Council and the London borough councils which took on their
statutory functions on April 1, 1965.

The Greater London Council's main responsibilities were for metropolitan roads, traffic management, refuse disposal, the fire service, land
drainage and flood protection, education in the inner London area
through a special committee, and building construction control in the
inner London area. It shared responsibility in planning and housing
matters with the London borough councils and the Common Council of
the City of London.

On the abolition of the Greater London Council on April 1, 1986, by
the Local Government Act 1985, its functions were distributed among the
remaining local authorities, other existing bodies and certain new
authorities.

Local authorities

London borough councils

28-02   There are 32 boroughs and they are listed in Schedule 1 to the London
Government Act 1963. The Queen-in-Council granted a charter of
incorporation of the inhabitants of each borough, and this charter deals
with such matters as the number of councillors and the division of the
borough into wards. Each borough elects a mayor and deputy mayor at
its annual meeting. The term of office of councillors is four years from the
election of 1978, and they all retire together.

The London borough councils are general purpose authorities and with **28-03** the abolition of the Greater London Council on April 1, 1986, they became solely responsible for local government administration in Greater London, outside the City and the Temples, apart from those functions allocated to the ad hoc authorities referred to below.

The City of London

The City of London Corporation is a body corporate by prescription. It **28-04** has a number of charters—the earliest was conferred by William I. The charters of Edward III (1341) and Richard II (1377 and 1383) recognised the right of the corporation to alter its own constitution by act of the Common Council. The following are the constituent elements in the government of the city.

(1) The Court of Common Hall. This consists of the Lord Mayor, sheriffs, aldermen and those freemen of the city who are liverymen of City Companies of at least one year's standing. The Court of Common Hall elects two sheriffs each year and nominates for the mayoralty two aldermen who have occupied the office of sheriff.

(2) The Court of Common Council. This is the principal governing body and consists of the Lord Mayor, aldermen and 159 common council men, who are elected annually at the wardmotes. These are assemblies at which all the inhabitants of the ward are entitled to be present, but only those statutorily qualified may vote.

(3) The Court of Aldermen. This consists of 26 aldermen, who occupy the office for life but who customarily resign not later than the age of 75 years. Twenty-five are elected, one by each of the 25 wards of the city, and one sits for the non-existent ward of Bridge-Without-Southwark. The Court of Alderman chooses the Recorder and exercises certain police and road traffic functions.

(4) The Lord Mayor. The Court of Aldermen appoints as Lord Mayor one of the two senior aldermen elected by the Court of Common Hall.

The internal composition and administrative arrangements of the City Corporation remained unchanged under the London Government Act 1963, except that it exercises all the functions of a London borough council. The Common Council thus retained its earlier functions and acquired others.

The Temples

The Inner Temple and the Middle Temple are small areas having **28-05** separate identities as local government areas for certain specific purposes, e.g. public health. For certain other purposes, e.g. food and drugs and weights and measures, the Temples are administered by the Common Council of the City of London.[1]

[1] See ss. 180, 198 and 201 of the Local Government Act 1972.

Ad hoc areas and authorities

The Inner London Education Authority

28-06   This authority was formerly a special committee of the Greater London Council comprising the members of that council for Inner London and one representative from each of the twelve Inner London boroughs and from the City Corporation. It was established as a separate corporate body, known until the abolition date as the Inner London Interim Education Authority, by section 18 of the Local Government Act 1985.[2] The Act provided that the authority should initially consist of the existing members who would continue to serve until directly elected members of the new authority took office. Ordinary elections, the first taking place in May 1986, are held every four years thereafter, at the same time as elections for London borough councillors. At the first elections two members are to be elected for each parliamentary constituency of the inner London area but subsequent elections are to be on the basis of one member for each electoral division.[3]

The authority must appoint a chairman and vice-chairman as the first business at the annual meeting of the authority and may pay them such allowances to meet the expenses of their office as it thinks reasonable.[4]

The authority precepts for its expenditure on the Inner London rating authorities[5] and is under a duty to consult them about its draft budget and main policy objectives and on school reorganisation proposals.[6] It is subject to rate limitation under Part I of the Rates Act 1984 and is eligible to receive block grant as a local authority under Part VI of the Local Government, Planning and Land Act 1980.[7] The authority is also subject to similar statutory provisions relating to borrowing, accounts and audit and financial administration as local authorities generally.[8] Other local authority provisions, subject to certain modifications, are applied to the Inner London Education Authority by Schedule 14 of the Local Government Act 1985.

The Secretary of State is empowered to review the exercise by the authority of its education functions and is required to lay before Parliament a report on any review before May 31, 1991.[9]

The outer London boroughs continue as education authorities in the remaining part of Greater London.

---

[2] See the Local Government Act 1985 (New Authorities) (Appointed Days) Order 1985 (S.I. 1985 No. 1283). See also the Local Government (Inner London Education Authority) Order 1985 (S.I. 1985 No. 1341).
[3] Local Government Act 1985, s. 19.
[4] *Ibid.* s. 20.
[5] *Ibid.* s. 68.
[6] *Ibid.* s. 21.
[7] *Ibid.* ss. 68, 69.
[8] *Ibid.* ss. 70–73.
[9] *Ibid.* s. 22.

The London Fire and Civil Defence Authority

This authority was established as a separate corporate body consisting **28-07** of one member appointed by the Common Council and one by each of the London borough councils under section 27 of and Schedule 10 to the Local Government Act 1985.[10] The Secretary of State may, after consultation with the constituent authorities, alter the size or composition of the authority having regard to the number of local government electors in the areas of the constituent authorities.[11] A member may be replaced at any time by a constituent council appointing him.[12]

The authority is required each year to appoint a chairman and vice–chairman from among its members and may pay them a reasonable allowance to meet the expenses of their office. It must also appoint a clerk to the authority and have regard to the desirability of that person being the chief officer of a constituent authority.[13]

The authority is responsible for the powers and duties formerly exercised by the Greater London Council under the Fire Services Acts 1947 to 1959, the Fire Precautions Act 1971, the Civil Defence (General Local Authority Functions) Regulations 1983 and other relevant legislation.

Its position as regards precepting, rate limitation, block grant, finance and the application of local authority provisions is similar to that outlined above for the Inner London Education Authority.

The London Residuary Body

This body was established as a corporate body under section 57 of and **28-08** Schedule 13 to the Local Government Act 1985.[14] It consists of five to ten members appointed by the Secretary of State who must appoint one of them to be chairman and may appoint one to be vice-chairman. One of the members is to be appointed by the Secretary of State from the membership of the London Co-ordinating Committee (see below) after consultation with that committee.

From April 1, 1986, the functions of the London Residuary Body include the following[15]:

(i) the assumption of all the rights and liabilities in respect of the external debt of the Greater London Council for which purpose each rating authority in the area, the Inner London Education Authority and the London Fire and Civil Defence Authority are deemed to have borrowed from the Residuary Body the sums

[10] See the Local Government Act 1985 (New Authorities) (Appointed Days) Order 1985 (S.I. 1985 No. 1283).
[11] Local Government Act 1985 s. 29.
[12] *Ibid.* s. 31.
[13] *Ibid.* s. 34.
[14] See the London Residuary Body (Appointed Day) Order 1985 (S.I. 1985 No. 1263).
[15] Local Government Act 1985, ss. 58–63.

specified in an order made by the Secretary of State in the terms specified in the order;

(ii) the making of redundancy and compensation payments to former Greater London Council staff;

(iii) the administration of the superannuation fund transferred from the Greater London Council and the payment of pensions;

(iv) the taking over of all property, rights and liabilities of the Greater London Council for which other provision is not made;

(v) the winding up of the accounts of the Greater London Council and their presenting for audit.

In exercising its functions the Residuary Body is required to comply with any directions given to it by the Secretary of State but failure to comply with any direction will not of itself invalidate any transaction entered into.[16]

The Residuary Body is required to use its best endeavours to complete its work as soon as practicable and in any event within five years of the abolition date. Where this cannot be done it must make arrangements for the transfer of relevant activities to another body or submit proposals to the Secretary of State for him to transfer them by order. Not later than four years after the abolition date the body must submit to the Secretary of State a scheme for its winding-up and the disposal of its remaining functions, property, rights and liabilities.[17]

The London Residuary Body is empowered by section 74 of the 1985 Act to make levies on the rating authorities in Greater London to meet its liabilities in respect of any financial year. The amount of the levy on each authority is determined in proportion to its population estimated by the Registrar General.

As with the Inner London Education Authority and the London Fire and Civil Defence Authority, many statutory provisions which apply to local authorities generally are applied to the London Residuary Body with appropriate modifications and adjustments.

London Regional Transport

28-09　　　Until June 29, 1984, the London Transport Executive was responsible for providing public passenger services in the Greater London area. Its members were appointed by the Greater London Council which also exercised a measure of control over general policy, fares and finance.

The London Regional Transport Act 1984 reconstituted the London Transport Executive as London Regional Transport and transferred control from the Greater London Council to the Secretary of State. Provision was also made for the establishment of a new consultative body, the London Regional Passengers Committee, to be appointed by the Secretary of State.

[16] Local Government Act 1985, s. 65.
[17] *Ibid.* s. 67.

Under section 50 of the 1984 Act, local authorities in the Greater London area may enter into arrangements with London Regional Transport, British Rail and independent transport service operators for travel concessions.

Police

The police authority for the metropolitan police district, which includes **28-10** Greater London apart from the City, is the Home Secretary. The Receiver of the Metropolitan Police who was constituted a corporation sole under the Metropolitan Police (Receiver) Act 1861, precepts on the rating authorities in the metropolitan police district for the expenses of the force.

The Common Council of the City of London is the police authority for the City.

Thames Regional Water Authority

This authority, which includes members appointed jointly by the **28-11** London borough councils and the City Corporation, is the water and sewerage authority for the Greater London area under the Water Act 1973.

Provision is made in section 11 of the Local Government Act 1985 for the transfer to the authority of the land drainage and flood prevention functions of the Greater London Council in the area known as the London Excluded Area, which comprises the bulk of Greater London and a small part of Surrey, by order made by the Secretary of State.[18] This brings the arrangements into line with the rest of the country.

London borough councils and the City Corporation have a number of independent functions in relation to water supplies and sewerage.[19]

Port of London Authority

This authority established in 1908 controls the docks and wharves up to **28-12** Teddington Lock.[20] The Common Council is the port health authority.

Distribution of functions

On the abolition of the Greater London Council the majority of its **28-13** functions apart from those transferred to ad hoc authorities as noted above, were transferred to the London borough councils and the Common Council. A joint committee of those authorities, known as the London Co-ordinating Committee, was set up as required by section 95 of the Local Government Act 1985 to co-ordinate the preparations for the transfer and to promote the making of arrangements, where appropriate,

---

[18] No order had been made at the time of going to press.
[19] See Local Government Act 1972, s. 181.
[20] Port of London Authority Act 1908.

for the joint discharge of functions under section 101 of the Local Government Act 1972.

Certain functions were made the subject of special provisions as follows.

Housing

28-14　　Under the London Government Act 1963, the Greater London Council was given the powers of a housing authority but by the abolition date the bulk of its housing stock had been transferred to the London borough councils by orders made by the Secretary of State under section 23 of the Act. Under these orders the Greater London Council retained certain rights and responsibilities in respect of the transferred properties. They included the right to nominate tenants to a proportion of lettings for a period, obligations to prepare and undertake programmes of certain types of repair and renovation and to make deficit payments to the transferee authorities.

Section 95 of the Local Government Act 1985 enables the Secretary of State by order to extinguish such rights and liabilities on or after the abolition date and transfer to himself the right to nominate tenants with power to delegate the right to any other authority or body. Where nomination rights were acquired by the Greater London Council in consideration of payments by that council, any outstanding liabilities on or after the abolition date become the responsibility of the London Residuary Body. That body also assumes responsibility under section 62 of the 1985 Act for outstanding housing advances made by the Greater London Council.

Planning

28-15　　Under section 3 of the Local Government Act 1985, the London borough councils and the Common Council became the sole local planning authority for their area. They were required by section 5 to establish by the abolition date a joint planning committee for Greater London to:

(a) consider and advise the authorities on matters of common interest relating to the planning and development of Greater London;
(b) inform the Secretary of State of the views of the authorities on such matters and matters on which he has requested their advice;
(c) inform the local planning authorities for areas in the vicinity of Greater London of their views on matters of common interest relating to planning and development.

The expenses of the joint committee incurred with the approval of not less than two-thirds of the constituent authorities are to be met by all of them in such proportions as they may decide or, if they cannot agree, by the Secretary of State.

The responsibilities of the Greater London Council with regard to listed buildings and conservation areas and its powers to undertake research and to publish information on the history, architecture and archeology of London, are transferred to the Historic Buildings and Monuments Commission for England by section 6 of and Schedule 2 to the 1985 Act.

Building

Building construction control in the Inner London area which was **28-16** previously dealt with by the Greater London Council under the London Building Acts 1930 to 1982 was transferred to the Inner London borough councils and the Common Council by section 16 of and Schedule 8, para. 14 to the Local Government Act 1985. Provision was made for the building regulations made under section 1 of the Building Act 1984, which operate throughout the rest of the country, to be applied to the Inner London area.[21]

Highways and road traffic

"Metropolitan roads" for which the Greater London Council was **28-17** previously responsible ceased to be such on the abolition date and became the responsibility of the London borough councils and the Common Council; the Secretary of State may by order direct that any one of these to be a trunk road.[22]

The Secretary of State may, after consulting the local authorities likely to be affected, designate a road in Greater London for the purpose of facilitating the movement of traffic. The local highway authority must then notify the Secretary of State of any proposal to exercise any power of traffic regulation and parking on such roads and may not exercise the power unless the Secretary of State approves the proposal or does not object within one month.[23]

The Secretary of State may issue guidance as to the exercise by councils of their traffic regulation powers in Greater London for the purpose of ensuring that they do not have any adverse effect on traffic or parking in the areas of other councils.[24]

Waste regulation and disposal

By section 9 of and Schedule 6 to the Local Government Act 1985, the **28-18** waste regulation and disposal functions of the Greater London Council were transferred to London borough councils and the Common Council. Where, however, the Secretary of State considers it advantageous for joint arrangements to be made, he is required by order to establish a

---

[21] Building Act 1984, s. 46 and Sched. 3, para. 3. See the Building (Inner London) Regulations 1985 (S.I. 1985 No 1936).
[22] Local Government Act 1985, s. 8 and Sched. 4.
[23] *Ibid.* s. 8 and Sched. 5, para. 5.
[24] *Ibid.* s. 8 and Sched. 5, para. 6.

single authority for the whole or part of the area except where satisfactory voluntary arrangements had been made by November 15, 1985.[25]

Grants to voluntary organisations

28–19 The London borough councils and the Common Council are empowered by section 48 of the Local Government Act 1985 to make a scheme for making grants to voluntary organisations whose activities will directly or indirectly benefit the whole of Greater London or any part of it extending beyond the area of any constituent council. Grants are made by one of the constituent councils designated for the purpose, and the constituent councils must contribute to the expenditure incurred, with the approval of at least two-thirds of them, in proportion to the populations of their respective areas. The total expenditure must not exceed the amount prescribed by the Secretary of State. The powers conferred by the section are not to be regarded as restricting the powers conferred under section 137 of the Local Government Act 1972.

Section 49 of the 1985 Act empowers the Secretary of State by order to provide for the making of grants by the London Residuary Body to charities wholly or primarily for the benefit of Greater London out of money received by it from the disposal of land.

Administration of justice

28–20 The system for the administration of justice in the metropolitan area was largely re-cast by the Administration of Justice Act 1964, consequent upon the changes in local government brought about by the London Government Act 1963. It made changes in the system of magistrates' courts in inner London, giving effect to recommendations of the Interdepartmental Committee on Magistrates' Courts in London[26] with regard to the integration of the work of the metropolitan stipendiary magistrates and justices of the peace in inner London.

Central Criminal Court

This court was formerly the Assize Court for Greater London. It was replaced by the Crown Court by the Courts Act 1971, but when it sits in the City of London it is still known as the Central Criminal Court and the Lord Mayor and any alderman of the City of London may sit with the judge.[27]

Commission areas

For other judicial purposes Greater London is divided into five "London commission areas," and each of these areas has a separate commission of the peace.[28]

[25] Local Government Act 1985, s. 10. See § 16–45.
[26] Cmnd. 1606.
[27] Courts Act 1971, s. 4(7).
[28] See the Justices of the Peace Act 1979, s. 2.

Magistrates' courts

The Act of 1979[29] deals with the organisation of magistrates' courts in **28-21** the inner London area. Lay justices share the criminal jurisdiction formerly exercised by the metropolitan stipendiary magistrates—before the 1964 reorganisation, two sets of courts had functioned independently, and criminal jurisdiction was exercised mainly by stipendiaries. The administration of magistrates' courts in inner London is governed by a committee of magistrates, consisting of lay magistrates and stipendiary magistrates. It has responsibility for the division of the area into petty sessional divisions, the employment of staff, the division of work between stipendiary and lay magistrates, the provision of instruction for justices, and other financial and administrative matters.

In the outer London area the service was administered by a separate **28-22** magistrates' courts committee funded by the Greater London Council for each of the four outer London Commission Areas. On the abolition of the Greater London Council the four area committees were dissolved and replaced by a separate magistrates' courts committee for each of the outer London boroughs, and the functions of the Greater London Council in respect of the service were transferred to the London borough councils by section 12 of the Local Government Act 1985.[30]

Coroners

The duty of appointing coroners in the Greater London area (outside **28-23** the City), formerly exercised by the Greater London Council under section 220 of the Local Government Act 1972, was transferred to the London borough councils by section 13 of the Local Government Act 1985. Appointments are subject to the approval of the Secretary of State and where a coroner's district includes two or more London boroughs, the Secretary of State may designate one of them to be responsible for the appointment after consultation with the other councils affected.

Lord lieutenant and sheriff

There is one lord lieutenant, one high sheriff for Greater London **28-24** (excluding the City), and an under-sheriff for each commission area.[31]

The City of London

The Lord Mayor and Aldermen of the City of London by virtue of a **28-25** charter granted by King George II are justices of the peace for the City, and a commission of the peace issues for the City as a county of itself by

[29] ss. 31 to 38 and s. 58.
[30] For transitional arrangements see the Local Government (Magistrates' Courts, etc.) Order 1985 (S.I. 1985 No. 1383).
[31] See Reserve Forces Act 1980, s. 130 and s. 19 of the Administration of Justice Act 1964, as amended by Sched. 30 of the Local Government Act 1972; also Sheriffs Act 1887 and the Local Government Act 1972, s. 219.

virtue of section 1(2) of the Justices of the Peace Act 1968 but under section 39 of the Justices of the Peace Act 1979 any of them may be excluded by the Lord Chancellor from the exercise of his functions as a justice. The Lord Mayor is chairman of the justices with the style of Chief Magistrate.

The Mayor's and City of London Court is a county court for the City and the Circuit judge assigned to it is known as the judge of the Mayor's and City of London Court.[32]

It is declared, for the removal of doubt, that the Inner Temple and Middle Temple are included in the City of London for the purposes of the law relating to the administration of justice, lieutenants, sheriffs and related matters.[33]

---

[32] See Courts Act 1971, s. 42.
[33] See Administration of Justices Act 1964, s. 26.

ALLOCATION OF PRINCIPAL FUNCTIONS

A. METROPOLITAN AREAS

All principal government functions are exercised by metropolitan district councils **29-01**
except the following:

Police	Metropolitan police authorities (*a*)
Fire	Metropolitan fire and civil defence
Civil Defence (*b*)	authorities
Passenger Transport	Metropolitan passenger transport authorities
Waste regulation and disposal	Greater Manchester and Merseyside Waste Disposal Authorities (*c*)

Notes
(*a*) The Northumbria police authority is the authority for the Tyne and Wear
   metropolitan county and the non-metropolitan county of Northumberland.
(*b*) Non-metropolitan district councils may supply information, provide assistance and establish an emergency centre.
(*c*) Waste disposal functions in Wigan are exercised by the district council and
   not the Greater Manchester Waste Disposal Authority.

B. NON-METROPOLITAN AREAS IN ENGLAND[1]

Non-metropolitan County Councils	*Non-metropolitan District Councils*
Education	
Youth Employment	
Personal Social Services	
Libraries	
Museums and art galleries (*a*)	Museums and art galleries (*a*)
Housing—	Housing—
Certain reserve powers	Provision
	Management
	Slum clearance
	House and area improvement
Town development (*a*)	Town development (*a*)
Planning—	Planning—
Structure plans	Local plans (*c*)
Development plan schemes (*b*)	
Development control (*d*)	Development control (*d*)
	Advertisement control
Derelict land (*a*)	Derelict land (*a*)
National parks	
Country parks (*a*)	Country parks (*a*)
Conservation areas (*a*)	Conservation areas (*a*)
Building preservation notices (*a*)	Building preservation notices (*a*)
	Listed building control

Tree preservation (a)	Tree preservation (a)
Acquisition and disposal of land for planning purposes, development or redevelopment (a)	Acquisition and disposal of land for planning purposes, development or redevelopment (a)
Footpaths and bridleways— Surveys	Footpaths and bridleways—
Creation, diversion and extinguishment orders (a)	Creation, diversion and extinguishment orders (a)
Maintenance (e)	
Protection (a)	Protection (a)
Signposting	
Transportation—	Transportation—
Transport planning	
Highways (e)	
Traffic	
All parking	Off-street parking (f)
Public transport (g)	Public transport undertakings (h)
Road safety	
Highway lighting	
Footway lighting (a)	Footway lighting (a)
Environmental health—	Environmental health—
Animal diseases	Food safety and hygiene
	Communicable disease
	Slaughterhouses
	Offices, shops and railway premises (j)
	Factories
	Home safety
	Water and sewerage (k)
Refuse disposal	Refuse collection
Consumer protection (e.g. weights and measures, trade descriptions, explosives, food and drugs)	Clean air
	Building regulations
	Coast protection
	Cemetries and crematoria
Police (l)	Markets and fairs
Fire (l)	By-laws
Swimming baths (a)	Swimming baths (a)
Physical training and recreation (a)	Physical training and recreation (a)
Parks and open spaces (a)	Parks and open spaces (a)
Smallholdings	Allotments
	Local licensing
Airports (a)	Airports (a)
Local lotteries (a)	Local lotteries (a)

¹This table is based on the table in DoE Circular 121/72.

Notes

  (a) Concurrent powers exercisable by county and district councils.
  (b) In consultation with district councils.
  (c) Except in national parks where counties are responsible. Responsibility for local plans subject to development plan schemes or structure plan.
  (d) Primarily a district council function except in the case of a national park or of "county matters" as defined in Schedule 16 to the Act.

(*e*) District councils may claim maintenance powers for footpaths, bridleways, and urban roads which are neither trunk roads nor classified roads.

(*f*) In accordance with the county transportation plan.

(*g*) Non-metropolitan counties have co-ordination functions.

(*h*) Some non-metropolitan districts under local Act powers.

(*j*) Fire precautions under the Offices, Shops and Railway Premises Act will be a county council responsibility.

(*k*) Through agency.

(*l*) Subject to amalgamation schemes.

Local authorities have power under section 101 of the Local Government Act 1972 to arrange for the discharge of their functions by any other authority.

Powers may be vested in joint boards under various Acts and the provisions of the Local Government Act 1972 may be applied to such boards under section 241 of the Act.

Many local authorities have acquired power to undertake other functions by means of local Acts.

C. Wales

The distribution of functions in Wales broadly follows the distribution of **29–02** functions in England, except that the following fall to district councils or may in certain circumstances be exercised by them: refuse disposal, disposal of abandoned vehicles, libraries, on and off-street car parking, food and drugs, weights and measures, and certain functions relating to agriculture listed under section 200 of the Local Government Act 1972.

PRINCIPAL POWERS AND DUTIES OF PARISH AND COMMUNITY COUNCILS

30–01

Function	*Powers and Duties*	*Statutory Provisions*
Allotments	Power to provide allotments. Duty to provide allotment gardens if demand unsatisfied	Small Holdings and Allotments Act 1908, ss. 23, 26 and 42
Baths and washhouses	Power to provide public baths, washhouses and bathing places	Public Health Act 1936, ss. 221, 222, 223 and 227
Burial grounds, cemeteries and crematoria	Power to provide	Local Government Act 1972, ss. 214 and 215. Parish Councils and Burial Authorities (Miscellaneous Provisions) Act 1970, s. 1
Bus shelters	Power to provide and maintain shelters	Local Government (Miscellaneous Provisions) Act 1953, s. 4
By-laws	Power to make by-laws in regard to— Pleasure grounds, etc	Public Health Act 1875, s. 164. Public Health Acts Amendment Act 1890, s. 44. Local Government Act 1972, s. 270 (1) and Sched. 14 para. 27
	Cycle parks	Road Traffic Regulation Act 1984, s. 57
	Baths and washhouses	Public Health Act 1936, s. 223 Local Government Act 1972, s. 270 and Sched. 14 para. 18
	Open spaces	Open Spaces Act 1906, s. 15
	Mortuaries and post-mortem rooms	Public Health Act 1936, s. 198
Charities	Duty to receive accounts of parochial charities	Charities Act 1960, s. 32. Charities Act 1985, s. 1
Clocks	Power to provide public clocks	Parish Councils Act 1957, s. 2
Closed churchyards	Powers as to maintenance	Local Government Act 1972, s. 215

Commons and common pastures	Powers in relation to inclosure and as to regulation and management	Inclosure Act 1845. Local Government Act 1894, s. 8(4). Smallholdings and Allotments Act 1908, s. 34
Conference facilities	Power to provide and encourage the use of facilities	Local Government Act 1972, s. 144
Community centres	Power to provide and equip buildings for use of clubs having athletic, social or educational objects	Local Government (Miscellaneous Provisions) Act 1976, s. 19
Drainage	Power to deal with ponds and ditches	Public Health Act 1936, s. 260
Education	Right to appoint school governor	Education Act 1980, s. 2
Entertainment and the arts	Provision of entertainment and the support of the arts	Local Government Act 1972, ss. 144 and 145
Gifts	Power to accept	Local Government Act 1972, s. 139
Highways	Power to repair and maintain footpaths and bridleways	Highways Act 1980, ss. 30, 43 and 50
	Power to light roads and public places	Parish Councils Act 1957, s. 3. Highways Act 1980, s. 301.
	Power to erect flagpoles and other structures for displaying decorations	Highways Act 1980, s. 144
	Provision of litter bins	Litter Act 1983, ss. 5, 6
	Power to provide parking places for bicycles, motor-cycles and other vehicles	Road Traffic Regulation Act 1984, ss. 57–60
	Power to acquire rights of way	Highways Act 1980, ss. 30, 72
	Power to provide roadside seats and shelters, and omnibus shelters	Parish Councils Act 1957, s. 1. Local Government (Miscellaneous Provisions) Act 1953, s. 4
	Consent of parish council required for stopping up or diversion of highway or for removal of the requirement of maintenance at public expense	Highways Act 1980, ss. 47, 116
	Power to complain to district council as to maintenance of highways or protection of rights of way and roadside wastes	Highways Act 1980, s. 130

Highways—*contd.*	Power to prosecute in respect of ploughing of footpaths and bridleways	Highways Act 1980, s. 134
	Power to provide traffic signs and other notices	Road Traffic Regulation Act 1984, s. 72
	Power as to roadside verges	Highways Act 1980, s. 96
Investments	Power to participate in schemes of collective investment	Trustee Investments Act 1961, s. 11
Land	Acquisition	Local Government Act 1972, s. 139
	Rights of way over land	Local Government Act 1894, s. 8(1)(*g*)
Litter	Provision of receptacles	Litter Act 1983, ss. 5, 6
Lotteries	Power to promote	Lotteries and Amusements Act 1976, s. 7
Mortuaries and post-mortem rooms	Power to provide mortuaries and post-mortem rooms	Public Health Act 1936, s. 198
Nuisances	Power to deal with offensive ditches	Public Health Act 1936, s. 260

30–02

Open spaces	Power to acquire land	Public Health Act 1875, s. 164. Local Government Act 1972, s. 270, Sched. 14, para. 27. Open Spaces Act 1906, ss, 9 and 10
Parish property and documents	Management and custody	Local Government Act 1972, s. 227
Postal and Telecommunications facilities	Power to pay the Post Office, British Telecommunications or any other public telecommunications operator any loss sustained in providing additional post or telegraph office or telecommunications facilities	Post Office Act 1953, s. 51. British Telecommunications Act 1981, Sched. 4, para. 12. Telecommunications Act 1984, s. 97
Public buildings and village halls	Power to provide buildings for offices and for public meetings and assemblies	Local Government Act 1972, s. 133. Local Government (Miscellaneous Provisions) Act 1976, s. 19
Public conveniences	Power to provide	Public Health Act 1936, s. 87

Recreation	Power to acquire land for recreation grounds, public walks and open spaces and to manage and control them	Local Government Act 1894, s. 6. Public Health Acts Amendment Act 1890, s. 44. Local Government Act 1972, s. 270 and Sched. 14, para. 27. Open Spaces Act 1906, ss. 9 and 10
	Power to provide gymnasiums, playing fields, holiday camps	Local Government (Miscellaneous Provisions) Act 1976, s. 19
	Provision of boating pools	Public Health Act 1961, s. 54
Town and country planning	Right to be notified of planning applications	Local Government Act 1972, Sched. 16, para. 20
Tourism	Power to encourage	Local Government Act 1972, s. 144
Village greens	Power to provide	Public Health Act 1875 s. 164. Local Government Act 1972, Sched. 14, para. 27
War memorials	Power to maintain, repair, protect and adapt war memorials	War Memorials (Local Authorities' Powers) Act 1923 s. 1, as amended by Local Government Act 1948, s. 133
Water supply	Power to utilise well, spring or stream and to provide facilities for obtaining water therefrom	Public Health Act 1936, ss. 125, 260

TABLE OF THE MORE COMMONLY USED SPECIFIC STATUTORY POWERS AUTHORISING THE PURCHASE OF LAND COMPULSORILY

31–01

Functions	Basic Statutory Provisions	Purposes
Aerodromes	Civil Aviation Act 1982, ss. 30, 41, 42	Provision of aerodromes. Purposes of civil aviation
Allotments	Small Holdings and Allotments Act 1908, ss. 25(1), 39 and Sched. 1, Part I (s. 36 as to London) as amended	Provision of allotments
Caravan sites	Caravan Sites and Control of Development Act 1960, s. 24	Purchase of sites
Cemeteries	Local Government Act 1972, s. 214(2), Sched. 26	For cemetery purposes
Children services	Children and Young Persons Act 1969, ss. 35 50, s. 68 Children and Young Persons Act 1963, s. 1 Children Act 1948, ss. 19, 56 Children Act 1975, ss. 1, 2	To carry out powers and duties under these statutes and s. 1 of the Children and Young Persons Act 1963

31–02

Civil defence and emergency services	Civil Defence Act 1948, s. 4	For the purposes of the Act
Coast protection	Coast Protection Act 1949, ss. 14, 27	Carrying out of coast protection work
Diseases of animals	Animal Health Act 1981, s. 55	Provision of wharves; provision of burial grounds for carcasses
Education	Education Act 1944, s. 90(1), as amended by the Education (Miscellaneous Provisions) Act 1948, s. 10	Land required for the purposes of any school or college or otherwise for the purposes of the Education Act

31–03

Fire services	Fire Services Act 1947, s. 3(5)	For the purposes of the Act
Food	Food Act 1984, s. 110	To carry out functions under the Act

Highways	Highways Act 1980, ss. 238 to 255	For construction and improvement of highways and other specified highway purposes
		Mitigating adverse effect of highway works or use
	Road Traffic Regulation Act 1984, s. 40	Provision of parking places
	Road Traffic Regulation Act 1984, s. 97	For discharge of functions relating to traffic wardens
Housing	Housing Act 1985, ss. 192, 300(3)	Purchase for temporary accommodation of houses unfit for human habitation
	Housing Act 1985, ss. 9(3), 17(3)–(4)	Purposes of Part V of the Act (provision of housing accommodation)
	Housing Act 1985, s. 290(3)–(4)	Land comprised in, or surrounded by or adjoining a clearance area
	Housing Act 1985, s. 255(1),	Land adjoining or within a general improvement area
	Housing Act 1985, s. 243(2)	Housing accommodation in housing action area
	Housing Act 1985, s. 227	Improvement of dwellings
Land drainage	Water Resources Act 1963, s. 65	For land drainage functions of water authorities
Markets	Food Act 1984, s. 110	To establish a market (but not to acquire an existing market)
Parks and recreation facilities and open spaces	Local Government (Miscellaneous Provisions) Act 1976, s. 19	Various recreational facilities, both indoor and outdoor
	National Parks and Access to the Countryside Act 1949, ss. 12(4), 13(8), 21, 53, 54 and 103(1), as amended by the Local Government, Planning and Land Act 1980, s. 1(7); Sched. 7, para. 1(1)	Provision of accommodation, camping sites, parking places, etc., in National Parks improvement of waterways for open-air recreation, provision of ferries for long-distance routes and nature reserves
	Caravan Sites and Control of Development Act 1960, s. 24	Provision of caravan sites
	National Parks and Access to the Countryside Act 1949, ss. 76, 77 and 103(1)	To secure public access for open-air recreation
	National Parks and Access to the Countryside Act 1949, s. 89	To enable trees to be planted to preserve or enhance the natural beauty of the land

	Countryside Act 1968, ss. 7, 9 and 10	For functions as to country parks and other related purposes
31-04 Planning and town development	Town and Country Planning Act 1971, ss. 112 to 114	Development, redevelopment, improvement and other planning purposes, land necessary for the public service, and listed buildings in need of repair
	Mineral Workings Act 1951, s. 17	Reclamation of ironstone land
	Town Development Act 1952, s. 6. Town and Country Planning Act 1971, Sched. 23	Purposes connected with town development
Police	Metropolitan Police Act 1886, ss. 2 and 4(11), as amended	For offices, police stations, houses and buildings required for the purposes of the Metropolitan Police
	Police Act 1964, s. 9	For the purpose of any of the functions of the police authority
Public health	Public Health Act 1936, s. 76	Provision of refuse tips
	Refuse Disposal (Amenity) Act 1978, s. 6(3)	For refuse disposal plant
	Refuse Disposal (Amenity) Act 1978, s. 1	Places for deposit, treatment and disposal of refuse
	Public Health Act 1936, s. 86	For cleansing stations
	Public Health Act 1936, s. 87, as amended by Local Government Act 1972, s. 180, Sched. 14, para. 9	Provision of public conveniences
	Public Health (Control of Disease) Act 1984, s. 27	Provision of disinfecting stations
	Public Health Act 1936, s. 198	Provision of mortuaries and post-mortem rooms
	Public Health Act 1936, ss. 221, 230	Provision of baths, washhouses, swimming baths and bathing places
	Local Government (Miscellaneous Provisions) Act 1976, s. 19	
Slaughterhouses	Slaughterhouses Act 1974, ss. 15, 18	Provision of public slaughterhouses and cold-air stores
	Local Government Act 1974, s. 35 and Sched. 6	

Social services	National Assistance Act 1948, s. 58 and Part III Mental Health Act 1959, s. 8 Health Services and Public Health Act 1968, Part II Employment and Training Act 1973, s. 40(1), Sched. 3, para. 3	Provision of accommodation for aged or infirm persons, temporary accommodation, workshops, etc., for disabled or mentally disordered
	National Health Service Act 1977, s. 21 and Sched. 8	Care of expectant and nursing mothers and young children, prevention of illness, care and aftercare, and related matters
Water	Water Act 1945, s. 24, as amended and extended by the Water Act 1948, s. 3	Purposes of water authorities
Water resources	Water Resources Act 1963, s. 65	To carry out the function of water authorities

TABLE OF PRINCIPAL LICENSING AND REGISTRATION FUNCTIONS

A. FUNCTIONS EXERCISED BY DISTRICT COUNCILS

32-01 *Nature of Licence*

Statutory Provisions and Statutory Instruments

Acupuncture, tattooing, ear-piercing and electrolysis	Local Government (Miscellaneous Provisions) Act 1982, ss. 13–17
Betting tracks	Betting, Gaming and Lotteries Act 1963, s. 6 and Sched. 3
Bingo and other group games	Lotteries and Amusements Act 1976, s. 16 and Sched. 3
Camping sites	Public Health Act 1936, s. 269
Caravan sites	Caravan Sites and Control of Development Act 1960
Cinemas and cinema clubs	Cinemas Act 1985, s. 1
Common lodging houses	Public Health Act 1936, ss. 235–241, 246–248
Dogs	Dog Licences Act 1959, s. 7 as amended by Post Office Act 1969 and Local Government Act 1972, s 213(1).
Dog breeding	Breeding of Dogs Act 1973, s. 1 as amended by the Local Government, Planning and Land Act 1980, s. 1(6); Sched. 6, para. 15; Sched. 34, Pt. VI
Filling materials: Registration of premises Licence in respect of premises where rag flock is manufactured or stored	Rag Flock and Other Filling Materials Act 1951, s. 2, as amended by the Local Government, Planning and Land Act 1980, s. 1(6); Sched. 6, para. 6
Food: Food hawkers and their premises	Food Act 1984, ss. 62–67
Food manufacturing premises (ice cream, sausages etc.)	Food Act 1984, ss. 16–19
Dairies (other than dairy farms) and dairymen	Food Act 1984, s. 34. Milk and Dairies (General) Regulations 1959 (S.I. 1959 No. 277), as amended, reg. 8
Game: To kill game.	Game Act, 1831, ss. 5, 6, 17, 18, 21–23
Gamekeeper to kill game	Game Licences Act 1860
Gamedealer	Customs and Inland Revenue Act 1883
Sell game to licensed dealer	Local Government Act 1894, ss. 21(3), 27
	Local Government Act 1972, s. 213(1)

Gaming machines not on licensed premises	Gaming Act 1968, s. 34 and Sched. 9, as amended by the Gaming Act (Variation of Monetary Limits) Order 1983 (S.I. 1983 No. 1740)
Hackney carriage and hackney carriage drivers	Public Health Act 1875, s. 171 Town Police Clauses Act 1847, ss. 37, 38, 42–68, as amended by the Local Government Act 1972, s. 180 and Sched. 14, paras. 24, 25 and the Local Government, Planning and Land Act 1980, s. 1(6) and Sched. 6, para. 1 Local Government (Miscellaneous Provisions) Act 1976, ss. 47, 51 Transport Act 1985, ss. 10–17
House to house collections	House to House Collections Act 1939, s. 2, as amended by the Local Government Act 1972, Sched. 29, para. 23
Kennels: Boarding establishments for cats or dogs	Animal Boarding Establishments Act 1963, s. 11, as amended by the Local Government Act 1974, Sched. 6, para. 17
Knackers yards	Slaughterhouses Act 1974, s. 1
Lotteries: Societies promoting	Lotteries and Amusements Act 1976, s. 5, Sched. 1
Moveable Dwellings	Public Health Act 1936, s. 269
Parking: off-street	Transport Act 1978, s. 11. Control of Off-Street Parking (England and Wales) Order 1978 (S.I. 1978 No. 1535)
Pet animal shops	Pet Animals Act 1951, s. 1, as amended by the Local Government Act 1974, Sched. 6, para. 8
Pleasure boats Boatmen	Public Health Acts (Amendment) Act 1907, s. 94, as amended by the Local Government Act 1974, Sched. 6, para. 1 Local Government, Planning and Land Act 1980, s. 186
Pool promoters' registration fee Continuation fee	Betting, Gaming and Lotteries Act 1963, s. 4 and Sched. 2
Poultry meat Licence authorising use of premises as a slaughterhouse or cutting premises	Food Act 1984, ss. 13, 118 The Poultry Meat (Hygiene) Regulations 1976 (S.I. 1976 No. 1209)
Private hire vehicles, operators and drivers	Local Government (Miscellaneous Provisions) Act 1976, ss. 48, 51, 55 Transport Act 1985, ss. 10–17

Private music, dancing and similar entertainment	Private Places of Entertainment (Licensing) Act 1967, s. 1, as amended by the Local Government Act 1972, Sched. 29, para. 27 and the Local Government (Miscellaneous Provisions) Act 1982, Sched. 2, paras. 2–4
Private places of entertainment	Private Places of Entertainment (Licensing) Act 1967, as amended by the Local Government (Miscellaneous Provisions) Act 1982, s. 1 and Sched. 2
Public Entertainments	Local Government (Miscellaneous Provisions) Act 1982, s. 1, Sched. 1
Refreshment houses which are open between 10 p.m. and 5 a.m.	Late Night Refreshment Houses Act 1969, s. 2, as amended by the Local Government Act 1972, s. 204 (9) and the Local Government Act 1974, Sched. 6, para. 24
Riding establishments	Riding Establishments Act 1964, s. 1, as amended by the Riding Establishments Act 1970 and the Local Government Act 1974, Sched. 6, para. 18
Scrap metal dealers	Scrap Metal Dealers Act 1964, s. 1
Sex Shops and Sex Cinemas	Local Government (Miscellaneous Provisions) Act 1982, s. 2, Sched. 3
Slaughterhouses	Slaughterhouses Act 1974, s. 1
Slaughtermen	Slaughterhouses Act 1974, ss. 39 and 40, as amended by the Local Government Act 1974, Sched. 6, para. 26 and the Animal Health Act 1981, Sched. 5
Street collections	Police, Factories, etc., (Miscellaneous Provisions) Act 1916, s. 5, as amended by Local Government Act 1972, s. 251 and Sched. 29
Street trading	Local Government (Miscellaneous Provisions) Act 1982, s. 3 and Sched. 4
Theatres	Theatres Act 1968, 2, 12 and Sched. 1, as amended by the Local Government Act 1972, s. 204(6) and the Local Government, Planning and Land Act 1980, s. 1(6); Sched. 6, para. 11; Sched. 34, Pt. VI
Wild animals	Dangerous Wild Animals Act 1976
Zoos	Zoo Licensing Act 1981

B. Functions Exercised by Non-Metropolitan County Councils and Fire
   Authorities

Cinema film stores	Celluloid and Cinema Films Act 1922, as amended by the Local Government Act 1972, Sched. 29, para. 15, S.I. 1974 No. 1841, and the Local Government Act 1985, Sched. 11, para. 6
	Order of Secretary of State dated 15.9.22 (S.R. & O. 1922 No. 1076)
	Celluloid and Cinematograph Films Act 1922 (Exemption) Regulations 1980 (S.I. 1980 No. 1314)
Sale of explosives including fireworks	Explosives Act 1875, ss. 15, 67, as amended by the Local Government Acts 1972, Sched. 29, para. 19 and 1985, Sched. 11, para. 3
Petroleum and carbide	Petroleum (Consolidation) Act 1928, ss. 1–4, as amended by the Local Government Act 1972, Sched. 29, para. 32, S.I. 1974 No. 1942 and the Local Government Act 1985, Sched. 11, para. 4
	Petroleum (Transfer of Licences) Act 1936, s. 1

C. Functions Exercised by Non-Metropolitan County and Metropolitan
   District Councils

Agencies for supply of nurses	Nurses Agencies Act 1957, s. 2, as amended by the Local Government Act 1972, Sched. 29, para. 30 and the Nurses, Midwives and Health Visitors Act 1979, Sched. 7, para. 9
	Nurses Agencies Regulations 1961 (S.I. 1961 No. 1214 as amended by S.I. 1984 No. 1400)
Employment of children in street trading	Children and Young Persons Act 1933, s. 20, as amended by the Children and Young Persons Act 1963, s. 35
Homes—residential homes for old persons, disabled, mentally disordered	Registered Homes Act 1984 Residential Care Homes Regulations 1984 (S.I. 1984 No. 1345)
Homes—residential homes for children	Children's Homes Act 1982 (from a date to be appointed)
Nurseries and child-minders	Nurseries and Child-Minders Regulation Act 1948
Performing animals	Performing Animals (Registration) Act 1925, as amended by the Local Government Act 1974, Sched. 6, para. 2, Sched. 8, and the Local Government Act 1985, Sched. 8, para. 17

32–02 appears to the right of the "Agencies for supply of nurses" entry.

Poisons—sale	Poisons Act 1972, s. 5, as amended by the Local Government, Planning and Land Act 1980, Sched. 6, para. 13, s. 11, as amended by the Local Government Act 1985, Sched. 8, para. 16
	Poisons List Order 1982 (S.I. 1982 No. 217)
	Poisons Rules 1982 (S.I. 1982 No. 218)
War charities and charities for disabled persons—registration	War Charities Act 1940, ss. 2, 10, as amended by the Local Government Act 1972, s. 210(8)
	National Assistance Act 1948, s. 41, as amended by the Local Government Act 1972, Sched. 23, para. 2(*a*) and the Registered Homes Act 1984, Sched. 1, para. 1

D. Functions Exercised by Police Authorities

32-03 Accommodation addresses	Official Secrets Act 1920, s. 5
Aliens	Immigration Act 1971, s. 4(3)
	The Immigration (Registration with Police) Regulations 1972 (S.I. 1972 No. 1758), as amended by S.I. 1982 Nos. 502 and 1024, and S.I. 1983 No. 442
Firearms	Firearms Act 1968, ss. 32 and 35
Shotguns	Firearms Act 1982
Firearms dealer	
Pedlars	Pedlars Act 1871, s. 5

APPENDIX 5

LIST OF PRINCIPAL BY-LAW MAKING POWERS

Function	Purpose of Subject-Matter of By-Law	Statutory Provisions	Confirming Authority
	Good rule and government	Local Government Act 1972, s. 235	Secretary of State for the Home Department
Aerodromes	Regulations for the use and operation of municipal aerodromes including the control of noise, vibration and pollution	Civil Aviation Act 1982, s. 32	Secretary of State for Trade
Allotments	As to letting, and generally	Small Holdings and Allotments Act 1908, s. 28 as amended by the Local Government, Planning and Land Act 1980, s. 1(5); Sched. 5; Sched. 34, Pt. V	Secretary of State for the Environment
Ancient monuments	As to access, preservation and protection	Ancient Monuments and Archaeological Areas Act 1979, s. 19	Secretary of State for the Environment
Animals	For the purposes of the Animal Health Act 1981	Animal Health Act 1981, s. 2	Minister of Agriculture, Fisheries and Food
Burials and cremation	Management, charges and use of mortuaries and post-mortem rooms	Public Health Act 1936, s. 198(1)	Secretary of State for the Environment
Cemeteries	Management thereof	Local Government Act 1972, s. 214(3), Sched. 26, para. 11	do.
Charities	For the regulation of street collections	Police, Factories (Miscellaneous Provisions) Act 1916, s. 5	Secretary of State for the Home Department

Function	Purpose of Subject-Matter of By-Law	Statutory Provisions	Confirming Authority
Children and young persons	Street trading by children and young persons	Children and Young Persons Act 1933, s. 20	Secretary of State for the Home Department
	Regulation of employment of children and persons under eighteen	Children and Young Persons Act 1933, ss. 18 and 19 (but see the Employment of Children Act 1973, which is not yet in force)	do.
Food	As to slaughterhouses and knackers' yards	Slaughterhouses Act 1974 s. 12 as amended by the Local Government, Planning and Land Act 1980, s. 194; Sched. 34, Pt. I	Minister of Agriculture, Fisheries and Food
	Securing sanitary and cleanly conditions and practices in connection with handling, wrapping and delivery of food and in connection with sale or exposure for sale of food in the open air	Food Act 1984, s. 15	Secretary of State for Social Services
	As to public slaughterhouses	Slaughterhouses Act 1974, s. 16 as amended by the Local Government, Planning and Land Act 1980, s. 194; Sched. 34, Pt. I	Minister of Agriculture, Fisheries and Food
Highways	Restricting the use of a road for the purpose of providing playground facilities for children	Road Traffic Regulation Act 1984, s. 31	Secretary of State for the Environment
	Regulation as to ferries	Ferries (Acquisition by Local Authorities) Act 1919, s. 2	do.
	New streets	Highways Act 1980, s. 186	do.
	Priority and queues in relation to persons waiting to enter public vehicles	Public Health Act 1925, s. 26	Secretary of State for the Home Department

Subject	Power	Act	Authority
	Prevention of danger from wireless apparatus liable to fall in any street or public place	Public Health Act 1925, s. 26	do.
	Regulation of hackney carriages	Public Health Act 1875, s. 171, Town Police Clauses Act 1847, s. 68	do.
	Regulation of the use of cabmen's shelters	Public Health Acts Amendment Act 1890, s. 40(2)	do.
	Parking places for bicycles and motor cycles	Road Traffic Regulation Act 1984, s. 57(7)	Secretary of State for the Environment
	Regulation of public conveniencies for road users	Highways Act 1980, s. 114(3)	do.
	Regulation as to persons using walkways	Highways Act 1980, s. 35(6)	do.
Housing	Management, use and regulation of houses provided by local authorities, and as to local authority lodging houses	Housing Act 1985, s. 23	do.
	As to underground rooms	Housing Act 1985, s. 281	do.
	Land held under the Housing Act 1985, s. 12	Local Government (Miscellaneous Provisions) Act 1976, s. 9	do.
Inland waters and waterways	Regulation of use	Transport Act 1968, s. 113 Water Resources Act 1963, s. 79 (to be amended by the Control of Pollution Act 1974, Sched. 4)	Secretary of State for the Environment or Minister of Agriculture, Fisheries and Food
Land drainage	Efficient working of drainage systems, drainage works against flooding	Land Drainage Act 1976, ss. 34, 98	Minister of Agriculture, Fisheries and Food
Libraries and museums	Regulation of use of libraries, museums, art galleries	Public Libraries and Museums Act 1964, s. 19	Secretary of State for Education and Science

Function	Purpose of Subject-Matter of By-Law	Statutory Provisions	Confirming Authority
Parks, recreational facilities and open spaces	Preservation of order and prevention of damage in National Parks and areas of outstanding natural beauty	National Parks and Access to the Countryside Act 1949, s. 90	Secretary of State for the Home Department
	The prevention of danger, obstruction and annoyance to persons using a seashore	Public Health Acts Amendment Act 1907, s. 82	do.
	Regulation of pleasure fairs and roller skating rinks	Public Health Act 1961, s. 75 (extended by the Local Government (Miscellaneous Provisions) Act 1976, s. 22)	do.
	Regulation of pleasure boats	Local Government, Planning and Land Act 1980, s. 185	do.
	Regulation of seaside pleasure boats	Public Health Act 1961, s. 76 (extended by the Local Government (Miscellaneous Provisions) Act 1976, s. 17)	do.
	Regulation of pleasure boats in parks and pleasure grounds	Public Health Acts Amendment Act 1890, s. 44(2)	do.
	Regulation of public walks, and pleasure grounds	Public Health Act 1875, s. 164	do.
	Regulation of ancient monuments	Ancient Monuments and Archaeological Areas Act 1979, s. 19	Secretary of State for the Environment
	Preservation of order, etc., in country parks	Countryside Act 1968, s. 41	Secretary of State for the Home Department
	Prevention of nuisance and preservation of order on commons	Commons Act 1899, ss. 1 and 10	do.
	Regulation of esplanades and promenades, including, inter alia, prescribing the nature of traffic for which they may be used, and regulating hawking and selling	Public Health Acts Amendment Act 1907, s. 83	do.

	Use of facilities in or near National Parks	Countryside Act 1968, s. 12(5)	Secretary of State for the Environment
	Regulation of lakes in National Parks	Countryside Act 1968, s. 13	do.
	Regulation of reservoirs and waterways for preservation of order, etc.	Highways Act 1980, s. 117(3)	do.
	Regulation of public conveniences for users of country roads		
	Regulation of open spaces and burial grounds, including preservation of order and prevention of nuisances	Open Spaces Act 1906, s. 15	Secretary of State for the Home Department
	Regulation of sailing, boating, bathing, fishing and works and services in country parks	Countryside Act 1968, s. 8(5)	Secretary of State for the Environment
	Regulation of picnic sites for motorists on trunk roads	Highways Act 1980, s. 113(7)	do.
Public health	As to hop-pickers and other persons doing similar work	Public Health Act 1936, s. 270	do.
	Regulation of fish frying and offensive trades	Public Health Act 1936, s. 108	do.
	As to common lodging houses	Public Health Act 1936, s. 240	do.
	As to public sanitary conveniences	Public Health Act 1936, s. 87(3)	do.
	Regulation of acupuncture, tattooing, ear-piercing and electrolysis	Local Government (Miscellaneous Provisions) Act 1982, ss. 14–16	
	Regulation of hairdressers and barbers	Public Health Act 1961, s. 77	Secretary of State for the Environment
	Regulation of public bathing including the areas and hours permitted	Public Health Act 1936, s. 231 (extended by the Local Government (Miscellaneous Provisions) Act 1976, s. 17)	Secretary of State for the Home Department

Function	Purpose of Subject-Matter of By-Law	Statutory Provisions	Confirming Authority
Public health —contd.	Regulation of swimming baths and bathing pools not under the management of local authority *inter alia* as to purity of water and prevention of accidents	Public Health Act 1936, s. 233	Secretary of State for the Environment
	Prevention of nuisance from snow, filth, etc., and from animals	Public Health Act 1936, s. 81	do.
	Regulating the removal of house refuse	Public Health Act 1936, s. 72(3), (4) (to be repealed by the Control of Pollution Act 1974, Sched. 4)	do.
	Regulating the removal through streets of offensive matter or liquid	Public Health Act 1936, s. 82	do.
	Regulation of the use of cabmen's shelters	Public Health Acts Amendment Act 1890, s. 40(2)	do.
	Regulating tents, vans, etc., used for human habitation	Public Health Act 1936, s. 268. Public Health (Control of Disease) Act 1984, s. 56	
Rivers	Prevention of pollution	Rivers (Prevention of Pollution) Act 1951, s. 5 (to be repealed by the Control of Pollution Act 1974, Sched. 4)	Secretary of State for Social Services
Water supply	Securing protection against the pollution of water	Water Act 1945, s. 18 (to be repealed by the Control of Pollution Act 1974, Sched. 4)	Secretary of State for the Environment and the Minister of Agriculture, Fisheries and Food
	Prevention of waste, undue consumption, misuse, or contamination of water, and as to water fittings	Water Act 1945, s. 17	do.

Water resources	Protection of resources	Water Resources Act 1963, s. 79 (to be amended by the Control of Pollution Act 1974 Sched. 4)	do.
	Regulation of lakes in National Parks	Countryside Act 1968, s. 13	Secretary of State for the Home Department
	Regulation of reservoirs	Countryside Act 1968, s. 22(6)	Secretary of State for the Environment
Weights and measures	Sale of solid fuel	Weights and Measures Act 1985, Sched. 5, para. 9	Secretary of State for Trade
Miscellaneous	Regulation of municipal baths and washhouses and bathing places	Public Health Act 1936, s. 223	Secretary of State for the Environment
	Regulations as to street collections (available to police authority)	Police, Factories, etc., (Miscellaneous Provisions), Act 1916, s. 5	Secretary of State for the Home Department
	Prevention of danger from whirligigs and swings driven by steam power, and from the use of firearms in shooting ranges and galleries	Public Health Acts Amendment Act 1890, s. 38 (repealed by the Public Health Act 1961, s. 75(7) (without prejudice to by-laws already in force))	do.
	Regulating the use or markets maintained by a local authority	Food Act 1984, s. 60	do.
	Relating to the provision of heat, hot air, hot water or steam	Local Government (Miscellaneous Provisions) Act 1976, s. 12	do.

APPENDIX 6

TABLE OF MAIN SPECIFIC GRANTS

Function	*Grant Provisions*
34-01 Administration of Justice—	
Expenses of Magistrates' Courts Committees	Justices of the Peace Act 1979, ss. 59 and 61
Crown Court— Cost of provision and upkeep of premises formerly used for assizes and quarter sessions	Courts Act 1971, s. 28 and Sched. 3, paras. 1, 4 and 9
Probation—revenue expenditure	Powers of Criminal Courts Act 1973, s. 51
Probation and bail hostels	Powers of Criminal Courts Act 1973, s. 51
Children— Provision of secure accommodation	Child Care Act 1980, s. 81
Civil defence— General functions	Civil Defence Act 1948, s. 3
Coast protection	Coast Protection Act 1949, s. 21
Consumer advice	Competition Act 1980, s. 20
Defence— Restoration of property used for temporary defence works	Requisitioned Land and War Works Act 1945, s. 52
Education— Student grants	Local Government Act 1974, s. 8
Careers service	Employment and Training Act 1973
Teacher training (in-service)	Education Acts 1962, s. 3(*a*); 1980, Sched. 5
Additional accommodation in educational establishments for unemployed people under schemes of Manpower Services Commission (M.S.C.)—capital grants	Employment and Training Act 1973, s. 2(2)(*d*)
Industrial language training scheme (M.S.C.)	Employment and Training Act 1973, s. 2(2)(*d*)
Technical and vocational education initiative (M.S.C.)—additional costs	Employment and Training Act 1973, s. 2(2)(*d*)
Youth training scheme—accredited centres (M.S.C.)	Employment and Training Act 1973, s. 2(2)(*d*)
Welsh language training	Education Act 1980, s. 21
Education support grants	Education (Grants and Awards) Act 1984

632

Emergencies and disasters—
Expenditure under s. 138, Local Government Act 1972

Ministerial statements

Employment—
Expenditure in pursuance of M.S.C. programmes to help unemployed find employment—community projects, training workshops, information technology centres, work experience on employers' premises, voluntary projects programmes

Employment and Training Act 1973, s. 2(2)(d)

Energy—
Energy efficiency demonstration projects

Science and Technology Act 1965, s. 5

European Community grants—
School milk and milk products

E.E.C. Regulations—Intervention Board for Agricultural Produce (IBAP)

Butter subsidy

E.E.C. Regulations—Intervention Board for Agricultural Produce (IBAP)

Regional development projects

E.E.C. Regulations—European Regional Development Fund (ERDF)

Projects for improvement of conditions for marketing and processing agricultural and fish products

E.E.C. Regulations—European Agriculture Guidance and Guarantee Fund (FEOGA)

Gypsies—
Provision of caravan sites

Local Government, Planning and Land Act 1980, s. 70

Harbours—
Harbour-related improvements and repairs which assist fishing industry

Fisheries Act 1955, s. 2

Highways and transport—
Advances for highway purposes

Highways Act 1980, s. 272

Transport supplementary grant

Local Government Act 1974, s. 6

Improved facilities for road transport in developmental or intermediate areas

Industrial Development Act, s. 13

Bus fuel duty

Finance Act 1965, s. 92, as amended by the Transport Act 1982, s. 62 and Public Passenger Vehicles Act 1981, ss. 1, 2

Historic buildings

Historic Buildings, etc., Act 1953, s. 5B. National Heritage Act 1983, Sched. 4, para. 7

Home insulation

Housing Act 1985, s. 521

Housing—
Housing subsidies

Housing Act 1985, ss. 421–427

Slum clearance subsidy

Housing Act 1985, ss. 312–313

Housing improvement grants	Housing Act 1985, Pt. XV
Agricultural housing	Housing Act 1985, Sched. 15, Pt II
Environmental improvements in housing action areas and general improvement areas	Housing Act 1985, ss. 245, 259
Improvements for sale scheme	Housing Act 1985, s. 429
Housing association grants	Housing Associations Act 1985, ss. 41–53
Reinstatement and repurchase of defective dwellings sold to private owners	Housing Act 1985, ss. 569–570
Housing benefit scheme	Social Security and Housing Benefits Act 1982
Home purchase assistance scheme	Housing Act 1985, ss. 445–450
Mortgage interest relief scheme (MIRAS)	Finance Act 1982, ss. 25–9, Sched. 7
Planning, development and industry— The acquisition, clearing and preliminary development of land acquired for the redevelopment of an area as a whole, relocation of population or industry or the replacement of open space	Town and Country Planning Act 1971, s. 250
Research and education	Town and Country Planning Act 1971, s. 253
Conservation areas, preservation or enhancement	Town and Country Planning (Amendment) Act 1972, s. 10. Local Government, Planning and Land Act 1980, Sched. 15, para. 27
Acquiring and carrying out works of reclamation or improvement of derelict land	Derelict Land Act 1982
Remedial operations on unstable tips	Mines and Quarries (Tips) Act 1969, s. 25
Town development	Town Development Act 1952, ss. 2 and 10
National Parks	Local Government Act 1974, s. 7
New towns—houses transferred to local authorities	New Towns Act 1981, s. 51
New towns—housing defects	New Towns Act 1981, s. 51A
Regional development—buildings and associated works	Industrial Development Act 1982, Pt. II, as substituted by Co-operative Development Agency and Industrial Development Act 1984
Enterprise zones	Local Government, Planning and Land Act 1980, s. 179 and Sched. 32, paras. 29, 30

Police—	
General	Police Act 1964, s. 31
Public health and land drainage—	
Smoke control	Clean Air Act 1956, s. 13. Housing Act 1964, s. 95
Port health services—medical examinations	Immigration Act 1971, s. 31
Land drainage improvements or new works carried out under ss. 30, 31, 91(6), 98, 99 and 100 of the Land Drainage Act 1976	Land Drainage Act 1976, s. 91
Rate Rebates	Local Government Planning and Land Act 1980, s. 69 (Disabled Persons)
	General—see under Housing benefit scheme
Rent officers service	Rent Act 1977, s. 63
Social needs—	
Expenditure incurred through existence of special need in any urban area	Local Government Grants (Social Needs) Act 1969, s. 1
Commonwealth immigrant population	Local Government Act 1966, s. 11
Smallholdings—	
Works or facilities of a capital nature (Investment grants)	Agriculture Act 1970, s. 29
Modernisation of farms in less favoured areas in accordance with E.E.C. directives (Development grants)	European Communities Act 1972, s. 2(2). Agriculture and Horticulture Development Regulations 1980 (S.I. 1980 No. 1298), as amended
Welfare services—	
Employment of blind, partially sighted and other disabled persons in sheltered workshops and industrial groups (M.S.C.)	Disabled Persons (Employment Act) 1944, s. 15(5)(c)
Employment of blind persons —home workers (M.S.C.)	Disabled Persons (Employment Act) 1944, s. 15(5)(c)
Resettlement units	Supplementary Benefits Act 1976, s. 30, Sched. 5. Social Security Act 1980, Sched. 2
Employment rehabilitation of disabled persons—capital grants (M.S.C.)	Employment and Training Act 1973, s. 2(2)(a)
Development of services for mentally handicapped (Wales only)	National Health Service Act 1977, s. 28B

INDEX

637

DEATHS,
registration of, 27–24
DEBENTURES,
issue of, 7–36
DECLARATION,
action for, 12–40
ultra vires acts, 1–19
DECLARATION OF INTEREST. *See* INTEREST
OF MEMBERS.
DECLARATORY JUDGMENT, 12–40
DEFAMATORY STATEMENTS,
defences, 4–13
newspapers, as to, 4–15
definition of, 4–12
privilege, 4–13
DEFAULT,
authorities, in, 11–16
education service, in, 11–17
DELEGATION,
committees, to, 4–49
joint committees, to, 4–51
officers, 4–54
DELEGATUS NON POTEST DELEGARE, 4–50
DEMAND NOTE FOR RATES, 8–30
DEMOLITION, WORKS OF, CONTROL OVER,
16–28
DEPARTMENT OF HEALTH AND SOCIAL
SECURITY,
food and drugs, responsibility for, 22–03
health services, duties as to, 18–03
DEPUTY CHAIRMEN OF COUNCILS, 4–02
DEPUTY MAYOR,
appointment of, 3–09
DERATING, 8–08
DERELICT LAND,
grants, for, 34–01
DEVELOPMENT. *See also* TOWN AND
COUNTRY PLANNING.
applications for consent, 19–17
consent for, 19–17
control of, 19–15
financial issues, 19–46
industrial building, control of, 19–22
meaning of, 19–15
office building, control of, 19–22
planning conditions, 19–23
unauthorised, enforcement provisions,
19–32
DEVELOPMENT CHARGE, 19–46
DEVELOPMENT GAINS TAX, 19–48
DEVELOPMENT PLANS,
application for development, and, 19–23
compulsory purchase under, 5–03
contents of, 19–06
functions of, 19–06
local plans, 19–11
objections to, 19–10
preparation of, 19–08, 19–09
purchase notices, and, 19–14
structure plans, 19–08, 19–09
unitary, 19–13

DEVELOPMENT PLANS—*cont.*
validity, testing of, 19–60
DIGNITIES,
former local authorities of, preservation
of, 3–11
DIGNITY, LOCAL OFFICERS OF,
preservation of, 3–11
DIRECT LABOUR ORGANISATIONS,
general provisions, 27–29
DIRECTIONS,
Ministers, by, 11–24
DIRECTOR OF PUBLIC PROSECUTIONS,
election petitions, at hearing of, 13–24
DIRECTOR OF SOCIAL SERVICES, 18–08
DISABILITY,
voting, from, 4–26
DISABLED PERSONS,
general provisions, as to, 18–12
DISASTERS,
expenditure, in connection with, 1–23,
7–08
DISCLOSURE OF INTEREST. *See* INTEREST OF
MEMBERS.
DISCRETION. *See also* JUDICIAL CONTROL.
abuse of, 12–20
fettering of, 12–15
mandamus, and, 12–37, 12–38
unreasonable exercise of,
powers of auditors, 7–19
DISCRETIONARY POWERS,
exercise of, 12–05
general policy, and, 12–15, 12–16
DISEASES OF ANIMALS,
contagious, control of, 4–59, 27–08
DISPOSAL OF LAND, 5–45
accounts, 5–46
capital money, application of, 7–07
moneys, 5–46
DISQUALIFICATION,
council membership, 13–08
DISTRESS,
for rates, 8–39
DISTRICT AUDIT. *See* AUDIT.
DISTRICT AUDITORS. *See* AUDITORS.
DISTRICT COUNCILS. *See also* LOCAL
AUTHORITIES *and* PRINCIPAL
COUNCILS.
additional powers obtainable by, 2–07
alterations in divisions, 3–14
change of name, 3–29
communities,
electoral arrangements, and, 3–25
review of, 3–25
community councils,
creation of, 3–06
compulsory purchase powers of, 5–02,
31–01
constitution of, 1–02, 3–02, 4–02
creation of, 1–01, 1–02, 3–02, 4–02
drainage powers, 23–29
expenses of, 7–02